ATLANTIC—LITTLE, BROWN BOOKS
ARE PUBLISHED BY
LITTLE, BROWN AND COMPANY
IN ASSOCIATION WITH
THE ATLANTIC MONTHLY PRESS

Published simultaneously
in Canada by McClelland and Stewart Limited

PRINTED IN THE UNITED STATES OF AMERICA BY
KINGSPORT PRESS, INC., KINGSPORT, TENNESSEE

JOHN ADAMS
and the
American Revolution

CATHERINE DRINKER BOWEN

AN ATLANTIC MONTHLY PRESS BOOK

LITTLE, BROWN AND COMPANY · BOSTON

1950

FOR

BARBARA REX

Whose eye with a manuscript is caustic and skillful, and whose friendship has survived the good chapters and the bad

CONTENTS

PART II

Attorney at Law. 1755–1768

PART III

The Approach of Revolution. 1768–1774

PART IV

The Continental Congress. 1774–1776

ILLUSTRATIONS

PROLOGUE

ON the Fourth of July, 1826, America celebrated its Jubilee — the Fiftieth Anniversary of Independence. John Adams, second President of the United States, died that day, aged ninety, while from Maine to Georgia bells rang and cannon boomed. And on that same day, Thomas Jefferson died before sunset in Virginia.

In their dying, in that swift, so aptly celebrated double departure, is something which shakes an American to the heart. It was not their great fame, their long lives or even the record of their work that made these two seem indestructible. It was their faith, their bounding, unquenchable hope in the future, their sure, immortal belief that mankind, if it so desired, could be free.

They were not alone in their faith. Theirs was the eighteenth century. The *Century of Enlightenment,* men called it proudly — the *Age of Reason,* when knowledge of the natural world was to break the bonds of man's primordial guilt, revealing that God himself was reasonable. With a prism, a telescope, Sir Isaac Newton had proclaimed it; the stars, the very heavens, sent down confirmation. Hell was vanquished. The universe moved by its own laws; the earthquake, the lightning and the pestilence no longer were God's punishment to earth. The riddle of his destiny was man's own to solve, by the joyful exercise of his free will. The awful catechism was reversed. God put the questions now, and in hope and eagerness men searched out answers, conquered the smallpox with a needle, threw down kings and fashioned governments to their very liking. "You will think me transported with Enthusiasm but I am not," John Adams wrote his wife the day after independence was declared — "I am well aware of the Toil and Blood and Treasure it will cost Us to maintain this Declaration, and support and defend these States. — Yet through all the Gloom I can see the Rays of ravishing Light and Glory. I can see that the End is more than worth all the Means. And

that Posterity will triumph in that Days Transaction, even altho We should rue it, which I trust in God We shall not."

Old John Adams, we call him today. *Old Sink or Swim*. These pages do not portray an old John Adams — though the old John was magnificent and deserves a volume. One book cannot cover those ninety years; it would be a mere chronicle, a list, a calendar of events, names, dates, with no space to tell why things happened and how the man felt who brought them to pass. In 1778, Adams went to France as Commissioner. Had he died at forty-two on that perilous trip across a wintry, enemy-infested ocean, he would already have done enough to merit immortality. We shall not follow him to the Court of Versailles, compare his services with Franklin's or describe his friendship with the young Jefferson who shared his household at Passy. What George III said to John at the palace in 1785, or what Abigail Adams — prim, delightful Puritan — thought of the Parisian ballet, is not our concern here. Nor is it part of our chronicle to describe the feud, long and fierce, between Jefferson and Adams, when the French Revolution divided them spiritually, nor how they fought for the Presidency in 1800 and Jefferson won, nor their eventual and noble reconciliation.

This book opens in October, 1745, when John Adams was ten years old. It closes in July of '76, when he was forty, with independence newly declared and the war with England only just begun. "What do we mean by the revolution?" John wrote at eighty. "The war with Britain? That was no part of the revolution; it was only the effect and consequence of it. The revolution was in the minds and hearts of the people, and this was effected from 1760 to 1775, in the course of fifteen years, before a drop of blood was shed at Lexington." [1]

Those fifteen years were the most important, the most significant, of John Adams's life. Among major political upheavals of history, it is said the American Revolution was the only one that succeeded wholly, the only one that did not run full cycle back to despotism — to a Napoleon and world conquest, a Kremlin and government by secret police. Months before the Declaration of Independence was launched, Adams showed the colonies how to write their separate constitutions. Setting down what he characteristically called A PLAN, he sent it to Virginia, New Hampshire, North Carolina, New Jersey. John Adams, in short, put a canvas bottom under the American

Revolution, so that when the colonies fell, they did not fall through to chaos, bloodshed and a new paternalism. "You and I," he wrote a member of the Congress in January of 1776, "have been sent into life at a time when the greatest lawgivers of antiquity would have wished to live. When, before the present epocha, had three millions of people full power and a fair opportunity to form and establish the wisest and happiest government that human wisdom can contrive?"

As a very young man, John Adams had a vision of a British commonwealth of nations, stretching across two oceans, an example, a challenge and an invitation to all who desired liberty under the law. He had lived through two French wars and had grown to manhood with the burning conviction that British rights, British freedom, the British constitution, must be cherished at all costs, even the cost of one's life. When he discovered his vision had been betrayed by Britain herself, when he knew this commonwealth must confine itself to one continent and the union with Britain be broken forever, he accepted the limitation with grief. "I go mourning in my Heart all the Day long," he said.

Serving both before and after the years of active revolution, Adams never changed his position; he was consistent throughout. If President Adams was a Federalist in 1800, Lawyer Adams of Braintree had been a Federalist in 1765. Independence and confederation were for him synonymous, the first contingent on the second. "What is an independency?" he wrote from Philadelphia in April, 1776. "Why, government in every colony, a confederation among them all. As to declarations, be patient. What signifies a Word?" By inclination a thoughtful man (with Woodrow Wilson surely the most scholarly of our presidents), Adams began early in life to examine the governments of the world, both past and present. Evidence led him to the conviction that sudden, violent revolutions are not fruitful to the cause of freedom. He never altered that position. "I adore gradual abolitions," he said. He loved order, loved the law. "I know not how it is," he wrote plaintively, "but mankind have an aversion to the science of government. Is it because the subject is too dry? To me, no romance is more entertaining."

For a man so inclined, it was not easy to throw himself into revolution. Here was no Sam Adams, no Tom Paine, born to defiance, from whose tongue and pen opposition poured inspired, and who ceased

functioning when the moment for opposition was past. John Adams was by disposition more architect than destroyer, far too candid to be trusted with the undercover plots that belong to revolution. "Concealment is not part of his nature," Jefferson said. "A man more perfectly honest never issued from the hands of his Creator."

John Adams's story is above all the biography of a political animal. "Do you recollect when it was you first became a politician?" Dr. Rush of Philadelphia asked him when they were old. . . . In the year 1745, John replied, at the age of ten, when New England men took ship for Nova Scotia to capture Louisburg from the French — and the next year, when d'Anville's great fleet sailed down the coast against Boston.

It is with these scenes, therefore, that our narrative opens — in that far-off, forgotten day when France was the enemy, Britain the well-loved protector and friend, and His Most Christian Majesty, Louis XV, the most powerful sovereign of Europe. We in America are strangers to our history in the period immediately preceding 1765. Stamp Act, Boston Massacre, Tea Party: these are familiar. With them the historical door flings open, our American tradition begins. We see a fat wicked king on a British throne, a fat wicked Lord North — both *sui generis,* sprung apparently from the foam, and breathing hatred for North America. On this side the ocean we see a crowd of gentlemen in knee breeches and cocked hats, signing Declarations or spurring black horses by night through country lanes. . . . "One if by land and two if by sea." . . . John Adams is among these gentlemen; that much we know.

Such well-worn trappings, the shoe buckles and snuff, the galloping scenery and "theater" of revolutionary days, have become stale to the point of spuriousness; they only obscure the human beings they are supposed to clothe. They are props, short cuts — and there is no short cut to historic realization. To make the acquaintance of a period is a slow and concentrated exercise; it cannot be hurried any more than prayer can be hurried. We must move deliberately, as life itself seems sometimes to move. We need to wander a little from our narrative. We need to pause, share our hero's anxiety when, young and in love, he climbs troubled among the rocks and trees of Braintree's North Common. Such procedure is our only antidote against the flood of pompous ancestral rhetoric, the stately thick brocaded curtain two centuries have drawn between us and our subject.

John Adams came from small and very quiet beginnings; their signature lay upon him to the end. No matter in what scenes of courtly ceremony he moved, his spirit, as has been said of another New England man, "dwelt always within the undecorated walls of his youth." The house where he was born still stands, and the small tidy house next door where he moved when he was married. It is necessary to know these houses, to make acquaintance with the wide sloping pastures that once lay round them, with the barns, the hills, the highway, the taverns and the Meeting-house of Braintree, Massachusetts.

In time and in space, that is where we first meet John Adams, aged ten. Some thirty years later, we leave him in very high company indeed — with Washington the soldier, Franklin the wise man and Jefferson the inspired trumpeter of freedom. It is the seventeenth of May, 1776. In Congress assembled, thirteen colonies have finally agreed to adopt governments independent of the crown. There remains a Declaration to be published, a confederation to be formed, a war to be fought. Yet Adams's greatest work is done; America is ready for independence. As we take our farewell, John sits alone in his lodginghouse bedroom, a short, plump figure, his bald head perspiring freely in the Philadelphia heat as he writes to his wife. *"When I consider the great Events which are passed, and that I may have been instrumental of touching Some Springs and turning Some Small Wheels, I feel an Awe upon my Mind, which is not easily described. Is it not a saying of Moses, 'Who am I, that I should go in and out before this great People?'"*

CATHERINE DRINKER BOWEN

BRYN MAWR, PENNSYLVANIA
July 10, 1949

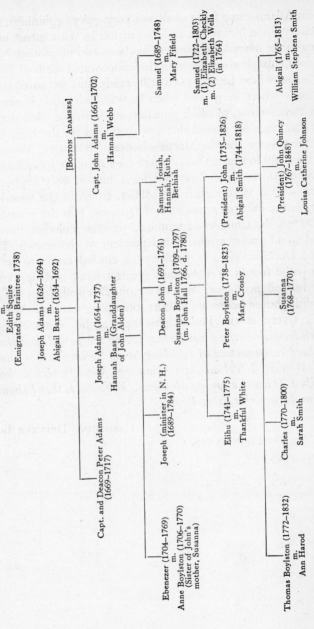

Henry Adams of England (1583–1646)
m.
Edith Squire
(Emigrated to Braintree 1738)

Joseph Adams (1626–1694)
m.
Abigail Baxter (1634–1692)

[BOSTON ADAMSES]

Capt. John Adams (1661–1702)
m.
Hannah Webb

Joseph Adams (1654–1737)
m.
Hannah Bass (Granddaughter
of John Alden)

Capt. and Deacon Peter Adams
(1669–1717)

Samuel (1689–1748)
m.
Mary Fifield

Samuel (1722–1803)
m. (1) Elizabeth Checkly
m. (2) Elizabeth Wells
(in 1764)

Deacon John (1691–1761)
m.
Susanna Boylston (1709–1797)
(m. John Hall 1766, d. 1780)

Joseph (minister in N. H.)
(1689–1784)

Samuel, Josiah,
Hannah, Ruth,
Bethiah

(President) John (1735–1826)
m.
Abigail Smith (1744–1818)

Abigail (1765–1813)
m.
William Stephens Smith

Ebenezer (1704–1769)
m.
Anne Boylston (1706–1770)
(Sister of John's
mother, Susanna)

Elihu (1741–1775)
m.
Thankful White

Peter Boylston (1738–1823)
m.
Mary Crosby

(President) John Quincy
(1767–1848)
m.
Louisa Catherine Johnson

Susanna
(1768–1770)

Charles (1770–1800)
m.
Sarah Smith

Thomas Boylston (1772–1832)
m.
Ann Harod

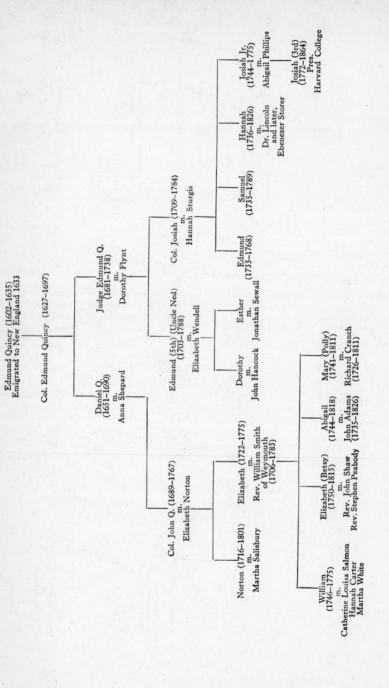

PART I

Braintree and Harvard. 1745-1755

CHAPTER ONE

*The god of battles fights for New
England against the French. Introducing
John Adams of Braintree, Massachusetts,
his father and others.*

ON a morning of early autumn, 1746, over the rim of a tossing,
wild Atlantic Ocean, the sun rose, a round red disk. Lost seemingly
in the immense gray waste, hidden from each other by mountainous
billows, ships wallowed, square-rigged, clumsy, plowing stubbornly
through the valleyed waters. A hundred transports jammed with
troops and forty ships of war belonging to His Most Christian Majesty, Louis XV of France.

Five weeks out of Brest, and already the water casks of d'Anville's flagship dripped scum and in a hundred holds the cattle were
dying. Seamen aloft on watch cursed in French the vastness of these
waters, wondering if they would ever again smell land and home,
wondering why they had 'listed in this American venture. They
knew vaguely of their destination — *Acadie;* some called it Nova
Scotia. But wherever it was and whatever it was, at the journey's end
lay fighting and a quick reward or fighting and a quick death. . . .

And if it happened that the seamen cursed in French, a dozen years
back they might have cursed in Spanish, in Dutch, in Swedish, English — a dozen tongues. For a century, ships like these had headed
westward across three thousand miles of ocean. At home their world
was at war, forever at war. Kings fought for their thrones and for
thrones that were not their own. On land and sea men battled in the
King's name or under their own flag as merchant-adventurers. They

fought for gold, for land and more land, for colonies, ports, rivers, for trees to build more ships and for the very fish that swam in seas as yet uncharted. But whether they called themselves pirates, merchant-adventurers or King's men, one thing was certain: their mission was predatory. To the captains, to the great commanders, the cause was sacred as the cause of King and Empire is always sacred. But to the seamen in the shrouds, to the homesick 'prentice below decks, the indentured servant, the settler and his wife dreaming of free land, it mattered little what monarchs at home lay dying, what kings rose up to don the purple.

Virginia . . . Florida . . . Pennsylvania . . . New England . . . In a dozen tongues the names were familiar. That within the compass of these names a nation was forming, the men on the ships had no slightest notion. They would have laughed at the idea. America was a land of many nations. America was hundreds of miles of unprotected coast line, thousands of miles of inland forest, plain and river land lying naked, ready for the taking.

The waters heaved, the deep was a billowy gray. Wallowing in three thousand miles of ocean, ships headed westward as the sun rose. Looking back over their shoulders, men saw it rise and turned their faces from it, waiting grimly, stubbornly for landfall.

On Beacon Hill the tar barrel sat high in its scaffolding, ready to flare when the first French ship was sighted. D'Anville's great fleet was heading down the coast. Smoke rose on Boston Common from the campfires of six thousand troops, Massachusetts men all, called by the Governor when the rumor struck early in September. They came from the military companies of Plymouth, Salem, Braintree, from Middlesex County, Hampshire County and west to Pittsfield in the Berkshires. Grizzled men in shabby uniforms from an earlier French war, men who had sailed on the famed *Province Galley* against Acadia when Anne was Queen of England, who talked tiresomely of weapons now outmoded. Young men in hunting shirts, carrying their own muskets, ignorant of fleets and armies, but who could hit a squirrel at fifty yards if the light was right. Veterans of the Louisburg campaign of '45, cocky and knowledgeable concerning this business of fighting Frenchmen.

And why not, when they had taken Louisburg from the French only fifteen months before? Louisburg fortress had been France's

pride, France's Gibraltar, its capture a glorious victory for New England troops. Louisburg fortress rose gray and proud from the barren hills of Cape Breton Island, guarding the Gulf of St. Lawrence, between Newfoundland and the great fishing bank. Cape Breton Island was the key to New France, to those huge northern dominions spreading westward up the St. Lawrence to the lakes, and beyond to the upper reaches of the Mississippi. A country vaster than France itself, deeply forested, rich in furs beyond a man's dream of riches.

Cape Breton Island was the key also to the British Empire in North America. It protected not only Nova Scotia but the whole coastal fishery, a fishery that New England knew — and London had begun to know — was more valuable than all the mines of Peru and Mexico. Those northern waters were an eternal nursery for some fifty thousand seamen, resourceful and daring, whom His Majesty King George the Second could call upon to man a warship as well as to harpoon a whale.

All this was familiar history to the troops on Boston Common that fall of '46. Concerning the Louisburg campaign, there was no end to the stories. Veterans told how, standing off Cape Breton in the frigates, they had loaded the big guns into whaleboats and steered landward through surf as wicked as any off Gloucester Point. Ashore they found one vast slimy bog from water's edge to the bare hills where Louisburg fortress rose high as Jericho. A hundred men to a gun, hitched like oxen they had dragged their armament inland by night through mud to their knees. If fog and rain had not covered them — and all agreed it was a cursed climate — they would have been shot down like dogs before they reached the hills. Forty-nine weary days of siege had been endured; nine thousand cannon balls poured into the town before the fortress surrendered.

And now by God it looked, the veterans said, as if they were due to fight the French again, and on home territory. Early in September a pinnace from the fishing fleet had brought the news, racing down from Cape Breton. Off the Grand Banks, French frigates had been sighted; the whalers bearing full-cargoed down from Greenland had seen them, the barques out for cod had seen them. A terrible city of ships, square-rigged, bristling with guns, the *fleur-de-lis* flying at the masthead. Under their towering poops, gulls wheeled screaming, and along the decks thousands of soldiers called to the fishermen

in outlandish popish tongues. Forty warships, a hundred transports . . . two hundred. There must be ten thousand soldiers on board — four thousand — fifteen thousand — commanded by that great warrior-admiral, the Duc d'Anville. . . . Nobody knew if they were headed for Cape Breton or Port Royal, but everyone knew why they were coming: to burn Boston and avenge Louisburg. Boston was the greatest single prize on the North American coast. Boston was the proudest city of the continent, with fifteen thousand inhabitants and over a thousand merchant sail of her own — not to mention the great fishing fleet. D'Anville's guns would burn Boston to her foundations and range unobstructed all the way south to the sugar islands.

Six thousand Massachusetts men were ready to stop them, and in Connecticut six thousand more awaited the call. From Kittery to Newport, men piled sandbags behind the sea walls, strengthened forts, moved powder barrels closer to the water front. If the wind continued to blow from the southwest, no hostile fleet bearing down from Cape Sable could enter Boston Harbor. Along hundreds of miles of coast line, at dawn and at sundown men watched the wind, praying the god of battles to keep it blowing from the southwest.

Ten miles south of Boston, the boy John Adams stood alone on a hilltop and gazed northward across Boston Bay. Behind him the farmhouses of Braintree nestled in their fields, straggling comfortably after the old Coast Road where it wandered down toward Plymouth. Under the boy's bare feet the rock was cold with morning; below him over bright October treetops the Bay spread blue and misty; the islands rose, still green with summer. From the clustered chimneys of Boston and Dorchester, smoke lifted, and beyond to the eastward, past Minot's Light a wide blue channel ran between the islands out to sea.

It was this channel the boy John Adams watched now, shading his eyes against the light, feeling in his face the northeast wind blowing down from Cape Sable across four hundred miles of ocean. Two days ago, the wind had dropped at sundown — the blessed southwest breeze that had held for eight days past. This morning when John woke it had been blowing from the northeast, a steadily increasing breeze with a blue sky, a warm sun and the air clear and salty. John's father, going out to the barn ahead of his son, had looked at the

heavens. A dry nor'easter, he had remarked, adding that it would blow like this for three days, most likely.

How could one's father be so casual, with a whole enemy fleet bearing down from Nova Scotia, sail upon sail, frigate upon frigate, its guns already trained on Boston? Wicked Frenchmen who worshiped the Pope and flung their Protestant enemies into dungeons or burned them alive. So John Adams had heard and so he believed. For weeks the neighbors had talked of nothing else, dropping into the farm kitchen after work to ask Mr. Adams what he thought about the situation. Mr. Adams was a town selectman and a church officer; in his hands was half the political business of Braintree. Uncle Ebenezer and Cousin Jonathan Webb came regularly, the Bass brothers, Thankful Marsh, Great-uncle Peter the maltster, and old Widow Belcher from across the road.

Dame Belcher had a school in her house; she had taught John Adams to read when he was six, before he went to the Free Latin School. John liked her, she was sharp as a crab apple, with a brief, pungent way of talking that enchanted him. Her family had been in Braintree almost as long as the Adamses. She supported Mr. Adams against the advice of half the neighborhood, who were determined, once the French fleet was sighted, to load their families in the farm carts and move westward — hide in the woods around Worcester until the French went away again. Why, down by Wollaston below Colonel Quincy's farm the beaches were altogether defenseless! A frigate could land six hundred men in no time at all; they would be swarming up the Coast Road before a man could barricade his door. . . . Hadn't Rumford, New Hampshire,* been attacked by a hundred Indians from Canada? Worse still, Fort Massachusetts up at Hoosick had surrendered to a party of French and Indians — nine hundred of them. It looked as if the French were aiming, this time, to sweep right down through New England.

Last evening in particular the talk had been vehement. Mr. Adams had remained silent a long time. Suddenly he got up, crossed the hearth and knocked out his pipe on the chimney. The movement was quick, unlike his usual deliberate good nature. "I am fifty-four," Mr. Adams said. "I have seen other French wars. Two of them, and lived through them." He paused, looked round the old kitchen, at the beams that lay along the ceiling, at the windows, black now with

* Now Maine.

evening, which faced directly on the highway. "They did not frighten my father out of Braintree, or my father's grandfather. The French were fighting us to the northeastward in '91, the year that I was born. They came to York with their Indians on snowshoes, killing and burning. My father's cousin saw it. We fought them again before I was twenty. Am I to leave now, because French ships are sighted four hundred miles to the eastward?"

He turned, spat in the fire. "I stay where I am, and take in my apple harvest until the French cut down my trees."

A clearing of throats was heard, a scraping of chairs. Men got up, walked to the door. "Neighbor Adams has the right of it. The mounseers can't drive us to the woods yet awhile." There was a jovial slapping of backs. Dame Belcher's voice, triumphant and a trifle cracked with age, told one of the Bass brothers that if he changed his mind again and moved westward she'd thank him to return the harrow he borrowed a month ago. . . .

John Adams ran up Penn's Hill whenever he could, and looked out to sea. He saw barque and brigantine, pinnace and dory move and shift across the Bay. But he saw no French ships of war. He knew what a frigate looked like. A year ago his father had taken him to Boston to see the frigate *Massachusetts* — New England's pride — when she returned victorious from the Louisburg expedition, carrying the iron cross from Louisburg market place.

Louisburg last year had been a glorious victory. Everyone conceded it. Never before had New England got full credit for beating the French. (Usually Old England took all the glory.) Privately, Mr. Adams, as a practical man, could not see that Louisburg had settled anything much. Here was Massachusetts, some eighteen months later, with a French fleet bearing down the coast, a worse threat than ever. To Mr. Adams it seemed we were forever fighting the French. In his lifetime we had fought Spain in Florida and the Carolinas, although news of those wars was vague. What could a man do but stick to his job and feed his family?

All summer Mr. Adams worked at his farm and in the winter at his trade of cordwainer. There was no use waiting and watching for alarms, for wars that came without warning, undeclared. Like as not the declaration took place in a far European city, and before the news fairly reached New England, some fortress, some blockhouse to the northward had been stormed and taken. The French, as every-

one knew, were diabolically clever at gaining Indian allies. Men were killed on sea and on land, neighbors died of the pestilence that came with armies. After a while a "peace" would be signed in Europe, trading recklessly the forts New England men had died to defend, the precious islands on whose shores the fishermen dried their cod. . . . King William's War, Queen Anne's War — and now King George's War. (In Europe they called it "the War of the Austrian Succession.") Three thousand miles of tossing wild Atlantic was not enough to keep imperial feuds from North American shores.

Mr. Adams had been a lieutenant in Braintree militia for years, having started his military career at the age of fifteen as drummer. He still retained some skill with the sticks, and if tactfully approached, could be induced to rap out a smart reveille on the kitchen chair. This sent all three sons, even the baby, into a transport of pleasure, but was indulged very seldom, Mrs. Adams complaining that it deafened her. The town powder was stored in a big chest in one of the farm sheds; young John was proud of this somewhat dangerous custody. On training days Mr. Adams still shouldered his musket and paraded the North Common with his neighbors. If the French should land in Boston this October of '46 — or land indeed on Braintree beaches — Mr. Adams was ready to take his musket from the chimney hook and march with the rest. Meanwhile, there were apples to pick, it was cider-making time and Mr. Adams had a reputation for the best cider in the North Precinct. He was, moreover, constable in Braintree, responsible for collecting taxes, and some of the South Precinct freeholders had not paid up this year. Merely because a French fleet might sail in tomorrow or next week or next month and burn up the town, Mr. Adams had no intention of excusing Moses Allen or his own cousin Ephraim Adams from this year's taxes. Besides, if he did he would have to pay the money himself.

Like his neighbors along the Coast Road, like his Braintree ancestors, Mr. Adams was a thrifty man. His land and the homestead had come gradually to him, part from his father, part by purchase. Mr. Adams treasured every inch of it — the farmhouse with its central chimney, steep-roofed, the clapboards weathered a soft uneven gray . . . the fields and orchard, the barns and cattle, the workshop where all winter Mr. Adams made harness, shoes, leather aprons and breeches for the country round. Cordwainer — a skilled trade — carried more prestige than shoemaker. . . .

A farm, a homestead, a loyal, vigorous wife who at thirty-seven was a very tornado of housewifely activity . . . Three sons to carry on his name when he was gone: John, Peter and small Elihu . . . It was enough for any man. Surely, the Lord would not take this from him now, would not suffer the French to destroy what he and others like him had built painfully, frugally, for a hundred years and more? But if Providence should order it that all this must perish, then, thought Mr. Adams, God's will be done.

Mr. Adams's Uncle Peter saw it a trifle differently where Providence was concerned. Uncle Peter was in his seventies, a deacon of the Congregational Meeting-house and an even stancher Calvinist than Mr. Adams. If God saw fit to lay His hand heavily on this countryside it was because, said Uncle Peter, His servants had not been faithful of late. They had gone whoring after strange gods. More than once, Uncle Peter hinted darkly that this French invasion was a direct message from on high to let Braintree know He disapproved the recent increase in Dr. Miller's Episcopalian congregation downtown. Braintree had been founded by Dissenters. Let them now give way so easily to the Church of England, with its London bishoprics, its tinsel show — so close to Romish practice — and they might well expect the Lord to send popish fleets to shatter Braintree steeple!

Mr. Adams was as faithful a Congregationalist as anyone. But he could not quite share his Uncle Peter's ferocity where the old faith was concerned. If the French were coming, they were coming because, like all the nations of Europe, they coveted more than they had. Meanwhile it was good the Governor had proclaimed a Fast Day to pray for deliverance from this present peril. Everywhere men observed it, thronging to the churches.

In Boston the Reverend Thomas Prince, from the high pulpit of the Old South Meeting-house, prayed before hundreds. The morning was clear and calm, people had walked to church through sunshine. "Deliver us from our enemy!" the minister implored. "Send Thy tempest, Lord, upon the waters to the eastward! Raise Thy right hand. Scatter the ships of our tormentors and drive them hence. Sink their proud frigates beneath the power of Thy winds!"

He had scarcely pronounced the words when the sun was gone and the morning darkened. All the church was in shadow. A wind shrieked round the walls, sudden, violent, hammering at the windows

with a giant hand. No man was in the steeple — afterward the sexton swore it — yet the great bell struck twice, a wild, uneven sound. Thomas Prince paused in his prayer, both arms raised. "We hear Thy voice, O Lord!" he thundered triumphantly. "We hear it! Thy breath is upon the waters to the eastward, even upon the deep. Thy bell tolls for the death of our enemies!" He bowed his head; when he looked up, tears streamed down his face. "Thine be the glory, Lord. Amen and amen!"

Amen and amen! said Massachusetts, her hope renewed. All the Province heard of this prayer and this answering tempest. Governor Shirley sent a sloop, the *Rising Sun*, northward for news. The *Rising Sun* found the French fleet south of Chebucto* and got chased for her pains. But she brought news so good it was miraculous — if one could believe it. The Rangers, a body of men commanded by Captain Gorham of Boston, had gone, the end of September, to reconnoiter. The Rangers were mostly Indians, the French took them for Canadians and talked freely. Two of the largest French frigates had sunk in a storm, they said, on the Isle of Sable. The whole fleet was nearly lost, the men very sick with scurvy or some pestilential fever. Their great admiral, the Duc d'Anville, was dead.

A week later the news was confirmed by other vessels entering Boston from the northeastward. D'Anville was indeed dead; it was said he had poisoned himself in grief and despair when he saw his men dying round him. Two thousand were already buried, four thousand were sick, and not above a thousand of the land forces remained on their feet. Vice-Admiral d'Estournelle had run himself through the heart with his sword. The few remaining ships, half-manned, were limping off to the southwestward, headed it was thought for the West Indies.

Pestilence, storm and sudden death — how directly and with what extraordinary vigor the Lord had answered New England prayers!

The country fell on its knees. Pharaoh's hosts overwhelmed in the Red Sea were no greater miracle. A paper with d'Anville's orders had been found, instructing him to take Cape Breton Island, then proceed to Boston — "lay that Town in Ashes and destroy all he could upon the Coast of North America; then proceed to the West Indies and distress the Islands."

Storm and pestilence — why, it was like the destruction of the

* Now Halifax Harbor.

Spanish Armada! Governor Shirley said so, to the Massachusetts Legislature assembled. Never had there been so direct an interference of Providence. "*Afflavit Deus*," said Shirley, "*et dissipantur* — The Lord caused the wind to blow and they were scattered." A day of Thanksgiving and prayer was proclaimed. From every pulpit the good news rang. Hip and thigh, the Lord had smitten the Philistines. There was no end to the joyful quotation: *If God be for us, who can be against us?*

On Boston Common the tents were struck. Massachusetts roads were dotted with militiamen walking homeward to Salem, Plymouth, Worcester and westward to the mountains of Berkshire. Some of them would be called again, said Shirley; the French would probably return in the spring. But the present danger was over; the stars in their courses had fought against Sisera.

And ten miles south of Boston in the little town of Braintree, Mr. Adams called his family to prayer and, kneeling in his work clothes beside his wife and sons, thanked a merciful Father for this most timely evidence of His favor.

John wanted to learn arithmetic, but Mr. Cleverly said he wasn't ready for it. Twelve, said Mr. Cleverly, was the age prescribed by Massachusetts school laws "for beginning arithmetic and making pens." *Ready?* John Adams was ready for anything. Dame Belcher had never bothered about school laws, or whether a person was "ready." She had started John at arithmetic when he was six, and had devised delightful problems about a boy who was given four red apples and eight bunches of fox grapes. Or if a man made ten runs in one game of rounders and twenty in another, what would be his average as a batter? At Dame Belcher's, a boy didn't sit still all day, longing to very sickness for the five-o'clock bell and freedom. On fine summer mornings Mrs. Belcher took the children out under her apple tree for lessons, gave them thick round ginger cookies from a crock. She taught John to sing old Scotch songs she said she had learned from her grandmother. She let him get up on his feet, too, and dance, with the clumsy feet of childhood, a solemn, joyful horn-pipe under the trees.

Most boys left dame school when they were seven, but John had begged to stay on a year or two, and his parents had complied. The boy seemed to be learning fast, and besides it was convenient. John could get in the wood before he left for school, help with the milking or give the oxen their feed. John was handy around the cattle and horses; his father noted with some amusement that the boy was handy also around the kitchen with his mother. He whittled pegs for her to hang her apron on inside the milkhouse door; he could build a fire in the kitchen hearth as deftly as a man. John took a pride in the house and the barns that was almost, his father remarked, like a man's pride.

And always, while John worked, he chattered, talking brightly, incessantly, of what he had learned at Dame Belcher's or what his cousin Nathan Webb had said or how he had beaten his cousin Boylston Adams at spelling even if Boylston was two years older. . . .

When John left Dame Belcher and went to school with Mr. Cleverly, his conversation at first was as bright and voluble as ever. John's parents could not have told just when it was the boy stopped talking, stopped confiding every detail of his day, begging his mother to hear him read and spell, or showing off his learning most mightily before his uncles when they dropped in after work. It was not that John stopped talking altogether. That would have been as unlikely

CHAPTER TWO

John Adams in school
and out.

THE celebrations over, the danger forgotten, John Adams with enormous reluctance went back to school, his brother Peter with him. The Adams farm was on the outskirts of town, the boys had about a mile to walk to the Free Latin School down by the Meeting-house. Years ago, John's uncle Joseph Adams had kept the school, before he got his appointment as a minister in New Hampshire. Now Mr. Cleverly was master. He was a Harvard graduate and a Church of England man and John Adams loathed him with a deep, unreasoning hatred that he dared not communicate to his father.

Every school morning, John and Peter left the farmhouse very early, pulling small Elihu after them by the hand. Elihu was nearly six years younger than John; he was fat, jolly and amenable. Just across the Coast Road they left Elihu at Dame Belcher's. John always lingered; Mrs. Belcher opened school with the children singing a psalm, and John loved to sing. Mrs. Belcher let him stand in the back of the room and sing as loud as he wished; his voice came out above all the others. It was worth being late to the Latin School, worth a caning, even. John Adams did not mind a caning now and then; at least there was action in it, and resistance. What John minded was inaction, the interminable sitting from eight to five with a Latin grammar in hand. Mr. Cleverly taught Latin and more Latin; it seemed the world of school had become one vast nightmare of Lily's *Latin Grammar*. Twenty-five kinds of nouns to be got by heart, not to speak of verbs and the awful labyrinth of conjugation.

John Adams" Book
Jan. 15 1727/8

1734 october 31 J was Married to Susanno Boylston
John Adams

october 19th 1735 Sabath day. John Adams the son of John
Adams and Susanna his wife was Born

1738 october 16th Peter Boylston Adams was Borne on Munday

May 29th 1741 Elihu Adams was Borne Friday

1764 Octr 25th John Adams the son above named was married to Abigail Smith.

1765 July 14th Abigail Adams, the Daughter of John Adams and Abigail his wife, was born (and it being Sabbath) was baptized in the afternoon, by Mr Smith, at Braintree

1767 July 11 John Quincy Adams son of John Adams and Abigail his wife, was born and it being Saturday was baptized the next day by Mr Wibirt at Braintree. the 6 little great grandfather for whom he was named, just dying when the 6 child was christened.

1768 Decr 28 Susanna, the Daughter of the above John and Abigail was born of a Wednesday at Boston and the next Sabbath 14 January 1769 was baptized by Dr Cooper. died Feb. 4th 1770

1770 May 29. Charles, son of said John and Abigail was born Thursday morning at Boston and the next Sabbath was baptized by Dr Cooper.

1772. Septr 15 Thomas Boylston Adams was born at Braintree and christened the next Sunday by Mr Wibirt. Mem. the 6 little great, great grandfather, one of the Name of Thomas Boylston, and built the old House at Brookline where my Mother was born, my Mother also had an Uncle of the same Name, the Father of the late Nich. Boylston Esq. & the present Thomas Boylston Merchant.

Reproduction of page from Willard's *Body of Divinity* in
which first Deacon Adams and then John inscribed family
events

as for him to stop breathing. Great-uncle Peter had once remarked that Johnny was the talkingest nephew he had — and he had about sixteen in the North Precinct alone. But after a year or two at the Latin School, Mrs. Adams had only to mention Mr. Cleverly for her eldest son's usually alert blue eyes to cloud, and he answered vaguely, as if he had been questioned in a foreign language.

Mrs. Adams was troubled. Competent, brisk and neat in all her household arrangements — and very voluble — when something was wrong Mrs. Adams said so and desired instant action, whether the action were well-considered or no. In all her responses she was far quicker and more passionate than her husband. She moved swiftly through the house in her bright homespun or calico, a small, plump woman with straight light-brown hair drawn smoothly over her ears. Her complexion was clear and high, and if she was quick to anger she was quick also to forgiveness; John had seen her cry and laugh within the space of three minutes. Her caps were spotless, and no one of her sons ever thought of her without something in her hand — a broom, a ladle, a spindle, a hank of wool.

Mr. Adams on the other hand was chunky and broad-shouldered, slow to talk, slow to laughter. It was to his mother that John ran with gossip of school and friends, of the small victories and defeats of childhood. And now this cheerful, confiding talk had somehow ceased. Mrs. Adams missed it. It was unnatural, she said, for Johnny to be cautious and close. But she could not make her husband share her worry. The boy did his work round the farm very well, Mr. Adams always replied. There had been no complaints from Cleverly, had there? He was a good boy, she was too fussy about him. Let him grow, that was all Johnny needed.

Mr. Adams himself had left school when he was twelve. He knew nothing whatever of Latin, had no measuring stick by which to gauge a boy's progress in learning. All his life, Mr. Adams had done his work and his duty; he expected his sons to do the same. The things John did at home he did well, with tremendous zest. Of course he would do well in school! Of course he would pass his examinations and go to the university according to schedule.

Before John Adams was so much as born, he had been destined for Harvard College and the Congregational ministry. A college education was the patrimony of an eldest son in New England; to the younger boys would go the farm and the homestead. Mr. Adams

himself had been quite content to stay home on the farm with his three brothers while the eldest — Joseph — went to Harvard. Joseph was a minister now in Newington, New Hampshire. Mr. Adams was proud of him, although privately he wished Joseph were not quite so long-winded, with his eternal quoting of Latin and his slavish imitation of Dr. Mather's pulpit manner. After all, Cotton Mather had been dead nearly twenty years. Nevertheless, it was a fine thing to have a minister in the family; Joseph was the first Braintree Adams ever to go to college. The others had been farmers and artisans like Mr. Adams — pious men who paid their debts, did their duty by the township and went down to a respectable grave as deacon or elder of the First Congregational Meeting-house.

Yet, obscure though they were, there ran through these people a strong but persistent inheritance that Mr. Adams himself possessed. He called it an "admiration of learning," and said he got it from his mother, who was a Bass of Braintree and never went to school at all. But she could read aloud, Mr. Adams said, like an angel from heaven; he was sure Dr. Mather himself had read Genesis and the Greater Catechism to no more effect. Unlike most of the Adams women, Mr. Adams's mother had not been strong and had died eventually of consumption. When a woman was not strong, she had time, Mr. Adams said, for learning.

Mr. Adams's wife was apt to greet this remark with a sniff. Her sister Anne was married to Mr. Adams's brother Ebenezer. They lived two miles down the Coast Road; Anne had already given birth to six. Mrs. Adams's own family, the Boylstons of Brookline, Massachusetts, were celebrated for learning. Or at least Uncle Zabdiel Boylston was celebrated, and for Mrs. Adams he set the Boylston tone. Uncle Zabdiel was a physician, known, at sixty-odd, far beyond the limits of Massachusetts Bay. It was he who, with Cotton Mather, had introduced the smallpox inoculation to Massachusetts in the terrible epidemic of 1721. Nearly every preacher in New England had fought him: if God sent the smallpox He sent it for a reason, and who was man to gainsay the divine punishment? All this scratching of the arm was nothing better than witchcraft. Dr. Boylston countered by inoculating first himself and then his only son. After that he went to London and inoculated the royal princesses. He was brave and he was learned, and he was one of the first men in North

America to be honored by a membership in the British Royal Society for Improving Natural Knowledge.

Mrs. Adams had a right to be proud of Uncle Zabdiel; the Adams genealogy boasted no one of like reputation. It was true that what the Adamses lacked in learning they made up for in strength and general fertility. They married twice or thrice; they lived to extraordinary old age, surviving whole waves of epidemic that swept the seacoast every summer: the throat distemper, the lung rot, the putrid fever and the smallpox. . . . With or without inoculation, Mr. Adams sometimes interjected when he grew tired of hearing about Uncle Zabdiel.

Mr. Adams liked to tell his sons about his own grandfather, Henry Adams. A booklover surely, Mr. Adams said. Henry had come over from England in the 1630's, bringing a wife and nine children — eight sons and a daughter. He was Braintree's first Town Clerk and he must, said Mr. Adams, have been a learned man because when he died he made express provision in his will for the dividing of his books among his children. That, added Mr. Adams with satisfaction, meant he had at least nine books. A man didn't have to go to Harvard College to figure that out, eh, Johnny? Nine books was eight more, certainly, than most Braintree families possessed in those old days. If they brought the Holy Bible in the ship with them, it was enough reading for men who had to clear a wilderness before they could plant their corn.

It was a pity the nine books had all vanished. Mr. Adams's own household had only two, besides the Bible. One of them was a big heavy volume called Willard's *Body of Divinity*, written by a vice president of Harvard. Mr. Adams kept it on the parlor table and entered on the flyleaf important family happenings: his own marriage in 1734 and the births of his three sons. On Sundays he liked to take it to the kitchen after breakfast and read aloud to the family, using his forefinger and going slowly, precisely, with no expression in his face beyond a kind of caution lest he lose his place. One day he hesitated so long over the word "immemorial" that John, unable to hold back, pronounced the word for him and then gasped, blushing furiously at his temerity. Mr. Adams looked up, thanked his son and remarked with a sigh that he looked forward to the day when Johnny would come home from the university and read aloud to

him. He hoped John would learn something of the French language at college; seeing we fought the French in Canada every generation it would prove useful.

Just down the road, Mr. Adams had a neighbor who could speak French — or pretended he could speak it, Mr. Adams said. Joseph Marsh was undeniably a well-informed man, always abreast of foreign news. Mr. Adams often sent John to borrow the Boston weekly newspaper from him. Marsh, a Harvard graduate and a bachelor, kept a tutoring school in his house. It irritated Mr. Adams slightly that Marsh, a man in his early thirties who had failed as a preacher and failed as a physician, saw fit to pronounce the Acadian place names in the French way instead of anglicizing them or taking them in one phonetic lump as did the rest of New England. The *Eel de Sab-le*, Marsh said, mincing it on his tongue. Marsh was knowledgeable certainly, but that was no reason for giving himself airs. Marsh's father, the Reverend Dr. Marsh, a man far more important in the community, had never set himself up to be so finikin. Joseph Marsh had let his father's farm go to seed. His mother and sisters worked the truck patch; they bought their meat from the neighbors. In the old days, people didn't live in that haphazard way. Life in New England was becoming too easy, Mr. Adams said.

In the intervals between backbreaking work with scythe and flail, Mr. Adams often pointed out to his sons how pleasant and easy life was nowadays. With the fields almost cleared of stone, with seed of every kind available over the store counter, with the Indians driven off or blessedly dead — by God's mercy — of the smallpox. Except, Mr. Adams added, what was left of the Ponkhapoags and Neponsets nearby, and they were harmless enough, though Colonel Quincy complained because they camped on his land in fishing season and broke up his fences for fuel. Their king, one Moses Pomham, came often to Penn's Hill, bringing with him his brother Aaron. Mr. Adams welcomed them, gave them food and beer. They were tall, strong Indians; their dark faces were lined and furrowed with wrinkles. Mr. Adams said they were very aged.

On these occasions Mrs. Adams was apt to vanish, returning to the kitchen afterward with a great show of brooms and soapy pails. A mile down the road was a wigwam of Ponkhapoags, swarming with dirty children, dogs, scrabbly-looking ponies. John liked to go there after school. The squaws gave him whortleberries, blackberries, wild

strawberries — plums and peaches too, from trees they had planted.

Great-uncle Peter remembered when Indians had been looked on with a far different eye. That ledge inside the big chimney, he told John — where it slanted off to meet the main flue. Did the boy know that in the old days Indians used this ledge to climb down from the roof? To keep them out, a smudge fire burned day and night.

It seemed to John, hearing these stories, that his forefathers had lived in Braintree forever. He would live there forever, too, he told himself. Surely, no place in the world was so friendly, no business anywhere so important as the business of farm and township that his father pursued!

As for the farmhouse, John had heard his father say it was built to last. Beneath the clapboard walls was solid brick and clay, the cellar was lined with stone. Under the floor of the long kitchen that served as living room, the wide pine boards were pegged to the trunks of huge chestnut trees set on field stones, and overhead the heavy summer beam was molded at the ends with lamb's-tongues. Mr. Adams said the old Braintree Puritans disapproved of figured molding; such trumpery and ornamentation was contrary to God's laws and the good life. He wondered who could have devised this beam. Mrs. Adams replied that the beam was plain enough in all conscience, like the rest of the cottage. She greatly desired, someday, to take the boys to Brookline to the mansion of their Uncle Zabdiel Boylston . . . a very elegant seat indeed, with furniture from London and nothing of the Puritan about it at all. . . .

John Adams did not stop to ask if his father's house were beautiful or plain. On the window sills he saw his mother's plants, fennel and chives and parsley, and on the kitchen hearth the skillets hung scoured and ready, each in its accustomed place. Just round the kitchen wall was a second fireplace, where Mr. Adams's friends gathered to smoke their evening pipes and talk over the newest candidate for town selectman or constable. The door opened to a tiny hallway, to the left of which the parlor loomed cold and stately. Once it had held a big four-poster bed, after the fashion of the last century, but Mrs. Adams had removed the bed and put her best tufted chair and footstool in its place. A steep and crooked stairway led to the two bedrooms, each with its fireplace. Elihu slept with his parents, John and Peter in a tiny room adjoining under the eaves.

Overhead in the big arched attic lived Joe, the hired man. Joe was a distant cousin whose parents had died when he was young.

Above John's bed the roof sloped steeply; sitting up, John could lay his hand against its rough boards. In spring and summer the rain drummed him to sleep with its long chorus and in winter the snow, driving from the eastward across the marshes, piled dark against the tiny window.

All this young John Adams took for granted — the warm hearth, the warm bed, the plentiful food that was laid before him. It was outside the walls that his real life lay. John roamed every foot of his father's acres, knew them intimately from western brook to eastern boundary. The long, sloping pastures behind the house where the sheep grazed, and where far off over the valley the hills of Milton rose against the sky. . . . The flat fields across the Coast Road, plowed for wheat; the west acres where the barley grew, and the Indian corn. . . . The truck patch beyond the kitchen door, the Stony Acres up Penn's Hill. His parents discussed selling the Stony Acres. They were good for nothing but sheep pasture, Mrs. Adams said. But somehow they never got round to selling. All his life, Mr. Adams had bought land, bit by bit, with money earned painfully and saved with greatest sacrifice. He could not bear to sell an inch of it. He would wait until John was ready for college, he said. The Stony Acres would pay the first college bond. . . .

When his father said this, John was silent, let the words pass over his head and retreated quickly to his own world, to the safe familiar place he had made for himself, where a boy need not think of Harvard College save as a sort of heavenly future — splendid but blessedly remote. Everything combined to tie John Adams to the land. Even Dame Belcher across the road was part of the conspiracy. She had got into the habit of giving the boy her grain to carry down to the mill for grinding. When he brought it back she handed him three pennies. "Save it, Johnny," she said solemnly. "Buy land with it. Do you hear?"

It was flattering to have Dame Belcher advise him this way, as one freeholder to another. John had seen his father buy land, right next door to the farmhouse where there was a second cottage, almost a twin. The two houses used one well. John had been nine when Mr. Adams bought the second cottage, quite old enough to understand the triumph in his father's face when he came in one morning carry-

ing the deed in his hand. Buying land, quite obviously, was part of life, like plowing in springtime and harvesting in summer.

But Mr. Cleverly's school was not part of life. Mr. Cleverly's school was something to be avoided, escaped, slipped out of by playing hooky, by being late or by begging to stay home and help with the haying. Vacations were haphazard; they came whenever individual fathers needed their sons at home, or when the township money ran low and it was decided to ship Mr. Cleverly to the South Precinct school for a month or two. Election week was always a holiday; so were Harvard Commencement week in July, Christmas, fast days, and training day once a month when Mr. Cleverly went down to the training field to practice the military art with his neighbors. And when escape failed, as it usually did, John Adams learned to endure. Even while crouched on that hard and backless bench with Lily's *Grammar* in hand, there were ways of escape. *The mind is its own place and in itself / Can make a heaven of hell, a hell of heaven.* . . . Satan himself had said that, in Mr. Milton's poem. Mr. Marsh often quoted it, told John to remember the words. They might come in handy, he said. John sat, by now, well in the back of the schoolroom. He was considered much too old for the *New England Primer* — but at least it had pictures. John borrowed the *Primer* from one of the little boys, propped it behind his *Latin Grammar* and, to pass the time, looked idly through the old familiar gruesome rhymes.

The frontispiece showed the features of His Majesty George II staring plumply out from under a curly wig. His Majesty had no crown in the engraving, but he was certainly very elegantly dressed. A page farther on, John came upon Adam himself, a far more important character, who, as all the world knew, had the honor of opening the alphabet:

In Adam's fall, We sinnèd all. . . . How miserable Adam looked in the drawing, standing naked by the tree, with the serpent coiled evilly, lording it over poor shivering Eve! All the way down the alphabet to **T**, death and hell-fire loomed — undeniably more exciting than Latin verbs. **T** fixed it irrevocably: *Time cuts down all, Both great and small.* Here Time with his hourglass stalked forward, winged and dreadful. Beside the letter **X** a coffin lay open, a man's head stuck out: *Xerxes must die, And so must you and I.* Next a fearful skeleton held an arrow over a child's head: *Youth forward*

slips, Death soonest nips. Johnny riffled the pages, looking for the picture of John Rogers. On page sixteen, Rogers the Dissenting martyr burned luridly at the stake while his nine children watched, clustered round their mother. How the flames flew and darted, how wicked the executioner looked in helmet and armor, and how the children's tears fell on their pinafores and poured to the ground! Gazing at this sweet rain, Johnny took up his pen and with a farmer's instinct, drew cabbages sprouting from the moistened spot.

The New England school laws prescribed large biweekly doses of the Westminster Catechism, that backbone of the Congregational faith. They used the Shorter Catechism — ironically so-called — re-edited by Calvinist divines who added large extra proportions of hell-fire, eternal punishment and torment. John Adams accepted it as one accepts bad weather on holidays, something that comes frequently and must be endured. It was Mr. Cleverly who suffered most under this stringent Dissenting medicine; as a Church of England man he would have preferred less of it. John Adams would have been surprised to learn that outside of school Mr. Cleverly was known, among Braintree's more worldly citizens, as very good company indeed. Unfortunately he hated schoolteaching, did it only to enable himself to eat, and simply existed at his desk through the day, waiting for the five-o'clock bell with the same desperation as his scholars. . . . Drawing the Catechism from his desk at the prescribed periods, Mr. Cleverly would begin in a voice hollow with boredom, *"What is the chief end of man?"* Fifty voices answered from the benches in monotonous singsong, "To glorify God and enjoy Him forever."

"And what," Cleverly went on, *"is the misery of that estate whereinto man fell?"*

Through open windows the high expressionless voice of childhood rolled: "All mankind, by their fall, lost communion with God, are under His wrath and curse, and so made liable to all the miseries of this life, to death itself, and to the pains of hell forever."

It would not have occurred to John Adams to question the Catechism as to sacredness, beauty or usefulness. Since he was four he had known those opening words by heart; his mother said the Catechism was a watering pot to shed good lessons. Dr. Mather had urged parents as well as schoolmasters to "drop something of the Catechism on the children, as honey from the rock." Small Elihu,

confused by this, had remarked loudly that he saw no honey and no watering spout in that book. John had laughed aloud, and his father's voice was sharp in reproval.

Young John Adams was always quick to laughter. Quick to anger too, and to tears when he was angry. And in spite of his contriving, there were times when Mr. Cleverly's school moved him to tears of helpless, angry boredom. There was so much he wanted to know — was none of it taught in school? Did the world of learning consist only of Latin and more Latin, and would Harvard College be but an extension of the same, with Greek and Hebrew verbs instead of Latin ones, with all the world shut out and farewell said to every exciting, quickened thing of earth and sky and sea?

One day after school, stopping at Joseph Marsh's for the newspaper, John inquired of Mr. Marsh if, in his private school here at home, he used Lily's *Latin Grammar?* Marsh shook his head. He was a tall man, very thin, a little stooped and pock-marked, with dark hair and eyes. Lily's *Grammar* was a disease, he said. An illness: New England had been afflicted with it for generations. It was one reason why he had given up teaching the Free Latin School just before Cleverly took it over. Cleverly was a man who thrived on routine, grew fat on it, Marsh said cheerfully. Now, here at home he could teach what he wished as he wished — and to whom he wished. But as for Lily's *Grammar*, even Cotton Mather had rebelled against it. Did Johnny know what Dr. Mather had said about the book? He said it prolonged the use of the ferule.

With his thumb, John stroked his bruised right palm and, vastly comforted, grinned up at Marsh. Marsh, observing the gesture, grinned back, but he frowned too. "I wish Joseph Cleverly joy of the rod," he said abruptly. He looked at John, a long look, quizzical, direct, a little hard. "I think," he said at last, "that you will survive Joseph Cleverly and his methods. You will survive even Lily's *Grammar*. . . . Here is the *Evening Post* for your father. I myself prefer the *News-Letter;* there seems a trifle more elasticity to it. Greet your excellent mother for me. Tell her I saw her uncle, Dr. Boylston, last week in Cambridge. He is interested in Professor Winthrop's new telescope and his findings concerning the transit of Mercury."

John felt two hands on his shoulders, a friendly push toward the door. "Get along now. And good luck to you, John Adams."

At home, John said nothing of this conversation, beyond delivering the messages. Concerning school he was, if anything, more silent than ever; when questioned he presented the same stubborn, impenetrable front. She had thought, Mrs. Adams said a little sadly, that a mother knew her children better as they grew older. But she was closer to Peter and small Elihu than she was to John. John gave her no chance at all for conversation. He was insatiably busy; Mrs. Adams remarked that she had never in her life seen a boy so busy, as long as the business did not concern the *Latin Grammar*. John had a whittling knife forever in his hand, a piece of pinewood he was carving into a dory, an Indian canoe. He couldn't wait to get down to Town Brook and launch it, or over to the beaches by Wollaston. John made linen kites and flew them; when the Creek froze in November he was first of all the neighborhood to know where the skating was smoothest and blackest.

Mr. Adams, going down to the west pasture, would find John cantering one of the horses bareback, round and round by the wall. Joe Bass had told him he could, John would shout joyfully. And when was his father going to let him have a horse of his own — could he have the next colt by Polly? John was passionately fond of riding and passionately fond of shooting. Whenever one of his uncles went out after grouse or heath hen, John was sure to know it beforehand and beg to go along. With the uncles it had become a standing joke, the way John Adams turned up mysteriously whenever a shooting expedition was toward. The boy had a nose for it, a witchly sixth sense. "Well, we're off!" Great-uncle Peter would tell his wife jovially, slinging his fowling piece over his shoulder. "We're only waiting for Johnny." And sure enough around the corner would come John, running — the boy never seemed to walk. "The partridge are feeding in the woods northeast of Bass's meadow," he would announce breathlessly. "Yesterday I saw three flocks. Uncle Peter, I can show you a short cut. . . ."

Great-uncle Peter, roaring with laughter, would whack the boy heartily on the rump, tell him to go home and study his Latin. But in the end he took John along, even at the expense of a later argument with the boy's mother. It was hard to resist young John. His enthusiasm bubbled up, a never-ending tide, and with it he had a canny, attractive little way of bargaining for favors begged or received. He had always something to offer. If Uncle Ebenezer, Uncle

Peter, Cousin Webb, would take him fishing, John knew where the smelts were running in Wollaston Brook. Only yesterday he had seen them so thick you could scoop them up in your hand. . . . And Tuesday afternoon in Penn's Woods near the hilltop he had heard a deer snort. Would Uncle Peter like to be shown just where? And did the roan pony perhaps need shoeing? He could ride him down to the smithy tomorrow after school and bring him back. . . .

John Adams lived very close to earth and all the things of earth. The soft warm hide of the cow against his forehead at milking time, the newborn calf staggering to its feet in the straw. The sow and her litter rolling muddy in the open sty, the choking, pungent dust that rose from the barn floor at threshing time. . . . On summer mornings the pasture grass was cool beneath his bare feet and at noon on the Coast Road the dust splashed soft and hot between his toes. And whether the breeze blew from the east, or southwest from the pine-scented hills, the boy had only to lift his head to know the sea was near. The Bay lay blue and wide, dotted with the sails of little fishing boats or the high white canvas of great vessels bearing eastward out to sea. John Adams loved the ships, went when he could to the small yards at Wollaston and watched the fishermen work at calking or mending their hulls. In the swamps one could hunt snapping turtles all summer and in the autumn, mushrooms and nuts on the flaming hills. In the marshes were minnows to be netted. How close the earth and how close the sea! The smell of sweet fern in the scorching summer noon, of new-mown hay, of low tide on the marshes. The hot pine woods gave off their breath, rising to his nostrils. The boy John Adams breathed the countryside, lived it, knew it with his ears and eyes and nose and all his senses.

What, compared with this, were books and learning? On the beaches of Wollaston John forgot the prison house of school. More and more he stayed away and, when nothing happened, became greatly daring. Mr. Cleverly, quite aware of the situation, preferred to overlook it; it was easier not to call the roll too closely. *Things* —the bright and vivid things of earth—these were what took up John Adams's days. "Little boats," he confessed later to a cousin, "watermills, windmills, whirligigs, birds' eggs, bows and arrows, singing, pricking tunes. . . ."

John Adams watched the world about him, learned its daily, homely message and found that message good.

John at church. He hears talk of politics both Dissenting and Episcopal. Introducing some Braintree preachers and, indirectly, Colonel Quincy and the Boston Adamses.

IF he was familiar with the things of earth, young John Adams was on astonishingly familiar terms also with the things of heaven and hell. Not only on Sundays and sermon days were John and his brothers instructed in religion. Morning, noon and night, on weekdays and holidays they were fed with the very milk of the Word. As deacon of the church, Mr. Adams sat on the honored bench under the pulpit with Great-uncle Peter, Colonel Quincy, Moses Belcher, Cousin Jonathan Webb and the ruling elders. The sight of these venerable heads in their familiar, holy place made John comfortably sure of what God looked like, comfortably sure that things would never change. Boys could grow to manhood, make their fortunes, sail perhaps to foreign lands and come home again to find these fathers sitting before the pulpit, sign manifest that right was right, virtue rewarded and the evildoer inevitably punished.

Mr. Adams himself would have said that to sit on the deacons' bench was far less important than to fear the Lord and do His bidding. But if he feared God in the old grim Calvinist way, Mr. Adams also loved Him in his heart and greatly desired his sons, he said, to have this sweet inheritance. He went about giving it to them in the directest way he knew, which was by constant exposure. Sabbath commenced at noon on Saturdays. On Sunday there was a service morning and afternoon, with sermons lasting from two to four hours,

and hour-long prayers heard standing — to kneel would have been popery. Small Elihu was permitted to sit with his mother, her warm skirts pulled over his knees. John and Peter sat in the gallery with the other boys, squirming, pushing their neighbors, shuffling their frozen feet — in winter the Meeting-house was cold as the jail. The Communion bread froze solid; when the Reverend Mr. Hancock broke it into the plate it rattled sadly, an awesome sound. On the gallery steps lurked the tithingman, ready with his stick when the boys became noisy or when stray dogs — oh blessed diversion! — slipped from their hiding place under the pews.

It would not, of course, have occurred to John Adams to complain of the cold or the hour-long prayers, of the nasal whine, led waveringly by the elders, that passed for psalm singing. Man, woman and child, it was a congregation to whom hardship was as natural as work, endurance a part of religion. The Meeting-house was not beautiful. It was bald and brown and plain. White-painted pews, mahogany guard rails, were in the future. The beauty of God's house lay rather in the spirit of man, in the upward surge of his most humble prayer and in the very comfortable assurance of God's present answer. If Mr. Hancock had much to say of hell he had even more to say of heaven; in proportion to the horrors of everlasting fire was the miracle of God's cooling hand. And if the enemy's sword did not forever threaten, forever wound — how then could man know, how recognize when it came, the healing touch of the Dove? The meadows of paradise were not dry, said Mr. Hancock — and said it in a six weeks' summer drought. The fields of paradise and all its pastures were watered by an everlasting wellspring. . . .

How good it was to hear these things! Great-uncle Peter, whose corn had been parched in the drought (it was planted on the hill), moved his head vigorously up and down. Mr. Hancock had baptized all three of the Adams boys, who were "children of the covenant" — born of parents already in the church. Hancock knew everyone in the congregation, their children, their farms, their crops. If on a summer evening the rainbow blazed wondrously above Penn's Hill, Mr. Hancock was sure to mention it as a sign of God's peculiar grace to Braintree. If hail destroyed the corn in the west field, the Adams boys would learn — if they had not been told already by their father — that God was angry with His servant and His servant must submit. And this public notice of one's personal

misfortunes was somehow comforting. In silent rows, men bowed their heads over a neighbor's broken corn, his hay spoiled by rain, his first-born who had died last night of the throat distemper. It was good to feel these prayers ascending, good to share one's sorrows with a Father on high and a neighbor in the next pew.

No community matter was outside the pastor's interest. As election week drew near in May, Mr. Hancock's congregation waited for him to tell them quite plainly which candidates he considered safe and godly men. (Over the border in Connecticut, there was a law requiring this service from the pulpit.) In these matters Mr. Hancock was amenable, glad to follow the advice of Mr. Adams and Colonel Quincy, who were experienced in politics. The Meeting-house was indeed the clearing place for news national and local. Few people saw the Boston newspapers regularly. Braintree was not a compact town; its fifteen hundred inhabitants, divided into three precincts for convenience in organizing the militia, lived widely scattered along the Coast Road. There was no "main street," no busy town center. Across from the Meeting-house on one side was the cemetery, lying naked and unfenced to the highway. To the east were the training field and one or two houses, spaced wide apart. An Episcopal church was to be found nearby with its doors left hospitably open. Not many people went in; Church of England missionaries had not made much headway in Braintree. A little farther south stood the gristmill in a hollow by Town Brook. There was of course the usual smithy, where a farmer or two passed the time of day while waiting for horse or oxen to be shod. Jedidiah Thayer kept a small store in his front room; one could buy needles, pins, a few West India dry goods.

Three taverns marked the crossroads leading out of town, but no stagecoach ran through the precincts, and there was no post office. Letters were carried by one's friends when they walked or rode the ten miles to Boston. In summer the journey was easy, but during the snows, the long spring muds, the town was as shut off as if it had been over the mountains. It was, indeed, quiet beyond imagining. Day after winter day the inhabitants heard no sound but the creak of heavy runners on snow, a driver's voice urging the slow oxen onward. Sunday church was a godsend in more ways than one. Here Mrs. Adams saw her friends and listened eagerly while Mr. Hancock read aloud the Governor's proclamations, warnings in

a smallpox year, details of local shipwrecks, criminals and crimes. "We hear from Topsham to the eastward," Hancock would begin, reading from his notes, "that on the twenty-sixth of August past, the Indians killed four men of that town within twenty rods of the garrison, and having scalped them, walked off in a very leisurely manner. They took a boy prisoner and scalped also a woman whom they left for dead, but she is on the recovery and like to do well. . . . O Lord," finished Mr. Hancock, "make us to see our end and the measure of our days, that we may know how frail we are."

When a marriage was proposed between the French Dauphin and "the Infanta Maria Antoinetta of Spain," Braintree congregations heard about it and shook their heads at this evidence of further alliance between popish enemies. Their pastor read aloud bits of important letters from England, France and Spain; all three countries, in 1747, were still busy fighting their war over the Austrian throne. Russia had come into it, under the Empress Elizabeth, and was ranged on England's side. New England always relished Russian news. Muscovian forests, it was said, were like our own forests to the westward, and about this beautiful barbaric empress and her wicked lovers the Shubins and Razumovskis there was a splendor that rolled pleasantly on New England tongues. To draw a pulpit moral was easy and took nothing from the story.

What sense of history young John Adams had, came not from the Latin School or Mr. Cleverly. No book of history entered those doors, and if Cleverly spoke of government it was the government of Greece or Rome. John Adams learned his English history at home, from his father's stories of the past, his father's part in local government. Or he learned it at church. In church there was a continuity; past and present merged, the stream was somehow bridged. The wanderings of the Israelites, as Mr. Hancock described them, were the perilous brave voyages of one's Puritan forefathers; the landing on Braintree beaches was the entrance, after persecution, to the promised land. The very psalms, as John sang them, seemed of today not yesterday:

> O give ye thanks unto the Lord,
>   Because that good is he;
> Because his loving-kindness lasts
>   To perpetuity.

So let the Lord's redeem'd say; whom
He freed from th' enemies' hands;
And gather'd them from East and West,
From South and Northern lands.

Then did they to Jehovah cry,
When they were in distress;
Who did them set at liberty
Out of their anguishes.

In such a way that was most right
He led them forth also;
That to a city which they might
Inhabit they might go.

O that men would Jehovah praise
For his great goodness then;
And for his workings wonderful
Unto the sons of men.

That was Psalm 107; it was Great-uncle Peter's favorite. Great-uncle Peter, born under a Stuart king, said he knew what persecution meant, even in North America. He had been a man grown when England, by the Glorious Revolution of 1688, rid herself of the Stuarts and put a Protestant ruler on the throne. But the danger was not over. Twice in this very century, the Stuarts had gathered their followers and fought to win back the crown — in 1710 with the Old Pretender and lately with Bonnie Prince Charlie. When the rebel lords of 1745 were captured — tried — hanged — drawn — quartered — Great-uncle Peter followed every detail of their punishment with a relish that at the same time awed and fascinated young John Adams, to whose generation Stuart tyranny was an old, forgotten tale. The Young Pretender — Bonnie Prince Charlie — *the king-over-the-water* — to John there was romance in the very names!

But when Mr. Adams talked about the Stuarts his face was grave, John noted, and he spoke of them not as the romantic past but as present danger. Had not Massachusetts been founded by men who left England to escape Stuart rule? . . . *Who did them set at liberty / Out of their anguishes.* Great-uncle Peter knew about those

anguishes, he said. He knew about James II and his infamous judge, Lord Jeffreys, who had made a travesty of British justice. Did Johnny realize, old Peter Adams demanded fiercely — did Peter realize — yes, and little Elihu too — what it meant to be a freeborn Englishman, free of Rome, free to worship as one chose, with no interference from Pope or crown? Let Spanish peasants, let miserable Frenchmen live in servile captivity to their Philips and Lewises. We, said Great-uncle Peter, *we* enjoy the liberties of Englishmen!

Mr. Hancock in his pulpit went even further. Massachusetts, he reminded his congregation, enjoyed all the privileges of the British constitution, plus her own charter. "Our invaluable Massachusetts charter," said Mr. Hancock proudly, "secures to us all the English liberties, besides some additional privileges which the common people in England have not."

When Mr. Hancock[1] died and the very young Reverend Lemuel Briant took his place, John Adams heard, if anything, more history than ever. Lemuel Briant was in his twenties and fresh out of Harvard. Had Mr. Adams or Great-uncle Peter dreamed how advanced in doctrinal views was their new shepherd they would have left the church before they elected him pastor. They looked on him as a young man of great powers with a slight tendency to wild talking that years and environment would soon control.

Lemuel Briant was, in fact, a free-will man who believed his neighbors could get to heaven by good works alone, dispensing altogether with the public avowal of faith and revelation that was the very core of Calvinism. John Adams and his brothers looked forward to these public confessions in church. Three times, young women had fainted when they rose to speak; it was exciting, and much relieved the general monotony.

If Lemuel Briant disliked this somewhat brutal evangelism, if he was repelled by the old Calvinist doctrine of determinism and hellfire, he did not say so at first; he had sense enough for caution. Infant damnation, salvation by election, were subjects too dangerous by far. Mr. Briant, eschewing the matter of tyranny in heaven, dwelt learnedly and even passionately upon possible tyranny on earth, instructing his parishioners as to the meaning of civil liberty, the divine right of resistance to civil tyranny. How were Englishmen governed? Mr. Briant demanded, leaning forward, his thin young hands grasping the pulpit rail. By His Majesty King George the Second —

and long might he reign! By the will of Parliament, yes. But above and beyond this was another, greater will, another law. God's law — *natural law*, the law of the people, granted them by heaven. Alone among governments of the world, the British constitution was founded not on the hereditary power of kings, but on a compact made originally between God and Moses or between God and man. This compact was the glorious inheritance of Englishmen. This was the people's law! And it was higher than parliaments, higher than kings. If Parliament and King did not obey, men had a right to rebel.

Mr. Briant's texts were biblical, but for proof he went to civil charter and statute, quoting John Locke and Milton — Sidney, Hooker, Hoadley, the great thinkers and martyrs of English liberty. Of Magna Carta he spoke often with a stubborn, joyful pride as though he himself had signed it. In reality, young Briant knew very little of what Magna Carta actually had meant to the barons of the thirteenth century. But to him and his Braintree parishioners, Magna Carta was a seal, a symbol of British freedom.

And if Briant's texts were historical, confirmation lay in all the air about him. On Boston streets this January of 1748, strange things were happening to freeborn Englishmen, things Mr. Briant declared foreign to the spirit of Magna Carta and the rights of British citizens under the constitution. The King's Navy being much depleted of sailors by French capture, His Majesty's lieutenants saw fit to kidnap Massachusetts citizens right off the streets of Boston, fling them in the black hold of frigates and put out to sea. Boston, in short, was experiencing what it called "a hot 'press." A British captain named Knowles, insufferably arrogant and very daring, had seized men in broad daylight, carpenter's apprentices and landsmen as well as sailors. Boston had fought back; the rioting lasted for weeks. Governor Shirley called out the King's troops. The very sight of them enraged the people; the Governor's mansion was threatened, then the Governor himself. Shirley was forced to flee for safety to Castle Island in the Harbor — an awful scandal against His Majesty's government.

Everyone in Braintree talked about it. In Lemuel Briant's congregation, young Gideon Newcomb sported a black eye, acquired when he drove a sled-load of fuel to Boston and was swept in spite of himself — he said — into the fighting. He had knocked down two British sailors, he added with satisfaction.

Nobody considered for a minute that Gideon Newcomb, in fighting the impressment evil, had raised his hand against King George. From Colonel Quincy to young John Adams, the congregation would have been horrified at the thought. This whole affair was, quite obviously, a case in point for the doctrines of civil liberty that Lemuel Briant was at such pains to define. If the King's power — ashore or at sea — was used tyrannically, to make slaves of British freemen, then it was the duty of British freemen in Boston or in Braintree to resist. King George himself would approve such resistance; Lemuel Briant was sure of it and so was his congregation. If the King's representative — the Royal Colonial Governor Shirley — misused his authority, Massachusetts was confident she had only to appeal directly to His Majesty, and all would be righted. Appeal and answer would take four months at the least. Meanwhile, one resisted.

New England had unbounded confidence in its King. He was their father, their ultimate champion in all matters of freedom and the fundamental rights. Not a man or boy in Braintree but would have used his fists to prove it. Braintree celebrated the King's Birthday with cannon bursts and the drinking of innumerable toasts, not to speak of Coronation Day each June. Royal fêtes at Windsor Castle, royal funerals or weddings were given whole pages in Boston news sheets. When King George's daughter married the Prince of Orange, Mrs. Adams of Braintree knew to marvelous exactness the costumes of the bridesmaids and which noble lord it was who had twenty-four diamonds for buttons.

John Adams grew up proud to be an Englishman. He had never seen a Frenchman or a Spaniard; automatically, they were to be despised. Hatred for the Pope he took for granted and in the Church of England lurked continual danger. These were the larger issues; for John Adams they were entirely uncomplicated. When Braintree's Episcopal church had been built in the 1720's at the instigation of Governor Shirley and the royal colonial party, Braintree was horror-struck. There being no Church of England rectors available, a Braintree man was dispatched to London for ordination. Great-uncle Peter gloomily foresaw an onslaught of lawn sleeves, incense, duckings, crossings, cringings, pardons-for-a-shilling, and all the things he said his forefathers had left England to escape. Most certainly, Christ Church would be the opening wedge. Next thing,

an Episcopal bishopric would be established in North America, taking its orders from crown and Canterbury. What then would become of the essential freedoms, of that separation of church and state which was the Dissenter's cardinal principle of liberty? Johnny's father and uncles feared an American bishopric even more than they feared the armies of France. A man could fight the French and Indians, could go out in the woods and avenge scalp with scalp. But if crown or Canterbury laid hands on the New England Dissenting church, there would be nothing for it but to leave home and migrate to the mountains and a new wilderness.

The Church of England had a powerful organization, called "the Society for the Propagation of the Gospel in Foreign Parts." It was a missionary organization for the making of good Episcopalians; the very name of it infuriated New England. Foreign parts, indeed! Braintree especially was sensitive. Were they, then, rude settlers living in tepees like the savages, that "missionaries" must be sent among them? A century ago their own ancestors had settled this country — missionaries themselves of the first water. With what blind and maddening arrogance the Church of England sent out its mandates!

But these high mandates and this Episcopal missionary zeal got nowhere; even Great-uncle Peter acknowledged it. No bishop appeared. Between Christ Church and the First Congregational Parish of Braintree, the division remained as plain, as unmergeable as the two sides of the Coast Road. It was a division social as well as theological. Governor Shirley had a summer mansion in Braintree; on Sundays he walked to Christ Church with his lady, splendid in a wine-colored coat, gold lace, gold-laced hat and white silk stockings. After all, it was pleasant to greet the Governor's splendid party and return His Excellency's bow with a touch of the finger to one's forehead.

John Adams's cousins and uncles and all the farmers, artisans and small traders of Braintree were Congregationalists to a man. The Church of England made up the aristocracy — landed squires like the Vassall family, rich West India planters who owned a mansion in Boston and a summer place in Braintree with rooms paneled in Santo Domingo mahogany. They had black slaves to wait on them — Pompey and Scipio, Psyche and Flora and Duchess; John Adams knew them all by name. Dr. Miller himself, rector of Christ Church, had a black boy named Cesar who followed after him through the streets, carrying the big parish Bible.

Although Braintree hated on principle the Church of England, there was no dislike of these Episcopal squires. They spent their money freely, lived well and laughed easily. They dressed in scarlet and gold, sent their sons to be educated in England. "Home," they called it, although many of them had never been to England. Or their sons went to Harvard, where they kept their favorite saddle horses and accepted as their due certain privileges of rank and social standing. The wealth of these families lay not in pasture, plows, oxen, smith or shop but in ships, commerce, foreign trade and foreign lands. One and all they belonged politically, of course, to the Governor's party, the party of King's Councillors and royal appointees. The Court party, it was called.

In New England it was natural that the propertied Episcopalians should stand for sound government and things as they were, leaving radicalism to the Dissenting faiths. The Church of England was homogeneous, doctrinally solid, perfectly secure in its theological principles. To Mr. Adams, observing this, it was a matter of regret that his own party was perpetually disturbed by factions. Within the Dissenting structure raged battles as bitter as any in Calvin's own hell. Since the great religious revival of 1735, New England had been torn and rent by these schisms. There were Old Lights and New Lights, Quietists, Enthusiasts, Separatists, Strict Congregationalists, Arminians, Socinians, Anti-Trinitarians, Antinomians. Braintree parish was well within the battle line; in Mr. Adams's house his sons heard angry ecclesiastical meetings, heard their parents discuss these matters when the elders were gone. At the age of twelve, John knew only that his father was right and the others — of course — wrong.

There was in truth a vitality in these Dissenters that flared and blazed with unquenchable fire. Individualistic to the core, each man would have burned for his own particular doctrine. The New England Calvinist, having been, as he considered it, hounded out of Europe for holding certain views, was determined to think for himself, make henceforth his own theological mistakes. More than he feared hardship, hunger, Indians, disease or war, he feared that someone would step in, tell him what to think about God and force him to think it. This viewpoint the New Englander called liberty of conscience, freedom to worship as one chose. What it resulted in was intolerance as rabid as any the immigrants had themselves

suffered in Europe. Because any theological deviation represented a threat to the new establishment, persecution became a virtue, intolerance a synonym for loyalty. Baptists had been banished, Quakers whipped at the cart's tail or hanged on Boston Common. Braintree still remembered how the Reverend Mr. Wheelwright, brother-in-law of Anne Hutchinson, had been forced out of his pastorate at Wollaston; in the end he left the Province. These things had happened long ago, but the spirit that prompted them was yet alive.

The New England Calvinist loved order, obeyed the law and had little complaint to make against the social system of Old England that came with him across the ocean. He did not, after the fashion of the later frontiersman, define "freedom" as a poor man's opportunity to rise above his neighbor. Indeed, the Braintree cobbler who turned out in laced hat and sword was derided, sneered at as a man who neither knew his station nor had the sense to take a proper pride in it. There was to be found in rural Massachusetts of the 1740's little resentment against what a man still called his betters.

John Adams, then, grew up in a community fiercely individualistic in religion, with a tradition that a man must die rather than submit to authority from Rome or from the Church of England. Yet this ferocious independence did not push beyond religious boundaries. There was no social revolution in Braintree and no need for it. Men owned their land, decided their taxes themselves in town meeting, appointed their own constables for collection and determined the penalties for infraction of laws.

In the actual governing of Braintree township, sectarianism was overlooked. Episcopal voters had their say as fairly as Congregationalists. Side by side in town meeting with the Adamses, the Marshes and the Fiskes, there sat the Episcopalian Millers, Vassalls, Cleverlys. Braintree had only one important squire who was a Congregationalist: Colonel Quincy of Mount Wollaston. Like the Adamses, the Quincys had been original settlers of Braintree, and for the last twenty years, Colonel John Quincy had represented the township in the Massachusetts General Court. Quincy was Colonel of the Suffolk Regiment — covering the whole County of Suffolk, of which Braintree was part. It was a very important post indeed; Mr. Adams served for a long time as Lieutenant under him. There was, in fact, no larger political figure in the township than Colonel Quincy; his estate comprised two hundred acres and he was on

familiar terms with the Governor and the Court party. He was said to be descended from the Norman *Sieurs de Quincy,* but his Congregationalism was unimpeachable by birth as well as conviction; he was the great-grandson of Thomas Shepard of Cambridge, most beloved of Massachusetts preachers.

Colonel Quincy looked the part and acted it too. There was nothing citified about him, none of the London elegance of Governor Shirley and his entourage. John Quincy was bluff, hearty, the very picture of a country squire, with his robust color, his strong, stout body and the way he sat his horse. The big mansion on the hill above Wollaston beach had its doors always open to a neighbor; food was plentiful, lavish, and came off the land. There was a flourishing tribe of Quincys, all busy in town affairs. Mr. Adams and the Colonel met in church and town meeting on terms of mutual respect and mutual liking. At election time especially, the Colonel was apt to send for Mr. Adams, pray him to ride over to Mount Wollaston for a pint of ale and a conference.

Mr. Adams's own political activities ran deep rather than wide. He too had been in local politics for over twenty years, but his ambition stopped short at the limits of Braintree township. He had no desire whatever to go on to Boston and the General Court with Colonel Quincy. The General Court was, of course, "The Great and General Court of Assembly" — the Massachusetts Legislature.

Massachusetts politics were still highly sectionalized. The counties that led the Province — or tried to lead it — were the thickly populated Middlesex and Suffolk,* comprising Boston, Cambridge and adjacent towns. England was doing all she could to keep manufactures from starting up in the colonies. But in Boston there was already a kind of industrialism. The mechanics and artisans, the men of ropewalk and shipyard had their secret clubs which were becoming a power in Boston politics. They were the radical element, the men who defied the royal government in the impressment riots and who in 1741 had stood behind the Land Bank. At their head, prime friend and organizer, was Captain Samuel Adams, second cousin to Mr. Adams of Braintree.

It was a strange kinship. The two men had little in common beyond their name and a deep loyalty to the Congregational religion. Mr. Adams of Braintree, like most of his country neighbors, looked

* Braintree (Quincy) is now in Norfolk County.

on city politicians as troublemakers, disturbers of good government. Boston men were uppity, all-knowing, and showed it. Captain Adams had even started a weekly newspaper, the *Independent Advertiser*. Joseph Marsh had got hold of the very first issue, in January of 1748, and sent it up the Coast Road to Mr. Adams. It was a bold-looking sheet, with an engraved female figure of Liberty at the top; its purpose was announced as nothing less than *to defend and state the Rights and Liberties of Mankind*.

Mr. Adams found this irritating in the extreme. "I see Cousin Adams of Boston has appointed himself to save the country," he remarked to his wife, folding the sheet sourly. It was well, he added, that the identity of the editors was guarded; government would not be grateful for this "salvation." Rumor had it that Captain Adams's son Samuel — Harvard, 1740 — was in the venture too. Mr. Adams told John he need not bring this *Advertiser* again from Mr. Marsh. The *Evening Post* had been good enough for him since 1700 and it was good enough for him now. He more than half suspected Joseph Marsh of sympathy with these defiant city schemers who were so eternally critical of the royal Provincial government. Cousin Adams of Boston had lost every cent he owned in the Land Bank swindle of '41.[2] Must he continue to support every antigovernment move the Boston people devised?

The boy John Adams had never laid eyes on his Boston cousin Samuel, who was thirteen years his senior, a Harvard graduate and a man in politics while Johnny was still struggling with Mr. Cleverly and the Latin School. Local Braintree politics was another matter. John took it for granted that one's father should be busy at election time, concerned over votes and assessments, over the question of the town lands. Should they continue to be held in common or distributed privately? The discussion was warm. The younger citizens said private ownership would increase productivity; people worked harder on their own land.

Mr. Adams had in truth an affinity for political responsibility, a gift for managing men. Colonel Quincy, nominating him for town constable, said Mr. Adams was the only tax collector he knew that could make a man smile when he handed over his money. It was not an easy office; most constables bought their way out of it. The five-pound fine was nothing compared to what one forfeited in making up uncollected monies.

Mr. Adams never bought his way out of it, and never lost money either. There was about him an honesty frank, deep-rooted, and somehow contagious. He had no trace of the pompousness so characteristic of small officialdom. By the time he was forty, Mr. Adams was bald to the ears. Going his rounds as tax collector, on warm days he had a way of taking off his wig and walking in a man's gate with his head as round and naked as a duck's egg. On the doorstep he would pause to put his wig on again; he was a man who believed in decorum. The wary taxpayer, opening the door, beheld Constable Adams with his hand extended, a smile on his face and his wig a trifle crooked. "Well, neighbor!" Mr. Adams would begin cheerfully. "It's tax time. . . . Cider time too, I see." He would lift his nose and wrinkle it, farmer that he was. "I hear you raised a fine crop of apples this year."

How could anyone refuse money to a man like that, whose blue eyes were steady as the everlasting hills and who had indubitably paid his own taxes weeks ago! Joseph Marsh told John that his father was a very Cicero at politics, a local Cicero without tongue, who had no need of oratory or scheming but accomplished his end by — well, merely by fixing his eye on the objective and walking toward it with his quiet, easy pace. If Mr. Adams had had a Harvard education, said Marsh, there was no telling where he would be by now.

Admiration between the two men was by no means mutual. These schoolmasters, said Mr. Adams, these thinkers-not-doers were entirely too glib concerning government and its "mistakes." It was positively dangerous to see two sides of everything the way Marsh did. Why, the man hesitated before setting the eggs under his hens! Should he eat them — should he hatch them? Marsh had changed his mind about being a preacher and changed it about being a physician. The theory of physic was most interesting, he said. But when he got out his scalpel to bleed somebody, he turned whiter than the patient, rushed from the room and out of the house altogether. There was no doubt whatever that Joseph Marsh knew how to get boys into Harvard College, even Mr. Adams conceded it. But Marsh took no interest in the land or anything that grew on it or under it, and did not hesitate to say so. His passionate intellectuality was matched only by the passion of his impatience.

As for politics, Mr. Adams would like, he said, to see Joseph

Marsh in town meeting for a change. Marsh would soon acknowledge that something beyond *talk* was necessary to get things done. Even to build ten feet of fence round the Common, let alone put through the large issues that beset a body like the General Court. Men had to yield, to listen to each other. Marsh would call it compromise, but *he* called it common sense, mutual consideration. It was true that Marsh was not strong physically; he was often laid up with gout or asthma. Such things were hard on a man, made him crotchety and unreasonable. But Mr. Adams was not sure it excused the savageness of Marsh's political talk or the undercurrent of sarcasm that went with it, which to Mr. Adams was distasteful, especially as Mrs. Adams was apt to laugh heartily at it. Mr. Adams found this unaccountable. His wife tried to explain it by saying that Joseph had a turn of phrase that startled her; she had never heard anything like it except from her uncle, Dr. Zabdiel Boylston of Brookline, who after all had moved in London circles and inoculated the royal princesses for smallpox. Men of the world were used to that quick manner of talking, where a person did not actually say out his thoughts but left much to inference and innuendo.

Mr. Adams said nothing to this. Lately, Marsh had been especially vindictive toward the royal government and even critical of the King, who he said was about to barter New England cheap in the European diplomatic market. Mr. Adams had been too busy on his farm, this summer of '48, to follow the foreign news closely. He knew that the War of the Austrian Succession was over and a peace about to be signed. But Marsh implied that England was planning to give Louisburg and all Cape Breton Island back to the French! It was unthinkable. New England blood was shed at Louisburg, nine hundred Massachusetts men were buried there. The mother country would never be so ungrateful; it was almost treason to suggest it.

"The mother country" — Marsh repeated it softly. He had strolled into the farmhouse kitchen one September evening with an arithmetic book for John, and at Mrs. Adams's invitation, sat down for a mug of ale. "*The mother country!*" Marsh, looking over his tankard, lifted one eyebrow in a way he had. "Three thousand miles of water is a long way for parental ties to reach. The umbilical cord is stretched a trifle thin. The peacemakers at Aix-la-Chapelle are not endeavoring to strengthen it. *Asini bipedes,* all of them. . . . Johnny, you know the Latin for two-legged jackasses? Spoiling one

country to enrich another — Ah, neighbor Adams, what deep mines men dig for gold! The mother country, you were pleased to call her. Shall we say — I am aware, Mrs. Adams, of straining my metaphor. Shall we say the child America is about to be abruptly weaned?"

CHAPTER FOUR

England signs a peace treaty and New England raises furious protest. "Britain's debt." John experiences a change of heart.

Concerning Louisburg, Joseph Marsh had prophesied truly. Late in the autumn, news came that a peace had been signed between England, France and Spain. At Aix-la-Chapelle, statesmen had bargained and swapped the territory of Europe with as little conscience — even Mr. Adams admitted it — as horse dealers at a fair. Most unforgivable of all, in exchange for Madras, a mere trading post of the East India Company, Breton Island had been restored to the French.

To Massachusetts, it was an outrage. The Province had lost some seven thousand men in this war, counting sickness and the epidemical fever brought home by the soldiers from Louisburg fortress. Great areas of farm land lay waste and uncultivated. Massachusetts was so depleted she had scarcely strength left to defend, she said, her own frontiers. Did London think, because a "peace" had been signed in Belgium, that the Mohawks around Albany would lay down the hatchet and become suddenly as tame as Delawares? The war was over but the enemy threat remained. Yet when a peace was signed and settlement made, New England was not so much as considered, let alone consulted.

After such treatment, what did Massachusetts, what did Braintree care for European kings and their European bargains? Sam Adams's paper was bitter: "Louisburg — a Place of Equal Importance to the Nation with Gibraltar! Louisburg, gained at the Expense of New

England blood, with the Ruin of half the Estates throughout the Province, is again to return to its former Masters as an equivalent for the Netherlands which is to our Nation NO EQUIVALENT AT ALL. I hope it will not be criminal in us to grieve and mourn our Country."

Our Country meant, of course, Massachusetts. Grief for his "Country" had made Sam Adams very daring; the umbilical cord was stretching perilously thin. Feeling ran high in Braintree as in Boston. Veterans from Louisburg swore they would fight no more for a mother country that bargained away the fruits of their toil and danger. The contemptuous indifference England had shown at the peace table was everywhere evident. British ships were anchored in the Bay below Colonel Quincy's farm; officers who came ashore were insolent, deliberately ignoring the most important social gradations as though New England men were so many head of cattle, one like another. They treated Colonel Quincy himself, people noted, with no more respect than they used to a green apprentice boy. The colonelcy of the Suffolk Regiment carried, to these whippersnapper British lieutenants, no more honor than the trade insignia of a blacksmith. Had the British Navy forgotten already that it was *our* militia, *our* seamen who dragged the guns uphill at Louisburg?

And what about the regimental commissions Massachusetts deserved and had waited for so long? Obviously, they had all been disposed of in England. Only one North American had been properly rewarded for his part in the campaign. William Pepperell of Kittery, Massachusetts,* merchant, and commander of our forces at Louisburg, was now Sir William, the first American-born baronet. It was humiliating. Massachusetts should already have flowered with baronets. "Strangers," exclaimed Sam Adams's paper, "reaped the reward! What an infatuation have we been under, when we who are the poorest of the King's Provinces, have been infinitely lavish with our Men and our Treasure!"

It was incredible that England would treat us so shabbily. And if Massachusetts was to have no share in the honors of conquest, then the least England could do was to pay back the money the Province had squandered on the Louisburg expedition — two hundred thousand pounds. "Britain's debt," Massachusetts called it. The Province was all but bankrupt. The government, trying to ease the situation,

* Now Maine.

flooded the country with paper money. Farmers, bringing their grain to market, never knew if they were to be paid in bills of the old tenor, the middle tenor, or the new. Trade was at a standstill; Boston shipwrights and mechanics were laid off by the hundreds and roamed the streets, looking for trouble. The *Independent Advertiser*, always the people's friend, printed angry verses:

The Sailor's Consolation upon the Prospect of a Peace

> Tho' Peace may discharge all our hands at a Jerk,
> And Trade may be wanting to set us to Work,
> Two Choices, my Lads, we shall have in reserve, —
> As Pyrates to hang, or as honest Men, starve.

As in all times of financial panic, a few men rolled up fortunes. Sam Adams's paper had an article about it. "Concerning Liberty and Equality," the piece was called, and it was far more outspoken than Mr. Briant had ever been in Braintree pulpit. The article was directed not against England or the Royal Colonial Government, but, quite simply, against the rich. "In every country and in every Government," it began, "particular Men may be too Rich." In itself this was an extraordinary notion, especially as the article mentioned no names, accused no one of dishonesty or peculation. It hinted that private wealth was a public concern; it even suggested that the Massachusetts Legislature should make public inquiry into private fortunes: "Certain monstrous, well-known fortunes," said the article, "that have been raised out of the Publick." And if anyone should put the question, Is it a crime to be rich? . . . "Yes!" answered the *Advertiser*. "*It is a crime to be rich at the Publick Expense, or to the danger of the Publick.*"

It was well that the Samuel Adamses, father and son, kept their editorial identity secret. In government circles — "Court" circles — heads were shaken gravely. Freedom of the press was a cherished British principle, but men could go too far. To quote John Locke on liberty was safe and proper. That pillar of British freedom had been dead nearly fifty years and anyway, he never advocated leveling principles. But if this *Advertiser* was going to stir up the lower classes, something must be done about it. To suppress the paper would not be easy. There was about its editors, whoever they

were, something diabolically clever — a deceptive candor, a trick of following their more daring articles with a letter of apology in the next issue, where the authors hoped they would not be considered "Mobbish or low," and where they declared impeccable loyalty to King George. As for His Majesty's Royal Colonial Government in Massachusetts Bay, the *Advertiser* was ready to defend it with the last drop of ink in the presses. . . .

North America had never seen a newssheet like this. Most newspapers were dry, formal, impersonal. Or they made clumsy attempts to ape the literary style of the London *Spectator*. But the *Advertiser* never fell into this dismal borrowed archness. It was as plain as a morning conversation, and it appealed to the most diverse sets of people. Women, hitherto ignored in editorial plans, liked the advice on *Nursing and Management of Children*, which the *Advertiser* quoted from a pamphlet got out by the Foundling Hospital. What it advised was very new: "Do not bundle up your Baby. Put him in a little flannel Waistcoat without Sleeves, and tye it loosely behind. Leave off his Shoes and Stockings in warm Weather and change his Cloathes every Day. Pay no heed to the old-fashioned Notion that clean Linnen and fresh Clothes rob Children of the nourishing Juices."

There were articles on sporting events in England. Around the docks, Boston mechanics bet high on the lady who undertook to drive her one-horse chair — quite alone — from Bath to London in eight hours. Eighty miles, the course was; she covered it in seven hours and fifty minutes.

There was something comic about South Boston apparently — a place whose name had only to be mentioned to raise a laugh. The *Advertiser*, after a list of solemn statistics, closed with the startling conclusion that there were

Married Pairs in South Boston, in all.............................872.
Married Pairs in South Boston, absolutely and entirely happy........ 9.

Shrewdly interspersed with these gossipy, easy articles were items showing the insolent behavior of British officers on Boston streets; Sam Adams never relaxed his propaganda. The matter of "Britain's debt" was hammered at week after week. Parliament had finally

granted the money. The question now was, How would it be distributed? The Massachusetts General Assembly was discussing the matter; the *Advertiser* printed abstracts of the proceedings, disguising them after the absurd manner of censorship in London newspapers when reporting parliamentary affairs: "The application of the P-rl--m--t--y Gr--t, now depending in our G-----l A------y, is very justly esteemed one of the most critical and momentous Affairs that ever engag'd the attention of the P--v--ce." [1]

Part of "Britain's debt" had actually arrived on Boston's Long Wharf in the shape of two hundred chests of hard Spanish dollars and a hundred barrels of copper coin. This was gratifying, but how would people know what the new money was worth? In terms of Spanish dollars, what would a farmer charge for a bushel of barley, and would his Massachusetts paper bills be redeemed? Farmers continued to hoard their grain, shopkeepers their latest shipments from Europe. One newspaper advertised a *Table for the ready turning of any Old Tenor Sum into Lawful Money. Very useful for Shopkeepers in the approaching critical Juncture of an Alteration of our Medium.* The table was rhymed as an aid to memory. People cut it out of the paper, remarking that a man would have to go to the university before he could do business under rules like these. Its very length was baffling:

A certain Rule & easy too,
To cast old Debts & make them new.

Take any Sum, divide by Ten
And add to that, one Third & then
Cast up those Sums & you will find
Its lawful Money to your Mind.

To make New Tenor lawful, first,
Take half the sum, and then you must
Add Eight Pence unto every Pound,
And so the Lawful Money's found.

To make Sterling-Money lawful,
Add just one Third, it is the Rule.
To make Lawful Money Sterling,
Take off one Fourth, it is the Thing.

The verses ended on an optimistic note:

> And now Old Tenor, fare you well,
> No more such Tatter'd Rags we'll tell:
> Now dollars pass & are made free,
> It is a Year of Jubilee.
>
> Let us therefore good Husbands be,
> And good old Times we soon shall see.

Suddenly, trade revived, confidence returned. Overnight, it seemed to happen. The instant men believed in their money, the counting of it was easy. The General Court, after talking about money for a year, finally passed a currency law. Thomas Hutchinson of Boston framed it. Hutchinson had been part of Massachusetts politics for twenty years, and his father and grandfather before him. He was a Harvard graduate, and rich, with a town house and a country place on Milton Hill which the Adams family passed whenever they rode to Boston. Town radicals mistrusted Hutchinson; the Boston Adamses blamed him for their bankruptcy because he had opposed the Land Bank. Twice, Hutchinson had saved New England's credit and got himself hated for his pains. Nevertheless he continued to advance; he was an ambitious man. This time, the General Court elected him to the Governor's Council. Even his enemies granted that Thomas Hutchinson knew more about finance than anyone in North America.

These events affected Braintree no more and no less than they affected the rest of Massachusetts. Mr. Adams had always been against paper credit, speculation, schemes for cheap money. In times of inflation he put what pounds sterling he had in the chest with the town powder and waited for them to resume value. When Mrs. Adams remarked that a powder barrel was an odd place to store money, her husband replied that if the whole currency system was going to blow up, the pounds sterling might as well go with it. He would leave these matters to the financial geniuses of Boston; the cows gave as good milk whether the pound sterling was down or up. Now that it was up, he could resume his trade of cordwainer; orders for harness were coming fast. His three sons had grown to

such usefulness round the place that he could afford to spend more time in the shop. Elihu at nine could milk a cow as dry as anybody; Peter was inclined to be dreamy but he could dream and pick apples at the same time. As to John, at fourteen he was almost as brisk as a man around the place.

Mr. Adams remarked on these things to his wife one day in August, a couple of months before John's fifteenth birthday. Complacently he added that with money so much easier, he no longer need worry about the bond for John's first year at Harvard. If they sold the Stony Acres —

"The Stony Acres!" Mrs. Adams said. She turned suddenly from her work at the kitchen table. In her voice was an immense scorn. She had heard enough of the Stony Acres these past three years. . . . It wasn't *money* that would keep John Adams from Harvard College. It was the boy himself: He never studied his lessons, never spoke of them, even. When had any schoolbook been seen in this house, saving Hodder's *Arithmetic* that Joseph Marsh had brought? What about Latin? Was his father blind then, with his talk of bonds and Stony Acres? Brisk! John was entirely too brisk about every living piece of business, as long as the business didn't concern the Latin School and the college examinations. . . . Before John was born, he had been destined for Harvard and the ministry. How many years had she heard about it! Did *wishing* put her sister Anne's boys in college? Did it win Joseph Adams his church in Newington, New Hampshire? How could a father be so easygoing where his son's entire future was concerned?

She was no Puritan, Mrs. Adams went on, her voice rising. She had no objection to gunning, sailboating, playing at quoits. Frolics and huskings, dances in the neighbors' barn were very well, provided a boy earned his fun. A boy? John was nearly a man grown! Where did he run to, these long summer evenings? His supper was scarcely in him when he was gone out the door. Gallanting the girls, that's where he was. Many a man married at eighteen — and then what of his career? Merely because John's father hadn't married till after he was thirty didn't mean his son would be equally slow. . . .

Mrs. Adams wiped her hands on her apron, came and stood before her husband. In ten minutes she had given voice to words that had festered in her heart some three years. She was shaken to the core,

yet her husband neither moved nor spoke. She noted, however, that his pipe had gone out; he made no effort to fill it. "What ails the boy?" Mrs. Adams demanded, harshly. "What ails your son? Has he no ambition? Are my sister's boys, are Ebenezer Adams's boys, to be educated at Harvard while John Adams stays here on the farm with no future beyond the cow barns and the tool shed?"

Mrs. Adams turned, walked swiftly to a cupboard, made a furious clatter with pail and dishes and came back, a little more hesitantly, to her husband. "Why do you not speak to him?" she asked. There was, suddenly, a desperate pleading in her voice. "Am I to do it then — his mother? Look at him! I tell you he is a child no longer. Yesterday I saw him tossing hay up to Joe Bass on the cart in forkfuls any man would be proud of. The days are passing. If nothing is done, I tell you, it will be too late."

Mr. Adams rose, his face was greatly troubled. "You need say no more. I have been very negligent. I am greatly to blame. I have favored the boy too much, perhaps."

Mrs. Adams, at this unexpected conclusion to her tirade, this sudden triumph, sank down on the nearest bench, burst into tears and threw her apron over her face. Mr. Adams laid his hand a moment on her shoulder. "I will move forward in this matter," he said. He paused. From back of the barn came the familiar sound of a ball thudding against a bat. Laying down his pipe, Mr. Adams went out the kitchen door.

Walking to the barn, he pondered what he was to say. Surely, it would not be difficult! John was a reasonable kind of person. It was true enough that lessons were never mentioned. Yet to Mr. Adams it had seemed that things were going well enough. Women had a way of digging out uncomfortable situations and harping on them, although it must be acknowledged that Susanna was usually right in the long run. . . .

Mr. Adams sighed. From behind the barn the bat[2] cracked again; there was a roar from John, the pound of running feet. Mr. Adams looked up; his face brightened. The farther he got from the kitchen, the more his spirits rose. Coming round the barn he saw his eldest son, bat in hand, waiting for Peter to retrieve the ball. John was twisting the bat, frowning in concentration.

For a minute or two, Mr. Adams stood watching. His wife had spoken truly, John was almost a man grown. He wasn't tall, not

above five feet six. But his shoulders were heavy, he was well-knit, muscular, very quick and sure in his movements. His color was naturally high; just now his face was red from exertion, his blue eyes blazed. His fine light brown hair had come untied at the neck, the black string hung down his shirt, hair blew loosely round his face.

Mr. Adams knew all at once that if his son would put one half the effort into his Latin that he put into his ball practice, he would be in Harvard in no time. . . . Suddenly, John hit the ball a tremendous crack; it sailed across the field in a straight, low, beautiful line. John, his face radiant, turned to his father.

Just in time, Mr. Adams checked the words *Well done.* "John," he said, "put down your bat. Peter, go to the house. I must talk to your brother. Seriously, John, about your studies. About the university."

John's face clouded instantly; his lips went together. He looked at the ground and did not move. In Mr. Adams's own face the blood rose slowly. Was this what his wife had meant? Was this the silence she had met so long, and was his son about to defy him with this tight-lipped, stubborn look, this wary sudden stillness? Mr. Adams raised his voice. John approached, trailing his bat, eyes on the ground.

"Very well," Mr. Adams said abruptly. "Very well! If you don't care to talk, John, neither do I. Your mother tells me you are behind in your Latin. Very far behind. Is that true?"

"Yes, Sir," John said.

Mr. Adams drew in his breath. "So!" he said. "If you won't study you can't go to the college. That is obvious. And if you don't go to the college, what then do you look to in life? You are nearly fifteen. At fifteen I was doing a man's work on my father's farm."

John stood perfectly still. The thought came to Mr. Adams that if his son did not speak, he would strike him. John thumped the bat against the ground and looked up, his nostrils spread. "Sir," he said, "I hate school. I hate Mr. Cleverly and his books. I don't want to go to the college."

"And what — " Mr. Adams found it hard to get the words out — "what *do* you want then? Put down that bat!"

John let the bat fall, stood stubbornly, hands drawn down at his sides. "I want to be a farmer," he said.

Anger left Mr. Adams as quickly as it had come. A kind of helplessness enveloped him, a panic he had never before experienced with
his sons. A farmer! But of course, he should have seen it. The boy had
it in him to be a farmer, more than either of his brothers. Perhaps he
had known it since the beginning. Perhaps that was why he had
never spoken. . . . To have John by him to the end, taking over,
as his own powers failed, the cares, the heavy labor, the burden. . . .
No wonder his eyes had been blinded; the ways of Satan were de-
vious and subtle. . . .

"No!" Mr. Adams said. He almost shouted it. "No! The farm is
for your brothers. My will is made, my testament inscribed. You
are to be a clergyman, a scholar. Don't you know your duty?"

He looked at his son, over whose face a peculiar expression had
stolen, no longer stubborn but unfathomable as ever. Was it possible the boy had read his thoughts, penetrated this disguise of anger?

"A farmer!" Mr. Adams repeated the words in a tone of deepest
scorn. "What do you know of farming, beyond galloping your colt
around the pasture, scaring the sheep?" He paused. "I'll show you
what it is to be a farmer."

Mr. Adams turned, strode to the house. John, picking up his bat,
walked slowly to the barn.

For the next few weeks, the Adams family lived in a state of siege,
an undeclared conflict that was acutely uncomfortable. John rarely
spoke. His mother made no attempt to intervene. Even Peter and
small Elihu were silent beneath the weight of this feud. Mr. Adams
piled farm work on his son, had him shovel manure by the ton,
take spade and mattock to dig a pond at the brook channel for the
cattle, clear dead trees from the wood lot for the winter's fuel. At
night after supper there was double ox harness to be cleaned and
oiled. One fearful day was spent, from sunup to supper, in the marshes
down by Penny Ferry, cutting grass for thatch. Father and son left
home at dawn, to stand for hours up to their ankles in marsh mud
under a blazing, relentless sun, thrusting their sickles at the tough
salt grasses. Mosquitoes swarmed about their heads and necks. It
was five o'clock before the grass was tied in bundles, the cart filled.
During the whole performance, Mr. Adams spoke scarcely a word,
but bent and swung his blade without surcease, seeming to mind the

mosquitoes no more than if they were so many clouds of mist about his shoulders.

That night, for the first time in his life, John was too tired to eat. After supper he fell asleep on the settle, collapsing suddenly, sprawled half on the floor, his mouth open, his face and lips swollen painfully. He roused to feel his shoulders shaken. "Well, John," his father's voice said, "are you satisfied with being a farmer?"

John staggered to his feet. "I like it very well, Sir," he said.

He walked to the back stairs, turned and stumbled slowly upward.

But even as John fell, half-dressed, upon his narrow bed, he knew he was defeated. He could not live like this, with all the family against him. Elihu himself had turned a reproachful face tonight, his round eyes swimming. Something must be done.

Next day John saw his father go off alone to the barn after breakfast, without a glance at his son, and no word of chores, of thatch or cattle. Mrs. Adams vanished to the cellar with her kitchenmaid to arrange shelves for preserves; the two boys were nowhere to be seen. John felt abandoned altogether. He wandered uncomfortably down the highway toward the village. Abreast of Mr. Marsh's house, for no particular reason he stopped, stood tracing a pattern in the dust with his bare toe. It was vacation time. Marsh's school was closed; the autumn term would begin in a week. An idea crept into John's mind. How fine it would be to go to school to Mr. Marsh! The notion hovered a moment and flitted. John knew his father did not like Mr. Marsh. Yet how pleasant was this old shabby house in the meadow, with the playing field behind! John had often seen Marsh's boys out there after school, kicking the football, or playing at rounders. . . .

In Mr. Marsh's presence nothing was dull, not even Latin. Marsh loved books and learning; so did his two sisters and his mother. Miss Anne had read Lord Clarendon's vast *History of England,* all six volumes. She was forever quoting it, quoting Milton, too. She made even the *Areopagitica* sound enchanting, not to speak of *Paradise Lost.* Old Mrs. Marsh had never learned Latin, and regretted it, she said. She had little tag ends of the language and used them jokingly, with much effect. "*Post nubile Phoebus*" — she would cry out to John on rainy days, from her upstairs window, as he passed on the way from school — "After clouds the sun!"

It had become a little game between them, matching Latin phrases; John searched them out beforehand in his book. He remembered one particular day when Peter and he had stopped in together and Mrs. Marsh called out, *"Par nobile fratrum —* A noble pair of brothers!" John, looking at Peter's streaked and dirty face, his own feet black with dust, had instantly quoted Horace, *"Pulvis et umbra sumus —* We are dust and shadows!" Mrs. Marsh had to have it translated, but Mr. Marsh roared with laughter, clapped John on the back and said the laurels were his by a length.

Standing now in the roadway, John thought of these things. A little path led straight to Marsh's door; the front step was shaded by two great buttonwoods. If the schoolmaster were at home, John knew he would be found back of the house, reading under a tree. . . . It came to John suddenly that his father would let him finish school with the devil himself, provided it got him into college. But perhaps Marsh's classes were full for the year, with no room for a new pupil? Perhaps Mr. Marsh had heard that John Adams was a poor scholar. Perhaps . . .

With his heel, John pushed angrily at a pebble. No matter if he were refused outright, he must talk to Marsh. Where else could he turn? He would not go back to Cleverly and the Latin School, not if he died for it. *I cannot have you confusing Cleverly with Cicero —* Marsh had said — *and the Braintree Latin School with the true realms of scholarship.* John remembered his face as he had said it, thin, pale, twisted with gout. Marsh had sworn outright. "God in His heaven knows the harm a dull schoolmaster can do!"

John's spirits rose unaccountably as he thought of it. He turned and walked slowly up the path. He had no actual plan in mind, no notion of what to say or how to begin. The front shutters were closed against the sun, the house looked empty. Stepping off the path, John walked round to the kitchen door. It was late afternoon, hot and still. High grass hid the playing field; the place had not felt a scythe blade in a month. Under the apple tree a long thin figure was stretched, dozing comfortably, hands under head. Marsh's feet were bare, his breeches buckles loosened at the knee. Across his chest a worn brown book lay open. John recognized it as Ovid. The boy stood perfectly still.

Marsh opened his eyes. "Well," he said easily, without hesitation. *"Amicus humani generis —* friend of man, what divine *afflatus* blows you here?"

John moved his toe in the grass. "*Dormitat Homeris,*" he replied, grinning.

Marsh laughed. "Hardly an answer," he said. "Still, one might call it a retort. Bonus *dormitat Homeris,* Johnny — Even the GOOD Homer nods! Am I, like Aristides the Just, to be grudged my full title by the citizenry?"

John did not speak. Marsh looked harder at him, took the book from his chest, rolled over and lay facing the boy. "Sit down," he said. His voice was kind. "Here, in the shade."

John sat down. From the highway, oxen lowed, and down the hill, frogs began their evening conversation. John crossed his legs tailor-wise, grasped a foot in each hand and rocked a little, forward and back. "Mr. Marsh," he said. "I told my father I would not go to the college. I said I hated books. I hate books and I hate Mr. Cleverly. It is true." John spoke slowly, his face very serious. He glanced away, then let his eyes meet Marsh's. "I want to be a farmer," he said abruptly, in a loud voice.

It was not what he intended to say at all. But to John's astonishment, Marsh did not appear in the least shocked by this extraordinary announcement. "A farmer?" he repeated. "Splendid! You will be able to tell me why my apple trees bear nothing but leaves. And will Harvard College prevent your being a farmer, pray? Dr. Wigglesworth, Professor of Divinity, has the two best milch cows in the Province. I told you not to confuse learning with Cleverly. Dr. Winthrop the astronomer has the noblest, nimblest wit in two continents. Will you be less of a farmer after making his acquaintance? He has a telescope twenty-four feet long. He will show you the planets in their orbs . . . Venus, and Mars. Saturn with its rings — the whole sky."

Marsh threw out his arm in a wide gesture. "Dr. Winthrop is father to mathematical inventions that Mr. Hodder, yes, and Jehiel Newcomb too, would go pale to contemplate. You have a turn for natural philosophy, John. Before relinquishing the university altogether, you might ask your mother's Uncle Boylston to show you Winthrop's apparatus chamber in Harvard Hall. He has a brass quadrant two feet across that belonged to Dr. Halley himself. He has instruments for surveying that the Braintree town fathers could use to much advantage — if they knew trigonometry from corn."

Marsh got up, dusted off his breeches. John rose with him. "Mr.

Marsh!" he said. "Will you take me in your school? Will you let me finish my schooling with you? That is what I came for, today." He repeated it. "That is what I came to ask you."

Marsh stooped, retrieved Ovid from the grass. John's breath was tight in his chest, all his body rigid. "Why yes, Johnny," Marsh said easily. "You may come to me to school. Of course your father desires it?"

Without waiting for a reply, Marsh turned to the house. His breeches dangled below his knees; the bare shanks were long and hairy. John stood as if rooted, his mouth open like an idiot, incapable of speech or motion. The ease of his triumph was incredible, he could not take it in. His head whirled. Never to see Mr. Cleverly again, never to sit on that bench, staring at a book he knew by heart and hated! . . . The sun danced in the sky, the frogs' croak swelled to a chorus of angels.

Marsh glanced carelessly over his shoulder. "Tell your good father we shall have his eldest son in Harvard College this day twelfth month," he said.

CHAPTER FIVE

John goes alone on a
hazardous journey.

O N June 6, 1751, the Boston *News-Letter* carried the customary annual notice signed, EDW. HOLYOKE, PRES. HARVARD–COLLEGE. . . . "The President and Tutors," it ran, "have agreed to attend to the business of the Examination of Fresh-men, on Friday and Saturday, the fifth and sixth Days of July next."

Far from dreading the day, John Adams looked forward to it. He had worked hard all winter — harder, in fact, than he had ever worked in his life. No miracle had occurred; John had not turned, in ten months, into a passionate booklover. Latin was still mere words on the page, so was rhetoric. John mastered them as he would learn to master a musket, a scythe, using his brain as he would use a muscle and, in spite of himself, enjoying the exercise. What he did, he did for Joseph Marsh. But his tutor never again talked intimately to him. If anything, he favored John less than the others and required more of him. This year, John was the only Braintree boy to take the Harvard examinations; the others were from Weymouth or Dorchester. Some, who boarded at the school, came from as far west as Worcester.

Friday, July sixth, dawned damp and threatening. A mist lay over the marshes; to the west the sky remained dark. John put on his best clothes, ate his breakfast and saddled the little mare which his father, pleased with his progress, had given him in January. John would let no one near her but himself.

He trotted comfortably down the road. Mr. Marsh had promised

to go with him to Harvard, take him to the appointed places and introduce him to President Holyoke and the tutors. They were to spend the night. As far as John could gather, the usual procedure was for a boy to be presented formally to the President and four tutors. Then two of the tutors examined him separately, ending with a final examination by the President. If the candidate was found acceptable, he was given a theme to write at home, the college rules to copy out, and the thing was done.

John tied his mare to the hitching post and hurried to Mr. Marsh's front door. To his surprise, old Mrs. Marsh opened to him. Her son was in bed, she said; his gout had come back in the night. John ran upstairs. Mr. Marsh, sitting up in bed, held his back with both hands. He couldn't dream of going out in such weather, he said. What if it rained? He would be bedridden for life and, besides, he could never mount a horse with this cursed pain. John would have to go alone. . . . And he needn't look like that, Marsh said, a most unusual exasperation in his voice. Nearly two dozen boys entered Harvard every year; he might add that not one trained by Joseph Marsh had ever been turned by. John was to lodge at Mrs. Hill's on the Charlestown Road, near Cambridge Square. He couldn't miss it, the house was painted red and had an odd little cupola. . . .

"What are you standing there for, boy!" Marsh roared suddenly, sinking back in bed, his face twisted. "You look as if all your brains had fled. Get along with you!" Muttering something about being late — as the day wore on the tutors got tired and touchy — better be among the first — Marsh waved his pupil from the room.

In horror, John walked downstairs and out, untied his horse and mounted. She turned her nose homeward; John let her go. The whole winter long, he had never visualized this examination without his tutor. For ten months, what Mr. Marsh told him to do, he had done. Mr. Marsh had led and he had followed gladly. Latin grammar had lost its sting; parsing Virgil with Mr. Marsh was almost a pleasure. . . .

And now, suddenly, there was no Mr. Marsh! He was alone. Why, John thought in desperation, he didn't even know his way to Harvard Hall, where the examinations were held! How would he wash his hands when he got there, where would he go to eat? As for the tutors who were to examine him, he didn't know one of the four. True, he had seen old Tutor Flynt once, at Colonel Quincy's when

he went there with his father. "Father Flynt," they called him; he had taught at Harvard upwards of fifty years and was related to the Quincys. But Flynt would never remember him. What were the tutors' names? Flynt, Hancock, Mayhew, Thomas Marsh. Thomas Marsh was a cousin of Mr. Marsh's. But that would do no good. Mr. Marsh hated his cousin. A psalm singer, Mr. Marsh said. One of your long-nosed Puritans. . . . Just as John left the room this morning, Mr. Marsh had murmured something about having spoken to one of the four tutors about John. . . . Which one was it? John racked his brains. In the confusion, the name had escaped him.

To go through this ordeal by himself was unthinkable. Facing the tutors would be bad enough. As for facing the President alone and unvouched for, John told himself he would sooner face King George II. A very prince among men, Marsh had called President Holyoke. Extremely handsome, with the bearing of a duke and a mind few dukes could equal.

Panic enveloped John. What did most boys do—did they go alone? He had never asked, there had been no need to ask. He would go home, tell his father Mr. Marsh was sick, make it clear he couldn't possibly go alone, that to go alone would be disastrous. He would only fail the examinations and be sent away disgraced.

The road curved, the Adams farmhouse came in sight. John pulled his horse up short. The sight of the low steep roof, the chimney smoking peacefully, brought him to his senses. Go home? It was out of the question! He was committed; for ten months he had been committed. Even if Mr. Marsh died, if he lay right back in his bed and gave up the ghost, he, John Adams, would have to go on to Cambridge. There flashed through John's mind a picture of the winter past, the months of reading, forcing, studying as he had not known he could study. Over it brooded the face of his teacher, pale, dark-eyed. . . .

If he refused to go today, his father would lay the blame on Mr. Marsh, would say he had not prepared John to stand alone. John himself had begged to have Marsh as teacher. It was his own decision. By the same token, this journey today was his own decision.

John Adams swore aloud, a good round oath. Swinging the mare abruptly, he dug his heels into her flanks. She broke into a canter, her nose toward Cambridge.

Leaving his horse at the Cambridge stables, John asked his way to Harvard Hall and went slowly up the steps. He found himself in a large, bare anteroom with a bench around the wall where boys sat waiting; there was a high desk with a man writing. The man wore a scholar's gown; he beckoned to John, told him to take his place with the others. John sat down. Directly opposite was a portrait in a gold frame. It showed a handsome gentleman of the old school, in a flowing wig and preacher's white bib and collar. John decided vaguely it must be Dr. Increase Mather or, anyway, one of the old Presidents of Harvard. Whoever it was, he looked formidable, uncompromising.

John glanced surreptitiously round the wall, counted the boys. Eighteen. He took out his handkerchief, dusted off his shoe buckles. The minute he had done it, the boy next him took out his handkerchief and dusted off his own. A very rash of shoe dusting broke out, all done in perfect silence. There were three doors in the room; it was immediately obvious which one led to the examiners' chamber. John kept his eye fixed on it. It opened. A young man in scholar's gown emerged, spoke to the man at the desk, who nodded to the boy nearest the door. The boy got up, followed the scholar and was instantly engulfed within the door, gone with a horrible finality. Like Jonah, John thought, swallowed into the whale's belly, slipping to strange and awful chambers. . . .

It occurred suddenly to John that his best blue suit with the metal buttons was to the last degree shabby. This morning when he put it on he had thought it very rich and tasty. He hugged his cocked hat under his arm. From time to time he shifted it; he must remember to keep it under his left arm so his right would be free if President Holyoke put out a hand. Did gentlemen in the great world shake hands, or did they merely nod as Governor Shirley nodded to Braintree citizens crossing the North Common on Sundays?

Any minute now, John knew he would be required to prove that he could *extempore read, construe and parse Tully, Virgil or Such like common Classical Authors; write true Latin in prose, be skill'd in making Latin verse, or at least in the Rules of Prosodia; and read, construe and parse ordinary Greek, as in the New Testament, Isocrates or Such like, and decline the paradigms of Greek nouns and Verbs.*

So ran the catalogue; John knew it by heart. But it was not his scholarship John feared today; Mr. Marsh had drilled him until he could answer routine examination questions in his sleep. Concerning these questions, Marsh was, in fact, extremely cynical. *Asinus bipedis* himself could get into Harvard, Marsh said, if he learned the proper tricks; let Johnny not imagine these examinations were a test of true scholarship. Harvard College desired students, they would let in anything with its face properly washed. . . . Marsh had been joking, of course; it was hard to tell if his jokes were truth or nonsense. . . . Mr. Marsh must have meant deportment; the sons of great men in the Province went to Harvard. Distinguished families like the Olivers and Hutchinsons . . . old Governor Belcher's son had gone there.

Looking across the room, John wondered which of these boys might be a Hutchinson, an Oliver, a Winthrop. . . . What if he made a fool of himself, before the tutors and the President? They would know him instantly for the country boy he was. Shifting his hat once more to the other arm, John crossed his feet, rubbed a shoe buckle against his white stocking. Another boy had gone in the door. Nobody came out. Were they examining two at a time? Were all the tutors there together, in that room? John thought again of Jonah, and decided to try prayer. His lips moved. . . .

The boy next him leaned suddenly near, asked John how old he was. "Fifteen," John said. "I'll be sixteen in October."

"I'm twelve," the boy said in a forlorn whisper.

John turned, looked full at him. Why, this was a mere child! Up to now, John had noted only that his neighbor's shoes were of the best quality and his shirt ruffle of finest cambric. Perhaps these candidates were not the young men of fashion and distinction he had imagined? After all, Cousin Joseph Adams had gone to Harvard and so had Cousin Eb. . . .

"Four boys have gone in," the little boy whispered. "I came early. The President went through that door, and the four Fellows. The President is very tall. Old Tutor Flynt's belly rumbled. I heard it." The ghost of a smile played on the little boy's face, and was gone. "You dassent — you dare not sit down with the President. You have to stand up, all the time. Did you know . . ."

The door opened, everyone froze. The little boy nudged John furiously. "It's for you," he said. John started, leaped to his feet;

the guide in the scholar's gown was beckoning. The whale's jaws yawned, and John passed through.

It was a beautiful room, paneled in walnut, with portraits on the walls. There was a big, polished desk; John found himself standing before it. Back of it sat the handsomest man John had ever seen. He wore a wig and black silk robe. Four men, also in scholars' gowns, stood nearby, chatting busily. The student who had led John in, bowed and disappeared. John moved his hat to his right arm, realized his mistake and stood paralyzed, afraid to move it back again.

President Holyoke bowed but did not extend his hand. John, letting out his breath, returned the bow. "Well, well!" Holyoke said, in a great booming voice. He glanced at a list in his hand. "John Adams, is it? Where are you from, Adams?"

John named his town. The President nodded. "Braintree — Ah yes! I have heard of your father from Colonel Quincy of that town. You have had several cousins graduated from the college, have you not?"

John looked up. Why, the President knew his father, knew Eb and Joseph! The four tutors had stopped talking; John felt their eyes on him. These men were not hostile. . . . One of the tutors spoke. "Sir?" John said. He realized suddenly that the question, which was in Latin, had been addressed to him.

Henry Flynt repeated his question. John answered quickly, in the same language. This was old Flynt's perennial joke; Marsh had prepared John for it. The four tutors smiled, President Holyoke smiled. John shifted his weight, stood very straight, looking at Flynt. Hancock put a question about rhetoric — something concerning paradigms. John faltered. "I don't know the answer," he said. His eyes fell, he clasped his hands tightly behind his back. Mr. Marsh had made very little of paradigms. Was this one of the catch questions?

John looked up boldly. "I know which page the answer is on," he said, "if I had the book."

Somebody laughed. The questioning continued; John's answers came more easily. He had almost begun to enjoy himself when Tutor Mayhew came forward. He was tall, gray-haired; Marsh had said he was the best man of the four, and that he would be John's tutor in his Freshman year. John was suddenly sure it was Mayhew that Mr. Marsh had spoken to in his behalf. Mayhew handed John

a paper with a long passage written in English. "Translate it into Latin," he said. The President spoke. "We are a little behind in our schedule, gentlemen. Suppose we let the boy do his translation here, while we proceed to the next candidate? It will save time." He indicated a table in the corner. "There is pen and ink."

John stood motionless. One glance at the paper had shown him a dozen words he could not translate. What was Latin for *morality?* All his new confidence left him. His hands trembled, he moistened his lips with his tongue. Terrified, he looked up, met Mayhew's eye.

Mayhew spoke to the President in Latin, very rapidly. John caught a word or two — *discipulus optabilis* — and Marsh's name. The President waved toward a door. Mayhew took John's arm. "Come with me, Adams," he said. "It will be quieter in my study."

They walked down the hall, turned into a pleasant room all tumbled about with books. The windows were tall and filmed with dust. "Here we are!" Mayhew said cheerfully. "And here is a dictionary. Perhaps you would like this Latin grammar for reference? I myself have never considered that a memory for nouns — especially memory under duress — was a criterion of potential scholarship. Sit here, by the window."

Mayhew turned to the door. "Your schoolmaster, Mr. Joseph Marsh, is an old friend of mine. He has spoken of you. We passed a pleasant evening together only last week. . . .

"It is well not to hurry these things," Mayhew said. "Take your own time, Adams."

He was gone. Drawing a breath that went down to his shoe buckles, John Adams reached for the dictionary.

*Harvard College in 1751. A Freshman
adapts himself to a new world.*

THE *university at Cambridge.* That was how people spoke of it. They called it "the Seminary," too, or "the colleges," which meant the three red brick buildings in which the entire student body — about ninety boys — lived, ate and studied. Harvard Hall, Stoughton College and Massachusetts Hall formed an open quadrangle round a well-trampled court, bare of trees save for one flourishing elm down by the fence.

The Province was proud of the three colleges, which were handsomely designed after the fashion of halls at Oxford and Cambridge, with long corridors upstairs into which the suites of bedroom and study opened. It was part of the English tradition that university students should live like gentlemen, and the founders of Harvard had themselves been university men.[1] In Harvard Hall (the students called it "Old Harvard") was a library of thirty-five hundred volumes, a collection extraordinary for the times. But it was the kitchen and butler's pantry that remained the focus of admiration for the neighborhood. Where else could one see such hearth fires, such monumental cook pots, such handsome large vessels of copper and pewter? Special laws were devised to keep students out of the kitchen, which was the only place in the country, excepting taverns, that was always warm in winter.

West of the colleges was a graceful, sturdy little brick Chapel, lately given to Harvard by a female admirer in London, whose family crest was blazoned in bright colors across the east pediment. Every

Sunday the student body walked out the college gate to worship in the old Congregational Church on the corner. Here Colonel Quincy's great-grandfather, the beloved Thomas Shepard, had once been pastor, and here, in the little burying-ground adjoining, rested men who had founded the Province. New England held no more hallowed spot.

All the way up and down the Charles River, the university owned property. Boston merchants often left Harvard an orchard or a cornfield in their wills. But the immediate ground on which the college functioned was only a few acres, fenced in and known as the yards, for the simple reason that they had once been part of Cowyard Row. This was a succession of fields in which were set down comfortably, without arrangement or design, the President's house, the two professors' houses, the Hebrew instructor's house and the pleasant mansion of the college steward, with its gambrel roof.

The whole establishment gave onto Cambridge Common, where four roads met around the green. Travelers from Boston came over the ferry to Charlestown — a penny if you were alone, twopence for a couple. Travelers from the west came up the Connecticut highway. There was Wood Street, and there was the long, tree-lined lane known as "the Way to the Parsonage." [2] It all looked very rural and neighborly. Harvard professors kept their own chickens and a cow; the President had a hayfield across the lane from his house, mowed during the summer by students. His orchard was fertilized, by generous order of the Corporation, "from the south privy."

Cambridge was, actually, a town no larger than Braintree, with a Common, a church or two, some shops and a tavern. For generations, the population (apart from the college) remained about fifteen hundred. Yet between the two towns was a difference wide as an ocean. Cambridge gave off an air of university distinction, great tradition and large affairs. At Commencement there were visitors from as far south as Philadelphia, not to speak of the Governor and his staff, and important members of the General Court.

For John Adams, it was an extraordinary fortune that plucked him out of a country village at the age of sixteen and set him down to spend four highly impressionable years at Harvard College. Considering the times, the university was astonishingly liberal. In science, or "natural philosophy," Europe itself held no better teacher than John Winthrop, who at thirty-seven was famous for his studies on

the transit of Venus, his observations on sunspots. His work in electricity was followed with greatest interest by Benjamin Franklin in Philadelphia; the two were lifelong friends. Winthrop's lectures were open to the public. And the public, lecture-hungry (Boston forbade theaters), came in droves, and in droves went away unconvinced by the professor's dry explanation of natural phenomena.

On the second floor of Harvard Hall, Winthrop had set up the first laboratory of experimental physics in America. Nothing like it had ever been seen. Boston spoke of it as "the Doctor's apparatus chamber," and looked on it with awe, pride, and, in strict Congregational circles, considerable mistrust. The long pendulum with which the professor demonstrated the new theories of terrestrial motion — was it not a flouting of other and older celestial laws, as described in Scripture? And the human skeleton hanging from the corner — where had Winthrop found it — had he robbed a grave? Surely, it was impious in the extreme so to flaunt these poor remains of man's mortal engine, when the soul that had once inhabited it had even now passed to a most glorious reward!

If it had not been for John Winthrop's name and lineage — as honored as any in New England — it is doubtful if the Massachusetts Legislature, which controlled the Harvard purse, and the Board of Overseers, which controlled Harvard policy, would have allowed the professor as much latitude as they did. John Winthrop was the fourth generation of his name in Massachusetts. His father was a Chief Justice; his great-granduncle had been a distinguished physicist in London, one of the founders of the Royal Society. Harvard had always a Winthrop on its undergraduate rolls; they were well-favored men, of a gentle, distinguished bearing.[3] And they were descended from the first Governor of Massachusetts, a founder of Harvard, whose portrait, dashing in starched ruff and pointed Elizabethan beard, hung in one of the college halls.

Professor John Winthrop, young, eager, possessing the scientist's calm and the scientist's detachment, bore the honors of his name and learning lightly. Graduated from Harvard at eighteen, he had filled the chair of mathematics and natural philosophy since he was twenty-four; the Overseers were quite aware that, if he resigned, there was no one in North America to fill his place. His subjects were mathematics, physics, astronomy and geography. It was difficult for President Holyoke to maneuver his science professor into gown

and wig. In the laboratory, Winthrop wore an old leather artisan's apron that covered his slight body to the neck; his thin fingers were stained with acid. Sometimes he forgot to take his apron off; students, meeting him as he walked homeward in the twilight, doffed their hats to the young savant who was not ashamed to look like a shoemaker.

Edward Wigglesworth, Professor of Divinity, controlled the other half of the Harvard curriculum — or rather, the other two thirds. Wigglesworth directed all teaching of the traditional subjects: Greek, Latin — reading in the classics; logic, rhetoric, ethics. It meant, actually, a division of the university into a college of science and a college of liberal arts, although as yet no one recognized it as such, and there were no elective studies except French. Wigglesworth, much older than Winthrop — he was nearly sixty — was, after his fashion, every bit as inspired a teacher. Deaf, shy and witty, Wigglesworth lived in an old pitch-roofed house east of the President's, with a wife and three healthy sons who could be heard shouting at him from halfway across the Yard. What Edward Wigglesworth had to say was, however, so much to the point that Cambridge was ready to shout for a reply — especially the Harvard Corporation,[4] which fervently desired his practical, common-sense advice, and was ready to ask for it in writing if necessary.

Wigglesworth occupied a powerful position; under his hand was the training of gospel ministers for Massachusetts. The Board of Overseers watched its professor of divinity with a jealous eye. A trifle vague in matters scientific, the Overseers were anything but vague when it came to the intricacies of Congregational doctrine. Thirty years before, they had chosen Wigglesworth for the newly endowed chair of divinity, partly because of his acknowledged brilliance — although even then he was very deaf — and partly because his grandfather was the Reverend Michael Wigglesworth of Malden.

Nevertheless, at his election, young Edward Wigglesworth had been most thoroughly catechized. Half the Harvard Board of Overseers were clergymen. The other half, who put aside theology all week in the rigorous competition of Boston trade, on these electoral occasions resumed a fierce and stubborn orthodoxy — particularly when the election concerned the chair of divinity. (John Winthrop they let off without examination, deciding, on the President's advice, that it was wiser not to press these things too hard with scientists.) Young Edward Wigglesworth stood patiently, his hand at his

ear, while the Overseers shouted at him. Did he assent to the Confession of Faith, according to the Westminster Catechism? And did he approve the ancient, sacred Harvard textbook, Dr. Ames's *Medulla Theologicae?*

Wigglesworth laid his hand on the Bible and swore agreement with the doctrines of predestination, the Holy Trinity, Christ's divinity, and that first and most difficult of Congregational doctrines, "special efficacious grace." Then he repeated his oath to the civil government of the Province and swore that he would "religiously observe the statutes of the Founder and all other laws and orders of the College."

The Overseers departed, satisfied; they seemed to have covered everything. But Edward Wigglesworth, moved to deeper self-examination, pursued his studies further and began to question these matters he had sworn to. Before a dozen years, he was graduating students like Jonathan Mayhew of the Class of '44, forerunner of Unitarianism, who overset the tables altogether and was barred from the Boston Association of Congregational Ministers. Wigglesworth even challenged the Five Points of Calvinism. "Examine these matters for yourselves," he told his students. "Believe in God, but remember it is man who makes doctrine. Think!"

It was a daring course, not easy to hold. Professors Wigglesworth and Winthrop set the tone of Harvard for sixty years — and they set it high. John Adams was wonderfully favored; America had no other institution that could have offered half so much. Only three other colleges existed. William and Mary, in Virginia, was an Episcopal school, serving the Southern colonies only, and as narrow in outlook as any Dissenting establishment had ever been.* The College of New Jersey was frankly revivalist, New Light in tendency, and, besides, it was only four years old. Dr. Franklin's academy at Philadelphia, designed on a broad platform, was as yet totally untried; its doors did not open until the year John Adams entered Harvard.

As for Yale College in Connecticut, it had been founded early in the century by Harvard graduates who viewed with alarm the liberal trend at Cambridge. Announcing itself openly as a seminary for the training of preachers, Yale held to the strictest Congregationalism and showed little interest, as yet, in science and the new experimental method. So Yale's enrollment went up, while Harvard's remained where it was; New England held stubbornly to the old religion.[5]

Harvard owed her liberal tone — and Winthrop and Wiggles-

* Jefferson's liberal Constitution was thirty years in the future.

worth their tenure as professors — largely to the tact and loyalty of President Holyoke, who knew how to persuade the Board of Overseers that Harvard professors had best be left to teach what and how they chose, provided they did not transgress the boundaries of Christian faith. On his election to the presidency in 1737, Holyoke himself had been suspected of doubtful orthodoxy. As a matter of fact he was not only liberal but courageous; the students called him "Old Guts," and it was a term of endearment. Rumor had it that Old Guts could face down, if necessary, the entire Massachusetts Legislature; he had the respect of Governor Shirley and the entire Hutchinson-Oliver tribe of political bigwigs.

Holyoke's Latin was superb; it rolled from his tongue at college ceremonies with a cadence not to be bettered — said Massachusetts — by any of your European scholars. Holyoke enjoyed taking over a class when the tutors were ill or absent. There was nothing that Holyoke did not put a hand to, including the care and cleaning of the clock on the face of Massachusetts Hall. When the clock stopped, the President climbed a ladder to look into it and did not scruple, at the year's end, to swell his very uncertain stipend by accepting, for his pains, twenty-six shillings eightpence, carefully entered in the college ledgers. At any time of the day or evening, Holyoke might be seen striding across the college yards, a large, ruddy man in his early sixties, his gown floating after him, a book under his arm. He wore a long, full, curly wig; over the gown his clergyman's bib stood out immaculate, stiff with starch. Everyone liked him, and everyone looked on him as invincible.

But in the privacy of his household, Old Guts was known more than once to give way. Flinging off wig and bib, he would sink down exhausted after a bout with parents, Overseers or Corporation. It was a dog's life, he told his wife in his loud, hearty voice. He would rather be Moses Richardson, the college carpenter, with no problems beyond where to find shingles for the privy roof. Mortification of spirit, the old Puritans held, was a fine thing; it kept down the sin of pride. "If any man wishes to be humbled or mortified," said Edward Holyoke — and the remark went round all Cambridge — "let him become President of Harvard College."

Of the trials that lay behind the management of the university, John Adams, Freshman, was happily unaware. He would be a Sopho-

more before Professors Winthrop and Wigglesworth admitted him to their classes. And as to Congregationalism, John accepted its tenets as he accepted noonday and the going down of the sun. Entering a new world, it was not for him to question its rules or its philosophy. It was his part to learn these rules, breathe this wider air, discover who, in this habitation of strangers, could be his friend.

Before term began in the autumn, all Freshmen were required to copy out the college laws, bring them to the Bursar and have them signed. Not until then was a boy truly admitted to the university. John did his copying (it was a long, careful job) at home on the kitchen table in August of 1751 after he took his entrance examinations. To his deep dismay, the first thing he saw was that students could not keep a gun. Cambridge countryside abounded in game — rabbit, squirrel, duck and woodcock in season. There were herons in the marshes by the river, and in November wild geese flew over the college chimneys. . . . How was he to exist, John demanded of his father, with birds to shoot and no gun to shoot them with? And see here, where it said that students must not fish, *or scate over deep waters!* What good was the Charles River lying near, with miles of clear black ice, and in summer the most delightful fishing and swimming?

There was page after page of script, divided into eight solemn, burdensome chapters. John read the chapter titles aloud to the family: "Concerning a Religious Virtuous Life." . . . *All scholars*, this chapter began, *shall behave themselves blamelessly*. . . . There was a chapter "Concerning Penal Laws," another "About the Scholars' Commons." There was a whole section "About the Steward, Cook and Butler." The last chapter, "Concerning Miscellaneous Matters," was worst of all: *Students must not go beyond the college fences without coat or gown*. . . .

"If you tell a lie at Harvard College," John said gloomily, "you are fined five shillings. Five shillings if you get drunk, unless it is 'very aggravated drunkenness,' in which case you are expelled." John took up the "Penal Laws" in his hand. "Twenty shillings for playing at cards or dice. Five shillings for frequenting Cambridge taverns. Fighting with, or striking, or willfully hurting any person, five shillings. Five or ten shillings for making tumultuous or indecent noises in town or college Yard. *Five shillings for swearing*."

Mr. Adams remarked that this Harvard education was likely to

prove expensive. John and his brothers had been making tumultuous and indecent noises for some half-dozen years, right here at home. Apparently it required more laws to govern a hundred boys than the whole of Braintree township. "John," said Mr. Adams, "keep the laws until they are proven unjust. Even then, do not disobey. As Constable of Braintree I have noted that rebellion is always extravagant. Prefer your petition, Johnny, and see the unjust laws be changed."

John laughed, but he knew his father was more than half in earnest. He had heard Mr. Adams say this before, when it concerned, not boys at school, but street fights in Boston over impressed sailors, riots in the time of the old Land Bank, matters of life and matters of money. "Your good citizen," said Mr. Adams, "knows that it requires more than riots to mend the law."

These Harvard rulings, John remarked, were out of date anyway. Cousin Nathan Webb, a Sophomore, said they had been composed twenty years ago, when some of the Old Puritans were still on the Board of Overseers. There was more bark than bite to them now. . . . And anyway, John added, with a cheerful rise of voice, the second paragraph of "Penal Laws" said those scholars who lived *within ten miles of Cambridge* could go home four days in a month. He wouldn't miss the fall gunning entirely.

Ten miles . . . ? Mr. Adams repeated. A crow could make it in ten miles over the treetops, but not John's mare Polly. By the road it was twelve miles if it was an ell. Let John tell the Harvard authorities it was ten miles to Braintree, and there went his first five shillings for lying. . . .

This was too much for Mrs. Adams, who, as the time drew near for John's departure, had taken to sudden silences, rapid blinkings, whenever Harvard was mentioned. "Over Milton Hill it is an easy ten miles to Cambridge," she said sharply. "At least, to Zekiel Harmon's smithy, and that is surely within the township limits. Mr. Adams, I will thank you not to conjure up nightmares. Or do you wish to bid our son a final farewell this autumn?"

Term began in mid-August. Mr. Adams drove John to Harvard in the farm cart with his box of clothes and his bedding. The bond of forty pounds was duly given, and five pounds cash paid to the steward. Uncle Joseph in New Hampshire had contributed — and so, surprisingly, had Uncle Ebenezer, who was known as a man that

did not part easily with his money. The Stony Acres had been sold at last. Mr. Adams bade his son good-by on the steps of Massachusetts Hall, where he was to live, then climbed in the cart and drove home, filled with a vast satisfaction. Tomorrow he could say to a neighbor, "I am lately returned from settling my son at Harvard College. He is preparing to be a minister of the gospel like his uncle, Dr. Joseph Adams of Newington, New Hampshire."

John, hedged suddenly with rules, customs, bell-ringings, admonitions and fines, did not stop to mourn or miss his freedom. He was too busy to mourn. Where lessons were concerned, he knew in a week that he was to have no trouble, for the present at least. The Freshman schedule differed little from his studies last year with Joseph Marsh: Latin, Greek, logic, rhetoric, ethics. Freshmen were taught entirely by the four tutors, each of whom, like a grammar-school teacher, took a section of the class through all subjects. John was assigned to Mayhew for the first term, Flynt for the next. Neither man, he soon learned, was as exacting as Marsh had been; after all, Marsh had taken him through two years' work in a winter. The tutors taught entirely by rote; the trick was to learn a page by heart and repeat it. But when he became a Sophomore and entered Winthrop's classes in physics, Wigglesworth's classes in divinity, John knew he would be hard put to it.

Every morning on his way to Mayhew's room, John passed the apparatus chamber on the second floor of Harvard Hall. At the door he lingered, watched Winthrop swing the brass orrery, demonstrate the movements of the heavenly bodies. On the long tables were crucibles and siphons, instruments for surveying and taking the difference of leveling. There was a variation compass, a model of the human veins filled with wax. Over all towered the great telescope, twenty-four feet long, its nose pointed toward the stars. On his first visit home, John talked endlessly of this treasure house. Peter and Elihu listened round-eyed, especially as to the skeleton. Was it a *big* man? they asked. How big? He would measure the tibia and femur and let them know exactly, John replied portentously. At least, he would if the janitor would let him in, sometime when he was alone in there, cleaning. The janitor was a Weymouth man, and very friendly. Next year, John added — *next* year he would have the run of the apparatus chamber. . . .

Next year — to John Adams, at sixteen, next year was as far off as eternity. Meanwhile, he moved cautiously among strangers. In his Freshman Class of twenty-four he knew nobody at all, on arrival. His cousins, the Webb boys, roomed in another hall. John was greatly pleased when Sam Quincy, Sophomore, came to his room not long after term began, with the neighborly purpose of enlightening John as to undergraduate *mores* — what was done and what was not done. Sam was from Braintree, a great-nephew of Mr. Adams's old friend, the Colonel. Lounging easily against the oaken paneling over the study fireplace — "Never mind the college laws," said Quincy, waving a lordly, careless hand. It was the college *customs* that mattered. The Sophomores would read them aloud in a public ceremony next week in Old Harvard. Meanwhile, if John didn't want to be run ragged by the Sophomores, he had best get a Senior protector. He might ask Sam's brother, Edmund Quincy. . . . And by the way, if John Hancock, a Sophomore, told Adams to take his wig to the barber for curling oftener than once a fortnight, let Adams come to *him*, Sam Quincy, and he would deal with the situation. Hancock seemed to have forgotten he was originally from Braintree himself; living in Boston had gone to his head. He had more clothes than anyone in college except a Junior from the West Indies who had arrived with six boxes and enough white linen shirts to dress a regiment. . . .

John listened with all-devouring attention. Quincy had an elegance about him, an impressive worldliness. John longed to achieve it, marked how Quincy wore his gown open, with the red plaid lining showing against his snowy shirt frill. He would wear his own that way, John thought, when he was a Sophomore and had a gown. Quincy left the room and John sat alone, his gaze on the empty fireplace. How endless, he thought, the academic hierarchy, with its mounting, sevenfold tiers! Next above the Sophomores came Junior and Senior Sophisters. Then came the men studying for their Masters' degrees, called Junior Bachelors, Middle and Senior Bachelors. As soon as a Senior Bachelor had recited his valedictory (in March of his last year), he was addressed, after the Oxford fashion, as "Sir." John's lips, in fantasy, already moved to a pleasant cadence: *Sir Adams.*

Above all these, of course, were the four tutors, who were bachelors, lived in hall and looked after discipline. As the Freshmen ranged

in age from Sam Dana, who was twelve (it was he that had spoken to John at the entrance examinations), to Josiah Goodhue, who was twenty-two, Tutor Mayhew, in his comfortable rooms at the end of John's hall, was constrained to act as both nurse and constable. Fines were levied on the older boys for breaking into Mayhew's private ale keg, on the younger for throwing footballs in his study window or climbing on the roof of Old Harvard to pick slate — an occupation which for some reason exercised a fascination over the whole undergraduate body. From the matter of tumultuous and indecent noises, John noted that the college reaped quite a little income. He was shocked at the easy manner with which boys forfeited five shillings or twenty; in the Adams family a cash expenditure of two dollars was discussed for days.

It was no wonder, however, that the college had trouble maintaining discipline. Having laid down laws impossibly severe, they placed some ninety boys under the charge of four overworked tutors whose only hope of peace was in leniency and the half-closed eye. Except for two hours of freedom on the playing field every afternoon, no provision was made for entertainment and the letting out of youthful steam. No female entered the college Yard except at Commencement, when the whole of Cambridge released its Puritan soul in a highly successful saturnalia. John's daily program was monastic in its severity. From five in the morning when the first bell rang, to nine at night when curfew called for lights out, *all scholars*, the laws said, were to *behave themselves blamelessly*.

Yet John felt neither confined nor put upon. If the bell rang at five and he had to rise in the cold dark — why, John had risen in the cold winter dark all his life. He rolled out of bed, flung on his clothes, groped for the fire tongs and coaxed up what embers were left in the study hearth. Then he woke his roommate, wrestled him out of bed, raced him to six o'clock prayers. If city boys complained of these Spartan hours, they were not Spartan to John Adams; after all, it was more fun to wake one's roommate at college than to drag one's brother out of bed and get wood from the shed to start the kitchen fire. . . .

Breakfast in Harvard Hall consisted of bread and beer. John broke his bread into a bowl and soaked it, managing a loaf sometimes, before he was through. Classes began at eight and stopped at twelve for dinner. What mattered it to John that the food was poor? He

could talk all he pleased; there were no parents to shut him up, no little brothers to admonish and hurry. He was waited on by fellow students; the long tables were laid with linen, changed twice a week by order of the Corporation. John ate his pound of meat and vegetables on a pewter plate, drank his half-pint of beer or milk from a pewter mug. (The last generation at Harvard had been content with vessels of leather.) To John Adams the arrangements were elegance itself. At home there was no cloth except for company, and as for mugs pewter or leather, one got used to the sourness. . . .

As soon as he had eaten, John bolted for the playfield back of the quadrangle for an hour of football, rounders or cricket. The river-banks were a source of perpetual, eager exploration. Once, John and Sam Quincy found an eagle's nest high in a dead pine tree. It took an hour to climb to it, and when they got there the nest proved no more than a great bundle of dried sticks, so huge they could not lift themselves around it to look in. That December was fearfully cold; the river froze solid for twenty-eight days. People walked across from Boston; the ferryman said he would starve if a thaw didn't come soon. The rule against skating was waived and boys swarmed out on the ice, their bright woolen mufflers flying, mittened fingers thrust inside their reefers. John covered miles in the clear afternoons, skimming past frozen banks where the marsh grass showed above the ice and even the crows hid in the thickets from the cold.

At two, everyone was supposed to go to his room and study until suppertime. But Tutor Mayhew was lenient; if a student did well, he was given an hour or two longer out of doors. At six, the bell rang for supper. Afterward, John studied by candlelight till curfew. Once a month, Mr. Adams sent the farm cart to Cambridge, laden with firewood. It wasn't half enough, John complained each time his brother arrived. Would Peter kindly tell them at home that this Harvard was the coldest place south of the Pole? Night after night the ink froze on his pen — how could a person be expected to sit still with a book? The evening always ended in wrestling, jumping about and general thumping. When slapping and prancing failed, John and his roommate crept to bed and shivered themselves into oblivion.

Early in January, college was dismissed for the usual winter vacation. This gave everyone six weeks to get warm. More important still, the poorer boys could teach school and earn a little money. There were towns around Boston that had no teaching at all except

what was supplied by Harvard vacations. John Adams went home with a bad cold. His mother looked at him in alarm. He was positively puny, and where were his fine red cheeks? If this was what Harvard College did to growing boys, she was not at all sure she approved the place. He was not a growing boy, John replied irritably. He had had his growth long ago. Even if five feet seven wasn't a giant, it was enough to keep one's head above the snow.

Toward the end of February, when John got ready to return to college, Mrs. Adams had a new cause for alarm. Smallpox had been announced in Boston. Mrs. Adams knew what smallpox meant; she had lived through the terrible epidemic of 1721. John had not been inoculated. More cases were being announced each week in the newspapers: what if the disease reached across the river to Cambridge? Surely, President Holyoke would excuse four or five weeks' absence for inoculation?

John shook his head; it would have required a worse threat than smallpox to keep him from Harvard. Spring was coming, the Freshman list would be posted and he would be assigned a permanent room and a permanent roommate. John hoped it would be Moses Hemmenway or Sam Locke. If they put an upperclassman with him, let it be Quincy or Daniel Treadwell.

Hemmenway and Locke were boys of John's own age, both studying for the ministry. They roomed on John's floor, the three were always together. Locke was a jolly, good-natured creature, sandy-haired and plump, who never seemed to study but did extraordinarily well in everything but mathematics. Hemmenway on the other hand was forever grinding away. He was ready to debate any subject, from the virtues of the Athenian republic (about which he knew very little) to the best method of making May flies for trout-fishing, about which he was extremely knowledgeable. "Take a brown mallard's feather," he would begin. "Whip it round your hook with silk. Then take the hackle of a cock's neck . . ."

Was there nothing, John Adams asked himself, that one could not learn at Harvard College? By now he knew, of course, all twenty-four members of his class. There was William Browne, studious, argumentative. There was David Sewall from York,* who intended to be a lawyer. A *rich* lawyer, he always added complacently. Hem-

---

* Then in Massachusetts. Now in Maine, as also Falmouth (Portland), where Jonathan Sewall lived.

menway and Locke, already inseparable companions, lived just down the corridor. Distinctions between Freshmen and Sophomores melted as the months advanced; in the class above were two of John's closest friends: Sam West of Barnstable, a big, kindly, slow-moving boy whose father was a physician, but who had been brought up on a farm. Last and most important was the Sophomore, Daniel Tread-well. John had never met anyone like Treadwell. He was just John's age, but he was far more mature, with a kind of unshakable intellectual balance. He was a brilliant student of mathematics; already, Professor Winthrop let him help in the laboratory, instructing the slower boys. He came from Portsmouth and was poor, earning his way by scholarships. Short and slight, so nearsighted he always seemed to be looking for something he could not find, young Tread-well challenged everything in the universe, and did it without defiance.

"So you are sure of God!" he said to John one afternoon when they were walking by the river. It was late April, a warm day of alternate showers and rain; the shining black branches seemed ready to burst into leaf. "And sure also," Treadwell went on, "of a blissful existence, *post scriptum,* up there?" He waved toward the soft blue sky. "How comfortable for you! I suppose your father told you, and that was enough. *I* am a skeptic, and do you know why? Because I can't see anything beyond five feet. Step off this pathway — four feet off — and unless you speak, I shall have to prove your identity by mathematical calculation. That makes a fellow pause before he believes everything the professors tell him."

John had never heard anyone mention immortality and God in such easy terms. Braintree too had its skeptics; John felt sure that Mr. Marsh was one, although he seldom mentioned religion. There were heretics in plenty at Braintree and there were atheists, too, like Mr. Gooch, who flaunted his unbelief, plowed his fields on a fast day in full sight of elders, deacons and the whole community on its way to church. But Treadwell did not flout anyone. He merely walked about in his nearsighted way, pricking the bubble of complacence when he found it, whether its owner were twelve or twenty. What he said was always funny; even the victim laughed. It was impossible to make Treadwell angry. To John Adams this was a miracle even more potent than William Browne's smooth shifts from white to black. John's own temper was quick; it welled up, boiling and rush-

A Prospect of the Colledges in Cambridge in New England

Harvard College in John's undergraduate days

The Burgis-Price View, 1743

ing from heart to tongue. How wonderful to be like Treadwell, so full of thought, so quick of utterance, yet never in trouble afterwards because of hasty, angry words!

Treadwell, Hemmenway, Locke, West, Sewall, Sam Quincy[6] — these were John's especial friends; it was with them he talked, walked, roamed the riverbank, argued the universe from immortality to fly-fishing. Like John, these boys had a New England background and like him they were good students. The first four, with John, led their class all the way through college. Outside this circle of intimates were the "foreign" students, on whom John and his friends looked with interest and a huge curiosity. Harvard always had five or six of these. They came from countries many weeks' journey away, such as the colonies of North and South Carolina, which to Massachusetts were more remote than Europe. (The London mail arrived at Boston with some regularity, but communication with these Southern provinces was haphazard and rare.)

One of John's classmates was from Albany, New York; his name was Philip Livingston. Sam Quincy, who always seemed to know such things, told John that the Livingstons were one of the old patroon families; they owned vast tracts of land, thousands upon thousands of acres, granted to their ancestors by a Stuart king. Philip had ridden to college with one servant, some two hundred miles. He knew more about Indians than anyone John had ever seen. Albany lay at the gateway to the Iroquois country; the wilderness was all about it. Yet Philip's family, said Quincy, lived like princes. Philip had formal, beautiful manners, an easy, assured carriage. John liked him yet felt shy in his presence, although the boy was friendly enough — as ready to talk crops and corn as John was, and to note when the President's hay was ripe for the scythe.

Then there was the student from Jamaica, an upperclassman, he of the magnificent wardrobe. Every six months, when one of his father's ships came in, the boy sent his linen home to be laundered. When it came back, box after box, everyone teased him. John heard Sam Quincy ask if a shop was about to be opened, with all these frilled shirts? Nevertheless John was impressed. He had never imagined such wealth and such a wardrobe. And there was, of course, John Vassall from the family of West India merchants who lived so romantically in Braintree in the summers, with their black slaves, their long shutters drawn against the noon heat. John felt a local

pride in the fact that it was Colonel Vassall who had donated the great telescope in Dr. Winthrop's apparatus chamber.

John Adams was never really intimate with these boys. They had money to spend, they boasted of rendezvous with girls in the forbidden houses along Cambridge lanes. Lacking the Puritan background altogether, they talked cockfighting and horse racing like veterans, and were forever being "admonished" and "degraded" in chapel for "drinking spirituous liquors" and being consequently late to morning prayers. They looked with horror on the New England Sunday and said so. At home, church lasted no time at all, and if it went on too long, their fathers were apt as not to rise, make a reproachful sign to the curate, march out the aisle and go on about their business or their pleasure.

But there was something very attractive about these "foreigners." They did not count their money or their words either, like New England people. They had a reckless, graceful way about them that could not, John knew, be imitated merely by taking thought. When the class lists were posted each spring, their names were sure to be at the top. The classes were graded, not according to scholastic ability, but according to the social standing of a boy's family. If your father was a governor, a judge, a prominent minister, you were ranked first and received, in consequence, the best rooms in hall, the upper seats at table, the first places in academic processions, and could help yourself first at commons. The system was natural enough to New England; it grew out of the traditional manner of seating people in church. Always, the Puritan fathers had assigned the front pews to the most prominent citizens.

At Harvard, the matter was determined each spring in Faculty Meeting. Every Freshman name was solemnly voted on — first place, fourth place, last place. The list was then beautifully inscribed and hung on a side wall of the Buttery, where boys came to buy groceries and stationery. This annual listing was a matter of furious excitement, not so much to the boys themselves, who accepted their rank with a good grace, but to their families. No sooner was the list posted than a flood of protests poured in. President Holyoke wished mightily that the grading depended on brains, color of hair, size of a boy's feet — anything but this vague and unholy thing called "social position." The places at top and bottom were unassailable; nobody could dispute a governor's son or a poor scholarship lad from

some obscure village. It was the middle rank that protested. "I am a justice of the peace for Essex County!" shouted one outraged father, stamping into Holyoke's office the morning after the lists were posted. "Why is my boy Sammy graded below a boy whose father has not been justice of the peace as long as I have, by three years and seven months?"

Old Tutor Flynt, sitting at his desk in the outer office, heard the roaring and decided he would not be President of Harvard for all the chamber rents in Massachusetts Hall — and whatever else the President got as salary when the Legislature remembered to grant it.

John Adams found himself fourteenth in a class of twenty-five. It was fair enough, he thought. Moses Hemmenway and Sam Locke were even further down, and Jacob Bailey, whom John liked very much, was end man. All three were studying for the ministry and all three were poor. Money, actually, did not count first in the ranking. (John Hancock, heir to the largest fortune in New England, had found himself, the year before, listed below Sam Quincy of Braintree and three below Henry Dwight, whose father had fought at Louisburg and was now a Chief Justice out in Hampshire County.)

John, taking the list home with him, was surprised at his mother's reaction. Mr. Adams showed no interest whatever, but Mrs. Adams, after some study, remarked that of course any son of hers would be satisfied with the station into which the Almighty had placed him at birth. Yet she would like to know just why, some years ago, Cousin Samuel Adams of Boston had ranked *fifth* in a class of twenty-two while her son ranked fourteenth?

It was entirely natural, Mr. Adams replied mildly. Samuel's father had been a member of the Massachusetts Legislature, justice of the peace, deacon of the church, town selectman. His house on Purchase Street, fronting the water, was a handsome mansion from anyone's accounting, although it was true the family had lost their money in '41.

She had thought, Mrs. Adams retorted, that mansions and money did not signify in this precious Freshman listing. As for being town selectman and deacon of the church, she knew *other* fathers who occupied these positions, even if *not* in Boston. What about relatives on the maternal side . . . Didn't they count at all?

The scene stayed in John's mind when he returned to college. His father, looking uncomfortable, had muttered darkly that he didn't

like this kind of talk. Holy Scripture held no such listings and rankings, heaven no such hierarchy. He had glanced severely at Mrs. Adams, as if he were about to quote the Beatitudes — John knew well that look. Suddenly he had smiled, changed his tone altogether. "Mrs. Adams," he said cheerfully, "in my opinion it is remarkable that John has landed as high up as fourteenth. Due, without shadow of doubt, to the Boylstons of Brookline. And especially to Uncle Zabdiel, who, after all, rendered the Province a very great service. . . . And the royal family too," he added with a smile, "when he inoculated the princesses for smallpox."

John had almost laughed aloud, the flattery was so palpable. Mrs. Adams, completely mollified, dropped the whole matter and went about her business, humming contentedly. How marvelously his father "managed" his mother! John thought suddenly, and for the first time in his life. He did not stop to ask if the management stemmed from expediency or love.

But as warm weather came on and the smallpox increased in Boston, Uncle Zabdiel's name came up again — not only in Braintree kitchen but at Harvard College. It looked as if the epidemic were going to be as bad as it had been in '21. Above one door after another the flag appeared — terrifying little ribbon that announced disease within. The city fathers, who during the first month had counseled calmness, urging the people not to discontinue coming to market, now issued a penalty of fifty pounds to anyone not reporting the disease. The newspapers announced that the Pesthouse was full. The Lieutenant Governor adjourned the General Court. Families poured into town for inoculation. Since those who invited smallpox by inoculation were quite as infectious as those who caught the disease "in the natural way," Boston selectmen forbade inoculation anywhere but at the Province Hospital or in one's own home.

The deaths mounted to hundreds. Preachers from their pulpits thundered the ancient argument: If God sent disease to scourge His people, what He desired was not inoculation but repentance! . . . In Harvard Chapel, President Holyoke reminded the students it was their duty to pray, as the preachers advised. But as *educated* Christians, it was their further duty to make careful inquiry into the operations of created causes, to seize the remedy offered, take every precaution for safety. He read aloud a piece from the *News-Letter*, written by Thomas Prince, the historian — by all odds, said Holyoke,

the most sensible scholar in Boston. The article defended inoculation, praised Dr. Zabdiel Boylston for his part in introducing the practice to Massachusetts. John was impressed. Until now he had regarded Great-uncle Boylston's fame as a mere family matter, a cherished myth of his mother's.

But prayer or no prayer, the disease spread across the River Charles, and on May seventh, 1752, President Holyoke dismissed the college. John Adams walked back to Braintree in the spring sunshine. He would arrive, he knew, just in time for spring plowing. And from what people said about smallpox, it would be September before he got back to Harvard.

*Harvard College (continued). Two great
teachers and their methods. John, a Sophomore, defends his position.*

"Upon the prikly bush of Logick grows
Of other Sciences the fragrant Rose."

PROFESSOR Edward Wigglesworth, finishing the quotation in
his light, slightly hollow, deaf voice, laid down his lecture notes and
smiled benignly at the Sophomore class in logic. It was his first
class of the year. Outside the windows, the leaves were dusty with
August; the morning was warm and there was a stillness in the air.
John Adams, sitting in the third row between his friends Locke and
Hemmenway, nudged them. This was Wigglesworth's favorite quotation; he was famous for it. . . .

A great physicist, the professor went on, had made that verse.
Charles Morton, a Harvard teacher of the last century, had seen the
shape of things to come, perceived that in assuming the new, scholars
must not foolishly discard the old. In this year of 1752, there were
men so dazzled by the experimental methods of Lord Bacon and the
great Mr. Newton, they forgot to use that other tried and ancient
tool of learning — logic. This morning he would like to say a word
or two about logic — *ars artificum et dictorum disciplina.*

Last year, continued Wigglesworth, the class, as Freshmen, had
gone through the elements of logic with their tutors. They had
studied Ramus's definitions. They knew the categories and what
makes a paradox, also the difference between themes simple, compound and universal. As for the syllogism — Wigglesworth smiled

again — of course, all twenty-four gentlemen had it at their tongues' end, whether dialectical, topical, modal or indirect.

The tool, then, was in their hands. It would be his care, for the ensuing three years, to see that every man learned to use this tool — so sharp-pointed, so deft and searching. Their textbooks would include Watts, an author eminently practical, who would point out how to read books to the greatest advantage; and Burgersdyk, the Dutch theorist and logician, one of the great scholars of the age. This morning, said Wigglesworth, he would like to read a line or two from Burgersdyk's Preface. And by the way, in *his* day at Harvard, Sophomores read Burgersdyk in Latin and called him *Burgersdiscius*. Let the class be thankful for this easy translation to the mother tongue. . . .

Wigglesworth opened the brown leather book. " 'What is more requisite,' " he read, " 'for acquiring the true knowledge of things, or more profitable and conducive to explaining the Essence of them, than the Science of Logick? By it we are enabl'd, with more ease, to unfold the Mysteries of Nature, and investigate the occult Qualities of things. *Let Democritus feign that Truth lies hidden at the Bottom of a well, Logick will dive and fetch it out.*' "

Putting down the book, Wigglesworth walked round to the front of the desk and stood easily, hands clasped behind his back, his gown billowing forward. The class, he said, was going directly from this room to Dr. Winthrop's apparatus chamber, where in due course its members would be introduced to such mysteries as the new mathematical method of *fluxions*,* brought to Harvard last year by Winthrop himself. In that ingenious chamber of engines, nothing was accepted on faith. All, all must be proven. No doubt the young gentlemen would be required to verify, by a kind of superior addition and subtraction, that the earth was round and revolved about the sun.

Well and good, said Professor Wigglesworth. Excellent discipline for the mind! But let the class remember that in these "proofs" was no disparagement of the great and universal arrangement of Almighty God who created heaven and earth. The eternal mysteries were mysteries still, despite the method of fluxions and the twenty-four-foot telescope. Wigglesworth, warming to his subject, began to pace back and forth before the class. *Moreover,* he said slowly,

* Calculus.

let these reverend Sophomores bear in mind that God in His infinite wisdom had opened more than one road to knowledge. The experimental method, introduced by Lord Bacon a century ago, begins with the facts — sensory facts that can be proven by eye, ear, touch — then proves the theory outward from these facts. Logic, on the other hand, pronounces a theory and then bores in, testing every step, endeavoring, by minutest and most merciless care, to break down that theory. Logic was a method tested through centuries. It was a way to knowledge. . . . "And a way to God," finished the professor, his face suddenly grave. Christian doctrine itself must be subjected to the test of logic. As professor of divinity it would be his business to show the class how, logically, to analyze the Scripture, and "find out the method of it." Let none consider this an easy assignment; he himself had spent some thirty years at it, and had by no means arrived at certainty. "We know nothing of God" — so one great scholar and divine had said — "but by putting some Logical notion upon him." Let the young gentlemen test, by experiment, the theories of the incomparable Mr. Newton. And by means of logic, let them test Christian doctrine itself.

There was a stir in the classroom. "Not Christian *faith*," the professor added quietly. "Faith responds to prayer rather than investigation." Christian *doctrine* was what he had in mind. Doctrine was the work of man. Were the Five Points of Calvinism, the Thirtynine Articles, arrived at by revelation — dictated from above like the laws on Sinai? There were those in New England who liked to think so. For his part, such an attitude suggested the sin of pride. Moreover, if the Five Points were worth swearing to, they were worth investigating; they could stand up to investigation quite as well as that theory of gravitation the class would soon be testing by pen and pendulum. . . .

"In short," finished Edward Wigglesworth, waving his hand genially in dismissal, "Almighty God has given us, in His wisdom, both heart and brain. Go now to my old friend, John Winthrop. Use the brain God gave you. But remember, it was God who gave it. Keep the faith! . . . Next Thursday at this hour, I shall examine you on the syllogism. Good morning."

From the tower of Harvard Hall, the bell rang. John Adams emerged with his friends into the August sunshine. Across the court Daniel Treadwell hallooed from the steps of Harvard Hall, peering

nearsightedly, his hand above his eyes. He had been waiting for them, he announced. He knew well what Wigglesworth had been saying; every autumn he gave this talk in defense of logic — especially to Sophomores who were about to be introduced to the apparatus chamber and the methods of Isaac Newton. "Upon the prikly bush of Logick grows" — Treadwell quoted the verse with relish. . . . And in the name of Petrus Ramus himself, what unspoken question inspired John Adams to scowl on so fine a morning? Had the professor's queries pierced too deep the tender mind of a future gospel minister? And in Braintree, did the church elders consign all thinkers to an infidel's hell?

By the way — Treadwell chattered on, as the four boys entered Harvard Hall — had Adams read *The Day of Doom,* by old Michael Wigglesworth, the Puritan preacher? With such ancestral pedigree, it was a wonder the professor dared talk so broadly of Calvinist doctrine. *The Day of Doom* would curdle the blood of even your moderate sinner; the very babes were bound hand and foot and flung into the burning lakes of hell. He himself had had to get pages of it by heart in the grammar school.

Pausing in the middle of the stairs as the boys trooped past, Treadwell flung out a dramatic arm —

> To lie in woe and undergo [*he chanted*]
> the direful pains of hell,
> And know withal, that there they shall
> for aye and ever dwell . . .

John wished mightily that Treadwell would lower his voice. If he wasn't careful, Treadwell would get himself up in Chapel for blasphemy, a matter that ranked in the Harvard Penal Laws with "robbery, fornication and other atrocious crimes."

"Well!" Treadwell continued cheerfully, as he walked down the hall a little ahead of John. "Come along, Adams. Let us see if Dr. Winthrop — and Isaac Newton — have a concern for the sweet logical doctrine of infant damnation."

John caught up with his friend. "You talk wildly, Daniel," he said. "I don't believe you are as atheistical as you pretend. But I wish I had half your cleverness at figures. . . . As for logic, let me tell you something. When I was a Freshman, I used to stand on the doorsill

of Winthrop's apparatus chamber, watching him swing the orrery or measure angles with the quadrant. I thought if I stood there long enough, he would ask me in. But he never did. He never even saw me. Now, when the bell rings, I enter that room of my own right."

John stopped dead in the hallway, looked gravely at Treadwell as the bell rang the hour. "All the logic in Aristotle," he said, "couldn't convince me as those machines" — John gestured toward the laboratory — "have convinced me already, though I do not know one third their uses."

It was a problem that belonged not only to John Adams, to Daniel Treadwell and Harvard College. This was a time when the entire Western World was striving to break through the boundaries of theological absolutism, the involuted logic of medieval scholasticism. The Puritans, it was true, had renounced the schoolmen, declaring their logical systems obscured the true nature of divine grace. Actually, however, this breaking away was no more than nominal; the struggle still existed. In New England it was evident in market place, pulpit and school. It appeared in the very practical argument concerning inoculation versus acceptance of disease as God's punishment. It showed itself in Braintree's Meeting-house over the doctrine of *"Determinism versus Free Will"* — a quarrel that was soon to lose young Lemuel Briant his pastorate.

At Harvard College, Professor Winthrop did not pause, as did his colleague Wigglesworth, to act as go-between, making a comfortable bridge between theology and the natural world. He simply presented the facts, let the student construct his own bridge. If this left many a young pilgrim stranded on the theological shore, Winthrop was oblivious to these castaways. It was his business to demonstrate the operations of science and the visible world, and he set out to do it the best way he was able. Professor Wigglesworth had been right when he said that in the apparatus chamber John Winthrop did not require his students to accept anything on faith. "Question and prove!" said Winthrop. "Ask, and find your answer in the facts." No phenomenon of nature was to pass unchallenged. Why had God put these questions, except for man to search out answers? To invent a theory and accept it *a priori* led to dogmatism. The more a man knew, the more humble he became. Infallibility as a doctrine was the pitfall of the scholar. The great Newton had not thought himself infallible.

So Winthrop told his classes in his precise, gentlemanly voice, waiting a moment or two afterward, for question or argument. When neither was forthcoming, or when Winthrop suspected a boy of cozening or insincerity, he had his own methods of rebuke. John had been in the class about a month when Winthrop mentioned, one morning, the theory of gravitation. "Do you believe it?" he asked the room at large. John stood hesitant, but four Sophomores near him nodded easy acquiescence. "Sheep!" said Winthrop icily to the four. "Newton did not believe it." He pointed to the pendulum hanging above a table. "Go prove it for yourselves, as Newton had to prove it."

John Adams, notebook in hand, moved to the apparatus. Across the room, Treadwell caught his eye and winked, jerking an eloquent thumb toward the offenders. Gravitation had always been a hard nut for undergraduates to crack. The great Newton had been dead less than thirty years — and who in North America but Winthrop and Dr. Franklin had read the *Principia?* One boy[1] went to his room and challenged the whole thing in his diary. "If the earth moves," he wrote, "I ask what the reason may be, why a cannon ball, when cast 50 feet in air, Descend in the same place from which it was Ejected. . . . Perhaps," the diary added plaintively, "you will answer."

There was a strong current of opinion to bolster the young man's doubts. A group of Junior Sophisters came solemnly to Winthrop. Would it not be valuable, they suggested, to institute public discussion of these matters? One set of student orators could expound the merits of the solar system as described by Copernicus, the other set could explain the Ptolemaic theory — not omitting, of course, the compromise theory of the great Danish astronomer, Tycho Brahe, who said the sun revolved around the earth, but the five planets revolved around the sun. From these discussions, the audience could determine for itself which system was the most reasonable.

"Discussions?" Winthrop said dryly. He had thought these were matters for demonstration rather than debate. Perhaps his good friend and colleague, Dr. Wigglesworth, would permit them to hold these "discussions" in his rooms, as far from the apparatus as possible, substituting logic for mathematics?

John loved it when the two professors chaffed each other in class, sending out oblique insults concerning each other's methods. As a matter of fact, although their teaching was so different, the two

pursued a like goal. And in spite of grumblings and threats from Overseers and Legislature, neither professor transgressed the aims for which Harvard existed. According to the statement of 1643, the college had been designed, not solely for the training of gospel ministers, but for *the advancement of all good literature, artes and sciences*. It was true the New England fathers had greatly desired an educated clergy and had looked to Harvard to supply it. But their broad purpose had indubitably been the advancement of knowledge, not only for individuals but for the New World. All the fanaticism of the Mathers, father and son, had not been able to make the college into a theological seminary.

. *The main end of the scholar's life and studies* (said the early *Harvard Rules and Precepts*) *is to know God and Jesus Christ which is eternall life. Therefore to lay Christ in the bottome is the only foundation of all sound knowledge and harmony.*

By John Adams's time, the words were gone officially from the college laws, yet their spirit brooded benignly over the establishment. *To know God and Jesus Christ which is eternall life* . . . As a principle of action, there was nothing here to preclude the deepest scholarship, the widest experimentation. Within the boundaries of such a law, both Winthrop in science and Wigglesworth in divinity could function freely; they were men who believed in God and were happy to make their faith manifest. John Winthrop searched out the Holy Spirit through the marvels of science and the new inductive method. The heavens still proclaimed the glory of God. The fact that telescope and calculus permitted men to trace the actual course of the planets did not detract from His glory but only enhanced it. For Winthrop, there was no war between scriptural authority and the experimental method. To those who attempted to create such a war he turned — if they were townspeople — an indifferent ear. If they were students, he referred them to textbook or apparatus.

Winthrop laid before his students, in the 1750's, the works of Robert Boyle, of Newton, Leibnitz, Halley — all dead, "and gone," said one pious Sophomore, "to their heavenly reward." Winthrop raised an eyebrow at this. In his opinion, these men had had their reward on earth also — God in His infinite wisdom seeing fit to grant to occasional mortals a very great and deep contentment in their earthly occupations.

John Adams, witness to this little scene, repeated the words silently: *A very great and deep contentment in their earthly occupations.* With what extraordinary aptness the phrase fitted Dr. Winthrop himself! The professor carried his head slightly to one side, with a gesture a little deprecating, as though he questioned not only the phenomena of nature, but — in spite of his celebrity — his own ability to solve them. He moved quickly, surely among his instruments. There was a brightness in his face. Cheerfulness, John would have called it, as though Winthrop were grateful to a providence that permitted him to investigate these mysteries.

And in this gratitude was a contagion even for the uninitiated. John liked to work with his hands; never before had he been encouraged to use them where study was concerned. In all the years of fruitless torment on the hard bench at Cleverly's Latin School, to *learn* had meant to be taught something from a book, accepting it because it was told. Even Mr. Marsh had perforce used this authoritarian method, though he cautioned John he did it only because time was short and college examinations would not wait upon true scholarship.

It was now, in his Sophomore year, that John began to read. Once started, he read voraciously, without plan or guidance. It was an appetite that grew with what it fed on. The Harvard library was used mostly by graduate students; about three fourths of the books were theological. The rules were stringent. A Sophomore could not enter the room but must have books passed out to him by the door, and only one book at a time. Such a ration, John complained to Perez Marsh the librarian (another Marsh cousin), was like one bite of beef at a time; it only made a man hungrier. Marsh relaxed his rules a little;[2] it became understood between them that John's cloak could hide two volumes, one under each arm, and that they would be returned on the morrow. John read the Greek historians — in translation — leaping furiously through Thucydides and Plutarch. He took down Clarendon's *History* in nightly gulps, paged through Newton, Boyle, Shakespeare's historical plays, begged Marsh to let him look through the *Transactions of the Royal Society*, of which the library had a complete file, and odd copies of the London *Spectator*. He read Dryden, and that manual of eighteenth-century philosophy, Pope's *Essay on Man.*

Half the time, John could not have told on Tuesday what he had

read on Monday. Perez Marsh asked him one day if appetite, in the Adamses of Braintree, never waited on digestion? Adams might recall to his benefit something Mr. Watts said, in his *Logick: Do not let your soul be a looking glass, that wheresoever you turn, it receives the Images of all Objects, but retains none.*

John laughed. But in spite of haphazard methods, he began to acquire a skill in reading — an ability to find at a glance what he was looking for on the page. Almost unconsciously, he searched for confirmation of what the professors said in class. In the laboratory, it was true, John had learned to go to instrument or mathematics for proof of the axiom as laid down. But so far, he had by no means achieved what Winthrop hoped a few at least among his students might achieve — knowledge by realization as well as by rote acceptance.

One afternoon, in March of his Sophomore year, John lingered in the laboratory after class. It was snowing outside, a miserable frozen drizzle that turned the Yard and buildings gray. John stood at a table, looking through Gravesande's *Natural Philosophy.* Gravesande was a Dutchman, a pupil of Isaac Newton. The work was in two folio volumes, very handsome, illustrated with beautiful, precise engravings of pendulums and siphons. John pored over them, standing on one foot and then the other. He liked the chapter titles, they seemed to range over infinity itself: *Of Air, and other Elastic Fluids.* . . . *Of Sight, where we shall speak of the Construction of the Eye.* . . . *Of the Opacity of Bodies.*

John turned back and began to read the author's preface. "Lay aside all feigned hypotheses," said Gravesande. "The properties of Body cannot be known *a priori;* we must therefore examine Body* itself. He only, who in Physics reasons from Phenomena, and pursues this Method inviolably to the best of his Powers, endeavors to follow the footsteps of Sir Isaac Newton; and not he who implicitly follows the opinion of any particular Person."

We must examine Body itself. The words rang in John's mind like a fire gong. He was astonished. How many times Dr. Winthrop had said this same thing! Francis Bacon had said it, Harvey, Isaac Newton — yet he, John Adams, had read and heard without comprehension. And now, at this chance phrase, he knew what these great men had

* Matter.

meant. Now suddenly his mind jerked open with a motion almost painful. . . .

The blood mounted to John's face. He must speak of this thing, he must talk, tell what he had found. . . . Dr. Winthrop stood across the laboratory at a tub under the window, washing a crucible. John walked swiftly to him. They were alone in the room. "Sir," John said, without preamble. "I have been reading. I found something, I made a — discovery. It was in Gravesande's preface."

Winthrop turned, looked in surprise at the boy before him. John's fine brown hair was rumpled, a strand had come loose from the black ribbon at the neck and hung over his ear. He stood balanced on the balls of his feet as if about to break into a run. "And what," Winthrop asked courteously, "does Gravesande say, Adams?"

For ten minutes, John talked; the professor sat on a stool and listened gravely. What John said was neither new nor especially clever, but it moved his teacher. This youth, with his clear steady eyes — he could not be above eighteen, Winthrop thought, looking at him with curiosity. How robust he seemed, and how quick! There was a constitutional stubbornness in him, a kind of violence that could be dangerous if not properly directed. This passion to communicate — the boy stood shaken with it to his toes. It was a quality born in a man, never to be denied though its owner perished for speaking. Winthrop had seen it before, in fools as well as wise men. But whatever this Adams boy was, whatever he might become, most certainly he was no fool. . . . What was the boy saying? Something about faith, conversion, the Congregational doctrine, something about logic versus proof by the methods of physical science. Winthrop gathered his attention, listened to the end.

"And so," the professor said when at last John was quiet, "you are to be a gospel minister, Adams! It is a fraternity that has included the world's best minds — and also its narrowest. Have you thought of teaching, after graduation, for a year or two, before making final decision?"

He was not at all sure of the future, John replied. He had not thought very definitely about the future; his father had laid that out for him, long ago. He knew only that today he had made a — a discovery. Winthrop rose, untied the strings of his leather apron. "What you have discovered today, Adams, is your own mind. That

is discovery enough for an afternoon. Go along now. And if you are late for supper, say the professor kept you."

In the spring of his Sophomore year, John was introduced to a little book that took him even farther on the road to understanding. *Essay concerning Human Understanding*, the book was called; John Locke had written it before the turn of the century. Professor Wigglesworth used it in his courses for Senior reading, but John picked it up one day in Oliver Wendell's room. The *Essay* did for mind what Newton had done for matter — took it off the shelf of medieval authoritarianism and looked at it by the plain light of day. Locke examined the soul, the will — speaking of them familiarly, as if they, like the circulation of the blood, were plain matters for investigation.

How, Locke demanded, do ideas originate in the mind? . . . At home in Braintree, John's family, with the rest of New England, took it for granted that man is born knowing, born with ideas stamped upon the mind. Not so! said Locke. All that we know, we know from experience. *We know heat because we have felt fire. We know white because we have seen sugar or snow.*

Why, this was Gravesande all over again, without the mathematics! . . . Above all, Locke examined memory. Is it, he asked, dependent on the will? Why then, when we are passive, do pictures from childhood flash suddenly upon us?

John Adams asked Wendell if he might borrow this volume, walked out with it and down the hall to his own room. Only this morning, he had had an experience such as Locke described. It had been a mild, sunny day, a foretaste of summer. Dr. Winthrop, as was his habit on pleasant mornings, had held his Senior seminar out of doors, under the big elm by Holden Chapel. John, passing the group not far off, had thought how pleasing it was. Like Plato's little senate under the blue Athenian sky. . . . Soon he, too, would be a Senior and sit among these favored ones.

And suddenly there flashed to his mind the picture of another group, another class held out of doors, under a tree — Dame Belcher's school, long ago on the Coast Road across from home. As plainly as if he had been a bystander, John saw his own figure, a small boy dancing solemn-faced under the trees, arms outspread in clumsy, childish joy. How far away this picture, and yet how close, how instantaneous the connection! John felt it with a rush of warmth. At

Dame Belcher's he had been happy, as he was happy now. All that he learned there, he learned with heart as well as mind. . . .

Again and again, John went back to Locke in the evenings, reading in his room. Here was an author who never advised but always questioned. Mercilessly, Locke probed the religious experience of revelation and conversion that John knew as part of Calvinist doctrine. The strength of a man's passions, said Locke, is no evidence of the rightness of his opinions. "Crooked things may be as stiff and inflexible as straight."

How different, all this, from the passionate and stubborn pronouncements of the deacon uncles round the fireplace at home in Braintree! Uncle Ebenezer, especially, never tested anything, either by his five senses or by reason. He simply laid down the law and then thought up a text from Scripture to "prove" it. Leaning over his study table in the failing afternoon, John read until the page was dim, then lighted his candle and went on. . . . *Whilst the parties of man cram their tenets down all men's throats whom they can get into their power, without permitting them to examine their truth or falsehood, and will not let truth have fair play in the world, nor men the liberty to search after it; what improvement can be expected? What greater light can be hoped for in the moral sciences?*

John paused, read the words a second time. His father and mother, his uncles — all of Braintree, it seemed — expected Deacon Adams's son to be a Congregational minister. John himself had by no means decided against it. Yet among the people he knew, Congregational ministers were most prone to "cram their tenets down all men's throats." Beyond argument and beyond proof, these men were sure of their theological premises. Yet how, thought John Adams, getting up and walking to the window, how could they be sure? The more one read, the more one doubted. Through this labyrinth of thought, this forest of eternal question, it would not be easy — nay, it would be impossible — to carry intact the faith of one's childhood.

In the matter of the Creation, for instance, he would have to be very sure before ordination. Every man, woman and child in New England knew the world had been created in the year 4047 B.C., that it took six days to do it and God rested on the seventh day. Newton's laws of celestial motion said nothing to the contrary, and yet . . in the study of physics and astronomy was surely something that inclined the mind to doubt. Dr. Franklin was rumored to be an atheist,

or at least a deist. Franklin, John remembered, was a friend of Professor Winthrop's. He would ask the professor if it were true about Franklin's atheism.

Next morning, John put his question, going early to class and finding the professor alone. Dr. Franklin, Winthrop replied, was an exceedingly wise man. He himself did not happen to be acquainted with any very wise atheists — although that, of course, was no proof they did not exist. Might he ask what had inspired this question on Adams's part? Was he, by chance, having difficulties with his conscience in matters of religious faith? Such difficulties were apt to start with Genesis 2.

John, astonished at the professor's perspicacity, replied that it was indeed the Creation which troubled him. Very natural, Winthrop rejoined. He himself, as a young man, had had much wrestling of soul concerning the Creation. A sentence or two in Gravesande's first volume gave the position of that justly celebrated mathematician on the matter. He thought he had it by heart. . . . *Physics do not meddle with the first Foundations of Things. The least examination of Nature will shew footsteps of Supreme Wisdom. That the World was created by God is a Position wherein Reason perfectly agrees with Scripture.*

Strong testimony surely, John replied. He wished his Uncle Ebenezer Adams could see it. . . . He had, John added apologetically, some very pious uncles at home. They were forever attacking him about these matters since he had come to Harvard College.

John copied the paragraph and took it to Braintree. Of all his uncles, Ebenezer was most suspicious where science was concerned, even though he had sent two sons to Harvard. Compared with Ebenezer, Mr. Adams was mild as milk in these matters. It was Uncle Eb who kept bringing up the question; he could not seem to let it rest. When John mentioned Dr. Winthrop or tried to tell about the apparatus chamber, Uncle Eb would not listen, but rose to his full height (he was a wizened little man, no taller than John) and roared, quoting Scripture, quoting *The Day of Doom* itself, reminding John with asperity that the grandsire of his precious Dr. Wigglesworth had written that poem. Did the professor of physics, in his highflying talks on the celestial system, ever recite the Reverend Michael Wigglesworth on Eternity?

It is a main great Oc-ean [*shouted Uncle Ebenezer*]
    withouten bank or bound,
A deep Abyss, wherein there is
    no bottom to be found.
This World hath stood now since the Flood,
    four thousand years, well near,
And had before endur-ed more
    than sixteen hundred year.

Now *that*, said Uncle Eb with triumphant finality, was a true description of the whole matter. He himself suspected there was something of the Arminian if not of the deistical about this Dr. John Winthrop. Astronomical studies inclined men that way. Look at Dr. Franklin; it was common knowledge that as a lad he had frequented deistical clubs in Boston. To think of Harvard giving the man an honorary degree in this year of our Lord, 1753! No doubt, Professor Winthrop was responsible; were not the two lifelong associates? The friends of religion and virtue would not be happy about this degree, in spite of the great discovery that Franklin claimed.

Uncle Ebenezer, looking defiantly at his nephew, demanded just what it was Dr. Franklin had discovered *this* time? He understood Professor Winthrop at the college trumpeted it as if the man had uncovered the original tablets on Mount Sinai. . . .

"Brother Eb," Mr. Adams broke in, mildly, "you talk very loud of matters with which we Adamses have not been intimate. What do you know of lightning, save that it killed your brindly cow five summers back?" He nodded encouragement to his son. "Go on, John. Tell us about the Doctor's discovery."

"Professor Winthrop says," John began carefully, quoting word for word what he had heard a week ago in class, "that Dr. Franklin has at last completed, by experiment, his grand discovery. It explains, on electrical principles, the phenomena of thunder gusts."

There was a brief silence. "Ho!" said Uncle Ebenezer. "And where does *that* bring us, pray? Of what use this grand discovery, except to make fine phrases?"

This was a poser for John, who had no more idea what use it was than Uncle Ebenezer. But, unlike Uncle Eb, John had heard the question propounded a dozen times. The Sophomore class itself, when Winthrop made his triumphant announcement, had been

wholly unimpressed. "Has any practical application, Sir, been suggested?" Sam Locke had asked.

"Uncle Eb," John said, "in Philadelphia they asked Dr. Franklin that question, *What use is it?* . . . 'What use,' Franklin said, 'is a newborn babe?' "

Mr. Adams, slapping his knee, burst into uproarious laughter and called his wife to come and hear what Dr. Franklin had said.

The truth was that Mr. Adams, who did not understand a tenth of the arguments John brought home from college, was immensely proud of him and very tired of his brother Eb's eternal badgering of the boy. The loan of ten pounds for tuition, already half repaid, surely did not entitle an uncle to such latitude. Time and again, Mr. Adams had wished John would turn on Ebenezer, but to hint it would have been a kind of betrayal of one's own generation. And now, without impudence, without defiance, John had done it. In Ebenezer's face the blood mounted. John sat seemingly unconcerned, one knee over the other, nursing his right ankle in a gesture he had. His round face was smooth, the blue eyes alert, his mouth drawn to one side in the little quirk that meant he was master of the situation and knew it.

Glancing at the two in turn, it occurred to Mr. Adams, with the suddenness of his own grand discovery, that his son was a man, and could hold his own with anyone.

CHAPTER EIGHT

*John is witness to strife in the church.
The Senior Discussion Club. A new
French war begins. John is graduated
from Harvard.*

IT WAS no wonder, that summer of 1753, that Uncle Ebenezer showed himself on the defensive. Braintree had got itself involved in an ecclesiastical battle of the bitterest kind; it entangled the entire Adams family. Uncle Ebenezer — and fully half of Braintree — declared that Lemuel Briant, now thirty-two years old, should be dismissed as pastor of the First Congregational Church. The charge was Arminianism,[1] or at least that was how the charge read in the beginning. But the controversy, having raged three painful years, had mounted until Briant was denounced not only as Arminian but Socinian, which meant he denied all Five Points of Calvinism, including the Trinity. He refused outright to teach the Westminster Catechism to children, with all its salutary reminders of the grave and of everlasting punishment beyond the grave. Indeed, he said boldly that he would be glad to "rase some of these doctrines out of the minds of Parents." Added to this, Briant denied "the Imputation of the Guilt of Adam's Sin to Posterity."

John Adams took no actual part in this quarrel, yet it affected him deeply. Coming home for vacation he found the whole town obsessed with the struggle. Not only in church but on Braintree Common John met it, and in the houses of his uncles and friends. At the blacksmith's, at the gristmill, at Jed Thayer's little dry-goods store, the name of Briant was sure to come up. Echoes of the talk followed

Mr. Adams to his workshop out by the barn, where the cured hides hung from the ceiling and the clean smell of polished leather met one at the entrance. In the late afternoon, neighbors, passing the Adams house on their way from work, had the habit of looking in at the shop. John had seen them all his life, lounging in their work clothes against the open door or on the benches, exchanging news from ship-yard or market, smoking, talking politics. Their rough easy laughter could be heard in the house.

Now they did not stop by at all, or their talk was tense and fitful. Mr. Adams himself had become strangely uncommunicative and gloomy. He was, in truth, torn asunder by the conflict between heart and conscience. He liked Lemuel Briant, who, apart from his indubitable mental brilliance, was warmhearted and friendly. (All the young of the parish were on Briant's side.) But as a deacon of the church, Mr. Adams was convinced that Briant must go. He had been elected pastor in the belief that he held theological views similar to those of the church elders. If, in the intervening six years, Briant had developed Arminian tendencies, it was his duty to announce the same openly and leave the church.

Mr. Adams, however, had never intended the thing to reach such proportions. Inevitably, it had turned from theology to personality and the insult direct. Ministers from five different towns met in solemn ecclesiastical state in the Adams parlor, compiled a lengthy report wherein Briant's character was condemned as "light and gay." The matter of his recent separation from his wife was discussed in detail, with a relish that made Mr. Adams acutely uncomfortable. Privately, Mr. Adams considered Mrs. Briant the most unpleasant, nagging woman in Braintree; she had taken advantage of her husband's present trouble to accuse him publicly of "several scandalous sins." Over Mr. Adams's remonstrance, the ecclesiastical report quoted her words.

From Great-uncle Peter to the Cousins Webb and Bass of Braintree, the Adams family had more than its share of deacons; it was natural they should be consulted. But it was Uncle Ebenezer, no deacon at all, who threw himself with utmost enthusiasm into the fray. The way Ebenezer was behaving, Mr. Adams said irritably, you might think Lemuel Briant owed him money. Ebenezer demanded outright that the deacons itemize publicly the "several scandalous sins" of which Briant was accused by his wife. *He*, said Eb-

enezer, knew how to compile such a list! Let it begin with that night last spring when Briant, in full view of the neighbors, had flung out of his house and disappeared up the road. He had not come back for five days. He gave out he was at Hingham, lodging with the minister there. Hingham indeed! said Ebenezer. *He* knew where Lemuel Briant had been, and it wasn't the Reverend Gay's house either.

It was an afternoon of early autumn when this particular conversation took place; John was home for his monthly visit. The three were alone in the workshop; dusk was coming on and Mr. Adams was preparing to close up for the night. Ebenezer perched on a stool by the door, gesticulating. John, sitting in the far corner, watched with rising impatience, first Ebenezer for his wild talk, then his father for permitting it. Mr. Adams's back was turned; he seemed busy over his tools.

Did the elders know, Ebenezer continued shrilly, about that little sick baby Briant kept visiting, over on the Weymouth Road? Had they ever stopped to ask whose baby it was? Its mother was a handsome young widow. . . . Was that, demanded Ebenezer, the way for a minister of God to behave?

Mr. Adams replied sharply that it was not a way for a member of God's congregation to behave either, spreading slander. For his part he didn't believe a word of it. Let Ebenezer mind his tongue, especially here in this shop or this house.

Ebenezer, waving an arm, loosed, at this, a whole stream of talk. John, watching spellbound, saw his father rise, bark three words at Ebenezer, heard Ebenezer scream back at him and saw Mr. Adams, fists clenched, advance on his brother. Ebenezer, knocking over the stool, backed out the door, shrieking that his brother was an Arminian himself then, and did he want the whole country to know it?

It all happened so quickly that John had scarcely time to rise from his chair before the door banged and Ebenezer was gone. Mr. Adams, returning, sank on the bench before his work-table, reached for a handkerchief and wiped the sweat from his forehead. John, paralyzed with astonishment, stood mute. Mr. Adams's face, usually so composed, so kind, had been white with anger; as he advanced on his brother he had sworn aloud, a deep, vicious curse such as John in his eighteen years had never heard from him. Now he sat breathing heavily. "There is an evil spirit abroad, in this thing," he said at last. "I have begun to hate my brother. I would have struck

him. God forgive me — is this the way to serve our Lord in His congregation?"

Staring through his knees at the floor — "John," Mr. Adams continued, "I am fearful for Lemuel Briant. He is ill, this trouble is likely to kill him. Have you seen him lately?"

Mr. Adams longed for reassurance, for his son to tell him all was well and he was imagining this danger to young Briant.

"Yes, I have seen him," John said slowly. "Yesterday, in the lane by the Meeting-house. He was alone, and walked with a cane. I hardly knew him. He looks an old man."

"Did you speak to him?"

"Yes," John said again. "I told him I had read the controversy, followed it in the newspapers. I told him I couldn't understand the fine theological points involved, but — "

John stopped abruptly. In these months of controversy he had been silent at home, had never told his father how he felt. Now it had to come out, the words burned in him and would not wait.

"I told Mr. Briant I was for him," John finished deliberately. He did not look at his father. "I told him my friends agreed."

There was silence in the shop. Mr. Adams, standing by his worktable, fumbled with the tools. Had his life depended on a word, he could not have spoken. After a moment he picked up his saddle knife, hung it against the wall. The gesture was a signal. Both men moved to the door. It was very still. Beyond to the westward the valley shimmered in the September afternoon. Over by the pasture the cows lowed; John heard his brother's voice, urging them through the gate.

"I'll go help Peter with the milking," John said quickly. "That cow Daisy is skittish as a young colt."

He turned from his father and was gone.

To Mr. Adams, the open defection of his eldest son was the last and hardest blow of all. He would have given much to be relieved of responsibility toward Briant. Would God, he told his wife bitterly that night, he had never been elected deacon! The truth was that Mr. Adams's withdrawal or support would have availed Lemuel Briant nothing at all. Briant was doomed before he started. He was a Unitarian, and New England would not be ready to accept Unitarianism for another hundred years. New England did not, as yet,

even use the name: they called it "anti-Trinitarianism," "Arminianism," "Socinianism," "deism." As a leader of the advance guard, Briant was to be by no means the only sacrifice.[2]

Before he went to Harvard, John Adams would have taken his father's side automatically. Now he could not take it. The more he read and heard, the more disgusted he became. Could not his father see that all these deacons and elders were behind the times? Ignorant men, with not half the brains or education of Lemuel Briant! Their arguments were lengthy and dogmatic, or else they went crazy altogether like Uncle Ebenezer, and resorted to slander. . . . Suppose he, John Adams, became a minister, a few years hence! Would he be blocked, thwarted, persecuted as Briant was persecuted? Uncle Eb was crazy, yes. But there was something in the local air that made such madness dangerously contagious. From deacon to town drunkard the infection spread.

The atmosphere at home was unbearable. John spent his vacations elsewhere as much as he could — with Mr. Marsh, a Briant sympathizer, with the Adamses' new tenants next door, young Dr. and Mrs. Savil. Marsh liked to walk to the North Common and watch the workmen blow out the rocks. They were carrying granite to Boston to build King's Chapel; the method was to make great fires round the boulders until the rock was thoroughly heated, when it split and could be pried out with crowbars. As the fires mounted, the boulders cracked and snapped like pistol shots. Mr. Marsh took huge pleasure in this, declaring it was the only form of contrived explosion he enjoyed; gunfire made him nervous. Besides, the whole scene reminded him of hell, and it was pleasurable to watch infernal fires without being scorched. Did not John think, Marsh inquired easily, that a Puritan Jehovah would assuredly cause the tormentors of Lemuel Briant to suffer, when their turn came, at least a little *singeing*?

John laughed aloud and felt relieved by his laughter. Marsh's gentle irony was comforting, after the passionate and stubborn wrangling of Uncle Ebenezer and the deacons. The Quincy tribe was on Briant's side too; old Colonel Quincy came out openly in his defense. John heard about it at Sam Quincy's house. Sam's father, a nephew of the Colonel, had bought the old Hancock parsonage. The place was gay with young people. Mr. Quincy complained that the house was far too small; he would build a new one as soon as the

times permitted. It was a frame building, three stories high, with not nearly enough fireplaces. From the outside at least it had an air of spareness and meager living that sat ill on the Quincy ménage, which was openhearted and boundlessly hospitable.

Sam Quincy, since his graduation from Harvard last spring, lived at home, as did Edmund, studying for his Master's degree. Then there was the youngest brother, Josiah, now ten and at school with Mr. Marsh. Josiah was cross-eyed and so was his father, but oddly enough this was not unattractive. When they were excited their eyes crossed more than ever. They had a way of lowering their heads when they talked, as if to see over their noses. John avoided looking directly at either of them, although he could have saved his pains, neither father nor son being in the least abashed by the infirmity.

There was a sister, too, a year younger than John Adams. Her name was Hannah; she had a tongue as quick as a lash. John had been afraid of her at first, although she was a little thing, always laughing, and very pretty with her dark hair and eyes. But when he found Hannah liked him, his shyness vanished. The girl was ready for any fun that came, from fishing expeditions to chestnut hunts in the autumn. John had seen her, out in the country, pick up her skirts and race her brother Josiah till her dark hair fell tumbling about her face. She could ride a horse as well as a man.

With the Quincys, there was no need to be forever defending something or attacking something. They took the world as it came. If a minister — if young Lemuel Briant — was being persecuted, why, it was outrageous, and they would do what they could to help him. But was it any reason, Hannah would exclaim, laughing, why they should not all go over to the frolic tonight at Uncle Ned Quincy's? There would be dancing — Uncle Ned had engaged fiddles and a flute. Cousin Esther was to be there, of course. John Adams must meet her. She had golden hair, said Hannah demurely. And besides, she knew how to keep an admiring silence before gentlemen. That was what gentlemen liked, was it not? asked Hannah, her bright brown eyes turned innocently up to John's.

John forgot Lemuel Briant and Uncle Ebenezer, forgot everything but himself and the good time he was having. He had not realized, at Harvard, how he missed in that monastic place, the fun, the frolics, the rides at night in the farm sledge when the stars were out.

Bells jingling . . . girls thrown shrieking against one as the horses rounded a corner . . . Cantering home by moonlight after a visit to the Quincys — had the world anything, John asked joyfully of the landscape at large, so pleasant as the companionship of a pretty girl?

Leaving his horse in the barn and bursting happily in his front door, John was met by the frozen and gloomy silence that had so long prevailed at home. It was Uncle Ebenezer's fate that disturbed Mr. Adams now. Ebenezer had actually been notified by the elders that he was barred from Communion at church, for the sin of scandal! Mr. Adams himself, with awful wrenchings of heart, had acquiesced in this decision in open meeting. Ebenezer had been given, beforehand, a chance to rise in church and confess his sin. Ebenezer's reply — that he would be damned first — had not been calculated to soften the hearts of the elders.

Mr. Adams felt it as a keen disgrace to the family. Besides, he was sorry for Ebenezer. To be debarred from God's table? It was unendurable, no matter what the provocation. Mr. Adams's emotions were shared by no one in the household. His wife, who cared more for her husband's peace of mind than she did for ten Lemuel Briants, had been tried almost beyond endurance by the whole affair. The fact that Ebenezer was her sister's husband did not make Mrs. Adams's position any easier. The morning the news arrived about Ebenezer's banishment from Communion, Mrs. Adams banged a heavy pewter spoon against the bowl where she was working and remarked loudly that thank God they had shut that man up at last. Then, catching sight of her husband's face, she went swiftly to him, put an arm about his shoulders and turned to her sons with a warning gesture.

John, with difficulty restraining a cheer, walked out of the house and across the yard to tell the Savils. It was wonderful, having such agreeable tenants next door. Elisha Savil, not quite thirty, was plump and easygoing, the best company in the world. He was a Harvard graduate and a physician, but he never seemed to get in the wood before a storm, and was immensely grateful to John for occasionally planing down a door that stuck, or puttying a windowpane. Mrs. Savil, ten years younger, a cousin of John's and as plump as her husband, was pretty and talkative, always full of gossip and avid for more.

The trouble was, said Dr. Savil when he heard about Uncle Eb-

enezer — the trouble was that Uncle Eb's defeat would be no help to Lemuel Briant, who in the past year had become a very ghost of a man, white, shattered, and scarcely able to stand in the pulpit. Did John know that Briant had sent in a request for his dismissal "on the grounds of ill health"?

The request was granted. Briant went away to Hingham where his friends were. The world saw him no more. A year later he was dead.

John was a Senior when he heard of Briant's death. He felt the old anger rise. So they had killed Lemuel Briant, with their eternal, self-righteous persecution! More than ever, John felt he could not preach from the Congregational pulpit. So much had happened in this past year that he had forgotten Lemuel Briant, or thought he had forgotten. In the months that had elapsed since Briant left Braintree, even Mr. Adams had ceased to mention his name. The talk now was all of the French, who had come south again from Canada — not by way of the Atlantic this time but far inland behind the mountains in the fur-trading country. They had penetrated boldly into Pennsylvania. At the junction of the Ohio and Allegheny Rivers — a spot strategic to the entire Ohio Valley — they had built a great fort,* named it after the Marquis Duquesne, new Governor-General of Canada, announcing defiantly that "the king, their master, commanded them to hold this country under the French flag." Boston newspapers at first had been full of it. Several hundred Virginia men under a young Lieutenant Washington had marched through swamp and wilderness over the mountains, built a stockade in the Great Meadows below the enemy. Fort Necessity, Washington called it. At Fort Necessity the Virginia troops had been beaten, driven back ignominiously.

That was four months ago, in July of '54. The threat was real, the danger great. Already, France held the Great Lakes region, the Champlain country down to Lake George. In the year '49 the French had sent one of their explorers far south into western Virginia, told him to bury leaden plates along the rivers, announcing possession. The Indians had been much impressed. The French were very clever at winning Indian allies, something immeasurably important to any nation with large holdings in North America. Without the good will of the Six Nations, especially the Iroquois and Mohawk tribes, the

* Now Pittsburgh.

colony of New York would be helpless against a long campaign.

Yet New England, after the initial surprise of Washington's defeat at the Great Meadows, was apathetic. The forks of the Ohio were many miles away. And as for Mohawks, let New York look to them. Massachusetts took a lofty tone. At Louisburg in '45 she had beat the French most gloriously. Others could meet this new problem. Were not Virginia, Pennsylvania, much closer to the danger?

Only a few men saw beyond the borders of their respective colonies: Governor Shirley of Massachusetts, Benjamin Franklin, Pownall, Governor Morris of Pennsylvania, Governors Dinwiddie and Glen in the south. They knew that no army could march overland from Canada without losing three quarters of its men on the way. But by water the continent was vulnerable from three points: The enemy could sail down from Nova Scotia by sea; they could fight their way, fort by fort, down the St. Lawrence to Lake George and the Hudson; they could bring an army from Lake Erie by the Ohio and Allegheny Rivers. There were indications that they planned to do it. To combat such a three-way movement over so vast a territory, the various colonial militia would by no means suffice. Trained troops were necessary. And England had trained troops, "regulars," well-equipped and seasoned, with experienced generals to lead them.

The question was, would Britain send these troops? Was she alive to the danger, and if so, did she care? Parliament might well refuse to finance a new French war in America. After all it would not hurt the British fur trade if the French had their share of Western territory. Could English fathers be induced to send their sons across an ocean to lead troops in a wilderness for a cause so remote?

In Braintree, Mr. Josiah Quincy was deeply concerned, ready to ask these questions of anyone who would listen. Mr. Quincy had spent many years in Europe, knew the North American situation from a broad angle. He was a friend and correspondent of Dr. Franklin, who a year ago had devised a plan of strong colonial union for better protection against the growing French menace. . . . Had John Adams heard of this plan, Mr. Quincy demanded one day in his living room at the old parsonage? He flung out the question as if he were addressing not a Harvard Senior, but town meeting and town meeting were hostile.

It was a November afternoon of 1754. John had walked down to

tea on invitation of Hannah. She was in the room, presiding over the tea table, very distracting in a dress of yellow wool, cut tight to her figure, with a wide, flowing skirt. Sam and Ned were there. Young Josiah lay sprawled on the floor before the fire, roasting chestnuts in a long-handled skillet. Outside, a northeast wind was blowing; the day had threatened snow. Crimson damask curtains were drawn against the dusk; the candles were lighted. Mr. Quincy turned in his high-backed chair. John's father, he remarked, was a man who knew matters of practical government. What did Mr. Adams think of this plan of union, proposed last June at Albany when Governor Shirley had gone out to treat with the Indians? Had John seen Dr. Franklin's motto for the colonies: JOIN OR DIE?

Yes, John replied. The Boston *Gazette* had printed the motto with the accompanying drawing, reproduced from a Philadelphia paper. A clever device of a snake, broken into parts. Each part bore the initials of a colony or section: New England, New York, Pennsylvania, North Carolina, South Carolina. Underneath was written in bold letters: JOIN OR DIE.

"The colonies," Mr. Quincy retorted bitterly, "seem to prefer the latter contingency."

It was true. When the Albany Plan had been put to vote in the various provincial Assemblies, one by one they had turned it down. Most of them protested that it gave too much power to the home government in England. Connecticut objected violently to the veto privilege of a President appointed by the crown. Benjamin Franklin, pondering these contrary opinions, declared them proof positive of how necessary some plan of union had become. When local sovereignties grew fixed and angry, it was imperative to find some kind of balance between them. England, moreover, had not so much as hinted at a declaration of war against the French. Suppose she left us to fend for ourselves, could we act at all unless we learned to act together?

Mr. Josiah Quincy, addressing his living room of young people, seized the tongs and poked angrily at the fire, looking over his nose. "How near must the French come," he demanded, "before the colonies forget their eternal boundary squabbles? And which is more important — a slice of the Green Mountains for Hampshire, or King Lewis's grenadiers walking down into Ticonderoga?"

"God in his heaven!" shouted Mr. Quincy suddenly, staring

straight at John — or what he thought was straight. John cleared his throat and looked away. "God in heaven! Here are three university men — Ned — Sam — John Adams. What does our precious Harvard College have to say about Franklin's plan of union and the French on the Ohio? Or does the Discussion Club" — Mr. Quincy's lip curled — "prefer to debate the governments of Greece and Rome, as it did in my time, keeping life on a high classical plane altogether?"

John smiled, but he was much struck by what Mr. Quincy had said. Walking home that night, guarding his lantern under his greatcoat — it had begun to snow in brief, gusty flurries — he went over the conversation in his mind. It was true, about Harvard's remoteness from the present scene. John was due back at college tomorrow. He had come to love the university, felt more at home there, sometimes, than in the farmhouse on the Coast Road.

As for the Harvard Discussion Club, John enjoyed it more than anything he had ever taken part in, or so he told himself now, climbing the hill toward home, his head lowered against the wind. He had not always enjoyed the club. As a Junior last year, he had been surprised to be invited to join. He was among the first four scholars in his class, but he knew himself as an awkward speaker, and the members were chosen for their skill in elocution and declamation. President Holyoke encouraged the use of rhetoric and graceful phrase, embellished with quotations from the classics. The boys read aloud the latest books and plays, which last they were careful to refer to as "dramatic compositions" — Massachusetts having just passed a new law forbidding stage plays.

When John's turn came to declaim for the first time, he had been terrified. His part was assigned to him: Oedipus's first speech from Pope's translation of the *Thebais*. John practiced for hours in his room, striding up and down, hurling out the words, now loud, now suddenly *pianissimo*. One gesture in particular he favored. Raising his right hand high, the index finger extended, he brought his arm down slowly until thumb and forefinger pointed directly at the middle man in an imaginary front row. This telling gesture John synchronized exactly with the climax of his hero's speech: "*Go, and a parent's heavy curses bear!*"

The club met in the library, with an audience of perhaps fifty. Several graduate students had been invited, as well as old Tutor Flynt, who after sixty years' service had resigned as a teacher but

lived nearby and liked to be included in these celebrations. John had practiced so hard and so long that he had forgotten his original terror — until his name was called and he rose. As he walked to the rostrum, his stomach turned over agonizingly. Panic gripped him from head to foot. He faced the audience, cleared his throat, opened his mouth. No sound emerged. He cleared his throat again, loudly. His eyes, fixed upward in a glassy stare, saw nothing, his arms stuck rigid to his sides. In a voice wholly unrecognizable, he began to speak, stumbled on toward the climax. As he approached it he gasped, inhaled noisily as if he were choking, then lifted his arm automatically above his head, brought it down slowly and pointed. . . .

There was a shout. "Don't shoot, Adams! . . . For God's sake spare a mother's son!"

Laughter broke like a hurricane in the room. Boys howled, wept, fell on each other's shoulders, leaned helpless over their knees, hugging their stomachs with expressions of agony. Even Tutor Flynt was in a state of collapse and made no effort at rescue. John, his notes crumpled in his hands, fled the rostrum in utter, completest defeat.

It had taken him months to forget it. Perhaps he would never, he thought, forget it. He knew his turn to speak would soon come round again. He practiced doggedly in his room with the door barricaded. This time he would speak his piece if the room burst into flames and the ceiling fell in. He would not be driven from that rostrum by the jeers of one man or fifty. He chose, from Shakespeare's *Coriolanus*, words of the hero's that breathed defiance in every line. The more John practiced, the more he felt at one with this soldier who refused to beg favors from the politicians.

The evening arrived. John rose and made his way to the rostrum. Even before he took his place, the titter started. John's palms were wet. The book, when he raised it, shook miserably in his hands. He began to read Coriolanus's speech to the tribune. The old soldier, scarred with battle, is a candidate for the consulship:

> What must I say?
> "I pray, sir" — Plague upon't. I cannot bring
> My tongue to such a pace. . . .

The titter increased. Sudden anger gripped John. He threw the book on the table and walked round to the front. Standing with his

legs apart, hands gripped behind him, head flung back, he began
Coriolanus's speech from memory:

> "Look, sir, my wounds!
> I got them in my country's service, when
> Some certain of your brethren roar'd and ran
> From the noise of our own drums."

Utterly careless as to effect, John spat each word as if every man
who heard it were his own personal, desperate antagonist:

> You common cry of curs! whose breath I hate
> As reek o' the rotten fens. . . .
> > Despising,
> For you, the city, thus I turn my back:
> *There is a world elsewhere.*

John finished and stood a moment in angry defiance, his round
face scarlet, his blue eyes flashing. With a reckless gesture he shook
the hair back from his brow, then swung round abruptly and
marched to his seat, to the sound of — what was this roaring, overwhelming noise? The audience was clapping, pounding its feet on the
floor! Friends rushed up, whacked John on the back. . . . "Adams!"
they cried. "You'll make the best speaker of us all, someday." . . .
"Coriolanus angry," Sam Locke told the room, "is surely better than
Oedipus scared."

John all but wept with surprise and pleasure. His collar was wilted,
his fine brown hair awry. The black ribbon at his neck had slipped
off altogether. John stuffed it in his pocket. He walked home across
the court, arm in arm with Locke and Sewall, singing a song convivial and forbidden. Tutor Mayhew, hearing it from his study,
smiled, and did not move from his chair.

In February, 1755, the longed-for British troops arrived. They
landed in Virginia, two regiments of regulars, commanded by the
English general, Braddock, a man of sixty with forty-five years'
military experience behind him. George II, it was true, had confessed
"an utter aversion" to sending his soldiers to fight in the New World.
But the colonies themselves had made it plain they would not bear
the total burden of a new French war, showing themselves far more

interested in local squabbles than in any threat to the frontier at large. In Pennsylvania, for instance, the Quaker Assembly was wholly taken up by its quarrel with the proprietary Penn family. Such meager troops as had been dispatched by New York and South Carolina refused, on arrival in the Duquesne territory, to obey the British commander, Colonel Innes. After Washington's defeat at Fort Necessity in the summer of '54, London saw that it must send troops to America or risk the loss of half a continent.

On the arrival of Braddock and his regiments in Virginia, Dinwiddie and four other colonial governors arranged to meet at Alexandria. Shirley went down from Massachusetts, De Lancey from New York, Morris from Pennsylvania, Sharpe from Maryland. Colonel William Johnson and Thomas Pownall were present as advisers. An extensive three-way campaign was planned: Braddock was to march against Duquesne at the forks of the Ohio, Johnson against Crown Point above Lake George, Colonel Monckton against Beausejour in Nova Scotia.

New England heard of the plans and was optimistic. Boston newssheets mentioned that young Washington was to accompany General Braddock as an aide-de-camp. True, the Virginian had been beaten in his one engagement with the enemy; some men called him impatient, reckless, and unpopular with the Indians. But his experience of the wilderness would be helpful in guiding the regulars over the Allegheny Mountains. No doubt they would take along plenty of Indian scouts; the French would surely be routed from the Ohio country.

At Harvard College John Adams heard the talk. Professor Winthrop in particular was full of it. John, busy about his own affairs, paid little attention. Commencement week approached, the days rushed forward. Senior recitations were finished; John was entitled now to the baccalaureate "Sir." Nobody used it except one or two Freshmen. The word, when it came, made John smile. He wished mightily that Treadwell had heard the Freshman from Barnstable address him as "Sir Adams." But Treadwell was gone, graduated last year and far away.

The final examinations were oral and not very difficult. John actually enjoyed himself. Professor Wigglesworth especially was entirely informal, kept John overtime and remarked, with his hand to his ear in the old gesture John knew so well, that it was a relief to

question someone with a good loud answering voice. As Commencement approached, Mrs. Adams showed much anxiety about John's clothes, and was highly relieved when he told her a new law had been passed by the Harvard Corporation, forbidding gold-laced coats or brocaded vests for Seniors. All his mother need do, said John, was mend the tear in his scholar's gown and supply a clean shirt. It was far more important to see that Peter and Elihu appeared in something respectable. And would somebody, John added pleadingly, please take Mr. Adams's wig to the barber before July 16? The hair hung down in strings; there was a worn patch at the back where he leaned his head against the kitchen settle. . . .

Mr. Adams, overhearing this exordium, remarked that Sir Adams need have no fear. His family would appear at Commencement strong in numbers and strong in finery; Mrs. Adams had been working over it for months. Uncle Joseph Adams was coming from Newington, New Hampshire. The Braintree uncles were to appear in force, including Ebenezer, who since Briant's death had shown a complete change of heart and desired greatly to be reinstated in the family affections. Ebenezer had gone to Boston and ordered a new hat for Commencement, three-cornered, with a bright purple cockade that looked, said Mr. Adams, like mourning for an emperor. When Mr. Adams asked what the cockade was for, Ebenezer replied that he didn't know, but he thought Johnny deserved it.

Mr. Marsh of course was coming, together with his two sisters and his mother. The old lady was tremendously taken up with the affair, said Mr. Adams. She had an ancient green satin gown and bonnet for the occasion. One day she had called him in to look at it, taken the bonnet from a box and put it on. It was stupendous. More like a tent than a lady's headdress, Mr. Adams added, what with ribbons and streamers and flaps and contraptions. He pitied the man that sat behind it. . . . Or did they seat ladies in the gallery at First Church? — he asked hopefully of John. . . . Anyway, old Mrs. Marsh had got into a habit lately of talking to herself when excited, letting out great deep-chested groans. He had heard her do it in Sabbath Meeting. So had the boys here.

"If she does it at Commencement," young Elihu broke in, "if she grunts out while John is making his Latin responses, Peter and I have a plan. We are going to cough very loud, both together, and drown her out. . . . Like this!" Elihu emitted a strangled roar.

John looked imploringly at his mother. Mrs. Adams, tossing her head, said she never heard such nonsense. Besides, she knew how to deal with old Madam Marsh. She would sit next to her, hold a hand over her mouth if necessary. "What bothers me," Mrs. Adams finished, suddenly serious, "is what is to become of you, John, after Commencement. Are you still thinking of teaching school for a year, before taking orders as a minister? And have you any immediate prospects of a place?"

John's heart sank. *What was he to do when he got out of college?* It was the question he dreaded above all questions. He had not the slightest idea what he was to do. He knew only that he must earn his living. He could not for another week, another day, remain dependent upon his family. The entire tribe of Adamses looked to him to distinguish himself, prove the worth of this long, expensive Harvard investment. When Mrs. Adams spoke, they all gazed at John expectantly. Peter and Elihu looked actually respectful.

"I have received no direct offers," John replied. In spite of himself he blushed, having received no offers direct or indirect. "But I hear they are looking for a schoolmaster in Worcester. The Reverend Thaddeus Maccarty of that town preached the Election Sermon in Boston this June. He is in Cambridge, looking over prospects."

Mr. Adams, whose good-natured pride in his son had never permitted him to share his wife's worries as to John's future, broke in delightedly at the mention of Maccarty's sermon. He had read part of it, he said, in the newspaper. *Scatter thou the People that delight in War.* . . . Meaning, of course, the French. . . . "Now *I*," said Mr. Adams, "fear greatly that it will be the *English* who are scattered, out on the Ohio."

Mrs. Adams gave an exclamation of impatience and moved away. Why could not men keep to the matter in hand? Why must they be always turning the talk to war or politics?

A day later, John returned to college.

Shortly before Commencement, an eloquent letter appeared in the Boston *Gazette*, addressed to the printers and signed with the initials of an unidentified citizen. It was dated July 14, 1755:

MESSIEURS EDES AND GILL,
    There is no one of our Red Letter Days that I spend with so great Satisfaction, as that at the Commencement in Cambridge. To see our

Youth bringing up to learning, to meet with an old Acquaintance and Friend — to see the universal Joy that is in every Countenance — to take a Pipe in the Cool of the Day — and to ride to the Ferry in a *Charlestown Hack*, is what strikes me with peculiar Pleasure.

But! When I come to the Ferry, the crowded Boats make me uneasy, and solicitous for their safe Passage. The Disorder at the Ferry-Wayes, more especiallay on the Boston side, is shocking. The last Commencement, I landed between 7 and 8 o'clock, but before I could get up on the Wayes (which was so crowded as to render the passing unsafe) two Gentlemen's Servants were thrown over, and not less than 20 of our poor Slaves (Male and Female) were thus injuriously served that Evening. The most astonishing Cursing and Swearing was continually sounding in my Ears. Women as they left the Boat, were indecently talk'd to, and some of them were immodestly handled.

That Part of the Town was in the utmost Disorder, and this effected by a Rabble that consisted of at least 200. Such Disorder! Such Confusion! is at no other Time to be perceived in the Town; No! not on Pope night.

The worthy Gentlemen, whose peculiar Business it is, to preserve Peace and good Order in the Town, will, I hope, bestir themselves; and some of them find their personal Attendance at the Ferry. For notwithstanding the two Constables that placed themselves there, the last Year, all this Confusion happened! I also hope they will not be offended at this modest Hint, for I have only in view, that we may in this particular be reformed.

Yours,
W. K.

The "modest Hint" was wholly futile; the gentleman might have spared himself the pains. Disorder was as much a part of Commencement as the tents on Cambridge Common, the sawdust in the grass, the broken jugs that lay behind the hedges next day. The Harvard Corporation did its best. Commencement came always on the second Wednesday in July. The Corporation had tried to transfer it to Friday, so people would go home and sober up for Sunday instead of prancing all over Cambridge for three frolicsome, fearsome days. But Massachusetts found this edict intolerable and said so in a loud concerted shout. The Corporation sighed, shrugged, and went back to glorious and traditional Wednesday.

The whole of Cambridge was transformed into one vast delightful pleasance, with booths, tents, acrobats, jugglers, drinking, fighting, dancing, love-making and general joy. Long before John Adams's time, poets had celebrated it:

Each successive Day
   Venus and *Bacchus* bear alternate sway.
The raking Tribe their lawless Games repeat,
   Nor can three Days their Baccanals compleat. . . .
Thus the loose Croud forbidden Pleasures seek,
   Drink HARVARD dry, and so conclude the Week.

The crowd began drifting into town on Monday. . . . There
were Indians with bows and arrows to shoot for coins; Negroes and
beggars; children in hordes, scattering across the grass like bits of
paper before arriving coaches and horseback riders; merchants and
members of the Governor's Council, splendid in brocades and the
gold-laced coats forbidden to Seniors. The roads leading to Cambridge were a cloud of dust, the Charlestown ferrymen at their wit's
end with the boats from Boston piled water-deep. People fell in and
were fished out, only to be knocked down again at the landing by the
crowd. Everybody laughed, joshing the pair of constables on the
pier who struggled hopelessly for order.

Visitors from far away lodged at inn or boardinghouse or out under a tree; they slept on three chairs when three chairs were available.
They drank ale and rum and flip and negus and Madeira; they made
innumerable speeches interlarded with innumerable bad puns. The
old boys, wigged, powdered, limping with gout, compared Harvard
of their day with Harvard of the moment, to the great disadvan-
tage of the latter, when boys — mere fops it seemed — lacked the
virility of their fathers who had rolled cannon balls off the roof of
Old Harvard and painted red the face of the clock on Massachusetts Hall.

The college authorities were forever publishing new sets of rules
to curb this riot and extravagance. They prohibited plum cake,
prohibited treating. Nobody paid the slightest attention. Windows
were broken, chairs were broken, heads were broken. Money ran
like water from the pockets of rich graduates to whom the Corporation had applied in vain for scholarships or maintenance. In short,
a Puritan community, lusty, hard-working, repressed for fifty-one
weeks, on the fifty-second simply rolled over Cambridge in a tide
of riotous joy.

The Adams family arrived early, coming from Braintree by way
of Milton Hill and Roxbury Crossing, avoiding the crowds at the

Charlestown Ferry. Dusty, hot and happy, they debouched on the Common, ten or twelve strong, counting the uncles, Joseph and Ebenezer, their wives, sons and daughters. The whole of Braintree seemed to be in Cambridge. The Quincys drove up a little before eleven o'clock, two families of them. The Webbs were there (Cousin Jonathan was to receive his Master's degree), and of course the four Marshes, the younger ladies totally eclipsed by their mother. Mrs. Marsh's green gown swept the earth; she had topped the bonnet with a plume. The effect was breath-taking, prodigious. Mr. Adams conceded he had done her wrong altogether; the old lady looked a very empress. She was in splendid fettle. Mr. Marsh had brought a stool for her; she sat on it outside the church, regally erect, waving gaily to friends and acquaintances.

Uncle Ebenezer came with Mr. Adams. His new cocked hat was too big for him; it kept slipping over his forehead, obscuring his eyebrows. Strangely agitated, talking continually, Ebenezer expressed himself as disapproving this noise and extravagance. All the same, he drank innumerable bumpers, and before nightfall was to be heard singing a song that amazed his brother. Young Peter and Elihu, aged sixteen and fourteen respectively, pleaded to remove their heavy homespun coats, were peremptorily refused, caught sight of the tents, heard the fiddles tuning and forgot instantly that it was hot and their backs itched.

Mrs. Adams wore light gray, her bonnet was lined with pink; she carried a pink silk fan. She looked prim — and very pretty, her sons told her. Mr. Adams was magnificent in a new broadcloth coat, full-skirted, brass-buttoned, which swept back to show his embroidered waistcoat (stitched by Mrs. Adams with infinite pains). His starched shirt frill stuck out, "like a frozen waterfall," he said, complaining that it tickled his chin. All this folderol, he grumbled repeatedly, was too much for a plain farmer like himself. But the family noted, when they reached Cambridge and finally got rid of the horses, that Mr. Adams never walked past a window without glancing in and adjusting his shirt frill with a look of vast satisfaction.

Commencement exercises were scheduled for eleven o'clock, in the old Meeting-house on the Common. They would last four hours or more; after that would come the feasting and festivities. Outside the church a hilarious crowd awaited the arrival of the Governor and his mounted escort; the Cambridge troops were lined up to greet

him, with flags and music. Mr. Adams, by arrangement, met Anthony Wibird on the church steps. Wibird was the new Braintree pastor, a Harvard graduate and a friendly young man. He had offered to look after the Adams family and find seats for them. Mrs. Adams, grasping old Mrs. Marsh tightly by an elbow, climbed to the gallery with the ladies. Peter and Elihu squeezed in with their cousin, Nathan Webb (Harvard, '54).

At last the church was filled. The bell in the steeple, which had been ringing for a full ten minutes, suddenly stopped. There was a stir at the door, delighted cheers from the crowd outside. Heads turned as at a wedding, and the procession marched slowly in.

The Seniors came first, two by two in their black gowns. They wore no hats, but one and all were handsomely pig-tailed and powdered. Nathan Webb whispered their names to the Adams boys as the procession moved forward: Cushing and Appleton, leading the march. William Browne next, walking with John Wentworth — David Sewall . . . Tristram Dalton . . . Sam Dana . . . Locke . . . Hemmenway. . . .* And toward the end, shorter than his partner, standing very straight, his gown a little open and swinging with his step, his face flushed and solemn, was brother John.

Mrs. Adams in the gallery drew a long breath and clutched the hand of her sister sitting on her left. Old Mrs. Marsh said, "Where is he?" in a loud voice. "*Where? Eh? I don't see Johnny.*" Behind the Seniors marched the Masters of Arts. Next came President Holyoke, tall and imposing, walking by himself. Then Professors Wigglesworth and Winthrop, followed by the four tutors. Last of all, in a blaze of red coats, swords and military boots, walked Governor Shirley with the Lieutenant-Governor and the Royal Council.

The important personages found seats on the platform; President Holyoke nodded pleasantly to the Seniors below the stage. There were prayers, a sermon. The first Latin orator walked up the steps, bowed to the *Honorandi*, the *Venerabilis* and the *Spectatissimi*, and began. Nobody but the professors understood more than an occasional word, but everyone smiled and nudged his neighbor. As orator succeeded orator, the whisper, "That's my son!" ran through the Meeting-house like a sigh. When John Adams mounted the stage the whole Adams family stiffened to fascinated horror and leaned

---

* Philip Livingston was sick, and received his degree *in absentia*.

forward, holding its breath. President Holyoke, looking genial, rose and addressed him:

"An libertas politica, in absentia restrictionis, consistat?"

John bowed. "No, Sir," he replied in Latin. "Political liberty does not consist in the absence of restrictions. Law is necessary to government." Holyoke put another question and another; John's voice, answering, was clear and confident. A dozen Adamses let out their breath like stuck balloons. Mr. Adams, hearing this Latin emerge smooth and easy from his Johnny's lips in the presence of two governors, His Excellency's Council and most of the wealth, beauty and ecclesiastical dignity of the Province, was unable to believe his ears. It was for this he had sold the Stony Acres, for this he had prayed and worked and waited. In Mr. Adams's eyes the tears welled, flowed hot and unheeded down his cheeks. Up in the gallery, his wife sobbed happily behind her fan.

John stepped from the platform. Mr. Adams blew his nose, leaned heavily against the pew back. A tall, dark gentleman in the pew ahead, in a clerical bib, turned to him and smiled, nodding toward the platform. It was the Reverend Dr. Maccarty from Worcester, who by order of the selectmen had been looking for a new schoolteacher, and who had just decided he had found one.

PART II

Attorney at Law. 1755-1768

CHAPTER NINE

Worcester and the school of affliction. John examines himself, examines the law—and decides on a career.

John Adams, in answer to his classmate, Jacob Bailey,[1] now pastor in a remote district of northwestern New Hampshire:

WORCESTER, *I know not what day.*

. . . I heartily sympathize with you in your affliction. I am myself confined to a like place of torment. When I compare the gay, the delightsome scenes of Harvard with the harsh and barbarous nature of sounds that now constantly grate my ears I can hardly imagine myself the same being that once revell'd in all the pleasures of an academical life.

Total and compleat Misery has succeeded so suddenly to total and compleat happiness, that all the Phylosophy I can muster can scarce support me under the amazing shock.

JOHN Adams had been in Worcester less than a month, and already he was sunk in a gloom deeper than his twenty years had ever experienced. With reason he used the word "shock." He was bewildered at the situation in which he found himself. It had happened so quickly. Immediately after Commencement the Reverend Mr. Maccarty had called at the farmhouse on Penn's Hill, made a definite offer which John accepted. Less than three weeks later — early in August — a messenger from Worcester appeared on horseback, leading a second horse for John. At sunrise next morning they had set out, covering the sixty miles westward in one day. John was given

board and lodging at Dr. Nahum Willard's — a physician — and almost before he could draw breath was at his desk in the schoolhouse, commencing the August term.

Worcester had a population of fifteen hundred, about the same as Braintree. John taught all the boys from town and the country round. His pupils ranged in age from five to fifteen. His school, facing the town green, was a one-room log house with the usual fireplace, the usual rows of worn benches and battered desks. No blackboard hung on the wall, no adornment of map or picture. John was handed a stack of dog-eared books; most of them he recognized from his own days at Mr. Cleverly's Latin School. John knew nothing of "pedagogy," he had no tricks to interest or amuse. Barehanded as it were, he faced a roomful of fifty squirming boys, all watching eagerly for the new master's vulnerable spot, prepared to torment or to obey him as the case might be.

Like most young bachelors, John had not the slightest interest in children or the slightest understanding of them. But he had grown up with two young brothers whom he had cuffed and cajoled since babyhood, and he carried a sort of sturdy, older-brother authority which the boys quickly felt and respected. As the weeks wore on and John grew established in his position, the problem became one of boredom rather than of discipline. The regime as prescribed was nothing short of horrible. School hours were long and very, very empty. At eight in the morning, John took his place at the high desk overlooking the room, read a passage from the Bible and heard his voice putting sonorous queries from the Westminster Catechism. Like a dream the words rose up from forgotten years of his childhood: *What is the chief end of man?* . . .

To John's mind came again the face of Mr. Cleverly, perched on his high platform long ago in Braintree. Had Cleverly been as bored as this? Impossible! Mr. Cleverly had been an old man — a cross old man. (As a matter of record, Cleverly had been in his thirties.) Such boredom went deep; it was felt almost as a sickness. It made a man ache all over, stiffened his very bones. For the first hour or two in the morning, John's scholars whispered and wriggled, kicked each other enthusiastically under the desk, then settled — it seemed to John — into a hopeless daze, their mouths hanging open like idiots'. After lunch the smallest ones fell asleep in their seats, slipped down, had to be wakened and propped up again. All fifty were forever

asking for escape to the privy outside. Their faces were dirty, their noses ran; one and all had a perpetual cold in the head.

Autumn progressed, and the room was always too hot or too cold. By noon each day when the hearth fire was high, a kind of steam arose from woolen garments into which fifty boys had been sewed against winter. The place smelled, John thought in disgust, like the animal cages on Boston wharves, where were displayed for a shilling, furry creatures that enterprising sea captains had carried home from foreign parts. John divided the room in sections as he remembered Mr. Cleverly had done, the smallest boys in front, the big boys behind. While one section recited, the others "studied" out loud, learning by rote whatever was placed before them, from spelling to Lily's *Latin Grammar*. The continual drone acted, hour upon hour, as soporific for teacher as well as pupils. John's eyes closed, he jerked himself awake, wondering desperately if some such buzzing drone did not accompany, in hell, the pangs of the tormented. . . . Was this, then, what New England spoke of so proudly as "education"?

There was no clock, merely a noon mark on the eastern window sill. At about quarter to five the room woke miraculously; the instant John raised his head to pronounce dismissal, the herd stampeded as if the building were on fire. The noisiest boy in school was Thaddeus Maccarty, son of the minister who had brought John to Worcester. At closing time, Tad was first on his feet. Down the middle aisle he charged, head lowered as if the Indians were after him, bowling over like tenpins the smallest boys in front. John, shutting his desk and making his own eager escape down the aisle after his scholars, had to hold himself furiously in check so as not to knock over more boys than Thaddeus.

Aside from the prison house of school, John found Worcester a pretty enough town, independent, far more self-sufficient than Braintree. Situated in the middle of Massachusetts, it had no Boston to depend on for supplies; there was as yet neither post office nor stagecoach. Round the Green, set back and shaded with great oaks and maples, were the houses of the principal citizens — Chandlers and Putnams and Paines and Willards and Bigelows. John, accustomed to the shorn hills of Braintree, admired the trees; writing home, he described them as "primeval." There was a new courthouse — Worcester was a county seat — a new jail with barred windows. Mr. Maccarty's Congregational Meeting-house reigned

supreme. Years ago, energetic Baptists had laid the foundation and rafters for a church; in the night, Worcester citizens, equally energetic, had risen and torn it down. They boasted about it to the new schoolmaster. John was disgusted at the pride in their voices.

Pleased with its young college-bred dominie, Worcester greeted John cordially when he passed along the Green on the way to school, shook hands with him in church on Sundays and invited him home to dinner. But in spite of the kindness of his landlord and neighbors, John was lonely, deeply homesick. He was ashamed of this feeling. Why could he not settle down, he asked himself, answer enthusiasm with enthusiasm? The new jail failed to move him. The whole place had an air wholly different, not only from Harvard College but from Braintree. As the weeks advanced, it came to John that the difference lay in Worcester's distance from the sea.

Only sixty miles west of Boston, this seemed almost a foreign country. Men's interests were not the same. To these people, news from the westward, from the frontier, was actually more important than news from Boston. One might have thought Europe did not exist. Dispatches from London, Madrid, Paris, that Braintree discussed so eagerly, here no one bothered to notice, although Boston newspapers were often brought in. What Worcester talked of was not the change of prime ministers in London or a shift in the Governor's Councilors at Boston, but the French war and what was happening up around Albany. The Connecticut River flowed down through Hampshire County to the immediate westward. Worcester spoke of this river as Braintree talked of Boston Bay, talked of Indians as if Indians were important, not just a dirty nuisance to be driven off one's land like stray cattle. Only seven years ago, the town had been raided by the Nipmucks, and before that for a hundred years men had walked to church with the butt of a musket resting in the palm.

John heard and saw, listened respectfully, made appropriate answers to stories of local history and local enterprise. But somehow he was not part of it and knew in his heart he never could be part of it. Here as a schoolmaster he was marking time. His future lay elsewhere, to the eastward, nearer the Atlantic Ocean and that vast world which lay beyond the ocean. This fierce proud inland provincialism of Worcester was admirable in itself, but it was not, John felt, something a man could aspire to. Moreover it had become

plain that the less he said about Boston and Harvard, the better. Worcester looked upon its new college-bred schoolmaster as a prize specimen, whose acquisition did the town credit. But this was no reason why the citizens should be forced to listen to Harvard talk or put up with Harvard airs.

John was thrown back violently on himself, spent long hours alone in his room at night, studying Greek with far more passion than he had ever shown at college. He had lost his identity. In blind desperation, he felt that study and study alone would re-establish it. He read every book he could find or borrow, copied page after page into a kind of diary he had begun to keep. Here also John confided his self-doubts, his fears, his mistakes of the day and his prayers for a better tomorrow. What was to become of him he had no notion beyond being certain that schoolkeeping was a mere stopgap to be endured, got through with until something better offered. John found himself, here in Worcester, in a hole. Fate had flung him into it, fate and the necessity of earning a living. He would climb out, he knew not how, but somehow.

There existed neither money nor connections to help him. For the first time in his life, John realized it. For the first time, the circumstances of his birth rose up to confront him, and he asked himself bluntly, what was his position?

The Adamses of Braintree were farmers, millers, cordwainers. The world took it for granted they would remain farmers and cordwainers, even if their sons, by dint of huge exertion, became ministers of the gospel, merchants, physicians, lawyers. The lines were drawn. Boston and Braintree were not the frontier, where name counted for nothing, brawn and courage for everything, and where a man might carve for himself such a career as the forest offered. Boston, Braintree and the Eastern coastal settlements had a social system as surely defined as any county or shire of old England. To Governor Shirley, to the Honorable Edmund Quincy, honest Braintree yeomen accorded a natural deference, tipping the hat, holding back at the church door that the squire and his lady might pass in ahead. The lines were drawn. Across them was but one road, one escape — the amassing of a vast fortune.

And suppose, thought John Adams, suppose he himself succeeded in piling up a fortune as great as the Hancocks of Boston, would he not still be John Adams of Braintree, honest farmer and

freeholder? It was a hurdle insurmountable. John saw it with a rush
of bitterness and bewilderment. His father's face rose before him,
kindly, patient, the face of a man content in his position, proud of the
acres he had won by the toil of his hands. There had been an incident
some years ago, when Mrs. Adams's father had died and the Boylstons of Brookline had come to Mr. Adams, asked him to purchase
their mansion and land so as to keep it in the family. Mr. Adams
had been much gratified that he was in a position to be applied to for
such favors. But he had refused. His own farmhold in Braintree
was sufficient responsibility for a man of his station in life, he said.

John remembered that his father had shown no desire to own
a mansion, sit in the squire's seat. And if the father was thus content,
why could not the son be content also? Why suddenly was he, John
Adams the younger, riddled with these questions, this anger, this
smoldering fierce resentment? Birth, money, position: he had
known of these things before. At college they had counted, John was
not blind to them. Yet his course there was not impeded because a
Sophomore from the West Indies had four dozen frilled shirts, or
because Hancock of Boston possessed three curly wigs and a brocaded waistcoat. Besides, President Holyoke had known of Deacon
Adams, and the name of Dr. Zabdiel Boylston was honored in academic circles.

But once a young man struck out alone to make a living, how
cruelly and inexorably his social position was exposed! As he con-
templated his position, John's mood veered from dejection and stubborn truculence to a reckless defiance. Influenced by some brief
triumph in company, some new friendship formed or flattering attention paid him, he swung upward to a soaring confidence in his own
ability, a pleasing illusion that brains and honest exertion outvalued,
in the end, the advantage of birth, money, position. At such times
John was apt to forget himself altogether and fall into the error of
castigating, to his new friends, the morals of gentlemen in laced hats,
gentlemen with five thousand pounds a year. Afterward in his room
he lashed at himself for his unbridled, foolish tongue. The laced hats
could not be put down by this method; it only exposed John Adams
the more. "I must never," he wrote angrily in his diary, "affect wit
upon laced waistcoats or large estates or their possessors. I now resolve for the future never to say an illnatured or an envious thing

concerning governors, judges, ministers, sheriffs, lawyers or any other honorable or lucrative offices or officers. . . ."

It was a large resolution. John Adams was fortunately unaware that he could never hold to it, unaware that even when he should have climbed to the highest office in the nation — a nation he had helped mightily to build — the laced waistcoats and the laced waistcoats alone would have power still (however foolishly) to cast him down.

Meanwhile he was twenty, marooned in Worcester with a living to get. Late in the autumn, Dr. Willard lent him a horse, and John rode home to Braintree for a brief visit. The exercise, the fresh air, the kindliness of his family's reception, their unflinching confidence in his future, gave John a new perspective. On the long journey back to Worcester, he resolved to do something to make his school less boring, more effectual. If a man were sunk in a hole, the least he could do was try to make the hole more bearable. At home on Wollaston beach John had picked up some cockleshells, an empty lobster claw. He tied them in a handkerchief and brought them to Worcester. He would set his scholars to collecting stones and minerals, tell them something of natural history, of the tides and stars, the solar system as he had learned it from Professor Winthrop. There was no reason also why the boys should not search for beetles and grubs, bring them to school and even dissect them after the fashion of the Harvard apparatus chamber.

The plan succeeded far beyond his hopes. There was something touching in the boys' response. From the biggest to the littlest, John's scholars arrived with boxes containing such treasures as three very dead beetles, a torpid snake, a toad scooped out of the Reverend Maccarty's well. . . . In spite of himself, John began to find his school less hateful. On spelling-bee days the rivalry became intense. John had instituted prizes (a bit of sugar candy, an old bent fishing hook from his own pocket). Afterward the outspelled team invariably sat down and cried heartily. John, as experience gained on him, kept in his desk a bundle of clean rags donated by his landlady, and summoned the defeated to have their noses wiped. "Caesar," he told Tad Maccarty one day after a particularly severe rout on the words "cough," "cuff" and "draught" — "Caesar leaned on Alexander's sepulchre and wept. Thaddeus, do you know why?"

Thaddeus looked up, shook his head. Three tears rolled down a well-marked furrow. "Because," John said — "here, blow *harder*, Tad! — because Caesar was nearly forty, and he knew that Alexander, before ever he was thirty, had conquered a whole world." [2]

Thaddeus, not comprehending this philosophy in the least, returned John's smile and went back to his seat, somehow comforted. Tad's father, the Reverend Mr. Maccarty, had been, of course, John's first friend in Worcester. John liked him, stopped in almost daily at his house which lay northward by the town brook. Maccarty was tall, excessively thin, with dark hair and eyes that were described as "penetrating." Actually they were not penetrating at all, Mr. Maccarty's character being made up more of kindness and genuine piety than penetration. He had a harsh, nasal voice, with which Sunday after Sunday he delivered sermons that were neither bright nor very dull. His wife, a harried, hospitable little woman, was always pregnant. (She presented her husband, in all, with fifteen children.) At the moment she had only six. She considered John starved at Dr. Willard's where he boarded, often urged him to share their own rather meager supper.

Mr. Maccarty had a great interest in local history; his enthusiasm was unbounded. He invited John for long walks about town, showed him the new courthouse from cellar to garret, the jail with the barred windows. Fresh straw lay on the floor. What was John's opinion of the New England penal laws, Maccarty asked. Did he believe punishment was for revenge? Or, according to the new Italian theory, for the moral regeneration of the prisoner? . . . Still talking, he led John out and up the common to the fulling mill by the bridge. At the door the smell of damp wool met them; men working in a cloud of steam shouted to each other above the rush of the mill wheel, the clack of the wooden shaft along the ceiling.

In the very middle of Worcester Green sat a long iron cannon, slightly askew on its pedestal. Maccarty said it was left over from the last French war. Worcester had sent as many as sixty-nine men to that war. A high proportion, Maccarty said proudly. Had Braintree done as well? The Almighty alone knew, the minister added, how soon Massachusetts would be called on for aid in this new trouble with the French. General Braddock's defeat at Fort Duquesne in July had been nothing short of disastrous. Out of eighty-six officers, sixty-three had fallen, including every officer on horseback except

one — Captain Washington of Virginia. The papers said he was only twenty-three; yet he had been left with a handful of men to guard four hundred miles of frontier.

Maccarty was especially interested in the French exiles from Acadia who lived a mile or so out of Worcester. The "Neutrals," they were called. The English had driven some seven thousand of them from Nova Scotia, fearing they might rise with the French. Worcester had only a handful. People liked them and were sorry for them; they were frugal, very handy about making farm implements. Maccarty bought a wooden rake from a bearded man who had a pretty, dark-eyed daughter. John tried to engage her in conversation but she had not a word of English.

Dr. Willard heard about this expedition stiffly, showed no sympathy for the pretty girl — who, John declared, had seemed "lonely and homesick." *Neutral* indeed! Willard said with a snort. No French person was to be trusted, be she handsome as Venus. Suppose the French got past Crown Point, pushed down Lake George to Hudson's River? For his part he didn't put a half-joe's confidence in the Albany men. Sell their souls to the Indians for a beaverskin any day, they would. . . .

"This whole Town," John wrote to his cousin Nathan Webb in Braintree, "is immersed in Politicks. Be not surprised that I am turned Politician. The Interests of Nations and all the Dira of War, make the subject of every conversation."

Laying down his quill, John looked with satisfaction on this last sentence. It was night; in his room the tiny fire smoked. . . . *The Interests of Nations and all the Dira of War.* It was an elegant bit, rhetorical in the best style without being too high-flown for a cousin with whom one had grown up. "I sit and hear," John continued, "and after having been led through a maze of sage observations I sometimes retire, and by laying things together, form some reflections pleasing to myself."

This time the reflections proved astonishingly prophetic. Was it possible, John went on, that someday the seat of empire would be transferred to America? "If we can remove the turbulent Gallicks," wrote John facetiously of the French on the St. Lawrence River, "our People according to the exactest Computations, will in another Century become more numerous than England itself. Since we have all the Naval Stores of the Nation in our hands it will be easy to

obtain the Mastery of the seas, and then the united force of all Europe will not be able to disunite us. *Divide et impera.*"

Divide and conquer. Throughout John's life the phrase would recur to him again and again. (In Philadelphia, nominating a Commander in Chief for the Continental Army. At Paris, begging French aid to fight a war. In Holland . . . London . . . in the White House at Washington, with half America cheering for Bonaparte, the other half cursing France and the French Revolution. In the bitter year of 1814, when even Massachusetts men, rather than fight "Mr. Madison's War," shouted "Quit the Union!")

Dr. Willard of Worcester did not share his young lodger's interest in these large post-bellum plans for political union. What concerned Willard was the immediate problem at hand to the northwestward. The French must be dislodged from the Champlain country. He swore he would join the next military expedition from Worcester as a surgeon — the army needed a good bonesetter. He had had notable success in fracture cases, he declared, by pouring rum over the splint. The spirits strengthened the bones. And besides, the fumes seemed to comfort the patient.

Willard was a bluff, hearty, energetic man who had never been to college, but who had an extensive practice in the county round. People were not particular about the university degrees of surgeons, provided they could let blood, apply plasters, set bones and deliver babies. Willard engaged John in enthusiastic discussion concerning the merits of purging over bleeding for fevers. He considered himself especially knowledgeable in the treatment of hysteria. To dissipate the melancholic humours, apply a dozen or so of leeches, he said. Order the patient five days in bed on water gruel, then send him to the wood lot — as he had his last patient — and let him chop down trees enough to fill the woodshed. . . . "Kill or cure is my motto," Willard added cheerfully.

In the downstairs office was a shelf of medical books: Sydenham, Dr. Cheyne, Van Swieten's *Commentaries on Boerhaave*. John went through them. Willard was delighted. Why could not John take up the practice of physic himself? He seemed to have a knack for it, or at least for talk of it. John considered this. The sooner he began training for a career — any career — the sooner he would be rid of schoolteaching, his foot on the ladder that led upward, out of this

hole. He liked the books on physic, yet the actual business of a surgeon revolted him. The atmosphere of a sickroom made him uneasy. As for letting blood, John felt sure he would be like Mr. Marsh of old and, scalpel in hand, turn green at the first incision. . . . The Adams family and most of John's friends took it for granted he was to be a minister. The Reverend Maccarty was calmly certain of it, discussed the matter as if it were *fait accompli.*

John himself was unable to believe in his gospel career. But he could not bring himself to say so until something else offered. As winter deepened and he settled into his surroundings, John became acquainted with a wholly different set of men — the county lawyers. Three quarters of Worcester got its living directly or indirectly from the square white courthouse on the Green. Here the Court of Common Pleas sat four times a year. In October, the Massachusetts Superior Court convened; in between were held General Sessions of the Peace, presided over by the county justices.

Local elections in May and October were periods of intense interest. The principal families campaigned for each other and each other's relatives, schemed to elect Cousin Gardner Chandler for Sheriff as though they voted for a Cromwell. These men talked law as glibly as if they had been trained in it, which they had not been. After one attendance at Quarterly Session, John, quick with new words, aired his vocabulary in a letter to a college friend.* What a lawyer's life might be at the peak he did not yet know, he said. But so far, it seemed no more than "a fumbling and raking amidst the rubbish of writs, indightments, pleas, ejectments, illatebration and 1000 other lignum Vitae words that have neither harmony nor meaning."

Truly, John went on, study of the law had lately become an avenue to the more important offices of state. In Massachusetts the Governor's Councilors were lawyers, so were the Admiralty Judges. Yet all the world knew a man was not appointed Judge of Admiralty from a simple farmhold in Braintree! "The winning of these offices," John stated candidly, "depends upon many circumstances of Birth and Fortune, not to mention capacity, which I have not, and I can have no hopes of being useful that way."

Back and forth John shuttled, aware that he must decide on a career. But no matter what he said or thought of the law, along with

* Charles Cushing, Harvard, 1755.

the rest of Worcester he found himself, that spring of '56, gravitating toward the courthouse and the men who frequented it. Among them the Chandlers were the reigning family. Judge Chandler Senior had the biggest house in town, was cousin or uncle or grandfather to everybody, knew politics far beyond the confines of Worcester. He had been to the Albany Congress of '54 with Franklin and Governor Shirley, and talked as fast and volubly as Mr. Josiah Quincy. He was a cheerful, friendly man, big and heavy, with a long Yankee nose and pleasant gray eyes. John had three Chandler boys in his school. The Judge liked to inquire about their progress, jokingly, as if the birch were a natural, healthy concomitant to the Latin language.

There was only one trained lawyer in Worcester. His name was James Putnam; he lived three doors from Judge Chandler, and had his office in a little one-room building on the Green. John had not yet met him. Putnam seemed forever away on circuit, or trying important cases in Boston and Cambridge. But one heard about him continually; his name kept cropping up. He was just turned thirty, people said. He had lived in Worcester only six years. But already his practice was wide, his position secure, and it had not been diminished by his marriage to Judge Chandler's daughter. Putnam came originally from Danvers on the east coast, had been graduated at Harvard in '46 and studied law with Judge Trowbridge in Cambridge. The town admired Putnam, but it was apparent they were also a little afraid of him. He had not the easy country ways of his in-laws the Chandlers, although he was sociable enough and liked to talk. John gathered that if, in conversation, one proved a trifle slow, Putnam would speak out his own answer — and not in terms calculated to make the listener more at ease.

John saw him first one evening at Judge Chandler's in a large company of men. Putnam stood before the fire, surrounded by listeners. Judge Chandler took John through the crowd and introduced him. Putnam bowed briefly and pleasantly, then resumed his conversation. But to John, lingering near, it soon became obvious why Worcester had talked of James Putnam. There was about him something arresting, something that caught the imagination. John saw a man of medium height, slim, with reddish hair and light-brown eyes that closed slightly as he talked. He wore a smooth, dark blue coat with silver buttons, spotless linen ruffles at the wrists. From time to time he took snuff delicately, from a thin silver box in his breast

pocket. He talked quickly, precisely, with a beautiful command of English. When he said something particularly clever he laughed softly, with an easy good nature. The company, at this brief sound, laughed too — but not before. Putnam's talk ranged from the law to natural philosophy, from Newton's *Principia* to religion. He had Morgan's *Moral Philosophy* at his tongue's end; he had read Clarke, Waterland, Emlyn, Leland's *Review of the Deistical Writers*.

John had never seen a man like this. Putnam wore his learning lightly, tossed off quips and quotations, mixed wisdom and nonsense as a juggler throws a string of balls over his wrist. The Reverend Maccarty had come in with John; the two stood together, listening. "It is my opinion," Putnam was saying, "that the Apostles were nothing more than a company of enthusiasts. We are told they spoke with different tongues, healed the sick, raised the dead. But we have only their word. What kind of evidence is that, after seventeen hundred years? A court of law would throw out their case, *nulli prosequi*."

He turned to John. "I have heard that our new schoolmaster rode to Worcester with a pair of books in his saddlebag that do not jibe well with strict Congregational doctrine."

John was startled. How could Mr. Putnam know he had traveled from Braintree with Bolingbroke's *Patriot King* as baggage? The circle was silent, waiting for the schoolmaster's reply. John gave a brief, polite little bow in acknowledgment of the sally, spoke quickly. "If I carry Bolingbroke in my saddlebags, Sir — why, after all, there was virtue in the world before there was orthodoxy in it."

The circle burst into laughter. "Hear, hear!" Dr. Willard called delightedly from the back of the room. "My lodger is a scholar, but I didn't know he was a wit. *There was virtue in the world before there was orthodoxy* . . . Capital, capital!"

John dared not catch Putnam's eye. The phrase was not his own. He had read it a week ago in *The Independent Whig* and copied it into his diary. Putnam's voice was amused. "All is grist, young Sir," he said, "that comes to a reader's mill."

John blushed, caught his tongue between his teeth. So Putnam knew *The Independent Whig*, as he knew Morgan, Clarke, Lord Bacon. Certain that he had made a fool of himself, John subsided utterly for the rest of the evening. After the party, alone in his room, he wrote miserably in his diary, "I can as easily still the tempest or

stop the rapid thunderbolt as command the motions and operations of my own mind. My brains seem constantly in as great confusion and wild disorder as Milton's chaos. Vanity, I am sensible, is my cardinal vice and folly. I am in continual danger, when in company of being led into an ignis fatuus chase by it, without the strictest caution and watch over myself. I never have any bright, refulgent ideas. Everything appears in my mind dim and obscure, like objects seen through a dirty glass or roiled water."

So wrote John Adams at twenty, with the Puritan introspection, the passionate self-questioning that was to be a trait of his sons and grandsons to the sixth generation. (As a matter of fact, James Putnam had been delighted with John's answer, thought only better of him for using so dashingly what he had read.) But John never enjoyed a triumph that he did not question, next day, right out of existence, pouring lavishly before a jealous God the libation of self-doubt. In a man of less energy and less virility, this introspection would have been dangerous; in John it acted as spur, as rowel pricking to new effort. . . . If yesterday's triumph today seemed insecure, John told himself it was because he had not applied himself to study, had wasted his time, his talents.

> I am resolved to rise with the sun [*he wrote now in his round clear hand*]. May I blush whenever I suffer one hour to pass unimproved. I will rouse up my mind and fix my attention; I will stand collected within myself and think upon what I read and what I see. I will strive with all my soul to be something more than persons who have had less advantages than myself.

A day or so later, to John's astonishment, Putnam called on him at Dr. Willard's, invited him to take tea at his house on the Green. John was quite beside himself with pleasure. For the next week his diary was filled with two names and two names only:

> *April 28. Wednesday*. Drank tea at Mr. Putnam's, walked with him to his farm, talked about nature.
> *Thursday*. Fast Day; heard Mr. Maccarty preach, spent the evening at Mr. Putnam's very sociably.
> *May 8. Saturday*. Went a-shooting with Mr. Putnam; drank tea with him and his lady.

On evenings after he had been in the country with Putnam, John forgot his introspection; the diary came alive. "The season is beyond expression delightful. The air is soft and yielding, filled with a ravishing fragrance. The trees put forth their leaves, and birds fill the spray. . . ." "There is a story around town that I am an Arminian."*

An Arminian. John set the words down easily, as a matter of little consequence. Yet it was a statement that would have shocked his father, shaken the old man indeed to the heart. Lemuel Briant had lost his church because the town of Braintree — and Deacon Adams — said he was an Arminian. John had come a long way in the last three years. Fortunately for him, most members of his school board were Arminians themselves; the Trinity was not popular in Worcester.

On the eleventh of May, court week arrived. The town welcomed it gladly, made a festival of it. Court week meant the end of winter, the end of snow and silence and the bitter unremitting cold. Around the Green, great trees moved softly against the sky, a faint burst of buds showed at their outermost branches. Court opened on Tuesday, to give the lawyers time to make their journey without breaking the Sabbath travel laws. They came by chaise and on horseback, their briefs and lawbooks in their saddlebags, their servants behind on horses borrowed from the spring plowing. One and all — judge, lawyer, plaintiff, defendant and juryman — were pleased to be in town, primed for courtroom triumphs or a little quick money from business picked up on the outside.

Refreshment booths appeared on the Green; at the corner on the highway, saddle horses stood in rows before Luke's tavern, awaiting the hostler. There was horse racing down the Leicester road, and in a roped-off arena young farmers wrestled and boxed while their sweethearts looked on, squealing frightened admiration. In the evening, fiddles played; young and old danced under the trees.

It was a school holiday; John was free as air the whole week. The weather was balmy, the oaks on Judge Chandler's lawn a shimmer of delicious pink, and along the brook by the fulling mill the willows drooped golden in the sun. "Rambled about all day, gaping and gazing," wrote John Adams in his diary the first day of court. At Dr.

* This last sentence is quoted not from the diary but from a letter to Charles Cushing.

Willard's, every bed was occupied. Mrs. Willard darted from kitchen to parlor like a woman distracted, calling John to help — bring wood for the fires, move the old chest from the milk house to the best bedroom so there would be a place for the gentlemen to lay their linen. Dr. Willard's nephew from nearby Lancaster, young Abel Willard, stayed in the house. John had known him slightly at Harvard. After graduation, Abel had studied law with the great Benjamin Pratt in Boston and had just been admitted to the bar. He was a quiet, modest fellow of twenty-three; John liked him immensely.

But among the galaxy of legal learning that arrived in Worcester that week, young Willard was a mere nobody. To everyone's surprise, Attorney General Trowbridge himself appeared; he usually reserved his visits for the October session. Trowbridge was in his late forties, known as a deep scholar of the law, an authority especially on real estate. Putnam had known him well since his student days. The Judge controlled the legal practice of three counties; rumor had it his frown could ruin any young lawyer. Putnam did not introduce John to Trowbridge, but John noted with curiosity the change in Putnam's manner the instant the Judge entered the room. It was all respectfulness and deference — an attitude, it was apparent, that went through to Putnam's backbone.

Trowbridge had the best law library in North America and expected his clerks to read in it. Not one of your overblown men of importance, said Putnam. Not one of your moneygrubbers who puts a clerk to copying deeds all day and never gives him a chance for study. The Judge was a heavy-set man, formal in bearing; he chose to preside in wig and gown after the English fashion. It gave a prestige to the simple Worcester courtroom, kept back the pettifogging and unlicensed practitioners with which the country abounded and who appeared in swarms for court week, hoping to come by a little business.

John went to court every day, listened while the lawyers pled their cases. There were the usual boundary-line disputes . . . One Ephraim Dyer had walled his south pasture "six foot over onto the Widow Baldwin's property." Somebody's horse had been found eating the apples from somebody else's tree or the grass from somebody's pasture. There was a case about an indentured servant named Moses Shove who had decamped before his time was up, and settled happily

in the employ of one Zebulon Thwaite "on the road to Cannadee." Zebulon refused to return him.

By the third morning when the cases were called, John no longer saw himself a mere spectator. Seated in his accustomed place in the third row, John became the lawyer for the plaintiff and the lawyer for the defense. When one of these, a Hampshire County man whose legal education had been gleaned apparently in the hayfield, made a blundering, palpable mistake in his Latin, John shuddered and turned to Willard a face as shocked as if he himself had said *respondENT superior* instead of *respondeat*.

It required no special knowledge to see that of all the lawyers, James Putnam was the most brilliant by far. No one had a chance against him. It was not done by witchery, by trickery or intimidation of witnesses. The veriest tyro, listening as Putnam built his careful, inexorable argument, felt that this man knew the law. He was cold as ice, his argument glittered with citations from Coke, Fortescue, Bracton. While the opposing lawyer talked, Putnam sat at the table below, perfectly composed, no muscle of his face moving, taking no notes. But when he got to his feet in turn, the light gray coat elegant under its silver buttons, the white ruffle falling below his cuff as he raised a hand in the familiar easy gesture, John felt the hackles rise on his neck. The questions Putnam asked of the witnesses brought out, in a way infinitely skillful, his side of the case. Yet how innocent the questions seemed as Putnam asked them, and how gentle he was with the witnesses! They did not fall into his trap; they leaped into it, urging as it were their horses to a gallop and jumping the hurdles gladly to land in Putnam's pit.

Young Abel Willard, sitting with John, shook his head. "Praise God this case concerns twenty shillings, not the plaintiff's life," he said. "James Putnam could get a man hanged for stroking his neighbor's cat."

Court sat all day, often did not rise till nine or ten at night. But whether it adjourned late or early, the lawyers moved as a man to the tavern or to the hospitable dining rooms in the big houses round the Green. Judge Chandler had four or five stopping with him. Mr. Putnam usually managed to secure Judge Trowbridge at suppertime. John trailed along after the company. Putnam seemed to have forgotten him altogether, but Maccarty and Dr. Willard had a speaking

acquaintance with everyone, and introduced John gladly. There were two men especially, who had no sooner been introduced than they began to seek John out, sitting by him in court, inviting him to the tavern for a glass of ale and, to John's surprise, asking his opinion of the day's cases as though he were an authority. They were known respectively as Colonel Doolittle and Mr. Baldwin. Doolittle was a prosperous merchant in the county. Baldwin, who lived in Lincoln, had been Register of Deeds for years and was familiar with local politics inside and out. Both men urged John to be a lawyer. He was positively born for it, they said.

John was flattered but a little embarrassed. Nevertheless the seed fell in fertile soil. Sitting at the tavern in the evenings while lawyers and judges drank their wine, John listened with new interest as the men reviewed the day's work or bargained with each other for the prompt trial of certain cases against the postponement of others. Sooner or later the talk turned to the war in the north, which during the winter months had been quiescent. The ice was gone now from Lake George and the Champlain country; fighting would be resumed on the upper Hudson. These men, John noted, spoke of the war in terms not of military strategy but of political results. Was it a trait of lawyers, to be interested in government? It began to be obvious that law and government were blood brothers; they functioned together, one grew out of the other.

"This year, this very year," Judge Chandler said, "will decide if the French shall drive us into the sea. Or if, as I have heard old Governor Belcher say, 'King George will be emperor of America.'"

Chandler had an extravagant, impulsive way of speaking. And yet, John thought, he had never heard so much good talk in his life, had never sat through so many suppers, shared so much punch and general conviviality. . . . And then of a sudden it was over. The lawyers were gone and all their entourage of servants, grooms, horses, hawkers, peddlers and hangers-on. Worcester Green was quiet once more; beyond John's schoolhouse the great oaks shed their quivering shade on Judge Chandler's lawn. In the evenings the Judge himself was to be found behind the house, mulching his strawberry bed instead of talking law.

Mr. Putnam vanished altogether; his wife said he had gone to Cambridge with Judge Trowbridge. John took up his duties at school, studied Greek, copied long extracts from sermons and visited Mr.

Maccarty. Court week seemed a vanished dream; John's spirits went down and stayed down. "I have no books, no time, no friends," he wrote mournfully in his diary. "I must therefore be contented to live and die an ignorant fellow."

In the middle of August, an express rider galloped in from Boston with news that England had declared war at last. It was high time; the situation on Lake George had gone from bad to worse. The French general, Montcalm, had captured the forts Oswego and George. If he proceeded down the Hudson and attacked Fort William Henry, the whole of Massachusetts would be endangered. From the courthouse steps Judge Chandler read the declaration of war to a crowd assembled on the Green.

On long afternoons when schoolkeeping seemed unendurable, John sometimes entertained himself with visions of Captain John Adams, epaulets on shoulders and sword at his side, swaggering out of Worcester at the head of a company of foot. But the prevailing social system by no means expected or desired its schoolmasters to go to war. Young men of university education seldom enlisted as privates; John had neither money nor influence to procure a command.

The current excitement increased John's restlessness, his fierce dissatisfaction with himself. The decision as to a career must be met. It could not be postponed another month, another week. There was no longer any serious thought of the ministry. Meeting that question squarely, John knew it must have been answered years ago, before ever he left college. Nor was he fitted to be a physician. The business of a merchant, with its close attention to ledgers, figures, accounts, loomed as sheer horror.

There remained the law. Examining himself closely, John could not say he felt a deep-seated call to the career of lawyer. But the law was all around him, here in Worcester. It was available, something he could begin at once. Before the third week of August, John made his decision: he would ask James Putnam to take him into his office as a student. He could continue his schoolteaching, make enough to keep him alive. And if in the end the law proved too much for him or too little, the study of it would have done him no harm.

If Putnam accepted him, John knew the plan would come, at home in Braintree, as no great shock. The family still assumed that John was headed for a gospel career. Yet surely, thought John, since

the Briant controversy Mr. Adams knew in his heart that his son
was lost to the ministry! As for his mother, John had heard her say
outright, the last time he was home, that while she loved God she
did not always love His representatives in the Congregational Church
as she had seen them.

The decision once made, John was in a frenzy of impatience to
proceed. Several times he walked up to Putnam's office but never
succeeded in finding that gentleman alone. When he finally cornered
Putnam, one very hot, still afternoon, and blurted out his request,
the lawyer showed no surprise and little apparent interest. He would
think it over, he said. He did not wish to make his decision today.

As a matter of fact, Putnam knew instantly that he would take
John Adams in his office. Moreover he planned to ask his wife if
Adams could move over from Dr. Willard's and board with them
for the ensuing two years. It would be stimulating to have someone
at the dinner table. In two years of marriage, Putnam had long ago
exhausted his pretty wife's stock of ideas and conversation.

But he said none of this to John. Instead, he inquired if Adams had
informed the Reverend Mr. Maccarty of his decision? The conversation was held at Putnam's front door, where John had found the lawyer sitting on the front step, taking the air in his shirt sleeves. Even
in that negligent costume, Putnam had an elegance about him. His
voice, slow and tired with the heat, was edgy. "Mr. Maccarty, *your
patron* . . ." he said, and there was something curt, sarcastic in his
tone. After perhaps five minutes' conversation, Putnam dismissed
John with a wave of the hand, bidding him call at the office tomorrow afternoon late, after school.

John walked slowly home. That night in his room, he reviewed the
conversation, word for word. Putnam had asked if John had informed his "honored father" of his decision, and had gone on to say
he understood Mr. Adams was an officer of the church. No doubt
Deacon Adams looked forward to seeing his eldest son in gown and
bib, exhorting his flock from a pulpit? "Lawyers in Worcester are
one thing — " Putnam said; his tone changed, he spoke earnestly —
"but have you any notion, Adams, what the Province at large thinks
of the profession? We are hated, mistrusted — and not without reason, considering the standards of the bar until recently. The town of
Boston never chose a lawyer to represent it at the General Court
until the year 1738, when they elected Mr. John Read. At the next
election they put him out."

John had never heard Putnam speak like this, with no trace of amusement or banter. "Sir," John replied with equal earnestness, "I had rather be dead than be a Congregational preacher. As for my father, he is an honest man. He will put my welfare above his own pride. What Mr. Maccarty thinks is no concern of mine. I have made my decision. I await yours, Sir, with — with utmost impatience," John had finished awkwardly.

There was nothing to do but wait, get through the next twenty-four hours as best he could. Punctually next day at five o'clock, John was at Putnam's office on the Green. It was the twenty-first of August, 1756, an afternoon cloudless and blazing. In a house far up the Green someone was practicing a fife; the sound came shrill and high above the drone of locusts. Putnam was alone in the little office, surrounded with books and papers. To John's delight he had a contract already drawn up; it called for two years of study. He invited John to live with him, the better to pursue his reading. "We can talk law in the evenings," Putnam said. His whole manner had changed, he was dazzlingly kind and affable.

"I shall have to go on with the school, Sir," John said.

He would indeed, Putnam replied. But the hundred-dollar fee could be paid at John's convenience. Beyond his board money, no charges would accrue.

John signed the contract; Putnam said he would have it witnessed on the morrow. These formalities over, Putnam put an arm across John's shoulders. "The occasion calls for a ceremony," he said pleasantly. If Adams would step over the road, to his house? The two crossed the Green; Putnam went up his front steps, led the way to the dining room. Mrs. Putnam had laid out a tray with two wine-glasses and a decanter. It was his best Madeira, James Putnam said, filling John's glass. Nothing less would do, today. He raised his glass. John Adams, raising his own, felt his hand tremble. Long afterward, he was to remember this scene. The big square room with its polished table and sideboard, the windows thrown wide. And beyond, up the Green, the high quick sound of a fife. . . .

Mr. Putnam moved a step forward, his glass touched John's. He bowed. John Adams, his throat suddenly constricted, returned the bow stiffly and raised the glass to his lips.

CHAPTER TEN

1756–1758. The law and the French war. John assumes a military mission.

August 32. Monday. Came to Mr. Putnam's and began law,
and studied not very closely this week.

IT WAS to be the last entry for two years; John had no time for
diaries. To live in James Putnam's house was a career in itself, leaving few moments for moods and self-reproaches. There was, at first,
scarcely time for study. When John was not teaching school he was
in Mr. Putnam's office over the way, sitting on a high stool copying,
in a careful scrivener's hand, deeds, writs, wills, pleadings or any long
document his master found convenient to present.

Putnam had about fifteen lawbooks, a good showing for days
when a lawyer's library could be carried in his saddlebags. (Harvard
itself had only twenty lawbooks.) Most of these volumes were a hundred years old, written by English judges who had sat on the bench
before Cromwell's time: the learned Dr. Cowell, Chief Justice
Finch who pronounced sentence on the regicides of Charles I, Sir
Matthew Hale, last of the great record-searching judges. And a century further back, Sir John Fortescue, who wrote his famous *History
of the Laws* for his royal pupil, the exiled Prince Edward.

Foremost among all these Records and Abridgments and Discourses and Histories was the huge folio volume of Coke's *Institutes*.
It included, as every student knew, Sir Edward Coke's *Commentaries upon Littleton* — greatest of lawbooks, very fountainhead of
knowledge. Within these yellow covers lay the records of some five
hundred years of English law. James Putnam put it in John's hands

the first day. "Abridge it," he said, heaving it down from the high shelf and laying it open on the desk. "Make a digest of it, in sections." Putnam had the grace to grin as he said it, blowing dust from the edges. It was like asking a man ignorant of Arabic to make a digest of the Koran.

John Adams did not grin. He leaned over the volume, on his face the look of a man about to run a race. When Putnam had gone, he turned the pages back to the beginning. The frontispiece was a large, handsome engraving of My Lord Coke himself in ruff and ermine, his narrow, bearded face intelligent, aristocratic. On the opposite page was an equally large engraving of Sir Thomas Littleton, kneeling on a cushion in his long robes and looking very medieval. From his mouth in a ribbon came the words, *Ung Dieu et ung Roy.*

One God and one King. John looked at the phrase in curiosity. "Do you know any French?" Putnam had asked abruptly before he left the office. "How much Latin have you?" He had gone on to tell a story of some miserable student in Benjamin Pratt's Boston office who was taken from Coke the first week and set back to studying Lily's *Latin Grammar.* John prayed it might not happen so with him. Coke, it was true, had put his *Institutes,* section by section, into three languages: first the Latin, then the French, then what purported to be English. But even the English was full of strange terms such as *service de chevaler.* Evidently, a true scholar in the law would do well to acquire at least an acquaintance with the French language.

The whole enormous pile of Coke's learning seemed to concern feudal tenures, beginning with a treatise "On Estates in Land and Tenements," then a treatise on "The Antiquity and Nature of Manors and Copyholds." Here the author, wandering back to the Saxons, became extremely involved and paused to remark engagingly that, perceiving himself "to be running into an inextricable labyrinth," he would "sail no longer in these unknown coasts but would hasten homewards."

And high time, too, John Adams thought. Amid all this *villein service, service de chevaler, fee simple and fee tail,* if My Lord Coke lost his way, what was to happen to John Adams of Braintree? "A lawyer," some long-dead Inner Temple man had remarked, "must have an iron head, a brazen face and a leaden breech." A true saying certainly; Putnam had often quoted it. And what had these ancient feudal customs to do, in God's name, with tenure of land in Massa-

chusetts in the year 1756? The Province had long ago abolished quitrent; men owned their land outright. And even where they rented it, they owed no villein service, no tilling of my Lord's soil, no rendering to the manor the first fruits of the harvest. . . . "Villein-service," read John: "as, to carry and recarry the Dung of his Lord out of the City, or out of his Lord's Manor, unto the Land of his Lord, and spread the same upon the Land, and such like." A female villein it seemed was called a "Niece"; the text announced that "a Niece, ravished by her Lord, might have an Appeal of Rape against him." Here in Worcester, only a month ago, a girl had been raped in Colonel Doolittle's barn by some passing stranger (described in John's diary as "a fine gentleman with laced hat and waistcoat and a sword"). The whole town had rung with it. Under feudal tenure, now, would the Colonel be liable?

No matter how remote from today this compilation of the great Coke might be, there was a fascination to the reading of it. Mastery of this book, thought John, might not make a man successful in the courts of New England. Yet surely, he who studied would end by knowing much of English history. Not that Coke told his facts as history. On the contrary, he had simply hurled his words on the page as they came to him, a vast, disorderly, dogmatic pile of statutes, customs, maxims, from which the reader must construct his own historical edifice. Perhaps this was why Abel Willard, speaking of the book, had complained so bitterly.

Generations later, students would be sighing over My Lord Coke. Daniel Webster was to declare he never understood a quarter of it. No boy of twenty could understand Coke, he said. Study of it had caused him to "despair, and almost give up the law for school teaching." Chief Justice Story as a young man tried to read Coke, tried twice and thrice. "I then set myself down," he confessed, "and wept bitterly." Thomas Jefferson admired it, mastered it — and referred to it afterward as "uncouth but cunning learning." And in London the great Lord Eldon advised his students to read Coke again and again, "as he who toils up that hill will have the world of law before him."

Toiling up his legal hill that summer of 1756, John found on Putnam's shelves nothing so solidly informative as Coke. Yet he discovered volumes that made far pleasanter reading. Lord Bacon wrote a flowing and elegant diction, Bolingbroke on the English constitu-

tion was easy to get through. There was an old treatise, written in the fifteen hundreds, called *Doctor and Student*. It was slim, light, easy to hold, and there was something charming about its simple, old-fashioned dialogue, where DOCTOR OF DIVINITY and STUDENT OF THE LAWS OF ENGLAND conversed together, seeking as it were a connection, a bridge from morality to law, from church to courthouse, from the authority of God to the authority of man.

It was a connection and a bridge much needed in the New World. Massachusetts clergymen, leaders in the Province since the first landings at Plymouth, were jealous of the rising power of the law courts, inclined to look upon lawyers as the devil's advocates. The DOCTOR OF DIVINITY did not think so at all. The laws of God and the laws of man were one, he said — interdependent, the second built upon the first. After the *law eternal* came the *law of reason and nature* which was written in the heart of every man and told him to "love good, hate evil, speak truth, do justice to all."

John found himself here in familiar pasture. From childhood he had sat in church and heard the minister expound "the laws of God and nature." Lemuel Briant, being politically minded, had referred these ideas straight to John Locke and the Glorious Revolution of 1688, but they were far older, went back indeed to Aristotle. . . . In New England, ecclesiastical and civil law were supposed to be entirely separate. But were they? Did not traces of ecclesiarchy overlap our civil courts? Massachusetts judges, if the English common law did not suit, fell back on Scripture, the codes of Isaiah or Deuteronomy. The famous Massachusetts "Body of Liberties," contrived in 1641, had built its criminal code squarely on the Mosaic law. Provincial judges were still inclined to give the opinions of Moses open preference over those of the Lord High Chancellor of England.

It was a situation entirely natural. New England was used to having clergymen as judges. Among the sixty-five men who landed originally at Plymouth, not one was a lawyer. As a matter of course, clergymen assumed the first leadership. Their education was superior; they were accustomed to authority and the ordering of ethical decisions for their flock. The early New England courts were by no means devoid of dignity; there was about them nothing of the rough justice of the frontier. Cases were deliberated with greatest care. John Winthrop, first Governor of Massachusetts, pre-

sided in wig and gown, preserving as best he could the majesty of the English courts. So did his son of the same name. Behind each of these men was a university education in the Old World.

But their immediate descendants had an upbringing altogether different, with neither time nor opportunity for a university education. Life in the New World was hard; a man's energy went to survival rather than book learning, either ecclesiastical or civil. By 1700, a change in the courts was indicated and very necessary. Settlements had spread, land had become valuable. Men were rich, now, beyond the boundaries of church membership and church authority. Lawsuits multiplied, developed complications too intricate for Congregational elders or even intelligent lay judges to solve. Men who had once stood up and argued their own cases now looked about for lawyers. The Province, which at first had not permitted attorneys to accept a fee, began to recognize the need for a professionally trained bar. In 1701 an order was passed, regulating the admission of lawyers to practice; the old English oath for attorneys was revived.

Such was the situation when John Adams began to study law. Nevertheless, it was small wonder Putnam had warned that the Province hated lawyers. The sudden need had given rise to pettifoggers, unlicensed and unlearned, who slipped past the oath and the regulations, swarming over the courts and preying on the natural-born litigiousness of New England men. During this confused and transitory era, law students had no body of American court reports to help them; a full generation would pass before the first of such collections was published. America was busy forming her own legal precedents, adapting the English law to her own pressing needs. And the process, as John Adams had divined, could not be hurried. It was heavily retarded by the fact that New England judges did not put their opinions in writing. Decisions delivered *ore tenus* were the rule. As late as 1799, the great Chancellor Kent of New York, taking office, was to declare, "We have no law of our own, and nobody knows what the law is."

All John had at his command were the scribbled notes of Putnam's own completed cases, a folder of reports and records Putnam had gathered on circuit. John was by no means aware that he was starved for material; he had quite as much to go on as any other law student of the day. Looking at the shelves above him it seemed, indeed, there was more law in this small Worcester office than one man

could master. John went laboriously through each volume whether he understood it or not. Where he could, he reduced the pages to brief headings and a general digest.

It was hard work, long and unremitting. Putnam gave his pupil little guidance and no praise. The evenings were too short for the amount of work John must cover. He took his books to the school-house, appointed monitors from among the older boys and snatched what study he could during recess or the lunch hour. Some time during the next two years he must prepare a dissertation for his Master's degree at Harvard. This was no very difficult matter; the requirements for graduate degrees were simple. John decided to write on government. His cousin Sam Adams of Boston had argued, one Commencement, the question "Whether it be lawful to resist the Supreme Magistrate, if the Commonwealth cannot be otherwise preserved." The Overseers and Faculty did not discourage such radical papers, so long as the speaker preserved the amenities — a proper respect toward the King's colonial officers who were in the audience. But John Adams preferred a subject more comprehensive. Looking over the possibilities, he chose a title: "Is Civil Government absolutely necessary for Men?"

With a flourish, John inscribed the words on a clean sheet of paper. Just when he would find time to develop this grave and important theme, he did not know; his intellectual schedule was already quite breathless.

What few moments remained of the evenings went in conversation with Mr. Putnam. This itself was no easy exercise, Putnam not being of the school that wants only a flattering listener. To James Putnam, conversation was a game that required a worthy opponent; John was hard put to it. At dinner, Putnam had not finished carving the roast when he was at it. Mrs. Putnam, pale and pretty, sat silent, her soft brown eyes fixed proudly on her husband. She had a little habit of nodding emphatically from time to time, as if she were part of the conversation. When Putnam caught her at it he frowned, or smiled his brief smile and, reaching out, patted her hand as if she were a child.

It took John Adams months to learn how to parry Mr. Putnam. What he could not get used to was the fact that Putnam did not argue from conviction at all. One evening the lawyer, when the wine was brought, began expatiating on what he called the nonsense talked

from the pulpit concerning immortality. Fortifying himself with quotations from Emlyn, Clarke and Bolingbroke, he wove an argument watertight and impenetrable, succeeding at last in making John agree with him. Putnam, at this, reached complacently for the decanter as if the argument were closed. "But Mr. Putnam," John said suddenly, "I thought you *believed* in an after life. I heard you tell Dr. Willard so, the second time I met you."

"Believed!" Putnam repeated. "What has belief to do with argument? Will belief win a case in court? What a simplicity is generated by the pure airs of Braintree! I shall have to acquire a new law clerk, before the Superior Court meets in the autumn."

Upstairs in his bedroom that night John, sitting with a shoe in his hand, saw before his face Putnam's image, smiling, bland, intelligent. That brief, crooked little quirk of the lip held an awful measure of contempt, of sarcasm, of a meaning deliberate yet so subtle it was gone before the victim was even sure he had interpreted it. What a shield against a wicked world! John Adams, whose passionate honesty left him defenseless as an oyster without a shell, felt sure he need only cultivate a smile like Putnam's to rid himself of all future discomfort in the presence of gold sleeve buttons, brocaded waistcoats and the squires of vast estates.

Next day, emerging from his bedroom to Worcester's main street and starting off for school across the Green, John copied Mr. Putnam's manner — his walk, easy, deliberate, graceful, his dashing way of putting on his hat, a little to the back and on one side, his light, careless bow that had in it the subtle contempt of his smile. After school that same day, greeting Mrs. Maccarty at her door, John did not shake hands warmly as was his custom but stopped short on the threshold, his hat under his arm, and bowed very slightly. His round face shone with health and the heat of a moist September evening; his blue eyes, usually wide open and alert, were partially closed by lids that drooped — John thought — with a lazy grace. Mrs. Maccarty, throwing him a startled glance, inquired if he were upset? Was there perhaps something on his stomach? Let him come in immediately; she would brew camomile tea. . . .

James Putnam on his part had as much difficulty adjusting to his lodger as his lodger had to him. Putnam was more than merely brilliant. He was a painstaking and perceptive student of the law who

found himself, here at Worcester, in a backwater too small for his talents. His contempt was no more than impatience, a longing for quarry worthy of his skill. In John Adams he had hoped for a companion as well as a pupil, and in part he found it. There was no question of John's mental ability — Putnam was amazed at the speed with which he went through Coke and Fortescue. And yet, Putnam told himself, this was the most incorrigibly unworldly youth of twenty-one he had ever encountered. It was true John came from a narrow farmhold in Braintree. But Braintree was not a wilderness. Did four years at the university count for nothing in the acquisition of at least a surface poise? John was impulsive, tense. All his gestures were clumsy. He went through a room like a camel, Putnam told his wife one night after John had excused himself and gone to bed, knocking over a small table on the way and carrying with it a Sèvres cup filled with hot chocolate. "If Adams," Putnam went on impatiently, "desires to move further than the Court of Common Pleas, he will have to develop something besides his brain. . . . Suppose he were to go to London to study at the Inns of Court! I would not dare procure for him a single introduction. If he were drawn into an argument he would leap to his feet and throw out his arm in one of those violent, meaningless gestures — " Putnam shot his own right arm forward, stiff as a board, and let it suddenly drop.

But he said nothing further. It was of no use to confide to Mrs. Putnam that John's most irksome trait was not his physical clumsiness but a guileless and stubborn insistence, in conversation, on basing every argument upon what was "right." No amount of ridicule seemed to penetrate this blind spot in his pupil. "Right by whose standards?" Putnam challenged wearily, again and again. "John, John, this world does not turn on its spindle by virtue of the acts of the Apostles."

At home in Braintree, John's decision to be a lawyer was received calmly, as he had hoped. Mr. Adams showed neither shock nor disappointment; Mrs. Adams confessed indeed that she had been looking for something like this. It was the uncles who demurred and more than demurred. Ebenezer, furious, declared he never would have lent the ten pounds for tuition had he known his nephew was to turn renegade. Uncle Joseph wrote from New Hampshire that he was deeply pained. John's own friends were eloquent in disapproval.

Richard Cranch in Braintree and John's classmate, Charles Cushing of Boston, begged him to reconsider, return to the ministry. John was making a serious mistake; he was "inconsiderate, rash."

When John wrote back his tone was reckless; it astonished his friends. "The point is now determined. I have cast myself wholly upon fortune. What her ladyship will be pleased to do with me, I can't say. The more danger, the greater glory." He was not without fears for the future, he continued in a strain more natural to him. But compared with his original dismay concerning a preacher's career, these fears were as nothing. Now he would be free of "ecclesiastical councils" such as the meetings in his father's house that had outlawed poor Lemuel Briant. The "diabolical malice" of what passed as "calvinistical good-nature" would have no further terrors. "I shall have liberty to think for myself without molesting others or being molested." And if he should succeed in the law, then — John finished triumphantly — ah, *then* he would think himself worthy of a louder triumph than if he headed the whole army of orthodox preachers!

John had a speaking acquaintance, by now, with the county judges who presided at Quarterly Sessions: Joseph Wilder, Nahum Ward, Edward Hartwell, Thomas Steele — men of ability, well thought of in the county. None was formally trained in the law, Steele being the only college graduate. In the May Session of 1757, when John had nearly completed his first year's study, Timothy Ruggles was appointed Judge of Common Pleas in Worcester. He was John's distant cousin, a stout, strong man of over six feet, who liked to boast that he practiced law not by the books but by rule of thumb and the common sense God gave him. He had fought at Crown Point under William Johnson, was known to three counties as Colonel. For a side line to the law, he kept a tavern on the Sandwich Road; he had been in politics some twenty years. At the courthouse John was pleased to be greeted as *Cousin*. But he longed for a man of his own age to talk to, and that spring of '57, he found him. . . .

Jonathan Sewall, brother of John's classmate David, was seven years John's senior, tall and fair-haired with the full, long Sewall face. He was imaginative, sensitive. He came from York, far to the northeastward, but just now he was studying law in nearby Lincoln with Judge Russell. His uncle was Stephen Sewall, Chief Justice of

the Massachusetts Superior Court, a descendant of the famous Judge Samuel Sewall who had condemned the witches in Salem. Jonathan liked to tell how the old Judge had stood up in Sabbath Meeting afterward and recanted, begging God's forgiveness humbly before his neighbors.

But Jonathan Sewall, for all his grand connections, was poor, and the fact was a bond between him and John Adams. Sewall's father was dead, friends had put him through Harvard College. He rode over from Lincoln to Quarter Sessions on a borrowed horse and if this were not available, walked the thirty miles. He was as pleased to discover John as John to discover him. The two liked each other immediately, spent hours alone in Putnam's little office among the books, windows open to the Green, talking and smoking. Sewall chewed tobacco and so, at this stage of his progress, did John. In comfort and friendship, plug in cheek, they discussed the lawyers and judges, their quirks and talents, planned their own futures. Sewall declared his eventual aim to be a seat on the admiralty court or the Governor's Council. What was John Adams's immediate goal?

Money! — John replied gloomily, without hesitation — Money was his goal. It had to be. How else could he get ahead in this world? It was all very well for a Massachusetts Sewall to talk of admiralty judgeships. But an Adams of Braintree would have to be worth five thousand pounds a year before he could make himself noticed by the gentlemen who dispensed colonial appointments and the King's favors. If he could become a good trial lawyer and an experienced, resourceful advocate in real estate and probate law, in ten years' time he might be able to marry and raise a family. After that would be soon enough to start dreaming of a judge's robes. And even then — John's lips drew in, he shook his head — even then it would be but a dream.

How much, Sewall put in after a moment, did John think Mr. Putnam was making? Eight hundred pounds a year — two thousand? . . . Speculation raged pleasantly in the little office. And while their careers awaited them so splendidly — why not, Sewall suggested, exchange the digests they made of Coke and Fortescue, carry on a correspondence, deliver as it were brief examinations to each other by letter? Sewall had, he confessed, especial trouble in distinctions between "trespass *de bonis*" and "trover." As to husbands' "rights of curtesy," he would never master them. What would John

Adams do if, for instance, he had to draw, entirely by himself, a special demurrer?

John spat vigorously out the window and remarked that he would rather not think about it. "James Putnam," John said, "loves special pleading. He would go twenty miles out of his way on foot to pick up a misjoinder. He pounces on a misjoinder as a fox on a rabbit. There is game in it as well as nourishment."

Sewall laughed; he was always laughing. John was an entertaining creature, he declared — in spite of a constitutional seriousness that approached the ferocious. "There meanders about your soul, John, a little capillary vein of — shall we call it satire? It breaks out when least expected." Startling to the beholder, Sewall went on, but it made for very good company.

John was pleased. Satire? Like Mr. Putnam, of course! John pulled his shirt sleeves smartly below his coat cuff, waved a hand languidly at Sewall, then laughed himself. . . . There were footsteps in the roadway. John got up and looked out. "Here comes Colonel Doolittle and Baldwin, our Register of Deeds," he said. "And that fellow Dyer. They will talk deism and the suffrage. Dyer is a stickler for what he calls equality. He says perfect equality of suffrage is necessary to liberty. Everyone must have a vote — lunatics, prisoners for debt, women. Every limitation of the suffrage is *anti-Christ*. His word, Sewall, not mine. He is a madman. Wait, you will see."

The men walked in, talking and laughing. Quite evidently, they had just come from the tavern; they were filled with well-being and forensic vigor. John gave up his chair, seated the others and stood lounging against the high desk, playing the host, watching with amusement as Dyer, scenting a new antagonist, opened his batteries.

"Sewall, eh?" he said. "An old name. An honored name, Sir! I take it you are a strict Congregationalist — no quarter for deists and equality men like myself. Now our friend Adams here is at least open to conversion. . . ."

John, standing against the desk, crossed one leg over the other, folded his arms and felt very much at home. How pleasant it was, he thought, here in the little office! The late afternoon sun struck low across the bookshelves, made a pattern on the dark, wide-planked floor. These three men were not the most important personages in the world, but they were here for no other reason than to see John Adams. They had sought him out, desired him as witness, as

host to their discussion. A glow of well-being filled John. He took from his pocket a pouch of tobacco, moved to Doolittle and offered it. . . . Sewall was already talking. "So you wish, Mr. Dyer, to give the suffrage to ladies and lunatics! Now, what would the Governor and his Council say to that?"

John seated himself on the table's edge, swinging one leg. He stuffed tobacco in his pipe, looked around the room, looked down, and smiled a fleeting, secret smile of satisfaction.

In July of 1757, ominous news of the war came to Worcester, news that was to put in the background all talk save talk of the French. Fort William Henry, at the southern end of Lake George, was in imminent danger of attack from Ticonderoga, forty miles to the northward. Rogers's New Hampshire scouts brought word that Montcalm had eight thousand men marshaled and ready; Fort William Henry had only two thousand. The English General Webb, at Fort Edward farther south, seemed oblivious to the danger and made no move to help. The main British army was far away in Nova Scotia waters. Lord Loudoun had elected the maneuver with a grand plan of joining forces with Lord Howe's five thousand regulars now on their way across the ocean. A splendid scheme, worked out on paper — but small help to the garrison at Fort William Henry that had not tasted meat in weeks.

Thomas Pownall, new Governor of Massachusetts, moved quickly. Without waiting for advice of crown or council, he ordered twenty-six Massachusetts regiments ready to march at a moment's warning. It was a high-handed proceeding, and in a proprietary government like Pennsylvania's, would have won severe reprimand. Expresses galloped out from Boston: Worcester was appointed headquarters for the rendezvous of all troops from the middle counties. Camp was established a few miles out of town, just west of Mr. Putnam's farm. The Green was suddenly overrun with countrymen walking in by twos and threes from Lancaster, Shrewsbury, Rutland, Lincoln, their muskets on their shoulders or "naked and begging arms," as Colonel Chandler's report had it. Excitement ran high. Day after day, dispatches came in from the northward, frantic calls for help. Colonel Chandler received the riders, sent orders instantly wherever troops were to be had. Worcester ran out of post riders. These damned farmers, said Colonel Chandler, wouldn't leave their hayfields in July

if the enemy were cannonading the courthouse itself. A man was needed to ride immediately to Providence, ask Governor Greene for troops. Rhode Island held onto its militia senselessly, Chandler complained. Were they waiting for the French fleet to sail into Newport before raising a defense?

John heard about it from Dr. Willard, whom he met on the main street, riding out to see a patient. Willard pulled up his horse, leaned down, asked John gravely if he knew anyone who would volunteer as messenger to Providence. John looked up quickly, caught his breath. "Do you mean me, Dr. Willard?" he asked. . . . "Why not?" Willard asked. He grasped John's hand, shook it heartily and rode on. In a state of high excitement, John turned, walked straight to Colonel Chandler's, knocked at the door and offered his services. There was no question of schoolkeeping or even of Putnam's permission to be absent from the office. This was war.

The Colonel was surprised. "You are accustomed to horses, Adams? I believe I have not seen you in the saddle."

Yes, John replied. Or at least, he knew horses as any farm boy knows them. . . . Then let him prepare to ride at daybreak, Chandler said.

Next morning it was still dark when Chandler himself pounded at John's bedroom door. The household was instantly roused. "Your horse is ready," Chandler said. John threw on his clothes, took papers and purse from the Colonel, snatched a bite of breakfast, vaulted on his horse in fine style and cantered out of town just as the sun rose over Quinsigamond Pond. Providence was a good forty miles. John rode hard, wishing he had a faster mount; this old mare was better suited to the plow than to express riding. Each time they cut across a bit of pasture she pulled perversely, lowered her head to the grass until John beat her from it with a stick.

All the same, it was superb to be out under the sky, posting away on military business. He would do this often, thought John. Perhaps Colonel Chandler would give him a regular commission — who knows! Men had received a lieutenant's insignia for lesser services than this.

John reached Providence by nightfall, only to learn that Governor Greene was in Newport, where the General Assembly was meeting. John snatched a few hours' sleep. At daybreak he found a fresh horse, got ready his papers in case he should be stopped by the

constable — it was Sunday — and rode southward through the green Narragansett country. John had never been outside of Massachusetts; he was surprised to see the people, on this pleasant Sunday, strolling about in their best finery as to a fair. The girls waved and John waved back, urging his horse gallantly to a gallop. No constable showed the slightest interest in calling him to halt.

Before long he began to wish mightily that somebody would stop him, no matter who. With reason, Colonel Chandler had asked if John could ride; since living in Worcester he had not been on a horse above three times a year when he rode home to Braintree. The saddle seemed suddenly filled with chestnut burrs; John shifted uneasily. His back ached, his legs ached, fiery pains darted from shoulder to calf. This morning the hostler had offered him choice of somebody's gaited mare and a two-year-old; John had grandly taken the two-year-old. The beast started and jumped like a new lamb at pasture; he shied at trees as if he had never seen a tree. John groaned, rising in the stirrups, cursing himself for being soft all over, a sedentary in time of war. As the sun rose to the meridian, dust rose with it. John had already begun to sniffle, he sneezed miserably at every stretch of sunny road.

Reaching a woods, the road narrowed to a trail; the horse picked his way over the logs as if he were dancing. The lofty shade was grateful after the hard trot and canter in the open. John mopped his face and neck with a handkerchief, sneezed and spat. Two horsemen appeared, riding toward him through the trees. Obviously, they were persons of importance. The older of the two, gray-haired, epauletted, wore a sword. John pulled his horse off the trail and hailed them. They stopped. "Are you from Newport?" John asked. "Is the Governor there?"

"What is your business with His Excellency?" the younger man asked stiffly.

He had messages to deliver, John replied. Military orders, from Colonel Chandler of Worcester.

The older man spoke at once. "I am Governor Greene. Produce your credentials."

He took the dispatches from John's hand, broke the seals, read them and shook his head gravely. This was a serious affair, far more serious than he had hitherto known. "The French," he said, "are determined to have this country."

Greene made a motion to his companion, suggested they dismount. He had further questions to ask about the news from Lake George. The three got down off their horses, sat on a log while the Governor put his queries. He was friendly, knew the Chandlers of Worcester well, he said. . . . Incredible, that four or five thousand Frenchmen, mostly Canadians and savages at that, could raise such an alarm through the country. . . . But Massachusetts would soon see that Rhode Island men were not behind in their duty. The answer to these — Greene tapped the dispatches — would be to march — yes, *march* through Worcester within the week.

The Governor pressed John to turn back with him to Providence, spend a few days at his house. He himself would send an express to Colonel Chandler. John was highly gratified at this invitation from a strange Excellency with a sword. War, it would seem, made all men brothers. . . . John hesitated, pulled himself together. Then he bowed as well as he could, sitting on a log. "I am honored, Sir," he said, and sneezed. "But I am eager to see Newport Island. I have never been outside my own Province of Massachusetts."

The Governor smiled. "All young men should travel beyond their own country. But you will have trouble, Mr. Adams, getting over the water at Conanicut. Every ferryman on the island is in his hayfield. New England cannot fight wars in July."

John got up stiffly, made his farewells, limped to his horse and rode slowly southward. At the ferry he waited interminably; the flies around the landing were awful. But once aboard the little shallop, John's spirits rose as the wind filled the sail. How delightful the sight and smell of the sea, after the dry airs of Worcester! He could never live inland permanently, John told himself with passion for the hundredth time since he had left Braintree two years ago. Did all men born by the sea bear this inevitable brand, this thirst for the damp salt air, the scream of gulls, the pebbles scraping down the little waves at the beach's edge? In Bristol Harbor the tide was low; the pungent odor of decayed clam rose to John's nostrils and he inhaled blissfully.

Three days later, John got home to Worcester, stumbling through Mr. Putnam's door late at night in the rain, more dead than alive. Putnam took one look, howled with laughter and called his wife to view — he said — the remains. "Our military hero!" Putnam

shouted. "Here, my friend, use my handkerchief. Yours looks exhausted, like yourself."

Mrs. Putnam glanced at John and did not laugh at all. She took him gently by the arm, led him up to bed and kept him there five days, plying him liberally with brandy and hot water, refusing pointblank to let Dr. Willard in the room to bleed him. John slept, sneezed, shivered and roasted alternately, waking with a start when he heard James Putnam's step on the stair, bracing himself miserably for the attack. He had started off so gloriously on his journey, filled with importance and military ardor! Was adventure to be rewarded, all his life long, with a cold in the head? Ever since his Freshman year at college, this had happened to him. Other men could sit out the night roistering, could take long journeys in the dead of winter, do all kinds of reckless, delightful things and come out unscathed. Raising rheumy eyes to Mr. Putnam, John agreed in a hoarse whisper that a law clerk had best keep to his books. . . .

In due time John returned to Putnam's office and resumed his studies. During the brief summer vacation from school, he did not go home to Braintree but stayed in Worcester, read hard and long, trying to catch up, cover as much ground as possible before the fall term opened in August. His time with Putnam would be over next summer, and with it his contract to teach school. John's distaste for schoolteaching had by no means decreased. Whatever fortune forced upon him in the future, he told himself, it would never, never be another school.

News from the north grew more alarming. On August third, an express galloped into town with news that Fort William Henry had surrendered to the French. Worse than that — the garrison had been massacred! The French general, Montcalm, had struggled at the risk of his life to hold back his Indian allies. But the savages, enraged at finding no booty in the fort, burst past him and cut down the unarmed militia as they filed out the gate. The New Hampshire troops at the end of the line had it worst of all; out of two hundred men, eighty were killed or captured.

It was the heaviest military disaster New England had ever suffered, and it woke the country. No matter if Montcalm had tried to stop his savages — anyone who knew Indians knew you couldn't bribe them with promises of plunder, incite them to raids and ter-

rorism along the border, and then stop them short with a gesture when the blood began to flow. Women lay murdered in the fort, their bowels ripped out and cast over their dead faces. Children's brains were dashed against trees, small bodies were sprawled and doubled on the ground. By God, said New England men — and said it in their newssheets — by God, it's time we ceased fighting fair, "fighting like Englishmen"! Time we began killing captives in our turn, just to show those devils. . . .

The Boston *Gazette* printed eyewitness accounts of the massacre, also a letter from Albany with a list of the equipment carried by every Frenchman that marched against the fort. People were amazed; one's own neighbors boasted no such wardrobe: "2 pair Indian shoes," the list read, "2 pair stocking, 1 pair spatterdashes, 1 pair breeches, 2 jackets, 1 large over-coat, 2 shirts and 2 caps and 1 hat. A pair of mittens. A tomahawk, 2 pocket knives, a scalping knife" — every woodsman carried a scalping knife — "a steel and flint. For every two men an ox, to every four a kettle and oyl cloth for a tent, with one blanket and a bearskin. To each man 12 day's provision of port wine and bread." All of this, the men pulled after them on little hand sleighs.

It was an impressive showing. Obviously, the French were not only dirty fighters but were coldly determined — as Governor Greene of Rhode Island had said — "to have this country." And the country knew it at last. The Worcester militia marched out, Colonel Chandler commanding. His brother Gardner, the sheriff, had a company; Luke Brown from the tavern was a lieutenant. Dr. Willard, true to his promise, went as surgeon. They were headed for Albany. Word from Governor Pownall had it the French would follow up their victory by an attack on Fort Edward, farther south. If the fort fell, the frontier would be defenseless, the whole of Massachusetts naked to the sea. Every man living west of the Connecticut River was ordered to drive in his cattle, destroy his wheel carriages — a terrible order in harvest time.

Mr. Putnam talked nothing but war. It was not the French he damned now, but the British generals that had let this thing happen. God knows, America needed them — but had any war been worse managed? Beginning two years ago with Braddock on the Ohio, what had these commanders achieved but defeat? General Webb at Fort Edward, sluggish in his quarters while Montcalm besieged

Fort William Henry fifteen miles away; Abercrombie at Lake George. "Mistress Nabbycrumby," his own men called him contemptuously. And above all, this new General Loudoun. Even Governor Shirley was incompetent in the field, although one must acknowledge he knew the wilderness.

It was true; Putnam was justified in everything he said. England had been incredibly careless concerning what she still called "the Canadian war." In London, high commissions in the North American command were looked on as plums for placemen and royal favorites. To many a nobleman, the Canadian wilds were an excellent disposal place for troublesome younger sons who would not settle down to a career. New England men, veterans of years of French and Indian fighting, were wild with anger when forced to march under some well-born, arrogant young Britisher who may have been brave enough, but who let his powder get wet overnight and who — with a Mohawk behind every tree — couldn't ram the powder down a muzzle-loader without reciting the manual of arms. John Adams's tall, tough, Indian-fighting cousin, Timothy Ruggles, although a colonel in his forties, at Crown Point had been compelled to fight under a twenty-two-year-old ensign that didn't know an Indian from a stump at ten rods. Ruggles had trouble preventing his men from turning their guns on the British instead of the French.

Up in Nova Scotia waters, Admiral Holbourne and his great British fleet proved useless. Most of the frigates were already destroyed by weather or taken by the French; the few ships that remained had turned tail for England. People began to say outright that we could fight the French better alone, without Great Britain. A new batch of British troops arrived in Boston Harbor; the House of Representatives flatly refused to vote them barracks and supplies. General Loudoun was bewildered. Instead of appearing in person and *requesting* the House of Representatives for barracks, he had sent an *order* for the quartering of troops — "as provided for by Parliament." On hearing the word "order," every New England back stiffened, every hand flung up to vote immediate *No!*

Governor Pownall, who understood his New England even though he was British born, tried to explain. Last month, he himself had gone to the House and asked humbly if the citizens "would be so good" as to provide barracks for a thousand Highlanders about to land. The House had agreed instantly. Then, right on the heels

of this tactical triumph, Loudoun, General *Lord* Loudoun, said Boston, spitting on the second word — saw fit to send an *order,* "according to act of Parliament."

But what kind of people was this, Loudoun asked, astonished, that hated the army which came to save it more than it feared the enemy at its western gate? The whole of Boston hurled itself against Loudoun's "orders." They were colonials, yes. But by God — or rather by Magna Carta and the British constitution — they swore no troops should be quartered on them without their consent! The *Gazette* carried passionate letters of protest in which the hand of Samuel Adams was visible. . . . *Oliver Cromwell with his Army destroy'd the British constitution. The ruin of Free States is generally imputed to the overgrown Power of Armies. Military Power is created by Civil Communities to protect not to govern them.*

Worcester County, reading this diatribe, shook its head. Oliver Cromwell indeed! If Boston were sixty miles farther west, she wouldn't take so high-handed a tone. No matter how badly Britain had behaved in the matter of generals, Massachusetts needed these trained troops. If the Suffolk County people didn't know it now, they would know it if Fort Edward fell and the French crossed the Connecticut River. Boston and her refined principles were a trifle suspect anyway, James Putnam said with some heat. Army supplies cost money. Was it Oliver Cromwell and military government the General Court objected to — or was it added levy for feeding troops?

Astonishing, the cupidity of man, James Putnam remarked further, one night at the dinner table. He laid down his carving knife and looked with distaste at the meat before him, as though the contemplation of human nature destroyed his appetite. . . . Boston, put in John Adams, was indeed greedy. But she was no greedier than Albany, if the stories one heard were true. Every frontier community traded guns and ammunition with Indians right over its own stockades. This was a scandal known since the first Plymouth landings. But the Albany men had been caught stripping their own dead and selling the clothes, with the blood still on them, to the Mohawks.

Putnam ignored this comment altogether. What an edifying spectacle does human nature present, he went on — if one stops to meditate upon it! Better not to meditate. Better to raise one's own company of foot and march with the rest.

James Putnam knew no more of the military art than did his law

clerk. But he was Colonel Chandler's son-in-law and a man of consequence in the county. On the last day of September therefore, with the insignia of a major on his sleeve, Putnam marched out of Worcester at the head of the town militia. They were bound for Westfield, fifty miles off, where they were to wait for the Hampshire troops to assemble, then stay encamped until orders came from the northwest. He would probably be home in a few weeks, Putnam said. If the French failed to attack Fort Edward, the militia would likely be dispersed; enlistments at the longest were for three months. Let John mind the office and the school until further notice.

Putnam returned in November; not long afterward, he was followed by the entire body of Worcester militia. The French, for some reason known only to heaven, had not followed up their victory. Montcalm's army was holed up for winter; Massachusetts could breathe again till spring.

Nevertheless, times were black, the danger only postponed. The winter must be used to raise and provision troops against the melting of the snow, when fighting would begin afresh. Boston blacksmiths advertised cannon shot for sale — *of various sizes, such as 9 lb. 6, 4, 3, 2, 1 lb. Also Swivel Shot, Star of Ring Shot, Langrige and Hand-Grenades; also Six and Four Pound Cannon.* One smith would undertake — he wrote in the *Gazette* — "to supply the Province with Bayonets, to be made Workmanlike, and of good Stuff; without which he knows they will no Ways answer the End for which they are to be made; but the Number cannot be set, till he knows the Space of Time which will be given to make 'em in."

People complained ceaselessly of the taxes. The *Gazette* advertised a pamphlet for sale at their office, composed by one POOR RICHARD, which answered the question, "Pray, Father Abraham, what think you of the Times? Won't the heavy Taxes quite ruin the Country?" POOR RICHARD said they would not, but POOR RICHARD was a voice crying alone. Soldiers straggled back from Albany. The army was sick, they said. In Boston, Samuel Adams was chosen Collector of Taxes. Just before the New Year, the *Gazette* tried to comfort its readers in cheery couplets:

> Fifty-seven to this poor nation
> Has been a year of sad vexation!
> Yet fifty-eight shall surely bring
> Honor, like Prussia's, to our King.

In all Europe, Prussia indeed seemed the only country that could be so congratulated. England herself was in a situation as critical as any in her history. The military reverses in North America were only a drop in a whole ocean of defeat. England was fighting the French in Germany and India. News reached America — it had been very long in coming — of a shocking disaster in India. The papers were full of it. At Calcutta, hundreds of captured English, both men and women, had been suffocated to death in a one-room military prison. They had been locked in at sundown, and next morning when the door was opened, scarcely anyone remained alive. The "Black Hole," the place was called. The "Black Hole of Calcutta."

England seemed to have no leadership, and there was corruption in high places. The people felt it. "Nothing can save us," an Englishman wrote despairingly. "We are about to be enslaved by our enemies, a fate we richly deserve. Our nation is made up of cowards and scoundrels."

It was at this moment that William Pitt returned to power — the strongest prime minister that had ever guided the foreign policy of the nation. "I believe," he said, "that I can save this nation, and that no one else can." In America his influence was felt with the first ship to cross the ocean. Pitt had appointed new commanders, men who knew how to listen and how to learn from the wild country where they fought — men young, incorruptible and brave. On land, Jeffrey Amherst, Howe, Wolfe. And by sea, Admiral Boscawen. From Governor Pownall of Massachusetts down to the youngest enlisted stripling in the Hudson River Territory, the colonies felt the change and took heart.

In July, 1758, Amherst and Wolfe captured Louisburg from the French after eight weeks of fighting.[1] In August, Colonel Bradstreet, a New England man, took Fort Frontenac, breaking the line of French communication between the St. Lawrence and the Ohio. In mid-September, General Amherst, with four thousand of his victorious troops from Louisburg, landed at Boston and camped on the Common for two days and nights. The celebrations were wonderful. Soldiers, sailors and civilians milled about the streets all night. The Commissioner of Excise noted with satisfaction that, entirely apart from illicit wines and spirits, the fall of Louisburg was toasted in no less than sixty thousand gallons of good Jamaica rum.

Then the troops marched westward for Lake George. On the

way they passed through Worcester. John Adams never forgot the sight. The army stayed overnight, camping on a hill behind the courthouse. The General himself lodged with Colonel Chandler; the town heard with pleasure how Amherst rambled with the Colonel over the whole of his farms, asking questions about American husbandry.

How different from General Lord Loudoun when he had passed this way, arrogant, unfriendly, with his troops committing every kind of thievery and depredation! Worcester, in truth, had dreaded this army of Amherst's. Now they saw four thousand men sit tidily on their hill, superbly disciplined. The officers walked into town, hoping to be invited to supper by the citizens. Bigelows and Paines and Willards and Chandlers took them in gladly; Mr. Putnam had two colonels and a major. In the evening, everyone went up the hill to see the Scotsmen in their plaids and listen to the wild music of bagpipes. On the strength of this good will, Worcester raised another company of militia; the men went out under Amherst with greatest confidence.

The tide had turned. New England saw hope ahead, felt her strength renewed. James Putnam no longer castigated the British generals. And as for his law clerk, who was within a few weeks of finishing his course as a student in the office — "I rejoiced," wrote John Adams, "that I was an Englishman, and gloried in the name of Briton!" [2]

CHAPTER ELEVEN

*John goes home to live, and finds difficulties
he has not expected.*

ON the first of October, 1758, a bright, windy morning, John Adams mounted his horse and set off for Braintree. His farewells had been made the night before. Mr. Maccarty had bestowed his good wishes, Mrs. Maccarty had kissed John heartily on the cheek and presented him with a woolen muffler she had knit herself. Little Tad wept openly. The Chandlers drank his health in the best milk punch. Dr. Willard, his arm around John's shoulder, remarked that beyond doubt his one-time lodger would some day wear a judge's robe, but he still considered bonesetting a happier choice of occupation.

The strange part of it was that John had no chance to say good-by to Mr. Putnam, who had vanished two days before. Mrs. Putnam said vaguely he had gone to Cambridge to see Judge Trowbridge, but it was John's private opinion that Putnam had not bothered to tell her where he was going. John left town without the Putnam blessing or a word of advice concerning his introduction to the Boston bar. How unlucky this neglect was to prove, John had as yet no notion. He only felt uncomfortable, as if he were disappearing with something still unsettled between him and his patron.

Mr. Adams had sent Joe Bass, the hired man, to Worcester with a horse for John. John was delighted; he mounted his horse in a high state of pleasure. As the two rode out of town the Green looked its prettiest. The trees had begun to turn; the big maples blazed in the early sunshine. Joe Bass expressed surprise that John showed no regret at leaving so flourishing a community. Braintree had no such

fulling mill, no grand courthouse. Wouldn't there be more law business here than at home? Last night at the tavern where he lay, the talk had been all of courts and court week, due in a week or so.

"Yes," John said; "there would be more business here." But he would not stay another day in Worcester County if James Putnam himself made an offer — which he had not. Home was where he was headed, and home was where he wanted to be. . . . It was true he had been asked to stay, from another quarter, John added. Two gentlemen had called at the office a fortnight ago with a very pretty proposition.

Jogging easily along the road, John reviewed the incident in his mind. The gentlemen had been Colonel Doolittle and Mr. Baldwin, the deist and equality man. Arriving one morning, strangely ceremonious, their wigs on and their coats buttoned up tight (most unusual for Baldwin), they had invited John to remain and practice law in Worcester. Why, Baldwin asked, should James Putnam and the Chandler family engross all available honors and emoluments? John Adams had made a place for himself, these three years. He might be surprised to learn that his name was known and esteemed in Worcester County. At Quarterly Sessions, people had taken note of him; he had made friends for himself. It was an assured thing that he could have the place of Register of Deeds at the next election. This would procure something handsome for the present, besides promising further business at the bar.

John had thanked the two men but refused without hesitation. Mr. Putnam and the Chandlers, he said, had treated him with much kindness. He had no wish to set himself up as rival. His own parents had invited him to live with them and practice law in Braintree. Colonel Doolittle, at this, shook his head decisively. Did Adams think for a minute that celebrated lawyers like Gridley, Pratt, Thacher, James Otis, would suffer the novelty of a country lawyer doing business only ten miles from Boston Court House? Why, they would gobble him up in a minute! It was preposterous to entertain such a plan.

John, who in the night watches had himself wondered if the notion were not thoroughly foolhardy, retorted with spirit that he already knew some of the gentlemen. (As a matter of fact he knew only Sam Quincy, Bob Paine and Charles Cushing, law students like himself who were not yet sworn at the bar.) "And besides," John

finished, flushing, "I believe these gentlemen have too much candor and generosity to injure a young man."

This noble sentiment struck the two visitors momentarily dumb. Mr. Baldwin was first to recover. Remarking that candor and generosity were characteristics he had not hitherto associated with lawyers, he asked dryly if John had ever encountered Benjamin Pratt of the Boston bar — One-legged Benjamin, whose bite followed close on his bark?

In the end they had parted pleasantly, Doolittle remarking that the opportunity would remain open, should John not be satisfied with his situation at home. . . . It was gratifying, John thought now, to have been invited to settle in Worcester, to know he had made a place for himself. Perhaps he had been too quick with his refusal. Perhaps Doolittle was right, and the great Boston lawyers would squeeze him out before he had his second client. . . . Yet today he could not seem to worry about the future. He was going home! That was future enough.

As the travelers neared Braintree on the morning of the second day, John's spirits soared. He sang, whistled, joked boisterously with Joe. Crossing the Neponset River below Milton Hill he caught sight of old Elijah Baxter, the mill keeper, standing by the mill house door. John whooped at him, rose in the saddle and waved as if to greet a dearest friend. Old Baxter, surprised, waved back, called his wife to come out and see who was riding home. At Crosby's tavern the travelers dismounted. John bought ale for them both, drank his own thirstily and received Tom Crosby's congratulations on his return.

Riding into Braintree, John looked about him with extraordinary interest. He felt as if he had been away a century, half expected great changes, half feared them. Each corner, each square foot brought back his childhood. On Mills's tavern the sign (a large green bear) was loose on its hinges and sagged outward, emitting the same rusty sigh with which it had answered to the wind for years. Leaning against a corner of the tavern wall was old John Scant, drunk as ever, though it was only ten in the morning. On the Congregational Meeting-house the steeple looked bitten off in the middle. Three years ago it had been struck by lightning and the top carried away. The weathervane had tumbled down; John's father had taken it home to straighten out the kinks. It must still be lying in the tool-

house, John thought indulgently, where it had lain since before he left Harvard College.

By the smithy stood a long cart, yoked to eight oxen and loaded with a boulder. "Braintree granite," Joe Bass said, "on its way to Boston." His tone was disapproving. "First thing a man knows, our whole Common will be dug up, right down to China. . . . That off fore-ox is badly galled in the withers," he finished with some satisfaction. "They won't get beyond Neponset River."

The old Hancock parsonage came in sight, where Sam Quincy lived. John slowed his horse to a walk. Perhaps Sam's sister Hannah would be in the garden. She must be all of twenty now and more beautiful than ever. But no Hannah appeared. The day was overcast, the wind had gone round to the east, a drizzle had commenced. Joe Bass shivered. But John spread his nostrils, drew a deep breath and remarked that it felt good and damp. He had been dried out in that inland place for three years. It would take a winter of east wind to soak him properly again.

From up the road a rushing, musical, familiar sound smote John's ear. It was Colonel Ned Quincy's waterfall. The Colonel had dammed up Town Brook, made a rustic bridge in sight of the highway, with a lovely cascade over which the willows drooped. Now in October, sumac flamed at the water's edge and the leaves of the alder were red and shiny in the rain. . . . Of all towns in North America — of all towns in the world — surely, thought John, this was the most beautiful, the friendliest!

John's welcome could not have been heartier if he had returned from Calcutta and the Black Hole itself. His parents met him at the gate. His mother, in her best flowered chintz, threw her arms around him, burst into happy tears. Mr. Adams looked hale and well, but — John noted with sudden surprise — old. Elihu appeared from the barn, rolling down his sleeves. At seventeen Elihu seemed a man grown, tall, wide-shouldered, with a voice that had gone deep in less than a year. Peter, now twenty, was quiet as ever; his dark eyes mild and dreamy. The two shook hands with their brother, told him he looked bobbish, positively weatherproof, which John interpreted rightly as meaning they were glad to see him. Demonstrations of affection did not come easily to the Adams men.

What demonstration there was, aside from Mrs. Adams, came less

from talk than from a quite monstrous celebration of eating. There were fresh-killed chickens for dinner, stuffed with chestnuts . . . oysters baked in butter . . . a haunch of venison that Elihu had brought in. There was ale and beer and cider; a ham — saved from the runt hog, Mr. Adams explained, that John had persuaded him to keep from the red sow's last litter.

The conversation, what there was of it, was jovial, consisting of local news and happenings round the farm. Polly Crosby was married. She had finally made up her mind, Elihu said, to take that German fellow from the glass works over by Weymouth. Betsy Thayer and Miss Hannah Quincy had stopped Mrs. Adams after church last Sunday to inquire when John would be home for good. . . . The black and white cow, Mr. Adams put in, had had twins in August as he had prophesied. "John," Mr. Adams said, "the floods last spring did much damage in the south ten. We'll have to brace up the wall by the barn. Best get at it presently, before the frost." John nodded. He would lend a hand, he said.

Looking round at his family, John felt vastly content. This was the talk he had heard all his life, here at home. It was easy, dutiful, there was a kind of health and innocence to it. Yet, undressing for bed that night, it occurred to John that no one, in all this conversation, had asked what his plans were. There had been no chance to tell about the offer to settle in Worcester, though John knew the incident would please his father. The entire family took it for granted they had a full-fledged lawyer in their midst. Clients would be swarming on the morrow, John's sign would swing merrily from the door. Mrs. Adams indeed had gone so far as to say John could receive clients in the parlor, which she had converted into a combination bedroom and office for him. Peter and Elihu slept upstairs now, in the second chamber. The only word John had managed to insert was that he could not practice law until he was sworn at the bar. He still had much studying to do, many things to learn, before he could consider himself an attorney, let alone a barrister. . . .

This had been met by total silence, broken by Peter, who said that six years' study ought to make a lawyer out of anybody. As to the swearing-in, couldn't Colonel Quincy do it, downtown? After all, he was Justice of the Peace, performed marriages and funerals. One more oath to administer would be, Peter implied, mere cockleshells to Colonel Quincy.

His family, John told himself, climbing into bed that first night, had not the slightest notion what lay ahead of him. He must go down to see Sam Quincy right away. Sam had just finished his course of legal study with Benjamin Pratt in Boston. Sam would know what to do and how to go about doing it.

A day later, John walked down to Mr. Josiah Quincy's house. He found Sam alone. Young Josiah was at Mr. Marsh's school, the rest of the family had gone to Boston shopping. Sam was delighted to see his old friend, drew him into a snug, curtained room he called his study, sat him down before the fire and brought out a bottle of his father's Madeira. The two sat grandly drinking it while they talked over old times at college. The day — how long ago! — when John had been a Freshman, and Sam had visited him in his room, told him not to let Hancock rag him. . . .

"As to getting sworn at the bar," Quincy said, "it will be simple enough." He himself was to be sworn early in November when the Superior Court met in Boston. Couldn't John arrange to ride in with him and be sworn that same day? "Of course," Quincy added, "you must go to Boston beforehand and present your letters and credentials from Mr. Putnam, stating the extent of your study, what books you have read and what progress you have made in the law."

The assurance with which Quincy offered this latter suggestion startled John into sudden evasive silence. He could not bring himself to confess that Putnam had let him come away with absolutely nothing in writing to show for his two years' study — no word of recommendation whatever. John left the Quincy mansion feeling extremely uneasy. Quincy had suggested John go to Boston ahead of time, any day now, and meet the leaders of the bar. "Come to the Town-house," Quincy had said, "the last week in October. I shall be there, listening to the cases. You will see everybody."

Two weeks remained before court met. John was worried, anxious. It was all very well for a Quincy to talk of "meeting the leaders of the Boston bar." But unless Sam himself would help, John wondered just how he was to achieve it. The first step, plainly, was to get himself to Boston Town-house, sit down at the lawyers' table as Quincy had instructed, and hope for the best.

On Tuesday, October twenty-fourth, John Adams rode his mare to Boston, across the narrow Neck, with marsh grass blowing on

either side. Then a mile across mud flats, where the gallows rose grim and mournful. At Town Gate the crowd of travelers multiplied; horses, ox teams, carts and chaises pressed to get through. John's mare pushed her way up the High Street to Cornhill, where the Town-house came in sight. Below, down the steep slope, the cobbled square was thronged with people to the water's edge. Under all was the continual sound of wheels lumbering over rough cobbles, the clop-clop of horses walking up the hill. Beyond the square, where the Long Wharf ran half a mile into the harbor, masts rose thick as trees, and the broad busy passage between was like another street.

John rode down the hill, left his horse at a hostler's and walked up the Town-house steps. The courtroom was on the first floor; upstairs were the chambers of the Governor's Council and House of Representatives. John knew his way, he had looked in here before. But entering the courtroom, he felt strange and awkward. ("Shy, under awe and concern," he wrote later in his diary.) It was ten in the morning, a case was in progress. A few spectators waited on the front row of benches, huddled together, whispering. Between the two presiding judges and the spectators was a large oval table with a green baize top, covered now with papers, ink pots and all the signs of business. Around it a dozen lawyers sat writing, talking to each other in low tones or, with their chairs pushed back, listening to the lawyer who was arguing, or the witness in the box.

It was this table on which John's eyes were fixed. Here, dressed in black gowns and powdered tie wigs, were the men he had journeyed to meet. Sam Quincy and Bob Paine sat at the far end in their ordinary clothes, taking notes. Standing hesitant in the aisle, John tried to catch their eye and failed, then walked forward and took a seat near Quincy.

Jeremiah Gridley was on his feet, arguing earnestly. At sixty, Gridley was known as "the father of the Boston bar." He had trained a score of lawyers, including at least four in the courtroom today. His office, just south of the Town-house, was a meeting place for young men interested in law and politics. Gridley lived in Muddy River. "Brookline" it was called now. He had represented that town in the General Court for the past three years. He had a forcible, rough manner of speech but he was impressive, used his words well. John knew that he was famous as a classical scholar; at one time he had edited a literary journal in Boston. Gridley used his whole body

when he spoke, lifting his right hand with its thick muscular wrist and bringing it down emphatically to make a point.

Gridley's famous pupil, James Otis, was at the lawyers' table. Young Paine in due course pointed him out by writing his name on a slip of paper and passing it to John. Otis was in his early thirties, with a strong, thick body like Gridley's, but in the very prime of health and vigor. All his movements were abrupt, jerky; he seemed always ready to burst into speech. John watched him with curiosity; even when writing busily with the quill, Otis turned from time to time and made extended remarks to his neighbor.

Otis's family came from Barnstable on the Cape and were well known throughout the Province; his grandfather had served nineteen years on the Governor's Council. Otis's father, a self-educated lawyer of the old school, John had met in Worcester. James Otis himself had lately moved to Boston and married the daughter of a rich merchant. Plainly, he was on the way to an outstanding career in both law and politics. Like his master Gridley, Otis was a student of the classics. Paine had said he was preparing a textbook in Latin prosody for use at Harvard College.

Mr. Oxenbridge Thacher sat quietly in his place, about six chairs from John. Above the black robe there was something gentle and benign about his face that set it apart. Thacher had studied theology, started his career as a preacher before he changed to the law. John found his eye straying again and again to Thacher's calm brow, his white hands folded motionless on the table before him.

Among them, one face and form engaged John's attention closest. It belonged to a thin, bent-looking man whose chair was pushed out to face the judges and whose hands rested on the bridge of a crutch. *One-legged Benjamin, whose bite follows close on his bark. . . .* Even without the crutches there would have been little doubt of his identity. Pratt's eyes were fixed on the floor, his face lined and twisted as though the meager frame which supported it suffered an agony that must at all times be kept under control. His shoulders were narrow; across them lay a greatcoat, although fires burned at both ends of the room and it was warm enough. John had the man's history in detail from his pupil, Sam Quincy. One-legged Benjamin had acquired the title at fifteen, when an accident severed his leg above the knee. Nobody knew his family; at Harvard his name had been last in the class list and he was penniless. But Mr.

Robert Auchmuty, the Scottish-born Judge of Admiralty (a great swell with a mansion, a chariot and a beautiful daughter), had taken him directly into his office.

Pratt had proved an extraordinary student, with a phenomenal memory. The pain from his severed leg was awful. Old Judge Auchmuty told of coming on him unobserved in the cold office of a winter's night, saw him leaning over his books with beads of sweat standing on his brow. In the end, Pratt had married Judge Auchmuty's daughter. His success at the bar had been immediate; he had been elected Boston Representative in the General Court and served thirteen consecutive years.

John Adams, sitting among the lawyers, went over the record in his mind, striving to be prepared before he should meet these men. All day he stayed in court and, before the judges rose, managed to get himself introduced to the four lawyers he desired most to know: Gridley, Pratt, Thacher and Otis. That night, John lodged in town and went with Sam Quincy to a *soirée*. It was his first evening party in Boston and far exceeded John's expectations. A mere item of candles, a myriad of them glowing from chandeliers and wall brackets, set him to counting on his fingers. He must tell the family at home. Why, there must be a hundred wax tapers — four hundred, five hundred. And the ladies! Satins and brocades, shimmering and shining in a rainbow of colors . . . bare necks and white arms, tiny feet in pointed slippers . . . clever maneuvering of fans and feathers! That night in his lodging-house room, John set it down in his diary as "the gayest company of gentlemen, the most spacious and elegant room and the finest row of ladies" that ever he had seen.

But when he got to bed, John could not sleep. The watchman's call disturbed him, the clocks and bells that told the hours, the shout and song of a drunken sailor who seemed to pass and repass the window a dozen times. . . . The events of the day were sharp in his mind. Sam Quincy's introductions in the courtroom had omitted entirely the fact that Mr. Adams was in Boston to get himself sworn at the bar. It would be necessary, John realized anxiously, to make a formal visit to every one of those men — Gridley, Pratt, Thacher, Otis — secure their support. Toward morning John slept fitfully, woke much too early, got up and dressed, ate breakfast at a nearby cookshop and walked the streets until nine o'clock. He had determined to call first on Jeremiah Gridley. If he could enlist even

some faint fraction of this great man's interest, the first step would be taken, the first skirmish won.

The morning sun struck across the brick wall of the old Townhouse as John walked up three steps to Gridley's office nearby, and lifted the knocker. The father of the Boston bar himself opened the door. John found himself directly in the office, a room much smaller than he had expected. A fire burned in the grate, the lawyer was alone. He greeted his visitor cordially, said of course he remembered him from young Quincy's introduction yesterday, and inquired if Adams were acquainted with Quincy's uncle, old Colonel John at Wollaston.

These pleasant preliminaries over, John went straight to the point. He had come for advice, he said. Would Mr. Gridley kindly point out what steps he must take for an introduction to the practice of law in Suffolk County?

"Get sworn," said Gridley promptly.

"I have no patron in this county," John replied with equal directness. His heart beat hard. Would Gridley quizz him as to why Mr. Putnam had given him no letter of recommendation? And what reply could he possibly make to this?

Jeremiah Gridley evinced no such intention. His manner continued courteous and kind. "I think I can recommend you to the court," he said. "We have become more strict in this matter. Each term the Justices are confronted with a half-dozen of pettifoggers, mere scriveners with a dash of law in their noddles, trying to pass as *bona fide* attorneys."

Gridley smiled, indicated a chair by the fire. "Sit down, Adams, and let me examine you as to your course of study with Mr. Putnam. What Latin books have you read, what French? Have you made a thorough study of rhetoric, logic and the rules of correct speech and grammar?"

The two seated themselves. What method of study had John pursued, Gridley began. . . . He had had to devise his own method, John replied, Mr. Putnam being often away for long intervals. He was not sure it could be called a method, though he had been at much pains with it. Enumerating the books he had read, John explained his system of making digests, reducing difficult pages to a paragraph or a line. He and a friend, Jonathan Sewall, pupil of Judge Russell, had exchanged letters at intervals, quizzing each other. Perhaps they

had not been very skillful at it, John added. But it made something definite to work toward, stations as it were on a long strange journey.

Gridley nodded. "The road to legal science is much easier now than when I set out. I was forced to begin with Coke-Littleton, quite by myself, and break through."

It was on the tip of John's tongue to say that he also had begun with Coke-Littleton quite by himself, and broken through. Instead, he inquired if a lawyer should study Greek? "Merely for the curiosity of it," Gridley replied. He himself read Greek because he liked it.

For more than an hour, the father of the bar plied John with questions in the law. The replies came quickly and well. To John it seemed, indeed, that he was talking more easily than ever in his life before. Problems, statements in Coke and Fortescue that had puzzled him, John heard himself unravel now as though some deep inner voice had given him the answers. Or had the answers lain there, he asked himself later — wanting only a wise and sympathetic listener to bring them to the surface?

Gridley rummaged in a drawer, brought out a bundle of letters, an old copybook. "Here is advice from the greatest authorities in England," he said. "Chief Justice Matthew Hale himself; Lord Reeve, the barrister who died ten years ago — worth, I might add, some twenty-three thousand pounds. They outline a method of studying the common law. The letter from Dr. Dickins of Cambridge University gives a plan for studying the civil law. This letter, I wrote myself to Mr. Robert Lightfoot when he came from London to serve as Judge of Vice Admiralty. He asked me for a plan to study the admiralty law." [1]

John took the letters and read them. In two entire years, James Putnam had not given him so much practical guidance. Gridley drew his chair closer to the fire. "A lawyer in our country," he said, "has far greater difficulties than in England, where a man need master only one branch of the law. Here, an attorney must be five men in one — counsellor, lawyer, solicitor, even scrivener. He must study common law, civil law, natural law, admiralty law. Such a program discourages many a young man."

Gridley looked sharply at John, who started to reply, thought better of it and merely nodded gravely. The old lawyer's tone changed. He spoke rapidly, as if the words were familiar and he had said them

before. But he spoke earnestly. "Pursue the study of law, young man, rather than the gain of it. Make money enough to keep out of the briars, but give your main attention to study. That is rule number one. Rule number two is: Don't marry early! A wife and family will allow you no time for study. And besides, marriage is expensive. In any event, you must not keep much company. A man who aims to be a lawyer must apply himself incessantly." Gridley repeated it. "Incessantly! The common law deserves your first attention. You must conquer the *Institutes*."

Gridley took out his watch, consulted it and rose abruptly, remarking that he was due in court within twenty minutes. Was Adams attending? They could walk across the square together. . . . "Mark what day the court adjourns to for judgments," Gridley said. "And come to town that morning to be sworn. I will recommend you to the judges. In the meantime," he continued cheerfully, "I will speak to the bar in your behalf. The court always inquires if the recommendation be with the consent of the bar."

Taking up his hat, Gridley flung a greatcoat over his shoulders, led the way across the square. To John Adams, entering the courtroom with the great Jeremiah Gridley was like entering heaven on the arm of Gabriel. As the two approached the lawyers' table, Sam Quincy and Bob Paine leaped to their feet, made a place for John and bowed deeply to Gridley, who walked on down to the bench to speak to Chief Justice Sewall.

Sitting at the lawyers' table, John took notes on the cases, feeling, as time went on, much easier in the courtroom, more at home. He would continue his visits this evening, he decided, beginning with Mr. Thacher, who looked somehow less formidable than Pratt and Otis. The day passed pleasantly enough. At about eight o'clock that evening, John found his way to Oxenbridge Thacher's house in the north end of town. A servant answered his knock, took his hat and coat. While John was straightening his neckcloth at a little mirror hung between candelabra, Thacher himself appeared from a room down the hall. He was a man of thirty-eight but looked older. His face was sensitive, scholarly; John had heard he was in doubtful health. Tonight he wore no wig. His brown hair, already marked with gray, waved from his forehead; there was a charming inflection to his voice. John identified himself, then opened with the question he had put to Gridley about introduction to the bar.

With an easy gesture, Thacher disposed of this part of the business and led the way to the family sitting room. Here he presented John to his wife and sister, kept him all evening and gave him tea at ten o'clock. The conversation soon left the law and ranged, John wrote afterward in his diary, over the whole universe, from original sin to the movements of the solar system and the extraordinary attainments of Mr. Jeremiah Gridley.

For John it was a wonderful evening; he enjoyed himself wholly. If he had been quick and accurate with Gridley, tonight he felt himself positively eloquent. With no hesitation, he heard himself expounding the philosophies of Jonathan Edwards, condemning the Genevan school as inimical to the findings of such experimentalists as Boyle and the great Sir Isaac Newton. Thacher listened courteously. The two ladies kept their eyes fixed on John, especially Mr. Thacher's sister, a gaunt-looking person of indeterminate age, who nodded and smiled enthusiastically from time to time. The only flaw came as John was taking leave. Thacher attended him to the door, stood politely while hat and coat were brought by the servant, wished John joy of the profession and then remarked in his silvery voice that the county already had as many lawyers as it could use.

This was dampening, certainly. John, walking through the dark streets to his lodging, considered it. Maybe Thacher hadn't really meant it; maybe he had meant something else? Trying hard to twist a very plain statement into a complicated one, John kicked at a stone in his way and decided not to think about it at all. Mr. Gridley had neither said nor hinted such a thing, and Gridley had more experience than a round dozen of Thachers. John reached his lodging, took a candle and climbed the stairs, undressed, crawled into a large and rather sagging four-posted bed and closed the curtains against a gale from the harbor that made the windows rattle. He drew a long breath of satisfaction. This had been a good day's work, surely. Tomorrow he would call on Pratt and Otis. He knew how to do these things now; he need not enter trembling like a schoolboy.

John slept soundly all night, woke next morning full of confidence and health. By nine o'clock he was on Benjamin Pratt's doorstep, lifting the great brass knocker with an easy hand.

Ten minutes later John emerged, his face red as fire, and plunged down the steps into the street. His fists were thrust deep in his

greatcoat pockets, wrath was in his heart. Hardly aware of where he was going, he charged headlong round the block, bowling over an elderly woman who looked like a bundle of rags, smelled strongly of spirits and, when John tried to pick her up, swore at him like a grenadier.

Benjamin Pratt could not have been ruder if he had rehearsed for it. A servant had opened the door, led John to a small, beautifully furnished anteroom. On the way, John had a glimpse, at the far end of the hall, of a dining room with a lady pouring tea from a silver pot. It had not increased John's comfort to learn from the servant that his master was at breakfast. After a few moments the servant returned, showed John into a large, handsome room lined with books and por-traits. Before the fire stood Mr. Pratt, leaning on his crutches. John went forward, smiling, bowed and put out his hand.

Mr. Pratt made no move whatever, but kept both hands occupied. In silence he heard John's little opening speech, which, with John's right hand dangling from the refusal of a greeting, did not emerge gracefully. Would Mr. Pratt, John finished, stumbling a little on the words, do him the honor to concur with Mr. Gridley and Mr. Thacher in recommending him to the bar?

Pratt's face remained exactly as it had been before John spoke. "Were you sworn at Worcester?" he asked abruptly.

"No, Sir," John said.

"Have you a letter from Mr. Putnam to the court?"

"No, Sir."

Pratt's mouth was a thin line. He made a movement of his body; a muscular spasm, brief but painful, crossed his face. "Had you been sworn at Worcester, you would be entitled to be sworn here. When a young gentleman goes from me to another county, I always write in his favor to the court where he is going."

The manner in which Pratt said this, more than the words, carried an assumption that perhaps Putnam had had his reasons for withhold-ing such favors. "As it is," Pratt continued, "there is nobody in the county to speak for you. Our information is only hearsay. I have *heard*" — Pratt stressed the word — "that you have made a proper proficiency in the science of law, and that you will do well for your-self in the profession. But I repeat, this is only hearsay."

John stood rooted to the spot. The blood rushed to his face, he

was almost suffocated with anger. The cool voice went on. "You have looked into the *Institutes*, I presume. How far have you gone with Coke-Littleton?"

Harmless words, but even James Putnam's voice could not carry such studied insult. John, retaining just sanity enough to keep from being swept into open conflict with Benjamin Pratt, answered briefly, bowed, turned on his heel and was gone. It required an hour's hard walking to cool off sufficiently to trust himself. Then he went to court, letting no word escape him as to the morning's episode. Pratt himself did not appear. It was Thursday, the last day of court. John planned to ride home tomorrow morning. Tonight he would call on Otis. There was all the more reason, since Pratt's refusal, to enlist as many supporters as he could. In fact, thought John Adams, his anger hardening now into cold resolve, he would visit every single lawyer of importance in Boston if it took him the rest of the month.

That afternoon, court rose early. Upon John's approaching James Otis to ask if he might wait upon him in the evening, the lawyer, to John's infinite surprise, took his arm and invited him to come right along to his office. Otis flung off his wig; his thick black hair sprung bristling from his scalp. He was noisy, laughed often, talked rapidly. There was about him something altogether magnetic and friendly that spread, John thought, like a thing tangible. No need of defenses here, a man could let himself go with James Otis. On the way from the Town-house they stopped for "a small draught of ale," as Otis expressed it. While John drank his pint, Otis managed to pour down two quarts. Then he wiped his hand on his sleeve, offered John a plug of tobacco and, with a hearty word to the barkeeper, walked out as if two quarts were his regular hourly consumption.

Once settled in the office, Otis inquired if John had called on Benjamin Pratt. When John hesitated and said yes, he had been there this morning at nine o'clock, Otis roared with laughter, clapped John on the shoulder and said he hoped One-legged Benjamin had not had him thrown into the street. Before eleven in the morning, Pratt was always savage. People said it had to do with his leg; the stump pained him. . . . As for introductions to the bar, he himself, said Otis, would be delighted to help; Adams need go no further. It was quite unnecessary to make these hazardous and difficult visits — Otis smiled — to any more Boston lawyers.

This happy counsel (which afterward proved highly injudicious) John accepted gladly. Taking his leave, he repaired to his lodging, found something to eat and went to bed. Next morning he rode home to Braintree, feeling as if he had been through the wars. In three years of effort and pushing, he told himself he had never pushed so cruelly hard as in the past few days. Thank God it was over. There remained, of course, the formality of the swearing-in. But that surely would be no hazard.

Trotting along the rutted road, John leaned to his saddlebags, felt to see they were safely strapped. Mr. Gridley had lent him the third edition of Van Muyden's *Institutes;* John was in mortal fear that something would happen to it. . . . The morning was fair and cold. The trees were almost bare, yet a glow of red hung to their branches; the fields were a rich autumnal brown. John's spirits rose; it occurred to him suddenly that he had earned a holiday. Court would not convene for ten days. He would make these days his own, use them as he pleased, enjoy himself. He hadn't taken a girl out since that summer when he had fancied himself in love with Polly Crosby. In Worcester there had been girls, of course. But the role of schoolmaster had forced him to live with extraordinary decorum. His every action was observed by the town, and the few times he had even cast an eye on a girl, talk about it had come to him later. Now, however, he was at home and could do as he pleased. He would look up every girl he had known in the old days, perhaps some he hadn't known. It was a delirious program. John urged his horse to a canter.

In the next eight days, John called on a different girl every evening, dragging his cousin Nathan Webb with him when he could. He did not care what age the girls were, John said — or if they were dull or bright, dark or fair. Variety was the thing. In the end, on the Sunday night before he was due in Boston, he went to the Quincys', where three words from Hannah made him forget instantaneously all the charmers in Suffolk County.

Hannah, when John came in, was seated at the far end of the drawing room, by the window. She got up and came forward, smiling. She wore a dress of bright crimson taffeta, long sleeved, with the neck cut square and low. As she moved across the room, her full skirt rustled, changing color in the candlelight. She looked at John out of wide dark eyes, looked down, looked away and gave him her hand as if she expected him to kiss it. John stood holding it awkwardly;

he had never bowed over a lady's hand in his life. (Nobody in Braintree, Massachusetts, kissed ladies' hands except maybe Governor Shirley in the old days, and the Vassall gentlemen over the west hill.) Besides, Hannah had known John Adams since he was a Freshman in Harvard and before, had run races with him in the fields, had dared him to ride her roan pony and had stood doubled up with laughter when the pony bucked him over its neck.

But this was not the same Hannah Quincy at all, this young lady who stood holding out her white hand! Three years had transformed Miss Quincy from a black-haired hoyden into a woman of the world, or so it seemed to John Adams, standing dazzled and foolish with the small smooth hand in his.

Hannah laughed, drew her hand away and dropped a curtsy in her wide-skirted bright dress. "This will never do, Lawyer Adams!" she said. "You have become a great scholar, no doubt. My brother Sam tells me you positively take pleasure in reading legal tomes in Latin. But you must have a few lessons in arguing your case before the ladies, or you will never win." Hannah turned, led the way into the room, looking back at John over her shoulder. "Would you care for an old friend as preceptress?"

That night, John went home in a dream. Of all the preceptorial programs life had yet offered, this was the most alluring by far. Unfortunately it could not be pursued immediately. On the morrow, a Monday, John was due in Boston for the swearing-in. But the ceremony would not take him away for more than a day and a night. As soon as he returned he would go down to the Quincys'. Perhaps it was as well to let a little time elapse. More politic and worldly-seeming.

Next morning, November sixth, John made an early start for Boston on horseback. It was snowing lightly, a raw cold day with the flakes driving in his face. John wore his red cloak, pulled the flaps of his three-cornered hat down over his ears until he had crossed the Neck and entered Town Gate, when he stopped and turned the hat stylishly up again. Mr. Gridley had told him to come directly to his office, they would go to court together. John felt secure in his program, but only because of Gridley's promised patronage.

It was a little after nine when John left his mare at the hostler's. Gridley's office, when he walked in, was cold and dark; the boy said

his master was not yet arrived from his home in Brookline. John waited, but Gridley never came. At half-past ten, John went alone to the courtroom. Everyone was in his place: Pratt, Otis, Oxenbridge Thacher, Dana, Benjamin Kent. There were three judges presiding. Sam Quincy, who was to be sworn with John, had come to town Saturday. He sat in the front row of the spectators' benches, looking very natty in a new suit of rich brown stuff with polished buttons. He beckoned to John, who walked down the aisle and sat beside him.

Nervously, John waited. Everything depended on Gridley. Pratt would not help him, that was certain. And in spite of James Otis's good will the other day, John did not feel sure of him either, when it came to the pinch. Thacher could be counted on, but that was not enough. The concurrence of the whole bar was necessary, and only Gridley could secure it.

In the Town-house tower the clock struck twelve times; from steeple after steeple the noon bells rang out. What if Quincy were sworn, John thought in panic, and he himself had no patron to speak for him? The pit of John's stomach seemed to give way; he sat rigid, trying to keep himself from looking back over his shoulder at the door.

Suddenly, the right-hand door opened. Gridley strode in and down the aisle, still in his greatcoat, his hat under his arm. He looked about until he spied John, when he nodded. John leaned back in his chair, took out a handkerchief and wiped his forehead. Mr. Gridley went straight to Pratt at the lawyers' table, leaned over him and said a few words, then moved to each lawyer in turn.

Afterward, John had the whole thing from Bob Paine, who was sitting within earshot. Everyone had been entirely acquiescent but Pratt, who had remarked, loud enough for all to hear: "Nobody knows him."

"Yes, they do," Gridley had replied at once, his tone perfectly firm and unruffled. "*I* know him. I have tried him. He is a very sensible fellow."

John himself heard the last three words, which were spoken in a clear, loud tone. He dug his toes into his boots, prayed that his face might not reveal what he was feeling. For John, this little scene had consumed half an hour — a day — a lifetime. Actually, it had not taken three minutes.

Gridley rose in his place at the head of the lawyers' table. "Mr. Quincy!" he said, and bowed. Quincy got up, moved forward to the judges' bench.

"Mr. Adams!" Gridley bowed again. John found himself on his feet. He walked out and stood beside Quincy, directly below Chief Justice Sewall on the bench.

"May it please your Honors," Gridley began. "I have two young gentlemen, Mr. Quincy and Mr. Adams, to present for the oath of an attorney. Of Mr. Quincy, it is enough for me to say he has lived three years with Mr. Pratt. Of Mr. Adams, as he is unknown to your Honors, it is necessary to say that he has lived between two and three years with Mr. Putnam of Worcester. He has a good character from all who are acquainted with him. He was with me the other day for several hours and I take it, he is well qualified to study the law by his scholarship. I gather that he has made a very considerable, a very great proficiency in the principles of the law. The clients' interests may be safely intrusted in his hands. I therefore recommend him, with the consent of the bar, to your Honors for the oath."

The Chief Justice ordered the clerk to swear the two gentlemen. John Adams and Samuel Quincy moved forward, laid their right hands on the open Bible and stood motionless while the clerk's voice, loud, rapid, monotonous, intoned the words of the oath. Outside, the storm had lifted, a pale sun streamed through the high windows of the courtroom:

You shall do no falsehood nor consent to any being done in the court. . . . You shall delay no man for lucre or malice, but you shall use yourself in the office of an attorney within the court according to the best of your learning and discretion, and with all good fidelity as well to the court and to the client. So help you God!

"Amen," said old Judge Sewall. "Amen," Gridley repeated, smiling.

One by one the lawyers came forward, shook the two young men by the hand. Adams and Quincy, according to the custom, invited them all to cross the square for a bowl of milk punch at Stone's tavern. "Docking the colt's tail," this ancient usage was called. Arm in arm with the mighty Jeremiah Gridley, John Adams walked down the Town-house steps, the noonday sun full upon his face, and in his heart a glory bright as any in the sky.

CHAPTER TWELVE

1758–1761. John Adams, attorney at law, experiences both defeat and victory. In the Quincy drawing room, fate arranges for him a narrow escape. The French war ends, and George III is King of England.

FOR John, the next three years were an anxious time. "Painful years," he was to call them later. He returned from Boston in the autumn of 1758, an accredited attorney with a long record of study behind him — six years, counting his Harvard education. His family and most of his Braintree friends looked on him as a man superbly equipped to defend his case tomorrow, today, before the Chief Justice of Massachusetts, the Governor's Council or if need be, the King himself.

But the picture John saw by no means fitted this pleasant frame. In the first place, how did a man acquire clients? Should he hang a shingle over the front door and proclaim his trade: JOHN ADAMS, ATTORNEY AT LAW? . . . John shuddered. The sign would wave in the wind, mocking him as he went in and out. "Do not be impatient," Mr. Gridley had cautioned before they parted on the day of the swearing-in. "Give life an opportunity to arrange itself, Adams. It is of no use to plunge at events, head on. Wait!"

Had Gridley said to him: Climb the mountains, defy the avalanche, cross the sea in an Indian canoe or translate the *Iliad* before Monday, John would have been delighted. But, *wait?* It was impossible. What

had he been doing those three years in Worcester, but wait? Now surely was the time for action, time to exert himself, become known, sought after. . . . But how? Should he begin here in Braintree — walk the lanes and byways, haunt the taverns, the smithy, the beaches where the fishermen docked at noon? Should he visit every house, converse with man, woman and child until his name, his face, his business were known? Should he return to Boston, renew his college friendships, mingle with the crowd "on Change" in the Town-house and make a reputation there? Should he contrive questions for the Boston lawyers after court, endeavor to impress them with his character and understanding?

"I feel vexed, fretted, chafed. The thought of no business mortifies, stings me," John wrote in his diary. "Shall I look out for a cause to speak to, and exert all the soul and all the body I own to cut a flash, strike amazement? In short, shall I walk a lingering, heavy pace, or shall I take one bold determined leap into the midst of fame, cash, and business?"

The cause to speak to appeared rather suddenly about six weeks after John had been sworn at the bar. It came in the corpulent form and ruddy face of a Mr. Field of Braintree, who walked up the road one fine December morning, knocked at the farmhouse door and, slightly out of breath, asked John Adams, Attorney, to make out a writ for a lawsuit he desired to reopen.

Field had already lost the suit once. John knew about it; he had sat through the trial downtown, with Colonel Quincy presiding. The case, like 90 per cent of Braintree's litigation, revolved around strayed cattle. A horse had broken into Field's pasture and stayed there a week, enjoying the clover. Field recognized the animal, a roan mare belonging to one Lambert, a newcomer to town. Knowing that a week's trespass would mean damages accruing, Field let the mare remain comfortably where she was, expecting to drive her to the public pound as was the custom, and collect. *Damage feasant:* it was a term familiar to Braintree.

But at the beginning of the second week Lambert appeared, climbed the pasture fence, stood on it, and without setting foot on Field's land waved his hat at his mare and drove her home, cheating Field of his damages. Field went straight to the sheriff, got out a warrant and haled Lambert into court for trespass.

What happened from then on was a trifle hazy, but Field lost the

case. Everyone in town knew about it. Field and Lambert cried
their wrongs and their rights from courtroom to market place. Braintree dearly loved a lawsuit; it was next best to horse races as opportunity for brisk and jovial betting. The general opinion was against
Lambert. In the first place he was a newcomer to town. In the second,
if he had wanted to drive his horse home, why hadn't he done it
sooner, not waited till the animal had eaten its fill of clover and then
waved his hat atop the fence right where Field could see him? . . .

All this had taken place in October. What Field wanted of John
Adams was a writ to reopen the case. A fresh approach would of
course be necessary. Mr. Adams, said Field, was to discover that
approach, make out a new writ stating the circumstances of the complaint and the Massachusetts law on which it could be based and
argued. "The writ must be skillfully drawn," Field said, leaning forward in his chair opposite John, both hands on his hickory cane, his
vest buttons straining across his wide belly. If there was anything
defective, Colonel Quincy would throw the case out of court. The
Colonel had said the damages would be fixed at ninepence — but the
loser would have to put forty shillings in the poor box. *Forty shillings!* Field pounded his cane on the floor. He would be damned before the almighty tribunal itself if he would put forty shillings in the
poor box with that knurly little rascal of a Lambert looking on and
crowing.

John listened, tried to make what sense he could of Field's story.
He felt uncertain, unsure of himself and the whole affair. But he was
not experienced enough to say so. He got up, stood by the table with
the papers spread upon it. "I will study the matter," he said a trifle
portentously, "and give my opinion in a day or two."

Field took his hat and went away, still talking. John looked over
the papers. He had never seen a writ based on this particular law of
the Province. *A declaration in trespass for a rescue.* . . . Field
wished to bring the case to trial Monday. This was Friday. How
unfortunate, John thought, that he could not get to Boston, consult
with Mr. Gridley, look up the Province law! At noon, John walked
into the living room. Mr. Adams was there, waiting for his midday
meal. John began to discuss the matter with him. Peter and Elihu
came in, stood by the fire in their work clothes, leaning against the
chimney. "I doubt if I am qualified to draw such a writ," John
finished, frowning. "If the writ is abated as defective my client will

be left with a large bill of costs. I am not familiar with the Province law."

Mrs. Adams appeared, from the kitchen. "Not know the law?" she said sharply. "After six years' study?" She set a dish on the table, stared across the room at her son. "This is the first piece of business that has come to you. If you refuse it, will another follow?"

Anger boiled through John. What did his mother know of a lawyer's business? He had not asked her opinion. He looked up, furious — and met the eyes of three men fixed silently on him. What Peter, Elihu and Mr. Adams thought was plain. Together these three had worked the farm, tended cattle, raked hay, slaughtered pigs, shoveled manure, done back-breaking manual labor year after year while John sat at his books. They had made no complaint; they had not begrudged what they gave. But it was John's turn to bring in a reward, prove these years of book learning, draw some money into the house. . . .

Three pairs of eyes were eloquent. John checked himself, held his peace. The family drew its chairs to the table, no more was said. But after dinner John went to his room, worked all afternoon at the writ and all next morning. He finished it, made a fair copy and carried it to Mr. Field, who expressed himself as delighted.

John shook hands with his client and made his way home, as uncomfortable as he had ever been in his life. He knew he had gone too fast with this business. He had, indeed, guessed at a large part of what he had written. What if the court abated the writ, threw it out as defective? Field would rage like a lion, spread the news far and wide. If only Mr. Putnam, in those Worcester years, had given some hints concerning practice, told him how to handle an importunate client, how to delay until he discovered if a case were worth taking. . . .

Ten days later, the worst happened. The writ was rejected; Field lost his suit. John's mortification was painful; he felt convinced the whole county rang with his defeat. Field was going round town cursing and consigning the whole affair to hell. How people must be laughing! What would Sam Quincy think, and the Colonel — and Hannah? Bob Paine in particular would pick this up, carry it to Boston and Worcester, make capital of it. Paine never missed a chance to take a fall out of John Adams. . . . Sitting alone in his room, staring out the window at the snowy December dusk, John swore he would not be caught like this again. He would be careful, go

slowly — What had Mr. Gridley said? *Wait!* . . . No reproaches of his family would henceforth drive him to accept a case without strictest consideration.

Peter and Elihu proved surprisingly respectful toward their brother's distress; Mr. Adams was philosophical about it. Even Mrs. Adams dismissed the affair as unimportant, now that it was over. There would be other opportunities, she said serenely. Braintree folk were forever at law with their neighbors. John let some days elapse, then walked down to see Hannah Quincy. She met him at the door in her dress of yellow wool, the sleeves pushed above her elbows. Her eyes were bright, her welcome as warm as if no such thing as lost causes existed. The drawing room was full of people. Ned Quincy and young Josiah were there, Jonathan Sewall from Cambridge, Hannah's cousin Esther Quincy from across the road.

Hannah drew John to a sofa, sat down by him. Mr. Field? — she said in her high, soft voice — How tiresome! She had forgotten him and his troubles long ago. Yes, her brother had told her of the writ. She only hoped Sam would lose *his* next case; he was insufferably puffed up since becoming an attorney — forever quoting Latin. Personally, she thought he didn't understand it himself, or else he simply invented it. Hannah moved her shoulders impatiently under the yellow dress. "I know some Latin. Josiah taught it me." She turned the full battery of her dark eyes on John. "*Puella amat puer,*" she said.

The effect was quite other than she had intended. "*Puella* what?" John returned immediately. "If your brother Josiah taught you that, he had best stay after school tomorrow. The object of the verb takes the accusative, in Latin. If you are trying to say the boy loves the girl . . . Or do you mean, possibly, the girl loves the boy?"

He stopped, blushing furiously. A peal of laughter had broken from Hannah. She was in fact doubled up with laughter. "John!" she gasped, wiping her eyes on a handkerchief she drew from her sleeve. "I believe you immune to the very oldest tricks in the repertory of womankind." She patted him lightly on the knee and called across the room to where her cousin Esther stood in a group of young people. "Esther!" she said gaily. "Lawyer Adams has a riddle, here, in the Latin grammar. Perhaps you can help us."

But the more Hannah laughed, with her dimple coming and going, her little white teeth shining, her head thrown back on its slim neck,

the deeper fell John Adams into the toils. There was, indeed, no defeat in Hannah's laughter; she was infinitely good-natured. She had a round dozen of beaux and managed them beautifully, giving neither too much nor too little. John spent nearly every Sunday evening at her house, stopped in during the week when he could think of an excuse, and often when he could not. He seldom saw her alone. Everyone came to the Quincys'; it was the most popular house in town, and Mr. Josiah the most jovial of hosts. He had always the latest news of Boston politics and the French war. John liked to talk to him. There would be no more fighting this winter; General Forbes's capture of Fort Duquesne on the Ohio had completed the autumn campaign. Now the Province would have time to assemble troops for the drive against Quebec next spring. Pitt as Prime Minister had changed the whole face of the war by the simple expedient of announcing that from now on the mother country would pay for everything. Almost unlimited credit was extended to New England. The Massachusetts General Court, which a year or two ago had refused even barrack room for British troops, now unbuttoned its purse, offered lavish bounties right and left to encourage enlistment. Pitt and England, England and Pitt, would pay for this war. *So fling thrift to the wind, boys!* said Massachusetts, nobly. *Buckle on your powder horns, sign up for three years or six. There's glory and hard money to be won!*

Mr. Quincy reviewed the situation excitedly, his eyes crossing more than ever. He took snuff until John wondered he did not choke. "New England men," he finished, blinking ferociously, "wear their hearts in their pockets. In their breeches pocket, Sir, buttoned double!"

"Better in the pocket than buried in the law," Hannah's voice said cheerfully. She stood by her father, leaning lightly against him.

And who, John wanted to ask, *wears his heart anywhere but on his sleeve, hereabouts?* Some hard-won caution stopped him. It was hopeless to engage Hannah in this kind of badinage; she was always victor. John said nothing, merely smiled and shook his head. Later, as he was leaving, Hannah took him aside, told him he already showed marked improvement. John had no need to ask, improvement at what? "Quite the air of a man of the world," Hannah added, raising a languid hand. "You are laughing at me, Hannah," John said. He caught her hand in both of his and to his own astonish-

ment, kissed it fiercely. Hannah, for once, was as surprised as John. She managed to curtsy, and without another word they parted.

John charged out of the house and up the hill in a state approaching exaltation. But when he reached his bedroom, closed the door, poked up the fire and took off his boots, his exhilaration seemed to ooze out with the snow that marked the floor boards where he had set his feet. Surely, Hannah had laughed at him tonight! Probably she was even now mimicking his uncouth gestures to her cousin Esther. John wrapped himself in a blanket, drew the little table to the fire, shook the ink bottle to see if the contents were frozen. "I have not," he wrote in his diary, "conversed enough with the world to behave rightly. I talk to Bob Paine about Greek; that makes him laugh. I talk to Samuel Quincy about resolution and being a great man, and study, and improving time, which makes him laugh. I talk to Ned Quincy about the folly of affecting to be a heretic, which makes him mad. I talk to Hannah and Esther about the folly of love, about despising it, pretend to be insensible of the tender passions — which makes them laugh."

It was possible, however, that John was too sure of his failures. Hannah had laughed at him, yes. John was in truth awkward, he could be stiff as a board. But there was something challenging about him and Hannah saw it — a masculine force, an aggressiveness that made itself felt even when John was silent. When he wanted to talk he could not be deflected by teasing, ridicule, or actual rudeness. And to make him laugh was a triumph; John threw back his head and shouted, his eyes tight shut, his cheeks scarlet. It had come to Hannah Quincy, now and again in the past weeks, that this John Adams — if ever he gave in, gave up, surrendered himself to a woman — would surrender with a thoroughness, a fierceness and an eventual loyalty which would ask much, very much in return. Hannah was by no means prepared to say she would give it. She had no plan, but she found herself watching the drawing room door on Sunday evenings, until the short, solid figure appeared. John had a way of standing on the threshold, his eyes glancing swiftly round the room, then fixing on someone to whom he moved instantly, without hesitation. If the someone were Mr. Quincy *père*, or Jonathan Sewall, Hannah knew John could be lost in conversation for an hour. So she watched, and when John appeared, rose and walked quickly to him.

Something was bound to happen; it wanted only opportunity. One

afternoon the two found themselves, by some miracle, alone in the
Quincy drawing room. It was nearly teatime but no one was at home,
the candles had not been brought. Between crimson damask curtains
the setting sun illumined the west windows; the room was shadowed,
quiet. John and Hannah sat on a sofa at the far end of the room, talking of Esther's engagement to Jonathan Sewall. Hannah remarked
how pleased they all were. Love had changed her cousin, softened
her.

John gazed at Hannah, whose face in the shadow was itself soft
and yielding. How beautiful she was, sitting so quietly, hands in her
lap. She seemed different today, her brittleness gone. A surge of
feeling swept over John. If Hannah made a move, if she so much as
lifted a finger . . .

Hannah turned slightly, stooped to arrange her dress. Her shoulder
brushed John's. He reached out, seized her by both arms. "Hannah,"
he said. "Hannah!"

There was sudden commotion in the hallway. The drawing room
door flung back; there were voices, the room was full of people. A
blast of fresh air blew in. "Well!" Esther said. "Where is everyone?
Why don't you light the candles? Hannah — is that you? It's so *dismal* in here!"

Half an hour later, John went home, profoundly shaken. In God's
name, he thought, what had he been about? In another moment
he would have taken Hannah in his arms, might even have asked
her to marry him! John stopped dead on the road, his face drawn in
dismay. He didn't want to marry Hannah Quincy or anyone else. He
had been bewitched altogether, spinning in the clouds, gone up like
a fireworks rocket. He couldn't possibly marry now. It was out of
the question. At twenty-three he was penniless, barely on the threshold of his career. Yet he had ridden directly at this situation, invited
it, let himself be drawn week by week closer to the abyss. Was
he completely lost in folly? — John asked himself, striding up the
frozen road, his breath emerging in angry steam. Hannah Quincy
didn't want to marry him any more than he wanted to marry her.
He would stake a wager on it. Yet she had most certainly been a
party to this somehow, somewhere. Hannah was adroit, skilled in
such matters.

John turned a corner. The farmhouse came in sight, nestling comfortably in the snow. A flock of rooks rose from behind the wood-

shed, flew off, calling raucously. Over the barn a star hung, sharp and blue. . . . *Do not marry early. Do not marry early.* . . . Whose voice was it? Mr. Gridley's, of course! That first day in his Boston office before the smoky fire. How could he have forgotten? He had put the words aside. *A wife and family will allow you no time for study . . . expensive . . . ruin your career.* With extraordinary clarity the scene came back. Gridley's face, outlined against the chimneypiece, had been earnest, impressive. . . .

A wife and family . . . a wife and family . . . All the way into the house and up the narrow stairs to his room the words pursued John, first with horror, then with a dawning satisfaction at his release. For it was a release. Providence itself had stepped in to save him. How powerful were a man's emotions and how they could catch him off guard! That night, John wrote with utmost seriousness in his diary. "I have been delivered from very dangerous shackles and left at liberty, if I will but mind my studies, of making a character and a fortune. I found a passion growing in my heart, that would have ate out every seed of ambition, every wise design or plan in my mind." [1]

And how was he to manage in the future? What was to prevent his being caught again, not tomorrow perhaps, but the day after tomorrow? Hannah Quincy on Monday would be as irresistible as Hannah on Sunday, no matter how stringently he argued with himself. What was to keep him from falling back into the toils? . . . Although, thought John with a sudden new worldliness of insight, Hannah very likely was as wary as he, by now. That motion toward him tonight had been the first involuntary, wholly unguarded action he had ever seen her take. . . .

He must map out his days — and his nights — with no loophole for error. Work alone could deliver him from this danger. He would pledge himself to the most intense, the deepest activity and discipline. John gripped his pen.

> Now let me collect my thoughts. Now let me form great habits of thinking, writing, speaking. Let love and vanity be extinguished, and the great passions of ambition, patriotism, break out and burn. Let little objects be neglected and forgot, and great ones engross, arouse and exalt my soul.

It was a program for a sage, an archangel. Oddly enough, John kept to it. He had meant every word of that large solemn passage. For a month, he did not return to the Quincys'. He laid out his days, hour by hour. . . . He would rise early, before sunup, light his fire, give the first hours to the *Institutes* as Gridley had advised, read Vinnius's notes in Latin, Van Muyden, Hoppius's *Commentaries on Justinian.* By ten o'clock he would shift to the admiralty law, study general treatises on naval laws and commerce. After noonday dinner he would look to his health, go out, "climb cliffs, walk in fields, by rivers and lakes." The evenings could be devoted to general reading such as Baxter's *Inquiry into the Human Soul,* Angeloni's *Letters* that Sam Quincy had lent him, Montesquieu, Bolingbroke and such books as he could borrow from the Harvard Library and elsewhere.

John's program began to grow by its own accretion. Rereading Locke's *Essay concerning Human Understanding,* he became absorbed in a study of the mental process itself. "Let me examine how men think," he wrote in the diary. "Let me search for the clue which led the great Shakespeare into the labyrinths of human nature." When he could, John attended court in Boston, Cambridge, Charlestown, carrying his large notebook with him. ("Commonplace Books," students called them then.) The dearth of lawbooks was perhaps his greatest difficulty. The Harvard Library had few, the new lending library in Boston still fewer. John trudged hopefully from office to office — Gridley's, Pratt's, Thacher's, Otis's — searching out authorities, piecing together what he had learned. His greatest find was a new publication he picked up at a bookseller's: Blackstone's *Analysis of the Laws of England,*[2] a series of lectures given at Oxford. Here for the first time a conscious connection was made between law and history; here the whole framework of society was examined in the light of the common law and of legislation past and present. No English-speaking university gave such a course; obviously, Mr. Blackstone was breaking ground.

How wonderful, John thought, to study under such a man! He wrote enthusiastically to Jonathan Sewall about the book and Sewall replied immediately, asking further particulars. John began also a serious correspondence with young Peter Chardon of Boston, begged him to report any interesting case he might hear in the courts, in the Governor's Council or even before the justices of the peace.

Ned Quincy and Bob Paine, disturbed by this wholehearted pre-

occupation of their colleague, took to baiting John in public, not always pleasantly. What was his aim — was he trying to outdistance the field? "You intend to be an authority in every branch of the law, I suppose?" Bob Paine asked sarcastically one day after court, before a group of lawyers. "Yes," John replied without hesitation. "I do." The men laughed, Paine the loudest. . . . That night in his room, John cursed himself for his simplicity. "Next time," he wrote angrily, "I will answer, 'No! Knowledge enough to keep out of fire and water is all that I aim at.'" [3]

From time to time, John saw Hannah Quincy. He was astonished at how freely they met. There was no constraint. All seemed pleasant, friendly. Now that John knew his mind and had laid his course, Hannah recognized it, laughed with him as easily as in the old far-off days when they were children together. Plainly, she herself preferred this relationship. John marveled. If one took the lead, maintained an attitude, were the bonds of friendship always so malleable? Was the matter, at bottom, a question of being the possessor of one's own soul?

At twenty-four, John was mature enough to see the need for balance. A man must be moderate, he told himself a trifle wryly, in study as in love, especially a man with his living to make. With remarkable objectivity John charged himself, in the diary, concerning his weakest points: "Avoid a gloomy countenance, a stiff behavior. Mix with the crowd in a tavern, in the meeting-house or training-field. Offer to change or sell, trade a horse. Converse and deal with mankind, move and stir from one scene of action and debate and business to another. These transitions will make study and debate and business not less profitable. In total retirement we are apt to smoke and trifle and drone it too much."

Clients began to come to the office on Penn's Hill. Their suits were small. When John was uncertain if a case were worth taking he made the client wait while he went to Boston and talked with Gridley or Otis. There was a case in Braintree about somebody's new felt hat that was not delivered by the hatmakers; there was what John recorded as "an action for an old horse versus Samuel Spear." John's fee could not have been above a few shillings. But he defended the old horse versus Samuel Spear with all the vigor that was in him, rose at dawn to rehearse his argument, climbed muttering through the woods all the way to the North Common and back.

John won the case, but argued it carefully a second time in his diary, noting his mistakes, the points he must watch for in future.

As experience grew, John became bolder, more confident, learned when to refuse a suit — and learned that refusing a suit does not necessarily mean losing a client. He began to enjoy his work in the courts, threw himself into it passionately. His cases were argued in Braintree, sometimes at Colonel Edmund Quincy's, sometimes in a room of the Meeting-house reserved for the purpose. John began to feel impatient with the pettiness of this service. These were not lawsuits, he told himself impatiently, but personal squabbles, aired in the courtroom as at a theater. And the "lawyers" were not lawyers at all, but wigmakers, shoemakers passing themselves off as writ drawers and attorneys. Their dishonesty turned the law into something small and shameful.

John said so, out loud in court, naming the culprits by name, never sparing them. "I would not have taken this case in the first place," he declared one morning before old Major Crosby and a roomful of spectators, "if I had not thought it my duty to put down the pettifogging deputy sheriff who drew the writ."

The courtroom stirred. John's voice rose. The town should be ashamed to permit such things! Good citizens were defrauded right and left, the widow and orphan cheated of their rightful protection by law. The place was so everlastingly quarrelsome there was actually a saying round the county, "as litigious as Braintree."

"Dirty and ridiculous litigations!" shouted John, his right arm raised, forefinger pointing at the culprit who stood below Major Crosby, notes in hand. "Against this evil the very earth groans and the stones cry out!"

It was the gesture that had brought down the house at Harvard in John's Senior year. But this time, the audience did not laugh. They sat silent, then nodded agreement, exchanging significant glances. Mr. Adams was right. And they liked the way he went at it, laying about him, smiting the wicked hip and thigh. There were scamps in plenty in the county, passing themselves off as lawyers, sucking the blood of innocent people. This young fellow was a proper son of his father, but cast in a sharper mold. Hadn't Deacon Adams served the town as selectman longer than any man alive except old Colonel Quincy? John Adams, that evening, was subject for conversation at more than one supper table. It had been a treat to see him rear up, ripping away about dirty lawsuits and pettifogging wig-

makers. He had faced down old Major Crosby, told him he was countenancing illegal practices, demanded if he had forgotten his oath to do justice between the parties according to law!

John himself decided he would like to discuss the matter with Mr. Gridley. Would it not be possible, with the support of the Boston bar, to draw up an agreement barring pettifoggers from court altogether?[4] Meanwhile John rode the circuit, attending court in Boston, Plymouth, Worcester, learning procedure, learning law, and above all, learning about his country. Wherever he went he made acquaintances — on the road, in taverns and inns, asking questions about the town, the country, local politics, the militia. From county to county, people looked differently on the French war. The enthusiasm of Essex was not matched in Bristol. The men of Salem and Marblehead regarded the struggle as a matter of recapturing the northern cod fisheries, while out in Middlesex and Worcester the issue turned on Indians, the fur trade, the imminent nearness of the frontier.

No wonder the Albany Plan of Union had failed five years ago, John thought. If even the counties in a province could not agree, it would require a more desperate war than this one to unite colony and colony. Mr. Josiah Quincy was inclined to blame the *impasse* entirely on Connecticut — a stiff-necked brotherhood of levelers, in his opinion. Connecticut, said Mr. Josiah, would sacrifice a hundred square miles of Massachusetts for a handspan within their own boundaries.

But there was one ambition every county had in common: a fervent, passionate, unremitting determination to improve its material status, its way of living, keep its houses warmer, enlarge the yearly harvest, enrich the soil, render the farm machines sturdier, quicker to answer to the hand. John Adams made no conscious note of these things. As citizen of a brave New World, he took it for granted a man would use every effort to better himself, raise his family to a higher level, discard the crude implements, the smoky chimneys, the leaky thatch of his forefathers. John's questions turned on husbandry, methods of farming: how to grow grapes for wine, how best to introduce red clover and other English grasses, how the new stocking looms worked and what was the principle of the machines in the coal mines of Newcastle that drew water from the bottom of the mines to the surface.

Problems of planting and soil, John absorbed easily. But the

machines baffled him. Tubes and globes, cocks that opened and shut? To comprehend them a man needed a mind as exact as Professor Winthrop's. In London they had a great pump, a huge affair that sucked water from the Thames right up to the chambers and garrets of dwelling houses. John heard about it on one of his trips. "By opening a cock," he wrote in wonder, "you may draw a pail of Thames water in any house of the city almost. But I do not remember the construction of the machine." He must go back, John added, ask again about this pump; watch the stocking looms once more and see if he could solve the puzzle.

John was not alone in his seeking. This was the eighteenth century. This was the Age of Enlightenment, the Age of Reason. Knowledge of the natural world was to set men free. Long ago, Lord Bacon had hinted it; Sir Isaac Newton had pointed the way. This universe, that for centuries had been God's dark secret, Newton had probed boldly with lighted taper. What he found suggested the system might be no mystery at all but God's very reasonable arrangement, proven not by Genesis 2 but by the downward movement of a stone, a feather, an apple. With a prism in his hand, man could explain light itself.

And it was man's duty to explain. It was man's duty to investigate every phenomenon of nature, utilize every resource of earth and sky, from the lowly worm that spit the silk to the lightning that ran down the string of Dr. Franklin's kite. Men felt this duty profoundly, proudly, almost as a religion. John Adams, child of his century, felt it too. For America, Dr. Franklin set the scientific tone. And in Cambridge, Massachusetts, Franklin's friend Professor Winthrop continued, from his apparatus chamber, to spread the gospel of empirical knowledge. Franklin himself had visited Braintree not long ago and stopped for tea at Colonel Quincy's by the waterfall. John had not seen him. But he heard about it, as did all the town. The conversation had turned upon the raising of grapes, the varieties of favorable soil. The great Doctor went back to Philadelphia, and three weeks later Colonel Quincy received two bundles of "Rhenish grape slips," one bundle sent by water, one by land. "Lest they should miscarry," Franklin wrote.

The Doctor, John heard, had searched seventy miles outside of Philadelphia for those vines. What trouble a great man takes to accomplish little things! Franklin had been interested, too, in the comet

that appeared over Boston that spring of '59. It was headed toward the east and had a very long tail.[5] Splendid and fiery, it streaked down toward the Harbor. People took it as a good omen. Surely the war would go well this summer. Surely, the French would be driven back!

The omen proved highly auspicious. On July 24, Sir William Johnson captured Niagara. Two days later, Amherst took Ticonderoga. There remained Quebec to fight for. *Quebec!* The word was on every tongue. The city was a great natural stronghold, the taking of it seemed impossible. From that rocky place had issued, for some seventy-five years, armed parties of French and Indians to kill and terrorize along hundreds of miles of border. Again and again the British had tried to storm it and failed miserably, retreating to the boats or the wilderness with their dead and wounded. Thousands of American lives had been lost before Quebec. Men had died of wounds, of fever; ships had been rammed, foundered, burned.

From England there arrived now, to take part in the great venture, the largest fleet ever to cross the Atlantic. Two hundred and seventy-seven vessels went up the St. Lawrence, with twenty thousand men as crew. Among them were prime seamen from Boston, hundreds of first-rate Yankee sailors — fishermen who knew the coasts, knew the tides, the shoals, the wind and weather, and who were bold to carry sail.

And on shore Pitt's new general, young James Wolfe who had fought so well at Louisburg, led nine thousand men to the attack, coming round by land on the hills above the harbor. Seven hundred American rangers were with Wolfe's troops. But this army — even Boston acknowledged it — was almost pure British. Eight thousand regulars, well-equipped — and well-trained, thanks to Amherst, in wilderness fighting . . . On the Plains of Abraham they met the enemy. Montcalm was mortally wounded. Wolfe was killed, but he had won the battle. From Eastport to Savannah, newspapers reared wavering, joyful headlines:

GOD BE PRAISED, QUEBECK IS IN ENGLISH HANDS!

Everywhere, men read it and rejoiced. Westward to the Connecticut River, west to the mountains, to Albany and the Hudson, men of farm and forest heard the news with grim satisfaction, remembering Fort William Henry and the women lying murdered behind the

stockade. Gloucester fisherman knew the Banks would be theirs again, to range as they pleased. And in Newport on moonlight nights, there was no more watching for French sail to round Gay Head or slide northward from Block Island across the Sound.

Quebec, of course, was not Canada. Montreal was still in enemy hands. But the French Navy was shattered, the great fortress taken. In Boston the boom of cannon was a heartfelt sound. Over the Bay in Braintree, people ran in the streets, shouting the news. The bells rang wildly, peal on peal — then soberly, summoning the citizens to church, to give thanks on their knees for a great deliverance.

Wolfe was the hero now. The papers carried long, flowery odes to the martyred general, so young, so brave, fallen "in defense of America." That, anyway, was how New England chose to see it, greatly pleased to praise a British soldier once more. For were we not all Englishmen, of one blood, one common heritage? New England praised Wolfe, praised the great statesman William Pitt who had sent us Wolfe and Amherst — sent fleets, armies, money, victory. This time, New England was not jealous. This time, she conceded the battle to Old England, claiming little glory for herself. Victory erased all complaints. "A peculiar harmony prevails through the Army," a correspondent wrote down from the battle area. "No Distinction is made between the Regulars, Provincials and Militia."

It was a love feast altogether. And as the days passed, newspapers were glad to revert to something besides war news. The very advertisements changed color. For the past five years, almost the only foreign merchandise listed had been French prize cargoes taken at sea and towed to Boston wharves or brought northward from Newport and Bristol. Silks, laces, Paris mantuas. All very fine, but it was reassuring to be offered the good solid British wares again. *Coals from Newcastle!* [the notices read] *Tin from the mines of Cornwall!*

In March of 1760, Boston had a fire. Boston was always on fire, the wooden houses went up like tinder. With no water hydrants, even the most smartly helmeted fire company was helpless to do much but chop down neighboring walls. This fire, however, surpassed all previous fires. "The greatest conflagration ever known in North America," said the *Gazette*. Whole blocks went up in smoke. Down at the Battery men worked furiously, throwing casks of powder into the harbor. The elegant Lieutenant Governor Hutchinson himself

was there in his shirt sleeves, heaving and rolling kegs. But the flames swept down the hill; the men fled, and with a roar heard plainly across the Bay in Braintree, the Battery blew up. There were a thousand homeless. Town meeting was called, shelter arranged for the destitute. Laws were passed for rebuilding the city: Boston, hereafter, was to have only slate or tiled roofs.

But even the worst disasters of peace are preferable to a state of war. After the taking of Quebec, the tone of Boston newspapers grew lighter. The foreign newsletters were filled with delightful gossip. The *Gazette* had a spicy bulletin from Paris announcing that Madame Pompadour had lost the love of the French King. "Lewis le Petit," the *Gazette* called him with fine sarcasm, to distinguish him from *le Grand Monarque*. They pronounced it Pett-it and it was an old joke, but Boston loved it. "La Pompadour constantly provides," the letter went on, "fresh beauties to distract Lewis from the people's discontent."

New England relished these morsels from the courts of France and Spain. Now that Quebec was taken, it was especially pleasing to fulminate over the immorality of papist life in general. Piquant bits from the Court at London were welcomed too. The *Gazette* nourished its subscribers on the amours of duchesses, in particular the suicide of a beautiful young lady of title who had tied herself to the foot of her bed and done away with herself in horrid fashion. Crossed in love, the *Gazette* said she was, printing her name discreetly with one capital letter and a series of blanks. During the war these gossipy foreign letters had been discontinued for notices of casualties, calls for troops or proclamations of fast days to pray for victory. Now there was time once more for frivolity, time for scandal to be enjoyed across three thousand miles of water. (Boston seldom printed its own scandals unless they had already passed through the criminal courts and the culprits were suitably rewarded with a day in the pillory, a loss of ears, or worse.)

In the summer of 1760, Governor Pownall left Massachusetts, sailed back to England, never to return. The papers barely mentioned it. Thomas Pownall had been in America only seven years. Yet he knew the colonial problem, the dilemma of empire as few men knew it. Throughout the French war he had been in frequent communication with Pitt, dispatching information concerning the temper of the people as well as the actual events of battle. Pownall saw that

Britain's colonies should be looked on as "external dominions, not subjects of the state but dissevered and distinct from the organized body which is called the kingdom of Great Britain."

Beyond Pitt himself, nobody listened to this oracle of a future Commonwealth. Massachusetts itself mistrusted Pownall, with his fine dress, his London manners, his way with the ladies which was strikingly successful in spite of a figure that was short and plump. Pownall, said Boston, was a fribble. When New England called a man a fribble, he was done; it was next thing to calling him a Parisian fop. Pownall, practical-minded prophet, sailed out of Boston Harbor; few guns celebrated his departure. Almost immediately, the town welcomed by cannon shot, bells and procession, his successor — the Governor who was to be a thorn in the side of Massachusetts for the next ten years . . . the man who, try though he might, would never understand colonials . . . the man who, endeavoring to serve two masters, would make one impolitic, arrogant move after another: that stubborn, intelligent, tactless, loyal servant of the King, Francis Bernard.

It was August when his ship arrived. All summer, the armies under Jeffrey Amherst had been closing in on Montreal. Early in September, three converging forces met on the Island itself. On the eighth of September, 1760, Montreal, and all Canada with it, surrendered to the British. The war was over.

The Boston *Gazette* printed "An Authentick Account of the Surrender, published by Authority." (A new departure for the *Gazette*, which hitherto had considered its own authority good enough.) And when the tales of heroism were told, the tales of fighting at sea and on land, the *Gazette's* tone turned jocose, as becomes the victor. Its front page carried a long *"Lamentation of Lewis le Petit for the Loss of his Ships."* The British Prime Minister had his share of glory. *"Mine Enemy,"* said the *Gazette*, which dearly loved a pun "has digged a deep, a fathomless P I T T."

There were rewards of victory more telling than glory. MEN OF MASSACHUSETTS! [The headlines were tall] THE FRENCH ARE GONE FOREVER. THINK OF THE COD FISHERIES! There could be no exaggerating the importance of this. Massachusetts could take its fishing fleets north to the Grand Bank once more, could dry its cod on Newfoundland beaches without dread of French raiders from behind the coves. Gone forever were the French

soldiers and their savage allies — and gone also the British troops
from North American soil. Redcoats; lobsterbacks had sailed away
to the eastward, down, down over the long horizon. *And may God
grant them a following wind!* said Boston, Newport, Plymouth, Bristol. The troops had brought victory; Massachusetts had tried to love
them. She heaved a sigh of pleasure to see them go.

It was rumored that some of the soldiers were to remain in
America and be granted lands. New England did not mind; there
were acres in plenty to the westward. Let the lobsterbacks try clearing the forest as New England men had cleared it. Let them handle
an ax, roll logs, build wagons. It would be good to be on hand when
these innocent ones launched their first dugout canoe on the rapids
above Schenectady.

But these were only bylights to the general rejoicing. From tidewater to inland lake, America praised God for victory, then praised
the King. *Long live George II, our Sovereign Lord, whose armies
have freed us from the Gallic yoke!*

His Majesty had not long to enjoy these felicitations. On the
twenty-fifth of October, 1760, he fell down on his palace floor and
was dead. New England heard it just after Christmas and chose to
feel sentimental. The King — he was seventy-seven — seemed to
take old times, old ways, along with him when he went. "Our good
old King is gone," people said to each other. The morals of George
II had been as light as those of any papist monarch on Boston's list,
and as for his honesty, it had not exceeded that of kings in general.
But in North America, bells tolled. Governor Bernard and his Massachusetts Council went into deep mourning; newspapers reported the
royal funeral in fullest, most luxurious detail. "The Royal Body,
carried by 12 Yeomen, was covered with a large Pall of purple Velvet and lined with purple silk, with a fine Holland Sheet, adorned
with ten large Escutcheons of the Imperial Arms, Painted on Satin,
under a Canopy of purple Velvet."

How grand a sight, thought Braintree, Boston, Plymouth, Worcester! The bells tolled grandly, sadly — then changed their tune and
rang joyful greeting to the new King. From the steps of courthouses,
meeting-houses, market houses all over North America, George III
was proclaimed. *Long live King George III! Long may he prosper!*

Long live George III, first English-born sovereign of his house
and scion of a Protestant succession. Twenty-two years old; slender,

vigorous . . . A very moral young man, the papers said, a proper English gentleman. A bachelor, ready to marry as the state advised. Ready to rule. Steady and persistent, so far, in all that he did. And eager — how eager! — for the prosperity of his "farms," as he called the American colonies.

1761 . . . The New Year was auspicious. France was beaten. Canada was ours. 1761 . . . and a new young King in the palace. *Peace to the world!* said Massachusetts, Pennsylvania, Virginia, Georgia. *Peace and prosperity for all.*

1761. Britain looks for revenue. James Otis makes a speech, and "the child Independence is born." Farewell to Deacon Adams.

AT the close of the Seven Years' War, the Province of Massachusetts rode proud and high. Money flowed; there was a boom. Cargoes crowded Boston wharves faster than they could be unloaded — no sooner unloaded than sold. Along the waterfront in sixteen great yards, ships were building; their thousand workmen had money to spend. The Province emerged from the war not impoverished but rich. And her domain was huge, sprawling from Cape Cod northward to Falmouth* . . . Castine . . . the St. John River and the territory of Quebec itself. Westward over the Berkshires, the Province reached almost to Lake Champlain.

Two hundred and fifty thousand souls inhabited this region. (The thirteen colonies combined had less than two million; Canada about eighty thousand.) Boston, with eighteen thousand, still called herself the Metropolis of North America, preferring not to notice that Philadelphia was crowding for the title.[1] Now that the French enemy was gone — or almost gone — the colonies could spread westward to the fertile Ohio Valley, to the great fur-trading territory beyond Detroit. A few daring souls such as Jonathan Mayhew of Boston prophesied that the colonies would someday reach to the shores of the Pacific itself! Countless millions would people this vast region. Of course, the Western Indians were a problem. But eventually, In-

* Now Portland, Maine.

dians were manipulated, or at least conveniently distributed, by treaty, gunpowder, smallpox, firewater or an opportune combination of all four.

It was a dazzling prospect, and not one to encourage colonial humility. Francis Bernard, the new Royal Governor, chose to remind the Massachusetts Assembly, in his very first speech, of their filial obligations. The present prosperity was derived, he said, from a proper "subjection" to Great Britain, without whose aid the colony would not now be a free people. No nation but Britain could have delivered North America from the power of France.

Subjection? The Assembly did not like the word. "Relation," they called it in their formal reply. "Our present freedom owes itself to our *relation* with Great Britain." The House of Representatives, in an outburst of good feeling, even used the phrase "filial obedience," which pleased Governor Bernard. It pleased also his henchman, Thomas Hutchinson, that elegant, handsome, ambitious, highly intelligent son of Massachusetts who by now had climbed not only to the Lieutenant Governorship but was commander of Castle William in Boston Harbor, Judge of Probate, member of the Governor's Council and Chief Justice of the Province. It was a lucrative plurality of offices. Because it combined the executive and judicial power in one man, it disturbed the Province slightly, when they came to think about it. But custom sanctioned such a combination; the Province was rather proud of Thomas Hutchinson. In 1761, his was the most powerful family in Massachusetts. The government was honeycombed with Hutchinsons; it was almost an oligarchy of Hutchinsons and Olivers, related by marriage or cousinship . . . and all rich, well-educated, worldly, and under signal obligations to his new and youthful Majesty, King George the Third.

While prosperity lasted, Massachusetts welcomed the royal patronage, accepted the King's appointees whether native or London-born. So did Virginia. These two colonies had given by far the greatest number of troops and money to the French war. But these two also, during the past seven years, had refused the mother country outright when she overstepped their Assembly's cherished right to vote its own taxes and appropriations. The refusals had been impudent, arrogant. Massachusetts and Virginia preferred to risk — so it seemed to England — military defeat from the French rather than a constitutional defeat in their own legislative chambers. Extraordinary in-

gratitude! said England. Had not the mother country herself created these elective Assemblies, generously endeavoring to give her colonies the same free government enjoyed at home under the British constitution?

But England, in truth, had never expected the colonial Assemblies to go so far. Gradually, these bodies had claimed privileges, assumed more "rights," until Massachusetts, indeed, looked on her government as a smaller version of the one at Westminster. The Royal Governor occupied the place of King. The Governor's Council of twenty-eight was the House of Lords. The Assembly, elected by the people, was the House of Commons. In England the Commons, after centuries of blood and struggle, had won from the sovereign, certain rights. These rights Massachusetts claimed for her own Assembly or Commons: the right to vote assent to Parliament-made laws and taxes, the right to initiate legislation. Great Britain by no means shared this view. Britain thought of the several provincial Assemblies not as Houses of Commons at all, but as something like municipal corporations, municipal councils, legally subordinate to Parliament. Would the municipal council of Leeds or Liverpool defy the Lords and Commons at Westminster? Most certainly not!

During the French war, England had overlooked colonial impudence; she was forced to overlook it. But now that North America no longer needed English troops and English guns, what might her people not say and do to defy the mother country, even rob her of rightful revenue? Perhaps it would be better to give Canada back to the French! In London the suggestion was not unpopular. "Awe of the French," wrote one noble lord to another in June of '61, "keeps our Colonys dependent upon the Mother Country." [2] The West Indian sugar trade brought in more money than all Canada's furs together. Why not, therefore, let the French remain in Canada and concentrate forces on the sugar islands? England had conquered the Island of Guadeloupe in '59. If she could take Martinique from the French, Havana and Manila from Spain, she could put France out of the sugar business entirely.

There was no overestimating the importance of sugar. It was the key to British commerce with the North American colonies. Sugar (or molasses) went from the West Indies to New England. New England turned it into rum ("Kill-devil," the commissioners of trade called it); sent the rum to Africa to pay for a cargo of slaves and

gold dust. Gold dust and most of the slaves were left at the islands in exchange for sugar. Thus the great triangle was completed: Rum, slaves, molasses . . . molasses, slaves, rum. Again, Britain was not reaping the rewards of this traffic.

Britain's Acts of Trade (passed by Parliament under the Stuart kings) said that colonial-owned cargoes must touch at a port of England before being sold, no matter what the eventual destination. In 1733, Britain had added the Molasses Act, putting a prohibitive tariff on every gallon of molasses brought from the French West Indies to North America.

New England evaded the Acts of Trade, disguised French sugar as English sugar, shifted brazenly the flags at her mastheads. Throughout the war, New England traded with the enemy, supplying slaves for the cane fields in exchange for the sugar, molasses, rum, that were the lifeblood of the triangular trade. By skillful bribery, New England skippers obtained licenses authorizing their vessels to proceed to the French islands under "flags of truce." *To exchange prisoners of war*, the skippers said. The ships sailed back to Boston, Newport, Plymouth, laden not with prisoners of war but with French sugar. Fraudulent papers, fraudulent flags were open business. Everyone knew, everyone closed an eye. Colonial governors themselves profited from the illicit trade; so did British customs officers at North American ports.[3]

And now that the war was over, this nefarious trafficking continued. Britain smarted under the rank injustice of it. British officers, returned from North America, told stories of colonial ladies parading on the Boston Mall, displaying silks and laces like so many duchesses. There were mansions of brick and stone three stories high, with splashing fountains in the garden. At ease in the summer shade sat the gay company, while black pages brought delicacies on silver trays: chilled purple grapes and little hot soft crabs, Madeira old and mellow as any in the cellars of a nobleman. And in Virginia, one met on country roads the chariots of great plantation owners, preceded by outriders in scarlet or green, six horses to the chariot, with the master's coat of arms emblazoned on the door.

It was not to be endured. *What was empire for?* demanded London, Liverpool, Bristol — the princes of Court and of trade. Since the first explorer had floated his ship down the tide with the blessing of Queen Elizabeth, the answer had been clear and unequivocal:

Empire was for the enrichment of the mother country. England, in 1761, had a stake of four million pounds in the American colonies, lent out by British merchants who had been promised their reward when the French war should end. The Canadian conquest was to make them rich. Instead, merchants noted bitterly, the Americans were piling up money that should be England's. In Great Britain, the public debt amounted to eighteen pounds per person; in America it was eighteen shillings. What a perversion of nature, what an overturning of the principle of empire! To London, Liverpool, Bristol, the thought was insupportable.

But in Boston, Massachusetts, hammers rang as the new mansions went up. Newspapers advertised *Tenements to lett, very convenient for small Family*. Such luxuries as white paints, oils, varnishes, sold before they could leave the Long Wharf. People desired their houses painted inside — even farmhouses. They were tired of floors laid on in homemade paint — a mixture of clay and fish oil that smelled like the beach at low tide and attracted flies in swarms. They were tired of bedroom walls washed with sludge made of the lime from crushed clamshells. Thinned with cattle drainings from the manure heap, the beautiful pale yellow mixture smelled even worse than the oiled floors.

Wash balls were advertised — French ones, perfumed. Tincture for the teeth, French chalk to remove stains from silk. *Umbrilloes for Ladies, of Oyl Cloth and Silk.*[4] One Charles Pelham announced the opening of a dancing school, to be held Mondays, Thursdays and Saturdays in the afternoon. The Boston *News-Letter,* half in jest and half in earnest, declared it as the highest mode, the very tip of taste, for gentlemen to be seen on the streets "with hair finely powdered, the Hatt under the Arm." Lavender kid gloves from Paris, a mauve satin waistcoat sprigged in flowers and a short French poniard carried carelessly in the hand would complete the picture of an *élégant.*

Boston, in short, was getting beyond itself altogether. And nearly every advertisement, every new importation of fripperies and lace, was followed by the notice of cargoes altogether different — but cargoes that paid for the luxuries advertised: *To be sold, a parcel of likely Negroes, from ten to twenty years, imported last week from Africa. . . . Just imported from Africa, a number of prime young Slaves, from the Windward Coast.*

Contraband sugar paid for the slaves. Again, the triangle was complete. It would not do, said England; it would not do at all. The time had come to stop this blatantly illegal commerce, this profiting at the expense of the mother country. The old Acts of Trade and Navigation Acts must be enforced. Smuggling must cease, and England reap a decent revenue from a colonial trade she had created, financed, and lately, defended against France.

But the enforcement of laws long dormant is not easy. One clear way would be to seize contraband goods, catch the lawbreakers redhanded aboard ship or in their warehouses. Legally, this required a warrant authorizing customs officers to enter and search. Governor Shirley of Massachusetts in his day (1755) had issued general search warrants for this purpose, called "writs of assistance." When the merchants disputed the legality of these warrants, Shirley had ordered the customs officers to apply to the Massachusetts Superior Court. The court, from then on, granted a number of writs of assistance. But no large seizures took place and there was little protest. George II died in October of 1760. Writs of assistance lapse automatically on a sovereign's death. Everyone assumed that new writs would not be asked for, now that the French war was over. After all, Shirley's writs had been directed chiefly at traffic with the enemy.

But no sooner was Montreal captured and Britain's victory secure than customs officers at Boston, armed with writs of assistance, began seizing illicit cargoes. In the autumn of 1760 they drew an especially spectacular prize, a shipment from Holland worth ten thousand pounds.

From Boston, Salem, Plymouth, a scream of anguish went up. It did not diminish when one Cockle, a minor customs official in Salem, applied to the Massachusetts Superior Court for writs of assistance in the name of the new King, George III. It seemed plain the move had been inspired from above, by Mr. Charles Paxton, Surveyor of Customs at Boston. In a week, Cockle's name was a synonym for robbing honest merchants (to be *cockled* out of one's profits). Why, howled the merchants with concerted voice, was Massachusetts thus singled for punishment? Rhode Island, where shipments absolutely princely came in on every tide, remained, for no reason at all, exempt from these disastrous seizures. Nothing had been said about search warrants for any colony but Massachusetts.

The shipping merchants went to Chief Justice Sewall. In England,

search warrants could be issued only by the Court of Exchequer. Had the Massachusetts Superior Court the authority, the powers, of a Court of Exchequer? If not, the writs of assistance were surely illegal.

The old judge hesitated. To his knowledge, the court's authority in this had never been determined. Perhaps the writs *were* illegal. Sixty-three merchants, emboldened by such expedient judicial doubt, petitioned the Massachusetts Court against the writs. The hearing was set for February, 1761.

After delivering this pleasing private opinion, old Sewall promptly died. In his place, the new Royal Governor, Francis Bernard, appointed Thomas Hutchinson. Political circles were aware that a judgeship had long ago been promised to James Otis's father, Colonel Otis. Rumor said that the son, when he heard of Hutchinson's appointment, stormed and raved, declared he "would set the Province in flames, though he perished in the fire." But James Otis aside, to have Thomas Hutchinson preside at this trial would not, the merchants knew, be auspicious.

Boston waited for February, while every day the talk grew louder, the indignation more furious. General search warrants, *writs of assistance?* They were more than illegal; they were unconstitutional, contrary to the rights of Englishmen! Proceedings worthy the reign of a Stuart tyrant rather than the enlightened policy of a George III! Was not an Englishman's home, his castle? If such things could happen, a man might as well go and live in France or Spain or Turkey, where despots ruled and the people had no rights, no constitution.

What, after all, *was* the British constitution? That priceless heritage of Englishmen was no mere list of rules and laws. It was not, in fact, written down at all. It was the ancient charters taken together, heritage of ten centuries' experience. The British constitution was Magna Carta. It was the Bill of Rights, won by the Glorious Revolution of 1688 that had put a Protestant king on the throne of England. The British constitution was John Locke and the *Treaties on Government*. It was Milton and the *Areopagitica;* it was Wycliffe, Sidney, Harrington and the illustrious martyrs to English liberty. The constitution was free speech, a free press, free elections. It was protestantism in religion as opposed to the Stuart kings and Rome. And New England, in the past hundred years, had managed to add a clause of her own: *separation of Church and State*.

In such broad constitutional definition, Massachusetts saw clause and principle outraged in this matter of the writs of assistance. When the Province decided a thing was unconstitutional, her feet were on firm ground at once, her sword sharp in the cause of righteousness. "Unconstitutional" meant contrary to the laws of nature and *right reason*, as Coke called it. "Unconstitutional" meant a violation of principles higher than Parliament, higher even than King! "Unconstitutional" was, in short, a word conveniently elastic. Massachusetts had used the word to good effect more than once in her history.[5] She prepared to use it now.

Legally, the writs case would hinge on whether the Massachusetts Court possessed the powers of the Court of Exchequer in England. But constitutionally, the enforcement of the writs violated two principles: an Englishman's right to have his home secure against search and seizure, and his right not to be taxed without his consent. Massachusetts did not question Parliament's authority to make laws for the regulation of colonial trade. An empire cannot exist without superintendence of commerce. What the Province objected to was revenue laws, excise taxes: any tax for the direct purpose of raising money for the government to use. Under the British constitution, excise taxes were looked on as a gift from Commons to King; they required the vote of the people's representatives.

It was a vital and important distinction. Excise taxes, taxes for revenue, were called *internal* legislation: *external* legislation meant laws for the general regulation of trade. As for external legislation: Massachusetts, in the past century, had accepted many acts contrived by Parliament to restrict colonial manufactures. She had accepted the Woolen Act of 1699, which said no woolen goods could be transported by water. (Since America had scarcely any roads, this effectually put a stop even to intercolonial trade: wool became contraband as soon as it had been carried over the first stream.) The Hat Act of 1732 forbade the exportation of American-made hats, restricted each hatmaker to two apprentices. The famous Iron Act of 1750 prohibited the erection of the slitting mills, plating forges and steel furnaces that had been springing up from Massachusetts to Virginia. The colonies could not so much as fashion a nail to shoe their draft animals. Send your iron to us raw, said England. Send us bar iron, pig iron. If your horse needs shoeing, why — suggested one jovial Lon-

don merchant — ship him over to Liverpool to be shod with British nails!

All this and more, North America had accepted without undue protest. Provided the revenue laws were not enforced, the colonies could afford to accept external regulation, no matter how bitter and how seemingly unjust. They knew the mother country had tried to balance restrictions on one commodity with bounties on another — a sugar tariff with a bounty on naval stores. But taxation for direct revenue America could not accept and continue to exist. "Commercial annihilation stares us in the face!" said the Hancocks, uncle and nephew; said the Wendells, Amorys, Grays, Lowells, Winslows. Surely, Britain did not desire the total destruction of American commerce? Keeping down the colonies would not keep up the empire. Was there no man on the London Board of Trade with eyes to see this fact? Was there no one in the Treasury Department to see it, no one in the admiralty courts, the vast network of London boards and committees responsible for the regulation of colonial trade?

The trouble was, said Massachusetts gloomily, these London boards and committees were totally ignorant concerning North America. No member of them visited the colonies. They were handed their positions as sinecures, political plums: their aim was to make the colonies profitable to England, keep the balance of trade in Britain's favor. To the Board of Trade, colonies existed to supply the mother country with raw materials. In exchange, the mother country sent out manufactured commodities. This was the mercantile system, by which the empire had functioned since the first Navigation Act was passed in 1651. *Trade and the Plantations*: in London the slogan still held. Britain desired her "Plantations" to be completely dependent for every manufactured garment worn, from shoes to hats.

But suppose, Massachusetts asked bleakly, in the autumn of 1760 — suppose the day came when the colonies no longer had money to pay for Britain's manufactured commodities? With prohibitive tariffs enforced, particularly the sugar tariff, Massachusetts families would be buying only the barest necessities. Commercial annihilation! . . . Cockle's application for writs was a test case. If Cockle won, Massachusetts was beaten to her knees.

"Paxton's Case," it was called, after the official who had ordered Cockle's writs prepared. Jeremiah Gridley was to argue for the

crown. His two former law students, James Otis and Oxenbridge
Thacher, had been engaged by the merchants to defend their petition.
Otis had resigned as Advocate General of Admiralty (a crown
appointment) in order to take the case. Both men refused payment.
"In such a case I despise all fees!" said Otis.

It would be a dramatic and extraordinary spectacle, master and
pupils facing each other before five judges of the Superior Court.
Nobody knew exactly why Jeremiah Gridley had agreed to take
the case against the colony. But Boston trusted Gridley and asked
no questions. The public was not to be admitted to the trial, only the
merchants who had signed the petition and a stated number of barristers. The Governor and his Council would of course be there.
The case was to be heard in the handsomest quarters the Province
could offer: the old Council Chamber upstairs in the Town-house.

When the great day arrived, John Adams and Samuel Quincy rode
to Boston together. Neither of them had yet been admitted as barristers; three full years of practice were required before a man could
wear the "long robe" — the black gown and powdered tie wig that
carried such prestige. But the court had been persuaded to overstep
a point, and the two young men were jubilant.

They rode out of Braintree the afternoon before the trial and spent
the night in town. Boston was deep in snow and ice. It was very cold;
the sun shone fitfully and there was a penetrating February dampness.
Adams and Quincy got to court early and found seats at the lawyers'
table. They had come none too soon; every barrister of Suffolk
and of Middlesex County was there — about twelve[6] of them.

The room filled quickly. Chairs had been brought for the merchants; they sat in three long rows with their hats in their hands,
talking busily. In a corner by the door, his shoulders pushed up by
his crutches, a greatcoat thrown over his shoulders, stood Benjamin
Pratt,[7] peering first to one side and then the other. (He had been
invited to represent the crown in this argument, but had declined.)
To men who approached him he responded with a curt nod and no
word of greeting. John, glancing at the wall clock, saw it was
barely nine and smiled a little, recalling a day when he himself had
approached One-legged Benjamin before eleven in the morning.

The audience rose respectfully as the judges filed in and took their

seats around the big fireplace. They were dressed in long robes of crimson English broadcloth, with wide white cambric bands. Immense judicial wigs fell over their shoulders. Usually the judges wore black for civil trials, red only for important criminal cases. But today, Governor Bernard and Thomas Hutchinson had desired an especially impressive effect.

And they had achieved it; the scene was brilliant altogether. This was Boston's historic Chamber. Here in this great square room with its nine long windows, its deep fireplace and glistening central chandelier, Sir William Pepperell had planned the Louisburg expedition of '45. Two full-length portraits hung on the walls, framed in gold, dominating the room by their splendor. James II and Charles II, imperial in ermine and purple, their robes sweeping the floor. Between parted velvet, the royal white silk legs were elegantly shaped, the tapered feet turned gracefully outward. The very bows on the white shoes bespoke majesty and pomp.

Everyone in the room knew the story of these portraits. They had been sent over from England in Thomas Pownall's time, donated to the Province of Massachusetts. If there was anything Massachusetts hated worse than the Pope and the devil, it was the Stuart kings and all they represented. Pownall had known it and never unrolled the canvases, but stored them in an attic and let them lie there, gathering dust. Bernard found them, had them cleaned, framed them magnificently and hung them in the Council Chamber.

It was an outrageous act, considering the tradition and temper of the people Bernard had been sent to govern. The two kings faced each other on this bright winter morning, despots who had sanctioned the infamous laws (so thought Massachusetts) that were today under discussion. John Adams, gazing at them, felt his gorge rise. He nudged Quincy's foot beneath the table, jerked his head eloquently toward the walls. Quincy looked up, shrugged his shoulders and to John's astonishment remarked, "Very handsome. Give off a rich effect, don't they?"

Had his friend described Satan himself as giving off a rich effect, John could not have been more shocked. But he had no time to reply. "*Oyez, oyez!*" the clerk said, pounding with his mace on the floor. . . . In their chairs the judges settled back. Jeremiah Gridley rose for the crown. John reached out a hand, chose the first of six care-

fully sharpened quills on the table before him. (What he put down was to constitute the only written account history would have of this trial.) As Gridley's argument began, John dipped his pen and wrote.

Gridley was lucid, reasonable. He quoted the Province law enacted by the General Court in 1699: "The Superior Court of Judicature shall have cognizance of all pleas and other matters, as fully to all intents and purposes as the Court of King's Bench, Common Pleas *and Exchequer*" (Gridley stressed the words) "within His Majesty's Kingdom of England."

It was true, Gridley went on calmly, that the law in this case took away "the common privileges of Englishmen." But was not this justified by "the necessity of the case and the benefit of the revenue"? Lacking revenue, Britain could not support her fleets and armies abroad, her ministers at home. Search warrants had always been granted, private houses broken into, for the purpose of catching thieves and murderers. Yet no man objected. Was not the collection of revenue quite as important to the body politic as was the apprehension of criminals? Citizens were indignant when collectors entered their houses, arrested them, destroyed their property without the usual benefits of law. But again, was not the speedy and effectual collection of public taxes of infinitely greater moment to the whole people than the liberty of any one individual?

Sixty-three merchants stiffened in their chairs. Sixty-three silent *No's* charged the air. John Adams stopped writing and looked up.

"If it is law in England," Gridley was saying, "it is law here, extended to this country by act of Parliament." For the writs there were precedents in plenty. Gridley cited them, bowed to the judges and sat down.

Oxenbridge Thacher stepped forward. Gridley's citation from the Province law was impossible to refute. Quite obviously, the Massachusetts Court did possess the powers of the British Court of Exchequer. "If it is law in England, it is law here," Gridley had said. . . . Thacher, in his cool, courteous voice, reminded the bench that even if writs of assistance were legal in England, here in the colonies they were much harder on the people, because "here are no lords or King, no restraining hand over the collectors." Whereas "at home" (in England) collectors seized goods "at their peril." Moreover, said Thacher, he had authority to show that writs of assistance were but

temporary warrants, special warrants that must be renewed for each search.

The merchants moved their heads in agreement. No one in North America objected to the issuance of special search warrants, which must be sworn to by an informer before they could be granted (thereby giving the shipper plenty of time to hide his contraband). . . . If Thacher could prove that the writs were special warrants, the business was safe. Thacher cited his authorities, but they were not decisive and the merchants recognized it uncomfortably. Thacher talked for half an hour, leaving unspoken the two great questions on which the case would rest: (1) Do acts of Parliament bind the colonies? (2) Are the writs void for unconstitutionality? . . . These were for Otis to answer. Everyone knew it, knew that Thacher was only preparing the way. . . . The silvery voice ceased, and Thacher went to his seat.

It was two o'clock in the afternoon when James Otis got up from his chair and strode forward to the judges. A button dangled from his brown coat. His shirt collar and ruffle were a mass of wrinkles; he had plucked and twisted them to ruins while he waited. There was violence in him and magnetism; the room felt it instantly. He was almost frightening; one had the feeling he might do or say something monstrous. His head was thrust forward on its short neck; he stood before the judges a moment, then began to walk up and down as he talked.

"This writ is against the fundamental principles of English law. . . . A man is as secure in his house as a prince in his castle. This is the Privilege of the House, and it obtains if a man be deeply in debt or if civil process be served against him. Only for felonies may an officer break and enter — and then by special, not general warrant. For general warrants there is only the precedent of the Star Chamber under the Stuarts. . . . All legal precedents are under control of the fundamental principles of English law."

Otis raised his voice. "An act against the constitution is void. An act against natural equity is void. If an act of Parliament should be passed in the very words of this petition for writs of assistance, it would be void. . . ."

The room stirred; a murmur ran from wall to wall. This was what the merchants had waited for. *An act against natural equity* is void. . . . Here was the ancient argument, by which New England had

held to her rights since the first charters. *The laws of God and nature. . . .* No parliament could stand against them, and no king. . . .

Otis was quoting Coke now, on Magna Carta: "If a man be taken or committed to prison *contra legem terrae,* against the law of the land, what remedy hath the party grieved? He may have an action grounded upon this great Charter. . . ."

On and on James Otis talked, until the room grew dark and candles were brought. Otis reviewed the Acts of Trade that were behind these writs, and the Acts of Navigation passed under Charles I, when Dutch ships, spreading over European waters, had threatened to engulf British trade altogether. The Acts were well enough in those days, when His Majesty's "plantations" had no ships of their own . . . "No goods from Asia, Africa or America to be brought into England, Ireland, or the Plantations" (so ran the first of the Acts), "save in English ships, the majority of each crew being English. . . ."

Otis went into great detail, ridiculed the well-known passage from the statute of 1663: "Nothing can be exported from the colonies, except to England, Wales, or *the Town of Berwick upon Tweed.*" Again and again he brought it in, making a travesty of it. *The Town of Berwick upon Tweed. . . .* Where in God's name, thought sixty-three merchants, was Berwick upon Tweed? They knew vaguely that in old times it had marked the limits of the realm, but must its name stand against their present traffic with the sugar islands? John Adams looked at Mr. Gridley, sitting directly below the great central chandelier. Everyone, from time to time, glanced at the old lawyer to see how he was taking this tongue-lashing from his one-time pupil.

But Gridley's face was impassive; he kept his eyes fixed on a point of the darkened window above the audience. As a matter of fact, he was filled with pride in both his pupils. ("I raised up two young eagles," he said afterward. "They pecked out both my eyes.")

". . . The infamous Molasses Act of the sixth year of George II!" Otis shouted . . . At last he was done. He had talked for nearly five hours. He bowed to the judges and walked slowly to his seat. Chief Justice Hutchinson, raising a hand, declared court adjourned until tomorrow; the room rose as the judges walked out. The crowd dissolved quickly into groups, into cliques of men talking rapidly, excitedly.

John Adams did not stop. He walked from the room, down the circular staircase and out into the winter evening. He was profoundly moved. Here, here was his cause to speak for! What Otis had said about the writs was the least part; the real significance lay in the arguments by which he had reached his point. . . . Man's right to liberty is inherent, inalienable as his right to live — and so with the right to his property, be it only the eel, the sculpin, the smelt he takes from his net. Bondservants have these rights, Otis had said. Negroes have them, even the poor slave against his master. . . .

It was a doctrine that held terror in it, leading one knew not where. When Otis pronounced the word "Negroes," the merchants had not looked happy. Massachusetts had five thousand Negro slaves, thirty thousand bondservants. But faces cleared when Otis made plain that his present application went no further than writs and shipping. . . .

Walking swiftly along Queen Street under the wintry stars, John did not try to split hairs, set point against point. He knew only that sentiments he had heard since childhood — pulpit sentiments, words from a book, words of theory — today had been applied to the problems of daily living and had thereby come to life, quickening his blood with a challenge rare and splendid. *Here this day, in the old Council Chamber,* John wrote fifty years later, *the child Independence was born.*[8]

But the five judges and Governor Bernard shared none of this fine sentiment. As for the word "independence," it did not occur to them. The British Parliament had power to bind the colonies. If writs of assistance were unconstitutional, they would have to be declared so in England, not Massachusetts. (To convince the five judges and Governor Bernard that Parliament could not legislate for America would require not argument but revolution.)

Paxton's Case continued. It was mostly recapitulation now, a recitation of precedent and source. The merchants waited. Legally, they were beaten and knew it. But constitutionally, Otis's points still held. It would all depend on Thomas Hutchinson.

On the third day, at noon, Chief Justice Hutchinson rose and faced the room. "The court thinks it proper," he said in his bland, quiet voice, "to continue consideration of the case until next term. In the meantime, the court will write to England and inquire what is

the practice at home, and what the grounds that underlie this practice."

The audience sat perfectly quiet, shocked to immobility. Wait for next term? Why that would not be till August! Writing to England and waiting for official reply was a matter of months. And why write to England at all — was this an appeal to the Privy Council? Hutchinson had not said so. Massachusetts had, of course, an agent in London to represent her, defend her interests in Parliament. But the present agent, William Bollan, was too much under Governor Bernard's influence to be relied on.

Meanwhile, were the writs to be enforced? If so, many a man present would be ruined long before summer. What of the cargoes landed yesterday, today? Sixty-three merchants knew that they were beaten. They rose from their chairs; an instant later, the courtroom was empty.

In coffeehouse and tavern the talk was angry, despairing. Thomas Hutchinson was the villain now. Not Jeremiah Gridley; he had but done his duty. And besides, had he not trained up the champion for the defense? Boston felt no animus against Gridley. It was Hutchinson who bore the brunt of their fury. Born and bred a Province man, Hutchinson had betrayed them. It was Hutchinson who had inspired this delay. Hutchinson alone knew how to contrive the defeat of Otis and the merchants — and to do it by delay rather than by overt action at a time when the coastal towns were worked to fever pitch. Thomas Hutchinson had served the Province more than twenty years, from the day Boston town meeting first voted him a selectman. From now on, he was no servant of Massachusetts. He was a servant of "prerogative." He was a courtier, a placeman. And his heart, said the merchants, was false.

If Thomas Hutchinson was Boston's villain, there was no doubt who the hero was. James Otis had lost the case at law — but he had won a principle that was higher than legality. In the Council Chamber, in the holy of holies, before five judges of the Superior Court and a royal governor, James Otis had asserted the rights of British subjects, defying the Parliament of Britain itself to abrogate those rights. The place for James Otis, henceforth, was the Massachusetts Assembly, as Representative for Boston. The May elections would soon be due; in political club and caucus the sachems laid their plans. Meanwhile, week after week, cargoes were seized as

contraband, huge fines imposed. The tariff on molasses was sixpence a gallon. Merchants, groaning, reached in their pockets and declared themselves ruined.

As election time drew near and the news spread to the westward counties, Massachusetts found itself divided. Western farmers and countrymen were wary of James Otis and his town radicals. The farmers had always been suspicious of Boston, jealous of city prestige. John Adams, riding to Worcester for court week, heard the judges of Common Pleas, heard Colonel Chandler, Mr. Putnam, the Willards and Paines and Mr. Maccarty, discuss Otis's candidacy. One and all, they were against him. "Out of this election," said old Brigadier Timothy Ruggles at the Chandler dinner table to the company assembled — "out of this election will arise a damned faction that will shake the Province to its foundation."

It was a true prophecy. The writs case itself — Paxton's Case — did not come up again in court until November. Then it was settled in a day, without reference to Hutchinson's correspondence with England or, indeed, any mention of it. The judges decided unanimously in favor of the writs. *Paxton's Case* was done, and belonged to history.

In Braintree, John Adams went about the business of making a living. Whether empires rose or fell, whether rich merchants became poor overnight, country clients must have their interests defended. Moreover, it was time for spring planting on the farm. John's father, at seventy, chose to look on himself as a very old man. He was increasingly dependent on his sons. Three years ago, when John returned from Worcester to live, Mr. Adams had announced that he was through with politics forever, through with holding public office. He was tired, he said. It was time for his sons to take his place.

At town meeting, he introduced John to the selectmen and officers. They received Deacon Adams's son as Deacon Adams wished, understood the significance of the introduction and declared cheerfully that it would be good to have a lawyer at hand when points of controversy arose, particularly the eternal and angry question of the division of town lands.

Nothing came of it however until March of 1761, a month after the writs trial. Sitting one night in town meeting, John was astounded to hear Dr. Savil, his neighbor on Penn's Hill, without a word of

warning, suddenly rise and nominate "John Adams, Junior," as Surveyor of Highways for the Township. John was not only astonished but furious. He had no time for such an office; moreover, he was entirely ignorant of surveying and highways. But he knew better than to protest, and in two minutes he was elected.

After the meeting, John waited for Savil, walked home with him, demanding angrily what Savil thought he was doing.

"Softly, neighbor, softly!" Savil said in his mild voice. "I did it to relieve you of election as constable. Every man must serve as constable or surveyor. The fine for refusal is large. And of two evils, surveying is the lesser."

John apologized. He hadn't known — he was apt to be hasty — he hoped he had not been rude. . . . Savil smiled. "John," he said, "you were hasty and you were also rude. I doubt if it is the last time you will show me those qualities of your temper. But I forgive you. My wife and I habitually forgive you. . . . Will you come this evening and read plays to us, as penance?"

That night, John crossed the yard with a volume of Shakespeare in his hand. He liked to read aloud. He read well, and the Savils often begged him this favor. John had his own set of Shakespeare now and was very proud of it. Eight volumes, published in London. Slowly, John was collecting a library; he was ambitious to own books, spent more money on them than he could afford. As to the surveyorship, once he found he could not escape it, he went at the job tooth and nail — "ploughing and ditching," he wrote in his diary, "and blowing rocks upon Penn's Hill, and building an entire bridge of stone below Dr. Miller's." The best workmen in Braintree constructed this bridge. Next spring the whole structure washed down with the floods. John salvaged the materials, had the bridge rebuilt. He was chagrined, expected censure. But the selectmen only said good-naturedly that bridges always got washed down in April. The workmen must have skimped the lime, filled the mortar with sand and taken the lime home for their own use. It was an old trick, well known to contractors.

Colonel Josiah Quincy donated fifty pounds for roadway repairs. But even that princely sum was wholly inadequate for what was needed. John, suddenly up to his neck in roadways, began inquiring round the county concerning methods of raising money for highway upkeep. What were the rates for paying builders, including their ox

teams, shovels, picks, tools? In Weymouth, Boston, Worcester, Roxbury, John asked these questions until in Roxbury he found a method that satisfied him. He copied this plan in full, adapted it to the problems of Braintree and reported it to town meeting, which received it with surprise, respect and a nearly unanimous vote in favor. "John," said Dr. Savil that night, "if you do not wish to hold office in Braintree, you are taking the wrong way to avoid it in future."

But whether he won or lost, whether his bridges were washed out by the floods or stood the test of centuries, whether the world called him fool or hero, John Adams had tasted public life. He had heard his name nominated, voted on, his plans argued in open meeting — and he was forever lost to privacy and peace. A new and pungent flavor was under his tongue, never to be supplanted by any taste, however tempting, soothing, healing. (At ninety, John would die with that flavor in his nostrils, aware also that a son in the White House, eighth President of the United States, held at his lips a cup as bitter.)

Looking about him in Braintree, John saw abuses and burned to rectify them, save his world, scourge the wicked and permit the righteous to receive their reward. He went about it with the clumsiness, the obstinacy, the tactlessness of a man doomed. His first crusade concerned drunkenness. John had long been scandalized by the amount of drinking in Braintree. There were taverns and dram houses to turn a man tipsy within fifty feet of the Meeting-house itself. After each town meeting, the selectmen adjourned to Brackett's and drank themselves foolish before suppertime. It was a situation, of course, that had existed for a hundred years. But never mind, thought John, if all New England condoned drunkenness, and Old England too. Reform must come, why not at once? Never mind also if the move made a hundred enemies. John knew who these enemies would be and told himself he cared not a whit. "Myrmidons, bull dogs, hounds, creatures, tools!" wrote the champion in his diary, raising his slingshot aloft.

He blocked out letters to the newspapers, marvelously eloquent. *Infernal dens*, he called the grogshops — *infamous seminaries, boxes of Pandora that spawn forth scum.* Not only was the health of citizens destroyed in these "brutal houses," but here the county elections were determined, the county nominations fixed beforehand. What

a scandal, what disgrace! "Here diseases, vicious habits, bastards and legislators are frequently begotten," wrote John, the blood rising to his face.

He went downtown, applied to the Court of Sessions, procured a committee of inquiry. After infinite labor he actually succeeded in wiping out the greater number of licensed taverns. It was an astonishing victory; such a thing had never happened in the whole of Suffolk County. Walking downtown, expecting congratulations, John was staggered at the "ill will" that met him on Braintree streets. He went home very thoughtful. "The Clarks hate," he recorded. "Mother Hubbard, Thayer, Lamb, Tirrell, J. Brackett. This is multiplying and propagating enemies fast. I shall have the ill will of the whole town. . . . Daniel White, Moses Adams. This will not do."

In no time at all the licenses, by some means or other, were renewed, the houses reinstated to the last and lowest den. John saw them filled with thirsty citizens and felt not only depressed but silly. His own family had followed the incident with mixed feelings. Mrs. Adams approved. She liked action, whether successful or no. But Mr. Adams shook his head. "You go too fast, John," he said. "A township is not to be pushed and shoved like a private person. Reform in politics comes slowly, slowly. For years I have said it." Mr. Adams smiled briefly, a gentle, benign, old man's smile that was gone as soon as it appeared. "You have not chosen to hear me."

Riding to Worcester that May of '61 to attend court, John thought of these things and of what his father had said. The old man had wisdom; there was no doubt of it. Not the wisdom of books but the wisdom of living. Lately, John had paid little attention to his father's advice, which irritated by its caution. Now he felt remorseful; he might at least pay the compliment of pretending to heed. What an awful thing, to grow old, lose control, authority! And yet, thought John as his horse walked the road and the May sun warmed his back — yet his father seemed content. Perhaps age diminished this fierce urge for authority, this desire, this thirst for men to listen to what one had to say.

Today John felt especially uneasy about his father. The old man had seemed poorly. He had risen stiffly from his chair and walked out the little front path to the highway to see John off, holding a hand to his head and complaining of dizziness. He was catching cold, he said. Never mind — it was nothing. They must not alarm

John's mother. Whenever there was an epidemic — and there was one now — Mrs. Adams grew panicky, sprinkled the house with sulphur, urged the boys to chew tobacco (which usually she hated), even smoked a pipe herself each evening before she went to bed, walking round and blowing smoke in every cranny, though she made faces and said it tasted rank. This particular epidemic was a throat distemper. It was very serious; fourteen people had died already in Braintree. Dr. Savil had lost two patients. Bleeding didn't help, he said, nor did purging. The disease began with a sore throat and violent pains in the head. If it spread downward to the lungs, hope was gone and the patient died within the week.

John shook himself, urged his horse to a trot. This was no way to be thinking on a fine day of May. Birds sang in the trees, loamy fields spread on either side and the corn showed green between the furrows. The wheat was tall and would soon be heading out.

Eight days later, when John returned home, his mother met him at the door. Her throat was wrapped in flannel. She coughed. Mr. Adams was most fearfully ill, she said. She led John, still in his boots and traveling clothes, upstairs to the sickroom. John's father lay in the four-posted bed. His eyes were closed, his arms outside the covers; his chest moved laboriously with a rapid, shallow breath. As John entered, the sick man opened his eyes, stared at his son, raised a hand and let it fall, then lapsed again into unconsciousness. So shocked was John at the alteration in his father's face and aspect that it was all he could do to refrain from falling on his knees by the bed. Mrs. Adams stood a little apart, by the window, weeping silently. The sight of her tears was awful to John. She had always been quick to laughter, quick also to anger, but John could not remember seeing her weep like this.

All that night and next day, Mr. Adams lay half conscious, his fingers drumming and plucking at the coverlet, his breath coming and going in light, quick gasps. Dr. Savil came and sat by him, holding the sick man's wrist. Peter and Elihu waited in their room across the hall or squatted on the narrow stairs, very much in the way, very desirous to be of help, and, like everyone, terribly helpless in the face of what was coming.

Just after sundown, Mr. Adams died. John was with him, his mother and two brothers were in the room. He went quietly, without struggle or apparent suffering. It was Mrs. Adams who knew

first that he was gone. With her eyes fastened on her husband's face, as they had been hour after hour, she seized his hand, and, crying out, fell on her knees by the bed.

Mrs. Adams, for the next two weeks, was a very sick woman. She was put instantly to bed. Before nightfall on the day of her husband's death, she was delirious with fever. She had caught the epidemic; the household feared for her life. Her sister Anne — Uncle Ebenezer's wife — came to care for her. The house seemed suddenly filled with people — aunts, cousins, uncles, offering aid and managing to be always underfoot. John himself took charge of his father's funeral.

Dr. and Mrs. Savil were infinitely kind; so was Parson Wibird. How beloved in this town his father had been! thought John. The neighbors came — farmers, fishermen, millers, squires — from Colonel John Quincy down to old Scant, the town drunkard, who broke blubbering in tears on the doorstep and stumbled off without managing a word beyond "respects." The women brought jellies and soups for Mrs. Adams; their husbands lingered to exchange, in lowered voices, stories about John's father. The famous story of old Levi Haskins and his boundary fence that had been quarreled over so long in town meeting. The story of Widow Crosby and the premium she claimed for her old lame black boar which she swore was sire to half the pigs in town. . . . Deacon Adams had settled that, too. He wasn't a talking man, the mourners said now. But when he had a mind to, Mr. Adams could persuade a person to anything.

Homely stories, with no trace of heroism — but to John they were stories infinitely touching. His father had been given wisdom to deal with people, knew when to be stern and when to be kind. Only once in his life could John remember seeing him lose his temper.

John acted now as attorney to settle Mr. Adams's estate. It was inventoried at £1330.9.8. The homestead where they lived went to Peter, the second son. (This had been determined long ago, when John chose a college education for patrimony.) To Elihu went the South Precinct land. John's portion was the little house next door where the Savils lived, and thirty acres — ten near the house, the rest on the farm.

Everyone was satisfied. The personal estate, indeed, was larger than John had expected. Groping for some way of declaring offi-

cially his gratitude — his respect and love for his father — John, in a kind of desperation, ended by turning the will over and writing on the back of it. What he said was stilted, as became a New England man:

> *This testator had a good education, though not at college, and was a very capable and useful man. In his early life he was an officer of militia, afterwards a deacon of the church, and a selectman of the town, almost all the business of the town being managed by him in that department for twenty years together; a man of strict piety, and great integrity; much esteemed and beloved wherever he was known, which was not far, his sphere of life not being extensive.*

Reading what he had written, John knew it said not a tithe of what was due. Yet it was a comfort, somehow, to have set down the plain words.

CHAPTER FOURTEEN

Abigail Smith

MRS. Adams — after an illness that would, her sons said, have killed three ordinary people — recovered, left her bed and went about the business of house and farm. She kept her feelings locked within herself; if she wept her sons did not see it. Grief did not interfere with her activity and she did not intend that it should. "The Lord gave and the Lord hath taken away," said Susanna Adams. "Blessed be the name of the Lord." It was her duty to surmount sorrow, show a cheerful countenance, render help to others that were afflicted. While the epidemic lasted, she went from house to house where the sick lay, carrying food, medicines. She was an excellent nurse, strong and capable.

Mrs. Adams was fifty-two and invincibly healthy. Elihu said she could outwork and outtalk them all. She did so now, in a manner almost appalling. It was as if the passion of her grief had outlet in restless, unceasing activity. John was astonished, not only at this quick return of energy after illness and shock, but at his mother's self-assertion, which was more marked than ever. Each detail of house and farm, Mrs. Adams seemed to think devolved on her alone. When her husband was alive, she had deferred to him in all outdoor matters, confining her authority to the household. Now, her sons could not plant a fruit tree without endless female direction as to just where the sapling should be put and how deep the hole be dug.

Of the three brothers, Elihu, the youngest, was the only one who could "manage" Mrs. Adams. At twenty, Elihu was as handsome and merry as ever. He teased his mother, cozened her into silence or even retreat. John observed his brother's success with admiration, but he

himself was far too close to his mother for such impudent tactics. He knew too well what she was thinking, knew instantly if she were gay or if she were anxious. Mother and son had the same quick temper, the same furious, deep energy, the same inevitable shifts from highest spirits to deepest gloom. And they both talked, at times, too much and far too indiscreetly. . . . Cozen his mother? John told himself he would as soon cozen a Bengal tiger.

There was no open strife, no quarreling. Merely — a house that in their father's time had held five Adamses comfortably enough now seemed too small for four. There was no reason why John could not move out, next door to his own house, and settle down. Dr. Savil had offered to leave. But John, on the day after his father died, had told Savil to stay where he was.

He began to regret this overhasty decision. The lease had been renewed for two years — "Unless you marry, John," Savil had added. John was twenty-six; most of his friends had married long ago. Three old bachelors, people said of the brothers, rallying them on their matrimonial elusiveness. Slippery as eels, said Uncle Ebenezer. Knew their way out of any net. John had never heard so much talk of marriage and giving in marriage. His father was no sooner in the grave than aunts, uncles and female cousins assumed quite openly that John would immediately "settle down." *Whoso findeth a wife, findeth a good thing*, Cousin Webb quoted smugly. Relatives developed a habit of running through the town register and discussing the likeliest candidates. Surely, John would choose a Braintree girl? It made things so pleasant and comfortable, when neighbors married. How about the young Widow Penniman, Uncle Ebenezer suggested with relish, his wizened little face alert with interest, his black eyes peering closely at his nephew. The Widow Penniman was a stout, handsome woman, with at least sixty acres of good farmland. Her south pasture lay only one field away from John's. If he bought the intervening land . . . Of course, added Uncle Ebenezer, there was quite a collection of little Pennimans attached. But as he remembered it, most of them were boys. With nearly a hundred acres to farm, John could use a baker's dozen of lads around the place. . . .

Uncle Ebenezer's wife shook her head disapprovingly. She was Mrs. Adams's sister, and a Boylston. Could nobody think beyond a *farm?* she asked impatiently. Surely, in John's professional journeys to Boston and elsewhere, he met young women of distinguished con-

nections, used to good society. Would it not aid his career to contract an alliance with a family of position and money? Solid worth
of female character was all very well, and so were a pretty face and
loving disposition. But were not these qualities to be found in houses
with Turkey carpets and fine plate as well as in the cots of the
obscure?

John's mother, oddly enough, took no overt part in this wife
choosing. But she referred often and in any company, to the domestic arrangements she would make when she had her first grandchild.
"Happy is the man with his quiver full," said Mrs. Adams, "his sons
like olive plants around his table."

These fervent and random metaphors were accompanied with a
sidelong glance at John, a toss of the head and an audible sniff. It
was becoming very difficult to resist this accumulated pressure from
relatives and friends, tactless and absurd though the suggestions
might be. The plain fact was that John, in every fiber of his being,
longed for a wife. In his heart he knew he had longed for one since
he was eighteen. He was a passionate man, and, so far, his passion
had not been fulfilled.[1] The long abstinence had caused him more
suffering than he was ready to admit.

Very early in life, John's parents had impressed on him the old
Puritan virtue of chastity. His father had not minced his words:
*Cursed be the fornicator, an abomination to the Lord . . . And the
Lord shall smite him in the knees, and in the legs, with a sore botch
. . . with the emerods, and with the scab of Egypt.* In his own
youth, said Mr. Adams, the Province punished fornication with
sixty stripes; *his* father had seen a man hanged for it. And if the
sinner escaped punishment on earth, there was no slightest doubt
but he would burn in hell. Mr. Adams quoted chapter and verse to
prove it.

John had been barely twelve when his father took him aside for
this grave and helpful little talk. As time passed, the boy noticed
that his friends, who had probably received like admonitions at
home or at church, seemed to take the matter with extraordinary
lightness. At any rate they pursued the girls enthusiastically when
opportunity presented. John marveled at their temerity, yet pitied
them the awful fate that would be theirs, either on this side the grave
or on the other. At thirteen, John inquired of several of his school-
mates if they knew what the emerods were; their ignorance only

caused the word to assume larger terrors. By the time John was a young man, the problem had taken on a moral rather than a purely punitive aspect. He dismissed the scab of Egypt to the dark recesses of his mind, told himself that illicit amours were of more danger to the soul than to the body. About such doings there clustered always the sins of deceit, lying, greed and cruelty. John ceased to discuss the matter with his friends. Their replies were apt to be ribald. Besides, conversation on the subject was itself disturbing and set the mind in dangerous directions.

John Adams was no fool, but a creature of basic common sense. Had he been less healthy, less essentially vigorous, his long abstinence might have warped or embittered him. As it was, this stringent discipline assumed, as time passed, an ample, romantic form. John fell in love and out of love; he "gallanted the girls," as he called it, "from Friday to Monday." Each lady of his heart was more ravishing than the last, more beautiful, more pure and unattainable, glowed brighter with the glorious attributes of woman. Naturally, these fragile images of perfection fell splintering one by one to the earth. Moreover, there was the ever-present danger of going too far; a man whose aim is marriage or nothing (and with John it was nothing) must recognize the boundary or stay away entirely.

Most ardently, John longed for female friendship and understanding as well as for the satisfactions of the flesh. At twenty-six, he held within him a whole ocean of potential fulfillment. Hannah Quincy had guessed aright: this man, when once he gave his love, would have very much to give — and would demand, in return, a loyalty complete and wholehearted, such as not every woman was equipped to offer. With Hannah, indeed, the entanglement might have been fatal. John owed his escape, he knew well, to pure luck and the opening of the Quincy front door.

Fortune, in John's lifetime, had not been lavish with her favors. ("It is my destiny," he had written at twenty-three, "to dig treasures with my own fingers. Nobody will lend me or sell me a pickaxe.") It was difficult for him to realize that he was free at last to marry, free to let down the bars that had stood so long between him and fulfillment. His father's death had removed, in one swift stroke, every objection to marriage. All Mr. Gridley's arguments, so incontrovertible three years ago, were gone. John was a man of substance, with a house and farm, a rapidly growing practice in the law. In his

mind, for the past several months, a plan had been forming, a plan that he scarcely, as yet, admitted to himself. He knew only that no matter what enchantress, what tempting lady of property the Adams family brought up in conversation, one figure remained in his mind and would not leave it — the small, slight figure of a girl of seventeen, dressed in brown, in gray, dressed primly. A girl with slim neat waist and graceful carriage, moving quietly through the rooms of Weymouth parsonage. A girl whose hands, at her household tasks, were deft and strong. Grave brown eyes and a clear pale skin . . . A girl whose voice was kind; a shy girl, elusive as a deer.

What was there in Abigail Smith to haunt a man, blotting from his mind all other images? Both her sisters were far more striking. Mary, the eldest, was an acknowledged beauty, used to the attention that was beauty's due. Betsy, at twelve, black-haired, dark-eyed and full of fun, was already as pretty as a ripe young apple. John had known the family for years. As a boy he had played in the cherry orchard behind the house, climbing the trees and throwing down the fruit to the sisters when Abigail had been no more than a baby. Parson Smith was a Harvard graduate, no intellectual but a man of dry country wit and easy volubility, very popular in the county, considered the best preacher round about. The Adams family had more than once driven over the hill and round the marshes to Weymouth to hear him preach, afterward stopping at the parsonage for a chat.

John liked to go there. The atmosphere was freer than in most minister's houses; the young people roamed in and out of the library; a visitor was permitted to take down any book from the shelves and browse away to his heart's content. The house stood on a hillside overlooking the highway. It was small and rather crowded, yet it had an air of welcome and large hospitality. Parson Smith, indeed, was known to his colleagues in the cloth as "the richest clergyman in the Province." Mrs. Smith, a tall, stout woman, still handsome, dressed herself in rich stuffs of an indeterminate color, plum or slate gray. Considered more than a little formidable, she was a Quincy, daughter of old Colonel John himself who had the big house at Mount Wollaston in Braintree. Colonel John, as all the world knew, was one of the most important men in Suffolk County. He had represented Braintree in the Massachusetts Legislature for forty consecutive years, had been a member of the Governor's Council and Speaker of the House

longer than anyone in Province history. Mr. Adams had helped him
to hatch more than one local political plan. Mrs. Smith was pleasantly
conscious of her Quincy connections, of her distinguished great-
grandsire the Reverend Thomas Shepard, a founder of the Province,
of the Nortons and the Tyngs and, farther still in the past, the *Sieurs
de Quincy* themselves, one of whom had written his signature to
Magna Carta.

Madam Smith, in short, was prepared to make her position plain
as the first matron of Weymouth and the surrounding neighborhood.
But she had not interfered with John's pleasure at visiting the parsonage, although there might well be interference if Mrs. Smith suspected what had come to be — John confessed it to himself — the
present object of his visits. The eldest sister, the beauty, was engaged
to John's friend Richard Cranch, and it was through Cranch that
John was now admitted to the house on terms of intimacy. Cranch
lived halfway between Braintree and Weymouth, at Germantown,
where he owned shares in the glassworks. He was in his late thirties,
already an established man of affairs and very much the gentleman,
born and bred in England, with a formality of manner that appealed
to Madam Smith. He was thoughtful, well read; John enjoyed his
friendship and when he had business in Weymouth, stayed overnight
at his house. It was natural that Cranch, on fine evenings, should in-
vite John to ride over to the parsonage when he called on Mary.

While Cranch and Mary communed in the parlor, John sat in the
library with the family and talked theology or farming with Mr.
Smith. He had been told the parson had a prejudice against lawyers.
But the Reverend Smith liked to talk about the law, encouraged
John to describe various court procedures in the Province, tell how
they differed from procedure in England. Young Betsy, during these
early evenings, hovered round her mother, being put through some
task of sewing or quilting, and begging for a game of backgammon
instead. In a corner, Abigail sat sewing, her brown head bent above
her work, the candlelight falling on her cheek. It seemed to John
that she had grown almost overnight from the spindly, awkward
girl he had known to a young woman, shy and silent it was true, yet
with a quiet self-containment that promised much, if a man could
but advance beyond the first barriers. Sitting at her work, Abigail
took no part in the talk, but sometimes John caught her listening, her
face raised, to his conversation with Mr. Smith. Often she did not

sew but sat with a book in her hands: Shakespeare, the poetry of Milton or Young, a copy of the London *Spectator* or books far more unusual for a girl: Tillotson's *Sermons*, the essays of John Locke or even the philosophical treatises of Butler and Berkeley.

It was Abigail's concern over these books that had first roused John's interest. He knew she had never been to school; her father had remarked a little vaguely that Abby as a child had been "too delicate" for the rough-and-tumble of the local seminary. The Latin School, of course, was closed to girls . . . And a good thing too, Madam Smith repeated at intervals: a formal education was worse than useless to the sex. It was unseemly that a young woman should study Latin, or any mathematics beyond what sufficed for simple household accounts. A girl's mother was the best judge of what she should know; reading, writing, sewing, baking, deportment could be learned at home. Moreover, said Mrs. Smith, Abigail's protracted visits at Wollaston with her grandparents, Colonel and Madam Quincy, gave opportunities few young women enjoyed. Abby had always been a favorite with both grandparents; the Colonel admitted her to evening parties at his mansion on terms of familiarity with the most exalted personages of town and court circles. Surely, a young woman could learn more of the world this way than from the pages of any book, however learned and philosophical!

When she said this, Abby's mother did not look at her daughter, nor did Abby look at her. But the maternal needle jabbed in and out of the tapestry frame in a way that told much. This, John saw, was a discourse already proven, brooking no argument.

One evening not long after Mrs. Smith had given voice to one of these homilies on female education, they were sitting in the library as usual, Mrs. Smith busy with her youngest, Abby in her corner. The parson got up to fetch a periodical. John left his chair, crossed the room to Abigail and inquired what she was reading. She held up the book; it was Locke on the *Human Understanding*. John smiled, looking down at the girl. The summer night was warm. On Abby's forehead, tiny beads of moisture shone; over one ear the brown hair curled tenderly. Her expression was serious, concentrated.

"A big book for such a little head," John said, taking the volume from her.

"You think so?" Abby replied, her voice low. She returned his

smile, but the color had come into her face and she moved her head impatiently. "Girls," she continued, "are not to know anything, I am told, beyond kitchen and parlor. Yet girls too may have their curiosity. And even a little head, Mr. Adams, may possess a longing for knowledge, or at least for understanding."

John was surprised; it was the first time Abigail had spoken three words to him together. Moreover it was obvious she intended the words for him alone. There had been no impudence in her tone and no coquetry, but a very passion of sincerity and something that John, reviewing the episode, recognized as a plea for help. It stirred him profoundly, not so much the words as the guarded, vibrant tone of Abby's voice, the way she moved her head, the sudden, startling intimacy with which she excluded parents and sister from her confession of faith.

No wonder, John thought, the girl had been at pains to speak softly; her appetite for reading must be an old point of friction between herself and her mother. He had been a fool to speak so patronizingly. He would make what amends he could, and speedily. The next time John went to Weymouth parsonage, he carried a book in his pocket — *The Independent Whig,* a small and favorite volume. When he entered the house with Richard Cranch, Abigail emerged from the dining room into the narrow hallway, some folded linen in her arms. She dropped a quick little curtsy and was about to pass up the stairs, but John stopped her. He took the book from his pocket. "Miss Abby," he began, "my apologies for what I said the other night. Will you accept this small volume? There is no book in my library more truthful — or at least, more outspoken. It contains my credo since college days: *There was virtue in the world before there was orthodoxy in it.*"

John bowed. He was smiling, but it was plain that he was deeply sincere in what he said. "It is a small book, but if it were twice the size it would not be too large for a head a man could admire greatly, were he given opportunity."

Abigail set her linen on a chair, took the book gravely and opened it. She read the title and smiled with pleasure, looking at John and coloring to the roots of her hair. John thought he had never seen anything so pretty in his life. How was it possible that he had sat, night after night, under the same roof with this enchanting creature, and had not recognized what he saw? When Abby blushed, her pale

skin came alive, the color ran and ebbed. "Oh!" she said warmly, drawing a quick breath, "Sir, Mr. Adams, it is a book I have much desired to see. My father says it is over liberal, and will not have it in the house."

Abby glanced toward the library door; her mother's voice could be heard within. She raised a hand in the slightest possible gesture of warning, her eyes meeting John's. And with that quick exchange, the two entered at once, and quite wordlessly, into a new relationship. John felt it with sudden high excitement. He did not move, and for an instant Abigail also stood perfectly still. In the scene there was nothing, actually, to remember. Yet John, afterward, could recall every detail: the narrow hallway with its bright figured paper, the dark newel post, the stair rail mounting upward, the sound of the clock on the landing whirring to strike eight. . . .

Abigail broke the silence. She curtsied again, her clear brown eyes shone. "I thank you most of all for the apology, which from so learned a gentleman" — Abby's face was demure — "was truly magnanimous."

She was gone up the stairs with a flash of skirts, running light as a bird. John, his face red as fire, his whole being exhilarated, entered the library, moved at once to Mrs. Smith, and standing before her, executed an elaborate bow. Madam Smith tried to return the bow over the top of her embroidery frame and succeeded only in knocking the whole thing from her lap. Betsy giggled outright, was sharply rebuked. There was a general scramble for colored wools and a pair of small scissors which John, after various acrobatics, located under Madam Smith's chair and returned to her with another, even deeper bow. Then he crossed the room to the parson, received his greeting with utmost warmth, almost shaking Mr. Smith's hand from his wrist. Seating himself, he inquired in a loud, hearty voice as to the state of things in the parish.

The parson responded with a flow of talk. John settled down to what proved a full hour's dissertation on the alarming possibility that an Episcopal bishopric might be established in·Cambridge. With the bishop's palace, said Mr. Smith indignantly, set up just round the corner from Harvard College! His voice droned on; after the first three sentences, John scarcely caught a word. Obviously, Abby was not coming back. Overhead a quick step passed and repassed. Was it Abby, and was her room directly above? Did she sleep with her sis-

ters, and why had he never noted the arrangements of the house? It seemed suddenly of the most profound importance that John should know where Abigail Smith slept, where she sat at table with the family and what she did with herself all day. What time did she rise in the morning, and were the windows of her chamber open at night or closed against the damp air from the marshes? When he took his leave and got outside, he would look up. . . . Abby had worn lace in her hair tonight, and a little bright blue ribbon. He did not remember having seen her, before, with anything in her hair. How could anyone say she was not as pretty as her sisters? Richard Cranch said Abigail was too thin, too pale; he preferred a more full-blown beauty. They were blind, thought John, ecstatically. Blind and stupid. . . .

He became aware that the parson was asking him a question, and it was not about the Episcopary at all. Oddly enough, Mr. Smith seemed to be talking about sheep. John caught the words, "Cotswold longwools," and then, with a start, Abigail's name. He leaned forward eagerly. At this sudden renewal of interest on the part of an audience which had seemed, to say the least, distracted, an expression of surprise stole over Mr. Smith's face; he hesitated slightly. "You wonder, Mr. Adams, that a young girl should be interested in sheep culture? As I was saying, my daughter greatly desired me to give up the Cotswold breed. She thinks the Leicesters better adapted to our New England pasturage."

Perhaps he should explain, the pastor went on with a smile, that his daughter had a most skillful hand with cattle. When she was ten, he had given her a lamb for a pet. Ever since, Abby had watched over his flock like any old Devon sheepman. She could spot a sick ewe from two fields away; at lambing time she was as much help as a man. Mr. Smith glanced across the room, his voice taking on the low tone Abby herself had used. . . . Or would be of help, he added, if Mrs. Smith did not believe a young woman belonged in the parlor rather than the barn. "Mrs. Smith is right, of course," the parson said with a sigh. "Yet I cannot bring myself to forgo the comfort of Abby's sympathy and really sound advice." He had twenty-six sheep, he finished. Twelve of them were Cotswolds.

John Adams, who hated sheep and had always left the care of his father's flock to Peter, flung himself fervently into the subject of sheep culture, racking his brains for what he could remember. He

had the desperate feeling that if he were ever to know Abigail better, he must make a friend of her father, and he could not begin too soon. Obviously, there was an understanding between father and daughter. "I hear," John said volubly, "that planters in Virginia have imported Merino sheep from Spain to cross with the native breeds. Would not a Merino ram improve your stock, Sir? Cotswolds are hardy, and the Spanish breed has a fine long wool." John paused. "I should like to see your Leicesters. Perhaps you would permit me, some day, to walk to the sheep pasture with you and ask further questions?"

John went home and spent the intervening two weeks chiefly in wondering how he could contrive it so that Abby would accompany them on this pilgrimage to the sheep. If he could have but one talk with her, away from her mother, away indeed from that busy household, sisters and all, John felt sure that something could be established between them. He had made a beginning; it must be followed immediately, before the advantage were lost. If Abby should be at home when he called for her father, he could, after he had greeted the family, suggest she go with them to the sheep pasture. Heaven grant her mother might not be within earshot! . . .

By the time John cantered out of Braintree over the long hill toward Weymouth, he had rehearsed the scene until it fell into perfect pattern. What was to happen after they got into the sheep pasture, John had no notion; his imagination stopped short at the first stile. He had a hazy idea that Mr. Smith would vanish, leaving him alone with Abby in the September dusk, half a mile from the house and from all human interference.

The afternoon was hot and still; huge clouds piled on the horizon and John's mare shook her head impatiently at the flies. A faint rumbling came from the western sky. John did not hear it. He had still a good two miles to ride. . . .

Alone in the pasture, Abigail would look at him, her lips parted. And then, and then . . .

What actually happened was that John rode up to the parsonage in a terrific thunderstorm, and entered the Smiths' front door drenched from head to foot. Abby, running to the hallway, insisted on taking his coat to dry it at the kitchen fire. Mrs. Smith was not at home, the parson said, emerging from his study, greeting John with much cordiality. She had gone to her father, Colonel Quincy at Wollaston, in the chaise with the two girls and their brother Wil-

liam. They would return before long. Obviously, a walk to the sheep pasture was impossible. Would not John step in his study? He had some pamphlets on sheep culture, just arrived from England.

John saw Abby disappear toward the kitchen at the end of the hall. The elation that had seized him when he learned the house was empty of all save the three of them changed to a sort of desperate determination. Muttering that he must get something from his coat pocket, John moved quickly after Abigail. He would speak to her, win some response, he knew not what or how. He was going to marry this girl. She must know it now and forever. The time was come, he could wait no longer.

The hall was dark from the storm; John could scarcely see the outlines of Abby's figure before him. There was a flash of lightning. Against the far window, rain was a bright silver sheet, then darkness again. Mr. Smith had vanished altogether. Perhaps he had gone into the study. John did not care. "Miss Abby!" John said. His voice was strained; it sounded almost angry. "Where are you going? Can't we take a walk together? Isn't it possible for us to go out somewhere?"

A roar of thunder interrupted him. All the clouds of heaven, obviously, were conspiring against him. Abigail stood motionless, a hand on the kitchen doorlatch. John reached out, his hand fell on his coat where it was bundled in her arms. Abby was trembling.

Afterward, Abby expressed surprise that John should have had the temerity to take her in his arms. She had dropped his coat on the floor with a great sigh and given her lips to him, warm and eager. "How could you have been so sure?" she asked, after the immemorial fashion of lovers. "Until then I had said nothing, nothing at all."

"I wasn't sure of anything," John answered, his heart swelling with happiness and pride, "except that you were not to leave me."

They had gone directly to the study; it had not occurred to them to do anything else. Mr. Smith was not nearly so astonished as they had expected. He rose from his chair, looked from one to the other, and grasping John's hand in both of his, shook it again and again. John apologized for his precipitancy. "I had not meant to speak to Miss Abby tonight," he said. "Sir, I would have spoken to you first, for your permission."

Mr. Smith took out a handkerchief and blew his nose. One arm was round his daughter's shoulders; he cleared his throat. "Life over-

takes us on occasion," he said. "One cannot always plan by the book. I am most happy, John. I am most happy for my daughter and for myself."

It was a full five minutes before anyone mentioned Mrs. Smith. When they did, they skirted round the issue politely, but with full understanding among the three. Mrs. Smith must have been delayed by the storm, her husband said finally. No doubt she would be back within the hour. He laid a friendly hand on John's shoulder. "I have not discussed this matter with my good lady. Possibly it will come as something of a surprise — I might almost say, a shock." He hesitated. "It might be wisest, John, if you were not here on her return. For such news, a mother needs preparation."

Mr. Smith looked at the window, against which the rain still beat in torrents. Abigail nodded quickly to John. "The storm is lessening," John replied cheerfully, as a clap of thunder shook the panes, "and Mr. Cranch looks for me on the hour." He took out his watch, consulted it solemnly. "I am already late." He bowed to father and daughter and turned to the hallway.

Taking up his hat, John opened the front door and stepped out on the pathway. Rain drove in his face, cool and sweet. He made his way across the lawn to the barn where his horse was tied. When he had gone halfway, the rain stopped suddenly, as if turned off at a tap. Across the highway the pasture was emerald green; there was a sound of water running from the barn eaves; on the ground, fallen apples lay among a drift of little broken leaves. The earth smelled of cider and crushed grapes. Clouds raced across the sky, long and jagged, streaming toward the sea. The wind had changed and came in fresh and sharp from the westward.

Harvest time, and the earth yielding her fruits. John raised his face and drew long, easy breaths. Climbing the slope to the barn he held himself erect; his body swung free. All his being was suffused with happiness and hope, his senses sharpened to the last degree. Each sigh, each sound of tree and earth and sky intensified itself tenfold, until John, without being in the least aware of it, understood each sight and sound: its meaning was clear, uncomplicated and wholly right.

Perhaps never in his life again would he be vouchsafed this sweet, convincing vision. John crossed the stable yard. Steam rose from the moist earth, on the damp barn floor his foot made a muffled sound.

about to say worthy of a Quincy, thought better of it and paused abruptly.

"Worthy of your father's daughter?" her husband finished. "Worthy of a Tyng, of a Shepard, of the *Sieurs de Quincy* themselves?"

At this cruel and unusual sarcasm from the husband of her bosom, Mrs. Smith sank on the pillows with her handkerchief again at her eyes. Her spouse, instantly remorseful, comforted her as best he could, reminding her that John was, after all, no pettifogging attorney but a Harvard graduate and a barrister of good standing in the Boston courts. Nor must they disregard the fact that a man so clever might go far in the Province, if his political sentiments were conformable. The Governor's favor was often extended to men of worth and intellect. The office of Attorney General might some day be open. He understood John had the patronage of Mr. Jeremiah Gridley.

Mrs. Smith was somewhat mollified by this. Nevertheless, it was tacitly established among the family that John was not to be left alone in the room with her, and that when the two were unavoidably together, the conversation must be kept from the subject of marriage. All John was able to effect was a promise, sealed solemnly by his ally, the parson, that the wedding would not be delayed beyond the autumn of 1764.

At Braintree, John's mother was wholly delighted with Abigail. So were the aunts and uncles. Mrs. Adams's sister, Anne (the Boylston), was in open ecstasies. "You could not have done better for yourself, John," she said complacently, pressing his arm as if they were conspirators. "There is not a family in the county more distinguished than the Quincys. In every respect, the connection will be a furtherance to your career."

John, though he thought his aunt a fool — he had always thought so — was by no means displeased by this praise of his beloved. Ever since their engagement, John had himself been amazed at the qualities revealed week after week by his future bride. He had fallen in love with a young deer, a shy elusive creature that sat in corners and hung down her head — "like a bulrush," John had written one evening when they were first engaged. Now he found himself about to be united to a woman who, though under twenty, could maintain her

position with the best of them, who managed a very difficult mother like a seasoned diplomat, and who even managed him, John Adams — he acknowledged it freely — with a loving skill that gave him great happiness.

John had not lived to be twenty-eight without knowing that his temper was short. Lately, he was aware that he had gained the reputation, around Braintree especially, of being stubborn and headstrong. It was a tendency that had grown on him with the increase of his business. How slow people were with their responses! John thought often, in irritation. They required six sentences where one would do; their minds turned heavily, like old wagon wheels lumbering up a hill road. A man could not stand there forever, waiting, while the wheels creaked round. . . .

Since his father's death, there had been no one to check John's impatience; it rose sometimes to open arrogance. The matter of the licensed taverns should have taught him a lesson. John thought it had, when he acknowledged in his diary the list of his new enemies. But listing enemies does not make friends. In Boston, Worcester, Cambridge, in the courthouse and among lawyers and politicians, John was well liked. Flattery was beyond his repertory, but when he admired a man, John let it be known instantly by his bearing. Unfortunately, this frankness extended also to those he did not like, of both sexes. Abigail remonstrated with him gently. "You frightened *me* for months, John," she said. "Even now, your manner drives me sometimes into silence. Have you not noticed?"

No, John said. He had not noticed. Abby was such a wonderfully sympathetic listener; when he was with her, his talk had the eloquence of an archangel. What was more, he could let his tongue run on with no after-worries. "How miraculous, Abby," John said, sighing, "to discover a person with whom one can make a thousand, thousand mistakes!"

As the months went by, the two contrived to meet at least once a week. Weymouth was only four miles from Braintree; John could be there in half an hour. But in the winter of 1764, they had a long separation. Smallpox broke out in Boston and Braintree. Mrs. Adams, who had lost her husband through an epidemic fever, declared herself terrified, and insisted that John go in to Boston for inoculation. Abigail's mother, on the other hand, disapproved of the treatment and would not permit any of her daughters to have it. John begged

and fought, offering to take Abigail to the hospital at Castle William himself and act as nurse. In the end he went off with a group of friends to be treated by a Dr. Perkins. They were shut up, five to a room, dieted, given powders, denied bread, milk and pudding, pricked and inoculated. Their heads ached, they burned with fever, broke out triumphantly, compared scabs and pustules after the traditional manner.[2]

At last the long quarantine was over and John, concerning whose health Abigail had greatly feared, returned to Braintree. But to John's dismay, he was no sooner settled at home than Abby was dispatched on a long visit to Boston. "My soul and body," wrote John gloomily, "have been thrown into disorder by your absence. A month or two would make me the most insufferable Cynic in the world. I see nothing but Faults, Follies, Frailties and Defects in anybody. People have lost all their good properties. But you who have always softened and warmed my heart shall restore my Benevolence as well as my Health and Tranquillity of mind. You shall polish and refine my Sentiments of Life and Manners, banish all the unsocial and ill-natured particles in my Composition and restore me to the happy Temper that can nourish a quick Discernment with a perfect Candour."

John knew well, by now, how deeply he needed Abigail Smith. ("You are teaching me kindness, dear Abby," he had said once.) Abby was indeed kind; she had none of the dreary, virtuous piety John had learned to associate with the good women of Braintree. There was a gaiety in Abigail that delighted John's very soul. Yet, at bottom, the girl was a serious creature, who believed that men and women were placed on earth not for their enjoyment but for a purpose. Man, created in the image of God, must fulfill his promise or become a blasphemy to his Maker.

With all his heart, John agreed. He could not have married a woman who did not share this philosophy. It was a Puritan inheritance. In the long road to heaven, man was accountable to God for every moment of his time; he must therefore "improve" that time, that day, that moment. An hour wasted was an hour's sin. The conviction was part of John and Abigail, running in their veins, to be transmitted to their progeny even of the fifth generation. It was a philosophy and a program that would sustain husband and wife through long separation, through ordeal most fiery (years while John

served the Congress at Philadelphia, years with an ocean between them). Separation was a decade in the future. Yet the future was implicit now in the meeting and the courtship of these two.

One morning in early autumn, Abigail took John to Wollaston to spend the day with her grandparents. The scene proved by no means so brilliant as Aunt Anne Adams had painted it. The company, gathered in the long dining room that opened on the terrace, consisted merely of Abigail's Uncle Norton Quincy, a quiet, easygoing man of forty-odd, her grandparents and two of her married aunts who had come to view the prospective bridegroom. The aunts took their leave after dinner, about four in the afternoon. Madam Quincy, a merry, talkative old lady, handsomely dressed in voluminous, rustling lavender and a cap with ribbons, excused herself and went upstairs to rest. Colonel Quincy suggested that the three of them, Abby, John and himself, stroll about the grounds and farm.

They went out; the Colonel walked between them, his ruddy face glowing with health and pleasure, his white hair, caught at the neck in a bag and narrow black ribbon, blowing a little in the wind. At seventy-four he was upright and sturdy, though he leaned at times on his cane and took John's arm if they had to traverse a rocky place. John thought he had never met so friendly a gentleman. No wonder the Colonel had held his place in the Legislature for nearly half a century! There was a largeness about him and about all his viewpoint. He spoke intimately, easily, of the Provincial Governors, from old Jonathan Belcher to the present Governor Bernard, describing them not as men of importance but as colleagues who had worked for him or against him in House and Council for this measure or that.

John, by now, had met many political bigwigs, from James Otis and Thomas Hutchinson down to Ezekiel Goldthwaite, the Boston Register of Deeds, and Mr. Greenleaf the sheriff. They were all strong partisans, either for the Governor's or for the people's party, for the conservative or the radical side. Colonel Quincy was a party man himself in so far as he strongly disapproved the writs of assistance and the possible passage by Parliament of a stamp act to tax legal documents. Yet he talked of these measures not as moral issues, in which one side was wholly righteous, the other inordinately wicked. He did not pass moral strictures at all, on either men or measures; he seemed rather to have passed beyond partisan fury and spoke of the good of the country as a whole. John was deeply impressed.

In the late afternoon sunshine, with a September breeze blowing from the Bay, his cherished trees and fields about him, the old man expanded on every subject from politics to horticulture. He stopped to gesticulate with his cane, pointing at each newly planted shrub or tree, explaining whence it had come and if he had obtained it from a neighboring colony or by special shipment from England.

In perfect amity, the three wandered over the bare hills below the mansion. Always, John noted, the Colonel included Abby in his talk, asking her frequent questions, waiting for the approval of her laugh. The very scene itself had a largeness about it. Like the Colonel's talk, there was a seeming lack of boundary that carried exhilaration. A mile below, down the long slope, across fields golden with autumn, the beach was a strip of dark wet shingle. Beyond the beach, the Bay reached eastward, deep blue, ridged with white where the rollers surged between the islands, driving in from the ocean. Every sail that entered or left Boston harbor could be seen from the windows of Wollaston mansion; the Colonel never walked out without his spyglass. He had it now and stopped to put it to his eye, remarking that the big sloop by Minot's Ledge must be one of Thomas Hancock's fleet. . . . Not nearly so much money in shipping, added the Colonel, since the Peace of Paris had put an end to privateering. Did John know that Mr. Josiah Quincy had got his fortune by privateering down around the sugar islands?

"Abby," said Colonel John, "let us rest here on the bench. Do you tell the story of Mr. Josiah Quincy and the Spanish frigate with the chests of gold."

The three sat down in a sheltered, sunny spot behind the orchard wall. Abby began to talk. She told her story eagerly, using her hands, moving her head and body as she spoke. John had never seen her so at ease or so delightful. Her brown fine hair blew across her face; something in her gesture when she raised a hand to her forehead enchanted John. There was a joy about her that was infectious, a nervous force he had not sensed before. Her story ranged beyond Mr. Josiah and his privateering schooner; Abby knew the history of privateering, was familiar with the Acts of Trade that made smuggling necessary. She did not hesitate to embellish her tale with pertinent historical and political details.

John was a little abashed at this skillful flow of narrative from one who had hitherto been content to let him do the talking — or con-

tent, certainly, to leave political explanation to his superior masculine intellect. More than once, Abby had tried to tell him there was something forbidding in his aspect, some lack of invitation that froze the words on her lips. "I can be more free with you in letters, John," she had said once, wistfully, "than when we are together."

John, at the time, had dismissed this as mere feminine coquetry. Only today was his mistake revealed. He knew it, uneasily, as a grave mistake. "Sir," he said to the Colonel as Abby's story was done, and the three rose to return to the house, "your presence is an inspiration to Miss Abby. I never heard her talk so well."

They were at the foot of a long flight of stone steps, leading to the garden. The old man took John's arm. "I am Abby's great admirer," he said. "I have enjoyed that role since she was three, and told me her first tale." He stopped to take breath. "Human beings need admiration and love," he said, "as plants need the sun."

On the twenty-fifth of October, 1764, John Adams and Abigail Smith were married from her father's house at Weymouth. All summer, week by week, the bride's belongings, her linens and blankets, her chests and furniture and modest trousseau of dresses, had been carted over the hill from Weymouth. Mr. Smith had given his daughter a handsome marriage portion; with it the two had purchased an orchard and a piece of land just down the slope from their barn. The little house itself was painted and refurbished to the last inch; John was very proud of it. It faced the highway bravely; Abigail had planted a lilac bush by the front step. It would surely bloom next year, she said. The old kitchen had been made over into an office for John, with a separate door cut in the side wall so that clients need not walk through the house.

Mrs. Adams had thrown herself into the marriage plans with all the energy of her nature. Her final act had been to purchase a superb piece of white imported satin and make her son a wedding waistcoat embroidered in gold thread. She asked John what pattern he preferred for the embroidery; John chose sprays of wheat to symbolize October and the harvest. When the waistcoat was finished and Mrs. Adams displayed it to the family assembled, John said something that became a byword in the household. He took the waistcoat gingerly in his fingers, unable to believe that he would soon wear so lightsome and shining a garment. Examining the em-

broidery closely while everyone waited, John traced with one finger the fat sprays and stalks. At last he came out with the remark, delivered in a voice full of feeling, that he wished to God all his wheat were equally free of the epidemic rust.

The family shouted with laughter. "John," Elihu gasped, wiping his eyes. "Is there no time for romance, even with the wedding vestments in hand?"

John felt himself blushing; he was glad Abigail had not been there to hear this remark. The plain fact was that having waited so long, he hardly dared let himself believe he was to have his bride at all, and so soon. The delay, the meetings and partings had become for both of them an increasing irritation. John had a way of flinging himself out of the parsonage door and down the path, his brow black as thunder, for all the world as if the parting were Abigail's fault and she had engineered it on purpose to hurt him. During the past spring and summer especially, there had been times when they deliberately avoided one another. "Shall I come and see you before you go?" Abigail had written, when John was getting ready for a journey. "No, I won't, for I want not again to experience what I this morning felt when you left." And again, when a winter storm had made the road impassable, John had suggested the accident was a blessing, "for keeping me at *my distance.*"

And now at last, the long constriction was over. The twenty-fifth of October dawned clear and cold. The rooms of Weymouth parsonage were dressed for the wedding in autumn foliage, sumach and maple branches, bright red and gold. There were bowls of fruit on the tables, yellow pears and big shiny apples, little round purple country grapes in festoons, and even some oranges, rather dried up, that Mr. Josiah Quincy had saved out of a shipment from Spain. John, in the dazed condition traditional with bridegrooms, thought he had never seen so many people in such a small space: Quincys, Nortons, Smiths, Tyngs, Adamses, Basses, chattered and stared. Abigail's bridal dress was of fine white challis, sprigged with little scarlet flowers. The bodice was tight, the neck cut square and edged with lace, the skirt enormous. John's legs were splendid in white silk stockings, the buckles of his shoes shone like the moon at high tide. His breeches were fawn-colored; above them the white satin waistcoat shimmered. His coat, long-skirted and fashionable, was of dark blue broadcloth, with silver buttons.

Altogether, people agreed, as wedding parties always agree, they made a very handsome couple. Aunt Anne Adams, surprisingly prim and speechless in the gay throng, stayed close by John's mother, noting each detail of dress, of entertainment, of food and drink and service, to carry later to a waiting Braintree world.

At last it was over. The sacred words were said, the happy vows exchanged. The bride was embraced, the groom congratulated. The bowls of punch were drained, the wedding meats devoured, the golden fruits were gone. Mrs. Smith had alternately wept and forgotten to weep. Mrs. Adams endeavored not to crow because she was gaining a daughter while Madam Smith was losing one. John's brothers told him the horse was ready on the highway just below the lawn; he went out and waited. Abigail, in her long scarlet riding cloak and hood, ran down the stairs from her chamber and out the door of her father's house. John mounted his horse, leaned down and swung his bride to the pillion behind him.

Then, with a salute to the throng by the parsonage door, Mr. and Mrs. John Adams rode triumphantly down the highway, headed northward for Braintree and home.

Great Britain, mistress of a new empire,
attempts imperial organization. Politics in
Massachusetts. Sam the Grand Incendiary.

JANUARY, 1765. Nearly four years had passed since James Otis argued against the writs of assistance, and two years since Britain signed the Peace of Paris and gained an empire. No European nation had ever achieved so large a conquest. And no European nation had accepted, at a peace table, such crushing terms as France had accepted at Paris in 1763. John Adams faced not only the changed personal life that comes to every married man, but beyond his household he faced a new world.

Between France and Britain a mortal rivalry was ended, a contest that had lasted a hundred and fifty years, raging over land and sea. Half the nations of the earth had been drawn into it: Spaniards, Prussians, Austrians, Dutchmen, Russians, soldiers of the southern islands and the northern cities, red Indians in America and jeweled nabobs in Bengal. The final phase was fought in America between 1754 and 1761. When France lost Canada, Louisiana and her North Atlantic fortresses, she gave up, at last, her place as leader in the European continental system.

Men were to speak of this long conflict as "the Seven Years' War," the "French and Indian War," the "Fourth Intercolonial War." But it was, in reality, the War for the Empire. If France had won, Americans would have found themselves herded between the Atlantic and the Appalachians, in a strip of land no bigger than Chile,

while outside their boundaries the French language and the French civilization spread over the continent.[1]

And now the long danger was ended. Great Britain was the leading naval and colonial power of the world. Her colonies reached from the Gulf of St. Lawrence to the farthermost limits of the southern West Indies. All Canada was hers, all land east of the Mississippi except the port of New Orleans (a town of five hundred), and a few settlements along the river. From the Great Lakes to the Gulf of Mexico, the long inland waterways were open at last. The seas were England's; her commerce could move unobstructed from continent to continent. Even in India, the French threat was gone — that threat, persistent and powerful, against which Britain's policy, over all her world, had been shaped for generations.

Now the aims of government must shift. The old policies of mercantilism were not sufficient for this huge collection of assorted peoples. Economically and politically the empire must be reorganized, strike new balances. "A New Arrangement," George III called it. Britain had a war to pay for, the Spanish to watch, half a world to govern and protect. In Canada, seventy thousand French-speaking subjects accepted their new allegiance without enthusiasm. And east of the land called Louisiana, between the Mississippi and Alleghenies, Britain had acquired a sprawling wilderness, reaching southward to the Gulf of Mexico. The Indians were a major problem. Should they be left to the designs of the traders, and were Indian lands to be seized by every band of frontiersmen with rum enough to befuddle the savages?

There was the commerce of the sugar islands to be regulated, and the great northern fisheries off Nova Scotia. Whalers from Nantucket — cod and mackerel fishermen from Marblehead, Gloucester, Newport, Boston — swarmed over these waters like locusts over Egypt; no fleet from England could rival them or even compete. New commercial rulings must be devised, new bounties offered, new restrictions enforced. Arrangements that satisfied Virginia were declared ruinous by merchants and speculators in England; trade restrictions welcomed by planters in the British West Indies were met in Massachusetts with angry protest and prophecies of ruin.

In London the Board of Trade, the Lords of Treasury and Admiralty and of the King's Privy Council, met in consultation. Agents were dispatched to travel through the colonies from Quebec to the

West Indies, and report on the best methods of regulating trade, raising a revenue and reforming the local governments. It would be well, perhaps, to reduce the memberships of the Legislative Assemblies, those hatcheries of defiance, and unite New Hampshire, Rhode Island and Massachusetts in one government.

Obviously also, North America must not be permitted suddenly to disarm, dismantle her forts and lie exposed and defenseless. British observers already reported the French busy building a navy; there was no telling how soon — ten years, fifteen years? — France might renew the attack. The thirteen colonies simply would not unite for the common defense; it was hopeless to persuade even two of them to act together. In the decade since Braddock's defeat on the Ohio it had become clear the disaster was due not to the old general's incompetence but largely to intercolonial jealousy. Local rivalries, local interests, mattered more than the common danger. At Albany in '54 it had been the same story, when Britain proposed a plan of colonial union for better protection against the French. The great patroon families of New York spent one day fighting the enemy, the next trading with them at vast profit. In Pennsylvania, when there was a war in the offing, a Quaker-ruled Legislature simply drew back, refusing not only militia but supplies for the British regulars. Maryland, when asked for supplies, sent eight hundred pounds of spoiled meat to Braddock's troops.

There was no relying on the colonies for their own concerted self-defense. British forces must be stationed permanently in North America: an army of twenty thousand regulars, well-trained, well-equipped. The colonies, properly taxed, could help pay for it.

Reasonable designs, thought England; there would be no trouble in carrying them out. (The Board of Trade had forgotten the little flurry in Boston over the writs of assistance.) They laid their plans openly, forwarded them confidently to America under the Royal Seal and Instructions. George Grenville was Prime Minister, Shelburne President of the Board of Trade. Pitt, the great Whig, was ill, hidden away at his country place, tormented with gout and scarcely able to hold a pen — for the North American colonies a fact unfortunate, tragic. Now, if ever, they needed a man of vision, a statesman whose dream of empire could be adjusted to the nature and circumstances of the peoples who inhabited this empire. George Grenville was not a man of vision but a man of zeal; if good bookkeeping could

save the nation he was well prepared to save it. He devised brilliant measures to bring in revenue, protect the nation's interests abroad.

A new "Currency Act" forbade further issues of paper money in the colonies. Merchants in Britain congratulated themselves. Inflation had followed the French war; colonial bills had depreciated greatly in value. Henceforth payment would be made in specie. And if gold was hard to come by, why, the Americans were ingenious and could dig for it somewhere. . . . The question of the Western lands was settled neatly by the Proclamation of 1763, establishing on the Allegheny ridge a line west of which no British subject could purchase land or settle.[2] The Revenue Act of '64 (in America called the "Molasses Act") reduced the tariff on sugar from sixpence a gallon to threepence, meanwhile providing much stricter enforcement, with no loophole for contraband and smuggling.

Grenville had conjured up an even surer device for colonial revenue — a stamp tax. He gave the colonial agents a year's advance notice before the bill would come up in Parliament. Every commercial and legal document — newspapers, ships' clearance papers, wills, deeds — must bear the King's stamp, paid for. A college diploma would cost two pounds, a newspaper, halfpenny. England herself paid stamp taxes; there was no reason why American colonials should object to them.

Surely, thought Grenville, Shelburne, and their painstaking boards and committees — surely, North America would welcome such simple, equitable methods of taxation? The stamp tax had the virtue of bearing alike on rich and poor; the Revenue Act was a reduction of tariff rather than an increase. How just and well-contrived were all these plans! Enough money would be raised to provide for the army that was to protect North America, with something left to pay the salaries of the Colonial Governors.

Busily, on paper, the ministry at London consolidated an empire. One thing, unfortunately, did not enter its nimble mind: Each of these beautifully laid measures for "reform" — Stamp Act, Molasses Act and Western Proclamation — contravened the deepest principles of American life. Parliament had only just begun to speak of these heterogeneous colonials as "Americans." How could there be national principles where there was no nation? (This mistake was to lose a continent for Britain.)

To protect merchant interests in England, Parliament prepared now to hem the Americans between mountains and sea as narrowly as France had once planned to restrict them. A young and vigorous country looked eastward for lines of trade across the Atlantic. Yet the Molasses Act would ruin her business with the islands, the key to all her ocean commerce. (Even threepence tax on sugar was prohibitive when strictly enforced.) If America looked over the mountains for goods to barter in a world exchange, the Proclamation of '63 shut the western door in her face, forbidding entrance to a continent she had begun to think of as part of her heritage and part of her domain. As for the Stamp Act, the colonies saw it as a flagrant instance of taxation without representation. To pay it, even a halfpenny of it, would remove them at once and forever from that condition of representative government they considered their due as Englishmen. Grenville's argument that the tax bore equally on rich and poor only made it hated by the many as well as the few.

The very reasons behind the taxation schemes — reasons which to Britain were not only just but self-evident — to America were insufferably irritating. New England considered she had more than paid her share in the French wars, as to both men and money. (Massachusetts had given more men and money than any three colonies put together.) As for this projected army, these twenty thousand regulars that were coming across the ocean — had anybody in North America asked for "protection"? *Defending, protecting and securing the said colonies and plantations,* the Stamp Act said. Protection from what? The French were gone, except from a few remote and negligible settlements. Twenty thousand regulars, indeed! Was this imposing force designed, New England inquired sarcastically, to keep at bay the Scatacook Indians, that warlike tribe of near thirty braves who sat scratching their fleas on the western border of Connecticut?

And how humiliating the measures to enforce these new schemes! Infractions of the Stamp Act were to be dealt with in the admiralty courts, which functioned without jury — where the judge, a royal appointee, reaped a commission on every fine and condemnation. To enforce the Molasses Act, British naval commanders in American waters were authorized to act as customs officers, with a fat percentage on each contraband seizure. Even Governor Bernard and Thomas Hutchinson, in anxious letters to the Lords of Trade, protested this sudden overarbitrary parenthood. It was poor policy

so to antagonize a people. The Molasses Act, said Bernard, had caused "a greater alarm in this country than the taking of Fort William Henry in 1757."

One by one the colonies sent in their protests: Rhode Island, Connecticut, New York, Virginia, Massachusetts. . . . They might have saved their pains. Not only was the American voice diluted by three thousand miles of ocean, but most of the colonial agents in England themselves had approved the stamp tax before the protests began to arrive. Benjamin Franklin, now in London as agent for Pennsylvania, had no notion of the effect the tax was to produce, and was ready to recommend various of his friends in America as stamp collectors — a position that promised three hundred pounds a year.

Not one of the petitions sent to England was read in Parliament that year of '64. James Otis's two pamphlets were among the most powerful, considered too startling even for consideration. Otis was still the acknowledged leader of the people's party in Boston. He had only to enter the House of Representatives for the whole meeting to break into spontaneous hand clapping and cheers. There was in this contagion something erratic, a little morbid. Otis's patriotism had begun to take strange forms. Personal antagonisms, bitter and sudden, unlooked-for shifts of policy bewildered his followers. He would scarcely let Oxenbridge Thacher rise on the floor of the House, and more than once shouted him rudely down. Yet Thacher had done great service against the Stamp Act by his own pamphlet. *The Sentiments of a British American*, Thacher called it.

British America: it was an old phrase but it carried a new meaning, the concept of a new relationship. Not the mother-child relationship but something like cousinship, something that would permit the child to grow to full stature. With a kind of pathetic hope, men seized upon the phrase and clung to it. How comfortably the words fitted the colonial tongue! British America — it was the word of compromise. But compromise, unfortunately, was not what Britain sought, once the Peace of Paris was signed. James Otis for all his violence came closer to the true note of prophecy. At the writs trial in '61, he had foreseen disaster in Britain's new policy, financial ruin for the Province of Massachusetts. (Beyond Massachusetts it had not been his business to look.)

And in January of 1765, Massachusetts found herself on the verge of a severe financial panic. One by one, great shipping houses closed

their doors. Men by the thousands were out of work. Scarcely had the farmers recovered from the terrible droughts of the preceding summer, when they found there was no market for their wheat. Land fell shockingly in value; grain rotted in the barns unsold. Moreover, 1764 had been a smallpox year, with city shops and markets closed for weeks on end. Half the population had moved out of town; there was no one to buy and little to sell.

And just when the country most needed guidance, valuable citizens chose this time to die. Mr. Thomas Hancock, richest merchant in Boston, worth seventy thousand pounds, walked into the Townhouse for a meeting of the Governor's Council, was stricken with apoplexy, carried to his house and perished there and then. People wondered if his heir — John Hancock, aged twenty-seven — had the good sense to administer this great fortune in such a way that the Provincial business would continue to profit by it.

To add to the general dismay, one roaring snowy winter night Harvard Hall caught fire. The General Court, meeting in the library upstairs because of the smallpox in Boston, had been lavish with their hearth fires; an overheated beam started the blaze. The alarm bells had barely begun to swing and men to run from their beds before the whole building — Boston's pride — was a wild red conflagration against the windy sky. Every book in the library was lost, and every beautiful machine in Professor Winthrop's apparatus chamber — twenty-four-foot telescope, brass orrery and all. Even the skeleton that dangled from the corner was reduced to a handful of ashy, powdered lime. What with Faneuil Hall burning in '61, and now Harvard Hall, it seemed that heaven desired to chastise Massachusetts in a very particular and bitter way.

On every side the talk was of taxes, potential ruin and how to save money. Always, England's name entered into the argument. There was a general agreement that no lambs would be slaughtered this year. With the wool, clothes could be spun at home, to prevent buying garments imported from Britain. No mourning would be worn except for nearest relatives; black gloves would not be given away at funerals. Everyone aired his pet thrift. "The reigning theme of the times," wrote A LADY, "is Oeconomy. We have laid aside Hoods and Scarfs at Funerals. Let us now lay aside the custom of feeing the Nurses of lying-in Women, when visiting. They follow one to the door, cringing and shew their anger if fee'd too low."

Politically, the confusion was great. People wavered, waiting to see what Parliament would do next spring when the Stamp Act came up for final vote; it had been pending nearly a year. Even Otis's Boston radicals differed among themselves, split into cliques and quarreled over small proposals, finding agreement only in a policy of thwarting the Court party at every turn. Governor Bernard, prompted from "home," proposed a census of Massachusetts, to be repeated annually. Nothing could have been more sensible or more necessary. But immediately, citizens wrote angrily to the newspapers. "Such a census," said one indignant letter, "would acquaint our enemies with our numbers. And also, it would aid the tax collectors."

Our enemies. Prudent citizens, reading the words, shook their heads. They were used to "faction," but this was going too far. Faction, indeed, had always existed in Massachusetts, divided roughly into what the Province called "the Court and Country parties." The Country party represented the farmers, the debtor class, the paper-money men, the radicals. Since 1761, it was true, leadership of the Country party had very definitely shifted to Boston. But the nomenclature did not change. These were the Dissenters, in politics as in religion. For seventy years they had called themselves "the Country party"; they were proud of the name.

As for the Court party, the Royal Governor and his entourage indeed constituted a kind of monarchical Court — owing their appointments to the King, dressing differently from the common people, living far more splendidly. Their shirt ruffles were of the finest lace, their coats of bright-colored velvet or English broadcloth. They carried swords (the mark of a gentleman), rode in chariots with servants in livery on the box.* The Court party, moreover, belonged to the Church of England; the Country party were Dissenters to a man.

So far, the Court party held a large majority in the Massachusetts House of Representatives. In the 1740's and 50's, Governor Shirley had built a powerful political machine; after him, Pownall and Bernard had been careful not to let it perish. There was an excellent rea-

---

* While it was true that lawyers had helped to rule the Province since earliest days, the profession of lawyer, to date, was placed only a degree above the grade of surgeon-barber, or physician. In 1765, not a lawyer in Massachusetts kept his own chariot; and when Daniel Leonard of Taunton finally attempted it, in the early seventies, he was jeered at in the streets; even his colleagues apologized for his pretensions.

son for this care. Royal Governors received their appointment from the King — but the House of Representatives voted their salary. If a Governor vetoed a popular bill, the House, as likely as not, would delay his salary month after month until the Governor agreed to right reason. (The bargain-and-sale plan, Franklin called this arrangement.) Royal Governors, therefore, were careful to parcel out to country gentlemen all over the Province, important judicial and military appointments. New England country squires loved the title of Judge or Colonel. As a result, large landowners like Brigadier Timothy Ruggles of Hardwick and the Chandler family of Worcester were stanch supporters of the Court party and saw to it that their counties sent loyal, obedient Representatives to the Legislative Assembly at Boston. Deputies, the counties still called their Representatives. And deputies were not expected to use their own discretion, but to act according to the written "Instructions" delivered them by their constituents at election time.

The House of Representatives, therefore, was honeycombed with Governor Bernard's henchmen. In actual numbers the House had, in 1765, one hundred and twenty. Of these, only four were elected by Boston: James Otis, Oxenbridge Thacher, Royall Tyler and Thomas Cushing. Four out of a hundred and twenty was a small minority to carry any measure against the Court party; the radicals were aware they must be doubly, triply active. James Otis was not lacking in zeal, but he most certainly lacked discretion. For the people's part it was fortunate that behind Otis, behind the eloquence and the oratory, stood a man of utmost patience and skill, a man born to be a politician.

Samuel Adams held, so far, no great public office; he was not even a member of the House. He was John's second cousin, thirteen years his senior, and he was to be one of the most important persons in John's life. "My brother Adams," John was to call him. Side by side with extraordinary success the two were to move and work for a common cause, playing each a very different hand, yet together making a team unrivaled. To old Governor Shirley of Massachusetts they became *this brace of Adamses*. ("Where this brace of Adamses comes from, I know not," Shirley grumbled in 1770 when Boston elected the pair to the Legislature. The remark went round, circulated assiduously by the Court party, which took it to mean the two were men of no birth, too obscure to be worthy of high elective office. *Par*

nobile fratrum, the opposition retorted quickly — A pair of noble brothers. The phrase stuck.)

With a close bond of blood and background — a New England Puritan ancestry — Sam and John Adams were profoundly different in character and outlook. Sam was a town man to his toes, bred by his father to city politics and the manipulation of men to a political end. He had been active on the radical side ever since the day he emerged from Harvard with his dissertation in hand: "Whether it be Lawful to Resist the Supreme Magistrate, if the Commonwealth Cannot Be Otherwise Preserved." At forty-two, he was a pleasant-looking man of slightly above medium height, with light blue eyes and fair complexion, a straight, high-bridged nose and bushy dark eyebrows. He was inveterately and hopelessly untidy about his dress. On his old brown coat the same spot appeared for weeks; his wife complained that if she sewed a button on his sleeve, he plucked it off deliberately before nightfall. When he consented to wear a wig, it looked as if he had slept in it; on warm days he left it off and his straight brown hair, already streaked with gray, was tucked behind his ears. He was never in a hurry, always had time to stop on King Street and hold converse with his friends. Yet his walk was quick and he held himself very straight; all Boston knew his red winter cloak. He had inherited a constitutional tremor of the head and hands; it came with agitation and was somehow shocking in a man whose face seldom betrayed annoyance or anger. When the tremor seized him, Sam was suddenly like an old man.

But in spite of spotted coat and rumpled wig, there was a dignity about Sam Adams. He was poor, with none of the sharp financial acumen traditional with Yankees. (Three times, the sheriff, a Court party man, had put the family estate up for auction. And three times, the town had refused to buy it away from Sam.) When his friends desired to lend him money, they had to approach the subject tactfully; Sam replied cheerfully that he had more than enough for his wants. Widowed in his thirties, he had lately married an agreeable young woman of good family who everyone said would look after him capably. With Surry, a freed slave girl of his mother's, and Queue, the big shaggy dog, Samuel Adams and his bride lived at the South End of Boston in the old residential section down by the docks. The property reached a hundred and fifty feet along the bay front. It had belonged to Sam's father and was flanked, by now,

with ropewalks; Sam was in the very midst of his friends. The house itself was rambling and dilapidated; the brown paint peeled off in flakes. There was a long garden full of fruit trees, and a dock and various outbuildings that went with the malt house, now disused and sagging by the roof. Young people liked to go to the Adamses'; they were hospitable, particularly to all such as needed help or shelter.

Not one of the radical leaders, from Otis to Thacher, knew the people as Sam Adams knew them; he was an invaluable ambassador from high to low. From South Battery to Gibbons's shipyard, among the artisans and mechanics, the riggers and carpenters, Sam had a thousand friends, could command a thousand votes. Sam's very shabbiness, his one and only ancient rusty coat, the fact that he never had money in his pocket, were all in his favor. Having no regular employment (Sam had failed at enough business ventures to convince himself and the town that he had better keep his hands out of trade), he was to be found in the mornings sitting on somebody's dock in conversation with the men while they took their eleven o'clock draught of ale. He was a witty talker when he chose to be; laughter followed him on the wharves and in the workmen's taverns. Yet he himself took only an occasional glass of ale and was a strict churchgoer, never missing Sunday meeting, morning or afternoon. His piety was deep and genuine; he was known among the more frivolous as "one of your narrow old Boston Puritans."

Yet somehow, people loved him the better for it; Sam did not ram his piety down other folks' throats. And because he was an essentially serious man, his smile, when it came, carried something flattering. He had a clear, remarkably sweet singing voice and was fond of music; among the workers he had formed a singing society that met regularly under his direction. He belonged to every political club and caucus in town; some of them had indeed been founded by his father.

In the year 1748, Sam Adams, writing to the *Independent Advertiser*, had protested England's part in the peace at Aix-la-Chapelle. Now he wrote for the *Advertiser's* spiritual successor, the Boston *Gazette*. And his output was amazing; he could not invent synonyms fast enough. He was A PURITAN; he was POPULUS, SINCERUS, DETERMINATUS, A BOSTONIAN — or, when he wished to be particularly sarcastic, A TORY. His pieces were instantly recognizable; they had a

little turn to them, even at their most venomous, that made people laugh. James Otis himself, whose pen was considered "hasty and rough," took all his writings to Sam Adams before publication. "To *que hew* them," Otis said. "To pour a little oil in them."

Lieutenant Governor Hutchinson had long known that the Adamses, first father then son, were his enemies. At the time of the Land Bank, Hutchinson's policy had ruined Sam's father financially; the son had not forgotten. Sam Adams, moreover, had a natural aversion for men of aristocratic tendency and appearance. Thomas Hutchinson was elegance itself.

But for all Sam's activity, it was not until the Stamp Act threatened that he found real ammunition for his guns. In the spring of 1764, Boston chose him as draftsman for the customary annual Instructions to the town's Representatives in the House. The four men were instructed to oppose the Stamp Tax in every way they could. And — here lay the sting for Hutchinson — they were urged to pass a law unseating any member of House or Council who accepted a post from the crown, also to refuse a salary to any judge who held another post beside his judgeship. Considering that Hutchinson, a member of the Council, was himself both Lieutenant Governor and Chief Justice by crown appointment, considering also that his brothers and cousins occupied like positions, Sam Adams's Instructions were the insult direct. They might as well have named Hutchinson outright and been done with it.

Sam Adams was not a member of the Legislature. Yet his power, indubitably, was growing; it could not be overlooked. In town meeting especially, he ruled supreme. And town meeting was taking on a significance it had not used to possess. A raffishly democratical organization, the Court party called it. At Faneuil Hall on town meeting day, the doorkeeper let men slip in to vote without asking if they had the required twenty pounds sterling behind their names. Court circles no longer dared persuade themselves that Sam Adams's poverty made him negligible politically, although it seemed absurd that men would trust the affairs of government to the hands of a bankrupt! For some eight years, Sam had been constable for Boston — the most popular tax collector the town had ever voted into office. Going from house to house with his worn black collector's pouch hanging from his shoulder, Sam lingered on many an insolvent doorstep to discuss the deplorable state of affairs in the Province since

Britain had threatened a stamp tax. Outrageous to the principles of British freedom! Sam said indignantly. He hoped the citizen would use his best efforts to combat the tax when election day came round.

Somehow, when Sam got home, the black pouch weighed no more than when he set out. The city fathers were alarmed. Looking into the public coffers they discovered Samuel Adams was seven thousand pounds in arrears with his returns. He was summoned before town meeting to explain this stunning default, summoned not once but repeatedly. Yet somehow, when the vote was called, Sam was always re-elected. The man seemed to have no pride, his enemies complained. He was willing to serve the town in any capacity — as chimney warden, fire inspector, committeeman for schools and for guarding against the spread of epidemics. For what he did, he expected, apparently, no reward. His very disregard of money held defiance in it, as though the man denied values his betters adored. Against such a creature, what weapons existed? Uneasily, with irritation, the Massachusetts Royal Government eyed this middle-aged insurgent, this maker of trouble — bankrupt, shabby, incorruptible and beloved of thousands.

Such was Mr. Samuel Adams, and such were the parties and factions in Massachusetts at the opening of 1765, that year which was to see John Adams's entrance on the political scene.

CHAPTER SIXTEEN

John Adams informs his countrymen on the Canon and Feudal Laws. There is riot in Boston. John writes the "Braintree Instructions." The first intercolonial congress meets in New York.

IN February, 1765, the British House of Commons passed the Stamp Act by a vote of 294 to 49. The debate was languid. ("Nothing of note in Parliament," wrote Horace Walpole, "except one slight day on the American taxes.") A Major Barré, who had fought under Wolfe in Canada, made a speech of violent championship for the Americans. "Those sons of liberty," he called them, declaring roundly that Britain owed more to America than America to Britain. Nobody listened: Barré, Dublin-born, the son of poor Huguenot immigrants, was looked on as *déclassé*, a disappointed man whose application for promotion had been refused by Pitt. It was to be expected he would side with the underdog. The Lords passed the bill. The King was alarmingly ill and could not write his name; men whispered the word "insanity." The Act therefore was signed by commission and put aboard the first packet at Dover.

The news reached Boston in May: *the Stamp Act was law, to take effect next November!* Church bells tolled; in the harbor a forest of flags slipped down to half-mast. John Adams, traveling the circuit far to the northward in Pownalborough, everywhere heard talk of the Stamp Act — talk no longer theoretical but striking very close to home. If, after the first of November, people refused to buy "the

King's stamps" — and with all his heart, John Adams believed they should refuse — then, not one piece of legal business could be transacted. What would happen? Would the courts close? Impossible! It would mean anarchy, lawlessness.

And what of the lawyers themselves? They would be without a profession, without business or occupation, without means of livelihood. Abigail was with child; the baby was to be born next month, in July. Two people would depend on John for support. If the courts closed, his career, his future, would be wrecked. He longed to get back to Boston, to Otis, Mr. Gridley and his cousin Samuel Adams. Up here in the country, men were conservative, very cautious in their statements, inclined to think Britain would never enforce the Act.

Riding down to Falmouth for the appellate court, John was relieved that he could talk to Jonathan Sewall, who lived in Falmouth and had most of the law practice roundabout; he was doing very well indeed. Since Worcester days, the two had often ridden circuit together, shared a room at crowded inns and sat up half the night discussing their cases and talking politics. There was no man John liked so well or with whom he felt so intimate. (*He called me John and I him Jonathan; and I often said to him, I wish my name were David.*)

John had not been a day in Falmouth when a coastal schooner brought Boston newspapers with the Virginia Resolves against the Stamp Act, reprinted. John bought a paper on the docks, took it to Sewall's house when he went to supper in the evening. The Virginia Legislature had been the only colonial Assembly in session when the Act reached America. One Patrick Henry promptly proposed seven Resolves. Henry was a new member of the House of Burgesses; a man under thirty, it was said, from Louisa County on the frontier; a young lawyer, with neither property nor connections. His Resolves were fiery beyond any official protest so far, especially the fifth: RESOLVED THEREFORE, *That the General Assembly of this Colony have the only and sole exclusive right and power to lay taxes and impositions upon the inhabitants of this Colony, and that every attempt to vest such power in any person or persons whatsoever other than the General Assembly aforesaid has a manifest tendency to destroy British as well as American freedom.*

This was stupendous; John marveled that an Assembly of landed proprietors had been willing to pass so daring a set of resolutions. He did not yet know that the fifth and seventh Resolves had been voted down by the Virginia House. Somehow they got in the mail with the others, and papers everywhere printed all seven as a unit. Nor did he know that Henry had been shouted down with the words *Treason, treason!* or the reply that had sprung from the young lawyer's lips. But Sewall's voice, when John finished reading, was cold; his long, intelligent face was bland and closed. It was a Sewall trait, when annoyed, not to frown but simply to freeze, shutting a sudden door against the antagonist.

"I am surprised at you, John!" Sewall said. "You stand there spouting lines like an actor. These Resolves flatter the human passions; they say what men desire to hear. Moreover, they savor strongly of independence. Even your friend Otis does not go so far. The reasoning is specious altogether. *No taxation without representation:* a fine-sounding phrase. But look at the facts! There are cities in England itself not represented in the Parliament. Manchester and Sheffield have no more direct representation than have Boston and Philadelphia. Wherefore then, must we howl so loud? On what do we ground our complaint?"

John's answer came quickly. Manchester and Sheffield lay almost next door to London: the Parliament would not dare to remain deaf to cries on her very doorstep. Whereas, both Lords and Commons could — and would — remain perfectly indifferent for months and years to the wishes of a population three thousand miles away. John looked sharply at his friend, told him he had not touched on the central question, that of allegiance. Even on her own side of the water, England had dominions that were not subject to Parliament. "Has the Isle of Jersey ever been taxed," John demanded — "or Guernsey, or Man?"

Sewall shrugged. "An empire must be financed. . . . These fine points of 'internal' and 'external' legislation are so much casuistry. As the Irish member said in Parliament: 'The colonies must be taxed. What a pother if the money be taken from their coat pocket or their waistcoat pocket!'"

A day or so later, riding south from Falmouth through the green spring woods, John, deeply thoughtful, recalled his friend's words. Sewall had spoken very bitterly of Otis, repeating gossip, slander

that had nothing to do with the issue at hand. . . . What part of his friend's words stemmed from conviction, John wondered now; what part from pique and disappointment? Five years ago, Sewall's uncle, the old Chief Justice, had died insolvent. Sewall had petitioned the General Court to pay his debts. Largely through Otis's influence, the petition had been refused. Ever since, Sewall had sneered openly at Otis and all his policies.

How easily a man's judgment was warped by circumstance! His father's words came back to John: *Satan makes the crooked to seem straight.* He himself must be very careful, in the dangerous times that were coming. He must pray to retain sanity, pray on his knees for an open, fair judgment of men and events. . . . Concerning the Stamp Act, there would be two ways to resist: the legal way, which was not to execute any document requiring the use of stamped paper, and the illegal way, which was to go on making out documents as if no Stamp Act existed. Which course would he take, which defend?

Riding homeward, mile after slow mile through the forest trail, John gazed upward to where blue sky opened briefly between the young green leaves. He could not envision his country of Massachusetts without courts of justice. He had a deep pride in the public tribunals; to this pride he had lately given testimony in three long letters to the Boston *Gazette.*[1] What he had said seemed very pertinent now. John tested it in his mind while his mare picked her way over the narrow trail, stepping round the great roots and shaking her head at the June black flies:

"The liberty, the unalienable, the indefeasible rights of men, the honor and dignity of human nature, the grandeur and glory of the public and the universal happiness of individuals, were never so skilfully consulted as in that most excellent monument of human art, the common law of England. No other nation has so admirable a system, not anywhere in history. To preserve it must be the responsibility of every citizen. Each step in the public administration of government concerns us nearly. The steady management of a good government is the most anxious, arduous and hazardous vocation on this side the grave. It becomes necessary to every subject to be in some degree a statesman, and to examine and judge for himself of the tendency of political principles and measures."

How aptly that sentiment fitted the present situation! The para-

graph that followed, the end paragraph of the piece, Abigail had admired greatly. It was a call to arms, she said, the color rising in her face. To civilian arms, arms without bloodshed. She had laid down her sewing and taken the page from John. Her voice came back to him, clear and slow: *Let us examine with a sober, a manly, a British and a Christian spirit. Let us neglect all party virulence and advert to facts. Let us believe no man to be infallible or impeccable in government, any more than in religion; take no man's word against evidence, nor implicitly adopt the sentiments of others who may be deceived themselves, or may be interested in deceiving us.*

This would be no easy course to follow now, John thought a trifle grimly. There was no telling what Boston men would do. He must talk with Otis and his cousin Samuel Adams; no doubt the political clubs and caucuses had already framed a course of action. It might be a good time to send his own paper, "On the Canon and Feudal Law," written last winter for Mr. Gridley's law club,[2] to the *Gazette* for publication; he would look it over and point it up to meet the present emergency. None of the pamphlets, protests and petitions against the Stamp Act, to date, had argued from a historical background. His own paper reviewed New England history from the first landing at Plymouth, showed how the old ecclesiastical and feudal laws had become outworn, and protested Britain's continued use of many phases of this system. Massachusetts people were shockingly ignorant of their own history. It would do them no harm to have a dose of it, provided he could persuade the Messrs. Edes and Gill to print a dissertation that leaned so heavily to the scholarly side. . . .

Meanwhile he desired desperately to get home to his wife. John had been away for a month. He had not worried about Abigail. After all, his mother lived next door, within a stone's throw of their bedroom window. But he had hated to leave Abby when her time was so near. John rode through Cambridge on a day early in June; each mile increased his impatience. The longer he remained away, the less he remembered Abigail as big with child. In his mind's eye he saw her as she had been before, slim and quick, moving about the house efficiently, proudly, as if she had been its mistress a dozen years. . . .

When John rode up to their door on Penn's Hill, Abby was out of the house and at his stirrup before he could dismount. She had

been watching for him, she said breathlessly, for days. Tears of welcome were in her eyes.

When John got down, Abby reached up her arms to him, and in the gesture, revealing her swollen, clumsy young body, was something infinitely touching. How pale she was! thought John. There were black shadows under her eyes, the whole expression of her face was altered; there was a look about her mouth that had not been there before. A rush of feeling surged over John: pity, love and a new sensation of awe. How inexorably nature moved forward to her ends! he thought with a catch of the breath. Nothing, nothing could stop it now, this suffering, this new life. . . .

Walking up the short path to the door, Abby clung to her husband's arm. John's heart contracted. At Marblehead last week, where he had tried a case in court, a lawyer had just lost his young wife in childbirth. . . . "Abby!" John said. He drew away and holding Abigail at arm's length, searched her face as though she were hiding something from him. "Abby, are you in health? Are you quite, quite well?"

"But of course I am well!" Abby said, astonished. She took John's hand, pressed it reassuringly in both of hers. They went in the house. John followed up the narrow, crooked stairs, Abby chattering all the way, telling of the work that had been done in her husband's absence — the cellar floor finished, the milkhouse ready. Yesterday, Elihu had come over and cleaned the well, Joe Bass had put new rafters in the hayloft. In their bedroom Abigail sat down heavily on a stool, knees spread, hands on her thighs to balance her. But she seemed unaware of her awkwardness, or proud of it — John could not tell which. In spite of her pallor there was a new confidence in Abby's face. She looked serious, pleased as she reviewed one by one the things accomplished.

John smiled, drew a long breath and felt his own confidence return tenfold. How extraordinary that his wife had no fears for the future! He had thought to reassure her, protect and strengthen her in her woman's weakness. And now it was she, all unconsciously, who poured into him the strength he needed.

On the fourteenth of July, the baby was born, a healthy little girl. They named her Abigail; Parson Smith rode over from Weymouth

to christen her. John spent two weeks at home, working in the fields with Joe Bass, getting in his hay, running cross fences, driving the cart to the pits for gravel. In the evenings he sat with his wife, admiring the baby and reading over with Abigail his essay "On the Canon and Feudal Law." He took the essay to James Otis in Boston, asked his advice about offering it to the *Gazette*. The dissertation was very plain writing, John said a trifle apologetically. Nothing of elegance in the style. But Mr. Gridley had pronounced it a strong plea for education. And in this crisis of the country's affairs, what but education could rouse the people to concerted resistance against the Stamp Act?

Otis, sitting in his office with his feet on the table and his coat off — it was a hot day in early August — remarked that if the essay proved as strong as John's letters in the *Gazette* about government, Edes and Gill would surely welcome it. He glanced at the opening paragraph: "Ignorance and inconsideration are the two great causes of the ruin of mankind. As knowledge is the best weapon against tyranny, so the first step toward a balance of powers is the education of the people."

"H'm!" Otis said. "Not quite so lively as your cousin Sam Adams's style. Did you read his last diatribe against Hutchinson in Monday's issue?" Without waiting for an answer, Otis read on, becoming more and more absorbed, breaking off frequently with an exclamation of surprise or approval. Finally he slapped the pages down on the table, swung his feet to the ground and seizing John's hand, wrung it furiously, announcing with a hearty oath that the essay was excellent. "We have had nothing to compare with it. This is history written from the heart. I had no notion, Adams, that you felt so strongly, or that you had thought this thing through to such an end."

Otis picked up a sheet, began to read aloud: *Government is a plain, simple, intelligible thing, founded in nature and reason, quite comprehensible by common sense. . . . The true source of all our suffering has been our timidity. . . . Let us dare to read, think, speak and write. Let every order and degree among the people arouse. . . . Let the pulpit resound. . . . Let the bar proclaim. . . . Let every sluice of knowledge be opened and set a-flowing. . . .*

Otis broke off, struck the pages with the back of his hand. "Your cousin Samuel, if I mistake not, will know how to put this to use." He reached for his coat and wig. "Come with me now, Adams. Let

me introduce you to the Messrs. Edes and Gill in their habitat among the ink and presses on Queen Street. Today is Friday; you can help us set the type. On Monday next you should see the first installment of your Dissertation on the Canon and the Feudal Law."

John's article was unsigned; the first installment took up two full pages out of the *Gazette's* total of four. John rode in town to get a copy, carried it home and presented it to Abigail, who sat downstairs in a low chair, her baby in her arms. She was pleased, spotted instantly a place where the printers omitted a sentence, and scolded accordingly. How impressive the article was in print, she said proudly. She wished John had signed his name, but after all it was not the fashion to sign one's own name in the newspapers. . . .

It would require four issues at least, John told her, to print the whole dissertation. By then, the author surely would be discovered. Meanwhile, August was nearly half gone and the first of November approached, when the Stamp Act would go into effect. Ever since the Act was passed, the Boston people had been restive; there were indications now that they were becoming ugly. After nightfall, men gathered in little knots on the street corners; Otis had seen three fights, he said, begun apparently over nothing at all. Householders barred their windows, kept their doors locked and would not say why.

On the fourteenth of August, early in the morning, citizens, walking to their business, were astonished to see, hanging from a big elm opposite the Boylston Market, an effigy of Mr. Andrew Oliver, Secretary of the Province, stuffed with straw and wearing a pair of yellow breeches. By it hung a large boot (for Lord Bute), with a devil peeping out the top. All day, people walked by, looking up in silence. Nobody laughed. This was no mere Pope's Day jest. There was something sinister here, something shameful. This foolish figure, swinging with painted, distorted face, represented a gentleman everyone knew by sight — Thomas Hutchinson's brother-in-law, a man high in the government of their own Province. No one touched the effigy, no one offered to take it down.

Just before dark a crowd began to collect, appearing from nowhere, from everywhere, drifting from alley and wharf, taking their places around the tree as at a signal. Someone cut down Oliver's figure; the crowd bore it to the Town-house, where the

Governor and Council sat upstairs, Oliver among them. Right through the building the crowd carried the figure; then surged down King Street, two thousand strong. On Oliver's private dock stood a small new building, said to be the new stamp office. Broadaxes appeared; in less than five minutes the building was laid flat to the ground. Cheering and yelling, the crowd roared on toward Fort Hill. Oliver's house was on the way; they broke the windows, swarmed through the rooms, smashing furniture, while the family hid terrified upstairs. Then they tore the garden to pieces, uprooted every flower and bush. At midnight they trailed up Fort Hill, singing, and burned Andrew Oliver in effigy.

From all accounts, this rising had not been a spontaneous thing. The mob had been led by forty or fifty decently dressed citizens; there had been purpose behind it. The *Gazette* gave a detailed account of the evening's performance. The morning after the riot, Sam Adams was found standing under the big elm, gazing up into the branches, shaking his head dolefully. Various respectable citizens approached, inquired if Mr. Adams knew who was responsible for the disgraceful effigies that had hung there? Sam lifted his hands and let them drop. "I wonder indeed," he said dreamily. "I must inquire."

"Liberty Tree," men called the elm, now. The *Gazette*, describing the riot, quoted Major Barré's speech in Parliament, defending the Americans and calling them "sons of liberty." America caught the phrase, seized on it as a slogan for citizens everywhere who protested the Stamp Act. In Connecticut the Sons of Liberty, five hundred strong, marched down the Wethersfield road after Jared Ingersoll, stamp collector, who was fleeing to the Hartford Legislature for safety. (He had accepted the office on the advice of Benjamin Franklin in London.) The crowd, led by three trumpeters and two militia officers in full regalia, overtook Ingersoll, ordered him to resign his office and produced pen and paper for his signature.

Ingersoll looked down the muzzles of two long muskets, heard the clashing of some five hundred staves. "The cause is not worth dying for," he remarked sensibly, and signed his name. "Put up your right hand," the leader of the crowd said, "and swear the signature was your own free act." This was too much for Ingersoll. He turned his back on the militiaman. "No!" he said stoutly, and waited. There was a murmur through the crowd, a brief conference of leaders.

"Well then," one of them said, "throw your hat in the air and shout three times, *Liberty and property, huzzah!*"

It was to become the password for a revolution. Liberty and property were synonymous. The great John Locke had said it a century before; now a new world must prove it. What a man owned was his, as his soul was his. No prince, no king, no parliament could take it from him without his consent. "Liberty and property!" cried Mr. Jared Ingersoll, tossing his elegant, three-cornered hat in the air — "Liberty and property! Huzzah! Huzzah! Huzzah!"

And if Britain would not respect American property, then by God, said Massachusetts men, they would not respect the property of Britons. Petition and protest had been spurned. Whose fault was this? Governor Bernard was English, born and bred in England. But his right-hand man was not born in Britain. Lieutenant Governor Thomas Hutchinson was a Massachusetts man who knew what Massachusetts wanted. Once he had been the most popular man in the Province. The first volume of his *History* was out. His days were devoted to the Provincial business, his nights to the second volume of this *History*. No one had served Massachusetts so long.

And yet, what part had he actually played in this affair of the Stamp Act? He *said* he was against it; declared he had pled with the Lords of Trade, with the colonial agent in London. Could Massachusetts trust him? In the past four years, since the writs case, whenever the Massachusetts House composed petitions to king, lords or commons, it had been Hutchinson, always Hutchinson, who "wiped out" (John wrote in his diary) "every spirited if not every sensible expression from these petitions." When the Province was ready to choose a new agent to look after its affairs in London, hadn't Hutchinson done what he could to get Jackson appointed? Jackson, secretary to Lord Grenville himself! It was like handing one's country to the enemy. About Thomas Hutchinson there was surely the taint of ambition, of a grasping, greedy nature. He controlled nearly every high crown appointment in the government. John enumerated them, a full page, with an indignant interrogation mark after each: "Has not the Lieutenant Governor grasped four of the most important offices in the Province into his own hands? Has not his brother-in-law, Oliver, Secretary of the Province, another of the greatest places? Is not a brother of Oliver a Judge of the Superior Court? Has not that

brother a son in the House, who is also a judge in one of the counties? Did not that son marry the daughter of another of the Judges of the Superior Court? Has not the Lieutenant Governor a brother, a Judge of the Pleas in Boston, and a namesake and near relation who is another judge? Has not the Lieutenant Governor a near relation who is Clerk of the House of Representatives? . . .

"Is not this ascendancy of one family," John concluded, "foundation sufficient on which to erect a tyranny? Is it not enough to excite jealousies among the people?"

It most certainly was enough. Everything told against Hutchinson. His personal elegance, the fastidiousness of his dress and manner, the rich appointments of his carriage and town house had once been a point of pride with the people; they had liked him better for it. Our Thomas Hutchinson, they had said, may be Province born and bred, but he is a match for any lord in London. . . . Now, these things told bitterly against him, aligned him with Bernard and the Lords of Trade, seemed to show plainly where his ambition lay.

One evening not long after the riot against Andrew Oliver, the crowd assembled again. They were very orderly this time, led by several merchants who had been friends of Hutchinson. Marching through town to his house on Garden Court, they surrounded it and called to him. "Come out," they said, "on the balcony above the street. Tell us you never wrote to England in favor of the Stamp Act. Tell us this yourself, and we will go away satisfied."

But Thomas Hutchinson sat silent in his study, doors and windows barred. His smooth brow was dark with anger, his hands, under muslin ruffles, grasped the desk edge. He had never written in favor of the Act. But no mob on earth had the right to demand explanations and declarations from Lieutenant Governor and Chief Justice Hutchinson. . . . He heard glass break, shouts — then a long silence while someone harangued the crowd. A neighbor in the next house, inspired, leaned from the window, called out that the Lieutenant Governor was away; shortly before nightfall he had left in his carriage for Unkity Hill, his house at Milton. There was more breaking of glass, the thud of a stone striking the wall below the study window. Then silence. The mob had gone.

They had gone, but they were not satisfied. Day after day, waiting for the ship from England to bring the hated stamps, Boston

looked for a victim. When Hutchinson's carriage rolled down King Street now, men turned and spat upon the cobbles. . . .

Monday, the twenty-sixth of August, was a day of breathless heat. Even after dark, no relief came. People sat on their doorsteps, fanning themselves, slapping at mosquitoes. Around nine o'clock, someone lighted a fire on the cobbles in front of Town-house, an odd thing to do on such a night. Sober citizens, seeing the flames against the sky, turned and went in their houses, barring the door. But from dark alleys and streets men drifted to the fire — stood round it idle, restless. Nothing remarkable had happened during the day, no signal had been given, no whistle heard — the long, shrill mob whistle that Boston knew and dreaded. But as the sun sank deeper and the Harbor islands and shore line darkened, there were five hundred men moving slowly down to the wharves, toward the house of Mr. Paxton, Surveyor of the Port.

Somebody knocked. Mr. Paxton, said the landlord, was not at home. Would the gentlemen like to adjourn to the tavern across the way, for a barrel of punch? The gentlemen would, and did, and Paxton's house was saved. . . . Three blocks away lived William Story, Register of Admiralty. The crowd broke his windows, stripped his house of books and papers, broke his furniture and rolled on through the streets to where the Comptroller of Customs lived. They forced their way into his cellar, struck the bung from every cask, sprawled on the floor and hilariously drank up the contents.

Singing and roaring, the crowd surged northward through town to Garden Court, came to a halt at the gateway before Thomas Hutchinson's three-storied mansion. Swarming over the lawn and up the steps, brandishing their axes, whooping like Indians, the mob split doors and windows and poured into the house, filling every room, shouting, cursing, yelling for Hutchinson, flinging open closet doors, searching to the very attic. Finding no one, the crowd slashed and ripped, tore down panels, broke walls and floors with their axes. Plates, portraits, dresses were flung out the window or torn to pieces and scattered on the floor. In Hutchinson's study, men climbed the shelves like monkeys to the ceiling, destroyed books and documents that it had taken thirty years to collect. Even the manuscript pages of *The History of Massachusetts* went out the window.[3]

Until dawn the crowd kept up its work. In the garden, trees were

hacked down, lay broken across the ravaged lawns and flower beds. Men swarmed to the roof, tore down the cupola, pulled away the slate and flung it to the ground. The Province had never known such savage destruction; had the Lieutenant Governor been there he would not have escaped with his life. Warned of the crowd's approach, he had hurried his family out by the garden gate, returned alone to the house. But his eldest daughter followed, clung to her father and swore she would not leave him. This was too much for Hutchinson. He fled with Peggy by the back door while the mob surged through the front.

Next morning was the first day of Superior Court. The room was jammed with spectators. Four judges sat in robe and wig when Chief Justice Hutchinson walked down the aisle in his shirt sleeves. Tears streamed down his face, his voice was broken. He begged his brethren to excuse his appearance . . . he had no other garment than was on his back . . . his family was in like condition. Hutchinson stepped to his place in the center of the bench. But instead of his expected charge to the Grand Jury, he turned to the people, spoke directly to them. "I call God to witness that I never in New England or Old, in Great Britain or America, aided or supported what is commonly called the Stamp Act, but did all in my power to prevent it. This is not declared through timidity; I have nothing to fear. They can only take away my life. . . . I hope all will see how easily the people may be deluded, inflamed, carried away with madness against an innocent man. . . . I pray God give us better hearts!"

This time, Boston was ashamed. And as the news spread through the colonies, all Massachusetts was ashamed. Town meeting was held, with Faneuil Hall full to overflowing. "Every face was gloomy," the *Gazette* reported, "and we believe every Heart affected." The leaders of the mob were arrested and charged with capital offense. One of them was "Captain" Mackintosh, who controlled the South End gang. In jail, Mackintosh protested loudly that he had thought he was doing God's service that night. Had not the Reverend Mayhew preached the day before from the text, *I would they were even cut off which trouble you?* Surely, the preacher could refer to no other than the Lieutenant Governor! No one in the Province had "troubled" them so much as Thomas Hutchinson.

The Reverend Jonathan Mayhew himself, when this conversation

was reported to him, wrote Hutchinson in greatest concern. If he could recall that sermon, he would do it at the loss of his whole estate. But the Lieutenant Governor, standing in his broken study with the wreck of a lifetime's work around him, read the Doctor's letter and dryly made a note for the next volume of his *History*, should it ever be written: "If the preacher had desired to keep the populace within bounds, he need only have quoted the Bible words that followed his incendiary verse: *For, Brethren, ye have been called unto liberty; only use not liberty for an occasion to the flesh.*

The Congregational clergy, it was plain, were making themselves a dangerous nuisance in this controversy with England. Whatever the purity of Mayhew's intentions, thought Hutchinson now, this was not the first time the clergy had intervened in Massachusetts politics. "The Black Regiment," Governor Bernard called them.

But if the Reverend Mayhew was ashamed, the town of Boston recovered all too quickly. Eight leaders of the mob awaited trial in prison. A crowd went to the jailer's house, took the keys from him and freed the prisoners. Town meeting, though it voted to put down all disorders in future, refused financial compensation to the Lieutenant Governor.

The people had made for themselves a powerful enemy. Thomas Hutchinson, previously, had consistently taken the position that, while Parliament had a right to tax the colonies, it would be wise not to insist on it. His tastes had always leaned toward control by an aristocracy. Now his mind was fixed; he knew he was right. The people were not fit to govern themselves. Massachusetts — and all the thirteen colonies — must be forced to recognize their subjection to Britain. Hutchinson, writing to London, advised Parliament that the oftener it reminded the colonies of this fact, the better.

When news came of the riot, John was down at Martha's Vineyard off the Cape, trying a long, difficult case. Riding home through the bright September weather, he rehearsed what he would do. Braintree must take a stand in this thing. The town, with fifteen hundred inhabitants, had only one Representative in the Legislature at Boston: Mr. Ebenezer Thayer (a citizen, by the way, who had once called John Adams, to his face, "a petty lawyer"). Ebenezer Thayer quite obviously needed a new set of Instructions from his constituents, to advise him what they desired done about the Stamp Act. And he

must have the Instructions immediately, while the Legislature was still in session at Boston, and before the stamps should arrive. Thayer must be told to vote against the Governor's request for troops to protect the stamp officers. Words formed themselves in John's mind. . . . "In all the calamities which have befallen our country, we have never felt so great a concern as now. . . . This tax is inconsistent with the spirit of the common law. . . . The public money of this country is the toil and labor of the people. . . . The Act has opened vast sources of new crimes, annexed prodigious penalties, all to be tried by courts of admiralty, without a jury, one judge alone presiding. . . ."

As soon as John reached home, he set the wheels in motion. The regular way to dispatch such Instructions was to call a town meeting, appoint a committee to write the Instructions, then call another meeting to approve them. Not waiting upon ceremony, John wrote out a full set of Instructions, appeared at town meeting with them rolled in his hand. Old Mr. Niles, the moderator, got up and explained the reason for the meeting. The country was in grave danger . . . A committee must be appointed to draw up new Instructions for Mr. Thayer at Boston.

This being voted in the affirmative, the selectmen invited John to walk to Mr. Niles's house with them. Once inside, John produced his Instructions; they were adopted without amendment and delivered to Thayer. Such Instructions, from the various counties, were nearly always published in the newspapers; John was not surprised to see his in the *Gazette*.

What did surprise him was the response of the Province. Forty towns read and adopted the "Braintree Instructions," with changes to suit the local needs. John was struck almost with awe at what he had done. This was no mere private intellectual speculation, this paper he had written for his townsmen — no essay on history or law, to be published in a newspaper at the editor's discretion. This was a public document, voted on and adopted by the people in lawful assemblage.

Of all John's careful, clear and simple paragraphs, the one that stirred people most was near the end. Its words were "worthy," one citizen wrote the newspaper, "to be wrote in letters of gold."

We further recommend [it read] *the most clear and explicit assertion and vindication of our rights and liberties to be entered on the public records, that the world may know, in the present and all fu-*

ture generations, that we have a clear knowledge and a just sense of them, and, with submission to Divine Providence, that we never can be slaves.

The Province of Massachusetts was not aware who had written the Braintree Instructions; they did not know who had written the essays "On the Canon and Feudal Law" [4] that now appeared Monday after Monday in the Boston *Gazette*. But they read the installments as they came out, studied them, speculated on who could have written them — probably, they said, Mr. Jeremiah Gridley of Boston; no one else knew enough legal history. When it came to serious essays, New England people could take fearful punishment; they had been trained to long theological newspaper controversies, not half so timely and applicable as these apparently simple arguments. Moreover, this author was somehow reassuring; he told the Province what it longed to hear: that its most fervent protests against Parliament were no new thing, no shocking innovation. The people were simply following, as Englishmen should, the great traditions of their ancestors who were bred to freedom.

And while Massachusetts read and digested what John Adams had written, John himself rode circuit in the Province, trying cases from Cape Ann to Pownalborough. In the past three years his practice had become extensive; he had clients in Plymouth County and Suffolk County, in Middlesex, Essex, Worcester. At Marblehead he had successfully defended the interests of Colonel Lee, of Mr. Hooper and the Messrs. King and Isaac Smith, "the three greatest exporters of fish," John recorded, "in the county of Essex." And always, outside of court as well as in, John asked his questions — avid with curiosity as to history, past and present. In port towns he went down to the ships, talked with the seamen employed by his clients — men of Nantucket and the Vineyard, men of Barnstable, Gloucester, Marblehead who sailed to Greenland for whale oil and seal, to the Banks for cod and mackerel. John Adams began to be known as a lawyer who won his cases, a man very knowledgeable concerning his "country" of Massachusetts.

Meanwhile the first of November approached, when the Stamp Act would take effect. . . . For the Province it was strange, this new feeling of sistership with Connecticut, Rhode Island, New Hampshire and New York. Always and forever, Massachusetts had quarreled with her neighbors, had bickered angrily over borders

and boundaries, sending her Governors to settle the difference, ready to send even her militia if need be. The Southern colonies had seemed as remote as Europe. But now, every post brought eager dispatches from the various representative Assemblies. "Power is a sad thing," wrote Philadelphia. "To talk of our being virtually represented in Parliament," said Georgia, "is an insult on the most common understanding." "It is an insult to common sense," replied the Middle States. "There ought to be no New England man," said Christopher Gadsden of South Carolina, "no New Yorker known on this continent, but all of us Americans."

Each coastal ship brought new encouragement, new strength. And not only colonial Assemblies but towns everywhere, sent messages: "By the citizens of Annapolis: *Resolved* . . ." By the citizens of Chestertown, Hartford, Newport, Plymouth . . . *Resolved* . . . "*Resolved* . . . *That with submission to Divine Providence, we never can be slaves.* . . ." Every one of these messages was printed in the *Gazette* and read from end to end of the Province.

And now, in the month of September, 1765, came a ship from England with news that the British ministry had changed hands. The great Pitt, America's friend, was in power once more. Bells pealed, bonfires blazed by night on the hilltops. But in the selfsame ship, the hated stamps arrived! Governor Bernard was in a quandary. Every inch of this stamped paper was dangerous as fused powder. What should he do with it? He was afraid to bring it ashore. Walking to the Town-house,* Bernard tactfully addressed the Legislature. He had no power to open the bales, he said. Would the House of Representatives please order or advise? For the moment, he was keeping the stamps at Castle Island in the Harbor.

The House replied with equal politeness. "We hope Your Excellency will excuse us if we cannot see our way clear to give you any advice or assistance herein. It might prove of ill consequence for us in any Way to interest ourselves in this Matter."

There was not the slightest doubt who had composed that paragraph. Sam Adams had just been elected Boston Representative to take the place of Oxenbridge Thacher, who was dead. And Samuel Adams's pen was smooth as a snake's tongue and as dangerous.

---

* To Bernard's disgust, Boston had begun to call this "the State House" — an elevated title, Bernard said, that gave too much importance to the representative bodies meeting there.

Governor Bernard reviewed the message with something like despair. What was he to do? If he was peremptory, the House stiffened like so many ramrods and shouted *No!* . . . If he requested them politely for "advice," they returned a queasy negative like this one. It came to Francis Bernard, not for the first time, that the office of Royal Colonial Governor was an impossible position, a very contradiction in terms. "Surely it is not known at Whitehall," wrote Bernard, "how weak & impotent the Authority of American Governors is in regard to Popular Tumults. For my part I am entirely at the Mercy of the Mob. The Power & Authority of Government is really at an end."

Week by week, the Boston *Gazette* raised its raucous voice. "An infamous paper," Bernard called it, "which has swarmed with Libells of the most atrocious kind." On the Monday after Bernard had addressed the House, the *Gazette*, wading deeper into infamy, parodied his speech about landing the stamps and opening the bales. There were more than a dozen verses, and the whole was signed by the Governor's initials backward: B. F.

> I now declare to all the Town,
> To rich and poor and great and small,
> To high and low and short and tall,
> That I've no order, warrant, might,
> Of whatsoever power, or right,
> To deal about th' aforesaid Papers,
> Or peep into th' enclosing wrappers,
> T' untie the Cords or ope the locks
> Of trunk or cafe or tierce or box. . . .

For days afterward, no citizen could empty a hamper of turnips in the market without someone's asking loudly if he had order, warrant, might or right, to ope the locks of trunk or box. Even James Otis's father, old Colonel Otis of Barnstable, was a trifle shocked by the *Gazette*. Did not this sheet, he wrote his son, "a Little overdo as to the *strick Truth* of things?"

But *strick Truths* are not always the most effectual distributors of newsprint. The *Gazette* let its fancy run. On the front page appeared what the editors chose to call an "advertisement." . . . "Stray'd away from Great Britain," it began, "the true old British Lyon. It is conjectur'd he swum across the Atlantick, having been seen of late in many of the Provinces of America. He is more than

Eighteen Hundred Years old, his Roar is awful, at which mighty
Monarchs having often trembled on their Thrones. It is thought that
he is ranging thro' America, as he has been heard to roar most terribly
at Virginia, New York, Rhode Island, Providence & Boston."

There was in this public ridicule, this loud rude laughter, something no Royal Governor of Massachusetts had experienced. Squibs
and handbills sold in the streets, anonymous notices tacked by night
on doorways were no new thing. But this newspaper voice had
power behind it; it was the expression of a thousand minds. In
England such practices were common; even a king was subject to
newspaper attack. But Boston was not London, Massachusetts was
not Britain. To Bernard, this ill-timed journalistic wit contained
something beyond impudence. (He was experiencing, in truth, the
growth of a formidable new power later to be called *public opinion;*
there was little wonder he could not recognize it.)

And now occurred something that was met in Court circles —
government circles — with utmost apprehension. On the seventh of
October, 1765, an intercolonial congress met in New York, to discuss
the Stamp Act. Massachusetts called it "a convention of committees
from the representative assemblies." Nothing in any colonial charter
authorized it, nothing in any commission from the crown. That the
colonies would act together had been counted impossible by the
mother country; no laws had been enacted against such a contingency. Without orders from home, Governor Bernard dared not try
to prevent the congress.

Only nine colonies sent delegates, it was true. But the twenty-eight
gentlemen who appeared in New York were by no means the riffraff
that the Court party liked to look on as representative of popular opposition to government. On the contrary, from Mr. Christopher
Gadsden of South Carolina to Brigadier Timothy Ruggles of Massachusetts, they were men of property and importance who carried
authority wherever they went.

Massachusetts sent, besides Ruggles, Oliver Partridge, a well-known
lawyer from the western counties — and James Otis. It was Otis,
indeed, who had proposed the congress in the first place. Ruggles
and Partridge were known as very conservative men. "Friends to
government," was how Thomas Hutchinson described them. Brigadier Ruggles was elected President of the congress, which sat for
eighteen days in New York's City Hall, framed an address to the

King, a petition to the House of Commons, and thirteen Resolves setting forth the rights of the colonies in their relation to the British Parliament. "All supplies to the crown being free gifts of the people" — so ran the Resolves — "it is the undoubted right of Englishmen that no taxes be imposed on them, but with their own consent, given personally or by their representatives."

This was too much for Brigadier Ruggles, who had not expected anything mutinous — beyond the fact that the very existence of such a congress was mutinous. He refused to sign and went home; so did Ogden of New Jersey. When Ruggles got back to Boston, the House of Representatives reprimanded him publicly. Ogden fared even worse: his image was hanged and burned.

The lines were drawn; the parties forming. Sam Adams, during Otis's absence at the congress, wrote a series of Resolves for the Massachusetts Assembly, also a lengthy *Address to the Governor.* Both were entered on the records and published in the newspapers — "so that," Sam Adams wrote, "a just sense of liberty, and the firm sentiments of loyalty may be transmitted to posterity."

There was little time left before the Act was to go into effect on November first. *To your tents, O Israel!* said the *Gazette,* its tone rising. *Now see to thine own house, David!* In the bottom right-hand corner of the front page, a box was kept for the King's stamp, marked with skull and crossbones where the stamp should go. Boston prepared for what might come. The town clerk ordered that "no Mulatto or Negro servants be abroad after 9 at night." A piece of scribbled paper was found tacked to a door on the Long Wharf; the *Gazette* copied it: "Liberty and Property and no Excise! The first of November is very nigh. Let not your courage cool, nor your resentment fail. Love your Liberty, and fight for it like men who know the value of it. God bless King George the third, King of Great Britain, & King and Lord of America. May his reign be long and glorious. God bless the British parliament with a happy and glorious understanding. . . . *Any merchant clearing out his vessel upon Stamp papers shall meet with our highest displeasure.*"

The *Gazette* made the most of this confused but urgent message; anything was good that added fuel to the fire. "We hear," the paper added, "that Numbers of young Persons in the Country are joining in Wedlock earlier than they intended, supposing that after the 1st of next Month, it will be difficult to have the Ceremony performed

without paying dearly for stamping." But the editors of the *Gazette*, and Sam Adams their adviser, did not desire a repetition of violence like that of August twenty-ninth. Ridicule served well enough. Even the Court party laughed, the affair was reaching such proportions. Half the world condemned the Stamp Act, without a notion of what it was. Peter Oliver, son of the judge, told of a Negro boy bade by his master to fetch something from the barn after dark. The boy refused to go. "Me 'fraid Massa Tamp Act he cotch me."

Then there was HUMPHREY PLOUGHBOY (probably Mr. Samuel Adams), who complained bitterly to the *Gazette:* "I can't sleep a nights one wink hardly, of late, I hear so much talk about the stamp act. I hate the thoughts of the first of November. I hope twill be a great storm, & black and gloomy weather, as our faces and hearts all will be. 'Tis worse than all the fifth of Novembers that ever was. I do say, I won't buy one shilling worth of anything that comes from Old England, till the stamp act is appealed."

October thirty-first, a Thursday, dawned bright and clear. That evening the sun sank, pink and misty, behind Beacon Hill. *The last day of liberty*, men called it, and watched for the morrow.

CHAPTER SEVENTEEN

*Boston requests the services of a Braintree
man. The country celebrates repeal, but
John Adams is skeptical. A son is born, a
domestic decision arrived at.*

O N November first at dawn, a bell tolled from the South Meeting-house, muffled, funereal. Men left their beds and went to the
window as steeple after steeple took up the melancholy sound. Down
the coast that day, from Maine to Georgia, mourning bells swung
slowly, marking the hours. New York had a funeral procession; "for
Liberty," they said. People went about their business, pausing sometimes as the minute guns boomed, announcing the death of liberty.
Ships in harbor struck their colors, and on Boston's Liberty Tree the
effigy of Grenville hung once more. In midafternoon the crowd,
strangely quiet, took it down, carried it to the gallows on the Neck,
hanged it, tore it apart and flung the limbs across gray windy water.

But there was no rioting. And what was more important, on Pope's
night, four days later, the North and South End gangs, instead of
fighting up and down the streets with brickbats, "affected an union"
— the *Gazette's* words — and marched together peaceably all evening, to the sound of music. It was wonderful to see "Captain"
Mackintosh in a brilliant new red and blue uniform, a little cane
resting on his elbow, leading his "troops," arm in arm with the highly
respectable General Brattle of Cambridge.

Thomas Hutchinson watched the procession with a narrowed and
thoughtful eye. These "troops" were the same men who had wrecked
his house and would have murdered him. But a mob under control

was a mob no longer. It was an instrument, almost an army. Sam Adams and Company, plainly, had entire control of this instrument. Was it possible the celebration tonight was put on as a show of strength? The situation in regard to the Stamp Act was no better; it was, in fact, worse. The stamps were still out at the Castle; the Governor dared not land them. The Custom House was closed, ships could neither load, unload, nor clear for departure. The probate office was shut, no wills could be drawn; the inferior courts had ceased to function all over the Province.

Obviously, the people had decided upon a policy of waiting. The resolutions and petitions of their Assembly had gone across the water; they still believed that King and Parliament would listen and reply favorably. Thomas Hutchinson knew better; so did Governor Bernard. So far, the King had given no sign either of yielding or of comprehending the seriousness of the situation. Bernard was aware that he must either act firmly as the King's servant or go home in disgrace to England. He took it upon himself, therefore, to go down to the State House. Standing before the Representatives at their last meeting before adjournment, he lectured them in his best paternal manner. It was fitting, he said, that he should remind them of his royal authority. Throughout the autumn he had kept silent, but the time might come when they would stand in need of him as advocate. "It is not prudent of you to cast off any of your natural and professed friends."

Pleased with what he had said, and pleased with the apparently respectful silence in which the House had heard him, the Governor walked out and home to Province House. Next Monday his complacence was rudely shattered. What the *Gazette*, in sixteen rhymed verses, had done to his dignified speech was past all contriving:

> Gentlemen of the Council & of the House,
> The last Part of the Session I have been still as a Mouse;
> Not forgetting the old Proverb, you well may think
> That the more some people Stir, the more they Stink. . . .
>
> . . . . it was fitting, & prudent, & wise
> For me to read you a long Catechise.
> As you call me Father you should behave like good Boys,
> Or else you'll all smart for the late horrid Noise.
> — (*Signed*) B. F.

Nor was Massachusetts content, this time, with ridicule. The *Gazette* even dared to address the King himself, in large black letters on the front page: **GREAT SIR, RETREAT, OR YOU ARE RUINED!** So preposterous a gesture should have been laughable — but it was not laughable. The merchants met, passed resolutions not to trade with Britain until the Stamp Act was repealed. They forced Andrew Oliver, Commissioner for Stamps, to come out under Liberty Tree in Hanover Square and sign his resignation. When he had done it they gave him three cheers, blew a whistle and had the square clear in three minutes, as if the scene had been rehearsed. In New York, Philadelphia, Maryland, Virginia, like scenes were enacted.

Out in Braintree, John Adams thought over the situation. Men's spirit seemed to outrun events. The actual affairs of the Province were in a complete muddle. Nobody knew what to do. Business was paralyzed. "I have not drawn a writ," John wrote in his diary, "since the first of November. Debtors grow insolent, creditors grow angry. The bar behaves like a flock of shot pigeons. They seem to be stopped, the net seems to be thrown over them; they have scarcely courage left to flounce and flutter."

And the effect on his own affairs was nothing short of disastrous. It could not, John pondered gloomily, have come at a worse time. "I was but just getting into my gears, just getting under sail, and an embargo is laid upon the ship." All his hard work was canceled at a stroke, all that he had labored for in the decade since he first entered Mr. Putnam's office and, green as grass, took down Coke from the shelves. John's pen was eloquent with indignation: "I have had poverty to struggle with, envy and jealousy and malice of enemies to encounter, no friends, or but few, to assist me. So that I have groped in dark obscurity, till of late, and had but just become known and gained a small degree of reputation, when this execrable project was set on foot for my ruin as well as that of America in general, and of Great Britain."

In God's name, thought John, why did not the bar take action, petition the Governor to open the courts, call town meeting in Boston or make a move of some sort? Why was James Otis silent, and Jeremiah Gridley and the rest? Must he sit here in the country and wait the thing out, idle and helpless?

Fourteen hours later, at noon next day, John heard a rider coming at a canter up the Post Road to his door. He went out as the man dis-

mounted. It was one of the Boston constables, a Mr. Clark. He had a letter for Mr. Adams, he said, producing it. John broke the seal:

SIR:

I am directed by the town to acquaint you that they have this day voted unanimously that Jeremiah Gridley, James Otis, and John Adams, Esquires, be applied to as counsel to appear before his Excellency the Governor in council, in support of their memorial* praying that the courts of law in this Province may be opened. A copy of said memorial will be handed to you on your coming to town.

I am, sir, your most obedient, humble servant,

WILLIAM COOPER, *Town Clerk*

BOSTON, *December* 18th, 1765

Clark followed John into his little office, warmed himself at the fire, took a glass of rum and water, some meat and bread — while John, carefully concealing the excitement and elation he felt at thus being chosen, wrote his brief acceptance and sealed it. When Clark had mounted his horse and gone, John opened the hall door and shouted for Abigail. She came running down the stairs; John told her what had happened. There was no time to lose, he said. The petition must be presented tomorrow; he had but a few hours to prepare his argument. Abby's gray eyes were sharp with excitement. She made no comment, but looked over her husband's head and began ticking things off on her fingers in the gesture he had come to know so well: "Two clean shirts," she said briskly. "Your blue coat must be brushed; there is lime on it from the henhouse. . . ."

John hurried back to his desk. What line should he follow tomorrow, standing with Gridley and Otis before the Governor and Council? Boston desired the Governor to open the courts and do business without using the King's stamps. If Bernard complied, he would be acting in direct opposition to his royal master, George III. Yet if he did not comply, he faced a Province of two hundred and fifty thousand souls in a state of anarchy. Government without the civil law courts was nothing short of anarchy, and Bernard knew it.

Should I, John thought, ground my argument on the legal maxim of *necessity?* He took down Coke from his shelves, Wood's *Institutes*, Holt's *Reports*, drew paper and ink toward him, made rapid notes: *The law forces no one to that which is impossible or vain . . .*

* A document containing a petition.

Things for necessity's sake are excepted out of a statute. Acts of Parliament impossible to perform, shall be judged void.

Or should he speak of natural equity and the constitution? There had been almost a surfeit of that lately; it was what the Governor, no doubt, expected to hear. "Common law is common right," John wrote. "The act of law never doth wrong. *Actus Dei nemini facit injuriam; actus legi nulli facit injuriam. . . .*"

The devil with Latin! John thought suddenly, throwing down his pen. He would speak plainly tomorrow, put his trust in the King's English. The Governor was no fool, stiff-necked though he had shown himself. Probably he too was looking for a loophole to extricate himself from an impossible, even a dangerous position. If Bernard brought the stamps to Boston, he risked his neck; the people might do worse to him than they had to Hutchinson. He had absolutely no protection for his person, night or day — unless one looked on the night watchman as protection, calling his rounds and shaking his rattle. . . . The first thing to do tomorrow, in that Council Chamber, John decided, was to watch Bernard's reaction while Gridley opened the argument, then base his own tactics accordingly.

John leaned back in his chair. The office windows were frosted thick against the candlelight, the fire was low but John felt no cold. How amazing, he thought, as his brain cleared and the incident stood before him for the first time in all its implications — how extraordinary, that Boston should have chosen him as pleader at such a critical time! Was it because of his articles "On the Canon and Feudal Law"? Gridley and Otis had been openly admiring of them. Was it because of the Braintree Instructions to the Representatives and their indubitable influence in the Province? Whatever the reason and whoever might be responsible for this nomination, it was the most important, the most significant thing, John told himself, that had happened in his thirty years. There was hazard in it as well as glory, should he acquit himself well. He would be throwing himself against the Governor, against Chief Justice Hutchinson and all the two represented. Would they look on it, John asked himself, as a final committing of himself — would this act cut him off from chance of advancement in courts whose judges were every one appointed by the crown?

How strangely fate moved to bring things about! At the very moment, almost, when he had been sitting alone, pondering on the

problem, the messenger had arrived at his door. Wasn't it Lord Bacon who spoke of secret, invisible laws of nature and communication, laws not discoverable by sense?

Next morning, snow lay white and dazzling on the fields as John, wrapped in his gray cloak, mounted his horse and set off along the road to Boston. He was in a hurry. He needed time to read and study the town's petition, check his citations with various books and reports in Gridley's office. But he made slow progress; the road was icy, the wind cruelly cold, although the sun shone brightly. As he rode along the narrow Neck, gusts of powdery snow struck John's face from the drifts around the fortification. Town Gate had two arched brick entrances, one for pedestrians, one for carts. Impatient, stiff with cold, John waited while a procession of wagons laden with firewood crept through before him. At midday he dined in Brackett's Tavern with Otis, Gridley, Kent, John Rowe the merchant. Afterward they made their way, single file, to the head of King Street between mountainous snowbanks to the Town-house. Upstairs in the Representatives' Room their friends awaited them. Sam Adams came forward immediately, his head shaking a little but his blue eyes alert. He greeted John warmly, took his arm and led him to a chair, remarking how pleased he was that Boston had named his "brother Adams" for this difficult, important affair. He hoped such an expression of respect would gain John's friendship permanently, for Boston? The event would undoubtedly increase his reputation at the bar. And the town of Braintree — here Sam smiled his sudden, warm smile, his face lighting — the town of Braintree, finding the eye of Boston on John Adams, would fix their political eye on him too, at the May elections. . . .

John glowed with pleasure; excitement mounted in him. While the others talked, he stood a little apart, rehearsing what he would say, going over the points in his mind. It was candlelight before he was summoned, with Gridley and Otis, across the narrow hall to the Council Chamber. About fifteen Council members sat round the big oval table, with the Governor in the center. On the walls the Stuart kings stood framed in gold, the royal purple dimmed a little in the candlelight. The three lawyers wore their barristers' gowns and powdered tie wigs, rolled above the ears. Bernard was dressed with his customary elegance in full white wig and black velvet coat heavily embroidered with silver. This evening he seemed relaxed, his manner

easy. He spoke pleasantly enough to the three lawyers, suggested they divide their argument carefully to avoid repetition. Otis and Gridley, replying, said they would endeavor not to repeat the arguments of "the gentleman who spoke first." After this they looked at John and were silent.

("Then it fell upon me," John wrote later, "without opportunity to consult any authorities, to open an argument upon a question that was never made before, and I wish I could hope it never would be made again: that is, whether the courts of law should be open or not.")

John stood across the table from the Governor, and without equivocation said what he thought. What he thought happened to be in direct contradiction to what the Parliament at Westminster thought, the ministry in Whitehall Street, and the King in his palace — not to speak of an Army and Navy that ruled half a world. But John said it in the clear, hard, slightly rapid voice that emerged always when he was greatly roused and his mind worked smoothly: "A Parliament of Great Britain can have no more right to tax the colonies than a Parliament of Paris. . . . The Stamp Act was made where we are in no sense represented, therefore it is no more binding upon us than an act which should oblige us to destroy one half our species. . . . The law, the King's writs, cannot be withheld from his subjects. Magna Carta says, *We deny no man justice, we delay no man justice.* Is not the closing of the courts, both denial and delay? To use the stamps is impossible — and the law forces no one to that which is 'impossible or vain.' "

No sooner had John sat down than Otis was on his feet. Tears ran down his face, his voice was broken, impassioned. . . . John, embarrassed, lowered his head and gazed at his hands, the short fingers gripping each knee. Tears would not move this Governor and this Council. They would laugh at tears. Otis had dined too well; a strong effluvium of rum surrounded him as he brushed by John. . . . "It is with great grief that I appear today before Your Excellency and Honors. A wicked and unfeeling Ministry hath caused a People, the most loyal and affectionate that ever King was blessed with, to groan under the most insupportable oppression. . . . The shutting of the courts is a total dissolution of government, an abdication. When the King closes the courts, he unkings himself. Nothing warrants it but war, invasion, rebellion or insurrections."

Fifteen minutes later, Gridley rose in turn, spoke reasonably, as one citizen to another. Suppose the ship with the stamps had sunk at the bottom of the sea. Would the Governor have closed the courts? There was not a syllable in the Stamp Act to hint that the courts must be closed if stamps were not obtainable. It was no default of Massachusetts that Parliament had passed a nonenforceable act. With the courts closed, a citizen's property was utterly unprotected. Better to be a barbarian of the woods than live in a state once under government, but now reduced to anarchy and confusion. . . .

Bernard heard him to the end. Their arguments were good, he told the three lawyers. But the gentlemen were, in his opinion, arguing before the wrong person. Such a petition should more properly be addressed to the judges themselves. It was not part of the executive power to advise the law courts. English judges, since the time of King John, had scorned to take advice from the crown. The Governor was the King's deputy. Tomorrow morning he would, however, discuss the town's petition and their argument with his Council. Meanwhile, it was late; let the meeting adjourn.

Next morning John Adams, Gridley and Otis repaired again to the State House, awaiting the Governor's final answer. It came at noon. He had no authority, Bernard said flatly, to open the courts "in the manner prayed for" (meaning, without using the King's stamps). At the next term of court, the town could renew its petition directly to the judges.

Plainly, the Governor was side-stepping, waiting for further news from England, further royal orders about the stamps. Or was he, James Otis put in dryly, waiting for the King's troops to arrive?

Town meeting was called in Faneuil Hall. The three lawyers gave their report to the people assembled, speaking each in turn — telling what he had said, and giving his opinion of the matter. Then John rode back to Braintree.

December 22 [*he wrote in his diary*]. At home with my family, thinking.

24. Tuesday. Spent the evening with my family, no other company.

25. Christmas. At home thinking, reading, searching, concerning the great pause and rest in business.

Again and again, John was to make this entry: "At home thinking." This business of the courts was only one phase, one facet of a great constitutional question: the question of allegiance, sovereignty, the limits of the realm, the basic relation of colonies to mother country. . . . If the King kept the courts closed, it was a removal of the King's protection from the people. Protection and allegiance were reciprocal. If protection were removed, would not the people remove their allegiance also? Where would such a horrid doctrine terminate? It would lead to treason! And there was no precedent, no guide to look to. In England the situation had not arisen since William the Conqueror. . . . Nay, wrote John — since King Lear!

The word "treason" was awful to John. His approach to the problem differed from that of his cousin Samuel and the Boston political clubs; it was not revolutionary but legalistic. John had a horror of the mob, a deep distaste for rabble rousing. He desired neither "independence" nor rebellion. With all his heart, John believed in the English law. Far from desiring to overthrow it, he wished to support the law in its deepest principles — principles that the British Parliament seemed to have forgotten as a man forgets sometimes his honor and the great traditions of his fathers.

Abigail expressed continued sympathy with all that John was doing and saying. More and more, John spoke of her as his "partner," his "friend," thanking God he had such high support at home and was not, like James Otis, bedeviled by a "ranting Tory wife." If Abigail had any criticism, it was that her husband moved too cautiously, was overprudent in the advice he gave the people's faction. John laughed at her. "You are fiery as a young grenadier, Abby," he said. Abigail was twenty-one; she had put on weight since the baby's birth. Color had come into her cheeks, she bore herself with authority, said what she thought without hesitation. She was much pleased over the stand her own father was taking in this controversy. Last Sunday in Weymouth he had preached the best sermon of his life, on the text, *Render unto Caesar* . . . It was entirely plain where his sympathies lay. Very different from the Reverend Ebenezer Gay of Hingham, who the self-same day had preached on passive obedience and submission. Passive obedience indeed! The very words enraged her, said Abigail, her gray eyes flashing. Did John know that Parson Gay had a club of young men who met regularly at his house to discuss the best

methods of using "passive obedience" to secure redress from Parliament?

What the preachers said and did was very important. In Braintree the Church of England faction was all for passive obedience. John's old schoolteacher, Mr. Cleverly, went round saying the British Parliament had entire right to tax America — he feared the King's ministers at home would be "stomachful," over this matter. Massachusetts had better lie low till spring and do nothing. . . .

Even Parson Wibird in Braintree had rendered himself suspect, when, on the last Sunday before New Year, he rose in his pulpit and announced the text, *Hear, O heavens, and give ear, O earth! I have nourished and brought up children, and they have rebelled against me.* But he twisted it round, John noted, as the sermon progressed, and came out on the right side.

> *1776. January 1, Wednesday.* This year [*so ran John's diary*] brings ruin or salvation to the British colonies. Britain and America are staring at each other, and they will probably stare more and more for some time. The spirit of liberty is everywhere triumphant. Such a union was never before known in America. . . . What will they say in England when they see the resolves of the American legislatures, the petitions from the united colonies, the resolutions of the merchants in Boston, New York, Philadelphia &c.?

What they said in England was soon evident. At the very moment John was writing, Lord Rockingham, the Prime Minister, was being bombarded with letters from indignant businessmen in Manchester, Liverpool and elsewhere. "Our trade is hurt," wrote the Honorable Member of Parliament for Yorkshire, angrily. "What the devil have you been doing? For our part, we don't pretend to understand your politics and American matters, but our trade is hurt. Pray remedy it, and a plague of you if you won't."

This was language any politician could understand. On the fourteenth of January, 1766, William Pitt drove in from the country, got himself, gout and all, to the House of Commons and by some miracle of the spirit, dragged himself to his feet and spoke for three hours.

"The Americans are the sons, not the bastards of England!" he said. . . . "The gentleman asks, when were the colonies emanci-

pated? But I desire to know, when they were made slaves. . . . The gentleman tells us, America is obstinate, America is almost in open rebellion. I rejoice that America has resisted. Three millions of people so dead to all the feelings of liberty, as voluntarily to submit to be slaves, would have been fit instruments to have made slaves of the rest. . . ."

Week after week, the Commons debated. In February, an American witness was called, stood up before the House and announced himself as "Franklin, of Philadelphia." . . .

Question: Can anything less than a military force carry the Stamp Act into execution?

Answer: I do not see how a military force can be applied to that purpose.

Q. Why may it not?

A. Suppose a military force sent into America, they will find nobody in arms; what then are they to do? They cannot force a man to take stamps who chooses to do without them. They will not find a rebellion; they may indeed make one.

Q. If the Act is not repealed, what do you think will be the consequences?

A. The total loss of the respect and affection the people of America bear to this country, and of all the commerce that depends on that respect and affection. . . .

Q. What used to be the pride of the Americas?

A. To indulge in the fashions and manufactures of Great Britain.

Q. What is now their pride?

A. To wear their old clothes over again till they can make new ones.

On the eighteenth of March, the Commons, by a vote of 273 to 167, repealed the Stamp Act. In the Lords the majority was only 34. The King, signing, drew his lips together. "It is a fatal compliance," he said.

America had the news in May. From Falmouth to Charleston, town vied with town in celebration. There were parades, speeches; people drank toasts to Pitt, Barré, Lord Camden. Annapolis burned an effigy of Discord, raised a garlanded pillar to Concord. Boston went wild with joy; there had not been such goings-on since Quebec was taken. At one in the morning the bells began to ring; music was heard in Tremont Street and along the Mall. On the Common the Sons of Liberty built a pyramid with 280 lamps; the newspapers

counted them proudly. Guns boomed from the North and South Batteries. Drums beat; south of the Common, Liberty Tree was gay with flags and bright-colored streamers. That night there were fireworks: "Rockets," the *Gazette* reported, "bee-hives, Serpents, wheels." Houses were lighted from cellar to attic. The *Gazette*, which had had the news a little in advance, published a warning: "Please, when you see a shop window not illumined, don't break the glass until you look closely. Shops having paper and woolen goods on display, dare not light a candle."

The grandest illumination of all was in John Hancock's big stone house opposite the Common. Outside, a stage was erected for fireworks. As the first wheel was set ablaze, two hogsheads of Madeira were rolled out and the crowd cheered. In Hancock's dining room, "the genteel part of town" drank their wine, and Sam Adams, standing at the window, gazing out with deepest satisfaction, waved both hands in greeting to his friends. These fireworks, this treat of Madeira, were his doing and he knew it. John Hancock should have been a Tory. His whole disposition, not to speak of his vast fortune, should have made him a conservative. But Sam had won him, had even succeeded in getting him elected to the Legislature — the biggest political triumph, to date, for the people's party: seventy thousand pounds to draw on if necessity asked.

Jonathan Mayhew, when Sunday came around, faced a congregation that filled West Church to the window sills. "Our soul is escaped as a bird from the snare of the fowlers," he said in his deep, expressive voice. "The snare is broken, and we are escaped." He went on to suggest, with the smile that always won his congregation, that it might be expedient, from now on, "to do something more and talk something less; everyone studying to be quiet and to do his own business, letting things return peaceably into their own channels."

People were determined to believe the strife was over. On both sides of the ocean, peace descended like a dove. "Let the past, like the falling out of Lovers," exclaimed one Englishman in London, "prove only the renewal of love." In Weymouth, Abigail Adams's father preached a sermon of Thanksgiving: "The Lord reigneth, let the earth rejoice, and the multitude of the isles be glad thereof." Parliament, of course, had been far from making a complete capitulation: there was the matter of the Declaratory Act, passed just before repeal — and passed unanimously — which stated in baldest terms that

Parliament had authority over the colonies "in all cases whatsoever." Even Pitt, the Great Commoner, America's champion, supported this declaration of unlimited sovereignty, himself stating that Parliament must *bind colonial trade, confine their manufactures, and exercise every power but that of taking money out of their pockets without consent.*

America chose to ignore this ominous signal, chose to regard the Declaratory Act as a mere saving of face: the Empire must not be expected to yield unconditionally. But John Adams looked on the sudden universal gladness with a skeptical eye. The Stamp Act was repealed; but anyone who read history knew that nations did not change their policies — and their hearts — overnight. In his diary, John copied the first paragraph of the Declaratory Act. "Query," he added: "What is the end and design of this bill?"

And why were not people more apprehensive concerning it? In America, despite repeal, the Court party retained its strength. Even in Braintree, the division was deep and unbridgeable, the struggle ready to break out again at any moment. John had just been made town selectman, after as bitter a political battle as was ever fought in the county. His opponent, Major Miller, was a Church of England man, a frank supporter of the Court party and of the doctrine of passive obedience. For the first time in Braintree history, the election centered on the people versus the crown; John's winning majority was ominously slight. Even his brothers worked unceasingly, canvassing, making the rounds, picking up votes. John himself took no part in the campaign, but he watched avidly every development and was openly triumphant when he won.

Nevertheless there was something disgusting, to John, in the uses men made, lately, of "liberty." They used it as a catch phrase, mouthed and shouted without comprehension. *Liberty!* What right had men to such words, unless they studied the true meaning? . . . One May Sunday, not long after his election, John and Abigail walked home together from Meeting. It was a beautiful, warm noontime, with the clouds soft and feathery above the hills, the trees showing the first faint delicate color. Not far from their house, at a place where three roads met, they came on a young buttonwood tree, newly planted, guarded by a little wooden fence. On it hung an inscription: "The Tree of Liberty, and cursed is he who cuts this tree!"

John stood frowning. He was not sure he approved these clandestine and — he noted — ungrammatical inscriptions, put up anonymously to rouse the people. The author could at least have used the subjunctive: "Cursed *be* he . . ." John turned to speak but Abby pulled his arm. "It is good to plant a tree to liberty," she said. She put out her hand and touched a branch. "How sturdy it is!" Abby paused, thinking. *"And the leaves of the tree,"* she quoted at last, *"were for the healing of the nations."*

The two walked home. John, as the days passed, forgot the incident. Whether he desired it or not, he was moving, in spirit, ever closer to Boston. Since the night John had argued Boston's petition before the Governor, Sam Adams's "Mohawks," as Bernard called them, sent frequent notes to Braintree by messenger: "The Sons of Liberty desire your company at Boston on Wednesday next. They want you to write inscriptions, one in favor of liberty, another with encomiums on King George, expressive of our loyalty. Pray let them be as short and expressive as possible. . . . Destroy this after reading it. Mr. Samuel Adams sends his compliments and desires you would come."

Mr. Samuel Adams, it was plain, was not letting the sun go down on liberty, repeal or no repeal. Among the Sons of Liberty, Sam had the most thorough understanding of the temper and character of the people, "though not," John wrote in his diary, "of the law and constitution." In all that John found most difficult, his cousin was adept. Sam made friends instantly, at the drop of a hat, and with the most diverse groups. Rich merchants like Hancock and John Rowe seemed enraptured with him — though one wore hereditary riches with the ease of a prince, the other was rough and self-made. Sam's way with such as Mackintosh and the highly independent, quick-tempered men of dock and ropewalk was to John nothing short of a miracle. His cousin never forced a conversation. Yet in a roomful of men, the largest group formed always around Samuel, who likely as not stood quite silent, listening, moving his head in assent, his eyes pleasant, receptive.

John knew that he would never be really intimate with his cousin as he was intimate with, for instance, Jonathan Sewall. Nobody knew Sam Adams intimately. He did not seem to desire close friends. Perhaps a man so influential, so manipulative, preferred not to make ties outside his family. And that his cousin was manipulative, John did

not wish to deny; Sam Adams had a very genius for enlisting strong young men to the party. If Hancock was Sam's acquisition, so was Josiah Quincy, Junior — at twenty-four a brilliant lawyer with a warm, ardent nature. John, of course, knew Josiah as the beautiful Hannah Quincy's youngest brother; John had been sworn at the bar with Josiah's older brother, Samuel. The squint in Josiah's brown eyes only made him more attractive. John was greatly drawn to him, touched when Josiah came to him across a room and peered, his head down, trying to focus. . . . And Joseph Warren the physician — the handsomest young man in Boston — Sam Adams had won him, too.

He himself had learned more, John thought, from watching Samuel Adams than a hundred books could teach. There was no questioning the man's integrity, the sincerity of his piety and of the Puritan austerity that sat so quaintly upon him. He was never seen to lose his temper, flare up, show irritation. Yet God knows, thought John, there was provocation enough, dealing with crowds as Sam did. "Staunch and stiff and strict and inflexible in the cause," John wrote, "but always for softness, delicacy and prudence, where they will do." Where Sam's subsistence was concerned and the making of a living, he was careless and unconcerned as a child. Heaven seemed to look after such men, provide their families with shelter, food and raiment. Yet if he was indifferent to his own financial career, Sam showed the most friendly interest in other men's advancement. At the last meeting of the Monday Club, he had come up to John and suggested he move his family to Boston! Sam had been insistent, very earnest and plausible, reminding John there had been a great mortality, during the past three years, among the Boston bar. Pratt was gone, and Oxenbridge Thacher. Jeremiah Gridley was failing, almost too ill for work in court. It would be an excellent time for John to step in and establish himself. "I wager," Sam said, "your practice will double in the first month. A lawyer who lives in Boston is not only more convenient to come by, but he has more standing, more reputation."

John knew it was true; he had himself been considering the move for some time. But he had said nothing to anyone, even to Abigail. "And your good lady, Mistress Adams," Sam continued — as if he read John's mind — "she would be happier here surely, during the heavy winter snows, than shut up alone in the country. You could be

with her more, not always on horseback. Ten miles is a long journey in the January storms."

Mr. Bollan's house on Brattle Street was empty of tenants, Sam said further. On the corner, it was — not far from the house that used to belong to Mrs. Adams's uncle, Dr. Zabdiel Boylston — across from the church and the house of William Cooper, Town Clerk for Boston. The White House, it was called. John knew the place, of course? A word in the right direction would secure it for renting; Sam would be glad to speak that word. There was space downstairs for a law office. John would find himself in the heart of town, not two blocks from Faneuil Hall, Town-house and the docks. . . .

At home, John put the proposition to Abigail. It did not come as a surprise, Abby said. She had been expecting it. She approved the plan. Let them wait only until the new baby was born next July. She would hate to leave the farm, especially the animals and her own little black lamb, a month old, now. But by that time, Abby added cheerfully, the lamb would be a great sheep, and she would not mind.

Very often, during the ensuing winter months, the two talked it over. His health, John said repeatedly, would never stand town life. John, whose constitution was to prove almost indestructible, had for years been certain, at intervals, that he was verging on a decline. He caught cold easily; undue excitement made him sniffle and wheeze. At such times he slept badly, tossing and coughing on his side of the bed. "Your health will bear town life very well," Abby told him a little dryly. "If I tell you you have the constitution of an ox, it will offend you."

In July of 1767, the baby was born, a boy, sturdy and strong. They named him John Quincy, after Abby's grandfather, the old Colonel on Wollaston Hill. The circumstances of his birth all but determined John to move to Boston. John had been on horseback, hurrying home from Plymouth court, half crazy for fear he would not arrive in time, although the calendar gave them another two weeks. On Hingham plain he had met Dr. Tufts in his chaise. "John Adams, stop!" the old doctor said. "Stop and hear me. You have a son."

John galloped home like a man demented, flung himself from his horse, bounded into the house and up the narrow steps to where his wife lay in their high bed, the child already at her breast. Dusty from traveling and smelling strongly of horse, John stood by the bed,

staring at the two. Tears of joy and relief ran down his face. Abby's dark hair was braided and lay over her shoulders; the baby smacked his mouth greedily, like a little animal.

Surely — John said much later — surely, if they lived in Boston, he need not be absent at the most important moments of their lives? His clients would live in the city, nearby. . . . He would suggest they go tomorrow, were it not for one thing. . . . "What is that?" Abby asked. "My mother," John replied. "With Elihu married and Peter about to take a wife, my mother will be alone in the homestead, with nothing to look forward to but the grave. . . . She is all of fifty-eight," John finished solemnly, his tone a little oracular. "We cannot abandon my mother in her old age."

Abby looked strangely at her husband. "Alone?" she repeated. "And old — your mother?" Abby was sewing, mending a shirt. She held up her needle, wet the thread and jabbed it expertly through the eye. "Your mother is a handsome lady. She has the vigor of a woman half her age."

John answered carelessly, "Now you mention it, my mother has been more terrifyingly vigorous this winter than ever." He frowned. "I never saw such a woman for suggesting improvements. She wants me to knock down the partition in her back kitchen for a new milk house to match our own."

Abby's bright eyes left her work, rested on her husband's face. "Your mother has a new dress," she said, "of peach-colored taffeta. And a peach-colored bonnet, trimmed with white satin ribbons. Have you not noted it? Mr. John Hall, last night, admired the costume excessively when he was here. Ladies — " Abby paused, finished with a touch of ribaldry highly surprising — "ladies do not wear satin ribbons to catch flies with."

John stared, then leaped from his chair. "In God's name!" he said. "Not Mr. Hall? Not my mother and old John Hall. . . . Abby!" John shouted indignantly. "Is my mother going to *marry* that old —— ?"

Abby looked serenely at her husband over her work. "There is no need to swear and rant," she said. "The thing is decided. He has admired her for years. Anyone but you, John, would have seen it long ago. But you had best let her tell you herself." Abby's face showed infinite satisfaction. "I have done all I could to further the match. Your mother will have companionship as she grows old.

You and your brothers have shown scant sympathy, to my way of thinking. Lieutenant Hall is a fine man; old widowers are very amiable toward womenkind. Moreover he has a commodious house. And if he works with his hands — why, have I not heard you say often that manual labor is ennobling?"

Abby folded her work, rose from her chair. "I might add," she finished, "that your mother's marriage will enable you to move your wife, your daughter and your son to Boston at our mutual convenience."

PART III

The Approach of Revolution.
1768-1774

CHAPTER EIGHTEEN

John Adams moves to Boston. The sloop
LIBERTY *precipitates a riot. John writes the*
"Boston Instructions" and the Court party
makes him a significant offer.

TOWARD the end of April, 1768, on a sharp, windy day, John Adams loaded his wagons and brought his wife, his family and a modest assortment of furniture to Boston. John rode his horse; Abigail sat in the two-wheeled wagon with the children and Sukey, their Negro servant. It was eleven in the morning before they were finally ready to start, and it seemed as if all Braintree were there to see them off. The town had not wanted them to go. When John refused to serve another year as selectman, Braintree voted him thanks for his services and recorded it in the books. It was a precedent; even his father had not been so honored.

It had been very hard to break away. John's roots went deep; in a hundred directions his lines were out. Abigail's friends were on every street and lane. John had not realized, until these last few weeks, how widely his wife, in her quiet way, had made herself known and loved. But now that the day and hour had come, John was impatient to be gone. How interminable, he thought, were these minuscule domestic arrangements and counterarrangements! Both of John's brothers were on hand; they had been most helpful. Mr. Hall, mercifully, had kept their mother away. John, already on his horse, watched the last desperate loading, the final flinging of an old featherbed over Abigail's spinet. John thought he had never in his life seen such a collection of disreputable-looking furniture. Set up

in the house, it had appeared nothing short of elegant. John's temper was not at its best in scenes of domestic confusion; by now he was almost frantic. Enthusiastic neighbors had brought their own libations and kept drinking John's health out in the middle of the road, or coming up and trying to shake his hand.

It did not improve John's temper to observe that Abigail, sitting in the wagon, seemed wholly undisturbed. "Mrs. Adams!" John said suddenly, in the loud, rapid voice he used to address public meetings. "Let us be off!" He wheeled his horse; the crowd cheered as the little cavalcade started north on the Post Road. The last thing John saw was old Joe Field, waving a beer mug and singing lustily the well-known song — a Tory song, John noted, introduced to the Province by Governor Bernard himself:

> Here's a health to all those that we love;
> Here's a health to all those that love us . . .

Abby had turned; she was waving back toward the house and the crowd and she was actually, to her husband's astonishment, singing the last lines of the song:

> Here's a health to all those that love them that love those
> That love those that love them that love us.

John grinned in spite of himself. They turned a corner. "Abby," John said, "after we are through Town Gate and into Marlborough Street, I would advise you to refrain from singing Tory verses."

Their house on Brattle Street was pleasant and roomy, three stories high, of brick, painted white. It had a little garden at the back with two pear trees and a rose arbor. John was very proud of his new establishment. The owner, Mr. Bollan the lawyer, British-born, lived in London now; he was popular with the people's party and had served the Province as agent, on and off, for years. John had his law office downstairs, with a door into the areaway. The house itself faced directly on Brattle Street and the big wooden church across the cobbled square. Not two blocks off, through the little alley called Dossett's Lane, was the Town-house where the Legislature met. Samuel Adams, thought Abigail, had been right about the White House being in the heart of Boston; they might as well have taken apartments in Faneuil Hall itself.

Sam had been right, too, about the move being good for John's practice. The increase in clients began almost the day John put his name on the office door. William Cooper, Town Clerk for Boston, strolled over from his house across the square, bringing a Mr. Avery who desired Mr. Adams's services for a conveyancing. Three well-known and prosperous fish exporters dropped round to see about the rule on prize goods. Sam Adams, calling to welcome his country cousins, declared quite openly that he saw no reason why John could not look after the vast Hancock interests far better than the "cringing Tory lawyers" to whom Hancock had been paying fees so far. He would drop the word within a week or so, said Sam genially.

Abigail, observing this continual coming and going, hearing from the garden the tinkle of the office bell, watched in wonder a husband who had feared town life might injure his health. John had never seemed so well; his appetite was prodigious, his cheeks were round and solid. He seemed altogether chunkier, stronger than ever, compounded of vigor, talk and movement. He was very careful of his appearance, meticulous about his linen, spoke sharply to the houseboy about polishing his boots and went regularly to have his wig dressed by the French barber, a Mr. Dehon. There was a new containment about him, a self-assurance bounding and cheerful.

To Abby herself the scene around them was a continual marvel. King Street lay very near, to the eastward. It led directly into the Long Wharf, which extended like another street half a mile into the Harbor, lined down one side with shops, booths, fish markets, liquor stores. All day the carts lumbered by, coming up laden from the ships or going down with produce from the country. There were hay wagons, huge, unwieldy; there was a perpetual procession of two-wheeled carts carrying firewood and kindling. And the fish! Abby smelled fish when she woke and when she went to bed; she smelled tarred rope within the walls of Meeting on Sundays. She was overwhelmed, at first, with the noise and dirt and confusion. Instead of Braintree's tiny population, almost every one of whom Abby knew by name and face, here were some eighteen thousand people, coming and going on their business or their pleasure, walking and talking, whistling their tunes on the streets, calling their wares, singing snatches late at night or shouting roughly if wheel caught against wheel in the narrow, crowded streets. The sailors in particu-

lar amused Abigail with their tarred pigtails, black wide-brimmed hats and belled blue trousers, their rolling easy gait. Here, so near the wharves, the streets were filled with them. They had a wild, profane way of speaking, but their phrases, catchy and colorful, permeated the speech of all Boston.

It was a month before Abigail learned to sleep. Below her window the watchman challenged passers-by. Abby, lying tense, waited for the answer, waited for the watchman's foot to proceed along the cobbles, the shake of his rattle as he intoned his cheerful message: *Past twelve o'clock and a clear night of stars.* . . . And the bells! They were the very voice of the city. They rang to open and close the markets; they pealed furiously for fires, tolled muffled for funerals. On Sundays they rang twice, calling everyone to Meeting. From the Brattle Street church across the square a great voice boomed at five each morning, calling Boston to rise. Abby, as the days went by, began to like these voices. They were friendly, she said. (She had not yet heard them ring for a riot and did not know the hoarse menace of that sound.) She had begun to recognize the different tones. Christ Church bell was lordly, New North was out of tune, King's Chapel deep and slow, as if it had a story to tell.

How like a woman's fancy, John thought. For himself he thought the bells horribly noisy, particularly the little handbells that tinkled along the streets, advertising wares, announcing dinnertime at the taverns. Brattle Square was hemmed and surrounded by taverns. Barricaded by them, Abigail said. What would happen, she asked, if John tried to repeat his Braintree crusade and do away with the Bunch of Grapes by the Town-house, or the Green Dragon, Chase's Distillery where the Sons of Liberty met, or Brackett's famous Cromwell Head Inn?

John laughed. "The Whigs would languish for want of a meeting place," he said. "Do you know, Abby, that no Tory will so much as set foot in the Cromwell Head door?"

When curfew rang at nine each evening, Abigail took her candle and went the rounds, locking doors, barring windows as she had never thought of doing in the country. The household was very busy. The baby was not a year old; little Abby nearly three. She was plump, with wide blue eyes, and looked like her father. Her prattle, her uneven small footsteps filled the house. John adored her, tried in every way possible to spoil her. She had a way of backing

down the long steps to the narrow front hallway. John, coming in, would stand and watch her patient progress, her starched skirts flaring above her stiff little drawers. When she reached the bottom and saw him she would scream with joy and leap to his arms.

Abigail herself was far from lonely. There were tradesmen to interview, shops and markets to visit, and all the endless business of domestic settling down to be achieved. Abby acquired a maid to help Sukey, a houseboy to carry wood for the fires and run errands for John from the office. Nor did Abigail lack friends in town. As a girl she had often visited in Boston with her uncles. Mercy Warren was here while the Legislature sat — Mercy Otis she had been, James Otis's sister. Abigail had known her for years; her husband, James Warren, was Representative from Plymouth. Esther Quincy was in Boston part of the year when her husband, Jonathan Sewall, brought her down from Falmouth. Jonathan was Attorney General of the Province now. He was a rich man; people said he made over three thousand pounds a year. He was still intimate with John, but there was no longer any doubt where Sewall's political sympathies lay. All his honors and appointments had come to him from Governor Bernard. Sewall was not belligerently Tory, and since repeal of the Stamp Act one could be friendly again with the government men.

Abby and John were pleased when Sewall appeared on their doorstep, his gold-headed stick under his arm, his handsome, three-tiered blue cape swinging from his shoulders. "All you need is a sword," John told him, "to be taken for a nobleman." When Abby knew Sewall was coming, she put on her best rose silk gown with the low square neck and short sleeves. It was drawn in with whalebone around the waist and showed her figure; lace came over the elbow. John loved it, watched his wife as she moved across the room; he thought she bore herself as well or better than any of your great town ladies. John did not say so aloud; it was not the New England way, to praise one's wife. But Abby, after four years of married life, felt her husband's eyes upon her, lifted her head and swung her skirts as she moved through the doorway. . . .

Although John lived at home instead of — as Abigail had been used to say — on horseback, his wife began to think she saw less of him than in Braintree. He was continually out, in court, at the Merchants' Exchange in Faneuil Hall, or across the square at Mr. William

Cooper's house. And when he came home, a gentleman or two came
with him and they retired to John's office, talking law or politics.
Josiah Quincy the younger came often; also Dr. Joseph Warren —
tall, reserved and very good-looking — whom John and Abigail had
adopted as their family physician. John Rowe the merchant came;
Sam Adams; James Otis from his office around the corner; Dr. Samuel Cooper, minister of Brattle Street church. And once or twice,
gorgeous in orange velvet coat and white silk stockings, John Hancock stopped in, smelling of soap and fresh linen.

There was much to discuss, concerning the country. In spite of
the repeal of the Stamp Act, things did not look well for the future.
To the people's deep disappointment, in London as well as America,
Pitt had accepted a peerage. The Great Commoner was gone, the
people said, and mourned their loss as if he had died. Lord Hillsborough was Secretary of State for the Colonies, and a worse choice
England could not have made. The new Chancellor of the Exchequer, Charles Townshend, had fortunately died soon after taking
office — but not soon enough. "Champagne Charley," they had
called him in the coffeehouses of London — the only man who could
make the House laugh on both sides of a question. Before he died,
Champagne Charley had pushed through Parliament new colonial
taxes on tea, glass, paper, painters' colors. The Townshend Acts, they
were called; their effect on America was to be as disastrous as the
Stamp Act. To enforce them, an American Board of Customs was
set up, with headquarters in Boston. Five Commissioners were appointed to cover the coast as far as Georgia. One of them was Mr.
Paxton, Surveyor of the Port of Boston, already the most hated Englishman in town.

London itself was going through a turmoil that amounted almost
to a Whig rebellion. (Boston, mistakenly, tried to take it for such.)
John Wilkes, gadfly of the Tories, had suddenly and stormily returned from his long Parisian exile and was being voted into Parliament by Middlesex — and turned angrily out of Parliament by the
Tories. The King himself was momentarily so unpopular he was
warned not to show his face outside Buckingham Palace; some observers said it looked as if George III had more loyal followers in
Boston than in London. Benjamin Franklin wrote from England that
within the year he had seen riots about corn, riots about elections,

"riots of colliers, riots of coal-heavers, riots of sawyers, of Wilkes-ites, of government chairmen, of smugglers."

The Boston *Gazette* looked on Wilkes as a hero, printed every word he said, recorded every rotten egg flung by his followers at the Lords temporal and spiritual. America put great store by these London riots, persuading herself that her English brothers across the sea had joined forces against a wicked Tory ministry. A new frontier township in Pennsylvania took the name of Wilkes-Barré, celebrating the two champions at a stroke. Nobody realized that John Wilkes was nothing more than an adventurer, not to be compared with such serious and devoted leaders as the American cause had produced.

John Dickinson of Philadelphia had lately written his stirring *Letters from a Farmer in Pennsylvania;* they were being printed everywhere. John Dickinson was no more a farmer than was John Hancock; he was a scholar and a gentleman, London-educated, with a handsome fortune. But he wrote plainly and beautifully, in an idiom the country could understand: *A perpetual jealousy respecting liberty is absolutely requisite in all free states. Liberty is never exposed to so much danger, as when the people believe there is the least.*

John Adams admired the FARMER's letters, read them aloud to Abigail. They were warm, John said, but they were reasonable. John himself hated demagoguery, inflammatory speeches. Living in Boston in the very midst of what Governor Bernard called "the faction," John had to use caution, or find himself altogether absorbed by the Sons of Liberty and their affairs. Dr. Warren had twice stopped by, asking him to go down to Faneuil Hall and "harangue town meeting." John had refused outright. "No!" he said. Haranguing was not his function. If the party needed public papers drafted, or constitutional arguments to back up what they did, he would be at their command. Had not the *Gazette*, for the past two winters, been filled with his pieces? In January of '66 he had written under the name of CLARENDON, and last winter he had carried on a tremendous newspaper controversy with Jonathan Sewall, who had taken it upon himself to defend Governor Bernard and his measures. Sewall had called himself PHILANTHROPOS; John had been GOVERNOR WINTHROP. John's articles had been so long and so detailed he wondered, he told Dr. Warren now, that readers would stomach them, For himself, no

subject was so absorbing, so altogether important, as the subject of government. But he would not cozen people. Indeed, he knew not how to flatter, cajole, make a serious subject attractive and easy.

Warren nodded gravely, the hint of a smile on his face. "Perhaps they do not read all that you write," he told John. "But solemnity becomes a statesman. The people wish their statesmen to be solemn."

John, observing events around him as the weeks went by, was by no means sure of this. To what flippant and even dangerous uses men put serious words, serious arguments! The Harvard students, a day or so past, had met and dedicated their own liberty tree on Cambridge Common, held a meeting under it and noisily voted the orders of their tutors to be "unconstitutional." Then they proceeded to break the tutors' windows. The Senior Class, marching to President Holyoke's office, actually petitioned to be sent to "the college at Connecticut" * and receive their degrees there! Everything, lately, was "unconstitutional," John noted sourly. There was some unnaturally cold weather that May. "Why," asked the *Gazette*, "is this weather like a late Act of Parliament for raising a revenue? *Because it is unconstitutional.*"

But if John Adams refused to rise to his feet and harangue the Boston mob to action, his promise to help with pen and paper would soon be put to the test. This year of '68 was to prove most significant in the Province's history. And Boston would lead the Province.

It began with the incident of Hancock's sloop, the *Liberty*, expected home from Madeira with a cargo of fine wines. The duty on such wines was seven pounds per tun. The time-honored procedure was for the customs men to board as the vessel docked, repair to the captain's cabin and sample the cargo with him, then tactfully vanish (for a consideration), while the cargo was unloaded out of sight and hearing.

But this time, it was rumored around town that Commissioner Paxton intended to use John Hancock and his sloop *Liberty* as an object lesson, knowing that Hancock would openly refuse to pay the duties. Both sides watched for the vessel to arrive. The day she was sighted rounding Point Allerton, the news spread quickly. At noon the *Liberty* docked at Hancock's wharf in the North End, down by King's Head Tavern. The customs man — Boston called him the "tide-waiter" — stepped aboard, and on his heels, Hancock's

* Yale.

agent. The usual libations were consumed in the captain's cabin, after which Hancock's agent made the usual delicate proposition concerning the cargo. This the tide-waiter refused flatly. The captain, rising with an oath, knocked the tide-waiter over, chair and all. Then he and the agent tied him securely and stowed him below. As soon as it was dark, the cargo, a hundred and twenty-seven pipes of wine, was unloaded in record time. (The captain, by the way, worked so furiously that he died next morning in his bed.)

Hancock's agent entered the cargo in the customs books as "four or five pipes of wine," swearing that was the whole of it. Such contraband doings were an old story; New England did not look on them as perjury. But on this occasion, there lay in Boston Harbor the British frigate *Romney*, a warship of fifty guns. Early in June, she had entered unannounced; she was anchored close to the docks, not more than two cable's lengths away. John Adams, from his bed at dawn, could hear the bugle blow and the boatswain's high whistle, calling the sailors on deck.

On Friday, June 10, around six o'clock, workmen from the shipyards and ropewalks, strolling home through the fine summer air, stopped at Hancock's dock to hear the news. They found the *Liberty* newly laden with oil and tar, as if for a journey outward. Surely then, she was not to be seized for false entry, and surely also, this was a signal victory for the town? The men stood about peaceably enough, joshing each other and pointing derisively with their pipes to where the *Romney* swung at anchor. Two officials from the Custom House chose this moment to appear, looking very purposeful. Sudden silence fell. The collector, Mr. Harrison, stepped aboard, walked to the mainmast and tacked up a printed paper; the King's arrow ➤ stood out black and strong. Hallowell, the other official, signaled the *Romney* and ordered the *Liberty's* crew to loose her docklines.

Two boatloads of sailors put out; it was plain they were coming for the *Liberty*. There was a growl from the crowd. "Leave Hancock's sloop be!" voices said. "No harm will come to her at her owner's dock. Is this a captured ship, a prize ship, and are we at war?" . . . Suddenly, as the *Romney's* sailors climbed to the dock, the place was a seething, roaring mass of angry men. Bricks flew; the customs officers, running for their lives, were hit, felled to the ground. A little pleasure sloop with an orange sail lay alongside the

dock, the property of one of the customs men. The crowd hauled it ashore, dragged it up Fish Street, through Brattle Square and past the burying-ground to Hancock's house, where they burned it in front of his door. It was midnight before the password went round: "To your tents!" — and Beacon Street was empty.

There was a rumor that Hancock was to be arrested, with bail fixed at a huge sum and the threat of ruinous penalties. Hancock asked John Adams if he would, in such case, serve as counsel. The trial was set for the autumn term of court. Obviously, it was to be a *cause célèbre*. John agreed to serve, well aware he would have to argue the constitutionality of the Revenue Act itself. Everyone in Boston knew immediately that John Adams was to plead for Hancock. On Tuesday, June 14th, town meeting was called; a petition was framed and sent by messenger to the Governor, asking him to have the warship *Romney* removed from the Harbor. It was voted that a new set of Instructions be given to the four Boston Representatives in the Legislature, telling them the town's wishes in this important crisis. John Adams was asked to draft the Instructions. He did it that same night, in his office, with the windows open to Brattle Square, the room filled with smoke, mosquitoes and politicians. In a corner, waiting quietly, sat Mr. Samuel Adams in his shirt sleeves.

By the time town meeting convened to hear their new Instructions to the Representatives, Boston was in a ferment of anger and anxiety. Four of the five Commissioners for Customs had already fled to the *Romney* for safety; now they were taken to Castle William* in the Harbor, their wives and children with them. They set up housekeeping in the barracks, swore they would stay there all summer unless Governor Gage in New York sent troops to Boston to keep order.

Word of this came ashore; Faneuil Hall could not hold the crowd. John's Instructions were read aloud twice, very slowly and distinctly, while the four Representatives sat listening:

> *To the Honourable James Otis, and Thomas Cushing, Esqrs; Mr. Samuel Adams, and John Hancock, Esq.*
>
> GENTLEMEN: With the utmost grief and concern, we find that, between our parent country and ourselves, the root of bitterness is yet

---

* Boston spoke of it as Fort William, Castle William or Castle Island. There were barracks for 1000 men; the Governor himself had apartments there and frequently took his family out for a week or two in summer.

alive. . . . Armed vessels have appeared in our harbor. The *Romney*, sent to overawe and terrify the inhabitants of this town, has, without instituting any libel or prosecution, removed in a hostile manner, a vessel lying at our wharf. . . . This warship has impressed sailors from our ships, against the act of Parliament passed in the 6th year of Queen Ann. [*John Adams never omitted chapter and verse.*] We hear that military forces are coming, to dragoon us into passive obedience. . . . It is our desire that you inquire into these rumors and that you put forward, in the House of Representatives, resolutions that every person who shall solicit or promote the importation of troops at this time, is an enemy to this town and province, a disturber of the peace, and good order of both. . . .

It is, however, our fixed resolution to maintain our loyalty and duty to our most gracious sovereign, a reverence and due subordination to the British parliament, as the supreme legislative in all cases of necessity. . . . At the same time it is our unalterable resolution, at all times to assert and vindicate our dear and invaluable rights and liberties, at the utmost hazard of our lives and fortunes. . . .

With the highest confidence, gentlemen, in your integrity, abilities and fortitude, we recommend that you exert yourselves for our relief.

Governor Francis Bernard, sitting in his pleasant study in Province House, read this document carefully, when it was brought round to him. Among these resolute and forthright phrases, the line that disturbed the Governor most was the one about due subordination to Parliament "in all cases of necessity." Why, that was no true submission! Who was to determine which cases were "cases of necessity"? And who had drafted these Instructions? Bernard asked his Lieutenant Governor, Thomas Hutchinson.

Still another Adams, Hutchinson replied wryly. A Mr. John Adams — the same lawyer, in fact, who had argued, before His Excellency, the town's petition to open the courts. He was a cousin of Samuel and newly moved to Boston.[1] John Hancock had engaged him as counsel for the case of the sloop *Liberty*.

The Governor's eyebrows went up. He remembered this Mr. Adams well, he said. His arguments that night in Council had been solidly grounded, although like all the people's polemics it had included some specious rhetoric about "natural rights" and "the constitution." Hancock could afford to choose his legal talent; this man must possess considerable ability? . . . Yes, Hutchinson replied. John Adams was a graduate of Harvard, trained under Jeremiah

Gridley, with more knowledge, people said, than his kinsman.* And in spite of this set of Instructions — which, after all, might merely be the expression of half a dozen firebrands such as Otis and Samuel Adams — John Adams was not yet, Hutchinson believed, wholly lost to the crown cause. The Attorney General, Mr. Jonathan Sewall, was an old and intimate friend of John Adams, a connection of his wife's. According to Sewall, his friend's character was not that of a demagogue, a Wilkes, a troublemaker. On the contrary, John Adams was a man of integrity and exemplary personal ambition, who by unstinting labor had raised himself from humble but honest beginnings, and was making a place for himself in the Province.

Governor Bernard looked thoughtful. There was no gainsaying the seriousness of the situation. The Court party had lost its majority in the House of Representatives. Bernard retained his power in the Council, or upper house, only by using his royal prerogative of vetoing new appointments. The defection of Hancock had been a serious blow. Joseph Hawley also had gone over. Hawley was Representative from Hampshire County, one of the most respected men in the western part of the Province.

Could not something be done before it was too late — Bernard asked now — to secure John Adams as a friend to government? Men even farther lost to reason had been won by judicious and timely application. . . . The office of King's Advocate was open, in the admiralty court — a post analogous to Attorney General in the Court of Common Pleas.

The appointment, Bernard went on, would serve a double purpose. It would be a politic way to wean Mr. Adams from the people's faction, and it would quiet the commonalty, whose confidence the man appeared to have. Because it was admiralty judges who convicted in cases of smuggling, hatred of these courts had become, of late, no less than fanatic. An Advocate General from their own ranks, someone the people felt they could trust, would reduce friction, the danger of rioting when unfavorable judgments were awarded. What, finished Governor Bernard, did Mr. Hutchinson think of John Adams's qualifications as Advocate General of Admiralty for Massachusetts?

---

* Quoted direct from Hutchinson's *History of Massachusetts*, Vol. III. See Chapter Note 1 for the full quotation, where Hutchinson compares the two Adamses.

One evening in June, 1768, not long after this very significant conversation, Abigail had just put the children to bed, when the front knocker sounded. A moment later, Sewall's voice was heard in the hall, greeting John. Abigail ran down, made her curtsy. He had come to dine, Sewall said cheerfully. Was he welcome as of old?

He was indeed, Abigail and John replied together. What a pleasure to see Jonathan Sewall in their house again! And how prosperous and handsome he was looking. . . . Surely that cinnamon coat, those fawn-colored breeches, must have been tailored in London? When Attorney General Sewall entered their door, Abby said gaily, with another curtsy, the place took on an air immediately, as if the nobility lived there. "And no duchess could grace the establishment better, Madam," Sewall replied gallantly, raising Abby by the hand. "It is a pity your husband persists in crossing rapiers with me, in the *Gazette*. Ah, John, my old friend, your zeal led you astray, as Governor Winthrop, last year! I think I pricked you, in that duel. I believe I drew first blood."

Sewall put an arm over John's shoulder as the two followed Abigail through the hall to the little garden behind the house. Dinner was laid on a table by the pear tree. The day had been hot, but in the late afternoon a fresh breeze had risen from the Bay. The three took their places at the table.

"I shall not forgive you," John told his friend cheerfully, "for taking the Governor's part. In your heart, Jonathan, you could not have credited what you wrote as Philanthropos. You forced me to compose a whole book, almost."

Sewall shook his head. "Verbosity is a weakness of lawyers. Years ago, in Worcester, I warned you against it."

Abigail, signaling Sukey to place the roast before her husband, looked at Sewall and laughed. "When my husband becomes verbose," she said, "will be a happy day for this house."

Sewall looked at Abby across the little table, a searching, kindly glance. "Does he ever tell you he loves you, Madam?" he asked. "Does he tell you how handsome you are in that rose-colored gown?"

Abby colored, looked at John with her eyes bright. All through dinner she was very gay. They ate mutton and fresh salmon, new potatoes sent in from Braintree, fresh homemade butter and some of Abigail's preserves. John went to the cellar himself and fetched

one of his bottles of fine Madeira. Holding his glass to the light, Sewall remarked that, speaking of Madeira, what did John think he could make of Hancock's suit next term? It would be tried, of course, in the admiralty court. "Between us, John," Sewall said lightly, "you haven't a leg to stand on."

A shade passed over John's face. "I confess," he said, "it keeps me awake at night. But I could not refuse the case. You know me too well, Jonathan, for me to·make any pretense. I have scant hope of winning, considering who brings the suit and the court where it is to be tried. Now, if I had a jury . . . But make no mistake, Jonathan, I believe government to be in the wrong, in this matter. An Englishman's property is not subject to confiscation and seizure without trial and prosecution. Of course you are aware the *Liberty* has been sold at government auction, converted into a coastal raider for the Custom House?"

Sewall put down his glass without replying. His air was suddenly serious. The conversation had taken a turn he had not looked for, and a turn highly disadvantageous to the purpose of his mission. He quickly put an end to it. "I have come for a reason tonight, John," he said. "I bear a message — a message very important to your welfare and future career." He glanced at Abigail. She rose instantly, saying she must see to the children abovestairs. John led Sewall through the house to his office. When they were alone and the door closed, Sewall began to speak. He was here, he said, at the request of Governor Bernard. The office of Advocate General was open, in the court of admiralty.

Sewall paused, smiled warmly and briefly at John, and continued. The Governor had inquired of gentlemen well qualified to give information — including one of great authority. (John knew instantly that Sewall meant Thomas Hutchinson.) The result of his inquiry was that "in point of talents, integrity, reputation and consequence at the bar, Mr. Adams was best entitled to the office." The Governor had determined, accordingly, to give it to him. But before writing the recommendation to His Majesty, whose signature of course was necessary, the Governor would like to know Mr. Adams's pleasure in this matter?

"I have quoted verbatim," Sewall said, smiling again. "I need not add how pleased I am to be the bearer of such tidings. And I might add, John, that the office is a sure introduction to the most lucrative

practice in the Province. Not to speak of its being a step to greater favors to come."

While Sewall was talking, John had sat motionless until he heard the words Advocate General of Admiralty. Then he looked up sharply, the color flooding his face. He raised a hand, pushed the hair from his forehead with a gesture almost violent. After that he kept his eyes on his friend's face throughout, not moving a muscle. Now he got up, walked to the fireplace and stood leaning his arm on the mantel, looking down at the hearth. As Sewall ceased speaking, a slight pause fell. It was a matter only of seconds; yet during it, a whole lifetime of conversation passed as it were between the two men. *Advocate General of Admiralty.* Both knew what this would mean to John and his family. Security for life. And more than security; it would mean immediate success, authority throughout the Province. Long ago, in Putnam's office at Worcester, Sewall had asked John what his ambition was, in the law. "To make my living," John had replied flatly. "I can never make a reputation that depends on crown patronage, Jonathan. I have neither blood nor wealth behind me."

And now it had happened. By this offer, the door was open to crown favor; the Advocate Generalcy would be only a beginning. Behind the Governor's patronage lay the power and prestige of Britain, all the places and appointments at a great king's disposal. Some of the most distinguished men in the Province had held the office: Benjamin Lynde, Governor Shirley. *Even James Otis had been Advocate General of Admiralty.* The thought struck suddenly into John's consciousness. Otis had no choice but to resign the position in '61, in order to argue the writs case. . . .

John drew a long breath, glanced at where Sewall sat quietly, his white silk legs crossed, swinging one elegantly booted foot. An easy confidence was on his pleasant, long, full face. Over the cinnamon-colored coat his shirt ruffle fell crisp and spotless.

"No," John said. "You knew it would be *no,* Jonathan." He moved impatiently as Sewall tried to intervene. "Do not think me ungrateful. You have done this for me; I see your hand plainly. You are my friend and you meant well. I tell myself you meant well. But you know my political principles. You know who my friends are." John looked straight at Sewall. With deep and sudden finality, he perceived that by this answer his course was charted, to-

night and forever. His voice was hard. "The Governor, also, knows who my friends are."

Sewall uncrossed his legs, took from his waistcoat pocket a slim snuffbox of tortoise shell, embossed in gold. "Your friends?" he said. "His Excellency mentioned that point to me, especially. He desired me to say that your political sentiments will be no objection. You will be at full liberty to entertain your own opinions, which — " Sewall's voice shifted almost imperceptibly — "which the Governor does not wish to influence by this position. He offers it merely because you are the man best qualified. He charged me to say that he relied, in this matter of politics, on your integrity."

This was almost too much for John. He gave a loud, distinct snort. *Jonathan, Jonathan,* he wanted to say, *do you take me for a fool as well as a knave?* But he could not say it. Sewall was wholly serious; there had been no banter in his voice, no loophole for the assumption that he looked on this offer as anything but the highest compliment. With a kind of helpless anger and at the same time a sinking sensation, a dark foreboding as of grief and loss, John knew that his friend was his friend no longer. Bernard and Hutchinson were bribing John Adams, and they had chosen Sewall as messenger. . . .

"So the Governor relies on my integrity," John said. He spoke coldly. "His Excellency goes far in the generosity and liberality of his sentiments. I have said I cannot accept this offer. Is it necessary to add, I cannot in honor or conscience accept it?" [2]

Sewall rose, adjusted his coat. There was no change in his voice; it was still friendly, persuasive. "You are too hasty, John. It is characteristic. You have allowed your emotions to become involved. There are others to consider in this matter." Sewall motioned with his eyes toward the floor above, whence the high brief wail of a child was heard. Snapping his snuffbox shut, Sewall put it in his pocket, indicated he was leaving. "I shall not take this as your final word."

John followed him to the door. "Give the office to Sam Fitch," he said, roughly. "Fitch is the Governor's man to his toes. There will be no trouble with Sam Fitch when the contraband rolls in."

Sewall laid a hand lightly on John's shoulder. Beyond the open door the noises of the city reached them. Above the darkened street the stars were very near. Down the block a lantern bobbed, then vanished as its owner turned a corner. "Pray convey my adieux to

your charming lady," Sewall said. "I shall return when you have talked it over with her. . . . Do not be proud, my old friend," Sewall added quickly, as John made a movement of dissent. "Remember that your decision will carry finality with it. The crown does not repeat its offers."

He was gone. John closed the door, drew the bolt and going upstairs to his wife, stated flatly and without comment, what had happened. The excitement, the anger that had sustained him was gone; he felt a little sick. "It is a bribe, of course," Abby said at once. She looked up from where she sat by their bedroom window; she had been waiting for him. "A very high bribe," she continued, "when one considers the implications. More will follow. You could be Chief Justice. The Court party thinks highly of John Adams." She grasped John's fingers in hers, pressed them briefly to her cheek. "My friend, my partner, they say you are an ambitious man. Is it not something of a satisfaction to be feared by the powerful?"

Three weeks later, Sewall was back. The Governor, he said, had sent for him again, told him the office must be filled. He desired an answer. John shook his head. "You have wasted the public time, Sewall." But John's anger, somehow, was gone, his manner natural again with his old friend. "Jonathan," he said, "we travel different roads, you and I. But I credit you with sincerity. It must be that you believe in what you do. You will accord me a like motive." John rocked on his heels, his hands hunching his coattails. "Mr. Putnam, in Worcester," John finished, "used to tell me, jeeringly — do you remember? — 'The pure airs of Braintree generate a great simplicity. . . .' The Court party should not count too highly on this quality, Jonathan. Let His Excellency be reminded — " John made a wide, quick gesture toward Boston, the streets and the Harbor — "let him be reminded that the Country party has removed, lately, to the very heart of town."

*Massachusetts calls a convention of towns. The
British troops arrive. Governor Bernard sails
for home. John Adams tries some very critical
cases, and receives a serenade
beneath his window.*

TOWARD the end of June, 1768, the Massachusetts circular
letter engrossed all minds. During the previous winter, the Assembly
had sent a communication to every colony, asking support against
the Townshend duties of '67, and the numerous restrictions and con-
demnations implied. Sam Adams had drafted the letter; it was a new
departure altogether and it had succeeded beyond his wildest dreams.
First the towns of Massachusetts, then the colonies as far south as
Georgia, responded enthusiastically. As each reply came in, the
Gazette published it; the one from Virginia was especially heart-
warming. "This is a glorious day!" Sam Adams cried out, reading
the message to the House of Representatives. It was extraordinary
to feel this sympathy from the sister colonies, to know they shared
a like hurt, a like indignation, and were willing to join forces. The
House was very proud of its circular letter.

But in London, Lord Hillsborough, Secretary of State for the
Colonies, was both angry and alarmed. Such concerted action was
wholly outside the law. To the empire it carried a far larger threat
than any mere local rioting, burning of effigies or pulling down
the gardens of customs officials. This circular letter would rouse the
whole continent. Hillsborough moved swiftly, took the letter to the

House of Lords. Henceforth, he said, Parliament must "grant nothing to the Americans except what they ask with a halter round their necks." A stinging reproof to Massachusetts was not enough; Hillsborough sent an immediate dispatch to each separate colony, commanding that the Massachusetts circular letter be treated "with the contempt it deserves."

Massachusetts's own particular message from Lord Hillsborough arrived in the still fateful month of June, and was promptly sent round by Bernard to the House of Representatives. The Clerk, Samuel Adams, read the message to a floor and gallery that sat tensely silent while their circular letter was denounced as "a flagitious attempt to disturb the public peace," a composition of a "most dangerous and factious tendency, calculated to inflame the minds of good subjects and promote unwarrantable combination." In His Majesty's name, the Massachusetts House was commanded to rescind the resolution that had given rise to the letter and repudiate publicly all that it had said.

Angry murmurs went around the gallery. Rescind the letter? Never! What would the other colonies think? Massachusetts had meant deeply, seriously, every word of that letter. Far from being the mere temporary expression of a rebellious impulse, as Hillsborough assumed, it was the combined sense of the Province lawfully assembled. Immediately, the House composed a reply to Hillsborough, a message also to Governor Bernard. Then the galleries were cleared, the doors closed and the vote taken. It was 92 to 17 against rescinding.

Next day, the Governor angrily dismissed the Assembly. The numbers 92 to 17 became a byword through the colonies. In song and verse the Famous Ninety-two were applauded; the Seventeen Slaves had their hats knocked off if they showed their heads on the streets. Paul Revere made a handsome silver bowl, inscribed to the memory of "the Glorious Ninety-two." The *Gazette*, in its very best style, carried a story about one of the Seventeen Slaves, who set off down the coast for Martha's Vineyard, on business. *Strick Truth* or no, the story was caught up, went from mouth to mouth like a fable. The way to Martha's Vineyard was by coastal vessel, but no self-respecting captain, it seems, would let the miserable Slave aboard. Finally he stowed away on an oyster sloop, "beneath a dirty Barral," and got as far as the Cape. Here the "honest

Ferryman" refused indignantly to take him across to the island. The miscreant would be there yet, said the *Gazette*, but an Indian squaw (a *squaw*, mind you, people repeated gleefully) eventually gave him a place in her canoe.

The fame of the Glorious Ninety-two spread wide. Petersham, New Hampshire,* dedicated a tree of liberty, burning Seventeen sticks and leaving Ninety-two branches to grow and flourish. The Philadelphia Legislature voted approval of the Massachusetts circular letter and sent a new song to the *Gazette*. Sam Adams's club liked to sing it.

> Now FARMER dear, we'll fill to you,
> May Heav'n its blessings show'r,
> As on the Glorious Ninety-two,
> And Seventeen devour.
>
> Mean abject Wretches! slaves ingrained,
> How dare you show your Faces?
> To latest days go drag your Chains!
> Like other Mules or Asses.

In his handsome study at Province House, Governor Bernard sat with his head in his hands. The windows were open; they looked down a grassy terrace to Marlborough Street. It was a pleasant, busy prospect on a perfect June day, but the Governor himself was far from pleased. On his table lay a copy of the *Gazette* — "the weekly Dung Barge," the Tories called it. It carried, today, the Assembly's petition to the King for Bernard's removal as Governor. Bernard pulled it toward him, his face wry. Eight years of the most difficult service in the King's entire civil list, and this was his reward. The petition was one long string of abuse. Every order that the King, Lord Hillsborough, or any of the ministry had dispatched — and Bernard in turn had delivered to the Massachusetts Legislature — was laid, not to the responsibility of its instigators and authors in England, but directly at Bernard's door. "He has treated our Representative body with contempt. . . . He has indiscreetly and wantonly exercised the prerogative of the Crown in the repeated negative of Counsellors of unblemished reputation. . . . He has been a principal instrument in procuring a military force . . ."

* Now in Massachusetts.

What could he do now, Bernard wondered helplessly. Almost since the day eight years ago, when he landed in Boston — and especially since the passage of the Stamp Act — he had tried desperately to make Parliament, the ministry, the Lords of Trade, understand the seriousness of the American situation. He had drawn up and sent to England tentative plans for reforming the American governments on a constitutional basis. "Take the Americans at their word," he had written as long ago as '65. "Let them send representatives to parliament: thirty for the continent, fifteen for the islands* would be sufficient. Let the relation of America to Britain be determined and ascertained by a solemn Recognition, so that the rights of the American governments, and their subordination to that of Great Britain, may no longer be a subject of doubt and disputation."

And for reply, what had London sent him? The Townshend Act; the Mutiny Act for the quartering of soldiers; the new courts of admiralty; scores of orders, commands, and "advices" that had mounted to an insuperable barrier between mother country and colonies. Whenever trouble threatened, London wrote ordering Bernard to "prorogue the rebellious Massachusetts Assembly and close its doors." England simply could not comprehend the power — and the intelligence — of this stubborn people. The ministry persisted in looking on the disorders, especially in Boston, as mere mob tumult. "On your side the ocean," Bernard had lately written home in desperation, "it is the prevailing opinion that America, if let alone, will come to herself, and return to the same sense of duty and obedience which she professed before. Discerning and considerate men on this side the water expect no such thing . . . An American Representation in Parliament, an incorporating Union is the only Provision which can prevent a Separation of the Colonies from Great Britain. If it is not done soon, it will be too late; & a Separation will take place at no great Distance of Time."

Bernard had begged to be allowed to sail home, make his personal report to Parliament. The ministry had replied that they were sorry he was uncomfortable in Massachusetts. If he pursued a firmer course with the populace and ceased "making Concessions," they were sure everything would come right. "How," Bernard replied, "would it have served his Majesty's cause, for me to have pro-

---

* The sugar islands, including Jamaica, the Bahamas, Barbadoes, the Windward and Leeward Islands.

voked the people, in whose power I was, to have knocked me on the head, or drove me out of town?"

Thomas Hutchinson said he wondered the Governor was still alive, after transmitting such peremptory messages from Hillsborough to the Massachusetts House. God grant, prayed Bernard, the King's troops would arrive soon from Halifax! No doubt Boston would blame him and Hutchinson for their arrival. The Province still clung to the belief that King George was on its side. Wicked, designing men (meaning Bernard, Hutchinson and the ministry at London) had prevented their petitions, prayers and resolutions from reaching the royal ear. "Sir," the Massachusetts House had written Bernard only this month, "we will consider his most sacred Majesty, under God, as our King, our best protector and common Father; and shall ever bear him true and faithful allegiance."

What could one do with colonials like these? The people's party liked to call themselves Whigs; they corresponded cozily with the rebellious Wilkesite Whigs in England — sent a huge green turtle to London, weighing, of course, the symbolic ninety-two pounds. They were comfortably convinced that they had a large and devoted following in Britain. An American had dined with John Wilkes in King's Bench Prison, and wrote to the *Gazette* that he and Wilkes had drunk toasts "to the King, to Liberty, the FARMER, and James Otis, Esquire, of Boston." . . . On Castle Island in Boston Harbor, four of the five Customs Commissioners (one had taken sides with the people) promenaded the battlements, staring out to sea, looking longingly for the King's troopships. . . . What a farce, thought Governor Bernard, for the government of Great Britain to hide from a small city of some eighteen thousand people!

Not for a minute did Bernard believe the whole Province was in a state of rebellion. But they would be soon, he told himself, if England continued her policy. The few who led "the faction" in Boston were of an extraordinarily energetic and persistent disposition. Otis and Sam Adams never let up — not for a day, not for an hour. Their infernal newspaper "stung like an adder," Bernard said. And that other Adams, the legal fellow, was lost also, now, to the forces of law and order. John Hancock, who should have been a Tory, was fixed as firmly to Sam Adams, Bernard told himself bitterly, as the rattles to the rattler's tail. The party would never lack money, with Hancock behind it.

A boy whistled in the street, loud and shrill. The Governor rose nervously from his desk. "Tom Cod, Tom Cod!" the boy called, and other voices took it up: "Tom Cod, have you had your supper?" Bernard winced. He loved codfish, often went to market himself and picked out a big fresh fish, brought it home in a basket covered with a cloth. The town had discovered this; morning and evening the jeering call sounded below his window.

In September, a British officer arrived in Boston. Before he had time to walk up to Province House and make his report, news went round that he had come to arrange quarters for the Halifax troops, due in three weeks or sooner. Next morning, high on the staff at the top of Beacon Hill sat a tar barrel, filled with turpentine, ready to be fired — ancient sign of the Province "when the first enemy ship is sighted."

Everyone saw it. *Enemy ships — the frigates of Great Britain?* There was in this small gesture, this innocent-looking black barrel atop a pole, something more openly hostile, people knew in their hearts, than any move the Province had yet made. Governor Bernard saw the barrel too, and would have done well to ignore the sight. Instead, stung by repeated accusations from London of "leniency and softness," Bernard sent for the town selectmen, peremptorily ordered them to pull the barrel down before sunset. Sheriff Greenleaf, with three or four volunteers — all very scared — crept up Beacon Hill at dinnertime when the Sons of Liberty were off the streets. At imminent danger of tar and feathers, which the *Gazette* was pleased to call "the modern method of Chastisement," they got the barrel down. That it proved to be an old, quite empty nail barrel did not make the Governor feel any better.

But in spite of such brave gestures from the "Boston faction," the popular party was in a state of profound discouragement. Two months ago, because they would not rescind the circular letter, their Legislature had been prorogued by the Governor, not to meet until the following January. The power of proroguing or dismissing the Assembly was the biggest weapon Royal Governors had in hand; they relied on it for all extraordinary circumstances, knowing it left the Province helpless to assemble beyond its separate town meetings. In this month of September, 1768, the people knew it was imperative they meet before the British troops arrived. Some strong, concerted

expression of resistance must be voted, published, circulated through Massachusetts to its most distant borders. The Province could not sit supinely while Boston suffered so deep a humiliation.

It was James Otis who thought of a way to assemble the people in spite of Royal Governors and their decrees. On the twelfth of September, a town meeting was called. It was held in Faneuil Hall and opened solemnly with a prayer by Dr. Samuel Cooper. With much stamping and clapping, Otis was elected Moderator. He got up, suggested an urgent message to be sent out to the towns of Massachusetts, calling a "convention" at Boston for the twenty-second of September, ten days hence. He had the letter here, already prepared, Otis said, producing it.

Everyone knew that such a proceeding was entirely outside the law. Calling a convention would be tantamount to summoning a session of the Legislature itself: no one but the Governor had power to convene the Legislature. But the vote was carried.

In a corner of the hall, stacked neatly against the wall, were four hundred muskets. Pointing to them, Otis reminded his audience of the old Massachusetts law requiring every citizen to have by him a musket, a pound of powder and a pound of bullets, for use "when danger threatened." Otis asked the meeting to vote arms for Boston "according to this law." After the vote was taken, the muskets would be distributed.

"But what danger?" a voice asked innocently. "What danger threatens?"

Sam Adams got slowly to his feet. "Have you not heard?" he replied gravely. "We arm against a French fleet, coming down from Halifax." A howl of laughter answered him, but Sam raised a hand for silence. Tuesday next, he said, should be set aside as a day of prayer, when all men might invoke divine aid under the wrongs they now were suffering. Would the meeting vote for such a fast day?

This was a new departure altogether. Boston had tried ridicule, tried violence, almost tried murder. Now Boston was going to try prayer, concerted prayer, thousands of men and women on their knees, each moment of communion increasing their resolve. No one but the Governor had authority to proclaim general fast days. But town meeting voted the day of prayer, voted to arm themselves "against a new French war," then voted to include a record of these motions in the letter going out to the towns, that all the Province

might know how Boston, with God's aid, was prepared to defend herself. Express riders were sent to carry the letter north, south and west.

Lord Barrington in England pronounced this town meeting to be guilty of "high Crimes and Misdemeanors, if not of Treason." Impeachment was suggested for the men responsible; it would be eminently fitting that five or six such examples be chosen "from Boston, the only place where there has been actual Crime." [1]

On the twenty-second of September, representatives from nearly a hundred towns arrived in Boston for the "convention." They met in Faneuil Hall, on a day of rain and wind, prepared to sit a fortnight if necessary. Following carefully the regular procedure of town meeting, they elected Otis as Moderator, Samuel Adams as Clerk. ("Government by convention": the people had found a new method of governing themselves. From now on, whenever they met with royal opposition, they would resort to it. Government by convention was to lead directly to the Continental Congress.)

On the second day of meeting, the delegates had barely reached their seats when Governor Bernard's message arrived: "Break up this unlawful assemblage and separate yourselves!" Locking the doors, the convention sat on, for five days more. Nothing they said or did was extreme; Massachusetts as a whole was by no means as radical as the town of Boston. But the fact that delegates from the conservative western counties were present at all was highly significant. While they were still sitting, the first troopship from Halifax was sighted off Nantasket. Next day, six ships of war came into Boston Bay.

The convention, its business over, broke up and went home, while from Town Dock to Castle Island the Harbor was loud with the rattle of anchor chains, the boom of guns from Fort William saluting His Majesty's Navy. On the first of October, twelve ships of war (counting armed schooners) lay broadside to the docks with springs on their cables, their guns ready to fire. At noon the troops began to land on Long Wharf. Seven hundred strong, they marched up King Street, Queen Street and through Tremont to the Common. Drums beat, fifes squealed. At their head, officers in scarlet coats walked with drawn swords, as though taking possession of a conquered town. Crowds lined the streets, silent, making no protest. Beyond mere moral resistance they were helpless and knew it. But

in the evening, the selectmen refused point-blank to house the regiments. The quartering of troops was against Magna Carta, against the common law of England. Let the soldiers stay on the Common, though even that was bad enough, said the selectmen, ruining the town's pasturage as it did. Already, most of the cows had run up over the Hill; their owners were out searching for them.

Colonel Dalrymple, the commanding officer, somehow got the doors open to Faneuil Hall and the State House and put some of his men there; the rest he distributed in a warehouse on Wheelwright's wharf, in Murray's barracks nearby, and in the Linen Manufactory House south of Milk Street. The main guard was stationed in King Street, directly opposite the State House; Dalrymple placed sentinels at the steps. Across the square, cannon pointed straight at the doors.

In a week or two, more troops arrived from Ireland; General Gage came up from New York to see to their disposal. When the last ship was emptied there were about four thousand soldiers, one to every four inhabitants. Boston reacted in sullen bewilderment. It was like living in a garrisoned town. The streets, the shops, the markets swarmed with soldiers. It was impossible to buy good fish or meat; the officers managed to take the best. The troops expressed themselves in raptures over the cheapness of Boston rum; the taverns did a huge business. As cold weather came on and the deep New England snows, the soldiers declared, shivering, that the only time a man felt warm in this cursed climate was when he was drunk, and acted accordingly.

Sunday, in the Province of Massachusetts, was traditionally quiet no matter what the provocation, with the streets empty even of pedestrians except those walking to church. Now the Sabbath was noisy with military parades. At Meeting time the bands played "Yankee Doodle"; locked windows in the churches could not keep out the sound. Nor was Boston used to the discipline of a regular army; the town found it hateful. One day, ten soldiers were whipped on the Common. Lines of people watched as the men, tied in a row, fell to their knees, screaming, their backs laid open and quivering. A deserter was caught, shot on the Common at seven in the morning and buried where he fell. It was the first military execution Boston had ever witnessed. When the volley sounded, Abigail Adams, standing back from her window, hands over her ears, swayed and nearly fainted.

Abigail and John, in Mr. Bollan's house, were in the very midst of the army. Each morning at dawn they woke to the drum and fife, the fall of marching feet, the crash of musket butts on cobbles. Directly below their window, Major Small's regiment went through its maneuvers; the commands rang out sharp. When John happened to come home after dark, sentinels challenged him at his own door. It was almost unendurable. "We shall have to move," John told Abby gloomily. "One of these nights I shall be tempted to break that sentinel's teeth, and it will not help the cause."

In December, another daughter was born to Abigail and John. She was a small child, pale and sickly. Susanna, they called her. The winter passed, a sad and anxious time. It was fearfully cold; in February the Harbor froze solid; people walked ashore from Castle Island on the ice. Beside the Long Wharf and Town Dock, masts and rigging dripped fat icicles. The British soldiers, altogether benumbed with cold, desired loudly and picturesquely to be sent to Greenland, Siberia — anywhere but Boston. The *Gazette* printed a forlorn letter from the town selectmen to Governor Bernard, saying someone must surely have "misrepresented us to the King." Otherwise, things would never have reached such a pass. Have the sentinels, A FREEMAN wrote the newspaper, a right to challenge the inhabitants? And if so, are not *manners* sometimes above the law? Must the sentinels be "so rude"?

The case of Hancock's sloop *Liberty* dragged on in the admiralty court, impossible to win and impossible, seemingly, to lose. "A painful drudgery," John called it. Jonathan Sewall, ironically enough, was Advocate General for the crown. The court seemed determined to summon the whole of Boston as witnesses, including the tradesmen from whom Hancock bought his groceries and his very ancient aunt, whose husband had made the original family fortune. Nobody could be found to testify against Hancock, although at least three hundred and fifty people had taken part in the riot. Perjury was flagrant. People said openly that because the admiralty courts were "unconstitutional," perjury therein was no crime. At the next term of Superior Court, Chief Justice Hutchinson took occasion, in one of his famous charges to the Grand Jury, to give specific warning against this crime of perjury "which strikes," he said, "at the very root of security in all society."

Newspapers followed Hancock's case in detail. The Boston *Eve-*

ning Post in particular discussed the various points of law. The prosecution had been based on an act of Parliament of 1765, imposing a duty of seven pounds per tun on wines imported from Madeira. John contended the law was unconstitutional — "made without our consent," he said. "My client, Mr. Hancock, never voted for it and he never voted for any man to make such a law for him." In England a bill could not become a law without consent of the people. The authors of the act themselves acknowledged this, then got round the point by declaring for consent by construction, by interpretation rather than by vote — a *virtual* consent. "This," John argued, "is deluding men with shadows instead of substance. Construction has made treason where the law made none. Whenever we leave principles and clear, positive laws, and wander after constructions, we get too far from fact and truth and nature. We are lost in the wild regions of imagination and possibility, where arbitrary power sits upon her brazen throne and governs with an iron scepter."

THE MERCHANTS OF BOSTON published "Observations" on the case. John's words came very close to home; their application was general. Parts of his argument were borrowed by the Massachusetts House of Representatives for use in their petitions and letters to the Governor. But on March 26, 1769, Jonathan Sewall announced that the case was dropped; His Majesty would prosecute no further. (He might have added that the spectacle of mass perjury day after day on the witness stand was not conducive to an obedient Massachusetts.) John Adams was glad to be done with the whole business. "I was thoroughly weary and disgusted," he wrote, "with the court, the officers of the crown, the cause, and even with the tyrannical bell that jangled me out of my house every morning." [2]

In April, John moved his family from Brattle Street up to Cold Lane by the Mill Pond. The house was not so comfortable as the old one, but at least it was farther from the soldiers. In May the General Court convened for its regular spring session, complaining that cannon pointed "at the very door of the State House where this Assembly is held." Boston town meeting sent Instructions to its Representatives, once more choosing John as draftsman. "The debates of our assembly must be free," John wrote. "Common decency as well as the honor and dignity of a free legislature will require a removal of those cannon and guards, as well as that clamorous parade which has been daily round our court house since the arrival of his

majesty's troops, and sometimes while the highest court of judicature has been sitting there, on the trial even of capital cases."

The Instructions were long and very plain. This time they sounded like John Adams; this time the whole tone was his.* In bitter protest against the juryless admiralty courts, John borrowed a paragraph or two from the brief he had used in Hancock's case. He cited my Lord Coke, quoted Magna Carta: *"No freeman shall be taken or imprisoned but by lawful judgment of his peers. . . .* Many of your fellow citizens, gentlemen," the Instructions went on, "have been worn out, within the year past, with attendance on these courts, in defence against informations for extravagant and enormous penalties."

Everyone in town meeting knew that no lawyer in the Province had spent so much time in admiralty court as John Adams. They knew also that he was to argue, this month of June, a suit far more notorious than Hancock's case of the sloop *Liberty*. It was an impressment case, and as such the eyes of all New England were turned upon it. Nothing roused Americans to greater fury than the Royal Navy's practice of kidnaping citizens, forcing them into service.

This, moreover, was to be a trial on capital charges: the lives of four men depended on the verdict. During the previous April the British frigate *Rose* had been cruising offshore, looking for sailors to augment her crew. (The Royal Navy seemed forever short of hands.) About six leagues from shore, the *Rose* stopped a Marblehead brigantine, bound home from Europe; the *Rose's* officers boarded her and tried to take off four men. They resisted, and a lieutenant from His Majesty's Navy was killed in the fight.

Four American sailors were accused of murder, and the case scheduled for a special court of vice-admiralty, created by act of Parliament to try cases of murder and piracy on the high seas. James Otis was engaged as senior counsel for the sailors, John as his assistant. But Otis, unfortunately, was going through what Boston called "one of his unlucid intervals," and would not even discuss the case, let alone appear in court. The whole burden rested on John. The court consisted of Governor Bernard, Governor Wentworth of New Hampshire, Chief Justice Hutchinson, Judge of Admiralty

---

* The Instructions (1769), in John's handwriting, may be seen in the Rare Book Room of the Boston Public Library.

Auchmuty, Commodore Hood (Commander of all British ships of war in American waters), and fifteen counselors from Massachusetts, New Hampshire and Rhode Island.

The day came; the court met. John presented his four separate pleas. They had taken him whole nights of care, study and deepest anxiety.* The witnesses were heard and cross-examined; there was no contradiction in their story: When the Marblehead brigantine was boarded by the British lieutenant and his men, the four American sailors selected for impressment retreated, with one Michael Corbet at their head, to the forepeak. Armed with nothing but knives and harpoons, they swore they would not be taken alive. . . . Let the British lieutenant step an inch beyond where he stood, Corbet shouted, and he was a dead man.

Young Lieutenant Panton, brave, disdainful and completely ignorant of the incredible skill of a whaling man with a harpoon, stepped forward. Instantly, blood gushed from his neck and he fell; Corbet's harpoon had severed his jugular vein as neatly as ever it struck a whale's right eye. The four seamen then proceeded to get very drunk on a keg of rum they had with them in the forepeak, and were taken prisoner.

That was the story. The witnesses told it well; even the British sailors from the *Rose* agreed in every circumstance.

"It then became my turn," John wrote afterward, "to speak in defence of the prisoners. I had taken more pains in that case than in any other, before or since; I had appealed to Heaven and earth; I had investigated all laws, human and divine; I had searched all authorities in the civil law, the law of nature and nations, the common law, history, practice, and everything that could have any relation to the subject. All my books were on the table before me, and I vainly felt as if I could shake the town and the world. A crowded audience attending, still as midnight, in eager expectation.

"I had scarcely risen and said, — May it please your Excellencies, and your Honors, my defence of the prisoners is, that the melancholy action for which they stand accused is justifiable homicide, and therefore no crime at all, — and produced one authority very plump to the purpose — when Hutchinson darted up and moved that the court should adjourn to the council chamber! No reason was given;

* For John's own original notes on this case, see *Works*, II, p. 526.

not a word was said; away marched their Excellencies to the council chamber."

John stood astounded. Court would resume next morning, Hutchinson had said. Was sentence to be given without defense counsel being heard at all? What lay behind this — why had the judges been at such pains to shut him up? John went home, carrying his books with him, and the thick piles of paper that made up his four separate pleas. That evening and most of the night he thought about what had happened: reviewed the scene, searching a clue. . . . Prominent among his lawbooks laid out on the table at the trial had been a bound set of the British *Statutes at Large* — the only complete set, John had reason to believe, on the continent. These lay open at a statute expressly prohibiting impressment in America — "almost the only British statute," John wrote later, "that included the word or idea of impressment. I was determined that if the law of God, of nature, of nations, of the common law of England could not preserve the lives of my clients, that statute should, if it could."

Chief Justice Hutchinson, from his place on the judges' dais just above, had leaned forward, peering down at the table and recognizing, John was certain, the book of statutes. Had this recognition played a part in Hutchinson's startled rise from the bench, his totally unexpected motion for adjournment? The Chief Justice knew, all the judges knew, that John's argument would be published in the *Gazette*, circulated through the Province and beyond, and with it the British statute prohibiting impressment.

At nine next morning, John was back in the courtroom. "Never," he wrote, "was a more gloomy assembly of countenances, painted with terror and horror, than the audience showed, expecting a sentence of death. The court appeared; the prisoners were ordered to the bar. The president arose, and pronounced the unanimous sentence of the court — that the killing of Lieutenant Panton was justifiable homicide in necessary self-defense. Auchmuty squealed out, 'The judgment of the Court is unanimous,' and not another word was said."

John was enormously relieved. His clients' lives were saved. But as he left the court and walked home he could not suppress a mounting chagrin that his work had all been wasted.[3] Days and nights of care and labor had gone into preparation for this argument — and then

the case was won without him! Long ago in Worcester, Jonathan Sewall had said it was foolish to work so hard, to waste oneself uselessly. "A man can win a race without stripping the skin from his feet," Sewall had said. John remembered it now, despondently.

But if John considered the case had been won without him, the Province of Massachusetts felt differently. To them John Adams of Boston, singlehanded, had saved the lives of four valiant Americans who had been attacked with intent to kidnap and impress. From now on, the people's party claimed John Adams as their lawyer.

It was flattering, certainly; yet it was not a position John craved. Not only was it unremitting, exhausting, but it brought in little or no money. The case of the four sailors had been almost a labor of love. John began to wonder, anxiously, if he had the right to give so much time and strength to the Sons of Liberty, although the cause lay so close to his heart and its principles were indubitably worthy of any sacrifice. But was a husband, a father, justified in sacrificing his family thus? The cause was certainly killing James Otis, if slow oncoming madness could be called death. For Samuel Adams on the other hand it was somehow different. Politics was Sam's avowed *métier*, his career and his life. Cousin Sam had confessed he never gave a thought to the financial morrow. Four thousand pounds in debt to Boston, he could sleep peacefully at night and let his good wife do the worrying — Sam called it the "managing" — while John Hancock or the Sons paid his debts by subscription.

Such inattention to material things was an excellent trait, perhaps, but one hardly possible to — John acknowledged it — a barrister, with a growing family to support and no money beyond what he earned in the law courts . . . Two small, helpless daughters and a son lived now in his house — a son to whom it was John's deep ambition to accord, when the boy should come of age, a position, a starting point far more favorable than his own had been at a comparable time of life. John Quincy Adams, when he emerged from Harvard, should not be forced to flounder among strangers in the country, unknown, unrecognized, teaching school for a pittance. With God's help, John Quincy Adams, if he proved worthy, should rank with the best of them, alongside of — well, not the Winthrops and the Saltonstalls perhaps, but the Cushings and Sewalls and Otises of this Massachusetts world.

John had forsworn the patronage of the crown and all that it implied of prestige and fortune. That much he had done for the cause of liberty; he would do it again tomorrow. But must he sacrifice everything, he asked himself now: his law practice, his means of livelihood, the advancement of his family? Again and again the question rose, revolved painfully in John's mind. His legal practice was excellent. In a year or two, if he applied himself as he should, he would have more cases per year than any lawyer in Massachusetts. . . .

Young men studying law came to John now, asked him to take them into his office as clerks. John took two, then worried lest his colleagues think him ostentatious. "What shall I do with two clerks at a time?" he wrote in his diary. "And what will the bar and the world say?" It was a responsibility to have the education of these young men in his hands. John remembered Mr. Putnam and his own desperate, lonely seeking among the lawbooks at Worcester. He must not neglect these students as he himself had been neglected. He must instruct them carefully, help them in their most difficult search. "For the advancement of these young men I can do little," John added. "For their education much, if I am not wanting to myself and them."

Summer came on, hot and very dry. The Province received notice that Governor Bernard was going home to England, "to lay before His Majesty the state of this Province." Massachusetts would have preferred other ambassadors; she knew well the color Bernard's story would take. Moreover, the King had "rewarded" Bernard with a baronetcy. "For his faithful service," the report read. This last, for the Province, was a vital blow. How much longer could they believe in the good will of a monarch who laid a laurel wreath upon the brow of their worst and bitterest enemy? . . . In Harvard College, someone cut the heart out of Bernard's portrait and left it hanging on the wall.

Late in July, the British warship *Rippon* arrived, sent up from Virginia to carry the Governor home. Bernard boarded her, leaving his wife and ten children to follow on the next packet. Just outside the Harbor, the *Rippon* was becalmed for a day and a night. Instead of the customary salvos of respect for a governor's departure, Bernard heard bells peal for joy, cannon boom in celebration. On Hancock's wharf the flags flew, and when the sun sank and dark came on, Bernard saw, high above Fort Hill, huge bonfires against the sky.

Boston, the *Gazette* announced next day, was "free of a scourge to this Province, a Curse to North America, and a Plague on the whole Empire of Britain."

Two weeks later, the Sons of Liberty, three hundred and fifty strong, celebrated the anniversary of August Fourteenth, 1765, when Boston had made her first public protest against the Stamp Act. There was a great procession through town; and then, in chariots and chaises, everyone drove out to Dorchester for what John Adams described as "a Feast." John went reluctantly, feeling, he said, as if it were his duty to be there. "Jealousies arise from little things, and many might suspect I was not hearty in the cause if I had been absent. Whereas none of them are more sincere and steadfast than I am."

But he had a good time in spite of himself. The guests sat out of doors, "at two tables," John wrote, "laid in the open field by the barn, with between three and four hundred plates, and an awning of sailcloth overhead." Mr. Philemon Dickinson* was there from Philadelphia and a Mr. Reed from New Jersey, "Both cool, reserved and guarded all day," John noted. Three pigs were barbecued; smoke floated deliciously from the charcoal pits where they swung. There was boiled codfish with egg sauce, chickens, deep blueberry pie, and a hogshead of Madeira that must surely, everyone said, have come from the sloop *Liberty*, it was so fine and mellow. The men sang a new song by Benjamin Church and then the FARMER's "Liberty Song." Sam Adams, standing on a chair, gave out the verses solo in a sweet, rather small voice, then waved his hands in genial leadership while the company thundered out the chorus:

[*Sam A.*] Come join hand in hand, brave Americans all,
    And rouse your bold hearts at fair LIBERTY's call;
    No *tyrannous* acts shall suppress your *just claim*,
    Or stain with *dishonour* AMERICA's name.
    Our worthy *forefathers*, let's give 'em a cheer,
    To *climates unknown* did courageously steer;
    Thro' *oceans* to *desarts* for *freedom* they came,
    And dying bequeath'd their *freedom* and *fame*.
        [*Chorus*: Now FARMER dear . . .]

---

* Brother to John Dickinson, who wrote the famous *Letters from a Farmer in Pennsylvania*.

[*Sam A.*] The *tree* their own hands had to liberty rear'd,
They liv'd to behold growing strong and rever'd;
With transport they cried, "Now our wishes we gain,
And our children shall gather the fruits of our pain."
[*Chorus*]
[*Sam A.*] This bumper I crown for our *sovereign's* health,
And this for *Britannia's* glory and wealth;
That wealth and that glory immortal may be,
If *she* is but *just* and if we are but *free*.

John lifted his face and roared with the rest. He loved to sing; at such times his round face became even rounder and pinker. A Mr. Balch, next on the program, entertained with his famous mimicry. There were forty-five toasts, beginning with the King and Queen and ending with "Strong halters, firm blocks and sharp axes to all such as deserve either." Nobody got drunk. "This," John wrote in a burst of enthusiasm, "is cultivating the sensations of freedom."

Such festivals, John thought, were indubitably promoted by Otis and Sam Adams to "tinge the minds of the people, render them fond of their leaders in the cause and bitter against all opposers." Nevertheless, pleasant as it had been today, doubt once more assailed John as to his own part in such celebrations. Defending the Sons in the admiralty courts was one thing; it was another to sit all afternoon in a field under an awning, drinking toasts and singing songs. And no matter how stringently John tried to resist, his days were more and more taken up by the cause. Even his Saturday afternoons were gone. Around one o'clock, somebody invariably stopped at the house and took him down to the *Gazette* office on Queen Street to help prepare Monday's paper. On the second floor above the press, in a room full of desks and tables littered with paper, ink and old newspapers, Otis and young Josiah Quincy were to be found writing, or busy with scissors and paste. Dr. Church was there, Dr. Joseph Warren and, of course, Sam Adams. John threw himself into the work, did his share with the others. But he did it with a kind of detachment, aware that it was not his natural function. "A curious employment," he wrote one night after such a session, "cooking up paragraphs, articles, occurrences, &c., working the political engine!"

Otis himself was becoming difficult, unpredictable, capricious in what he said and did. Often it was hard to tell if he were drunk or

sober. Along the streets he walked with his head down, muttering, sometimes raising his head to stare wildly, letting out some ejaculation or oath. His friends tried to protect him, walked home with him after a meeting of the political clubs and left him only outside his door. One evening in September, 1769, Otis got into a brawl at the British Coffee House, a favorite haunt of army officers and Court party men. It was a serious affair; Otis was carried home with a deep wound in the head. He engaged John Adams as counsel, took the matter to court and sued his assailant, a customhouse official named Robinson. John won from the jury a three thousand pounds award. When Otis refused to take a penny of it, declaring that insults to honor and patriotism could not be assuaged by gold, the Province applauded mightily, reinstated their hero in his former place of esteem and tried not to believe he would get himself into another such fracas before the year was out.

Nevertheless, men hesitated to engage Otis as legal adviser. Young Josiah Quincy, looking through the cases listed for the current term of Superior Court, saw that he himself had 9 cases, John Adams 60, and James Otis only 4. John grieved for his friend, noted in his diary each change for the better or worse. "Otis is in a confusion; he loses himself, rambles and wanders like a ship without a helm. Tonight he attempted to tell a story which may at any time be told in three minutes with all the graces it is capable of, but he took an hour. I fear he is not in his perfect mind. I tremble, I mourn for the man and his country. Many others mourn over him, with tears in their eyes."

The Province loved James Otis, mad or sane. So did John; to make this farewell by inches, as it were, was very painful. How many years he had known and admired the man! John recalled the first time he had seen Otis — that October morning of '58 in Boston's courtroom when John had ridden from Braintree to make the acquaintance of the bar. Otis had been young then, forceful, pungent in all he said and did. Now, only eleven years later, he was an object of pity. He looked an old man, the very ruin of greatness.

Gridley, Thacher, Otis, Benjamin Pratt — the names ran darkly through John's mind. *One-legged Benjamin, whose bite followed close on his bark.* . . . Dead and in their graves, all but Otis, whose very existence was a tragedy. Other men had risen, stood now in their places; the world would soon forget them. How brief life was and how precarious! A man must use every minute, every dis-

cipline to achieve even a small success, a small portion of wisdom before life made an end. There was no doubt that Oxenbridge Thacher as well as Otis had fallen a sacrifice to his country; it was well known that Thacher had worked himself into a consumption at the time of the Stamp Act. He himself, John thought now, must be very watchful; he must not allow his feelings to master him. In his way he knew himself to be as impulsive, as quick to anger as Otis himself. He must use discipline, preserve his health, spend more time in the open air, take walks and exercise, avoid crowded meetings and late hours.

Perhaps it was nothing more than fatigue; but whatever the reason, John's depression deepened as November arrived, and with it the first flurries of snow. He did not see, John told Abigail, how they could live through another winter with the British troops in the city. A comet appeared in the eastern sky; this time people looked on it as a bad omen. If it came between us and the sun, dire things would follow. Professor Winthrop of Harvard wrote to the *Gazette*. Comets weren't bad omens, he said severely. They did not blow up unexpectedly like Guy Fawkes's gunpowder, or plunge from the sky and land red-hot in people's backyards. Comets were natural phenomena, their motions predictable. . . . Nobody believed him.

John went off to the country, riding circuit again, very pleased to be out of town. The bare fields, windswept, lonely, the wide country sky were somehow comforting. Even the work in court was a welcome change, having no possible connection with politics. In Salem, John had a murder case. A young married woman had died after giving birth to a baby in her mother-in-law's house. Neighbors, suspicious because the dead girl had been hustled too quickly into her grave, had caused the body to be exhumed. In the presence of a huge, excited crowd, the dead girl was laid on a table in Salem courthouse, the suspected murderess was ordered to approach, touch the body on the neck. If the flesh showed color under her finger, she was guilty. It was the ancient medieval ordeal by touch, and it was never again to be used in America. The woman refused the ordeal, was indicted; her son secured John as lawyer.

John won his case, got the woman acquitted, then rode out of Salem and southward toward Boston. How awful to know that superstition and witchcraft still had a hold in one's own country, in modern times, in a century of enlightenment! Without his help, the woman

would have been hanged. John got home to Boston about sunset, dog tired. At the Charlestown ferry his horse balked, tossed his head and indicated a plain preference for the road to Cambridge and Braintree. . . . Standing in the heavy flatboat, holding his horse's bridle in the fading light, John wondered, as the shoreline approached, why he had ever left Penn's Hill, the farm and all the healthful, quiet pursuits of field and pasture. He had come to town to make his reputation in the law, make a name and possibly a fortune for himself and his family. In a way, he was succeeding — but at what expense! His peace of mind was gone. He had let himself be drawn into Boston politics, Provincial politics, to such an extent that he was carrying two full-time professions. It was more than any one man could stand, John told himself with a sense almost of desperation. His head ached, a little hacking cough had begun to bother him. . . .

Surely, the Sons of Liberty did not need him as much as he had let himself believe? Probably he had persuaded himself of his indispensability; men were liable to this kind of self-delusion. Someone else would serve quite as well. The ranks of life close quickly; Samuel Adams could discover patriots in a desert.

It was after dark when John rode down Hanover Street and turned north to Cold Lane. He left his horse at the livery stable on the corner and walked home, his head down. A British sentry challenged him. John gave his name and destination sharply; once more he had the impulse to knock the man down. Abigail opened the door, led her husband upstairs and put him to bed like a child, without waiting for an account of his journey. John fell at once into a troubled sleep in which the sound of drums beat dimly, mournfully.

An hour later he woke to music below his window. There were violins and a flute, men's voices, with one baritone, strong and true, rising above the rest. John sat up, bewildered. Abigail was standing by the window. "It's the Sons of Liberty," she said, "serenading you. They were here twice while you were away."

John went to the window in his nightshirt, threw it open, leaned out. There was a joyful greeting from the darkness below. Torches flared as the song rose again:

> JOHN ADAMS dear, we sing to you,
> May Heav'n its blessings show'r,
> As on the Glorious Ninety-two,
> And Seventeen devour . . .

John had never been so surprised in his life. The Sons of Liberty, he thought, singing to *me?* Far off on the Common, between intervals of the song, a drum beat. The voices rose louder, drowning the sound. "Abby!" John said. "Abby, listen! They are singing my name." He dressed quickly, ran down and let the singers in, took them to the dining room, gave them ale and cider from Braintree. There were about fifteen men, mostly mechanics and artisans. John knew five of them by name — Swift, Crafts, Henry Bass, George Trott, Mr. Edes the printer.

They had missed him, they told John politely, while he was off on his law business; they liked him within calling distance. They feared for the town this coming winter, with these damned red-coated soldiers mulling round the streets. Tonight they had come to show their respect and love. John Adams had done much for the cause; they hoped he was aware of their true gratitude? "We trust we have not disturbed your household tonight," Trott said, speaking carefully, managing to achieve a magnificent and unaccustomed formality — as if, John thought, amused and touched, he were addressing a bishop.

It was late, someone said, moving toward the door. They would go now and leave Mr. Adams's household to sleep in peace. But they would come again, from time to time, to show their good will, their very real need for his friendship.

*The Boston Massacre, March 5, 1770.
John accepts a guinea from the Irish
Infant, and Samuel Adams comes to him
with a little suggestion.*

EVEN a minor prophet could have foretold that trouble was to come to Boston. All appeals to England had failed; the new Prime Minister, Lord North, showed no disposition to understand American problems. "The drunken ragamuffins of a vociferous mob," he said, "are exalted into equal importance with men of judgment, morals and property. I can never acquiesce in the absurd opinion that all men are equal."

Few people in Massachusetts believed or even desired all men to be equal, but they did not like being referred to as a "vociferous mob." Feeling against the Townshend duties mounted. The Non-importation Association had powerful members among American merchants in coastal cities as far south as Georgia; they were extremely severe on men of business who broke the agreement by importing British goods for sale. Non-importation was the last remaining weapon. Loss of trade might rouse London merchants, Liverpool shippers, to force through Parliament a repeal of the Townshend Act.

The Boston *Gazette* each Monday printed prominently the names of such renegade traders as were discovered in New England. Thomas Hutchinson's two sons, Thomas and Elisha, were accused, forced to disgorge a whole warehouse of valuable cargo. The New York Association publicly charged John Hancock himself with permitting his ships to carry British goods. In the *Gazette*, Hancock

published indignant denial. But there was good reason for suspicion; certain "friends to Liberty" whose voices had been loudest at parades and bonfires, showed great ingenuity in smuggling British merchandise to port for future sale. They bribed British army officers for use of their names, caused large consignments of goods to be directed to them from England as if ordered for the troops. Such cargoes as were discovered by Association members were sent back on the next ship to Britain — a move very effective on the other side of the ocean. An Englishman wrote from London that ten thousand pounds of goods shipped back unsold had more influence on Parliament than a hundred thousand pounds of merchandise seized by the Sons and held in Boston warehouses against repeal.

American protest once more took violent form. Off Newport one July night the Sons swarmed out in rowboats to the sloop *Liberty* — now a customs raider — burned and scuttled her. In October a customs informer was tarred and feathered, carried on a rail through Boston streets. When John Mein, the Tory printer, exposed in his newspaper certain New England "Saints" who he said were violating their own Non-importation Association, he was attacked on Boston Common by twenty liberty boys and only by sheer luck escaped with his life.

The crown party in turn employed every weapon at its command. Because all judicial appointments were crown-made, most judges of the Superior Court were what Chief Justice Hutchinson still called "friends to government." It was no surprise to anyone when at the November term of court (1769), Josiah Quincy, Junior, was refused the title of Barrister. Young Quincy had taken no part in the riots, but he was, the Bench announced indignantly, far too "active in the opposition." *Wilkes Quincy*, the people called young Josiah now. Wilkes Quincy walked out of Superior Court with his golden head high, carrying the judicial reprimand like a coronet. He would manage quite as well, he told his colleagues of the Monday Night Club, "unsanctified and uninspired by the pomp and magic of the Long Robe." Moreover, he added, these troubles would not last forever; letters from England gave indication the Townshend duties would be repealed after the New Year. But it would not do to let the news out: the Sons might relax their vigilance. John Adams had an office near Quincy's, in King Street next door to what Boston now called the State House. The two had argued several cases in

partnership; the combination was proving most successful and both men enjoyed it.

Jonathan Sewall was appointed Judge of Admiralty for Nova Scotia, with a salary of six hundred pounds sterling a year and little work attached. (He still held, as well, the office of Attorney General of Massachusetts.) Chief Justice Hutchinson, traveling the quarterly circuit, grew even warmer and more hortatory in his addresses to the Grand Jury. In Worcester, Northampton and far-off Pittsfield on the western border, he took occasion to administer sharp rebuke. On these occasions, Hutchinson was more careful than ever to dress in full judicial regalia, with robe, white bands and shoulder-length wig. When his carriage approached a town, the sheriff with a white mace came out to meet him, escorted him ceremonially to the courthouse, and back to his inn when court rose at sunset or later. Concerning "riots, routs and unlawful assemblies," the Chief Justice gave especially solemn warning: "You gentlemen who live in country-towns seldom hear of these things. But we who live in trading-towns see, feel and hear often — that there is going to be a Rumpus, as it is called — a cant Word for a Riot."

John Adams read Hutchinson's jury lectures, pondered them, mulled them over angrily in his diary. Nothing the Chief Justice said was actually beyond the rights and duties of a judge, yet his continual harping on the crimes of treason, libel, rioting and unlawful assemblage was palpable propaganda. Hutchinson was using his high office for political purposes. Something must be done to circumvent him.

The bench, in truth, was the Tory party's last stand, the only really influential forum left open. In Boston proper, the liberty party had achieved nearly undisputed control. The four Representatives from the town — Otis, Sam Adams, Hancock and Cushing — began to set the political tone for the Province. (Even in Connecticut, the liberty party waited for directions from "the Boston seat.") Nevertheless, Hutchinson himself was still a well liked and powerful figure, particularly in the western counties. John Adams, riding circuit, had seen enough to prove it. In this business of influencing the populace, Samuel Adams insisted that a hair made the difference between success and failure, between the people's *yes* and its *no.* Thomas Hutchinson was a skillful man, intelligent, reflective. He had

the manners and dress of a prince, and a smile, when he chose to use it, that could disarm the dourest Yankee farmer in the mountain counties. Boston was in a dangerous mood, ready at any moment to burst into open conflict with the British troops. It was of utmost importance that the county towns, the country population, be kept in sympathy with the cause. Boston might well have need of help from outside — and very soon. That Thomas Hutchinson knew it and was using his judicial office to break down everywhere the spirit of rebellion, was plain.

As February arrived and the winter's snow piled deeper and dirtier along the gutters of Boston, tension seemed to mount, men's tempers were stretched unbearably. Early evenings saw the streets filled with young boys, rough, noisy, ready for trouble, quick with their jeering whistles and even quicker with snowballs, chunks of ice. Sober citizens had an uneasy suspicion that some of these boys were paid to insult or intimidate merchants who broke the Non-importation agreement. John himself was sure of it, although no one had told him outright. The thought was shocking. There was something terribly wrong, even sinister, about the deliberate employment of youth for such purposes. Not only was it corrupting to the boys themselves, but it was a weapon that, once unleashed, might get beyond control.

Thus far, in spite of riots, the scuttling of ships and wrecking of gentlemen's libraries, no blood had been shed. It was a fact amazing, and one in which the more thoughtful Sons of Liberty took pride. Massachusetts was by nature a peace-loving community. Even Governor Bernard, harassed by open rebellion, by open hatred and personal insult, had testified to this. At the time of the stamp riots, a visiting Englishman had asked Bernard one day, in the Council Chamber, how he dared walk the streets of Boston alone and unprotected. "The Massachusetts is not a bloodthirsty people," Bernard replied gravely, and the remark went around.

But the most peaceable community can be driven beyond control, and John, watching as the winter days went by, was anxiously aware of it. Not only were the troops a continued irritant, but the colonial position itself had become untenable, unworkable. Even if Parliament repealed the Townshend duties, it would probably be done with strings attached, as in the case of the Stamp Act. In God's name, John asked himself desperately, what were they thinking about, in White-

hall and Westminster? Men like Camden, Shelburne, Pitt, Burke, had shown understanding of the situation. Why did they not rouse themselves, exert their influence? Once American blood was shed, it might well be — John acknowledged with a shudder — too late.

John was greatly worried about matters at home in his own family. The baby Susanna, a year old at Christmas, had been sickly since birth. Now, in spite of all they could do, she grew worse. Abigail scarcely left the room; in the night, John waked to see her bending over the cradle or holding the child in her arms. Dr. Warren came often, suggested in vain every kind of gruel and feeding. It became plain the baby would not live through the winter.

By February she was dead. John's brothers brought the big farm sled in from Braintree; together the three men lifted the little coffin above the runners, drove it sorrowfully over the hard-packed snow to the burying ground beside Braintree Meeting-house. Abigail, prostrate with grief, exhausted with continual nursing, was too ill to go. Moreover, she was pregnant again, a baby was expected late in May. John, with Peter and Elihu, lowered the small wooden box from the sled. The ground was frozen hard as a stone; to dig a grave was impossible. Elihu fetched pine boughs and covered the coffin high. He would watch daily, he said, and when the thaw came he would return immediately and bury the child. All three men wept as they left the churchyard and walked slowly to the sled.

At home, John noted anxiously that Abigail, usually so resilient, so quick to rebound from illness or sorrow and so competent about the house, was not herself. She made no outcry and no complaint, but was unnaturally quiet, almost listless. John, coming home in the winter afternoons, would find her sitting in the dark by the window, gazing out, hands in her lap. When he tried gently to divert her, engage her in conversation, she turned away her head; John knew she did it to hide her tears. He felt lost and anxious; he had not realized how deeply he had come to count on Abby's good spirits, her strong, healthy response to all the demands of life. John felt uneasy, leaving her alone in the house with her two maids. The new houseboy was unreliable, always running into the street on some pretext, never at hand when needed.

On the twenty-second of February, John, walking up Middle Street on his way from some legal business near Hancock's wharf, saw a painted wooden head on a post, set up before Mr. Theophilus Lillie's

shop. It signified that Mr. Lillie had broken the Non-importation agreement, and no one was to buy from him. John stopped, deciphered three additional names painted clumsily below the head, then walked on. There was nothing new or particularly alarming about the incident; such signs were often to be seen around town. They were removed when the guilty merchant acknowledged his fault, forfeited his imported goods and swore publicly to observe the rules in the future.

But later that same afternoon, Mr. Lillie's nearest neighbor, Ebenezer Richardson, a customs informer and tide-waiter, came home from work and saw the sign. Without a moment's hesitation he took hold of the post, shook it angrily, dashed into his house, reappeared with an ax and took a swing at the base of the post. He had not struck three blows when a shrill whistle was heard and the street swarmed with boys. They hurled icy snowballs at Richardson, drove him inside, surrounded his house, flung stones and brickbats through the glass panes. Suddenly, at an upstairs window, Richardson appeared with a loaded musket. "By God!" he shouted. "I'll make a lane through you!" He aimed at the crowd and fired; the boys fell back instantly. In the cleared space a lad lay dead in the street.

Men came running from every direction. With a roar the crowd swept forward and into Richardson's house, seized him, put a halter round his neck, dragged him out and through the streets toward Fort Hill. On the way, by some miracle, he was deposited alive in the stone jail by the new Court House.

On the twenty-seventh of February, a great public funeral was held for the dead boy. (His name was Snyder; he was the son of a poor German immigrant.) John Adams walked behind the coffin with the rest. The day was cruelly cold. A light snow fell and the wind blew in hard from the east. The procession started under Liberty Tree and made its way north to the Town-house, then up to the burying ground by the Common. The line reached, John said afterward, nearly a quarter of a mile. It seemed endless, comprising young and old, high and low, women and girls as well as men. John Hancock was there, dressed from head to foot in richest black; Rowe the merchant marched with young Mr. Oliver Wendell. The Congregational clergy were out in force: Dr. Samuel Cooper of Brattle Street church, Dr. Eliot of the New North Meeting-house. Just ahead of John, hat in hand, his long white locks blown back and

wet with snow, walked Dr. Charles Chauncy of the First Church, senior minister of Boston.

All the boys in town had turned out; they walked two by two before their friend's coffin, very quiet and solemn. John had never beheld such a funeral. It was a sober, impressive sight, hundreds of citizens following the coffin of a poor untutored lad whose name few had known before, yet whose blood might well prove the first sacrifice to a great and common cause. The very orderliness of the affair added hugely to its significance. The procession came together quietly, marched in silence except for the tolling of bells. And when the grave was filled and the last prayer said, the crowds dispersed quickly, leaving the streets clear and empty as though nothing unusual had occurred.

In not one of these solemn communal gestures, these threats against the King's peace, did the troops intervene. When crowds collected, the red-coated sentinels vanished from the streets like snow in the sun. Quite obviously, they had orders to vanish. Their officers were in a position not only dangerous but absurd. British law forbade them to give the command to fire without permission from Hutchinson or someone in civil authority. The sentinels, consequently, were instructed to let almost anything pass rather than provoke open conflict. When thieves broke into Mr. Gray's house and the justice of the peace next day questioned the red-coated sentinel, the sentinel replied that yes, he saw two men force a window. How could he help it? He was posted on that very corner. "And did you challenge them?" the justice persisted. "No." "Why not?" Because, the soldier said stubbornly, he had orders to do nothing "which might deprive a man of his liberty."

The story circulated, losing nothing in the telling; it did not tend to make the Sons of Liberty less defiant. The soldiers were tormented on every hand; the provocation to retaliate was almost unendurable. "Bloody backs, bloody backs!" boys screamed after them in the streets. "Lobsters for sale. . . . Lo-obsters, who'll buy?" The soldiers cursed and spat. "Yankees!" they called back. "Damned mohairs. . . . Boogers!" John Adams, passing the guard on Water Street by Murray's barracks, himself sharply rebuked three urchins who were throwing ice at the sentry. Why there had not been an explosion long ago, nobody knew. Everyone expected it and dreaded the moment. In London, Benjamin Franklin wrote Dr. Cooper of the

Brattle Street church that he had been "in constant panic" since he heard of troops assembling in Boston.

The soldiers, poorly paid and idle, were eager for work that would bring them in a little money. One day — it was Friday, the second of March — three privates from the 29th Regiment strolled by Gray's ropewalk, just around the corner from their barracks. It was the eleven o'clock lunch hour; workmen had come out to take the air. One of them — a big fellow, a notorious brawler — approached the soldiers as they sauntered by, asked pleasantly enough if they wanted work for their spare time. Yes, one soldier replied; he would be glad to have work. The ropewalker replied softly, persuasively, while his friends watched in perfect silence. Whatever work he offered and in whatever words,[1] the uproar was instant and violent, raging until the bell rang to call the ropewalkers back to the yard. Nobody was seriously hurt; the ropewalkers won the fight, which had been ten to three anyway. But next Monday morning a poster appeared, tacked up around the water front:

BOSTON, *March* 5, 1770
This is to Inform the Rebellious People in Boston that the Soldyers in the 14th and 29th Regiments are determined to Joine together and defend themselves against all who shall Oppose them.
Signed, the SOLDYERS OF THE 14TH AND 29TH REGIMENTS.

No one ever found out who posted the sign, but there was more than a suspicion that it had not been the soldiers. Someone in Boston was trying to provoke an incident; someone, obviously, had decided there was no other way to get rid of the troops, get them out of town forever. It was impossible to make public protest. The Legislature, which had been due to convene in January, had been prorogued by Acting Governor Hutchinson until March 15. He had ordered it moreover to meet in Cambridge, safely out of the scene of possible conflict. The four Boston Representatives — Sam Adams, Otis, Hancock and Cushing — knew that even if they succeeded in putting through a resolution of protest against the presence of the troops, there was no likelihood it would be heard or regarded. The lines were tightening. On Monday, March 5, the tension snapped.

There was a layer of ice on the ground that morning; during the day a few inches of snow fell. In the afternoon the sky cleared, and

with sunset a young moon appeared over Beacon Hill, shining very bright, throwing shadows along the streets. Parties of boys, apprentices, soldiers, stood about; there seemed more than the usual crowd, cursing and jeering. From Murray's barracks, in Water Street, a party of ten or twelve soldiers emerged, armed with clubs and cutlasses. They were out for a stroll, they said. A small crowd of citizens collected near the wooden church on Brattle Square. Most of them had canes and heavy cudgels which they struck and clashed together noisily.

At a little after eight o'clock, Captain Goldfinch of the Army crossed King Street on his way to Murray's barracks. A sentinel was stationed as usual on the corner by the Custom House. As the Captain passed, a barber's boy whistled through his fingers and called out — with embellishments — that the Captain owed his master for dressing his hair. The sentinel gave chase, whacked the boy with the butt of his musket. The boy set up a howl calculated to raise the dead. By now the crowd before Murray's barracks had begun scuffling with the soldiers on guard, pelting them with snowballs and ice. Captain Goldfinch ordered his men within, shut the yard gate and promised the crowd that no more soldiers would be let out that night.

Quiet ensued, and things might have stayed quiet had the situation been let alone. But someone hoisted a boy through a window of the Brick Church at the North End of town, told him to climb the belfry and ring the bell as if for fire. The bell pealed wildly, and at the sound, men ran into the streets, carrying fire bags and buckets. (In this city of wooden houses the fire hazard was great; scarcely a week passed without one or two dwellings burning to the ground.) "Where is the fire?" people asked. "The bells did not tell the direction." "There is no fire," sober citizens replied. "There was a slight rumpus with the soldiers, but they are ordered to quarters. Go home, every man." King Street once more was empty; the same lone sentinel, firelock on shoulder, paced unmolested before the Custom House. But in Dock Square, just below, a man was addressing a gathering crowd; his voice could be heard a block away. (This was the mysterious stranger who was to figure so largely in the case — never identified, but always described as a "tall large man in red cloak and white wig.") As the man ceased speaking there was a cheer and the cry, "To the main guard!"

At about the same time — a little after nine — another crowd

moved toward King Street from the direction of Royal Exchange Lane. As they reached the sentinel by the Custom House, someone shouted, "Here is the soldier that struck the barber's boy!"

"Kill the soldier, kill the damned coward, kill him, knock him down!" voices cried. The sentinel, backing up the steps of the Custom House, shoved the rammer down his musket and primed it. Chunks of wood were thrown at him; pieces of ice, sharp-edged and heavy. The sentinel, dodging for his life, shouted for help. Captain Preston of the main guard heard him from Murray's barracks, sent a file of seven men across the square, headed by a very young, very flustered officer. The eight crossed the icy cobbles on the trot, pushed the crowd aside with threats from their bayonets and formed a half-circle round the sentry box. The crowd continued to jeer and hurl ice. Captain Preston himself appeared, ordered his men to prime and load.

There were now nine soldiers on the steps, counting Preston. The crowd before them numbered perhaps a hundred, whooping, cursing, whistling piercingly between their fingers and throwing anything that came to hand — clubs, oyster shells, icy snowballs. The big ropewalker — the man who had put the question last Friday on Gray's wharf — was much in evidence with his friends. "Damn you for cowards!" the crowd yelled at the soldiers. "Let's see you fire! . . . You dare not fire. . . . Lobsters! . . . Bloody backs! . . . Let's burn the sentry box. . . . Come on boys. . . . *Lobsters!* Who buys lo-obsters tonight?"

One of the soldiers, struck by a missile, lost his footing and fell; his gun flew out of his hand. No one heard the order to fire, though many afterward swore they heard it and that it came from Captain Preston. The eight soldiers, one after another, fired their muskets into the crowd. When the smoke cleared, five men lay sprawled on the snow — three dead, the others mortally wounded. For a brief moment the crowd seemed frozen motionless, silent with horror. Then the stillness was broken by the thud and rattle of rammers as the soldiers pounded a new charge down the muzzles of their guns.

Captain Preston ordered his men to withdraw across the street. The people surged forward, dragged their dead to cover, carried the wounded men away. Drums began to beat; soldiers from the 29th Regiment marched into the square, formed two platoons around the main guard. A third company took up position by the northeast

corner of the State House and at command, dropped to one knee in the position for street firing.

Suddenly, all over the city, bells began to ring the alarm. The streets were full of men carrying cudgels, knives, any weapon they could find, running toward Dock Square. The cry of "fire" was drowned in another cry: "To arms! *Town-born, turn out!*" In his house at the north end of town, Governor Hutchinson heard the bell in the Brick Church nearby. Almost before he could reach his front door, men were on the steps, breathless with news. The Governor must come immediately to King Street, "or the town will be all in blood." Making his way with difficulty to the market place in Dock Square, Hutchinson found himself in a pushing, dense, excited throng, all carrying cutlasses or heavy sticks and calling for guns, muskets. Hutchinson did his best to make himself heard, climbed the steps of a dwelling house and tried to compel attention from the people. He was pushed roughly into the street; almost fell, heard his name spoken with a curse.

From a nearby doorway, friendly hands reached out, drew Hutchinson to safety. The Governor let himself be led through the house, then slipped out and into King Street by a private way. The square was jammed with people, apparently waiting for Hutchinson, expecting him. He was forced bodily into the State House, up the stairs to the Council Chamber and out onto the balcony. In the moonlight he faced a seething, roaring, angry mass that filled the square and one side of the street. On the other side the soldiers stood or kneeled, their muskets primed and pointed. Behind Hutchinson the lighted windows threw him boldly into silhouette. The crowd, sighting him, was silent; on their upturned faces the moon shone almost bright as day. Hutchinson stood a moment and waited.

"Go home," he said at last. "Let the law settle this thing! Let the law have its course. I myself will live and die by the law. Let you also keep to this principle. Blood has been shed; awful work was done this night. Tomorrow there will be an inquiry. . . ."

"Tonight!" the crowd roared back. "Preston . . . Preston . . . Where is Captain Preston? Arrest him! Get the soldiers off the streets!"

Hutchinson, raising both hands, tried to speak, to say he had no authority over the soldiers, could not give orders to the military. . . . An angry roar cut him short; the crowd surged forward.

Colonel Dalrymple, Commander in Chief of British troops in Boston, stepped suddenly out to the balcony, spoke rapidly to Hutchinson. His men would take Captain Preston and the soldiers to the jail, where they would be safer than in the barracks; Preston had already suffered physical abuse from the people. He himself would order every soldier off the streets. . . .

In a few moments the soldiers by the State House rose from their kneeling posture; the order "Shoulder arms!" was heard. The troops marched to barracks while the people fell back to let them pass. The crowd began slowly to disperse. By three o'clock in the morning it was over; the streets empty save for a guard of citizens — about a hundred men who had formed themselves into a watch and patrolled slowly about King Street, the square and the docks.

When the first alarm bell rang, John Adams had been down at the South End of Boston with his political club, which met that night at the house of Mr. Henderson Inches. Supposing the alarm to be for fire, the members snatched up their hats and cloaks and went out to help. It took John some time to make his way to King Street. As he went he tried to learn what he could — the soldiers had fired on the inhabitants, killed some and wounded others; expresses had been sent out of Boston to warn the countryside. John's immediate concern was to get home to his wife. Should there be more shooting, the danger of fire would be great. Little Abby, aged four, no doubt was already terrified; the fire bells always frightened her. John Quincy was a heavy, strong child; his mother could scarcely lift him. Most certainly she must not lift him now, in her condition, and run out on the icy street. . . .

John arrived at the State House in one of those lulls that come in scenes of riot; he saw nothing but the soldiers grouped around their cannon on the corner. He crossed Cornhill and began to run down Boylston Alley, his cloak thrown over one shoulder, his hat jammed on the back of his head. It was dark in the narrow way, the moon hidden by rooftops. John's lantern was out — as a matter of fact, he had not taken time to light it. He held it from him as he ran.

In Brattle Square, he checked himself to a walk. Two companies of regulars were drawn up before the big church; in the moonlight John could see their bayonets glitter. They took up the whole side of the street, leaving only a few feet for passengers. John walked

by the line, almost under their guns, terribly anxious lest they challenge him, refuse to let him proceed. Many of the officers knew him by sight; Major Small might be among them. . . .

He passed safely by. At home he found Abigail upstairs with the children, the house surprisingly peaceful and calm. Of course she had been frightened, Abby said. But she had got little Abby to bed and to sleep. John Quincy as usual had cried to go out and see the guns go off; she had had to be sharp with him to make him obey. Up here at the North End of town the noise had not been great, once the bells stopped ringing. Indeed, she had heard nothing beyond the bells and the actual firing.

John and Abigail went to bed, got what sleep they could. Next morning early, John walked to his office by the State House door. Already the streets were full of people. Many were obviously from the country; they carried muskets; their clothes in bundles were tied ludicrously to the barrels. Someone must have sent for them in the night, John thought. He remembered hearing Molineux, the new captain of the liberty boys, say something about dispatching expresses to Roxbury and Dorchester to warn the countryside.

In front of John's office a little crowd was waiting. Benjamin Edes of the *Gazette* was there, Crafts the painter and Swift of the North Enders. John took them inside with him. "How many were killed last night?" he asked quickly. "Four," Ben Edes replied. "One was Sam Gray, the ropewalker that started the fight Friday morning on the docks. Crispus Attucks was killed, the big mulatto. You must have seen him around town, Mr. Adams. The two others were simply standing in the street looking on — one a lad of seventeen. Patrick Carr the Irishman is dying at his house of a gunshot wound. Dr. Warren is with him. Captain Preston is in jail. They have been questioning him all night; there is no doubt he gave the command to fire."

"When the crowd dispersed at three this morning," Edes went on, "we tried to countermand the order we had sent the Sons in the neighboring towns, asking for help and arms. But we were too late. The people are flocking to town; have you seen them, with bundles on their muskets?"

"Get them out of town," John replied roughly. "Get them home. Where is Sam Adams? We had best organize a citizens' watch for tonight. There will be more trouble when the sun goes down."

He had scarcely finished speaking when there was a rapid knock

at the street door. A man stumbled in, his clothes torn, tears streaming down his face. John recognized him immediately as Mr. Forester, a friend of the British officers — surely, the last person John expected to see in his office at such a moment and in such a condition. Around town Forester was known as "the Irish Infant," a good-natured man who liked to take his dram at the British Coffee House. John spoke quickly to Ben Edes, who moved at once to help clear the office, get the men out of the door and off the stoop. John turned the key in the lock.

Forester, breathing hard, sat down and was silent a moment, struggling for composure. He came directly from Captain Preston in prison, he said at last. He bore a message, a solemn message from a very unfortunate man. Preston's life was in danger; he desperately needed a lawyer. No one would help him. Preston was in terrible condition, bruised all over, his face and eyes swollen and black. Since three this morning they had questioned him; he had had no sleep all night. None of them had slept, Forester added, his fingers twisting nervously. Preston's examiners were trying to make him say it was he who had given the fatal order to fire into the crowd. . . .

"As God is my witness," Forester said, gripping the arms of his chair, his eyes wide with distress, "as God is my witness, Preston is an innocent man! His soldiers were defending their lives from the mob. . . . Mr. Adams, were you in King Street last night? Did you see what happened?"

John shook his head shortly, made no answer. "Why are you here, Mr. Forester?" he said at last.

"They will try Preston within ten days," Forester said. "He has no one to defend him. Mr. Adams, would you consider — will you take his case?"

Forester almost sobbed; the words came out in a rush. Already this morning he had called on three of the crown lawyers* — naturally, he went first to them. They would not defend Preston, would not even touch the case. Mr. Auchmuty, the admiralty judge, was the only one who would listen. Auchmuty said he would act for Preston on one condition: if John Adams of the people's faction would serve as counsel with him. "After that I went to Mr. Josiah Quincy, Junior, next door to you," Forester continued. "The eight soldiers are in

---

* For the political implications of the ensuing trial, see Notes for Chapter Twenty-one.

jail, too, for murder. Mr. Quincy gave the same answer as Auchmuty. He will defend Captain Preston if you will act with him."

Forester raised his eyes wildly; John watched him without speaking. . . . So the crown lawyers would not defend Preston! Their own man, and they dared not. They were afraid of the mob. Thousands would be on the streets today, hundreds had already gathered round the stone jail. Coming down Queen Street this morning, John had heard a name called again and again, in a kind of roaring chant. Now he knew the name had been Preston. . . .

Color rose in John's face. So far, he had felt nothing but anxiety, a great dread and horror that such things could come to pass in his own town, his own country. Now, suddenly, he was angry. Here in Massachusetts Bay, where the English law gave everyone fair judgment by trial of his peers — here a man, an Englishman, lay in jail in peril of his life, and the bar denied him counsel! Auchmuty the Younger — John knew him well. He had lately been named Judge of Admiralty for all New England. He was a confirmed, even a bitter Tory and very much of a swell, driving his own coach and four, trading blatantly on the reputation of his distinguished father. He was not a college graduate; John had little respect for his knowledge of the law. (Jeremiah Gridley, John remembered now, had been openly scornful on the subject.) Yet Auchmuty was an able advocate in his way, a good jury lawyer, quick with his tongue and capable of an eloquent appeal. With someone behind him to bolster his dramatics by sound legal props, Auchmuty might do well for Preston. No doubt all the judges would be scared to death of the mob — except Hutchinson, who would naturally refuse to serve anyway. As for Josiah Quincy, at twenty-six, he was a clever lawyer and a very eloquent man. But he was furiously impulsive, apt to let his feelings run away with him in court. As likely as not he would rise at the trial and orate to the bench on the meaning of "liberty."

Forester was talking. "Captain Preston is innocent," he repeated. Tears rolled down his face. "You will excuse me, Mr. Adams . . . Before God in heaven, Preston acted in self-defense! He is an innocent man."

"That," John said coldly, "must be ascertained at his trial."

Forester drew a long, shuddering breath and sat upright; he seemed afraid to speak. Outside in the street the clamor increased; the square before the State House was filling with people. A man ran heavily

past the window; there were shouts. There flashed through John's mind the scene at Salem courthouse last autumn. . . . An old woman, gray-haired, haggard, accused of murder. *Ordeal by touch.* The people would have hanged her, not on evidence but on superstition . . .

I will take this case, John thought suddenly. *I will defend Preston if it is the last thing I do.* . . . And he would use no tricks of the trade. No sophistry, no lurid adjectives. No trembling voice or pointing of the finger at a hypnotized jury. Fact, evidence and the law would try Captain Preston. There were things at stake greater than a man's life — greater than nine men's lives, for if he defended Preston he must *ipso facto* defend the soldiers with him. And if what he had gathered since morning were true, this would prove as important a case as had been tried in any court of any country in the world.

John was suddenly swept with emotion, almost with awe, at the thing he had undertaken. The implications of it staggered him, towered higher than he could see. He got up, cleared his throat. "If Captain Preston," he said, "thinks he cannot have a fair trial without my help, then he shall have it. Here is my hand."

Forester sprang forward, seized John's hand and wrung it. Then he dug in three different pockets and brought up, after some struggle, a single guinea. He held it out. "A retaining fee," he said, his face entirely serious. John took the money with equal seriousness, bowed gravely. If he never received another cent for this most difficult, perhaps impossible task, both men knew the coin was binding. Avoiding a second wringing of the hand, John opened the door, bade Forester good morning and saw him down the steps.

The crowd by the door had increased; they pressed forward. "It's the Irish Infant," someone said. "It's him all right!" Benjamin Edes of the *Gazette* stepped out; close behind him was Swift of the North End gang. "What's the Irish Infant coming to *you* for, Mr. Adams?" Swift asked roughly.

John stood on the steps; his eyes went from face to face. "Forester came to me from the jail," he said. "Ben Edes, you may tell whom you please that I have agreed to act as counsel for Captain Preston, who is held for murder. You may say also that I shall defend the British soldiers lying in the stone jail under capital charges."

There was a murmur from the little crowd. The sweat trickled down from his armpits but John stood a moment longer, rocking

on his heels. His hands were behind his back, his coattails bunched forward; if he was afraid he did not show it. The light of battle was in his eye; he looked ready to take on all comers. "If you desire more information," he finished abruptly, "you will know where to find me." He turned, stepped into his office and shut the door.

The news ran through town like lightning. By noon that same day — March 6 — Boston knew that John Adams and Josiah Quincy, Junior, were to act as counsel for the defense of Preston and the soldiers. When John went home to dinner, he was stopped by a score of indignant Sons of Liberty. Was it true he had undertaken to defend those *murderers?* John replied hotly that he had engaged to defend men who were assumed innocent until the law had proved them guilty. John had expected hostility from the Sons; his blood rose to meet it. What disturbed him far more was the quite open congratulation from crown sympathizers. "Nine Tories out of ten," John told Abigail gloomily as they ate their dinner, "are convinced I have come over to their side, and Josiah Quincy with me."

Meanwhile the streets remained full of people. At eleven that morning, while John was still in his office, a great mass meeting had assembled at Faneuil Hall.[2] Sam Adams asked Dr. Cooper to open with a prayer. Already, a message had gone to Governor Hutchinson, urging him to remove both regiments from town — the 29th, which had fired on the people last night, and the 14th, stationed in the Manufactory House just east of Tremont Street. No answer had been received. A committee of fifteen was appointed now, with Sam Adams at their head, to go in person to Council Chamber in the State House and tell the Governor that if the soldiers were not withdrawn to Castle William immediately, the town could not answer for the consequences. Sam Adams and his committee walked out into crowded streets; the people in Faneuil Hall sat patiently and waited for their return.

They waited until three o'clock. By that time, Faneuil Hall, with a capacity for thirteen hundred, could not hold the crowd. Three thousand strong, they poured out and over the hill to Old South Meeting-house. Sam Adams and his committee emerged at last from the State House and their conference with the Governor. . . . Hutchinson had refused their petition, using the old excuse that he had "no authority to give orders to the king's troops." One regiment

only, the 29th, would be removed, to Castle Island. The 14th would stay in Boston until orders came from General Gage in New York.

Sam Adams, making his way toward the Old South church, passed slowly through a solid lane of people that parted to let him by. As he walked he turned his head rapidly from right to left. "Both regiments or none!" he repeated, over and over. "Stand out for both regiments or none!" Inside the church he called the meeting to order, read from a piece of paper the Governor's exact words about the troops and their removal. "Is it your pleasure to assent to the Governor's decision?" Sam asked. "Is it the town's desire that the 14th regiment remain? Let the vote be taken, *viva voce. Both regiments or none* — is that your pleasure?"

Three thousand voices shouted *Ay!* . . . The roar filled the church; outside on the streets the crowd took it up. (Only one voice, small but piercing, shouted *Nay!* three times at the very beginning when it could be heard — *Nay! Nay! Nay!* — and the clerk recorded it.)

A light snow was falling when Sam Adams and his committee of fifteen left the mass meeting to carry the town's vote back to Governor Hutchinson. Upstairs in the State House they found a full Council of twenty-eight seated behind the big oval table. Scarlet winter cloaks were thrown over the chairs; the Councilors were in full dress, with swords, powdered wigs, coats laced in gold. From the walls the Stuart kings still looked proudly down. Hutchinson rose as the committee entered. Samuel Adams, his gray hair tucked behind his ears, a rusty hat under his arm and his coat more wrinkled than ever, walked to the Council table, stretched out an arm and pointed boldly at the Governor. His hand shook, but his voice was strong and clear. If His Excellency had authority to remove one regiment, he had authority to remove two. The people demanded it. *Both regiments or none!* Fifteen thousand men were ready to rise throughout the Province. By noon tomorrow they would march to the relief of Boston. At this very moment, three thousand armed men waited in the Old South; a thousand more had already come in from the countryside. They would not wait much longer.

("It was then," Sam Adams himself wrote afterward, "I observed the Governor's knees to tremble.[3] I thought I saw his face grow pale, and I enjoyed the sight.")

Hutchinson sat down abruptly, held a whispered conference with his Council. Colonel Dalrymple stepped to the table. It would be wise, he said in a low voice, to remove both regiments. The people were in deadly earnest . . . Moreover it was true they were armed; he had seen them this morning on the streets. . . .

Hutchinson nodded curtly to Sam Adams. "Tell the people we grant their petition. Both regiments will be removed from town."

Sam Adams bowed briefly, made a sign to his committee and was gone. He went immediately to the Old South Meeting-house. It was nearly dark, but no one had left the meeting. In absolute silence, Sam walked up the aisle to the front and, turning, gave the news of his victory. It seemed as though a sigh of relief ran through the multitude; they did not cheer. They had had enough of noise and bloodshed. The meeting stayed on, organized a civilian night watch. It would be some days before the troops could be moved from their barracks, and no soul desired further riots, not even Samuel Adams. Citizens were to take turns at guard.

On the second night, March 7, John Adams himself set off from Cold Lane with musket and bayonet, broadsword and cartridge box. Until dawn he paced behind the State House, a little tin lantern strapped to his breast, his gun over his shoulder, the butt end in his mittened hand. The night was cold, with a bitter, damp east wind, but John enjoyed every minute of it. Since youth he had secretly hankered after the life military. (This was the closest he would ever come to it.) And he would be damned, John told himself firmly, if he was going to come down with a sore throat and sniffles in the morning. He did not know when he had felt so peaceful, his mind so much at rest. How simple, how plain to take up one's firelock and go where one was told! Arriving there, how satisfying to face right, face left at the captain's orders! John's captain was Adino Paddock the coachmaker, famous for setting out, lately, a row of English elms opposite his dwelling on the Mall by the Common; Boston watched their growth solicitously.

Pacing from the Custom House to Cornhill across the square, John turned his corners smartly, clicking his heels in the solitude as if Colonel Dalrymple himself were witness, and not merely a young moon that sailed serenely over the Court House chimneys to the west. John forgot the trial of the soldiers — or if he remembered, it was in terms of victory, not anxiety.

As the moon sank and the sky paled above the Harbor and the docks, John saluted his relief — it was the Reverend Samuel Cooper from Brattle Square — blew out his lantern and walked home. His peace of mind did not outlast the doffing of his cartridge box and broadsword. The sun was not fully risen, but on the way home, John had seen lights come on in the houses; there was already movement in the streets. Abigail came from bed to greet her husband. She had kept up the fire in their bedroom, she said. There was a hot drink on the hob; John had better take it and get some sleep; his ears looked frozen. Abby began to rub them briskly. John looked at her and sneezed; his military enthusiasm had vanished completely with the closing of the front door. He felt exhausted. "If Preston's trial is not postponed," he said suddenly, with complete irrelevance and the hollow voice of gloom, "we shall have no chance at all. No judge will sit, no jury dare give fair verdict."

John went slowly up to bed. The worst of it was, he told himself, that Sam Adams and the Sons of Liberty were all for immediate trial, now, in the March term of court. Sam was doing everything he could to force the issue.

It was true. That same afternoon — Thursday, March 8 — a huge and solemn funeral was held for the men killed by the soldiers. "Martyrs of a horrid Massacre," Boston had learned to call the dead men. The streets were a solid mass of people; six deep the mourners marched behind the coffins, to the tolling of every Congregational bell in Boston. Somebody saw to it that the bells rang also in Dorchester, Roxbury, and Cambridge. Nothing could have been more designedly dramatic. The four hearses came together in King Street at the place of the shooting; they were guarded by the civilian watch, with fixed bayonets.

John, walking in procession with the rest, felt sincere mourning for the dead men, all of whom were young and had their lives before them. Yet his feelings were necessarily mixed. He was well aware that every tolling bell, every tear, every solemn processional footfall would make his ordeal harder when the "murderers" came to court. Against this mass grief, this deep concerted fury, what would fact and the evidence avail to save the lives of his nine clients? Although it was plainly out of their way, the leaders took the funeral procession straight past the jail, under the barred windows where Preston lay. Most certainly, there was intention here. At the burying ground, as

the last of the four coffins was lowered, John looked up, caught the eye of Josiah Quincy who was standing near. Neither man allowed the least hint of expression to cross his face, but both knew instantly what the other was thinking.

On the twenty-seventh of March, Boston, worn out with drama, had a welcome moment of comic relief. His Majesty's 14th and 29th Regiments of Foot, solemnly escorted by the liberty boys, marched to the Long Wharf and embarked for Castle William, across green wintry water. The Sons were jubilant, the troops very glum. That brief march from barracks to wharf had been most humiliating. Side by side with their commanding officer marched Will Molineux, captain of the Sons. He wore a red and blue uniform left over from the last Pope's Day parade; his musket looked as if it had survived the Siege of Louisburg. His three-cornered hat, set at an angle far from conventional, flaunted a Wilkes cockade. From time to time he bowed genially to the crowd, which responded with a roar of delight. All Boston was on the streets; the windows were open and festooned with ladies in their brightest ribbons. Small boys in hordes ran along the gutters, scrambling into step with the army. Hup! they screamed. Hup, hup, hup! *Who buys lobsters?*

Never, thought His Majesty's soldiers bitterly, could they hold up their heads again. They were right. . . . *Sam Adams's two regiments*, Lord North dubbed them in London when he heard the story. And Sam Adams's two regiments they remained.

The Boston selectmen, prodded busily by Samuel Adams, prepared a report of the "Massacre" for British consumption; they did not trust either Thomas Hutchinson or Commanding Officer Dalrymple as correspondent to Parliament or King. Ninety-six witnesses were rounded up, a sworn statement taken from each. John Hodgson, the only shorthand writer in Boston, walked about holding his right wrist and asking plaintively if he was to be crippled for life in this cause? The ninety-six depositions were dispatched immediately to London, together with a twenty-two-page report — *A Short Narrative of the horrid Massacre in Boston, perpetrated in the evening of the fifth day of March, 1770, by soldiers of the Twenty-ninth Regiment . . . with some observations on the state of things prior to that catastrophe.*

The whole was, of course, published and distributed throughout

the Province. The *Narrative* itself was beautifully written, enough to wring the heart with the wrongs of the slaughtered Bostonians. It was prefaced by a bold and skillful introduction which had the signature, among others, of John's friend, Dr. Warren.

John Adams and Josiah Quincy, locking the office door, went over the whole thing carefully. Of the ninety-six witnesses, ninety-four made it appear that the fault lay entirely with the soldiers; the reader had an instant picture of a peaceful citizenry fallen upon in the night by bloodthirsty grenadiers. Nothing was said of the lone British sentry who, at the beginning of the fray, had stood his post, dodging oyster shells and chunks of ice until he called in desperation for the guard to save his life. Of the two witnesses favorable to the soldiers, one was Dr. Church of Boston who gave his post-mortem examination of the mulatto, Crispus Attucks. The other, Number 96, was proven in three careful footnotes to be a paid hireling of the crown and a liar to boot.

The depositions made vivid reading. "No doubt," John told young Quincy grimly, "we shall have these fellows on the stand against us. Perhaps all ninety-four of them. . . . Listen to this: 'I, William LeBaron, of lawful age, testify and say . . . I saw about thirteen or fourteen soldiers appear in King Street near the watch-house, with their drawn swords, cutlasses and bayonets, calling out, "Where are the damned boogers, cowards, where are your liberty boys"; at which time there was not more than eight or ten persons in King Street. One of the soldiers came up to me, damned me, and made several passes at me with a drawn sword, the last of which the sword went between my arm and breast, and then I run, as I had nothing to defend myself, and was pursued by a soldier with a naked bayonet, who swore he would run me through; at which time your deponent cried fire! and soon after the bells rung, and further your deponent sayeth not.' "

Josiah Quincy looked despondently at his senior associate. "Ninety-four witnesses, and all liars — or else they saw things through eyes more crossed than mine." Quincy held the paper at arm's length, began in his turn to read: " 'I, Robert Polley . . . was going home with my friends, when I met in Boylston Alley eight or nine soldiers, armed with drawn swords and cutlasses. One had a tongs, another a shovel, with which they assaulted us. One of them said, "*Where are the sons of bitches, by Jesus let them come.*" '

" 'I, Samuel Atwood . . . met ten or twelve soldiers armed with drawn cutlasses and bayonets. Your deponent asked if they meant to murder people? They answered, "Yes by God, root and branch," saying, "here is one of them"; with that one of them struck the deponent with a club: the deponent being unarmed—' "

John cut his partner short. "Enough!" he said. "From Plymouth to Pittsfield, the Province is reading this fine tale. Our only hope is in postponement of the trial. In six months, men can forget even their own lies."

Quincy agreed. For the first time in their legal careers, the two found themselves in complete harmony with Governor Hutchinson, who by skillful manipulation finally succeeded in deferring the trials until the August term of court. This meant they might not come up until October; court term lasted until all cases were off the docket. Hutchinson, in truth, was greatly pleased that John Adams was to be counsel for the accused. Himself convinced the soldiers had acted in self-defense, Hutchinson was determined, should the jury convict, to urge the King's pardon for all eight men. Such a gesture he was aware would put his own life in danger. On the other hand, John Adams's skill, his standing with the people, together with a certain stubborn, fearless honesty the man seemed to possess, might actually persuade the jury to bring in a verdict of acquittal, or, at least, manslaughter, something no crown lawyer could achieve. Already, Captain Preston in prison was receiving anonymous letters, warning that if the King should pardon him, the walls of Boston jail would not hold against the people's wrath. Thomas Hutchinson far preferred acquittal achieved by John Adams to a pardon achieved by himself.

Samuel Adams too was pleased at Preston's choice of counsel, but for very different reasons. No matter when the trial was held or what the outcome, there was bound to be some very deep delving into the events of Monday, March 5. Who, for instance, was the "tall large man in the Boston red cloak, that harangued the people in Dock Square"? And who had posted the previous Friday's notice, signed by the soldiers of the two regiments, stating they were planning to revenge themselves for the morning fight at the ropewalk? With all his heart, Sam Adams wished to see Preston hanged — but most fervently also he wished to avoid the slightest evidence of collusion

by the town in this "horrid Massacre." Had Preston and the soldiers engaged only crown lawyers to defend them, Boston would have had no protection against possibly damaging disclosures, unnecessarily prolonged cross-examination of witnesses. John Adams and Josiah Quincy were to try not the town of Boston, but eight men indicted for murder. And should the two lawyers, in the heat of forensic vigor, forget this point, it could be nicely drawn to their attention out of court.

John himself, as time passed, faced the forthcoming battle with every ounce of pugnacity in him. He needed it; everywhere, he felt hostility. Arriving home one evening, he found a window broken; Abigail showed him two stones she had picked up in the room. "They are only small stones," she said quickly. "That is why I kept them to show you. You must not fear to leave me; I am the equal of any three rowdy boys. I know they were boys; I saw one of them disappear round the corner."

The incident only served to whet John's anger; he began to feel an appetite for the oncoming ordeal. He trusted he knew enough of the art of cross-examination, he told Josiah Quincy, to make a fool of any Boston liar on the stand. The prosecution already had ninety-four witnesses, if they intended to use the men who made the printed depositions. The town must be scoured for an equal number of defense witnesses. John himself began to spend much time in King Street and Dock Square, searching the very cobbles as oracle, he said. Again and again he walked over the scene of the shooting, paced the distance between the Custom House and Murray's barracks, noted how the light fell at eight o'clock in the evening, at nine o'clock, ten o'clock — and entered it carefully in his little book.

It made things no easier that John's junior counsel, in the month of April, was wholly taken up with another murder trial, and had little time to discuss the affair of the soldiers. Josiah Quincy was desperately arguing in court for the life of Richardson, the customs informer who, a few weeks before the "Massacre," had fired from his window and killed the twelve-year-old boy, Snyder. Josiah's older brother, Samuel Quincy, was arguing against him for the prosecution. The outcome would have profound effect on the soldiers' trials next fall. The same laws would be referred to, the same plea made of

self-defense. If Josiah Quincy lost the case, if his client Richardson were convicted of murder, the jury and judges next autumn would be that much harder to influence for leniency or acquittal.

Quincy lost his case. When the jury brought in a verdict of guilty, the courtroom, jammed to the windows with spectators, gave a great shout. On a technicality, the judges managed to delay sentence; hurried Richardson back to jail. The Governor urgently wrote to England for the King's pardon. (Whatever Hutchinson lacked, it was not courage.) "I am absolutely alone," he wrote General Gage in New York. "No single person of my Council or any other person in authority affording me the least support. If the people are disposed to any measure, nothing more is necessary than for the multitude to assemble; nobody dares oppose them or call them to account."

On the career and future of John Adams, Richardson's conviction had another effect, immediate, far-reaching and totally unforeseen. James Otis, pondering apparently on Richardson's fate and the crime that had led to it, walked upstairs in his town house and tried to duplicate the events. Standing at a window he fired off six guns, one after another, accompanied by sportive whoops. This was too much; even his warmest admirers could no longer pretend that James Otis was sane; they agreed it was impossible to conceal his condition further. Sam Adams called on him, told him gently that he must resign his place as Boston Representative to the General Court. Otis complied.

Sam Adams left the house sadly; this was one of the hardest tasks he had put upon himself. Not only was he devoted to Otis, but it was awful to think of the liberty party without him. They needed his eloquence and spirit — and even more, they needed his knowledge of British law. Every new dispute with the Governor brought up important constitutional questions; since Oxenbridge Thacher's death, Otis had been the one to solve them. Moreover, by birth and connections, Otis was the equal in respectability of anyone in Boston. Well did Sam Adams know the value of this.

But there was no doubt who was the man to fill Otis's place.[4] One morning late in May, Sam Adams strolled casually into John's office by the State House steps. "Your name is up for nomination as Representative," he said. John merely shrugged. "A pleasant gesture, Cousin," he replied. "Due no doubt entirely to your good offices. I thank you. But the thing is impossible; I would not poll ten votes.

The whole town knows I am to defend Preston and the soldiers. I am the most unpopular man in Boston. This morning on Queen Street a mudball missed my ear by inches. Last night, passing the Custom House, I heard the riot whistle three times, and somebody behind the wall asked why I had left my red coat at home. . . . You might as well nominate Captain Preston. Besides, they tell me Ruddock is your man."

Ruddock was a rich merchant who had worked his way to fortune — a fact that would make for popularity with high and low. But Sam shook his head. John Adams, unpopular? — he repeated — No! Mud-slinging boys were one thing, even mud-slinging *liberty* boys. But voters, actual voters were something else. Only freeholders voted: men with an estate of forty pounds sterling. And the freeholders of Boston, soldiers' trial or no soldiers' trial, trusted and liked John Adams. As for Ruddock, yes, he was up for election; it wouldn't do to have only one name. The party needed rich merchants, and it pleased Ruddock to see his name in nomination. But let John wait till Wednesday, when the final vote was taken. He would see, said Sam Adams genially, what he would see.

Taking up his old brown hat, Sam blew at it, clapped it on, walked out and down King Street to the wharves where his friends were. John sat alone in his office, thinking. The idea of his being elected was preposterous. Yet Samuel Adams was not in the habit of making preposterous political suggestions. How long had this plan been afoot, if it was a plan? Immediately after Otis's resignation from the House of Representatives, James Bowdoin the merchant had been elected in his place. Bowdoin was a man of much importance; his fortune was greater even than John Hancock's. A few days later, Bowdoin had been sent on to the upper house as Councilor, thereby insuring even more influence in that august body for the liberty side, and leaving the fourth seat in the House again vacant. Had Sam already put these new wheels in motion? — John wondered. And was he at the moment occupied, down along the wharves and ropewalks, with the business of securing votes?

It was incredible, John thought; Boston had never sent an outsider like himself to represent it in the Legislature. Why, the four Boston seats were guarded with bitterest jealousy! Everyone knew that John Adams had lived in town but a scant two years. Today, Sam had said the liberty side needed a "knowledgeable legal adviser,

one that great merchants like Rowe and Hancock could respect."
Something in the way he said it made John's mind fly back. . . .
Once before, Sam had hinted it would be well if John were in the
Massachusetts Legislature. The scene came back as if it were yesterday. It was in the Town-house, in December of '65, just after John,
with Otis and Jeremiah Gridley, had petitioned Governor Bernard
to open the courts in defiance of the Stamp Act. Sam had congratulated his cousin on being chosen by Boston for this most important
business, and in an emphatic voice had added that Braintree, as a
result, no doubt had its eye on John for the coming elections in
May. . . .

That was five years ago. But Sam Adams, where politics were
concerned, was the most persistent man in North America. . . . As
the implications of the thing began to widen, John, appalled, stared
before him at his office wall. The people's cause, the cause of liberty,
lay very close to his heart. For it he had made many sacrifices; he
was ready to make many more. Yet before God, thought John, he
had never intended to make politics his career. And to be Boston
member of the General Court, in these troubled days, was most
certainly a career. The Legislature was no half-time affair. Membership absorbed a man's whole time; absorbed — John thought
with a stab of real panic — a man's whole mind, energy, emotions.
Look at James Otis! Until he threw himself into politics, Otis had
been the most prosperous and respected lawyer in the Province; he
had inherited Gridley's mantle by virtue of sheer ability, knowledge
and worth. . . . Gradually he had lost everything to the cause: clients, money, his living — and now his mind. For indubitably it was
politics that had unsettled Otis's mind; his emotions were not equal to
the strain. Otis, John considered, was a man of tender nature, quick,
impulsive; he had not Samuel Adams's extraordinary cool strength.
Nothing upset Sam, neither personal abuse nor rioting nor danger.
And bankruptcy upset him least of all. . . .

"But bankruptcy," John thought grimly, "would upset *me* more
than a little." And should he be elected to the Legislature, where in
the name of thrift would he find money to clothe and educate his
family? As it was, he had little enough time for clients, and the soldiers' trial had absorbed what was left of that. Rising abruptly from
his chair, John shook his shoulders as if to rid himself of nightmare. . . . Of course he would not be elected — what had he been

thinking of! This was some scheme or machination of Cousin Sam's; it was even possible that John's name was being used as a pawn to play off against Ruddock. The workings of the political engine had always been beyond John; the first political office he ever held, that of Surveyor of Roads in Braintree, had come to him unsought and even unwanted.

John closed the office shutters and moved about the little room, preparing to leave for the night. Why was it, he thought, suddenly exasperated — why, when all he honestly desired from life was to be a good lawyer, make a decent fortune for himself and family, collect a library, improve the farm at Penn's Hill and educate his children — why must he be forever thrust into large, harassing jobs which he never, left alone, would dream of undertaking? This business of Representative was not of his choosing in any sense. Nobody had asked him if he desired the post. They knew better than to ask him, John thought sourly, walking down his office steps into King Street.

*Boston votes for a new Representative
and John rides north on circuit. The trial
of Captain Preston.*

ELECTION Day came on Wednesday, June 6. Early that afternoon, John sat alone in his office, while a few blocks away in Faneuil Hall the citizens of Boston met to cast their votes for Representative. The windows were open, a pleasant breeze blew up from the Bay. All day there had been noise and movement in the street outside. Men passed by, talking and laughing. Twice, John thought he heard his name spoken.

The week or so since Sam Adams's visit had passed for John with incredible rapidity; in his own household, world-shaking events had taken place. On the twenty-ninth of May, Abigail had given birth to a second son, a long thin baby with an insatiable appetite and gray eyes like his mother's. They had christened him Charles. Far from exhausting Abigail, the baby's birth had somehow restored her; she was gaining strength rapidly. As for Charles, he grew fatter almost under the eye. Thinking of the two now, John felt reassured, content.

But the feeling did not, he knew uneasily, extend beyond the four walls of his house. In an hour or two the meeting at Faneuil Hall would break up. That he should win the election, John considered preposterous; he retained the profound conviction that his defense of the British soldiers had made him the most unpopular man in Boston. He wondered wryly if he would receive any votes at all beyond Sam Adams's, Josiah Quincy's and a few others of his friends and

associates. It would not be pleasant to face defeat and repudiation at the hands of the very men who for so long had come to him for help and advice.

John got up, went to his bookshelves and took down a new volume by the Marquess di Beccaria: *Crimes and Punishments*. It would be good to sit quietly and renew one's spirit with study. Beccaria's book, published in 1764, was scarcely known on this side of the ocean; John had written to London for it. In these times of violence, when men's tongues called loudly for "justice" (and their hearts called for revenge), it was heartening to read this Italian philosopher, with his faith in humanity, his respect for the value of human life. Crime, said Beccaria, was due largely to environment; punishment should aim to reform the criminal rather than avenge the victim.

With all his heart, John agreed. And until this cursed affair with the soldiers, the whole Province, John told himself, would have shared his opinion.[1] Old Governor Bernard had been right — *the Massachusetts was not a bloodthirsty people*. But the climate was altered now: eye for eye, tooth for tooth, was what the Province looked for. In pulpit as well as newspapers there was much talk of "Moses and his laws." Preachers cited with relish God's words to Noah after the Flood: *Whoso sheddeth man's blood, by man shall his blood be shed.*

His own wise and gentle father, John remembered, had brought him up, after the New England fashion, on this murderous Old Testament doctrine. It was going to be very, very difficult to explain to a Massachusetts jury the difference between murder and manslaughter, tell them what was meant by "the benignity of the English law." Yet to make such explanation successfully was his only hope, and the only hope of nine men indicted for murder. Young Quincy said the jury would not listen to abstruse definitions; he said they would go to sleep, or turn surly from tedium. . . . John did not believe it. "Plain men too have curiosity," he told Quincy sharply. "They read my essays on the Canon and Feudal Law. Compared with those bits of long-winded historical evidence, what I shall have to say of manslaughter will be to the last degree exciting."

Since the morning of March 6, when John gave his hand to the Irish Infant and pledged himself to the defense of Preston, Beccaria's book had scarcely left him. There was one passage in particu-

lar to which the pages fell open: *If, by supporting the rights of mankind and of invincible truth, I shall contribute to save from the agonies of death one unfortunate victim of tyranny, or of ignorance equally fatal, his blessing and tears of transport will be sufficient consolation to me for the contempt of all mankind.*

John repeated the words in his quiet office; they seemed to fall on his heart like a blessing, a benediction that took the sting from what he had pledged himself to do. . . . Talking with his cousin Samuel and others, John had tried to laugh off the remembrance of mud that spattered his cheek in the streets . . . whistles, catcalls. . . . "Who buys lobsters, John Adams?" a voice had whined softly last night from behind a hedge. Sharp as a sword, the words had pierced John's breast; he had been sick with anger and hurt. . . . *If, by supporting the rights of invincible truth, I shall save from the agonies of death one unfortunate victim* . . .

From Brattle Street church steeple the clock struck twice, and across the street a tavern bell sounded for dinner. John sat wholly absorbed. With a pen he underlined phrases in his book, finding comfort in the small, simple act.

There was sudden commotion in the street outside — voices, a knock at the office door. Josiah Quincy burst in, his fair hair on end, his thin face flushed, his eyes crossed hopelessly with excitement. "I am just come from the meeting!" he said breathlessly. He stopped, coughed, leaned against the door. "You are elected! You beat Ruddock four to one. Don't you want to know the vote? Out of 536 votes cast, 418 were for you. . . . What have you been doing? Why, you haven't got your wig on! . . . Come, where is your hat? Here, let me help you. The people want your acceptance. They want to see you. I told Sam Adams I would fetch you. They cheered for you, three times three. Didn't you hear your name?"

Journal of the House of Representatives of Massachusetts Bay

1770. June 6. John Adams, Esq. returned a member from Boston. Upon his making an appearance in the House it was ordered: That Mr. Hancock attend Mr. Adams to the gentlemen appointed to administer the oaths.

Who reported that he had taken the oaths and subscribed the declaration required by act of parliament, and then Mr. Adams took his seat in the House.

It was nearly eight that evening when John got home to Cold Lane. He had been carried triumphantly from town meeting to tavern and the occasion celebrated with toasts, congratulations and one brief but heartfelt speech from Sam Adams. Then he had been hurried across the river to Cambridge, where the Legislature was meeting, and formally inducted. Touched and deeply gratified by these marks of trust and affection, John was nevertheless deeply uneasy. Had he done wrong to let the House proceed so fast? And in God's name how had it happened anyway? He had not lifted a finger to get himself elected. There was no doubt that Sam Adams's fine hand had been behind all this. In the crowd at the tavern, among the warm congratulations in the House itself, Sam had been everywhere evident — affable, easy, assured. In all John's thinking, he had never envisioned the business as a triumph. Yet the people had made it into a triumph, into a salute and a reward.

But would Abigail look on it as a triumph? What would she say, how would she receive this overwhelming sudden change in their life together? Stepping from the Charlestown Ferry, John said farewell to his colleagues and turned alone down Prince Street toward home. Most fervently he desired the shelter of his house, wished to be alone and think this thing out. It would be Abigail, he told himself remorsefully, who bore the brunt. She would have less money to look forward to; their manner of living must be drastically curtailed. Moreover, it would mean that Abby saw even less of him than she did now. He would be forever in Cambridge, and when the House finally rose he would have to spend each waking hour at his law office, trying to earn money for their bread and sustenance. . . .

John wished profoundly that he had prepared his wife, talked over with her the possibilities of this election. But he had not believed in it himself; it had not seemed worthy of serious discussion. Abigail was no novice at city politics. She knew well the usual preliminaries to election — the angling for votes, the visits to ropewalk and wharf at the eleven o'clock lunch hour, the careful Sabbath attendance at various Congregational meeting-houses. James Otis, when up for election the first time, had been advised to go to church at least once in each of the twelve wards of Boston, and to be sure to employ plenty of artisans round his house — have the chimneys relined, the roof shingled, take all his kegs and barrels to the hooper whether they needed hoops or no.

Abby knew all of this, and knew that John had not made one such pre-election move. Consequently she would be wholly unprepared. . . . John opened his front door, walked in and straight upstairs. The new baby was only eight days old; Abby still kept to her chamber although she professed herself impatient to be downstairs again and out in the world. John found her sitting in the big flowered rocking chair, dressed in a loose blue morning gown, her brown hair piled high on her head. He crossed the room and without pause for a greeting, stood close before her and began to speak. "I was elected Boston Representative today," he said. "The vote was four to one." John's voice, as always when excited, was loud; he gave his wife no chance to reply. "I believe — I fear you know what it means, Abby. Danger aside, I have thrown away my prospects as a barrister. I had last year more business than any lawyer in Massachusetts. I have worked long and hard for such a position. From now on, no crown man will trust me with a case. Moreover, my time will be taken up, and my energies. We shall be poor. . . . I have — Abby, can you forgive me? I have deliberately doomed you and my children" — John made a sweeping, rough, dramatic gesture — "to a life of poverty and danger."

To John's intense consternation, Abby flung both hands over her face and burst into tears. Then she reached for a handkerchief, blew her nose. "Forgive me, John," she said. "I cry easily, these days." She smiled, reached out a hand. "How foolish you are, my dearest partner! I am very proud of you. It does not come as a great surprise. Josiah Quincy told me ten days past that you would be elected. You seemed not to wish to discuss it; you have been so taken up with the soldiers' trials. . . . If I was upset, it was at your manner, not at what you had to say."

Abigail rose, still holding her husband's hand. Her face was grave and at the same time, tender. "Let me share what comes with you always, John. I fear nothing but our parting, nothing at all. I know well the dangers of this position. But you have done right. And I believe," she finished simply, "that for our future, we must trust in Providence."

The Legislature continued to meet outside of Boston, in Cambridge where Hutchinson had exiled it. Professor Winthrop, John's old teacher, had offered the Philosophy Chamber in Harvard Hall as

an assembly room. Across the corridor was Winthrop's new laboratory; from where he sat John could see the crucibles and the big telescope. Passing the door one morning he caught sight of a skeleton hanging in a corner and smiled, remembering things past. Most Harvard students were rabid partisans for the liberty side. They slipped in and stood lining the walls to hear the debates; sometimes John found himself escorted to the ferry by a little band of Senior Sophisters in their gowns, cheering and talking and asking questions.

John was exceedingly busy; the post of legal adviser to the House and Council was an arduous one. If tactical moves were originated by Sam Adams, Dr. Warren, Joseph Hawley, it was John who decided the legislative and constitutional questions. The House was in the midst of an angry, endless controversy with Governor Hutchinson, trying by every means to force him to take the Assembly back to Boston. Not only was this exile openly humiliating but it was very inconvenient. There were no bridges to Boston and the ferries were slow and uncertain.

The Townshend duties had been repealed at last — with, as John had prophesied, the inevitable string attached. This time it was a duty on tea. Everywhere, American merchants tightened the Non-importation rules. Hutchinson, still Acting Governor but expecting daily his full commission from the King, addressed the House in his best manner, reminding them of his long and devoted service to Boston and begging co-operation. The House listened coldly, then replied with a polite and stubborn message opposing Hutchinson's every suggestion. John Adams was on the committee that drafted it. He was, indeed, on so many committees, drafted and signed so many letters and resolutions, that ex-Governor Bernard in London was asked, he wrote Hutchinson, "who this *John* Adams was?" . . . "I gave," Bernard continued stiffly, "as favorable an answer as I could, but not such as would have justified the appointment to him of an office of trust."

Hutchinson granted the House a recess. John prepared immediately to go off on circuit. In the next eight weeks, he told Abigail, he must make money enough to carry them till Christmas. As soon as the General Court reconvened in September he would be wholly taken up with that and the soldiers' trials, which were due in October. He had cases to plead in Salem, Newbury, Portsmouth, Biddeford

and all the way to the easternmost limit of the courts, at Falmouth in Casco Bay.

The minute he was across the ferry and out of Boston a load seemed to fall from John's shoulders and his spirits rose. He drove his little two-wheeled sulky northward along the dusty road, noting the coming crops with a farmer's eye. The corn was no more than a foot high; here and there, hills were missing. There had been heavy cold rains at planting time; John hoped his own corn at Penn's Hill had not been injured so much as this. At Salem tavern he found a note from Goldthwaite, once Register of Boston, inviting him to dine at two o'clock "under the shady trees by the pond, upon fish and bacon and pease, with half a dozen as clever fellows as ever were born. As to the Madeira, nothing can come up to it. We'll give a genteel dinner and fix you off on your journey."

John went, and enjoyed himself hugely. He was eager to know what the people north of Boston thought of the political situation. Here in Salem, men seemed convinced that a British army was due to arrive. Ten regiments at least, and many line-of-battle ships. Did Mr. Adams think the people as a whole would support this armament or oppose it? . . . John shook his head. Let his Salem friends repeat the question when he passed through on his return journey. By then he would know more about the temper of the Province.

When dinner was done, the gentlemen escorted John to his little carriage and bade him a hearty farewell. John bowled off down the road in the late afternoon shadows, resolved to note and learn all he could. The indications, at first, were encouraging. At Wenham Inn, John was greeted by a signboard depicting the face of William Pitt. *Entertainment for the Sons of Liberty* was written underneath. But the farther north he went, the more conservative John found the spirit of the countryside. Driving through York he caught a glimpse of his Harvard classmate, David Sewall, walking in his garden. John stopped only for a greeting, then drove on. Sewall was not of the liberty side. Indeed, it appeared that most of the established families hereabouts were crown men. They were afraid for their commissions. John's landlord had told him about it that morning. "Rather than run the hazard of losing business," he had said, "these men would ruin the country."

John was in no way surprised; after all, a Province of two hundred and fifty thousand souls was naturally slow to move, slow to change

its habits. The Boston Representatives must be reminded of this fact; they must not try to urge the horse beyond its will. South of Boston, on the other hand, people were far more resentful toward England. The week before he started on this journey, John had been at Plymouth trying a case. Eating breakfast at the inn, he had noticed a man get up and go outside. When John went out himself, he found his horse all saddled and bridled at the stoop. The stranger held John's stirrup while he mounted. "Mr. Adams," he said, "as a man of liberty I respect you. God bless you! I'll stand by you while I live, and from hence to Cape Cod you won't find ten men amiss."

But up here in the remote country, men were slow to let themselves become involved in these larger issues, although John found them surprisingly well informed. Moving from town to town, arguing his cases, dining afterward with the judges, talking with landlords, gospel ministers, artisans, farmers, John kept careful record of what he heard and saw. Not all of his researches were political. John was by nature an inveterate sightseer; people felt it, and showed him eagerly their peculiar treasures. The children of one tavernkeeper had a pet crow. "A sight I never saw before," John wrote wonderingly in his diary. "The head and bill are monstrous, the legs and claws long and sprawling. But," John added, suddenly conscious of the frivolity of such recordings, "the young crow is not an object that will interest posterity."

And while John drove northward on his long journey, Abigail moved the family once more, this time back to Brattle Square. She was uneasy about returning to the center of town. Their new house was across the street from the Meeting-house. Abby found the friendship of the pastor, Dr. Samuel Cooper, very comforting. She had so much rather, she told him, have remained at the North End, especially until the soldiers' trials were over. But their landlord had wanted the Cold Lane house for himself, and she could find no other. Every riot that might take place next winter, every crowd that assembled would gather almost under her windows. Did Dr. Cooper think her husband's life would be in danger next October, when the trials opened?

No, Cooper replied. It would have been in great danger, had the trials not been postponed. But the temper of Boston had cooled; he for one believed men were far more ready to listen to reason and to give the soldiers a fair hearing.

John got home late in August and was swept once more into the business of the Legislature. Two gentlemen from the Virginia House of Burgesses visited the Assembly; John talked with them at length. In Virginia, the Governor and judges received large revenues from tobacco, granted them in the reign of Charles II. As a result, the executive and judicial departments were dangerously independent of the people's money and therefore of the people's wishes; the Governor called the Assembly only when he pleased, sometimes not more than twice a year. A warped and insidious situation, John said at once. The people of Massachusetts must guard carefully their right to pay Governor and judges from the Provincial, not the King's, purse.

When October came, John and Josiah Quincy spent most of the month rounding up witnesses. There were to be three trials: that of Captain Preston; then the trial of the eight soldiers; then a third trial of six Boston citizens, partisans of the soldiers, who were said to have fired on the crowd from the Custom House windows. Captain Preston's trial was set for October 24; his lawyers were Robert Auchmuty, John Adams and Josiah Quincy. Auchmuty, by virtue of his age and position as Judge of Admiralty, had been named senior counsel. The three lawyers met daily, planned between them the conduct of the case. Auchmuty was to do most of the talking, Josiah Quincy would examine and cross-examine the witnesses. John himself was to put his energies into the actual legalistic aspect. Of the three men, he had by far the widest knowledge of the law.

It was the second trial — that of the eight soldiers — for which Boston reserved its most vengeful feeling. And well John knew it. Far more than they hated Preston, the people hated these soldiers, all eight of whom were known by name and face to that part of Boston which lived down near the barracks. The soldiers' guns had done the actual killing; Preston himself had held no weapon in his hand. Nevertheless from the legal point of view, Preston's trial, coming first, would be the pivot on which the thing swung. If it could be proved that a sentry on duty has the right to defend himself even to the point of killing, then Preston would be justified in giving the order to shoot, and the question of whether or no he gave such an order would lose its significance.

It was around this point that John determined to build his defense. With infinite care he had searched out, during the past months,

statute and precedent, the rules that govern homicide, the difference between homicide justifiable, excusable and felonious. Patiently he went over it with Auchmuty. What were the facts that could reduce murder to manslaughter? It was of the utmost importance, John said, that Auchmuty explain to the jury at the very outset that a sentry's post is his castle. To attack him is, by English law, an illegal act. And the prisoners were to be tried, not by the law of Massachusetts or the laws of God and Moses but by the English common law. Moreover, a party of soldiers sent by their commanding officer to a sentry's relief constitute a body lawfully assembled. If assaulted, they may defend themselves even to the death of the opponents. And if any of them does an illegal action, he alone is accountable. Whereas they who attack are illegally assembled; together they are accountable for each one's separate action. These were points unknown in Massachusetts, where the people were convinced that a soldier in time of peace was forbidden by law to fire on a citizen no matter what the provocation.

It was a pity, John added grimly, that old Justice Lynde was to preside at the trials instead of Thomas Hutchinson. No one knew better than Hutchinson what constituted legal and illegal assemblies, what a riot was, or a "rumpus." Had Auchmuty, John asked, read any of Hutchinson's charges to the grand jury in the past five years, since the stamp troubles? . . . No, Auchmuty said, he had not.

Privately, John was surprised and much relieved, he told Josiah Quincy later, at the older lawyer's response, his willingness to take direction. Auchmuty displayed actual humility, seemed only too glad to receive points of law from John and showed little ambition to take the front of the stage when the day of trial should come. Quincy replied cheerfully that for his part he was far from surprised. Why should any crown man wish to expose his neck to the mob's halter? In spite of a noticeable cooling-off of anger, God only knew what the people of Boston were already planning in the way of revenge, should the verdict be acquittal.

"It will be acquittal," John said confidently, "provided we secure an impartial jury. We must not accept one town-born man on the panel. We will challenge them from sunup to dark, if the judges do not balk. . . . And concerning the town, I have a bit of advice for you also, Mr. 'Wilkes' Quincy. Unless events take some extraordinary and unforeseen turn, we shall have opportunity to make sad fools

out of the prosecution's witnesses. Before we are done they will be battered black and blue. You, Josiah, are a man of zeal. In the heat and inspiration of your cross-questioning, do not, my young friend, press your examination beyond the necessities of the case."

John paused, looked straight at Quincy, who, for want of ability to look straight back, raised his blue eyes and squinted desperately. "We have enough evidence to acquit our client six times over," John said. "Remember that we are trying, not the town of Boston, but Captain Preston of His Majesty's army. It is by no means our business to track down citizens who may be guilty of inciting riot. Our effort must be directed toward proving the innocence of our client. All England certainly — and perhaps all Europe — will be watching these trials. It will serve our enemies well if we publish proof that the people's cause in America is led by a mere mob, by a riotous and irresponsible water-front rabble."

He could not stress the point too strongly, John continued. Let Josiah remember it and plot his course accordingly.

Josiah replied a trifle ruefully that Mr. Sam Adams had been giving him the same advice. Of course it was right — even irrefutable. But it was bound to skim the cream from the performance, especially when they came to the trial of the eight soldiers.

John cut the conversation short. "Cases at law," he said stiffly, "are often won by what is left unsaid."

Josiah nodded, sighing. In truth his position was far from easy. To begin with, he had lost Richardson's case last April, arguing against his own brother Samuel. Now, Samuel was to oppose him once more, as counsel for the prosecution of the soldiers. There was bitter feeling between the two. People said Sam Quincy had turned Tory from jealousy of his younger brother's brilliance, his popularity with the people. In Braintree their father, Colonel Josiah, was beside himself with grief and anxiety. It was bad enough to have his older son a Tory, without Josiah going over to the crown by defending the British soldiers. "Those criminals!" the Colonel wrote angrily. "Good God! Is it possible you have become their advocate?"

When the day came at last that brought "*Rex* versus *Preston*" to the docket, the lawyers for the defense went early to the courtroom in Queen Street, seated themselves at the table below the bench and arranged their books and papers. The opposing lawyers arrived: Samuel Quincy and Robert Treat Paine. Bob Paine, as John had

always called him, was Solicitor General now, a substitute for Attorney General Jonathan Sewall, who was absent in Nova Scotia.[2] Paine was black-eyed, with a narrow, sensitive face. He was intelligent and well educated, but constitutionally dull — a man, John said, who could make even murder tedious. As for Sam Quincy, he had not his younger brother's brilliance but he was capable of constructing a sound and solid argument; he was not an adversary to sneer at.

The courtroom filled quickly with spectators; the four judges swept in, awful in the red robes that signified a trial on capital charges. Captain Preston, looking pale under his dark hair — he wore no wig — was led to the bar under guard. The indictment was read, the prisoner pronounced his plea: NOT GUILTY. The jurors were called, challenged peremptorily or for cause; twelve were finally chosen and sworn. Justice Peter Oliver leaned forward, rapped for order and addressed the courtroom. His voice was angry, his handsome face indignant. For presiding at this trial, his life had been threatened; anonymous letters were left at his door. It was an outrage, a disgrace to a civilized community. No threat on earth could force him to relinquish his duty. . . . Oliver leaned back in his chair, nodded to old Chief Justice Lynde. Samuel Quincy rose for the prosecution and the trial began.

The prosecutor had not talked fifteen minutes when John's heart expanded within him and he told himself that unless something very unexpected happened — such as Bob Paine's being suddenly inspired from above or a battery of Congregational preachers deciding overnight to act as crown witnesses — the case was won for the defense. Sam Quincy talked for two hours. And every word he said, the courtroom already knew by heart. He went over the scene of the riot, motion by motion as it were, reading from the written page, his head bent. His voice took on a droning quality; the jury fidgeted, plucked at their clothes, leaned down to scratch their ankles. The third man from the left kept pushing back his wig as if it were too tight; every time he did it his neighbor nudged him, indicating with a jerk of his head the four judges under their huge shoulder wigs.

As the day wore on it became obvious the trial was going to move very slowly. At noon, to everyone's intense surprise, Judge Lynde adjourned court for an hour, then adjourned again at five, saying the jury would be detained overnight in the Court House. It was unprecedented: capital trials in Massachusetts went on all day and all

night until a verdict was reached. Twelve noon and five o'clock were the hours when Boston laborers were free and on the streets. Were the judges really fearful for their lives then, the audience asked each other? Governor Hutchinson declared that, had he been presiding, he would not have permitted adjournment.

Day after day the trial continued. When Auchmuty's turn came to speak, he rose quite above himself and carried away the honors, singlehanded. John was enormously relieved. There had been times, during the past few weeks, when both he and Josiah Quincy had wondered if Auchmuty would go through with it at all. (Even Colonel Dalrymple wrote Gage that he feared Auchmuty's last-minute defection.) But Auchmuty did very well indeed. Using every one of John's carefully prepared arguments, he pounded away at the jury on points of law and the rules governing homicide charges until even the two Hingham jurymen, whom John considered by all odds the thickest-headed yokels in six counties, nodded solemn understanding.

John himself did not stop to consider whose was the glory. He was far too busy. Bob Paine produced his witnesses for the prosecution and examined them competently. But the testimony was thin, and nothing Paine said or did could make it solider, with its picture of a brutal soldiery rampaging on peaceful streets, calling for innocent blood. By the third day, John was sure of a favorable verdict.

But his troubles were by no means over. What began to bother him now was the conduct of a member of his own team. Young Josiah Quincy had become altogether skittish and overbold. During the fourth afternoon, on his feet for the cross-examination, Josiah went quite crazy with enthusiasm and either forgot or disregarded completely all warnings given out by the brace of Adamses, the *par nobile fratrum*. So skillfully did Josiah proceed and so frank were the answers he elicited, that it began to appear that Preston never commanded the troops to fire! In a minute moreover it might be revealed who it was that had ordered the alarm bells rung, why two different groups had converged around nine o'clock by the Custom House, and other matters extremely damaging not only to the town of Boston but to the cause of liberty.

John, reaching forward where he sat, tapped his young partner on the shoulder. Quincy turned, faltered, nodded his fair head in agreement and went on with the questioning. (Of the five lawyers

present, Quincy was the only one without the barrister's wig and gown.) But Josiah, like an eager bird dog in the field, soon forgot caution; ten minutes later he was sharp once more on the scent. This time it looked as if even the identity of the man in the red cloak might be revealed, his name published to all the world. Bounding to his feet, John begged the court's permission for a brief adjournment, took his colleague out in the corridor and told him peremptorily that if he didn't keep his mouth shut and use some discretion, he, John Adams, would leave him and Auchmuty to finish the case by themselves. Did Josiah care nothing for the reputation of Massachusetts and the people's cause?

Josiah, deeply contrite, almost weeping indeed, promised to restrain himself in future. The business had got away from him somehow, he said; it had begun to lead him, instead of he it. . . . He was as good as his word; John had no more trouble on that score. But when court rose that same evening, Captain Preston and his friends, much alarmed, sought out John. Why had he stopped Mr. Quincy, whose examination of the witnesses had been most skillful and effectual? Was it possible that Mr. Adams, their mainstay in the defense, was turning on them? No! John replied coldly — it was not possible. Sufficient evidence had already been given to clear Captain Preston and obtain a favorable verdict. But let it be remembered that he for one had undertaken this case in a spirit of impartiality, because he believed an accused man should have full benefit of the law. He must be permitted to conduct the trial in such a spirit or not at all. John's eyes blazed as he said it; he stalked angrily from the room.

But in spite of these minor hazards and skirmishes, the jury at the end of six days brought in a verdict of NOT GUILTY.* Preston's life was saved; the defense had won hands down. For John Adams and Josiah Quincy the acquittal was a triumph and they felt it as such.[3] Boston, however, reacted sullenly; Preston dared not show his face on the streets. Moreover, relatives of the "murdered men" (Boston clung to the phrase) signified they were going to sue him for damages. Preston wrote General Gage that he would like to "go to the Jerseys in order to escape these endless lawsuits but my counsel as-

---

* There is no record of John's speech at this trial. Mr. Hodgson, the shorthand writer, declaring himself exhausted with taking depositions for the 96 original witnesses, refused his services. For sources see Bibliography and Note 3, this chapter.

sure me, I shall not be safer there than here, so that I have been forced to shut myself up in Castle William, where I hope to receive your orders." [4]

It was the last day of October when Preston was acquitted; the trial of the eight soldiers was set for November 27. John wished it were nearer; he had a deep and fervent desire to be done with this business forever. Most certainly Preston's acquittal would make the next ordeal easier, but John was by no means sure of the outcome. For many reasons it was a more difficult business than Preston's. During the intervening weeks John had no time to rest, scarcely time, indeed, to breathe. The Legislature was in session at Cambridge; John had been excused attendance only for the immediate time of Preston's trial. The day the Legislature adjourned, Joseph Hawley of Worcester County appeared at John's house with a sheaf of papers for his approval, another resolution against the Governor, a renewal of the petition to move the Assembly back to Boston. It seemed to John he was always on the ferry. Abigail packed his lunch in a cabbage leaf and tied it with string — rye bread, meat and cheese, a bag of plums from Penn's Hill which John shared with the ferryman at Charlestown Crossing.

During Preston's trial the Boston *Gazette* had been mercifully silent, even after acquittal. This was the more surprising in that the town's reputation had come out of the affair not a little tarnished, in spite of John's exertions to safeguard it. Affidavits had been procured from members of the 29th Regiment now in "the Jerseys." These were especially damaging. General Gage remarked they proved "the people of Boston to be the most Vile Sett of Beings in the whole Creation." At the very end of the trial, old Justice Lynde, addressing the jury, had said gravely that he was "happy to find, after such strict examination, the conduct of the prisoner appears in so fair a light. Yet I feel myself deeply affected, that this affair turns out *so much to the disgrace of every person concerned against him, and so much to the shame of the town in general.*"

It soon became obvious the *Gazette* had been saving its fire. Preston's acquittal had greatly increased the general desire for vengeance against the eight soldiers. On the Monday before their trial, the paper came out with a nicely timed blast. . . . "Is it then a dream, — murder on the 5th of March, with the dogs greedily licking human

blood in King-Street? Some say that righteous Heaven will avenge it. And what says the Law of God, *Whoso sheddeth Man's blood, by Man shall his Blood be shed!*" *

John, reading the paper that evening at home, swore roundly. The worst of it was, the *Gazette* quoted not only the Bible but a sermon given yesterday in First Church. The Reverend Dr. Chauncy, senior minister of Boston, had risen in the pulpit, his white locks serene about his ears. In a shocked voice he announced there was a rumor around town that should the soldiers be convicted of murder, a reprieve would be granted them. Even the suspicion of so base a move must be suppressed, the minister insisted. It was an indignity, a scandalous reproach upon Governor Hutchinson. "Surely he would not counter-act the operation of the law, both of God and man! Surely he would not suffer the town and land to lie under the defilement of blood! Surely he would not make himself a partaker in the guilt of murder, by putting a stop to the shedding of their blood, who have murderously spilt the blood of others!"

The *Gazette* quoted luxuriously from Chauncy's sermon, the word *blood* illuminating every sentence. John thrust the paper from him. If Sam Adams, Joseph Warren and the Sons, together with every Congregational minister of Boston, planned to hammer away at this theme all during the trials, then the good work of education achieved with Preston's jury would have to be done over again. . . .

This time, John thought in weary, desperate anger, he would do it himself. He was, he told himself, well equipped. By now he knew the rules governing homicide better than he knew the Lord's Prayer.

CHAPTER TWENTY-TWO

Trial of the British Soldiers.

O N Tuesday, November 27, the Superior Court of Judicature convened once more on Queen Street. This time, the audience overflowed, pressed on the doors outside, begging admittance. Ethics aside, no matter who won or lost, this was to be the greatest show ever staged in Boston. People came in from the country, brought their lunch and ate it in the taverns or shivering on the nearby Common, leaving friends and relatives to hold their seats in the courtroom. (Mr. Hodgson the shorthand writer complained that he had scarce room to move his right elbow.)

The judges walked in and took their places, majestic in red. All four were distinguished men, well known to the Province: Justice Cushing was seventy-five, Chief Justice Lynde over seventy. The two had presided years before, when James Otis argued against the writs of assistance. Justice Trowbridge was the most learned judge in Massachusetts, a serious, melancholy man. He had taught law to James Putnam; John had known him since Worcester days. The fourth judge, Peter Oliver, was a roaring Tory, good-looking, tall and heavy; he wore the scarlet robe and wig with style. Oliver had always been something of a grandee. When he rode on circuit he went in coach and four, with outriders and postillions, his coat of arms blazoned on the door.

Samuel Quincy and Robert Treat Paine, as before, were the lawyers for the prosecution. John and Josiah Quincy had an assistant in the person of Sampson Blowers, a young man in his twenties engaged by Preston's friends to help with the enormous work of digging

up witnesses and taking affidavits. (All in all, the crown was to produce thirty-two witnesses, the defense, fifty-one.)

The eight soldiers were led to the bar; their red coats made a
blaze of color in the room. Their faces were set, without expression,
and pale from confinement. They stood with their backs to the audience while the clerk read the indictment: "William Wemms, William
M'Cauley, Matthew Killroy, Hugh Montgomery, James Hartegan,
Hugh White, William Warren and John Carrol, *not having the fear
of God before their eyes, but being moved and seduced by the instigation of the devil and their own wicked hearts, did, on the fifth day
of this instant March, with force and arms, feloniously, wilfully and
of their malice aforethought . . .*"

They were charged, specifically, as principals and accessories
in the murder of five citizens. The dead were (1) Maverick, a seven-
teen-year-old apprentice boy shot fatally a few minutes after he had
shouted at the soldiers, "Fire away, you damned lobsterbacks"; (2)
Sam Gray, the tough ropewalker who three days before the Massacre had offered the soldier a job (the nature of which was to come
out strong at the trial); (3) Crispus Attucks, the huge, knock-kneed
mulatto of forty-seven who seemed to have done more rioting than
any other six men together; (4) James Caldwell, a sailor from a
Massachusetts coasting vessel; and (5) the innocent bystander, Patrick Carr, known as "the Irish teague," who had lingered ten days
after he was shot in the breast, suffering horribly.

Everyone in the courtroom — everyone in Boston — was familiar
with these facts before the trial began. A large part of the audience
had been acquainted with the dead men, and knew also the soldiers
by name and face. Two were particularly well known and hated:
Matthew Killroy, who killed young Maverick, was notorious as a
surly, quarrelsome character; and Hugh Montgomery, the soldier
who had borne the worst barrage of oyster shells and ice and who
had been knocked to the ground before firing his gun.

To the indictment, the prisoners answered one by one, NOT
GUILTY! And the clerk replied solemnly, in the immemorial words of
the English law, "*God send you a good deliverance!*" The talesmen
came forward to be challenged by the prisoners and their counsel. It
was a business of utmost importance. John was determined to include
no partisan, no spokesman for those who might have incited the

Massacre. Before John was done, thirty jurors had been rejected. Among the twelve who finally walked to the box, there was not a Boston man, a fact that was to bring on a diatribe of bitterest abuse from the *Gazette*. They were all countrymen, from Roxbury, Dedham, Milton, Hingham — and one, Isaiah Thayer, from Braintree: John Adams knew him well.

"Good men and true," the clerk said, "stand together and hearken to your evidence!"

There was a stir in the courtroom. It was a dark morning; outside the windows, snow was falling. There were two fires in the courtroom but the audience shivered in winter cloaks and gloves. Samuel Quincy rose and opened for the crown. The cause today, he said, was perhaps "the greatest that had yet come before a tribunal in this part of the British dominions, a cause grounded on the most melancholy event that has ever taken place on the continent of America." Praying the jury, by virtue of their oath and their duty, to examine the evidence impartially, without passion or prejudice, Samuel Quincy produced the witnesses for the prosecution and began to question them.

Their testimony took all that day and the next. They easily identified the prisoners as the soldiers who had fired on the people; what they said was almost a replica of the original ninety-six depositions gathered by Sam Adams and his friends. . . . "There came seven soldiers from the main guard without any coats on, driving along, swearing and cursing and damning like wild creatures, saying 'Damn 'em we are seven . . . by Jesus let them come . . . damned Yankee boogers, slay them all.' " . . . The morning after the riot, Private Killroy's bayonet was thick with dried blood to three inches from the point.

John, at the lawyer's table, wrote busily, taking down the evidence, underlining what seemed most important.* Nothing new was revealed, although the prosecution obviously was going to make capital of the dried blood on Killroy's bayonet. It was Thursday morning before Samuel Quincy was ready to sum up the evidence: Eight soldiers had fired on the citizens. But except for Killroy, who shot the apprentice boy, and Montgomery, who fired first and probably

---

* John's notes of the evidence, his digest of Josiah Quincy's opening speech for the defense, and notes for his own brief, can be seen in his handwriting at the Boston Public Library.

killed Crispus Attucks, the evidence was not precise as to who had killed whom. Killroy was proven to have been in the fight at the ropewalks the previous Friday; moreover, he had been heard to say — in cold blood, quite sober — that "ever since he landed in Boston he had wished for a chance to fire on the inhabitants."

Resting his case, Samuel Quincy instructed the jury as to the law. "I remember," he said, "at the last trial [Preston's], my brother Adams made this observation, that 'Man is a social creature; his feelings, his passions, are contagious.' * In the events of March fifth, there was food indeed for the passions to feed on; murder was done *sedato animo*, in cold blood."

It was shortly after nine in the morning when Samuel Quincy began to speak; he kept on for more than an hour. He spoke well, far better than he had against Captain Preston. There were, he began, two things to prove: (1) the identity of the prisoners, together with the fact that they committed the acts·charged in the indictment. And (2) the motivation that lay behind these acts. . . . Reviewing the testimony of his witnesses, Quincy proved the first point satisfactorily and at some length. Then he took up the question of motive — the provocation, what he called "the circumstances that lay behind the act."

"What species of homicide is this?" he demanded. And was there, in law, such a thing as *voluntary manslaughter?* He reminded the jury that the question had been asked today from the bench itself. He had never seen in any book or record, a decision based on voluntary manslaughter. "A person cannot justify killing if he can by any means make his escape. He should endeavor to take himself out of the way before he kills the person attacking him."

Judge Trowbridge interrupted. "You are anticipating the defense," he said. The four judges conferred, agreed that counsel in opening a case cannot be permitted to anticipate what may be urged on the other side. Quincy gathered up his papers. He had more to say, he told the court; but he deferred to their objection. Also, he could wish that the fatigues of yesterday, and the circumstances of his family, had permitted him "to arrange the evidence more particular." On the evidence so far, the facts against the prisoners were fully proven. Quincy turned to the jury. "Until something turns up to re-

---

* This quotation, from Samuel Quincy's speech, is all we have of John's defense of Preston.

move from your minds the force of that evidence, you must pronounce the prisoners GUILTY."

In the jury box twelve good men and true watched Sam Quincy
take his seat. Their faces indicated nothing. What he said had been
proper, orderly, reasonable — and lacked fire altogether. The jury
did not desire pyrotechnics; no jury ever does. But lack of fire im-
plies lack of conviction; the Solicitor for the Crown had not carried
conviction in his tone. Moreover, Sam Adams's printed *Narrative of
the Massacre,* together with the original depositions of the ninety-six
witnesses, had long ago made the prosecution side of the case familiar
to everyone. There was little Quincy could have added: it was the
defense which was the unknown quantity. And it was the defense
for which audience, jury, bench and prisoners waited impatiently.

Quincy had scarcely seated himself when his younger brother was
on his feet, almost visibly trembling with eagerness. John watched
his young associate narrowly. He himself was to sum up the case,
after Josiah had examined the crown's evidence and called the witnesses for the defense. Josiah was beautifully prepared; he and John
together had gone over every scrap of evidence, worked the thing out
laboriously, minutely. ("We must test each argument," John had
said, "as though it were written in a foreign language.") If Josiah
kept his head, the next day or two would see the building of a strong,
impregnable platform for John to stand on when the trial should be
near its close. . . .

As Josiah Quincy bowed to the judges, chairs scraped, the audience
craned its neck, whispering. The jury sat up, seemed to shake themselves like twelve dogs emerging from deep water. Outside, the storm
had spent itself; it was a clear day of sparkling snow, with the wind
sharp from the northwest. The sun sent long, dusty shafts down from
the eastern windows. . . . There was about Josiah Quincy something hugely engaging. He was neither tall nor handsome; he was
cross-eyed and he coughed — but these things seemed only to add
to his attractiveness. Perhaps his charm lay in his youth, his fair hair
and high color, his clear, soft voice and slim figure — or the knowledge that he was doomed. One of the Quincy brothers had already
died of consumption; Josiah had been heard to say he had only a few
years to live, and he was going, with God's help, to live them deeply.

On this Thursday morning he lived as deeply, perhaps, as he ever

would again. Conviction rang and quivered through all he said, febrile, highly contagious. . . . There was a prejudice in this country, Josiah began. that said a soldier's life was not as valuable as a citizen's. But the law did not think so — and it was with the law they were concerned today. This whole continent, moreover, considered its rights and liberties invaded, its chains already forged by the parliament of England, its fetters prepared. And now, behold! — soldiers arriving to fasten, rivet the shackles of this bondage! . . . But with the justness of these fears, Quincy told the jury, "you and I have nothing to do in this place. You are here as jurymen not as statesmen . . .

"Gentlemen," said Josiah Quincy, "great pains have been taken by different men with different views, to involve the character, the conduct and reputation of Boston in the present issue. *Boston and its inhabitants have no more to do with this cause than you or any other members of the community.* You are therefore by no means to blend two things so essentially different as the guilt and innocence of this town and the prisoners together."

John Adams, sitting in his usual place at the lawyers' table, gave a scarcely perceptible motion of the head. . . . Good! . . . Josiah was making honorable amends; this time he would need no tap on the shoulder. . . . "We must steel ourselves," Quincy went on, "against passions which contaminate the fountain of justice. Our present decision will be scanned, perhaps, through all Europe. We must not forget that we ourselves will have a reflective hour, an hour in which we shall view things through a different medium — when the pulse will no longer beat with the tumults of the day — when the conscious pang of having betrayed truth, justice and integrity shall bite like a serpent and sting like an adder!"

Again there was movement in the audience. Heads nodded solemnly, faces turned toward the jury. Young Josiah, arguing against passion, had already raised the temperature of the courtroom considerably. A call to arms could not have stirred them more. The spectators glowed with the desire to do justice at its most romantic. Appeal to the New England conscience, John thought, looking round him, and you appeal to its heart. Let Josiah not overdo it, now, at the outset. Let him save his fire a little. The jury was red-hot and ready for the molding. . . . They cooled off visibly as Josiah launched into a painstaking review of the crown evidence; they

perked up again as witnesses for the defense were called and began
one by one — over fifty of them — to review the events of the fatal
evening.

Every witness was well known to someone in the audience — as
relative, servant, physician, friend. What more fascinating than to
see how one's apprentice boy or one's cousin Shubael conducted himself under examination? It was by all odds the best show ever staged
in Boston, its stake the lives of eight men. . . .

BENJAMIN LEE, *sworn:* As I stood by the sentinel; there was a barber's
boy came up and pointed to the sentinel and said there is a son of a bitch
that knocked me down; on his saying this, the people immediately cried
out, kill him, kill him, knock him down.

DANIEL CORNWALL, *sworn:* I saw them throwing oyster shells and snow
balls at the sentry at the Custom-house door, he was on the steps. Some
were hallooing out, let us burn the sentry box, let us heave it over-board,
but they did neither. Just before the soldiers fired, I heard the people say,
damn you, fire, you bloody backs.
QUESTION: *What number of people were there about the sentinel?*
Near two hundred boys and men.
Were they pressing on the sentry?
Yes they were. They said fire, damn you, fire, fire you lobsters, fire,
you dare not fire.

Inexorably, the testimony piled up. Witness by witness the town
was incriminating itself, digging its own deep pit. . . .

JOHN BULKELY, *sworn:* I went to Mr. Josiah Quincy's office near the
main-guard; there was a prodigious noise in King Street. I apprehended
the sentinel was in danger. Capt. Preston was before the office, and
appeared in a great flutter of spirits. I knew not he was captain of
the day. A very young officer commanded the guard; I pitied his situation.
A person came to Capt. Preston and said they were killing the sentinel;
Capt. Preston said, damn you, why do you not turn out; he spoke
roughly to them.

The testimony took up all Friday and Saturday. Perhaps the most

damaging witness was Dr. Jeffries, the surgeon who had attended Patrick Carr, "the Irish teague," before he died:

After dressing his wounds, I advised him never to go again into quarrels and riots; he said he was very sorry he did go. He told me also, he was a native of Ireland, that he had frequently seen mobs, and soldiers called upon to quell them; that he had seen soldiers fire often on the people in Ireland, but had never seen them bear half so much before they fired in his life.

JOSIAH QUINCY: *How long did he live after he received his wound?*
Ten days.
When had you the last conversation with him?
About four o'clock in the afternoon preceding the night in which he died, and he then particularly said he forgave the man, whoever he was, that shot him; he was satisfied he had no malice, but fired to defend himself.

When the last witness had said his say and retreated, it was five o'clock on Saturday afternoon. (The trial had begun the previous Saturday morning.) Court rose, the jury was led out to be locked up over the week end. The spectators stood, stretched themselves and walked into the winter dusk. Among them the more ardent Sons of Liberty were conspicuous by their absence; the thing had become too uncomfortable, too painful altogether. The Sons stayed away, but they were neither idle nor passive. Half a block from the courtroom, at the *Gazette* office, pens flew. Should the verdict be acquittal — and the evidence pointed that way — Sam Adams, Joseph Warren, Will Molineux and the Messrs. Edes and Gill had no intention of letting their beloved town of Boston go down smirched and blasted to posterity. There were other ways to try murder than in court. . . .

On Monday morning, December second, at nine o'clock, Josiah Quincy began summing up the evidence for the defense. How differently the jury must feel, he exclaimed, since they heard this testimony! He was sure they no longer thirsted for the application of certain ancient laws, much hammered at around town of late: *Whoso sheddeth man's blood, by man shall his blood be shed.* . . .

Josiah, having talked this morning a solid hour, and having been on his feet the previous week for three entire days, drew a long, quivering breath and prepared to make an end. He quoted "the

sagacious Mr. Locke" on the English law; he quoted Shakespeare: "The quality of mercy is not strained." Stretching out his right hand he invoked upon the jury, in a hypnotic whisper, the eventual benediction of those in jeopardy for their lives: "May their blessing come upon you! May the blessing of 'him who is not faulty to die' descend and rest upon you and your posterity!"

The soft, ringing voice ceased; there was silence in the courtroom. Josiah Quincy sat down. The audience turned moist eyes upon the jury, who looked dazedly at one another. After such blazing rhetoric, what was left for Mr. John Adams? There really seemed nothing more to say. Yet the clock over the judge's head told only half-past ten in the morning and Mr. Adams, senior counsel for the defense, had not spoken beyond his preliminary challenge of the jury. Already the jury felt exhausted. Sunday in the courthouse had not rested them. They had wrangled ceaselessly over the testimony of the witnesses, coming back stubbornly to the conclusion — taught them since childhood, imbibed with their mother's milk — that "blood had been shed and for it blood must atone." Josiah Quincy had mentioned the point this morning it was true. But after all, he was a very young man. Who was he to set aside the laws of God and Moses? In the liberty party, it was well known, were many outright atheists.

Mr. John Adams on the contrary, was in his middle years. (John was just turned thirty-five, but in his barrister's wig and gown he looked older.) It was well known he seldom missed a Sabbath Meeting. It was known also that he was a great partisan for the liberty side and had been elected to fill James Otis's seat in the Massachusetts Legislature. The incident of his stopping Josiah Quincy's cross-examination in Preston's trial had made a great impression. People said John Adams was not to be turned from his course by either passion or partisanship.

The clock in the courtroom struck eleven as John stood up to close for the defense. The very manner of his rising was reassuring. He was so plain in what he did, taking his time, drawing no long breaths, making no preliminary gesture or preparation. How neat he was in his black gown, the white bib and collar freshly laundered! Under the curled gray wig his face had a workaday, morning look. And his voice, when he began to speak, carried a quality more of energy than anything else, although it was evident he was deeply concerned.

"May it please your Honors," John began, "and you, gentlemen

of the jury: I am for the prisoners at the bar, and shall apologize for it only in the words of the Marquis of Beccaria: *If I can be but the instrument of preserving one life, his blessing and tears of transport shall be a sufficient consolation to me, for the contempt of all mankind.*"

Audience and jury turned instinctively to the prisoners' box, where eight men waited, dressed in the uniform of the British army. Hitherto the prisoners had sat nearly motionless. But at John's words, so unexpected, so moving after days and hours of testimony concerning blows, wounds, anger, hatred and death, the men shifted their position, exchanged glances. It was as if a new breath had blown into the room, bringing hope not only of justice but of mercy, kindness, the restoration of the faith man has in man.* Somehow, in these long days of argument and counter-argument, of witnesses by the dozen and by the score, the prisoners had been overlooked. The spectators had come to regard the trial as something like a chess game, calculating the next move, setting witness against witness, ready to bet good money on the outcome and forgetting, as the hours passed, that the lives of eight men hung on the issue. . . .

"As the prisoners stand before you for their lives," John was saying, "it may be proper to recollect with what temper the law requires that we should proceed to this trial. . . . The form of proceeding at their arraignment, has discovered that the spirit of the law upon such occasions is conformable to humanity, to common sense and feeling; that it is all benignity and candor. And the trial commences with the prayer of the court, expressed by the clerk to the supreme judge of judges, empires and worlds: *God send you a good deliverance.*"

John Adams of Braintree knew his jury, God-fearing men all. And in the jury's mind in turn there was no doubt by now that the Senior Counsel for the Defense called upon the Supreme Being with the fear of God in his own heart. No atheism here, no newfangled deistical casuistry. This was a plain man like themselves, to whom an oath taken was sacred. . . .

"In the rules laid down by the greatest English judges, who have

---

* In the *Works*, John's grandson, Charles Francis Adams, as careful and austere an editor as the nineteenth century affords, goes so far as to say that John's opening words that day "spread a thrill through the auditory," adding that individuals present carried to the end of their lives "a most vivid recollection" of the incident. (*Works* I, pp. 111-112.)

been the brightest of mankind," the strong, even voice continued, "we are to look upon it as more beneficial that many guilty persons should escape unpunished, than that one innocent person should suffer. I will read the words of the law itself. The rules I shall produce to you from Lord Chief Justice Hale, whose character as a Christian no man will dispute. . . ." Here John read the law in Latin, explained it. "I grant it as a first principle," he continued, "that the eight prisoners at the bar had better all be acquitted, though we should admit them all to be guilty, than that any one of them should by your verdict be found guilty, being innocent."

John paused. There was a sound from the prisoners' box. The accused men sat in two rows. The far man in the last row, Matthew Killroy, was seen to lay both hands over his face. . . . "The action before you now is homicide," John went on. "But it is not criminal in all cases for one man to slay another. Had the prisoners been on the plains of Abraham and slain one hundred Frenchmen, the English law would have considered it as a commendable action, virtuous and praiseworthy."

In the clear, measured voice of a teacher, John instructed the jury in the three kinds of homicide: justifiable, excusable, felonious. If felonious, it might be murder or manslaughter. "God Almighty, whose laws we cannot alter," said John, "has planted in every man the quality of self-love, the first and strongest principle of our nature. Religion has commanded us to love our neighbor as ourselves — but not" — John smiled briefly — "not *better* than ourselves. Common sense directs the law of England here. If two persons are cast away at sea, and get on a plank (a case put by Sir Francis Bacon), and the plank is insufficient to hold them both, the one hath a right to push the other off to save himself."

The jury seemed to assent. "We talk much," John continued, "of *liberty and property*. But if we cut up the law of self-defense, we cut away the foundation of both." John took a step nearer the jury. "Place yourselves in the situation of Killroy or the sentry, with the bells ringing — and you know well there is no fire — the people shouting, huzzaing and making the mob whistle as they call it. Let a boy make this whistle in the street, and it is no formidable thing, but when made by a multitude it is a most hideous shriek, almost as terrible as an Indian yell. The people are crying, Kill them! kill them! knock them down! — and heaving snow balls, oyster shells, clubs,

white birch sticks three and a half inches in diameter. . . . Consider yourselves in this situation and then judge if a reasonable man would not consider they were going to kill him."

Reaching for his book, John read aloud sections of the law on self-defense: "He who on an assault retreats to the wall beyond which he can go no further before he kills the other, is judged by the law to act upon unavoidable necessity. . . . And an officer who kills one that insults him in the execution of his office may justify the fact."

Human beings, said John, amid the shocks of fortune and the whirls of passion are liable to run into riots and tumults. "There are church quakes and state quakes in the moral and political world, as well as earthquakes, storms and tempests in the physical." For some time it had been obvious that a quake of severe proportions was due in Boston. But no matter what its wrongs, Boston was not yet justified in open warfare with the soldiery. "If heaven, in its anger," said John, "shall ever permit the time to come when, by means of an abandoned administration at home, and the outrages of the soldiers here, the bond of parental affection and filial duty shall be shaken loose, then the American and British soldier must fight it out upon the principles of the law of nature and of nations. But such a time is not arrived, and every virtuous Briton and American prays it never may. Till then, we must try causes in the tribunals of justice, by the law of the land. . . .

"I do not mean," John added firmly, "to apply the word rebel on this occasion. I have no reason to suppose that there ever was a *rebel* in Boston, at least among the natives of the country."

Justice Peter Oliver, Tory, raised his eyebrows sharply under the great white wig. To his mind the town of Boston had been a hotbed of rebellion since the year 1761. *This word, rebellion, it had froze them up, as fish are in a pond* (Justice Oliver recalled his Shakespeare).

"Suppose," John was saying, "the people who made this attack on the sentry had nothing more in their intention than to take him off his post. Suppose they intended to go a little farther and tar and feather him, or to ride him (as the phrase is in *Hudibras*), he would have had a good right to stand upon his defense, the defense of his liberty. And if he could not preserve that without hazard to his own life, he would be warranted in depriving those of life who were en-

deavoring to deprive him of his. That is a point I would not give up for my right hand, nay for my life."

John reminded the court that one of the challenged jurymen, at the outset of the trial, had been refused because, while he believed Captain Preston innocent, "innocent blood had been shed, and somebody ought to hang for it." John quoted him, adding that he feared many others had formed such an opinion. "I do not take it to be a rule," said John, "that where innocent blood is shed, the person must die. . . . Here are two persons, the father and the son, go out a-hunting, they take different roads, the father hears a rushing in the bushes. . . ."

The courtroom, the jury, pricked up its ears. Who among them but had taken his gun on his shoulder and gone a-hunting out Milton way with his son, his brother, his friend? Suppose one of them, hearing a movement in the bushes, had fired and killed his son! It would be innocent blood taken, yet the father ought not to die for it. Any man knew that. If the soldiers, defending their lives — Mr. Adams was saying — had killed innocent men, the Bible, the laws of England, did not intend them to die for it. . . .

"The law," John went on, "considers a man as capable of bearing any thing and every thing but blows. I may reproach a man as much as I please; I may call him a thief, robber, traitor, scoundrel, coward, lobster, bloody back. And if he kills me it will be murder, if nothing else but words precede. But if from giving him such kind of language I proceed to take him by the nose, or fillip him on the forehead, that is an assault, that is a blow. The law will not oblige a man to stand still and bear it. There is the distinction: *hands off, touch me not!* As soon as you touch me, if I run you through the heart it is but manslaughter. The utility of this distinction, the more you think of it, the more you will be satisfied with it. It is an assault whenever a blow is struck, let it be ever so slight. And sometimes even without a blow. Every snow ball, oyster shell, cake of ice or bit of cinder thrown that night at the sentinel and the party of soldiers was an assault upon them whether it hit any of them or not."

John turned to the lawyers' table, gathered up his papers with an air of finality. "I have endeavored," he said, "to produce the best authorities, give you the rules of law in their words, for I desire not to advance anything of my own. I choose to lay down the rules of law from authorities which cannot be disputed."

Above old Justice Lynde's head the wall clock struck a slow five, and outside in Brattle Street steeple the bell clanged. The judges rose and moved from the room, but the audience lingered. A people whose only public entertainment had consisted, since childhood, of listening to sermons, election speeches and the famous Boston Thursday Lecture, dispersed slowly to their homes, discussing the case as they walked through the cold December dusk.

John had, in truth, put a different face on things today, with his insistence on the law, his quoting of authorities, followed always by his own careful translation into plain, understandable terms. If Josiah Quincy with his impassioned rhetoric, his young ardor and headlong oratory had fired their imaginations, John Adams had touched their hearts and minds. What was more to the point perhaps, he had reawakened their common sense, something that had been — men acknowledged it — more than a little dormant since the Massacre. People were tired of violence and threat; they were tired indeed of their long-cherished anger. They wished for peaceful days and nights, the return of brisk commerce and busy trade. The 14th Regiment was still at Castle William. Outside in the Harbor lay a dozen ships of war. Their presence colored everything. It was impossible to forget them, with their buglings and boatswain's whistles, their running up of flags, their salutes by cannon at sundown. When the trials were over, if the soldiers were acquitted, perhaps the frigates and the armies would go away.

How much longer, people wondered, would John Adams speak, tomorrow? There remained, also, Robert Treat Paine to close for the prosecution. And the four judges would have something to say, especially Justice Peter Oliver. More than once, Judge Oliver had looked as if he were about to interrupt John Adams, read him some kind of lecture.

On Tuesday morning, December 4, at nine o'clock, John proceeded to the examination and review of the defense testimony. The jury, by now, had had its fill of such examination. So had the spectators; they hunched down on their benches, prepared for boredom. They soon sat up again, listening to an account of the riot that was almost more exciting than the fight itself. . . .

Twelve American sailors with clubs, said John — big clubs cut from hedges — had attacked the British soldiers. What were the soldiers to do, stand still and wait to see if the sailors would knock their

brains out? "Between soldiers and sailors," John added, "there is such an antipathy they fight as naturally when they meet, as the elephant and rhinoceros." Montgomery in particular was "smote with a club and knocked down." As soon as he could rise and take up his firelock, another club, thrown from afar, struck his breast. "Do you expect," John asked the jury bluntly, "that he should behave like a stoic philosopher, lost in apathy? Patient as Epictetus while his master was breaking his legs with a cudgel?"

John's voice was suddenly hard, decisive. "It is impossible you should find this man guilty of murder," he said.

John looked hard and searchingly at the jury. After days of testimony, he felt his point was proven, his clients safe if they were ever to be safe. Before proceeding to his final review, there was something he had to say and he was determined to say it. The entire defense had turned on proving that the soldiers had been attacked, were defending their lives when they fired on the crowd. It was time now to show what John himself believed — that this assault on the soldiers had been made not by the whole of Boston, but by a mob, a rabble, a mere fraction of the populace — and a fraction of which the Province and the friends of freedom should be far from proud. Almost more than they hated the word "rebel," the Sons of Liberty hated the word "mob": to use it was tantamount to a blow in the face. John prepared to use it now.

"We have been entertained," he began, "with a great variety of phrases, to avoid calling this sort of people a mob. Some call them shavers, some call them geniuses. The plain English is, gentlemen, most probably a motley rabble of saucy boys, Irish teagues and outlandish jack tars. And why we should scruple to call such a set of people a mob, I can't conceive, unless the name is too respectable for them. The sun is not about to stand still or go out, nor the rivers to dry up, because there was a mob in Boston on the fifth of March that attacked a party of soldiers. Such things are not new in the world nor in the British dominions, though they are comparative rarities and novelties in this town. Indeed, from the nature of things, soldiers quartered in a populous town will always occasion two mobs where they prevent one. They are wretched conservators of the peace!"

Twelve jurymen, country born and bred, listened in stolid approval. John went rapidly on, entered into a minute and merciless

consideration of every witness the crown had produced, then once more reviewed the testimony for the defense. It was four in the afternoon when he got through. It was moreover the ninth consecutive day of the trial, not counting two Sundays. The jury was exhausted; so were spectators, judges, prisoners. (John himself did not yet recognize his own deep fatigue, although in the past hour something had happened to his voice; it was difficult to make himself heard.) Everyone, by this time — probably including the judges — knew more about the homicide laws than they had expected to know in their respective lifetimes.

John laid down his notes and glanced at the jury, which moved restively, bracing itself for the inevitable peroration, the throbbing emotional appeal they had learned to expect. But John made no such appeal. "Facts," he said, "are stubborn things. And whatever may be our wishes, our inclinations or the dictates of our passion, they cannot alter the state of facts and evidence. Nor is the law less stable than the fact. The law, in all vicissitudes of government, fluctuations of the passions or flights of enthusiasm, will preserve a steady, undeviating course; it will not bend to the uncertain wishes, imaginations and wanton tempers of men. To use the words of a great and worthy man, a patriot and an hero, an enlightened friend of mankind and a martyr to liberty—I mean Algernon Sidney: *The law no passion can disturb. 'Tis void of desire and fear, lust and anger. 'Tis written reason, retaining some measure of the divine perfection. It commands that which is good and punishes evil in all, whether rich or poor, high or low. 'Tis deaf, inexorable, inflexible.*"

John moved closer to the jury and made a great effort to speak clearly. "The law," he said, "on the one hand is inexorable to the cries and lamentations of the prisoners. On the other it is deaf, deaf as an adder to the clamors of the populace. . . . Gentlemen, to your candor and justice I submit the prisoners and their cause."

He turned and walked to his seat, mopping his face with a large red India handkerchief. Robert Treat Paine got up to close for the crown. Mr. Hodgson the shorthand writer gave an audible groan and wriggled his right hand, holding the wrist. Then he leaned back in his chair, looked round the courtroom with glazed and hopeless eye. He was through and he did not care who knew it. Paine spoke well, far outdoing his associate, Sam Quincy. But the jury, by this time, had absorbed, they considered wearily, more law, more facts and

more summings up than mortal ears should be asked to absorb in a
year, let alone two weeks. Mr. Hodgson was not alone in his rebellion; if the jury listened they gave no evidence of it.

Robert Treat Paine, who was no fool, and well versed moreover in
the ways of juries, made an end as quickly as he could. Justice Lynde
adjourned court, to meet next morning for the judges' charge to the
jury. Everyone went home. At eight o'clock on Wednesday morning most of Boston, with wife and neighbor, was in the courtroom or
waiting outside. Mr. Hodgson, refreshed, took up his pen. Judge
Trowbridge spoke first and at much length; it was the longest charge,
he said, that he had ever given any jury. He spoke of "riot and rebellion," and he did not scruple to use the word "treason," adding
that "the law in that regard should be more generally known here
than it seems to be." The two oldest judges, Cushing and Lynde,
added little to what Trowbridge had said.

It was Judge Peter Oliver's words that made the profoundest impression. This, he told the jury, was "the most solemn trial he ever
set in judgment upon." Pains had been taken "to exculpate this town"
from guilt; outrageous attempts made to prejudice the Province
against the prisoners at the bar — especially one newspaper article
published the day before the trial came on, which had libeled the
court as well as the prisoners. "I think," said Judge Oliver indignantly, his dark eyes flashing under the huge wig, "I never saw
greater malignity of heart expressed in any one piece, a malignity
blacker than ever was expressed by the savages of the wilderness."
This riot, the judge went on, had been perpetrated "by villains" —
men heard to damn in public His Majesty himself. As for the "tall
man in the Boston red cloak and white wig," whoever he was, the
calling out of the main guard and consequent attack on the soldiers
were the result of his speech to the people. . . . "That tall man,"
Judge Oliver finished, his voice booming to the four corners of the
room, "is guilty in the sight of God, of the murder of the five men
mentioned in the indictment. And although he may never be brought
to a court of justice here, yet unless he flies speedily to the city of
refuge, the Supreme Avenger of innocent blood will surely overtake
him!"

Peter Oliver, arranging his robes regally about him, leaned back in
his chair. He had said his say. The next trial that he would like to see
would be in London, and it would result in Sam Adams's head grac-

ing the spikes of Tyburn gate. (It had already been suggested that Samuel Adams be sent to England to be tried for treason.)

The jury withdrew. They were gone two hours and a half. John Adams, who had looked for a quick verdict, felt sick with anxiety. Judge Oliver's almost venomous address could not change the verdict — but it might cause serious, dangerous trouble among the Boston Sons in case of acquittal. . . . They had already been forced to accept a measure of guilt and humiliation at John's own hands. But it was one thing for John Adams, Representative in the Legislature, to call that crowd of citizens on March 5 a "mob"; it was another for a crown judge in a scarlet robe to rear up and say it from the bench . . . The Sons of Liberty were not famous for patience. . . . Six of the prisoners, John felt sure would be acquitted, but he was much worried over Killroy and Montgomery. Should the jury find them guilty of manslaughter, he would ask benefit of clergy; he and Josiah Quincy had long ago agreed to that. (Benefit of clergy was an ancient English law that permitted the clergy to demand trial by an ecclesiastical court which could not inflict the death penalty. Today, in 1770, benefit of clergy had been extended to all who could read and write. Those to whom it was granted were branded in the thumb and discharged immediately.)

A door behind the bench opened; the jury was returning. They stood while the foreman, Joseph Mayo of Roxbury, gave the verdict: "William Wemms, James Hartegan, William M'Cauley, Hugh White, William Warren and John Carrol: NOT GUILTY! . . . Matthew Killroy and Hugh Montgomery, NOT GUILTY of murder, but GUILTY of manslaughter."

As the foreman's voice ceased, John rose instantly and asked benefit of clergy for Killroy and Montgomery. The judges granted it. (No doubt they had expected the move.) The six innocent men were discharged and left the courtroom. The iron was brought and heated at the open fire. Killroy and Montgomery stood up. The courtroom rose with them, stretching eagerly on tiptoe. Old Justice Lynde, rapping angrily with his gavel, bade all but the prisoners to be seated. Only the front rows saw the branding, saw the two men stretch out their hand and receive the hot iron on their thumb. The judges rose, the trial was over.

John Adams, gathering up his papers, walked to the prisoners' room. They seized his hand, crowded round him. "God bless you,

Mr. Adams!" they cried. "We owe our lives to you and Mr. Quincy. You are an honest man and a clever one."

"And by God, a brave one!" somebody said roughly.

Matthew Killroy, considered by all odds the toughest of the eight, sat in his chair, weeping openly. Tears of joy and relief poured down his face, his sobs alternated with desperate curses on his own lack of manhood for crying. Montgomery held up his branded thumb. "A small price to pay for our lives, Sir," he told John with a grin.

John took the man's hand in his, examined the burned thumb. "I am sorry for this," he said. He did not add that he had seriously considered — and repudiated — the idea of pleading with the judges to excuse Montgomery and Killroy from the branding. Too complete a victory might result in a later and far more dangerous verdict and punishment from the town of Boston. "What had we best do now, Mr. Adams?" someone asked. "Do you think we shall be safe on the streets?"

"No!" John said shortly. "You will not be safe. Get yourselves conducted under guard to the wharf and the Castle." . . . "And you, Sir?" William Wemms asked. He was the most intelligent of the eight; throughout the trial he had been their spokesman when necessary. "Will your life be safe?"

John turned to leave the room. "You forget, gentlemen," he said wearily, "that you have been acquitted by a jury of my countrymen. Boston is my home."

John's voice was bitter; everyone in the room felt it. He shook each man again by the hand, left quickly and walked from the courthouse.

It was dark in the street outside. John trudged home, holding his lantern before him. Where his light fell, snow was dirty. The weather had turned suddenly warm but there was a dampness in the air. John shivered, holding his head down, hugging his long cloak tighter to his body. . . . Next week the third trial was due — that of the four Tory sympathizers accused of firing on the crowd from the Custom House windows. It would be a mere farce; nobody had shot a gun from the Custom House. The Grand Jury should have seen through such flimsy fabrication in the first place. The whole thing could be exposed in half an hour.

And half an hour, John thought, dragging leaden feet over the cobblestones of Dossett's Lane, would be about all he was equal to.

His very bones were numb. He would go right up to bed, ask Abigail to bring him a hot rum toddy. . . . This, today, had been what the world calls victory. He had won his case, he had saved the lives of eight men. Yet he felt no relief, let alone elation. Victory! A man looked forward to it as though the event would change his life, alter the very climate of the day, enhance the aspect of sun or stars, charge his spirit with some mysterious and lasting power to make all future problems easy.

Yet when victory came, it changed nothing, nothing at all. The east wind was as penetrating, the procession of minutes as inexorable toward the morrow. Victory presented herself, and all a man thought of was hot rum toddy. Women knew this. Women never deluded themselves. Perhaps it was because they looked forward to no triumphs of their own beyond the triumphs of hearth and nursery. . . . Thank God, John thought, climbing three steps to his front door — thank God he need not explain himself to Abigail, pretend that moral victory kept a man's feet warm on a cold night. Abby knew how he felt by the sound of his step on the stair. She had told him so.

Laying his hand on the heavy brass latch, John opened the door of his house and went in.

CHAPTER TWENTY - THREE

"Farewell politics." John retires from public life, takes a journey for his health and decides to make his fortune in the law courts. But his friends decide otherwise.

JOHN proved right about the third trial; the jury acquitted all four prisoners without leaving their seats. The prosecution produced only two witnesses, both easily discredited. One of them, a French servant boy, very glib with his broken English, was so palpably lying that he ended by winning for himself an hour in the pillory with twenty-five stripes for perjury.

The case was closed, the trials ended. John was mortally glad of it; this had been hard labor. He told himself he had come out of it with ten guineas' reward,[1] a clear conscience and a very sore chest. The hoarseness that had begun to plague him increased; it hurt to breathe deeply and he had an intermittent pain in his side. Abigail noted with alarm that her husband had little appetite for his dinner — a sure sign of disturbance in a man who usually ate with relish.

It was not the mere work on the trials that had fatigued John. It was the position in which he found himself, now that the battle was over and won. More than ever, John believed that Britain had put the colonies in an impossible position and that the colonies must resist to the very limit of their constitutional power. Yet the Sons of Liberty hinted broadly that John had gone against them. (To the end of his days, John would be refuting the charge that he turned against the people's cause in the year 1770.) In the nighttime, handbills were secretly posted on the State House door: *The Court hath cheated*

*the injur'd people with a meer Shew of Justice. Let us rise up at the
great call of Nature and free the world from Domestic Tyrants!*

On the other hand the crown men blandly took it for granted that
John had come over to their side, although not by word or sign had
he given them reason so to think. . . . Had ever man maneuvered
himself into such a position? John asked his wife desperately, that
January of 1771. Before God and his conscience he had done right.
He had followed the oath of his calling, defended nine innocent men
in the face of great odds, not to speak of great personal risk. And
what was the result? He found himself misunderstood by both sides.
The friends to liberty looked at him askance; the "friends to government" had adopted him as a favorite son.

It was enough to turn a man's stomach, John said one night at
table. He looked in disgust at his plate of beef and greens, coughed,
and laid a hand on his chest. "Most certainly, my health is failing,"
he told Abby where she sat beyond the candles. "I am going into a
decline. I cannot make a speech in court without my chest hurting
and my throat tightening as if someone closed a hand around it." He
pushed back his chair, thrust a leg before him, gazing somberly at a
well-filled white cotton stocking. "My flesh is falling away. I have
scarce strength enough to mount a horse." He looked at Abby and
when he got no response, continued in a hollow voice: "I have not
told you before; I didn't wish to alarm you. But I think I am not
long for this world. I must put my affairs in order."

Abby helped herself to more pudding. "You are not dying, my
dear," she said, serenely. "And your legs look very well. I have always thought you had a handsome leg. A little less flesh is becoming."
She smiled, then laid down her spoon and was suddenly serious. "But
you need a rest, John. You need the country air. You could breathe
freely enough if we left this town and this town's politics. It is not
honest work in the courts that lies so heavy on your breast. It is your
friends. They have been tearing at you like wolves. Do you think I
haven't seen it?" Abby met her husband's eye, spoke urgently. "Our
lease on this house is up in April. Let's go home, John! Home to
Braintree."

John shook his head. He could not by any possibility leave Boston,
he said. God only knew — John sighed — how he longed for his
fields and meadows, for the pines and rocks, the clear sweet air of
Penn's Hill. But he had wasted almost a year on these infernal trials.

He had a living to make. Did Abby think money rained down from the sky like manna of old? Here they were, approaching middle age — he would be thirty-six next birthday. They had three helpless children to support — two of them boys who must be educated, sent to Harvard College. "Have you no ambition for your sons?" John demanded hoarsely.

Abigail sat unmoved by this tirade. She came back inexorably, after the manner of woman, to the point at hand. "You could ride your horse to Boston each day," she said. "And ride home again at night if you wished. No doubt Josiah Quincy would be glad to share an office with you, somewhere near the Court House. Your two clerks could take care of details."

John rose from the dinner table. "I tell you I am too ill to mount a horse," he repeated; "let alone ride ten miles twice a day."

He left the room without further discussion. But Abby's words, the blessed, healing suggestion of home, stayed with him, a loophole for comfort. Looking about him, John saw the crown party, only four weeks after the last Massacre trial, enjoying complete and unmitigated triumph, not alone in Massachusetts but throughout America. It was the quickest about-face he had ever beheld in the political world. The Massacre had everywhere jolted "men of fortune, men of the better sort" into shocked realization that their country was drifting under the rule of King Mob and they had better do something about it. Now that the Townshend duties were removed, merchants had no need to band together in resistance to Britain. New York, then Philadelphia, then Charleston abandoned the Non-importation agreement. In Boston, large importers like Isaac Low and even Thomas Cushing, Speaker of the House, agreed quite frankly that it was time to stop quarreling with England about taxation, colonial liberties and "high points about the supreme authority of Parliament." John Hancock deserted altogether, advertising his British merchandise blatantly in the very pages of the *Gazette:*

John Hancock
Informs the Public

That after the most strict Compliance with the Non-Importation Agreement during its Continuance he has received by the Ship Lydia, Captain Scott,

An Assortment of Goods, which he will sell Wholesale, at the very

lowest Rates, at his Store, No. 4, East End of Faneuil-Hall Market, where constant Attendance will be given, and the Favours of his Customers duly acknowledg'd.

Boston shops were filled with tempting merchandise from England: house paints and figured wallpapers; window glass, English desks and furniture; *Walnut Chairs with Turkey-work Bottoms;* Scotch carpets; mirrors, *Glass Sconces for the Mantelpiece,* luster ware; gloves, beaver hats, woolens and satins and brocades; crimson capes and riding cloaks. And as always when times were right and the ocean free for shipping, the repeated, necessary and somehow symbolic advertisement of *Coals from New Castle.*

When the Queen's Birthday came round, Boston celebrated with jovial booming of cannon, fireworks on the Common, a big evening celebration. John's friend, Rowe the merchant, hitherto a stanch friend to the people, attended. "A very grand Assembly at Concert Hall," he wrote in his diary. "The Governor and all the Best People in town, a General Coalition so that Harmony, Peace and Friendship will once more be established in Boston. (Very Good Dancing and Good Musick but very Bad Wine and Punch.)"

Hutchinson's popularity returned in a flood. The "rising sun," men called him now. Once more the tribe of Hutchinson-Oliver rode high, once more dispensed the King's favors to the faithful. The people, it seemed, were coming to their senses at last. If Parliament, thought Hutchinson, could refrain from passing some bungling new restrictive legislation, Massachusetts and her sisters would soon be back where they had been before the French were driven from Canada in '61 — dependent, dutiful, loyal. "We have not been so quiet these five years," Hutchinson wrote to England. "Our incendiaries of the lower order have quite disappeared. The people about the country have certainly altered their conduct, and in this town, if it were not for two or three Adamses, we should do well enough."

At the South End of Boston, Mr. Samuel Adams, *Grand Incendiary, Matchiavel of Chaos, Master of the Puppets,* sat with his friends and took stock of the situation. Things looked extremely black. The Whig party was falling to pieces; there seemed nothing to hold it together. But Sam believed he could still count, in a Province of two hundred and fifty thousand, seven thousand souls who would scorn to bow the "Knee of Servility." *Resistance* — to Samuel

Adams it was the very breath of life. Seven thousand was no great number. Yet what had Lord Bacon said? "A few that are stiff do tire out a greater number that are more moderate." Sam intended to see that the seven thousand remained very stiff indeed. "It is a good maxim in Politicks as well as War, to put and keep the Enemy in the wrong." . . . It was an excellent motto; Sam would miss no chance, in this year of 1771, to remind the people that the enemy was still among them. . . .

In January, five weeks after the Massacre trials, Sam launched a series of articles in the *Gazette*, signed VINDEX. They were careful, suave — and wholly venomous. Designed as proof that the soldiers should have been hanged, what they really amounted to was a brand-new trial, with Sam Adams as judge, jury and counsel for the prosecution. . . . Why, demanded VINDEX, were there no Boston men upon the jury, not even one? Why had so much pains been taken to complete a jury of countrymen? Court had been adjourned at noon and sunset each day. Was it possible the judges were afraid to meet honest men on the streets? (Only guilty souls, VINDEX inferred, felt such fears.) . . . The soldier Killroy's bayonet had been bloody three inches from the point, a fact rather slurred over by counsel. . . . VINDEX took up the defense testimony point by point, hinting mysteriously that the witnesses had told only half they knew. How fortunate for Captain Preston that he was not tried by court-martial! "He would not," said VINDEX, "so luckily have escaped."

As climax, VINDEX recalled that as the trials opened, defense counsel had been at pains to quote from the English law, a phrase directed toward the prisoners: *May God send you a good deliverance.* . . . He would like, said VINDEX, to make that same prayer now, for the three juries: *On their own day of trial before the Eternal Judge, may God send them good deliverance!*

John Adams, reading this in his study on King Street, let the paper fall from his hand and sat staring at the wall. *May God send you a good deliverance!* He himself had quoted the line. He would have risked his life for those words and Sam Adams knew it. . . . Was propaganda then to stop at nothing, even the complete distortion of truth? Was the people's cause so hopeless it must be bolstered by such shameful props?

Abigail, entering the room, picked up the paper and began to read.

John sat slumped in his chair; he did not speak. But his wife, a moment later, broke the silence angrily. This was an outrage! she said. It was a thing not to be believed — a betrayal of friendship, a breach of faith and nothing less. "What are you going to do?" Abby persisted. "These pieces will be read from end to end of Massachusetts. Will you write a refutation?"

John shook his head slowly. His wife's indignation, her wholehearted condemnation of Sam Adams had acted somehow as a brake to his own gathering resentment. "I need time," he said. "Time to think. Sam Adams — I always loved him. I always revered him. You say he was my friend. I am not sure —" John paused — "I am not sure if it is important, whether Sam Adams is my friend. He is the people's friend. . . . Abby, it can't be these articles are aimed at me, personally. I cannot believe it. The man doesn't think the way you think, the way I think. Sam Adams lives for the cause. Money, reputation, hope of advancement — nothing matters to him. For the cause, Sam would — I believe he would take his daughter Hannah and throw her in Boston Bay." John stopped, struggling for words. "Abby, Sam Adams doesn't see any farther than the cause," he said.

A few days later, John met his cousin by chance, just outside the State House door. Sam took pains to stop, passed the time of day and asked pleasantly after little John Quincy as he always did. Then he remarked that he hoped John's pen, now the work on the trials was over, would find time to be active again.

Not a word was said about VINDEX. John, walking on alone, even had the distinct and astonishing sensation that Sam had wanted him to mention the articles, applaud them as a politic gesture. . . . How, John wondered in weary bewilderment, could anyone remain angry with a man like that? His singlemindedness amounted to a kind of primal innocence. Yet God knows the man had guile enough. . . . Climbing the Court House steps, his green lawyer's bag over his shoulder, John told himself doggedly that he would stay here in Boston, tend to his legal business and see if things did not straighten out, between him and the Sons. He had always been too sensitive to criticism. A man's fiber must be resilient, tough. It must not, John told himself severely, give way under every adverse turn of circumstance.

March fifth arrived, first anniversary of the Boston Massacre. John

had dreaded the day, and dared to hope that his cousin would let it pass in silence. Surely, the VINDEX articles had sufficed the cause of vengeance! But it was not to be. The *Gazette* came out rimmed in broad bands of black as for a king's death. "Remember this day!" it said, forbearing only to add, "And keep it holy." At noon the church bells began to toll and kept it up for an hour. When the first stroke sounded, John had just come from court and sat down at his office desk. He knew instantly what it meant, and moved instinctively to the window, as though he expected to find commotion outside, men hurrying, running wildly with weapons in their hands. But King Street was empty in the pale noon sunshine, and over wet roofs the red brick chimneys of the Court House rose broad and solid against the sky.

Turning from the window, John began to pace the floor as one after another the bells spoke out in the long funeral rhythm, muffled, slow. Anger once more welled up in John. This indeed was outrageous, intolerable; this was propaganda, naked and unashamed. Sam Adams could have chosen no more powerful weapon; to New England its church bells were the very voice of God. "Revenge!" the bells said, striking, repeating. *Revenge!*

Revenge is a kind of wild justice, which the more a man's nature runs to, the more law ought to weed it out. Bacon's words came back to John; he repeated them bitterly, as a man recalls words of wisdom that come too late. *Law!* What was the law to men who would use such weapons to such an end? John shook his head, trying to rid his ears of the sound; the strokes of the bells were painful as if they beat within his own skull. And with each tolling, each long intolerable moment of clang and echo, John's horror grew. It was more than anger now; it approached despair. . . . That voice, nearest and loudest, was Brattle Street Meeting-house across the street. Even Dr. Cooper, his good friend and his wife's friend, had acquiesced in this outrage. . . . That bell, flat, a little rapid, was from the Brick Church at the North End, where the boy had rung the first alarm on the fatal night. How the bells brought back the scene! Brattle Square, with the soldiers drawn up in line, their bayonets fixed and glinting in the moonlight. . . . That giant voice, deeper, slower, would be the biggest bell of all, from the Old South Meeting-house. . . . REVENGE, REVENGE!

John sank in the chair before his desk and stayed there, motionless,

until the hour was done. Then he crossed the room, opened the hall door and climbed the stairs of his house slowly, with the heavy, uncertain gait of a sick man. In the little sitting room he found his wife sitting by her work table quite idle, hands in her lap. John went to her. His face was pale, his voice very tired. "Abby," he said. "We can't stay here. We can't live here. I can't endure it. You heard the bells."

Abby nodded; her gray eyes were kind. "Of course you can't endure it! You are not called upon to endure it, John dear. We'll go home to Braintree, where we belong. We are countryfolk, you and I. These people" — Abbey made a gesture toward the window and the street — "don't think as we do; they don't look at life as we do. Didn't you say so yourself?" Abby rose, took her husband's hand, smiled gravely. "I have learned skill, these last years, in moving household furniture. If you will ask your brother Elihu to help me, we can be at home for spring plowing."

> *April 18. Thursday*. Fast Day. Still, calm, happy Braintree.
> No journeys to make to Cambridge, no General Court to
> attend. I divide my time between law and husbandry. Farewell politics!

So wrote John in his diary, six days after his arrival at Penn's Hill. How good it was to be home! How quiet the country world outside his window, how bright the April sunshine! And how delicious, in the early morning, to step from one's front door to a yard shining with dew, warm with homely sounds — the lowing of cattle from the barn, the barking of Abby's little dog begging to be released, the foolish hoarse welcome of the ducks waddling forward in a line to be fed. John's very heart felt restored. He was only ten miles from Boston, yet he seemed blissfully separated from the shadow that had followed him so long. Over these fields, these green and rocky pastures where every step and turn brought back his childhood — what benign spirit presided? In peace and gratitude John asked himself the question.

He did not ride back and forth each day to Boston as Abigail had planned, but took lodgings with old Mrs. Bollan, kept his horse at a nearby hostler's and went home as often as he could. His new office was in Queen Street, almost directly across from the new Court

House; Josiah Quincy had rooms adjoining. And John's law practice, to his infinite satisfaction and surprise, took a sudden leap for the better. The great influx of trade from England gave rise to varied and almost endless litigation. There were old debts to settle, contracts, indentures to be drawn. John had more cases than he could handle. Poor James Otis, though rational again, had lost all his business; John was much pleased to be able to turn over to him eighteen clients, four from Boston, the others from the town of Wrentham. Every day confirmed him in the rightness of his decision to leave Boston. From the blessed, healthful vantage point of home, the entire prospect took on a different color. "The people of Boston deserve better treatment from mankind than they meet with," John wrote. "I wish to God it were in my power to serve them. But my wishes for them are impotent, my endeavors fruitless."

Sam Adams, that spring, had fallen on evil days. In the May elections he ran again for one of Boston's four Representatives — and would have lost had it not been for the almost heroic exertions of the North End Caucus Club. A week later, nominated as Register of Deeds for Boston, Sam was ignominiously defeated in favor of the old Tory warhorse, Ezekiel Goldthwaite. Sam himself took it philosophically. "I am *in* fashion and *out* of fashion, as the whim goes," he said resignedly.

But John could not seem to shake off the episode so lightly. He was shocked, disillusioned by this new evidence of fickleness on the people's part. . . . Sam Adams, who a year ago had a thousand friends . . . Sam, whose name had been cheered in the streets . . . defeated, supplanted by a fawning toady who got his bread by licking the boots of the great! "The victors crow like dunghill cocks," John wrote. His depression returned, as black and deep as if it had never left him. At night he came home cross, stalked into the house scarcely greeting the children, and began a long monologue of abuse against Boston and Boston men. Twice, little Abby, listening at her mother's skirts, burst into sudden tears — and John, frowning blackly at the child, flung himself from the room, his shame at his own behavior making him angrier than ever.

Abigail stood it for two weeks, then put on her bonnet and paid a visit to old Dr. Thayer down the hill. Next evening the good doctor put in his appearance at Penn's Hill, went over John, pressed a wigged and rather dirty head against his heart, wrote a prescription

and looked solemnly at his patient over his spectacles. "You are subject," he said gravely, "to weak muscle and lax fiber, which leads to serious irritability of the spleen. This kind of disorder can increase rapidly, rendering a man unfit for business altogether. You must remove yourself immediately from" — the doctor paused significantly — "from Boston. Your office, I understand, is in Queen Street near the docks, a crowded area. With so much refuse burning . . . ships unloading . . . deleterious gases fix the air, thicken its liquids, affect the solids . . . derange the animal economy in the most notable manner."

Dr. Thayer paused to let this sink in. "You must go west immediately. I prescribe a visit to Stafford Springs in Connecticut. The waters there contain a chalybeate principle which your system needs. In short, the springs will cure you." .

Two days later John mounted his horse, said a gloomy farewell to his family and headed alone for the southwestward.

He traveled by way of Worcester, stopping over Sunday at Mr. Putnam's house, at that gentleman's urgent invitation. To John's surprise, the whole town turned out to make him welcome. His former pupils were grown men now. Tad Maccarty was a physician; Nat Chandler, large and quite fat, was studying law in Leicester nearby. Mrs. Maccarty still had five out of her fifteen children living at home. The entire population was Tory; they ranted and raved against Boston and the mob. Old Dr. Willard, especially, inveighed against "Captain" Mackintosh and his "lieutenants of liberty tree." Mr. Putnam was more icily sarcastic than ever.

John arrived at Stafford on a Tuesday. He arranged for his lodging and went immediately to the springs. Near them, one Mr. Childs had built a little station where were housed, John wrote later, "the halt, the lame, the vapory, the hypochondriac, the scrofulous." It was not the most engaging company in which to drink and bathe, especially as the pool itself was tiny. Threading his way gingerly between the halt and the scrofulous, John looked down at the water. It was clear and limpid, gushing out from under a hill; a little wooden gutter carried it down to the pool. The boards were stained yellow, John noted, as were the rocks and stones at the bottom. Mrs. Childs emerged from somewhere, handed John a glass mug, badly cracked and held together with putty. John took it, smelled at it, stooped to the spring and drank. The water tasted of iron and made him gag.

Then he laid off his outer clothes and plunged in the icy water, slipping on the yellow pebbles. He emerged, gasping and shivering, gave Mr. Childs eight pence, plunged again, came out, gave Mr. Childs another eight pence and got into his breeches as fast as he could.

Riding back to his lodgings, John ate his dinner and looked around for someone to talk to. He found nobody and went mournfully to bed. Next morning a Dr. McKinstry of Taunton turned up; John seized eagerly upon him. McKinstry — a slow, ponderous-looking man in steel-rimmed spectacles — professed himself delighted to converse with Mr. John Adams on the science of government. Now, take the Roman Empire, McKinstry began heartily. It came to its destruction as soon as the people got set against the nobles, like Wilkes in England. They went right on quarreling till Brutus — "a great man, Brutus," said the doctor — "carried everything before him and enslaved 'em all!"

John cleared his throat. "You mean Caesar, don't you, Doctor?"

"No," McKinstry replied firmly, shaking his head. "I said Brutus and I mean Brutus. Brutus conquered the Roman Empire and enslaved 'em all."

For two full days, John enjoyed the steady company of Dr. McKinstry, whose ideas about the universe were, John said, "enthusiastical enough to give a fund of entertainment." Nevertheless, John's homesickness increased by the hour. "I grow weary of this idle, romantic jaunt," he wrote. "I want to see my wife, my children, my farm, oxen, cows, fences, walls, workmen, office, books and clerks. I want to hear the news and politics of the day. But here I am, listening each night to landlord reading a chapter of the Bible in the kitchen, and holding prayers with his family in the genuine tone of a Puritan."

On the fourth day, John could endure it no longer. He dared not go home until his time was up. But at least he could abandon that cursed chilly spring and see something of the country roundabout. "Chalybeate principle" indeed! It was nothing but iron; you could buy the same thing from any Boston chemist in a bottle. Besides, the sight of that sick throng — blind people, people with the itch and people with the lung rot — was itself enough to put a man into a decline.

John got on his horse, said a glad farewell to his pious landlord and headed south along the Connecticut River toward Hartford. He was charmed with what he saw. The broad river was shining, placid;

the great road beside it ran clear down to New York! "Here is the finest ride in America," John confessed. "I wish Connecticut river flowed through Braintree." The black-loamed fields of the river valley were rich and fertile. Colts ran in the green meadows; the crops of grain and corn were thick and high. "This morning I rode through paradise," wrote John, then paused to define paradise after his own especial fashion: "The land will yield two crops of English grass, and two tons and a half at each crop with plenty of afterfeed besides, if nicely managed and properly dunged."

But paradise, for John, would never lie far from home. When finally he trotted up the Post Road and clattered into his own barn, he greeted his wife and children with the enthusiasm of a traveler returned from China. "Let me die here, on these scrubby hills," he told Abigail, seizing her, swinging her off her feet while the children screamed with pleasure. "Let me dwindle into ten declines, shrink to skin and bones — but let me never again suffer such banishment! My brains have been barren and my soul starved."

Yet something had restored John, no matter what he said. His wife saw it and rejoiced. His face was smooth and round again, his color had returned, the look of strain was gone. His carping and complaining had vanished like marsh mist under the morning sun. Everything pleased him. He sat patiently while his daughter Abby read her primer, correcting and encouraging; he took small Charles by the hand and led him across the grass to the duck yard, conversing volubly all the way.

Abby watched the little procession contentedly from the doorway. John was very kind. . . . But she must not let herself forget this episode of illness. She must be wary. If she saw the condition returning she must bring John immediately back to Braintree, no matter where his business required him to be. To her husband, Braintree was more healing, Abby knew well, than any chalybeate spring or balsam prescribed by the physician. Abby turned her eyes to the westward, where across the green valley, Milton hills rose faintly purple against the afternoon sun. These hills, she thought; *these fortunate fields* . . . God grant John might never leave them for long. God grant he might spend his days in peace, at home where his heart lay.

On the fifteenth of September, 1772, a third son was born to Abigail and John; they named him Thomas Boylston. He was a

plump, hearty little boy with round cheeks like his father's and a
head as bald as an egg; John laughed whenever he looked at him.
It occurred to John that his family was swelling to vast proportions;
there was no telling where this would end. With a shudder he
thought of Mrs. Maccarty in Worcester and her brood of fifteen.
Abigail reminded him soothingly that these things ran in families. She
herself had only two sisters and a brother; the Adams family was
even smaller. Perhaps little Tommy would be the end, for them.

Perhaps he would, John said dubiously. Yet the situation was one
to make a father sit down and take stock of his property and prospects. . . . At thirty-seven, John owned the house in Braintree and
some sixty-eight acres of farmland,[2] part of it excellent, part dry
and worthless. He had paid off his debt to Colonel Quincy for the
twenty acres of salt marsh by the creek and he had paid two hundred and fifty pounds, old tenor, toward the purchase of the Queen
Street house in Boston where he had his office. Three hundred
pounds remained in savings. It was not much, considering his age
and how hard he had worked. "My season for acquiring knowledge
is past," John wrote in his diary. "For the remainder of my days I
shall decline in sense, spirit and activity. Yet I have my own and
my children's fortune to make."

He wondered what Abigail would think if he suggested moving
back to town. They had been in the country sixteen months; there
was no doubt they both were healthier and happier for it. On the
other hand it was hard, having to ride ten miles in the winter
weather. They could keep the farm for a summer home; it would
not be extravagant.

When John finally broached the subject, his wife met it with her
usual serenity. She had been considering it herself, she said. John's
business had increased to the point where he really ought to be in
town. Moreover, in a few years, John Quincy would be ready for
the Latin School. He was far too clever a child to be held back by
the stultifying methods of Braintree's droning schoolmasters. All
three boys, in fact, would be better off at the Boston Latin School.
The reasons for their leaving town no longer existed: There had
been no riot or excitement in Boston for the past two years; she
saw no reason why there should be in the future.

"And now that I am out of politics," John added, "there will be
far less strain and fatigue in town life."

Abby said nothing to this last, merely remarking that her strength had returned very quickly after little Tommy's birth. She could be ready to move before Christmas.

On the twenty-fifth of November, accordingly, Abigail, with three children, a babe in arms, two maids and a houseboy, followed by the farm cart with a load of firewood, pumpkins, onions and turnips, arrived in Queen Street to join her husband. The new house was much too small. John's office took up the best room downstairs; there were a tiny hall, a dining room and a parlor. Upstairs the new baby slept with his parents; Charles in a trundle bed beneath. The other two children shared a room; the maids were in the attic and the houseboy boarded round the corner.

They were like rabbits in a warren, Abigail said cheerfully. But she did not care, so long as they were together. She reminded John that since the year '68 they had moved five mortal times. Most certainly they appeared settled at last, John answered contentedly.

> I am disengaged from public affairs [*he wrote in his diary*] and now have nothing to do but to mind my office, my clerks and my children. I hope I have profited by retirement and reflection, and learned in what manner to live in Boston. I must remember temperance, exercise, peace of mind. Above all things I must avoid politics, political clubs, town meetings, General Court &c. &c. I must spend my evenings in my office or with my family, and with as little company as possible.

John paused, laid down his pen and drew a long sigh of satisfaction. Then for no especial reason he took up the quill again. Perhaps he feared his own contentment; perhaps his Puritan ancestors looked over his shoulder.

> **Beware** [*he wrote in large, firm letters*] **of idleness, luxury, and all vanity, folly and vice!**

Scarcely had the ink dried on these admirable sentiments when John's new happiness, together with his firm renouncement of the life political, received a nasty jolt. The episode itself was small but its implications were large. James Otis was responsible. It happened one morning when John stopped in at the printing office to see about having some legal documents copied. He stood a moment talking

with Ben Edes and his partner Mr. Gill; Paul Revere was there too, he came often to hear the early news. The talk turned on the local militia and the new training program, urged by Sam Adams since the Massacre. Lately there had been a surprising response. Last training day, said Paul Revere, the turnout had been very large. It was John Adams who was truly responsible for this, Ben Edes put in. At the trials John had proven to the whole Province that un-trained mobs cannot compete with regular troops. . . .

It was at this moment that James Otis stepped in — "his eyes fishy and fiery," John said later, "looking and acting wildly." Otis listened a moment, then turned suddenly on John. "Soldiers?" he said. "*You* will never make a soldier. You can only talk about it. You have the head for strategy — but not the heart for fighting." Otis repeated it scornfully, his face twisted in a grimace. "Not the heart. I have searched your heart. Tired with one year's service as Representative, dancing from Boston to Braintree and from Braintree to Boston. Moping about the streets of this town as hipped as Father Flynt at ninety. *You* don't care for anything but to get money enough to carry you smoothly through this world!"

Otis stopped as suddenly as he had began. His face was purple, his eyes started from his head. Without waiting for reply, he cracked his riding whip against his boot, gave a whoop like a hunting halloa and dashed from the door. Nobody said anything. Ben Edes shrugged his shoulders, Paul Revere seemed suddenly busy tying a cord round a bundle on the table. Mr. Gill walked to the back of the room. They were embarrassed to speechlessness — very sorry for Otis, who was obviously mad or drunk or both.

John mumbled something, took his leave and walked the few steps to his office. He felt both angry and deeply wounded. What Otis said had hurt him less than the silence of the three men. Did the whole town then think of him in such base terms, as a mere money-grubber? Were his former services to the cause forgotten? After all, Edes and Gill, and Revere too for that matter, spent their days at their various businesses, earning a living. . . . John sat down at his diary, reviewed his public services to date, trying to persuade him-self that he cared no whit for what James Otis said or thought.

> I thank God my mind is prepared for whatever can be said of me. The storm shall blow over me in silence.

No storm ever blew over John Adams in silence. This one only renewed his stubborn determination to have nothing more to do with politics and politicians. One December evening not long afterward, he sat working in his office. It was a cold, clear night of stars. Snow had fallen during the day, the windowpanes were frosted thick and John had built a roaring fire in the hearth. At about eight o'clock, the knocker sounded; John rose and went to the door. On the steps beneath the iron lamp stood Mr. Samuel Adams, beside him his trusty henchman, Mr. Pemberton. Snow blew from the street against Sam's red cloak, his hat was powdered with it; as he entered he took it off, shook it vigorously.

John greeted his visitors, laid their cloaks aside, drew up chairs before the fire. He was infinitely surprised to see them — and he felt also infinitely cautious. What did Sam Adams want, and why had he brought along Pemberton, of all people? Pemberton was an extremist, hand in glove with such men as Molineux and "Captain" Mackintosh. *I must be very careful,* John thought. *I must not commit myself.* . . .

Sam sat down, stretched his feet toward the hearth and moved his toes comfortably inside his boots. "We are come," he said cheerfully, "to bid you welcome to Boston. The Sons of Liberty have missed you. Our ranks as you know are something depleted." Sam's rare smile flashed out. "But we are not here in a private capacity. We come as deputies from the Boston standing committee. They have unanimously named you, John, as orator at Faneuil Hall for March fifth next."

Sam raised a hand as John looked up. "We have been very provident about our plans, as you can see. We have come three months beforehand. We know you as a man who likes to make long and thoughtful preparation."

John sat perfectly silent, playing for time. His thoughts whirled, he kept his eyes on the ground. Orator for Massacre Day? In God's name, what was the purpose of this? Was it possible the Sons did not know how he felt about the trials, about the verdict, the celebrations last year, the articles in the *Gazette* . . . the bells. . . . Was this, tonight, one of Sam's plots, something contrived? . . . Most certainly it was a flank attack, a surprise assault. One thing John knew: he must not be put on the defensive. He must not let Sam lead him into argument.

John's manner was formal. "I thank the town of Boston," he said, inclining a little from the waist, "and I thank you also, gentlemen. But I must beg to be excused. I am out of politics forever."

Nobody answered him. Nobody spoke at all. Sam Adams sat easily, eyes on his boots in the firelight. Pemberton cleared his throat, looked intently at the window. A feeling of desperation came over John. . . . Sam Adams glanced up. "What are your real reasons, John?" he asked softly.

John rose from his chair; his voice was hard, decisive. "You desire March fifth* as a martyr's day for Massachusetts," he said. "Possibly that is compatible with a verdict which found the soldiers absolutely innocent. There is a nice distinction here, a distinction the world does not seem capable of making. I see no reason why I should make it for them. I defended the soldiers. The world knows where I stand."

John stopped abruptly, looked straight at Sam. "You know it too," he said.

Sam got up slowly, so did Pemberton. Neither appeared in the least abashed, let alone angry. "Well, John," Sam said, taking up his hat with the old familiar motion of flicking imaginary dust from the crown, "I always said you were no trimmer. The Sons like to say you are a stubborn fellow." Sam moved to the door, laid a hand on the latch and turned. "Good night, my friend; sleep well. . . . And you will keep our visit a secret."

The door closed. John drew a hand across his forehead; he was sweating as if he had run a race. He blew out the candles, banked the fire and, leaving his office, went upstairs to bed. . . . Two days later, he heard that Pemberton was going about calling him "the proudest and cunningest fellow he ever knew." John was not sure if it were praise or insult, nor did he care. He only knew that his refusal, the stand he had taken before Sam Adams, had eased his mind enormously. Perhaps, when March fifth came round, he might even attend the ceremony at Faneuil Hall, listen to whatever orator they might choose. After all, Boston men had lost their lives on that fatal night. The town had a right to mourn them, provided it mourned without revenge. . . .

* To the riot of March 5, 1770, the liberty boys succeeded in fastening the name of Massacre forever, though only five men were killed. Colonel Dalrymple of the 29th Regiment called it a "scuffle." One British historian, Henry Belcher, refers to it in his book as "the little *émeute* in 1770."

1773. January the first, being Friday. I never was happier in my whole life than I have been since I returned to Boston. I feel easy and composed and contented. My resolutions to devote myself to the pleasures, the studies, the business and the duties of private life are a source of ease and comfort to me that I scarcely ever experienced before. A head full of schemes and a heart full of anxiety are incompatible with any degree of happiness. Peace, be still, my once anxious heart.

So wrote John on New Year's Day, at the age of thirty-seven. It was well for him that he could not look ahead. Less than a week later he would be head over heels in politics. And this time he was to jump in very deep. From this final plunge he would not emerge for some thirty winters.

Representative from Massachusetts to the Continental Congress . . . Commissioner to the Court of France . . . Peace Commissioner to England . . . Agent in Holland to negotiate a loan . . . Minister to the Court of Saint James's in London . . . Vice President . . . President of the United States of America . . .

Not until a new century dawned would John Adams find himself again a private citizen. Not until that day when, leaving the White House after four stormy, bitter years as President, he would ride north to Braintree and, sitting down in peace beneath his roof-tree, inscribe himself at last — and with what deep relief — as FARMER JOHN OF STONY FIELDS.

The King's grant and the Massachusetts judges. Sam Adams and the Hutchinson letters. "The Tea that bainfull weed arrives." Parliament closes the Port of Boston, and Massachusetts elects delegates to a Congress.

JANUARY, 1773. America had enjoyed three years of peace. With the Townshend duties gone, merchants grew fat on their ocean trade. True, the tea tax remained, but smuggling was always profitable; New England drank more tea than ever. In Massachusetts the Court party flourished; Thomas Hutchinson's star still rode high. Harmony and prosperity reigned.

Sam Adams did not call it harmony and prosperity. To him it was apathy and corruption, luxury and licentious living. A Puritan to his marrow, Sam looked on the old asceticism as a paramount New England virtue. It stung him that Boston citizens actually gave balls, card parties, routs, evening assemblies, invited Hutchinsons and Olivers to drink their punch, share the delicacies of their table. Yet nothing Sam did could change the situation, neither tolling of bells on Massacre Day, nor eloquent harpings upon past injuries and future dangers. Only Britain herself could break this spell, only some fresh move by Lord North, some rash blunder of the ministry or new threat against the colonies.

The ministry complied. With a perversity almost unbelievable, Britain, this year of '73, moved toward the destruction of her empire. Lord North decided to "reform" the law courts of Massachusetts.

Suddenly, the Province received news that her five judges of the Superior Court henceforth would be paid by the crown, not the people.

The Tories moved swiftly to consolidate this gain. The thing was a mere matter of convenience, they told the people persuasively, in newspaper, pamphlet and Legislature. Instead of the Massachusetts House of Representatives' voting the judges' salaries as hitherto, the bench would be paid outright from monies collected by the crown Commissioners of Customs. The Provincial treasury would be the richer, the Provincial economy would benefit, and the judges themselves receive considerably more money.

Had Lord North aimed at it, he could have done nothing to lure John Adams back into politics more swiftly. What had King James, of infamous memory, said to his Parliament? *You make the laws. Let me make the judges.* Massachusetts judges were crown appointees. The only control the people had over them was in granting or withholding their annual salaries. The Governor was already completely dependent on the crown, the Council almost entirely so. If the judges were made so too, then what part of government, John asked himself, would be left to the people? *Executive and judicial branches must be kept separate, inviolate* . . . John's entire political life to date had been built on this principle: his writing of the "Braintree Instructions" back in '65, his arguing with Governor Bernard for opening the courts without the King's stamps, his essay on the Canon and Feudal Law and even, obliquely, his defense of the British soldiers after the Massacre.

No longer a member of the House of Representatives, John took the only forum left open to him — the newspapers. On Monday, January 4, 1773, the Boston *Gazette* published the first of eight articles on the independence of English judges — articles concealed by no pseudonym, neither VINDEX nor CANDIDUS nor VALERIUS PUBLICOLA, but signed in bold capital letters: JOHN ADAMS. From first to last they explored the nature of government, of empire, of the makeup and procedure of English courts of justice under free constitutional rule. . . . *Judges are the servants of the people and should be paid by the people.* It was a statement that should need no arguing; behind it lay the law, the records, "the whole torrent of history." No English judge holds his commission for life, without the words *quamdiu se bene gesserit* — during his good behavior.

John quoted every authority from Bracton to Blackstone, adding a score of others that nobody ever heard of. He swept off into Latin, making no concession whatever to the popular taste. "And now I go on," he remarked from time to time, "with my delightful work of quotation." From Monday to Monday the articles grew longer until, at the end, the *Gazette* had room for scarcely anything else. The printers reduced the size of their type. John himself began to wonder if his pieces were not "a trifle tedious." His style was surely deteriorating. He had not his former "elegance of expression."

To the Province of Massachusetts, John's articles did not need to be elegant or even entirely comprehensible. By their sheer weight they swept down the Tory argument. The grand historic names, the strings of learned quotations, the long involved paragraphs said what the Province needed to hear. The very sight of those close printed pages was convincing. Here were set forth the people's rights, their privileges by charter, custom and the great traditions of England.

Sam Adams was inspired, about this time, by a device, an invention all his own — a small and seemingly innocent plan of public correspondence between the towns and counties of Massachusetts. Let each town, Sam suggested, form a Committee of Correspondence, to write to neighboring towns and tell how the citizens felt about British taxation and such immediate problems. And let all the towns begin by reporting to the central, Boston Committee on "the sense of the people concerning the judges' salaries."

Never had Sam struck a surer note. The response was immediate and overwhelming. (The Committees of Correspondence were to be Sam's greatest contribution to the American Revolution. They led directly to the Continental Congress in the fall of '74.) In long scrolls, signed and sealed, the towns' Resolves arrived in Boston, sent not by a score of Committees but by a hundred. From Eastham, Stoughtenham, Winchendon; from Salisbury on the Merrimack; from Ipswich, Plymouth, Leicester, Spencer, the messages came. "Death is more eligible than slavery," wrote Marlborough. From Gorham: "The swords which we whet and brightened for our enemies are not yet grown rusty." From Kittery (Maine): "We offer our lives as a sacrifice in the glorious cause of liberty." In Chatham on Cape Cod the fishermen stayed home a day from their boats to attend town meeting. "Our civil and religious principles," they

wrote, "are the sweetest and most essential part of our lives, without which the remainder is scarcely worth preserving." Woolwich declared their answer "not perfect in spelling or the words placed," but solemn and hearty in the cause. And from Lenox in the Berkshire Hills the farmers declared, "As we are in a remote wilderness corner of the earth, we know little. But neither nature nor the God of nature requires us to crouch, Issachar-like, between the two burdens of poverty and slavery."

Governor Hutchinson was at first blind to what was happening. *Committees of Correspondence* — the very title was slow and did not sound rebellious. "It is such a foolish scheme," Hutchinson wrote to England, "that the faction must necessarily make themselves ridiculous." But as the towns' Resolves rolled in to Boston, Hutchinson knew suddenly that of all the moves yet made against government, this was the most sinister. These self-appointed Committees were nothing less than a system of government formed to operate entirely without royal sanction. Like the old Convention of Towns invented by James Otis in the crisis of '68, when the British troops were about to arrive, the Committees of Correspondence could function even when the Legislature had been dissolved by the Governor. They went beyond impudence; they were greatly, dangerously effective. "The foulest, subtlest and most venomous serpent," said a Tory lawyer, "that ever issued from the egg of sedition." [1] Suppose, thought Hutchinson, the Committees should spread beyond Massachusetts? Suppose, instead of being merely intertown, they became intercolonial?

Hutchinson saw that he must face it down. In full meeting of the Massachusetts Legislature he must bring the underlying issue into the open: the issue, not alone of judges' salaries, of taxation or of the King's troops on Boston soil, but the issue of allegiance to Britain. The venture might cost him his governorship. Neither King nor ministry acknowledged the existence of such an issue. Hutchinson determined to risk it.

In January of 1773, just when John's articles on the judiciary were in full swing, Hutchinson, dressed for the occasion in rich black with a silver-embroidered waistcoat, walked into the State House, faced the Legislature and stepped immediately off into deepest waters: "I know of no line that can be drawn between the *supreme authority of Parliament and the total independence of the colonies.*" The Mas-

sachusetts House of Representatives, furthermore, had arbitrarily assumed, of late, the name of *Commons*. An impossible nomenclature! said Hutchinson. Under one king, two legislatures could not exist — a parliament in England and a parliament in Massachusetts. It was unthinkable: such a condition would make two realms as distinct as the governments of England and Scotland "before the union."

Hutchinson's address was printed, and on both sides of the ocean the repercussions were tremendous. In England the ministry was outraged. The supremacy of Parliament needed no defense! It was intrinsic, absolute, not a "question" to be introduced in local colonial legislatures by a Royal Governor. Hutchinson had been foolhardy enough to ask the people for a reply, begged them not to be hasty but to consider well what they said. John Adams himself was astonished. "I stand amazed at the Governor for forcing on this controversy," he wrote. "He will not be thanked. His ruin and destruction must spring out of it either from the Ministry and Parliament on one hand, or from his countrymen on the other. He has reduced himself to a most ridiculous state of distress. He seems in the utmost agony."

The House sat down to prepare its answer. Sam Adams drafted it, with the help of Dr. Warren and Joseph Hawley of Northampton County (the most important politician in western Massachusetts). The document emerged from Sam's pen, long, flowery, passionate in its declamation of the people's rights. Sam was pleased with his handiwork. But Hawley the lawyer, a slow man and judicious, was uncomfortable. The thing was too romantical by far. These grand declarations of liberty, this copious quoting of Mr. Locke, would get them nowhere. The ministry in London would scoff at such; they were altogether sick of the word "liberty." * The committee, at Hawley's instance, carried the paper to John, who took a week to revise it. The next step would be to submit it to the House for approval.

John was not entirely satisfied, but the paper was surely improved. What Hawley had called "the roses and flowers" were out of it and good constitutional props were under it. Properly understood, the doctrine of allegiance, in no sense, said John, precluded two

* Hawley was right. Soame Jenyns, Member of Parliament from Cambridgeshire, said the term "liberty" had become "synonymous for blasphemy, bawdry, treason, libels, strong beer and cider."

legislatures from existing in one empire, under one king. . . . As for drawing a line, as Governor Hutchinson suggested, between the supreme authority of Parliament and "the total independence of the colonies" — that would be so arduous an undertaking the Representatives could not even think of proposing to do it *without the consent of all the colonies, in Congress.*

This last assertion was so extreme and so completely unexpected that Sam Adams had trouble getting the paper voted through the House at all. The members balked. In a congress? — they repeated, astonished. "A *general* congress?" The very hint or suggestion of an intercolonial congress would blow the Governor sky-high like a charge of powder — not to mention the Parliament of Britain. But one February day when the clouds let down sleet over knee-high snowdrifts along Boston streets, certain members of the House who loved their comfort stayed at home, and Samuel Adams pushed his paper through. Less than a week later, in Virginia, the House of Burgesses voted to make the Committees of Correspondence intercolonial.

March passed, and April. In Massachusetts the breach in the people's party had closed. Hancock and Sam Adams made up their two-year quarrel: to prove it to the world, Hancock had Copley paint twin-size portraits of himself and Sam, hung them side by side in his parlor. Cushing, Hancock, Sam Adams, Phillips were sure of their annual re-election as Boston Representatives; they saw to it that the House nominated John Adams as Member of Council.* On the twenty-fifth of May, John heard he was elected. Two days later the Governor vetoed his name. The news was brought by a delegation from the House, accompanied by Dr. Cooper of the Brattle Street church. Cooper offered friendly consolation. It was too bad, he said. Not only was this a setback to the party but it was an indubitable check to John's own career. To be a Member of Council was a feather in any man's cap.

John interrupted him. "A check?" he repeated. To his own surprise his voice emerged loud and derisive. "By my soul, Dr. Cooper, I think I take pride in it. The Governor's veto is no check but a *boost.*"

The company, which knew its Bunyan, laughed at the old word

---

* The Governor's Council had 28 members, elected by the House of Representatives. It corresponded to the present Senate.

so sharply, newly used. The phrase caught on, traveled about the Province, delighting people. John was to hear it wherever he went. The Governor's veto, that fearful weapon of condemnation? — "No check but a boost." Sam Adams in particular admired the phrase; he could not have devised a better one himself.

And now, in the early summer of 1773, there dropped into Sam's hand what he recognized instantly as the most beautiful piece of propaganda to date. It came unexpectedly, falling out of the skies: a package of Thomas Hutchinson's old letters, obtained somehow in London by Benjamin Franklin and sent confidentially to the radical leaders in Boston. (Just how Franklin got hold of this entirely private correspondence was never revealed, but in London a duel was fought over the affair. Franklin was accused of thievery, interrogated by the Privy Council at a most humiliating public session, and deprived of his office as Postmaster General of the Colonies.)

To Sam Adams it mattered little what happened to Franklin.[2] At long last he had a weapon that could utterly destroy his enemy in Massachusetts. True, the letters said nothing that Hutchinson had not many times implied in public speech and message to the Legislature. Yet implication is very different from outright statement. These were private letters, written to a friend in England in the crucial years of '68 and '69; in them Hutchinson spoke out, revealed plainly his scorn of the people, his mistrust of their ability to rule themselves. The very tone was maddening in its condescension, its conscious superiority. Hutchinson spoke of "Otis and his creatures, alarmed and frightened"; "the licentiousness of such as call themselves sons of liberty"; "our scandalous newspapers," "our incendiaries."

Properly utilized, this would be enough and more than enough. Despite utmost effort, outside of Boston, Sam had never yet succeeded in making Massachusetts hate Thomas Hutchinson. The Governor's popularity remained a barrier, a block to wholehearted rebellion. *As chief justice for two years after our first disorders* [so ran a sentence in the letters] *I kept the grand jury tolerably well to their duty.* . . . It was true, and by "keeping the grand juries to their duty," Hutchinson had controlled the counties represented by these juries. It was the rural districts that Sam Adams considered most recalcitrant. The country people liked Hutchinson the better for being an aristocrat, took pride in his distinguished appearance as

Chief Justice, admired his coach and four rumbling grandly up to their town commons. Everybody knew what Hutchinson had done for Massachusetts. Twice he had rescued the Province's currency (and economy) from disaster. He had gone to England in 1740 to settle the boundary line between Massachusetts and New Hampshire; he had been commissioner at the Albany Congress of '54. For nearly forty years he had served: as a member of the House, the Council, as Chief Justice, then Governor. Now, in this spring of '73, he was down at Hartford trying to adjust the ancient, angry dispute with New York over the boundary lines.

But Franklin's precious package contained ammunition to blast the whole tribe of Hutchinson-Oliver. There were letters equally offensive, written by Hutchinson's brother-in-law, Andrew Oliver, now Lieutenant Governor. At a stroke, Sam hoped to wipe out the dynasty. The thing would affect Chief Justice Peter Oliver too, and the Governor's brother, Judge Foster Hutchinson. None of them could withstand this blow, if it were properly prepared, the sword nicely edged. *Ignorant though they be* [Hutchinson had written] *yet the heads of Boston town meeting influence all public measures. . . . The town of Boston passed a number of weak but very criminal votes. . . . As the prospect of British revenge became more certain* [this was in '68, when the troops landed in Boston], *the people's courage abated in proportion.*

Franklin had entrusted the correspondence "to six or seven of the people's leaders." John Adams was one of the chosen. Reading the letters alone in his house, it seemed to him impossible that these sentiments could have come from the pen of a Massachusetts man. "Bone of our bone!" John wrote. "Born and educated among us. Vile serpent!" . . . What would Sam do with this correspondence, how would he present it to the public?

Sam took his time. He began by preparing the Province for a startling and dreadful revelation. Week by week the *Gazette* hammered at it until the moment was exactly ripe. On June 16, Sam stood before the Legislature and read the letters aloud. The House reacted immediately, passed a set of Resolves that held Hutchinson and Oliver responsible for every destructive measure the British ministry had undertaken against Massachusetts, beginning with the Stamp Act and leading to the "arrival of a fleet and army into His Majesty's loyal Province." The last Resolve — number fourteen — prayed

the King to remove Hutchinson and Oliver from the government forever.

The document was published, entire, in the *Gazette*. Two days later, Sam released the actual letters. They appeared under the heading, BORN AND EDUCATED AMONG Us, and the editorial pen had been very busy. Sam had taken whole sentences from their context and printed them alone, mixing his own words with Hutchinson's. The reader could not tell which man was writing, and the Governor's remarks took on special and sinister meaning. All summer long the thing continued, until men five hundred miles away who had scarcely heard of Hutchinson, looked on his name with loathing.

One paragraph in particular seemed to offend most deeply. Hutchinson had written it in 1769, four years after the Boston mob had destroyed his house, his garden, his library, and a *History of Massachusetts* that was the labor of a lifetime: *I never think without pain* [it ran] *of the measures necessary for the peace and good order of the colonies. There must be an abridgment of what are called English liberties. I doubt whether it is possible to project a system of government in which a colony 3000 miles distant shall enjoy all the liberty of the parent state.*

The lines themselves were no more than the sorrowful statement of a thoughtful, courageous, and mistaken man. Sam Adams did not tamper with them. Yet after the impetus Sam had given them, the frame he made for them, the words stood out, charged with a dreadful and portentous message.

It was the end of Thomas Hutchinson. As for Lieutenant Governor Andrew Oliver, the affair killed him. He died suddenly in his house outside of Boston — of a broken heart, his friends said. Hancock and his Boston cadets escorted the body to the burying ground, according to convention. After all, Oliver had held office in the Province almost thirty years. But the people followed after his coffin in the street, jeering, hooting, and when the grave was closed a voice cried out, "May Thomas Hutchinson be next!"

In the autumn of 1773, Samuel Adams, looking about him, could congratulate himself on work well done. His fellow countrymen were roused from their three-year torpor; the spark was ignited, it needed only fuel from England to work it into a blaze. In the matter of resistance to tyranny, Sam greatly desired that Massachusetts

should lead all the colonies, and that Boston should lead Massachusetts.

This time, Sam was not kept waiting. News arrived from London that Parliament and the British East India Company had made a new and profitable arrangement about tea. Smuggled Holland tea had, it seemed, ruined the great East India Company. Seven years' accumulation of tea leaves lay rotting in its London warehouses; the Company was hopelessly in debt to the British government. As a way out of this highly undesirable situation, Parliament had reduced the price of tea from twenty shillings a pound to ten, permitted the East India Company to export and sell directly to America in its own vessels, with no need to stop at British ports. The government retained, however, the tax of threepence a pound. America, thought Parliament, would not be able to resist good bohea sold so cheap. Surplus merchandise would be unloaded in the colonies; American merchants, acting as middlemen, would be cut out of the market; smuggling merchants would be ruined and Britain would collect her tax at last. More than a thousand chests of tea were immediately dispatched to the Company's consignees in Charleston, Philadelphia, New York and Boston. Britain congratulated herself on a clever *coup*.

This time, the ministry succeeded in uniting all interests against them. The big colonial merchants saw financial ruin ahead: why should not a tea monopoly be followed by other monopolies equally disastrous? The political radicals in their turn read slavery and submission in the payment of the tax. All parties agreed the tea must not be landed. New York and Philadelphia forced the consignees to promise they would not handle the tea on arrival; the ships' captains would simply be instructed to swing round outside the harbor and head back for England.

But in Boston the consignees turned suddenly stubborn. (Two of them were sons of Thomas Hutchinson.) Defying all threat of tar and feathers, they refused to sign away their commissions, even when a crowd of thousands assembled around Liberty Tree and summoned them by bell and proclamation. Hutchinson himself declared he would not sign an order to send the tea ships back to England unless he first had a receipt from the Custom House, saying the duty had been lawfully paid.

A way out, it was true, existed. The ships could anchor beyond Castle William, thus avoiding the port and the port duty; their

captains could quietly be instructed to go on home as they had come. But this would forfeit the chance for a magnificent patriotic gesture. Boston must set an example for the continent; and Sam Adams intended to see she did it properly. When the first tea ship came in sight, the Boston Committee of Correspondence summoned its captain to town, told him to tie up at the wharf and land all his cargo except the tea.

These maneuvers took, from first to last, nearly two months. Meanwhile the Sons used every effort and every well-learned technique to rouse not only Boston but the whole of Massachusetts. Messengers from the Correspondence Committees rode far and long. On November 30 a great meeting was held in Old South Meeting-house. People poured in from outlying districts. A night watch was instituted, citizens were armed, instructed how to answer if the bells sounded. Post riders spread the alarm to neighboring towns. The tea must not be landed!

Abigail Adams to her friend Mercy Warren of Plymouth

BOSTON, *December* 5, 1773.

The Tea that bainfull weed is arrived. Great and I hope effectual opposition has been made to the landing of it. The proceedings of our Citizens have been united spirited and firm. The flame is kindled and like lightning it catches from Soul to Soul. I tremble when I think what must be the direfull consequences. And in this Town must the Scene of action lay, my Heart beats at every Whistle I hear, and I dare not openly express half my fears.*

On Friday, December 17, the tea was liable to seizure by the Custom House for nonpayment of duties. Hutchinson continued to refuse clearance papers. The ships must not leave the Harbor until the duty was paid, he said. On Thursday morning a last appeal was sent to him at his house in Milton, eight miles away. A meeting was called for three that afternoon, to hear his answer. Some seven thousand people came, crowding into the Old South church or standing outside in a cold, drizzling rain. The three ships — the *Dartmouth*, the *Beaver*, the *Eleanor* — had moved to the inner Harbor. They were

* This is Abigail's own delightful spelling, quoted from the *Warren-Adams Letters*, edited by W. C. Ford.

tied by long cables to Griffin's wharf. As evening approached they swung down with the tide. At sunset the rain ceased, a clear wind rose, and over the chimneypots of Boston the moon appeared through rifts of flying, wintry clouds.

It had been dark an hour before the messenger returned with Hutchinson's answer: *Clearance for the tea ships is refused.* Sam Adams read the message, then addressed the people briefly: "This meeting can do nothing more to save the country," he said. The words were a signal to the crowd outside. Instantly a warwhoop was heard, and the general shout, "To the docks!" Several hundred men, most of them disguised by prearrangement in Indian paint and feathers,[3] headed north for Griffin's wharf, boarded the three ships and dumped three hundred and forty-two chests of tea into the Harbor.

Not a life was lost, not a man hurt, no drop of blood was shed. In the moonlight a vast crowd assembled on the dock, watched almost in silence while the "Mohawks" did their work. The stillness was extraordinary; the crash of hatchets could plainly be heard across the line of water, and occasional perspiring grunts as men tipped the heavy boxes over the bulwarks. Admiral Montagu's two frigates lay in the outer Harbor, but the tide was on the ebb and they did not try to approach. None of the "Mohawks" kept so much as a fistful of tea for himself; one or two who tried it were quickly and summarily dissuaded. When morning came, tea marked the edge of high tide on beaches as far south as Nantasket. . . . One Mohawk, it was true, found his shoes full of tea when he got home; he put a little of it in a jar as a souvenir.*

John Adams heard the news at noon of the seventeenth, on his way home from attending court at Plymouth. His reaction was swift and, for a man who loved the law, extraordinary. Eighteen thousand pounds' worth of property had been destroyed in the night by a crowd of men dressed and painted like Indians. John might have been expected to condemn the whole thing out of hand, as he had condemned other riots. But he did not. His mind leaped forward. Here had been no violence, no drunken cruelty, no "mean movement for private revenge," aimed at a particular individual the mob happened to despise. This time, the target was the British ministry, the Parlia-

---

* It was Major Melville, whose grandson wrote *Moby Dick*.

ment of England itself. This time the punishment suited the offense.

"This is the most magnificent movement of all," John wrote that night in his diary. "There is a dignity, a majesty, a sublimity in this last effort of the patriots that I greatly admire. The people should never rise without doing something to be remembered, something notable and striking. This destruction of the tea is so bold, so daring, so firm, intrepid and inflexible, and it must have so important consequences, and so lasting, that I cannot but consider it an epocha in history. . . . Many persons wish that as many dead carcasses were floating in the harbor, as there are chests of tea. What measures will the ministry take? Will they punish us? How? By quartering troops upon us? by annulling our charter? by laying on more duties? by restraining our trade? By sacrifice of individuals? or how?"

It would be five months before America could know the answer. The winter passage required six to eight weeks each way, and Parliament needed time to act. Meanwhile the liberty party must strengthen itself throughout Massachusetts, secure its position against the blow that was sure to come. Five hundred barrels of gunpowder were purchased, stored in Boston and Charlestown arsenals. Military companies were reorganized, chose new officers and commenced a stricter course of training. But all this was mere bravado; Sam Adams himself confessed it. Of what use five hundred barrels of powder and a few honorary captainships against the armies and fleets of England?

What shall we do to be saved? . . . John Adams heard the question on every side. To him it was not the military but the civil end of the liberty party that needed consolidating, strengthening, in these brief critical months. More than ever the people must be assured of a share in government. Their courts of justice must be free of crown influence, their judges independent and secure. The matter of the judicial salaries had reached a pitch actually dangerous. Chief Justice Peter Oliver — brother of Andrew Oliver — had declared himself only too pleased to accept the King's grant, proud and happy to take a salary from his sovereign. (The other four judges had yielded to popular pressure and refused.) The House of Representatives was in session; they sent urgent messages to Oliver, desiring a pledge that he would refuse the King's grant or resign his judgeship. Each time, Oliver returned a haughty negative. Even from the bench he boasted that he would not yield, adding flatly that no man could live for six months on what the Provincial Legislature paid its judges in a year.

There was truth enough in the last statement. Not without reason had Jonathan's uncle, old Chief Justice Sewall, died in penury. But this was no time for royal judges to be lashing out arrogantly from the bench. Around town John heard ugly talk: "Captain" Mackintosh, Thomas Young, Pemberton and others hinted that if Peter Oliver held out, then by God the branches of Liberty Tree were stout enough to bear the weight even of a Chief Justice of Massachusetts.

Immediate action was necessary to forestall the people; Peter Oliver must be got off the bench by some move short of violence. For the judges personally, John had real respect and said so. On circuit he had dined with them often, drunk port with them, discussed everything from Greek verbs to feudal tenure. Judge Trowbridge had been his friend since Worcester days. Peter Oliver, aside from his politics, was a most amiable creature, intelligent, quick, with pleasant manners, a superb conversationalist. But even had John hated them, all five, the judges symbolized the law; their robes, their persons, were sacred. If the people seized their own Chief Justice, carted him in tar and feathers to Liberty Tree and put him to death, what then would remain of government but anarchy, the hopeless, irretrievable tyranny of mob rule? ("The poor people themselves," John was to write later concerning this affair, "who by secret manoeuvres are excited to insurrection, are seldom aware of the purposes for which they are set in motion, or of the consequences which may happen to themselves. When once heated and in full career, they can neither manage themselves nor be regulated by others.")

What then was to be done? England had a constitutional procedure for removing judges from the bench: impeachment. The House of Commons impeached, the Lords tried the case with the Lord Chancellor presiding. The process was long and very difficult. History, John knew, had few such cases to show even in England; America had none at all. No Massachusetts judge had ever been impeached. No machinery, no precedent existed. They certainly could not carry Peter Oliver to the British House of Commons for impeachment! Yet if they attempted it here, Governor Hutchinson would use every means in his power to block it.

John decided the Province must try it anyway, precedent or no precedent. Let the Massachusetts Legislature assume the powers of a complete Parliament, with the House of Representatives as Commons, the Council as Lords. For years the General Court had tried to rise to this status. Now let them assume it in one bold swoop and

see what happened. John proposed the plan one day early in February, 1774, dining in Cambridge at the house of Samuel Winthrop, Clerk of the Superior Court. Five or six members of the Legislature were present, also Dr. Cooper of Brattle Street Church and Dr. Winthrop, John's old professor of mathematics and astronomy, who had lately been offered the presidency of Harvard and had refused.

John's suggestion was received with astonishment and much grave shaking of heads. It was impossible, it could not be done, there was no precedent, nobody in either House would know how to set such a thing in motion. ("All harps," John said later, "were on the willow; the storm was terrible, no blue sky to be discovered.") John went home; he was aware he had chosen his audience well. The news spread instantly. Next morning, callers began to drop in at the office. Robert Treat Paine came — "grief and terror in his face," John said. Hawley of Northampton followed. "If the Commons in England is the grand inquest of the nation," John told them reassuringly, "then the House of Representatives is the grand inquest of our Province. Try it. What can you lose?"

On the fourteenth of February, the Massachusetts House of Representatives, meeting in Boston, formally impeached Chief Justice Peter Oliver for *high crimes and misdemeanors against the people of Massachusetts Bay*. John himself drew up the articles of impeachment, after the English parliamentary form. They were presented to Governor Hutchinson, who refused to have anything to do with them, refused to preside at such a "trial" or indeed to come to the Council at all. This was a "mere mock Parliament," he said angrily. He would not countenance it!

The House went ahead without him. By the traditional strategic assumption that the Governor had been present in Council — "presumptively present," was how Sam Adams put it — they entered the impeachment in their official *Journals*, then published it, together with much pertinent comment, in the newspapers, and circulated it industriously throughout the Province. The remaining move, the ultimate decision, must be left to the people of Massachusetts. Neither Sam nor John dared prophesy whether they would rise to the occasion.

The test came at the next session of Superior Court. John saw it happen — at Boston Court House, at Worcester and at Plymouth. He said afterward the scene "filled his eyes and heart," and that he

wept as he stood by the lawyers' table and watched his countrymen, "those honest freeholders, in the moment of their fiery trial." Chief Justice Oliver, sitting in his robes, called Grand and Petit Jurors to approach the bench and take the oath. One by one they refused. "What is the matter?" Oliver demanded as the men came forward to the bar and stood stubbornly, lips closed. "Are all of you Quakers that you cannot take an oath?" "No sir," they answered. "The Chief Justice of this court stands impeached of high crimes and misdemeanors, and of a conspiracy against our rights as written in our charter. We cannot serve under him. We will not take the oath."

It was the end. John had builded better than he knew. The court never met again under royal jurisdiction. More than a year later, John, in Congress at Philadelphia, was to hear that Massachusetts had organized her own Superior Court of Judicature, with five judges appointed by the people. As Chief Justice, the Province had named John Adams.

Meanwhile, five months had elapsed since the Boston Tea Party. The Province still waited to hear its fate. The news from England came on May tenth, 1774. It proved dreadful beyond previous imagining: Parliament had ordered the Port of Boston shut up, blockaded altogether. The city was to be starved into submission, her channels lined with warships: no food or fuel could enter except by the narrow neck of land to the westward. The *Boston Port Bill*,[4] the measure was called. Parliament had passed it almost unanimously. Even Major Barré had voted to punish Boston. Members of the House of Commons had shouted that Boston was a "nest of locusts" and should be "knocked about the ears of its most insolent inhabitants." "I wish the Bostonians were at the devil," said the Lords. "They are likely to be a continual plague to us."

Boston — why was it always Boston that broke the King's peace? New York had sent their tea ships back, the contents unharmed. But Boston must needs dump the cargo into the sea, wantonly and willfully destroy eighteen thousand pounds' worth of British property, in full view of two royal frigates anchored down the Bay. Boston, said London's *Morning Chronicle*, was a "canker worm in the heart of America, a rotten limb which (if suffered to remain) will inevitably destroy the whole body of that extensive country."

The Port Bill was to go into effect on the first of June. This left

Boston only three weeks of freedom. A great body meeting* was held in Faneuil Hall; the crowd got down on its knees and prayed for help. Samuel Adams read the Bill aloud: WHEREAS, *dangerous commotions and insurrections have been fomented and raised in the town of Boston by divers ill-affected persons, to the subversion of His Majesty's government and the utter destruction of the public peace.* BE IT ENACTED, *that no vessel, lighter, boat or bottom, no goods, wares or merchandise whatever . . . be transported or carried, discharged or brought from any other country. . . .*

Immediately, the Boston Committee of Correspondence translated the Bill into briefer language, added some thoughts of its own, got the whole signed by eight neighboring towns and sent the protest to the South by rider:

They have ordered our port to be entirely shut up, leaving us barely so much of the means of subsistence as to keep us from perishing with cold and hunger. A fleet of British ships of war is to block up our harbor until we shall make restitution to the East India Company, and obedience is paid to the laws and authority of Great Britain, and the revenue duly collected. . . .

The single question then is, whether you consider Boston as now suffering in the common cause, and sensibly feel and resent the injury offered to her.

We desire your answer by the bearer; and after assuring you that, not in the least intimidated by this inhuman treatment, we are still determined to maintain to the utmost of our abilities the rights of Americans, we are, gentlemen, your friends and fellow-countrymen. . . .

Three days later, on May 13, His Majesty's Ship *Lively* sailed into harbor, seven weeks out of Liverpool. She brought a new Governor for Massachusetts: Thomas Hutchinson was going "home" at last. "By His Majesty's most gracious condescension," Hutchinson had told the Massachusetts House, he had received "discretionary leave." He hoped soon to return to a Province that had learned wisdom from experience. . . . On May 17, a day of rain and wind, Governor Thomas Gage, Commander in Chief of British Forces in America, amid the booming of cannon and the squeal of fifes, made his formal landing from the *Lively*. Three regiments were shortly to arrive —

* A mass meeting, as distinguished from a regular town meeting summoned by the sheriff.

and God only knew, said Boston, how many after that. But the *Gazette*, seeking comfortable words, hastened to inform its readers that "our worthy citizen, Mr. Paul Revere," was by now well on his way "with important Letters to the Southern Colonies."

There was nothing to do but wait. Boston could not move alone; she had tried solitary rebellion at the Massacre, and it had been a most dismal failure. It was rumored moreover that other punitive measures would follow: the Port Bill was only the first of a series of Acts designed to crush all resistance.

Annual Election Day fell on May 24: this at least was something Parliament had not yet seen fit to tamper with. The Massachusetts House of Representatives, in a last desperate move, canceled all but ten of the old Councilors and sent in eighteen new names. Governor Gage, with Thomas Hutchinson looking over his shoulder, drew his pen through thirteen of them, including the name of John Adams.

It was the largest slaughter of elected men the Province had ever seen. "Thirteen dead men" the slang phrase had it.

On the first of June, at high noon, the Port of Boston was officially closed. By now all the continent had the news, and the continent observed the day in mourning. Shops drew their shutters, bells tolled. In Philadelphia even the Episcopal Church muffled her clappers and only the Quakers withheld a sign. It was a weekday, but people thronged the churches, heard fiery sermons from texts wonderfully expressive. "Pulpits," wrote one indignant Tory, "were converted into Gutters of Sedition. The Clergy quite unlearned the Gospel & substituted Politicks in its Stead." Virginia kept fast day; her churches were filled.

Weary messengers rode into Boston, bringing sympathy and strength. "Don't pay for an ounce of the damned tea!" wrote Christopher Gadsden, shipping rice to Boston as a gift from the planters of Carolina. "Our hearts are warmed with affection for you," wrote Norfolk, itself dangerously exposed to ships of war. "Be assured we consider you as suffering in the common cause and look upon ourselves as bound by the most sacred ties to support you." Best of all was the voice of Colonel Washington of the Virginia militia, who had addressed the House of Burgesses in one brief, plain and highly characteristic sentence: "If need be I will raise one thousand men, subsist them at my own expense and march myself at their head to the relief of Boston."

On the second of June, Boston received, by ship from England, the expected Acts of Parliament. She read them with horror. The first Act, "for the suppression of riots and tumults in Massachusetts Bay," ordered all disturbers of the King's peace to be transported out of the Province for trial, either to England or some place designated by the Royal Governor. "The Murder Bill," Boston called it at once, and knew Sam Adams would be first to go. . . . The second Act, "for better regulating the government of Massachusetts Bay and purging their constitution of all its crudities," * tied the Province hand and foot forever. Members of Council were to be crown appointees — no more elections by the House of Representatives. The same with all judges and officers of the courts. Even jurors must be chosen by the Sheriff. After August first ensuing, no town meetings could be held anywhere in Massachusetts without the Governor's consent in writing. One Assembly of the people could be summoned during the year, on the annual Election Day provided for in the Massachusetts charter.

Not only, it became plain, was Boston to be starved into submission; she was to be bitterly humiliated, rendered utterly powerless. Drums from the Common reminded her of it six times a day, as the King's regiments began to arrive. The *Gazette* printed the two Acts of Parliament, then printed beside them words from the Bible and from the poets.

They that be slain with the Sword are better than they that be slain with hunger.

> Our necks are under persecution. . . . Britons arise!
> And know you have the virtue to be mov'd.

> What man can do against them, NOT AFRAID,
> As shall amaze their proudest persecutors.

General Gage had not yet closed off the Neck. The arched brick gates were thronged with incoming carts, laden with gifts for Boston. Marblehead sent two hundred and twenty-four quintals of "good eating fish, one and three quarter casks of olive oil and thirty-

* The last phrase was Lord North's, spoken on introducing the bill. See Note 4 for further information about the Acts and the Quebec Act that followed them.

nine pounds, five shillings and sixpence in cash." Salem, ancient
shipping rival of Boston, dispatched warm assurance, in the form of
an official Resolve that she would not take advantage of "her sister's
situation." Farmington, Connecticut, sent four hundred bushels of
rye and Indian corn; Wethersfield matched it. Old Israel Putnam of
Connecticut, stout veteran of the French wars, appeared one very
hot day behind 130 sheep he had driven all the way from home —
nearly a hundred miles.

Meanwhile Boston herself did more than pray and write to the
newspapers. The time was very short. After August first, no more
meetings could be held, no assemblies of any kind without royal warrant. On the fifth of June, the Committee of Correspondence sent
out a plan for economic war with Britain. It took the form of a
Solemn League and Covenant that went beyond any boycotts
hitherto attempted. This time, Sam Adams desired the whole continent to swear not only against importation of British goods but
against exportation also, until the Port Act should be repealed. (He
was to be disappointed; the continent did not approve the Solemn
League and Covenant.)

Two days later, the Massachusetts Legislature convened at Salem,
twenty miles north of Boston, whence Parliament had exiled it. The
Province was not yet under complete military government. General
Gage greatly desired what co-operation he could win from the
people, and there was much business to be done. But Gage changed
his official residence from Boston to Danvers, four miles from Salem.
It was necessary to observe closely each move of that nest of locusts,
that hatching place for traitors, the Massachusetts House of Representatives.

On the seventeenth of June, John Adams acted as moderator of a
town meeting in Faneuil Hall. The assembly was large and very
rowdy. Everyone agreed quickly not to pay for the destroyed tea,
and to send out a letter of thanks to the sister colonies for help and
encouragement. Then Josiah Quincy got up, proposed that common tables be instituted to feed the Boston poor, and that those present share their own food and money for the purpose. Instantly, the
meeting turned sour. There were whistles, catcalls and most vociferous *No's*. John Adams, stepping to the edge of the platform, put
up a hand for silence and got it. Angrily he told the meeting it should
be ashamed of itself. . . . Was lip service all they had now for

patriotism? Milton had the proper words to describe this audience! . . . In his strong, deliberate, slightly harsh voice John proceeded to quote them — "Owls and cuckoos, asses, apes, and dogs." *

A roar of good-natured laughter answered him; the shaft had hit home. John rapped for order. "We will now reconsider the motion for common tables," he said.[5]

Meanwhile, that same afternoon, Sam Adams in Salem was putting to the House of Representatives a motion: *That a General Congress of deputies meet at Philadelphia to consult together upon the present state of the colonies, and to deliberate and determine upon wise and proper measures for the recovery and establishment of their just rights and liberties, civil and religious.*

Much careful planning had been necessary to prepare the House for this meeting and this motion of Sam's. Tory members were induced, whenever feasible, to stay away. Daniel Leonard, the Tory lawyer, was at home innocently working on a case; his friend Robert Paine had assured him the House had nothing important under discussion today. Absolute secrecy, of course, was imperative. Should General Gage get wind of the proceedings, he would dissolve the Legislature instantly. About a dozen Tory members had turned up. As it was not possible to keep them out, the only alternative was to keep them in. Sam stationed watchmen at the doors: after the meeting started, no one must enter and no one must leave.

The House heard the motion concerning a General Congress at Philadelphia; a buzz of conversation followed. Toward the back of the room a member rose unnoticed, made his way to the door. "Let me out," he said quietly to the doorkeeper, pressing both hands to his stomach. "I am going to be sick." **

The doorkeeper let him through and the man fled like a deer to the Governor at Danvers, while the House passed, by a vote of 120 to 12, the motion for a General Congress. Five delegates from Massachusetts were named and agreed on: Thomas Cushing, James Bow-

---

* I did but prompt the age to quit their clogs
By the known rules of ancient liberty,
When straight a barbarous noise environs me
Of owls and cuckoos, asses, apes and dogs.

— Sonnet XII, "On the Detraction which Followed Upon My Writing Certain Treatises."

** Abigail's friend Mercy Otis Warren, in her *History of Massachusetts*, says the gentleman "pleaded the necessities of nature."

doin, Samuel Adams, John Adams and Robert Treat Paine. The next question was what monies to appropriate: the delegates must not be expected to accomplish such a journey from their private purses. . . .

There was sudden noise in the street outside, a loud pounding on the doors. It was the Governor's messenger. "Open in the King's name!" he shouted. "By order of His Excellency the Governor, this meeting is dissolved!"

A crowd began to collect around the pillared portico. The door-keeper slipped the Governor's message through a window. Sam Adams walked unhurriedly down the aisle, picked up the message, read it and spoke through the door to the watchman. "Stand your ground!" he said.[6] The meeting went on with its business. Five hundred pounds sterling was granted to the Philadelphia delegates as expenses. Meanwhile the Governor's messenger, in despair of a proper audience, delivered His Excellency's orders, complete with preamble, body and finale, to the assembled crowd of bystanders, who received it with a hearty cheer.

A few moments later a bar rattled in its bolt, doors were thrown open and the members poured out. Twelve of them walked close together in a little huddle; they were observed to look very glum. One hundred and twenty others, flushed with victory and excitement, glanced ostentatiously at the Governor's messenger, touched their hats jauntily. Then, descending the wide steps and making their way through a jubilant crowd of Salem citizens, they mounted their horses and turned southward toward Boston in the June sunshine.

It was the last Provincial Assembly ever to convene in Massachusetts under the royal authority.

PART IV

The Continental Congress. 1774-1776

CHAPTER TWENTY-FIVE

"There is a new and grand scene open before me . . ."

There is a new and grand scene open before me, a Congress. This will be an assembly of the wisest men upon the continent, who are Americans in principle. I feel myself unequal to this business.

—DIARY: *June* 20, 1774

ON a hot, dry morning of August, 1774, a coach and four swung round a corner east of Beacon Hill. With a clatter of horses, a squeal of brakes, a thunder of iron-shod wheels against cobblestones, it drew up before the handsome mansion of Thomas Cushing, Speaker of the Massachusetts House and delegate to the Grand Congress at Philadelphia. This was Wednesday the tenth. Today the great departure was to take place; the deputies were even now assembling in Cushing's hallway. The neighborhood was in a holiday mood. Cook, mistress, shopkeeper, apprentice boy — all Bromfield's Lane turned out to watch the coach roll by.

The coach itself was a splendid affair, newly painted and polished, the wheels outlined in red and yellow. Ignoring the threats of the driver, the crowd pressed forward, peered inside, exclaiming at the red silk curtains that framed the windows, the red cushions on the seats, the leather hand loops conveniently placed for the delegates when the coach lurched. The four chestnut horses were fresh and sleek; a groom sat beside the driver. Behind perched two black footmen in livery, their arms folded stylishly, a pleased grin on their faces. They were, somebody remarked, John Hancock's servants. The

coach was his too; he had lent it for the purpose. There was disagreement. No, a voice said. It was Mr. James Bowdoin's; Hancock's coach was smaller, and lower-slung.

Four mounted servants, well armed, rode alongside. As they pulled up, one of the horses reared, wheeling. The crowd, delighted, joshed the rider, asking where he got his white gaiters and if he could load and aim those flintlock pistols without getting down first and tying his horse to a post. . . .

Cushing's house was filled with people. All the delegates were there except Sam Adams, who was never late and always leisurely. John Adams, with Robert Paine, Hancock, Josiah Quincy and a dozen Sons of Liberty, stood in the dining room, looking out the windows at the crowd. On the table behind them were pitchers of ale, platters of bread and cheese, melons, plums, dried currants. The gathering was noisy, excited; there was laughter, hearty greeting of friend and colleague.

Abigail Adams waited with the other women in the parlor across the hall. She had on her best dress of white summer chintz, printed gaily with little red and blue flowers. Her bonnet was white too, tied with a blue ribbon under her chin. Already the taffeta bow had begun to darken with moisture in the heat, but Abby did not care. She was very quiet. Early this morning, she and John had said their farewells in their chamber; since then it seemed to Abby that all speech was gone from her. She sat numb as the women chattered, smiled politely when she was addressed, turned her head mechanically. But her gray eyes were dark, and when she raised a hand to smooth her brown hair under the bonnet, her fingers trembled. . . . "They will be gone two months at the most," someone said.

Two months? That was not long. John had often been away three weeks at a time on circuit. It was not the solitude that Abby dreaded. She was used to solitude; she liked her quiet country life with the four children. She was to live in Braintree while he was gone. "You will be safer there," John had said. "Boston will be an armed camp by September." . . . Safer . . . they would be safer. . . . John would not be safe in Philadelphia, no matter what he tried to tell her. Suppose Governor Gage should seize the four delegates today, on the outskirts of town? Sam Adams's head was forfeit, so was Cushing's. There was no telling when they might all be taken, sent to England and tried for treason. Five British regiments were encamped on Bos-

ton Common. Abby prayed that the coach, on its way to Cambridge Ferry, would avoid Tremont Street, not drive right by the troops. She had seen a letter John had written lately to Joseph Hawley: "Sydney died on the scaffold, Harrington in jail. Politics are an ordeal path among red hot ploughshares. Who then would be a politician for the sake of running about bare foot among them? Yet somebody must."

Sydney died on the scaffold. . . . The words went through Abby's head, shutting out the talk, the laughter around her. If John died, she would not wish to live a day, an hour. She had told him so two nights ago in desperation, and he had replied gravely that it was wrong to think such thoughts. They were not young lovers, blind to the world and to duty. She was nearly thirty, he would be thirty-nine in October. She must remember the children.

Abby clutched her handkerchief tighter. It would not do to let her fears be seen. When the final moment came and the coach clattered off, she must not weep or give a sign. All summer she had borne up wonderfully. To break down now would be the worst thing she could do for her husband. Since his election as delegate last June, John had been terribly depressed, fearful lest he might not be equal to the task before him, and as usual, perfectly frank about his fears. Abby had seen gloomy letters — to James Warren at Plymouth, to Hawley out beyond Worcester. If only he had more time to study, before the Congress met, John had said repeatedly. Time to learn something about the great men in the Court of the British King, time to study the character and feeling of the English people. New England education had told him none of these things, so necessary in the larger political world where he was going.

For two long months, Abigail had summoned all her resources, all her energy and love to comfort her husband, give him back his belief in himself. If the four delegates knew little about London and the island of England — surely, she had said stoutly, they were not more ignorant than England was about America. Let them be bold and stand up for what was right! And the more she said it, the more Abby's heart quailed within her. She was, in fact, exhausted with her role. Of all husbands upon earth, John Adams, she told herself, could descend deepest into the slough of self-doubt. Abby longed to snatch off her brave mask, sit down and cry, cling to her husband, beg him not to go. There was plenty to be done here at home in the political

way. James Warren was not going to Philadelphia, nor was Hancock, nor Josiah Quincy. John had never been outside New England. Now he would move in scenes strange to her, walk in foreign streets, sleep in rooms she had never seen. Soon he would write familiarly of names she had not heard before.

Premonition swept over Abby, a feeling sharp, physical, shaking her suddenly as if life itself were being torn from her piecemeal. She pressed her hands on her thighs and looked down. Was this the beginning of a real separation, a life apart for herself and her husband? From this day noon, all their familiar ways together were destroyed. The pattern was erased, the shape of days and hours they had built around their intimacy through the years — so dearly won, so closely cherished. Would it return, could it ever return?

Sitting against the wall in Mrs. Tom Cushing's parlor, Abigail tried to put the black vision from her. She had forgotten, she told herself, to pack John's second-best waistcoat, the canary one with the brown edging. In Philadelphia, would he take care to have his head shaved regularly, keep his wig in order? There was comfort in the remembrance of these small homely details. Looking up, Abby saw a woman come through the hall door. It was Mrs. Sam Adams; she walked straight to Abigail, took her hand. "My dear," she said with her kind, easy manner. "My husband said I was to find you and stay with you until the coach left."

In the street they were cheering. "Sam Adams!" they said. "There he is. . . . *Sam Adams!* Huzzah for the Congress! Huzzah! Huzzah!" There was a general movement toward the front door. Abby rose, made her way to the hall; Mrs. Sam Adams followed. Abby saw John come toward her through the crowd, felt his hands strong around her wrists, his breath on her cheek, heard him speak briefly and managed to reply. John left her, walked to the street door. There was a roar from the crowd outside. "Come this way," Mrs. Sam Adams said. "Look, they are getting in the coach! There goes your husband. They are cheering his name. Do you hear?"

"John Adams!" the crowd shouted happily. "Cushing! John Adams! . . . Sam Adams! Huzzah for the Congress. Huzzah!"

Horses' hoofs struck aaginst stone; heavy wheels rolled, a door slammed. The crowd roared again. . . . "They could have taken the north ferry to Cambridge," a woman's voice said, high, excited. "But they didn't. They will drive straight down Tremont Street,

not twenty feet from the soldiers. Isn't it glorious? Mrs. Adams, are you not proud of your brave husband?"

Abby looked at the speaker and nodded gravely, her eyes quite dry.

By four that afternoon the coach had left Watertown[1] and was headed southwestward on the highway to Connecticut. For the deputies, this departure from Boston had been an experience almost overwhelming. At least a hundred friends and well-wishers, in carriages or on horseback, had escorted them over the ferry and down the road. Molineux and Dr. Warren rode alongside the coach, crowding close, leaning from their saddles to shout greetings through the windows and stirring up a dust that was nothing short of prodigious. John sneezed till the tears streamed down his face, then mopped his eyes and returned the greetings as best he could. . . . At Watertown a banquet awaited them, out under the trees. There were speeches, toasts, cheers, and at the end a solemn prayer by Dr. Cooper. John had not dreamed the Province contained so much concentrated good will. If only, he thought fervently — if only Abby could see and hear this evidence of strong support for their venture and their cause!

When the last toast was drunk and the coach door slammed upon the last farewell, the four delegates threw themselves back in their narrow, cushioned seats, dazed and numb. All, that is, but Sam Adams, who seemed composed as ever. He took off his wig, wiped his face and neck with a handkerchief. What had pleased him most, he said, was the drive this morning down the Mall through lines of cheering citizens in full view of the British regiments on the Common. Did not the gentlemen agree that had been a pretty touch, prettily arranged by the Committee?

John nodded. Then he looked hard at his cousin, gave an exclamation. "You are the most gorgeous apparition in New England," he said. "Claret-colored coat! Ruffles! John Hancock himself was never so magnificent. You put us all to shame. May I be so bold as to ask where you acquired that gold-headed cane? All day I have been consumed to put the question."

Sam flicked dust off the sleeve of a brand-new broadcloth coat, looked complacently at his shining silver shoe buckles. Surely, his Brother Adams had heard about this costume? The whole of it had been presented anonymously. Hatters, tailors, shoemakers had been

knocking at his door for weeks past. New wig, new cocked hat, red cloak (it was in his trunk, strapped outside). Two pairs of shoes, six pairs of silk hose, these silver buckles, a pair of gold knee buckles. . . . Sam reached out an arm. His sleeve buttons, like the gold-headed cane, were stamped with the emblem of the Sons of Liberty. Then it was obvious, John said at once, where the gift came from. He was not sure, Sam replied. The tailor had revealed nothing beyond a hint that the "gentlemen" had desired Mr. Sam Adams not to appear shabby in Philadelphia. Whoever sent the wardrobe, Sam added, looking very pleased, had also begun yesterday to put a new roof on his barn and repair the steps from his private wharf down to the water.

John offered congratulations. Privately, he marveled at the simplicity with which his cousin received these gifts. Sam thrust a hand in his breeches pocket, produced a gold johannes. Someone had presented him with fifteen of these, he said — or was it twenty? "For my needs on the journey," he finished. "Was it not kind? Does it not show a good faith in what we are about to accomplish?"

John almost laughed aloud. The gold pieces would have burned his own pocket like so many slivers of hot steel. He fell silent, thinking. There was more to this than met the eye. Sam was quite right in assuming the gift had been directed not so much at him personally as toward the honor of Massachusetts. John had heard their delegation described by a Tory as "men of desperate fortunes with nothing to lose." This gift to Sam proved that even the Sons of Liberty realized the importance of a respectable representation at Philadelphia. The New York delegation had men of large fortunes and estates. One of the Maryland men, Mr. Carroll of Carrollton, was said to possess a hundred thousand pounds sterling and would come into more. Among the Virginians were gentlemen of property. It was a great pity their own fifth delegate, James Bowdoin, had refused to come along. His wife was ill of a fever and he would not leave Boston. Bowdoin's estate was larger even than Hancock's. These things mattered; they influenced unthinking people.

John's fears, his doubts of the summer, returned, casting a shadow over the triumph of the day. He glanced narrowly at his companions. Which of them, including himself, had so much as seen a British Minister of State, or even a Member of Parliament? Sam Adams had never been outside Massachusetts in his life. Bob Paine, it

was true, had traveled in his youth — to Spain and England for his health, and to the Carolinas, not to mention a trip to Greenland aboard a whaler. He had brought home a fine fund of information about rice plantations, Spanish vineyards, how to imbed a harpoon in a whale's right eye and the strange marital customs of the Esquimos. But it was hardly information that would help the Congress win disputes with the Lords North and Dartmouth. Would God they had a Franklin to guide them! But that man of wisdom and worldly experience was still in London, with no prospect of immediate return.

True, the four delegates knew the problems of Massachusetts intimately, thoroughly. They knew how to run the Province from town meeting outward; they were familiar with the constitutional phases of this great quarrel. All were graduates of Harvard. But they lacked — there was no doubt of it — extensive knowledge of "the realm." They were ignorant of the ramifications of West Indian commerce; they had no broad picture of trade laws and policy throughout the empire. . . . Suppose this Grand Congress should fail in the eyes of the whole continent, fizzle out with nothing to show beyond the usual humble petitions to Parliament? It was not the contempt of America John dreaded, he confessed to himself; it was the despair and disappointment of his own country of Massachusetts.

The coach gave a lurch. John's shoulder hit the wall. Paine fell over him, apologized briefly and resumed his seat. . . . John's thoughts went on. In Maine this summer, where he had ridden on his last circuit to finish up some cases, the country had swarmed with Tories and lukewarm liberty men. It was the latter John found hardest to bear. They had baited him continually about "the Boston mob and Sam Adams's Mohawks," until John, who hated mobbing as he hated the devil, found himself defending Captain Mackintosh like a brother. There was no getting away from it, the notion still prevailed among all parties that the crown side drew the persons of gentility and distinction. "*The better sort*, the *wiser few*," John had written home, were considered to be on one side. "The Multitude, the Vulgar, the Herd, the Rabble the Mob only are on the other. So difficult is it for the frail, feeble Mind of Man to shake itself loose from all Prejudice and Habits."

A scene came back to John as the coach rolled on. . . . In Falmouth lived Jonathan Sewall, still John's oldest, closest friend. Nothing had ever really come between them — neither the offer of the

admiralty post for John nor Sewall's Tory articles in the *Gazette*. Wherever they met the two drew together naturally, bound by ties of their youth, their days of struggle and study. Sewall was the most congenial companion John had ever known. (*He always called me John and I him Jonathan; and I often said to him, I wish my name were David.*)

After court one July day at Falmouth, Sewall had taken John aside, invited him to walk on the hills above the sea. They had climbed high, sat at the summit on a warm rock, smoking their pipes. Even up here among the rocks and bayberry, Sewall, immaculate as always, had a look of belonging to the scene — something John admired infinitely and could never emulate. "John," Sewall had said, "I want to talk to you about Philadelphia. About this Congress, this grand gesture, this venture you are about to embark on. . . . I wish you would not go. I wish it deeply, sincerely, and I hope you will listen to me, for old friendship's sake. I won't repeat that you will ruin your career, nor that men of property and standing are not on your side. I am aware such argument carries no weight with you. . . . What I desire you to see, to look at clearly, with no rosy Lockeian mist before your eyes, is the actual situation. Britain's power is secure, irresistible. She will never alter her system. For ten years and longer, you and your friends have been trying to make her alter it. She has not moved an inch. Your faction will drive this country to a civil war. And where will your Sons of Liberty be then, before the fleets and armies of an empire? I don't speak of your personal safety, the safety of your wife and children. But your country — what will happen to it? Think of this, my friend. Think of it well. You will tear your country apart, rend it in two, set brother against brother."

He had turned to John, looked directly at him. "I use large words — war . . . duty . . . patriotism. But it is your own welfare I have at heart today, my old friend. James Bowdoin has withdrawn from the delegation. You can withdraw too, without shame or apology. There is still time."

John had been profoundly moved. There was no questioning his friend's sincerity, the disinterestedness of his motive. The two men sat silent. Words struggled upward in John, words born of long and bitterest thought, of painful doubt and indecision. Yet he could not speak. Sewall would not understand. . . . From far below, the sound

of surf came faintly. A gull swooped, his wings flashed against the afternoon sky. *War . . . their country's peril . . . the setting of brother against brother . . .* Not one of these questions but John had put to his Maker again and again, alone on his knees in his chamber. Did Jonathan not know, could he not sense how awful had been the struggle that brought him to decision? *I go mourning in my Heart all the Day long, though I say nothing,* John had written. *I feel unutterable anxiety. God grant us wisdom and fortitude! Should this country submit, what infamy and ruin! Death in any form is less terrible!*

Around the northern headland a sail appeared, and another. The fishing fleet was coming home. John got up, took a few steps and halted before his friend. He felt no anger, only a deep sadness, the sense of loss. "Jonathan," he said, "you make it very hard. You strive for my salvation in your own way, and I thank you. But between your way and mine there is a gulf as wide as" — John flung out an arm — "an ocean. I am going to the Congress with my friends." He repeated it, *"With my friends."*

John stared out to sea. "Much that you say is true," he continued. "Britain will never alter her system. And by that same token we shall not alter ours. I have crossed over my river. I have passed my Rubicon. I will never change. Sink or swim,* live or die, survive or perish, I am with my country from this day on."

Sewall rose instantly. Both men knew it was the end, yet neither held out his hand. As though by agreement they parted, going separate ways down the hill to the town.[2]

As he thought of it now in the coach, pain shot once more through John's breast, quick and bitter. He lowered his head, looking at his hands spread on his knees. *The sharpest thorn on which I ever set my foot,* he thought.

Outside, the driver cursed; the off fore-horse had stumbled. Brakes screamed as the great wheels lumbered downhill.

Hartford, Middletown, Wallingford, New Haven . . . Crowds met the coach outside of town, escorted it in, banqueted the "Boston Committee," toasted them, informed them on particulars of local commerce that would prove useful at the Congress. . . . Connecticut sent thirty thousand bushels of flaxseed annually to New York

---

* John's nickname in history, "Old Sink or Swim," derives from this conversation. For further data on Sewall and the fate of this friendship, see Note 2.

for export, in exchange for salt. Should the colonies sign a Non-exportation Agreement, Connecticut could make the seed into oil at profit; she had many oil mills. On the other hand, she exported a great number of horses and cattle to the West Indies; to dispose of these animals elsewhere might prove impossible.

The business of the Congress was to center largely on matters of trade. Short of war, the only effectual protest against Britain's system of empire would be boycott. It was not going to be easy to persuade the colonies to relinquish their various export businesses. Each province would hold out for its especial product. It was important for the delegates to tabulate these interests, learn them, acquire an over-all perspective. Here in Connecticut it was perfectly understood that no New England delegate would urge independence. Massachusetts had been careful, in her June Resolves declaring for a Congress, to include a paragraph praying for *the restoration of that union & harmony between Great Britain and the colonies most ardently desired by all good men.*

As the delegation entered New Haven, church bells were set ringing; cannon boomed. Men, women and children crowded to doors and windows, "as if to see a coronation," John wrote. Even Mr. Jared Ingersoll, Tory Judge of Admiralty, came to call. He was the famous defiant Stamp Master of '65, and by way of being a great swell. His politeness to the Massachusetts men astonished John, who put it down as indication of the strong leveling trend in Connecticut. The delegates went sightseeing. John noted there were three Congregational churches to one Episcopalian. . . . In the burying-yard the grave of Dixwell the regicide* was kept significantly fresh with flowers. . . . A Mr. Douglass had a fine garden of fruit, a muskmelon seventeen inches long, a huge watermelon "whose inside looked as if it was painted." Someone hinted that the great parade, the bells, the salute of cannon at their arrival had been engineered by Mr. Ingersoll and his friends, to divert the people from putting up a liberty pole hung with the usual images.

It was not easy, these days, to distinguish friend from enemy. Driving out of New Haven, John remarked on the fact. Yes, Cushing replied instantly; they were going into strange country, they must be exceedingly cautious. Cushing was known as the sharpest intelli-

* One of the judges who convicted Charles I, and great-grandfather of Justice O. W. Holmes's wife, Fanny Dixwell Holmes.

gence man in the liberty party, with a marked talent for securing advance information about Britain's next move. Concerning policy in Philadelphia and their own part in shaping it, no advice could be better, Cushing reminded his colleagues now, than Hawley's letter to John Adams. It contained messages for each of the four men, advice pointed and characteristically frank. Sam Adams, indeed, said they ought to read it aloud every morning before breakfast. He himself preferred morning prayers and always held them, at home. Failing prayers, Hawley's words would do pretty well.

There is an opinion which does in some degree obtain in the other colonies [*Hawley had written*] that the Massachusetts gentlemen, and especially of the town of Boston, do affect to dictate and take the lead in continental measures; that we are apt, from an inward vanity and self-conceit, to assume big and haughty airs. Now I pray that everything in the conduct and behavior of our gentlemen which might tend to beget or strengthen such an opinion, might be most carefully avoided. It is highly probable, in my opinion, that you will meet gentlemen from several of the other colonies, fully equal to yourselves or any of you, in their knowledge of great Britain, the colonies, law, history, government, commerce, &c. I know there are very able men there. And by what we from time to time see in the public papers, and what our assembly and committees have received from the assemblies and committees of the more southern colonies, we must be satisfied that they have men of as much sense and literature as any we can or ever could boast of.

Sam Adams quoted the last sentence now in the coach. "It is meant for you, of course, John," he said solemnly. "*Sense and literature!* What possible foundation is there for the notion that I, for instance, could desire Massachusetts to 'dictate and take the lead in continental measures'?"

The three men roared with laughter. Sam laughed softly with them, shaking his head in mock disagreement. Yet Hawley, of course, was right and Sam knew it. It was of primary importance that the deputies, both Northern and Southern, assume the larger viewpoint, pool the private in the public interest, the provincial in the continental. Such indeed was the purpose of this Congress, which was in no sense a legislative body. It had no power to raise money, conscript an army, declare either war or independence, even if it had a will to do so. This was merely a congress of ambassadors, a meeting of twelve

collective minds (thirteen, if Georgia decided to send deputies) to sound out and publish the common opinion and the common purpose. The very name — "congress" — revealed the nature of the gathering. The word had always connoted a meeting of ambassadors or delegates from sovereign states, just as the word "convention," in earlier English history, had meant an irregular meeting of Parliament. James Otis's Convention of Towns in '68 had been a case in point; the Congress at Philadelphia was another. (Few men spoke of it, so far, as "the Continental Congress." That would come later. At the moment it was known everywhere as the General Congress, the Congress of Deputies, the Grand Congress, or simply the Congress at Philadelphia.)

In such a gathering, tact would be of utmost importance. Daring, innovation, were to be avoided. The New England colonies had a reputation for radicalism, republicanism, the leveling spirit. Rumor had it that the Boston faction actually desired independence — a notion abhorrent to every colony except perhaps Virginia. (How abhorrent, the Massachusetts men would very soon learn.)

Milford, Stratford, and the wobbly plank bridge over the Housatonic . . . The coach rolled on. John was coated with dust — "inside as well as out," he told Bob Paine. The taste of dust was in his mouth, the smell of it in his nostrils. Cushing complained that he was sore and bruised from head to foot. He had been flung about this cursed coach like a football; their much-vaunted Connecticut highway was no smoother than a pair of wheel ruts through a pasture. John was surprised at his own lack of fatigue. He felt wonderful. "If Camden, Chatham, Richmond and St. Asaph had travelled through the country," he recorded, "they could not have been entertained with greater demonstrations of respect than Cushing, Paine and the brace of Adamses have been."

Each night after the others turned in, John sat writing industriously in his diary, avid for every detail of the countryside and people, curious as a traveler to Cochin China . . . Kingsbridge, with Uncas River running before the tavern door . . . How splendid the great country seats along the road! Now they were only ten miles from New York . . . Five miles . . . Hell Gate was a "whirlpool . . . at certain times of the tide, water rushes into a large cavern under the rocks."

On Saturday morning, August twentieth, the travelers drove into the town of New York, just ten days out of Boston.

The Massachusetts men stayed a week in New York, with scarcely a moment to themselves. They were dined, breakfasted, wined, argued with, denounced and praised. This was a city about the size of Boston, with eighteen thousand inhabitants. But the Province of New York had only two hundred thousand, not nearly so many as Massachusetts. John and his colleagues were escorted around the Battery — "the fort," John called it. The view of "Hudson's River," the East River, Long Island and New Jersey was very fine. They saw a shipyard, several markets; walked up "the Broad Way, a handsome street, very wide, and in a right line from one end of the city to the other." These streets were vastly more regular than in Boston, John noted. The houses were grander too, and neater. Most of them were painted, even the brick buildings. John saw the stone prison, gazed upon His Majesty's statue on horseback, "very large, very high, made of solid lead and gilded with gold." On the streets, people pointed at "the gentlemen from Massachusetts."

Everywhere, talk was of the Congress. On the night of their arrival, John stayed till midnight at the tavern, discussing politics. . . . New York was overwhelmingly conservative. It was only lately that its Committee of fifty-one had managed by skillful, patient maneuver to put through some resolutions on the liberty side. The two great families in the Province were the Livingstons and De Lanceys; nothing could be done without the support of one or the other. A young Mr. John Jay, just twenty-nine, delegate to the Congress, was married to a Livingston.* Jay was a lawyer — a hard student and a good speaker, John was told. Throughout New York Province the Episcopalians were very powerful. . . .

The day after their arrival, a Sunday, John and Sam went together to the Presbyterian Church and heard a rousing sermon on hell. ("Spoken without notes," John recorded admiringly.) But the singing was most distressing. These Presbyterians hadn't yet given

---

* This was the great family of Scotch Dissenters that settled at Albany a hundred years before. Their manor covered 160,000 acres; they were allied by marriage with the powerful and aristocratic Van Rensselaers and Schuylers. John's college mate, Philip Livingston of Albany, undoubtedly belonged to the family; he died in 1756.

up "the old way"; they sang through their noses, with "all the drawling, quavering discord in the world." After church, Mr. Morin Scott introduced himself — a lawyer, leader of the liberty party in the city. Would the travelers breakfast with him next morning at his house in the country?

John was enchanted with Morin Scott's establishment. "Hudson's River" flowed below the garden. In a "fine, airy entry," the ladies of the family came forward — "dressed to receive us," John recorded with infinite satisfaction. He himself rose magnificently to the occasion, bowed deeply to Madam Scott, a trifle less deeply to three young ladies who might have been nieces, and all but kissed the hand of a dowager, dressed in rustling slate-gray silk, who proved later to be the paid companion. They moved into a front room. . . . "A more elegant breakfast I never saw . . . Rich plate, a very large silver coffee-pot, a very large silver tea-pot, napkins of the very finest materials, toast and bread and butter in great perfection. After breakfast a plate of beautiful peaches and another of plums and a muskmelon."

The Massachusetts men were lodged near the Battery, at a private house. Four New York delegates called to pay their respects, the Messrs. Livingston, Duane, Low and Alsop. John looked hard at them, seeking to read their characters for future reference. Livingston was a "downright, straight-forward man," Alsop a "soft, sweet man." Duane had a "sly, surveying eye, a little squint-eyed, between forty and forty-five, very sensible and artful." He was in correspondence with London, and told John with much assurance that it was idle to count upon winning friends in England.

So it went, day by day — and day by day John's diary grew more caustic. . . . The Livingstons were supported entirely by income from their estates. They were all rich. Some were "very sensible." The Congress was to have two of this family as delegates. The second one, Philip, nearly twenty years older than John, was a "great, rapid, rough mortal," who was fond of saying that if England should turn the colonies adrift, they would instantly go to civil war among themselves to determine which colony should govern the rest.

The brace of Adamses began to lose patience with the town of New York. There was too much of this dining and wining and coffee drinking; these Episcopalians lived too well. Of course, hospitality provided a way to meet people, learn local politics, feel out the sense

of the Province. But Sam was repelled by the luxury, and John wanted time to visit the booksellers and King's College where his old college friend, Daniel Treadwell, had taught mathematics before he died. One morning, when the four Massachusetts men were expected to dine on Long Island with still another Livingston, the two Adamses sent word they were fatigued . . . the day was raw and wet . . . they prayed to be excused.

No sooner were the others out of sight than the *par nobile fratrum* sallied forth. First they went to Trinity Churchyard and paid their respects to the grave of that good Massachusetts man, Mr. Benjamin Pratt, who in '61 had left home to become Chief Justice of New York — *One-legged Benjamin, whose bite followed close on his bark*. John stood long, looking down at the stone. Benjamin Pratt had all but turned him out of his parlor in the year '58 when, fresh from Worcester, John had come as supplicant. Pratt had taught him much, some of it very bitter. He would not forget. . . . The Yorkers, Sam said easily as they walked away, had not liked One-legged Benjamin overly well, although they said his mind, his memory, were prodigious. . . . Well, if he died lonely it served the man right for deserting his own country of Massachusetts, Sam finished.

St. Paul's Church nearby had cost eighteen thousand pounds, York money, and it boasted a piazza with stone pillars. But neither inside nor out did it equal, both Adamses agreed, Dr. Cooper's church on Brattle Square at home. At King's College they watched Dr. Clossy conduct experiments with his pupils, "to prove the elasticity of the air." But the college had only forty students and one building; it was not to be compared with Harvard.

On Friday morning they were to leave. John, recovering from the first bedazzlement of the traveler, set down his impressions as became a Massachusetts man. "For all the opulence and splendor of this city," he wrote in the diary, "there is very little good breeding to be found. We have been treated with an assiduous respect. But I have not seen one real gentleman, one well-bred man since I came to town. At their entertainments there is no conversation that is agreeable. There is no modesty, no attention one to another. They talk very loud, very fast, and all together. If they ask you a question, before you can utter three words of your answer, they will break out upon you again and talk away."

Friday dawned hot and still, with a haze over the river. The dele-

gates crossed at Paulus Hook, then "Hackinsack Ferry," Newark
Ferry, and midday dinner at "Elizabethtown." That afternoon they
drove twenty miles, slept the night at Brunswick. It was noon on
Saturday before they reached "Prince-town." . . . Nassau Hall College, wrote John, was a stone building standing on a hill, with a fine
prospect round it. Every chamber in the hall had three windows and
every study, one window; it was very commodious and airy. The
President, Dr. Witherspoon, proved as high a Son of Liberty as any
in America and declared his students were of like mind. Could
not the Congress raise money to hire writers for the British newspapers, Witherspoon suggested — men who could explain the truth,
cut down British prejudice against us? The Virginians, he went on,
were enraptured with two of their delegates, whom they boasted as
the Cicero and Demosthenes of the age. Richard Henry Lee and
Patrick Henry, their names were.

Privately, John hoped the Congress would not produce too many
orators. Oratory always slowed up procedure. . . .

On Monday the four men drove to the river, boarded a barge and
drifted pleasantly down the Delaware, the coach following by road.
At Trenton they breakfasted and went on by the highway. The day
was lovely. Rain had mercifully settled the dust; the wide fields lay
fresh and green. "One vast champaign," John called it. . . . Bristol.
. . . Burlington. . . . Along the road came three huge wagons, the
like of which John had never seen. "Passage wagons," he called them,
designed to carry much baggage and many travelers. Painted red,
they had four wheels; arched covers of sailcloth protected them.* At
Frankford the delegates were met by a large escort of carriages and
gentlemen on horseback. John was particular to learn their names:
Mr. Thomas Mifflin of Philadelphia, Mr. McKean "of the Lower
Counties" (Delaware) . . . The two New Hampshire delegates
were with them, and a Mr. Rutledge of Carolina — "a young, smart,
spirited body, very high for liberty." They had scarcely been introduced when Rutledge announced in a loud voice that he did not trust
the King's word for an instant. Startled, John looked at his colleagues. Was this the cautious attitude they had been led to expect
outside of New England? In Boston's Green Dragon Tavern, one
could not hear worse!

* Probably Conestoga wagons.

There was a general rearrangement of carriages and occupants, and the parade drove in to Philadelphia, coming to a stop before the London Coffee House at Front and Market Streets. "The most genteel tavern in America," John called it, chagrined that he must enter it for the first time all dusty, hot and disheveled. But the supper was superb, and as the evening progressed, more and more gentlemen poured in to greet the Massachusetts men. Mr. McKean told John they looked for fifty-six delegates at the Congress. Of these, twenty-two were lawyers — which would, John decided a trifle grimly, make their business both easier and harder. He knew how to deal with lawyers, yet they were talking men, apt, when action was needed, to waste their energies in detailed discussion. Someone whose name John did not catch warned him against "the famous Dr. Smith, provost of the Pennsylvania College — a soft, polite, insinuating creature, with ambitions toward an American Episcopate and a pair of lawn sleeves for himself."

By ten o'clock John, already dizzy with travel, the motion of the coach still ringing in his head, found himself blinded with smoke, half-deafened with talk, noise, the shifting of the crowd from table to table. At the shank of the evening, the door swung open and Charles Thomson walked in. "The Sam Adams of Philadelphia," John called him. A striking-looking man, thin, with piercing, deepset eyes, wearing his own hair cut short above the ears. He was about to marry a lady with five thousand pounds sterling and he was, it seemed, the very life of the cause of liberty in Pennsylvania.

Toward midnight the Massachusetts men were escorted to their lodgings on Arch Street near the river.[3] A week remained before the Congress would hold its first session. John set out to learn the town and its ways. He liked Philadelphia, felt immediately drawn to it, although the heat was violent beyond any heat John had ever experienced. Even in the morning the air lay heavy, breathless, and the mosquitoes were nothing short of infernal.

This was the largest city on the continent, with thirty thousand inhabitants. It was paved and lighted; you walked on brick. The citizens complained because there were no bridges. But the ferries ran constantly. "Horse boats," the people called them: horses walked in a circle, turning a capstan which made the wheels move. John thought it very ingenious. A mailcoach, justly called the *Flying Ma-*

chine, made the trip to New York in only two days. The coastwise shipping was tremendous; Philadelphia was a great shipbuilding center; its annual tonnage far exceeded Boston's.

People lived well — dined late, at three or four in the afternoon, had supper at seven and sometimes tea at six besides. It seemed to John the Philadelphians were always eating. And they did not begin dinner with a thrifty plate of yellow New England mush to dull the edge of appetite. Even the plain Friends ate like princes. At Mr. Miers Fisher's one day, John had for dinner "ducks, hams, chickens, beef, pig, tarts, creams, custards, jellies, foods, trifles, floating islands, beer, porter, punch, wine — and a long etc." After dark the guests hurried home to avoid the night air, which was dangerous hereabout. With sundown a miasma arose, an effluvia that caused bilious fevers — due, John learned, to the great number of millponds round the city.

The days passed quickly. On Sunday morning John went to the Presbyterian Church, the nearest approach to his own Congregational Meeting-house. Looking round, it appeared a trifle grubby; the sermon was dull and long. "Neither a very numerous nor a very polite assembly," John confessed. Strolling into Christ Church later, he found it a "more noble building, a genteeler congregation," with a fine organ, a choir that sang most sweetly, and no Calvinist intoning through the nose. No doubt about it, these Episcopalians could ravish a man's spirit. Great-uncle Peter had been right, long ago in Braintree. One must be on guard against such incantations. John ventured further, to the Romish Chapel itself. "Grandmother church," he called it, half repelled, half tranced by the color, the music, the rich dress of the priest, the wax candles and the images. "I wonder," he wrote earnestly in the diary, "how Luther ever broke the spell."

Here in these Southern colonies was no homogeneity of religion as in New England. Quakers, Episcopalians, Roman Catholics, German Lutherans and a half-dozen other sects rubbed shoulders. It might prove a serious stumbling block to the Congress. There was no subject on which men felt more passionately; religion and politics were by no means separate. How, for instance, would Mr. Carroll of Maryland, a devout Roman Catholic, feel about the Quebec Act,* against which New England planned to frame a spirited official pro-

---

* The Quebec Act, passed by Parliament on June 22, 1774, guaranteed freedom of religion for French Catholics in Canada. Further particulars are given in Note 4 for Chapter Twenty-four.

test? Could Mr. Carroll and Sam Adams, for instance, manage to agree on anything at all, with this fierce chasm of religion between them? Sam must be warned before Congress met, advised to keep his Dissenting principles to himself.

John had seen little of his cousin here in Philadelphia. Cushing said he spent his time down around the docks at Front Street, making the acquaintance of the mechanics and carpenters, the riggers and craftsmen whom Charles Thomson was doing his best to mold into a political influence. Philadelphia had its radical party, but the lines were drawn differently from the way they were at home. It was hard for a stranger to disentangle the threads; a man's religious affiliation gave little clue to his politics. In Boston it was taken for granted that all Church of England men were Tories; Sam Adams's "Black Regiment" of Congregational ministers had been the backbone of the liberty party for years.

Here in Pennsylvania, however, the Dissenting faiths — Quakers, Presbyterians, German Lutherans, Moravians — by no means stood as a solid block in support of the liberty side. Old Israel Pemberton, known as "the King of the Quakers" — the Indians called him "King of Wampum" — was dead set against a stoppage of trade with Britain, or indeed any move that threatened to break communication with the mother country. On the other hand, the genteel Episcopalian congregation of Christ Church, which John had permitted himself to admire, included in its number many true and outspoken friends of liberty. It was an important matter, something to be studied now and after the Congress should meet.

Joseph Galloway led the conservatives at the moment. He was a man of large fortune, an old hand at politics, very popular with what remained of the Quaker political machine. John met him and mistrusted instantly his "air of reserve, design and cunning." With Dr. Franklin still in London, the Philadelphian best known to New England was, of course, the FARMER, Mr. John Dickinson. He called on the Massachusetts men one afternoon, driving up in his own coach with four beautiful horses. He had been laid up with gout, he said, or he would have come sooner to pay his respects; he was subject to hectic complaints. "He is but a shadow," John wrote. "Tall, slender as a reed, pale as ashes. One would think at first sight he could not live a month. Yet upon more attentive inspection he looks as if the springs of life were strong enough to last many years."

It was a little difficult to ascertain just where Dickinson stood. In local Pennsylvania politics, he had always been rabidly conservative — against breaking up the old proprietary government of the Penn family. Yet in the year '68, his famous *Letters from a Farmer in Pennsylvania* had had deep and widespread influence against Britain's iniquitous "system." Not a delegate to the Congress, he was chairman of the Philadelphia Committee of Correspondence. But he greatly desired reconciliation with England, and after the Boston Port Bill he had refused to go further than friendly expressions of sympathy.

It was most important to know these men, sift grain from chaff, discover which in the Congress were to be merely loud talkers and which wielded real influence with their constituents at home. Day by day the delegates drifted into town. Georgia was the only colony not represented. So far, the Massachusetts men found themselves happiest with the gentlemen from Virginia. John set them down as "the most spirited and consistent of all." Peyton Randolph was "a large, well-looking man"; Mr. Bland, "learned and bookish," swore stoutly that he would have come to the Congress if it had been held in Jericho. Benjamin Harrison said he would have walked all the way if necessary. Richard Henry Lee — "tall, spare, a deep thinker" — had a brother who was High Sheriff of London. The numbers of people represented at this Congress, Lee told the Massachusetts men, he computed at about "two millions two hundred thousand." Britain's revenue from them was at least eighty thousand pounds sterling. Something to bear in mind, Lee said, if the Congress should commence discussing a commercial blockade.

Mr. Lynch of South Carolina had brought his wife and daughter to Philadelphia. He was a "solid, firm, judicious man"; John was greatly pleased with him. Colonel Washington had not yet made his appearance. He had much business to settle, his friends said, on his plantation, which was large, with many hundred Negroes. But he would surely be here for the first session on Monday.

To the New England men, discussing the situation late at night in their rooms when the company had gone, it was plain that Virginia and Massachusetts were to lead the liberty party, while Pennsylvania and New York worked their hardest for accommodation with Britain and for business as usual on land and sea. Pennsylvania had a tribe of men exactly like the Hutchinson supporters at home — persons who loved the royal government and all its symbols, desired harmony

at any price. "Men," said John angrily, "whose weather vane pointed always to their private interest." Galloway, Dr. Smith of the Pennsylvania College, stood just where the Hutchinson faction had stood in 1754. They had not moved forward an inch. Moreover it had begun to be obvious that every colony harbored such a set of people.

But what a noble quantity of burgundy these Southern gentlemen could consume in an evening! John was amazed and admiring, his diary thick with convivial entries. "Went with Mr. Barrell to his store, drank punch, eat dried sprats. . . . Spent the evening at Mr. Mifflin's, drank sentiments till eleven o'clock. . . . At Mr. Powel's, a most sinful feast again. Curds and creams, jellies, sweetmeats, twenty sorts of tarts, fools, trifles, floating island, whipped sillabubs. Parmesan cheese, punch, wine, porter, beer. . . . Later, at evening, climbed the steeple of Christ's Church from which we had a clear and full view of the whole city, and of Delaware River."

Christ Church steeple was tall, the stone steps high and rough. Up in the gathering summer dusk went the Parmesan cheese, the punch, the wine, the porter, the sillabubs. This Congress, John told himself, puffing audibly, possessed gentlemen of firm constitutions, not lightly dismayed.

CHAPTER TWENTY-SIX

The Congress meets.

FROM Christ Church belfry and St. Peter's, from Romish Chapel and Lutheran, from Presbyterian steeple to the high tower of the State House, Philadelphia's bells pealed welcome to the Congress. Forty-four gentlemen, handsome in powdered wigs, knee breeches and smart black three-cornered hats, crossed the little cobbled court from Chestnut Street to the high, white-painted doorway of Carpenters' Hall. It was ten in the morning of Monday, September 5, a fine clear day with the heat mercifully lifted and a fresh breeze blowing across the Northern Liberties. The delegates were in good spirits, talkative, friendly. They had met by appointment at the City Tavern and walked in a body through the streets while passers-by fell back, gazing in open curiosity at the distinguished strangers, often giving them greeting or salute.

The business of the moment was to examine Carpenters' Hall, decide if it was to be the meeting place of Congress. Joseph Galloway, Speaker of the Pennsylvania Assembly, was expected to make a formal offer of the State House,* two short blocks up the street — a building three times as large, very spacious and beautiful within. The question and the choice had a significance far beyond material convenience. As leader of the moderate party, Galloway's influence would be stronger in the traditional atmosphere of the State House. To him, the official home of a great Province seemed the logical, dignified place for this Congress to convene. Carpenters' Hall on the other hand was a private building, belonging to the Carpenters'

* Later Independence Hall.

Company, a guild formed early in the century and by now very powerful in city politics. To choose it as permanent meeting place would be an open concession to the mechanics and laborers, the extreme liberty men who in Galloway's view were already too influential in government affairs.

Carpenters' Hall was new, only lately opened for use. From cornerstone to cupola it was the handiwork of the Carpenters themselves, and they were justly proud of it. Their Company numbered some of the best architects and craftsmen on the continent. It was a two-story brick building, designed in the classic style. A broad flight of steps led to a perfectly proportioned doorway, flanked with square pilasters. Above, the second-story windows were long and arched, supported by small white ornamental columns. Round to the left, between the garden wall and the building, stood an iron pump with a long handle. A dozen boys and women were gathered near it with their pails. The Carpenters' well was famous, used by houses for blocks around.

Climbing the steps, the delegates entered the hall and exclaimed in pleasure. To the right, a charming balustraded staircase curved upward to committee rooms. The ground floor was divided in two chambers.[1] The westerly one, looking toward the State House, was lined with glazed bookcases that housed the collection of the Library Company. Between the two rooms a wide hallway ran through the building, ending in a splendid fanlighted doorway giving on the yard. . . . The members could walk up and down this hall, someone suggested, for the purpose of private discussion — so necessary in political conventions when disagreement threatens.

The East Room was the one proposed for Congress. The door was open, the delegates filed in. They found a cheerful, small, bright chamber, its walls painted a light buff, with a low, white-paneled fireplace. Morning sun poured through the big windows. There were a desk for the chairman and rows of hickory armchairs, painted black — made by the Carpenters, the delegates were told; most commodious, especially for large gentlemen. Benjamin Harrison of Virginia, whose bulk was magnificent, let himself down into one.

"But this is a fine light chamber, surely!" the Virginia men exclaimed. Gadsden of South Carolina agreed; so did McKean and Rodney. Sam Adams said nothing, neither did John. The Massachusetts contingent preferred to remain very, very silent. But Joseph Gallo-

way, choosing a seat of vantage in a corner, frowned. Whence came
this sudden concerted enthusiasm for the Carpenters' Hall? Was it
possible his offer of the State House was to be refused? If so, it
would be a slap in the face not only for him personally but for the
whole conservative faction.

The members settled down, the various delegations in groups together. John, in his chair between Sam Adams and Cushing, reflected
that the room was certainly small. Yet its air of intimacy was not only
agreeable but somehow reassuring. Looking about him, John was
pleased to recognize two thirds of the faces. The Massachusetts men
had done well to come a week early; acquaintance with one's colleagues gave one a sense of confidence. All the members, of course,
had not arrived. The North Carolina deputies were still on the road;
communities everywhere continued to elect representatives. Among
forty-odd delegates, the extreme liberty men could be counted,
John noted ruefully, on one's fingers: Richard Henry Lee, Patrick
Henry, Colonel Washington; Gadsden of South Carolina, Roger
Sherman of Connecticut, Governor Hopkins of Rhode Island. Stephen Hopkins was the veteran of this convention. Since the Albany
Congress of '54, he had been shouting defiance at Britain. He was
a fine-looking old man who wore the sober Quaker's dress and broad-
brimmed hat; his gray hair hung to his shoulders. John had always
admired him; Hopkins could be counted on to speak out when
plain speech was needed.

But with so large a conservative majority against them, the liberty
men were aware they must be discreet, work diligently to win supporters. They had no definite program. At most they hoped to
achieve a blockade of trade with Britain: some plan of "commercial
non-intercourse" strong enough, severe enough, to force repeal of
the Intolerable Acts, a lifting of the Boston blockade and a change of
the system of colonial taxation. At the worst they feared Congress
might rise, in the end, having achieved nothing beyond petitions to
Parliament, memorials to the King and humble appeals to the ministers at London. Sam Adams of course wished for unutterable things,
but he was wise enough to know he would not get them. John himself was mistrustful of the efficacy of a commercial blockade. "When
Demosthenes," he wrote James Warren, "went Ambassador from
Athens to the other States of Greece, to excite a Confederacy against
Phillip, he did not go to propose a Non-Importation or Non-Con-

sumption Agreement!!! . . . Somewhat a little more Sublime and
Mettlesome, would come from Such Kind of Spirits. However, we
must fast and pray, bear and forbear."

Bear and forbear. . . . In Carpenters' Hall someone was speaking,
putting a question: Did this Hall satisfy the gentlemen? . . . There
was murmur of approval, and although Duane and Jay, the New
York moderates, rose to object, the motion was made and quickly
seconded: Carpenters' Hall was to be the home of Congress. Mortification showed plainly in Galloway's face. Peyton Randolph of
Virginia was unanimously chosen as President or Chairman; he
bowed his thanks and walked to the desk — a plump, slow-moving
gentleman of fifty-three who looked sixty in his powdered wig.
Members noted approvingly that he was dressed in plain stuff of
American manufacture.

Thomas Lynch of South Carolina rose next to propose, as Secretary of the Congress, "a gentleman of family, fortune and character
in this city, Mr. Charles Thomson." In his chair by the window, Galloway started, his long upper lip drew down. Thomson, the Sam
Adams of Philadelphia? Why, Thomson was not even a member of
the Congress (thanks largely to Galloway's own pre-election efforts). Again Duane and Jay objected and lost the vote: Thomson
was named Secretary and a messenger sent into the city to find and
fetch him. Galloway glanced angrily at the Massachusetts men. This
morning's work, it was plain, could not have been accomplished
without much preliminary maneuvering out of doors. In future he
must be more watchful. There was small doubt who was behind this
sinister choice of both Hall and Secretary.

Peyton Randolph, calling for order, requested the delegations to
stand in turn while their credentials were read. The two New Hampshire men were first, with Major Sullivan as spokesman. Sullivan
was tall, muscular, owed his military title to the militia; at home
he was known as a successful and highly disputatious lawyer. The
New Hampshire deputies had been elected, Congress heard now,
by "85 Deputies of the several towns, meeting at Exeter." Their instructions were "to devise, consult, and adopt measures to secure
and perpetuate their rights, and to restore that peace, harmony and
mutual confidence which once subsisted between the parent country and her Colonies."

Massachusetts came next. Once more the phrase was repeated:

The restoration of that union & harmony . . . most ardently desired by all good men . . . This Congress, John Adams reflected dryly, did not lack reminders concerning its essential purpose. *Union & harmony . . .* Much water had run under the bridge since the writing of these various Instructions, early in the summer. The past two months had seen tarrings, featherings, riots, ugly disturbances throughout the continent. The political temper had advanced. On the journey from Boston, John had been surprised, at first, when the Tories gathered to bid them Godspeed. But what other position could a Tory take? Either the Congress was an act of rebellion and should be broken up (something no Royal Governor felt powerful enough to attempt), or the Tories must take the position that this Congress was gathering for pacific purposes.

Rhode Island . . . Connecticut . . . The delegations rose in their turn. Roger Sherman's gray-brown hair was cut short all round, above the ears. He looked plain, strong, unbendable as oak. Connecticut made no mention of peace or harmony. . . . New York (now, here was a strange-sounding election! No House of Representatives, no Convention of Towns or Committee of Correspondence had chosen these deputies. *By duly certifyed polls, taken by proper persons in seven wards, it appears that James Duane, John Jay, Philip Livingston . . .*) New York had no Instructions at all. Evidently, her constituents preferred not to commit themselves to a program. New Jersey . . . Pennsylvania . . . *"For establishing union & harmony,"* said Pennsylvania's spokesman, sonorously.

Of them all, the fiercest Instructions came from the small territory known as the "Lower Counties on Delaware": Newcastle, Kent and Sussex. Thomas McKean's voice, reciting them, was vehement; plainly, he was enjoying himself. McKean was an old hand at conventions; he had been a member of the Stamp Act Congress in '65. He was an erect man of about forty, carefully dressed and wigged, with a slim figure and a quick, nervous way of moving. He spoke well . . . *For taking away the property of the Colonists without their consent. For new-modelling the government of the Massachusetts-Bay . . .*

Wonderful, thought the Massachusetts men, how the colonies hammered away about Boston, the blockade, the Intolerable Acts, the judges robbed of independence! John wished suddenly that his

wife could hear these words. How heartened she would be! No matter what Congress finally achieved or did not achieve, something invaluable, amazing, had already been accomplished. These Instructions proved it. The people's determination had balked at no obstacle: Governor Wentworth of New Hampshire (John's old college friend) had done his level best to prevent the election of delegates from his province; yet here they were, two stout New Hampshire men, sitting not three chairs away. . . . Several New England delegates had refused to come, even after election: Bowdoin of Boston and Johnson of Connecticut. Johnson's excuse had been that he could not leave his legal clients.

South Carolina was last to speak. Her Instructions were superb: *"The acts and bills of Parliament in regard to Massachusetts Bay affect the whole Continent of America."* As the words emerged, John could scarcely forbear to cheer. Peyton Randolph ordered the doors locked; the real business of Congress was about to begin. Utmost secrecy must be maintained. The members pledged themselves not to divulge by word or letter what went on. . . . It was suggested that a committee be appointed to discuss procedure.

John Adams rose. "How are the delegates to vote?" he asked. "By colonies, one vote to a colony? Or by the poll?" (By the poll meant counting heads, with a majority winning.)

It was the question of questions, beside which all other procedure dwindled to unimportance. Congress was bound by the instructions of its constituents. Yet the various delegations by no means represented their colonies fairly as to numbers. Massachusetts, with a population estimated at nearly two hundred and fifty thousand, had only four deputies. New York, with a lesser population, had five; so did poor, small, thinly populated New Jersey. There was no guarantee that nearby colonies like New York or Maryland would not send a dozen extra deputies, any day, to sway the vote for some particular measure. Virginia in all her majesty most assuredly expected to wield larger influence than some small province whose voice, so far, had scarcely been raised for liberty. Virginia was rich and powerful in her own right. Her seven delegates — with one exception — represented large tidewater plantations, shippers of tobacco to Europe and England.

Patrick Henry spoke out, for the mighty colony of Virginia. Im-

portant precedents were about to be established, he said. In the councils of America it would be a great injustice if a little colony were given the same weight as a great one.

Major Sullivan of New Hampshire was instantly on his feet. His voice was rough, loud: "A little colony has its stake as well as a great one!" Governor Ward of Rhode Island was quick to agree. "We come," he said, "if necessary to make a sacrifice of our all. By such sacrifice the weakest colony would suffer as much as the greatest."

The New Jersey men nodded vehemently. Benjamin Harrison of Virginia stood up. He was a large, slow, luxurious-looking gentleman, beautifully dressed in smooth blue broadcloth, his wig faultlessly curled and powdered. His plantations, as everyone knew, were immense; he had been a member of the House of Burgesses for a quarter of a century. "My province must be granted her proper share of influence," he boomed sententiously. "If disrespect be put upon my countrymen, I am very apprehensive we shall not see them at another convention."

Patrick Henry, who had listened restlessly to his colleague, sprang to his feet. "We must vote by the poll," he said, reversing instantly his former stand. "Not by colonies! To vote by colonies will defeat the purpose of this Congress." He spoke directly to Harrison. "Where are now your landmarks, your boundaries of colonies? We are in a state of nature, Sir!"

A state of nature.[2] Every man in the room knew the phrase, yet today it struck with most startling effect. In each mind was instantly a vision conjured up by the great John Locke: Man in his original state, denizen of the forest, innocent of control. Man in his political infancy, ready to make new compacts, new arrangements of government and sovereignty. In a state of nature, man owed allegiance to none but God, and stood ready to make his "original compact" under no eye but God's. . . . It was a concept that had demolished the divine right of kings, swept a Stuart off his throne. No one present denied its value. Yet the delegates had by no means expected to have recourse to it here in Philadelphia, and on the first day of meeting.

The room was silent, every eye on the speaker. They saw a lean man just under forty, dressed in a plain suit of parson's gray, his brown wig unpowdered, carelessly arranged. Henry's forehead was

high, his brows dark and straight. His eyes, blue and very bright, were set deep in his head. About his narrow face was something burning, intense, something dedicated, that left no room for self-indulgence. (Henry did not pronounce his words as Harrison did, or Washington — but flatly, with a little drawl, after the manner of the frontier. "Man's natteral parts," he had been heard to say, "are much improved by larnin'.")

Patrick Henry had been a member of the Virginia House of Burgesses a full nine years. He represented an element greatly feared: the rough unorganized democracy of the border. Yet he had won and held the respect of his colleagues. They were proud of him, of his orator's tongue, his fire, of his extraordinary command of any assemblage once he began to speak, be it courtroom or legislature. Now they glanced complacently about the room. Even Benjamin Harrison, about to be refuted, looked pleased. *See now this meteor from Virginia!* he seemed to say. *Gaze on this bright comet from the greatest colony in North America!*

Henry's right hand was raised. "Let freemen be represented by numbers alone!" he said. "Throughout the continent, government is dissolved. Landmarks are dissolved!" He repeated himself. "Where are now your boundaries? The distinctions between Virginians, Pennsylvanians, New Yorkers, New Englanders are no more. *I am not a Virginian but an American!*"

For a moment he stood motionless, letting his gaze sweep the room. Then he subsided to his chair, took out a handkerchief and wiped his face vigorously. Forty-three delegates sat spellbound, hypnotized altogether. It was crazy, what they had just heard; they knew well it was crazy. An American — in God's name what was that? *Government is dissolved* . . . Well, it wasn't dissolved, not by the length of a constitution. As for landmarks and boundaries, since morning in this little room, men had become more conscious of boundaries than ever in their lives. Boundaries lay rigid between the delegations, tight, crippling as chains, well-nigh impassable. . . . Madness, what this voice had said. Yet in this madness and this man, by God there was contagion!

A chair moved, someone coughed, there was a murmur of voices. Thomas Lynch rose, for the planters of Carolina. He was in his forties, a little heavy and slow. ("A solid, firm, judicious man," John had called him.) "I differ from the gentleman from Virginia," Lynch

said courteously. "Something more than numbers must be considered. *Property* must be considered. A compound of numbers and property should determine the influence of each colony."

John Jay of New York spoke next. He was a slight, youthful figure. Already there was in his face and bearing something composed, thoughtful, palpably disinterested, something that commanded respect. "I cannot yet think all government is at an end," he said reasonably. "We are here not to frame a new constitution but to correct the faults of an old one. At this point it is hopeless to determine the comparative wealth, the exact populations of the various colonies. That would be the work of months."

Let the Congress, Jay finished, give one vote to each colony. But let not this method be entered on the *Journals* as a precedent. Let it be a temporary, working arrangement.

The President of Congress rose behind his desk. It was three o'clock; an adjournment was moved. The delegates left their places and, filing through the door into the hallway, went out and down the steps, crossed the little court and walked home to dinner.

Miss Jane Port's house was on Arch Street near Front, about five blocks from Carpenters' Hall. Arrived at their doorstep, the Massachusetts men, pausing, could see, over the rise of ground that hid the river, the masts of a great schooner moving to the wharf. Heavy carts rolled down Front Street; there was a smell of tar. Sailors' voices shouted from the docks. . . . Things had gone well today, Sam Adams said with satisfaction. Their party had won on two counts — the Carpenters' Hall as meeting place, and Charles Thomson for Secretary. Their work out of doors last week had not been in vain. "I hope," Sam added cheerfully, "that Mr. Joseph Galloway is enjoying his dinner. I trust his appetite is not impaired. As we parted today, I bade him a polite adieu."

The others laughed. But how lofty and to the point had been Mr. Henry's speech! John remarked. He had taken notes; they were in his pocket. The man's voice was like an angel's; it went through to the bone. Sam shrugged. Very fine, he agreed. Too strong, of course, for the Congress to swallow. Yet an excellent tonic for certain members. He hoped sincerely it would fortify those whose blood was thin.

Sam spoke pleasantly. But he looked tired, his head and hands

shook. A large grease spot had appeared by the second button of the beautiful claret-colored coat; the skirts were mussed as if Congress had sat a year. "I am much concerned," Sam went on gravely, "over this fanatic fear of our New England religion. It means more than appears on the surface. The Southern men actually believe we Congregationalists have ambitions to rule the continent. I am sure of it. Something must be done, else there will be real division."

The four agreed. Still talking, they went in the door. The dark hall smelled strongly of cabbage; it was steamy, close. Miss Jane Port, their landlady, magnificent in side curls and a high starched cap with purple ribbons, darted from a doorway and sank to the floor before them in a curtsy. Startled, the men bowed vaguely, and followed each other up the stairs.

Congress, next morning, proceeded to its business quietly, with as much regularity as if these forty-odd strangers had been meeting every day for months. Jay's motion of yesterday was seconded: the vote would be one to a colony. No member, it was decided, would speak more than once on the same point without leave. It was resolved to name two grand committees, one to state the rights of the colonies, the other to examine and report on matters of trade and taxation.

When all this was accomplished — it took, with other procedure, until two o'clock — Cushing of Massachusetts came forward with a proposal. In view of the seriousness of the emergency, he moved that Congress be opened tomorrow with a prayer. Such was the practice in the British Parliament and in various legislative bodies here on the continent. The Romans too had the custom of addressing the Supreme Being in their Senate, to ask His blessing over their deliberations.

John Jay spoke immediately, in strong disapproval. Who could deliver a prayer in this place — an Episcopalian, a Quaker, a Congregationalist, a Presbyterian, an Anabaptist? It was now that Sam Adams stood up. His voice was soft, his manner pleasingly diffident. He was a stranger in Philadelphia, he began. But might he suggest, for such a prayer, a Philadelphia clergyman, Mr. Duché of the Episcopal Church? He himself was of a different religious persuasion. But he hoped he was no bigot. He could hear a prayer from a gen-

tleman of piety and virtue who was at the same time a friend to his country. He had ascertained that Mr. Duché was all of these things.

Every eye opened wide. Sam Adams, moving for an Episcopal prayer? Then it was possible the New England orthodoxy was not so ambitious, unyielding, as they had been led to believe. . . .

The motion for Duché was carried without objection. The room broke into talk. In the midst of it there was a knock at the door. An express rider was admitted. He had an urgent dispatch for the Congress, he said. From Massachusetts. . . . President Randolph took the paper, broke the seal. Alarm showed on his face. He read the message aloud: Gage's soldiers had seized the powder stores "at some town near Boston." The people had risen — six men were killed. All the country was in arms, down to Connecticut. . . . British cannon had fired on Boston the whole night.

The room sat as if stunned. Every head turned toward the Massachusetts men. "What town?" Cushing asked. Was it Charlestown? Five hundred pounds of powder were stored there. How had the fight started? . . . In the streets? Who fired first, the troops or the people?

The messenger shook his head. He knew nothing beyond the message he carried. The room broke into talk. Horror and dismay were on every face. *War!* The word went from mouth to mouth. Congress adjourned; the members hurried to the street. Ten minutes later, the State House bell tolled muffled, and from across the city, bell towers answered one by one. All day the mournful sound continued. Philadelphia was disorganized, business suspended. The Massachusetts men had little sleep that night. Next morning, walking to Congress, they were stopped again and again. "Is it war?" people asked fearfully. "Does this mean war?"

It was a dull, warm day, the air heavy, lifeless. In Carpenters' Hall the delegates took their seats. Until this rumor was confirmed they must proceed to their business, not be shocked into panic. But the news had most certainly raised the temper of Congress. . . . The door opened; the Reverend Mr. Duché walked slowly up the aisle. His black silk robe was bordered with velvet; a clerk behind him carried the Bible. Men looked up, it was obvious they were glad to see him; this was a morning when every heart desired prayer. Watching narrowly, Sam Adams was well pleased. Among the

Southern Episcopalians were some of the warmest friends to liberty on the continent.

In the silence, flies buzzed at the windows; on the wall the sun, appearing briefly, made a sharp pattern and faded. Duché took his place before the desk, opened the prayerbook and after reading prayers, looked up, pausing; then announced the Psalter for the Seventh Day, the Thirty-fifth Psalm. He had a voice of great sweetness and warmth; he read slowly, with no show of dramatics:

Plead thou my cause, O Lord, with them that strive with me, and fight thou against them that fight against me.

Lay hand upon the shield and buckler, and stand up to help me.

The effect was electric. Men bowed their heads and wept. Surely, these sacred words had been written for this day, for this company and this hour! . . . The clear voice read on:

Bring forth the spear, and stop the way against them that pursue me: say unto my soul, I am thy salvation.

For they have privily laid their net to destroy me without a cause; yea, even without a cause have they made a pit for my soul.

False witnesses did rise up: they laid to my charge things that I knew not.

They rewarded me evil for good, to the great discomfort of my soul.

I behaved myself as though it had been my friend or my brother; I went heavily, as one that mourneth for his mother.

Lord, how long wilt thou look upon this? O deliver my soul from the calamities which they bring on me, and my darling from the lions.

So will I give thee thanks in the great congregation; I will praise thee among much people.

Closing the book, Duché broke into an extemporaneous prayer. The members fell to their knees. When his voice ceased, they took their seats again, renewed, heartened.

Congress, rising in a body, gave the clergyman a vote of thanks. "One of the most sublime, catholic, well-adapted prayers I ever heard," wrote Governor Ward of Rhode Island that night, himself a Baptist. A masterly stroke, this move of the New England men, it was everywhere conceded. A generous gesture, one that would be well rewarded.

Two days later, on Thursday, a fresh express rode in from Mas-

sachusetts. The rumor of bombardment was false.* Boston was safe! General Gage had indeed tried to seize the powder at Charlestown, and had placed guns on Boston Neck — something the Province had been dreading for months. The countryside, aroused, had gathered its militia; twenty thousand men were ready to march on Boston. But after making sure their powder stores were safe, they had disbanded without a shot fired. . . . Philadelphia repeated it joyfully. *Not a shot fired!* No blood shed, no lives lost! The relief was profound. Joyful bells pealed across the city. Congress, released from nightmare, breathed freely, and locking its doors, talked once more of policy and peace, of *the restoration of that union & harmony between Great Britain and the colonies most ardently desired.*

Very shortly afterward, John had a letter from Abigail, describing the "Powder Alarm," as men called it now. Already, John had heard three times from Abby, vivid letters that he kept by him; letters telling of the children . . . of John Quincy, who was reading Rollins's *Ancient History* aloud to her . . . of the cows, patient sufferers from the drought . . . of the meeting of towns in Suffolk County . . . and of Abby's great longing for her husband's return. The political news she gave was full and explicit; John began to depend on it, he told her, above all his letters from the North, even James Warren's. . . . Royal warrants had been sent out from Boston, Abby wrote, summoning juries for the courts. Not six miles from town the messenger was overtaken by sixty liberty men on horseback who forced him to get down and burn the warrants before their eyes. . . . Governor Gage was mounting cannon on Beacon Hill, digging entrenchments, throwing up breastworks. . . . As for the Powder Alarm, would John like to hear how it had affected Braintree?

"On Sunday," Abby wrote under date of September 14, "a soldier was seen lurking about the common, supposed to be a Spy, but most likely a Deserter. . . . At about 8 o'clock a Sunday Evening there passed by here about 200 Men, preceded by a horse-cart and marched down to the powder house whence they took the powder and carried to the other parish and there secreted it — I opened

---

* Galloway believed that this rumor, like the "Suffolk Resolves" of slightly later date, was deliberately arranged by Sam Adams — a man who, Galloway wrote, "eats little, drinks little, sleeps little, thinks much, and is most decisive and indefatigable in his objects." — GALLOWAY: *Historical and Political Reflections on the Rise and Progress of the American Rebellion.* (London, 1780.)

the window upon there return. they passed without any Noise, not a word among them till they came against this house, when some of them perceiving me, asked me if I wanted any powder — I replied not since it was in such good hands. The reason they gave for taking it, was that we had so many Tories here they dare not trust us with it."

When they left the farmhouse, Abby went on, the men built a fire to burn the Sheriff's warrants. Circling the blaze, "they called a vote whether they should huzza, but it being Sunday evening, it passed in the negative." As for the Braintree Tories, not one but was hiding his head. The town was "as high as you can well imagine, and if necessary would soon be in arms." The Church of England parson had thought the men were coming after him instead of the powder! "He ran up garret they say . . . an other jumpt out of his window and hid among the corn whilst a third crept under his bord fence and told his beads."

The days passed. New delegates appeared in Congress: Johnson and Tilghman from Maryland, Wisner from Orange County in New York, George Ross from Pennsylvania, and the North Carolina delegation of three. John and Sam Adams represented Massachusetts on the grand committee to prepare a "Declaration of Rights." There were twenty-two members. They sat in an upstairs room in Carpenters' Hall and met every morning, working very hard, sometimes all day. To ascertain and express the united sense of twelve colonies on this matter of rights was difficult in the extreme. Easy enough to agree that the Intolerable Acts must be repealed, and the Boston Port Bill. After all, it was to protest these measures that Congress had convened in the first place. But when it came to political theory, to the basic principles of sovereignty and allegiance, the committee reached a deadlock. Were the colonies to base their rights wholly on the British constitution and the colonial charters? Or should they include the law of nature?

The *law of nature*, like the *state of nature*, was as familiar as the days of the week. The "incomparable Mr. Locke" had defined it; so had Grotius, Harrington, Burlamaqui, Montesquieu, and other great writers on government. The law of nature meant God's law, by which man is born to liberty. By the law of nature, the right to personal liberty was coexistent with man; it was his proud, divine

inheritance. No parliament, no king, could wrest it from him. "I was very strenuous for retaining and insisting on the Law of Nature," John wrote afterward, "as a Resource to which we might be driven by Parliament much sooner than we expected."

But the others were mistrustful. The law of nature was vague, all-embracing; it lent itself to dangerous, rebellious doctrine. In the end, after hours of debate, persuasion and reassurance, the moderates gave in. *The deputies declare* [so read the clause as finally agreed on] *that the inhabitants of the English Colonies in North America, by the immutable laws of nature, the principles of the English constitution and the several charters or compacts have the following rights:*

RESOLVED, N.C.D. 1. *That they are entitled to life, liberty, & property, and they have never ceded to any sovereign power whatever, a right to dispose of either without their consent.*

Any sovereign power whatever . . . The phrase was conciliatory; it could refer to France as well as England. After all, it was scarcely a decade since the colonies had ceased fighting France. . . . *Liberty & property:* in men's minds the words were complementary; one set off the other. Even Sam Adams believed it. A man had a right to his land, to his harvest that was the fruit of his toil, to his chest of clothes, his savings great or small. Rich and poor alike possessed this right, and government existed to safeguard it. A man's right to his property was as sacred as the right to his soul. No sovereign power could take it from him, neither parliament nor king nor — Sam would have added — the great East India Tea Company.

Not without reason had the Stamp Masters of '65 been forced, at peril of their lives, to chant that phrase under Liberty Tree: *Life, liberty and property! Huzzah! Huzzah! Huzzah!* And it was still the watchword; men were ready to die for it. (To alter it by a word would require the passage of two years' time.) Now, in late September of '74, some two dozen hard-working gentlemen sat at a table on the second floor of Carpenters' Hall and hammered out, line for line, paragraph by paragraph, the "Declaration of Rights" for America. . . .

CLAUSE 4: *What authority should be ceded to Parliament?* Should Parliament be permitted to regulate the trade of the empire, and with what restrictions? . . . The New Yorkers attacked the question as if it were new, never broached before. Two Adamses exchanged glances. John stretched his neck, fingered a stock wilted and very

damp around the edges. . . . Since the year '61, he and his cousin
had thrashed out this problem of parliamentary authority, laboring
by speech, pamphlet and newspaper to convince their countrymen
in Massachusetts. In God's name, they thought now, must they begin again at this late date to convince their countrymen in North
America? A subcommittee was formed, to reduce the thing to
smaller, more manageable terms. The talk commenced all over
again; it spun on and on. At last the elder Rutledge turned to John.
"Adams," he said, "we must agree on something. I like your expression, *the necessity of the case.*"

Picking up a pen, Rutledge handed it to John. "Here," he said,
"see if you can't produce something to unite us."

John drew a sheet of paper to him. (*Compromise!* he thought.
This is the hour for compromise.) He sat a moment, wrote briefly,
gave the paper back to Rutledge. *Deny Parliament's authority as a
matter of right*, it said in effect, *but consent to it as a matter of
necessity.*

Rutledge read the lines, handed them round the table. John's
clause satisfied nobody. But in desperation the subcommittee passed
it, reported it to the grand committee, which reported it to Congress
— which proceeded to debate the entire composition of both committees, word for word.

Long before the debate was finished — about a week, indeed, after
the committees had begun their work — something happened to
strengthen enormously the radical side. This time it was no rumor,
no sensational tale of blood and battle. Paul Revere rode down from
Massachusetts, bearing the resolutions passed by the convention of
towns in Suffolk. Suffolk County was Boston's county, the heart of
the Province; Sam Adams had been waiting for these Resolves. The
scroll was long, covering many pages. Peyton Randolph began to
read aloud. The room sat very quiet, recognizing instantly the importance of what they heard.

The "Suffolk Resolves" were the boldest statement ever made on
the continent. They spoke of Britain in terms of utmost violence:
. . . *The arbitrary will of a licentious minister . . . The streets of
Boston thronged with military executioners . . . A murderous law
is framed to shelter villains from the hand of justice . . . Our enemies have flattered themselves that they shall make an easy prey of
this numerous, brave and hardy people, from the apprehension that*

they are unacquainted with military discipline. We therefore advise . . .

What Suffolk County advised was even more to the point than her lurid language. Let a strong militia be formed, with every town and district "exerting utmost diligence to acquaint themselves with the art of war." The late acts of Parliament were to be disobeyed, all taxes paid henceforth not to Britain but to the treasury of a provincial independent government, hereby formed. The British-made judges were "under undue influence" and must be wholly disregarded. CLAUSE 14 committed Suffolk County to a thorough program of commercial nonintercourse with Britain, both as to outgoing and incoming goods — *with additions, alterations and exceptions only as the General Congress of the colonies may agree to.*

John, listening intently, wondered who had drafted these Resolves. It must have been Dr. Warren of Boston, or Josiah Quincy. About the preamble there was a tone of deepest seriousness, a consciousness of destiny, a sense of mission. *On the fortitude, the wisdom and exertions of this important day is suspended the fate of this new world, and of unborn millions. To us our venerable progenitors bequeathed the dearbought inheritance of liberty, to our care and protection they consigned it, and the most sacred obligations are upon us to transmit the glorious purchase, unfettered by power, unclogged with shackles, to our innocent and beloved offspring.*

Four Massachusetts men, sitting bolt upright, felt their heartbeats quicken. They scarcely dared look about them. It seemed impossible that Congress would put its approval to such a statement and such a program. . . . *We cheerfully acknowledge George the Third to be our rightful sovereign* . . . Randolph continued to read. (Ah, this might help!) . . . *and heartily recommend to all persons of this community, not to engage in any routs, riots or licentious attacks upon the properties of any persons whatsoever; but by a steady, manly, uniform and persevering opposition, to convince our enemies that in a cause so solemn, our conduct shall be such as to merit the approbation of the wise, and the admiration of the brave and free of every age and of every country.*

Randolph's voice ceased. The room burst into spontaneous applause. Men rose from their seats, hurried to the Massachusetts delegates, seized them by the hand, congratulating them. In the general confusion, nobody noticed Galloway and Duane, silent in their cor-

ner. Congress passed a vote of full approval, entered it in the *Journals* as unanimous, over the stringent protest of Duane and Galloway. "For Congress to countenance such a statement," Galloway said furiously, "is tantamount to a complete declaration of war." Overruled, he and Duane wrote out personal certificates of disapproval, signed them and exchanged the papers.

And while these loyal gestures to empire were making, four Massachusetts men, the plaudits of Congress ringing in their ears, walked out of Carpenters' Hall and home across the city in the afternoon sunshine, almost overwhelmed with joy.

"One of the happiest days of my life," John wrote that night in his diary. "This day convinced me that America will support the Massachusetts or perish with her."

Galloway proposes a dangerous plan, and the liberty party creates the "Continental Association." John says a cheerful farewell to Philadelphia.

THE Massachusetts men dared not show their triumph openly. The battle was far from won. The moderates were strong, they had no intention of letting the New England radicals walk away with the Congress. Galloway, Duane, John Jay, the Rutledges, sharpened their defenses — made bitter issue over proposals which to the Massachusetts men were ancient history, long ago argued out and accepted. John vented his impatience in a barrage of letters homeward.

"Tedious, indeed is our Business, Slow as Snails," he complained to Abigail on September 25. "I have not been used to such Ways. We Sit only before Dinner. We dine at four O'clock. We are crowded with a Levee in the Evening — Fifty Gent^n meeting together, all Strangers, are not acquainted with Each other's Language, Ideas, Views, Designs. They are therefore jealous of each other — fear full, timid, Skittish."

In the afternoons when Congress rose early, John was relieved to get away by himself, stroll out Chestnut Street to the Common or westward along the green slopes above Schuylkill River. His was a nature that needed solitude as it needed food and drink. John's mind was extraordinarily sensitive to intellectual impressions, almost painfully so. He knew what a man would say before the words left his mouth. But he needed time, release of pressure, to let the ideas, the arguments, sink in — arrange themselves, become part of him.

Some men — Sam Adams, Patrick Henry, Richard Henry Lee —
achieved this process in company. John envied them their ability to
think and write in a smoky, aromatic roomful of talking, argumentative humanity. They seemed to reach conclusions as well or better
with the pressure, the movement, of actual flesh and blood about
them. It stimulated them, put spark to their tinder, caused the bright
eruption of their best and fullest thoughts.

It was not so with John. *At home without company, thinking, pondering* — the diary said it very often. John would always have this
necessity. And when pressure became inescapable, he fell sick —
caught cold, lost his voice, ran a fever, was forced to his chamber and
his bed until solitude renewed him. Here in Philadelphia he took care
to slip from Carpenters' Hall a little early or a little late, walking
quickly so none would see him go. He had not covered four blocks
when the pressure began to lift and peace stole down — lighting on
his shoulder, John thought smiling, like a dove. Beneath the bright
uncrowded sky he could move at his own pace, blissfully aware
that among these passing strangers no eye would seek his in sympathy or in anger. John's breath came slow and deep, he lifted his
head, watching a hawk's flight high above the river. . . .

The fall days were fine now, neither hot nor cold; Philadelphia
lived its life sociably on the streets. Along the brick footways, boys
played pitch-penny. Housewives, their work done, sat on benches
placed before their doors, exchanging gossip, stitching at their shell-
work and enjoying the air. On warm afternoons, men and boys still
swam in the Delaware. John liked to sit on the bank and watch them.
There was one Quaker, a broad, fat, jolly man, who tied a big paper
kite to his wrist and let it pull him across the river while he floated
grandly on his back. Whenever he appeared a crowd gathered, betting enthusiastically on how long it would take him. Philadelphia
women were pretty, John noted. The serving maids wore their
petticoats short, displaying a neat ankle. The ladies had wide flat
crowned hats called "skimmers." On very bright days they laid green
masks over their faces, held them by a little bar between their teeth.
Some even carried parasols, though it was considered rather French
and affected. The Reverend Duché caused much comment by walking out on rainy days with an oiled linen "umbrilloe" over his head.

John stopped at a draper's shop and bought Abigail a silk camlet
mantua of a pretty blue color he knew would become her. He toyed

also with the notion of taking her a red capuchin cape, but decided to wait until cold weather made the choice wider. Abby loved bright colors, but she was timid about wearing them. Once he had told her quite sharply that the colors of a mouse did not become her. Slate-gray worsted, he had said, suited neither her face nor her spirit. Abby had surprised him by blushing with pleasure like a girl. As he remembered it, John's heart twisted in sudden, almost painful longing. He thought morosely that if he were in Spain he could not be farther from his wife. The scene here was so foreign, so different he could not attempt to describe it nor repeat again and again how continual business, continual company kept him from writing the long letters he composed in his thoughts.

The dinner parties continued, and the evening meetings in tavern and club. John spent much time with the Virginia men, and with the radicals from Delaware, Thomas McKean and Caesar Rodney. The next move must be for a commercial blockade against Britain. (No one spoke of it as a blockade; the word was not yet invented. Colonel Boycott would not raise his Irish head for another century. Non-consumption, non-exportation, non-importation were the words used.) To put through such a plan was imperative. No lesser move would force the ministry to back down — and to force them to back down was the whole purpose of this Congress. Declarations of Rights and Humble Petitions, Parliament could throw in the scrapheap unread. But neither Lords nor Commons would dare ignore an arbitrary sudden cessation of the American trade. More than seventy members of Parliament owned plantations in the West Indies; these men would not sit by and see themselves ruined. British merchants had large interests in Virginia tobacco, Carolina rice and naval stores. John Adams, who in August had scoffed at commercial nonintercourse as being too mild a measure, saw it now as the only hope of the colonies, short of war.

The Southern colonies would be first to suffer from such a blockade. Virginia and the Carolinas had scarcely any market beyond England, whereas the Northern colonies traded with all Europe. The non-exportation men decided to split the scheme, not ask Congress to swallow it all at once. They put through a preliminary measure for non-importation — Galloway himself voted for it — and a mild plan to distribute handbills "requesting" people to order no more goods until Congress settled its policy.

But Galloway had no intention of letting the thing go further. He was ready with a plan of his own. Months ago he had prepared it, with the help of Governor William Franklin of New Jersey and others. If his scheme succeeded, there would be no more talk of a blockade, and the extreme liberty party would look very silly indeed. Galloway was neither a traitor nor a fool; he was an experienced politician who knew what worked and what did not work. An intimate friend of Dr. Franklin, he was in close correspondence with the provincial agents in London, understood the point of view on both sides of the water.

What Galloway desired was some kind of American constitution that would unite the colonies without separating them from Britain. Everyone in Congress knew that such a plan had been proposed at Albany in '54; everyone regretted its failure. Congress would welcome any workable plan for colonial union. The sticking-point would come at the union with Britain and the terms that must necessarily be its condition. For no matter how vehemently it was denied, Galloway knew there existed in the Congress — and therefore in the colonies — a strong and desperate conviction that should Britain not back down in her demands, independence was the only answer, even if it brought total ruin. Fifty-six men were met in order to avert that ruin if they could. They were ready for suggestions. The field lay fallow, awaiting the seed.

On the twenty-eighth of September, Joseph Galloway rose and asked leave to present two Resolves for a *Political Union between the Colonies and the Mother-State*. Producing a sheaf of papers, he stood up and began to read. His voice was agreeable; in his smooth, light gray coat and powdered wig he bore himself easily, with confidence. His thin face was delicate, alert. Even John Adams, who at the word "Mother-State" had bristled angrily, acknowledged to himself the man could talk.

The room gave strict attention as the plan unfolded. . . . Each colony was to retain its present constitution, the whole to be administered by a Grand Council of Representatives, chosen every three years by the people of each colony, and a President-General appointed by the King.

So far, so good. Even Massachusetts did not object to a crown-appointed President and still desired George III as sovereign. . . . But what a cold-looking man this Galloway was, John reflected. The

long upper lip was stubborn, haughty. There was no candor here, no frankness but a thinness of spirit, some pale note of caution. *Persons lightly dipped*, John thought, *not grain'd in generous honesty*. . . .

"The Grand American Council," Galloway was saying, "shall hold and exercise all the like rights, liberties and privileges as are held and exercised by and in the House of Commons of Great Britain."

Heads nodded, glances were exchanged. The New York delegation smiled openly, looking about them. Should this plan go through, they could go home and tell their constituents the danger of financial ruin was over, and the danger of war. . . . "The President-General and the Grand Council," Galloway continued in the same even voice, "shall be an inferior and distinct branch of the British legislature, united and incorporated with it. . . . All general acts and statutes shall be transmitted to the Parliament of Great Britain. *The assent of both Parliament and Council shall be requisite to the validity of such acts or statutes.*"

The assent of Parliament. John almost cursed outright. The four words invalidated the whole plan, showed it for what it was — a farce, a sham, a most dangerous illusion. How clever Galloway was! The way he put it, the thing had seemed an equable arrangement altogether, a step forward not back. Gadsden of South Carolina cleared his throat, loudly and rudely. Colonel Washington, his grave face impassive, shifted in his seat. The Virginia men looked hopefully at Patrick Henry.

Galloway laid down his neat sheaf of papers, but went right on talking. . . . In the last war, the colonies had come near to being destroyed by France. And why? Because the colonies were disunited. "There must be a union of wills and strength. I am as much a friend to liberty as any that exists. No man shall go further in point of fortune or in point of blood. But we are totally independent of each other. A State must be animated by one soul. Every government — patriarchal, monarchial, aristocratical or democratical, must have a supreme legislature." Galloway leaned forward, the tone of his voice changed: "RESOLVED," he said, reading from a paper, "*That the Congress will apply to his Majesty for a redress of grievances under which his faithful subjects in America labour; and assure him, that the Colonies hold in abhorrence the idea of being considered independent communities on the British government, and most ardently desire*

*the establishment of a Political Union, not only among themselves,
but with the Mother-State."*

Galloway sat down. There was a murmur of approval. Duane and
Jay rose to express their support; Edward Rutledge, the South Carolina conservative, seconded them. "I think it an almost perfect plan,"
he said. Old Stephen Hopkins applauded. (He had been at Albany in
'54, and this plan was very like Franklin's.) But Hopkins's colleague
from Rhode Island, Governor Ward, opposed it. So did Patrick
Henry, with his usual vehemence. Yet John, listening, did not admire
what Henry said . . . something about being ruled by the *representatives of representatives,* something about Britain's system of
bribery in government, and how our own representatives would perhaps be corrupted. . . . John himself did not rise to speak. And as
the day wore on and the debate continued, hot and rapid, he saw
that the room was about evenly divided, pro and con. There was great
danger Galloway might actually prevail, his plan win a majority of
votes. If that happened the New England men, the Virginia men,
could go on home, defeated.

Yet still John did not speak. Words were useless now and logic was
useless. Galloway's own logic had been clearer than anything the opposition was putting forward. They had come too far for talk. This
matter was not to be settled by logic and reason. The division was
deeper — a matter of emotional bias, of a man's outlook toward
government and toward life, predetermined, unalterable. . . . When
the count was taken, six colonies against five voted, not for repudiation, not for acceptance, but to let the plan "lie on the table for
future consideration."

Two Adamses, meeting outside in the afternoon sunshine, mopped
their brows. What a narrow escape! Fortunately, the world would
not know how close it was. When Charles Thomson could not write
Resolved unan. in the records, he simply stopped with the word
Resolved; and if a motion was defeated he did not record it at all.
Walking slowly across the city to their lodgings, Sam was very
thoughtful. John offered consolation. "One vote is as good as twelve,
cousin, for all practical purposes," he said. Let Sam recall the tremendous decisions of history that had been decided by a single vote.
In the year '45, the great Louisburg expedition, proposed in the
Massachusetts Council by Governor Shirley, had gone through by
only one vote. . . . John stepped carefully around a pile of bricks

and dirt on the footway. "The Virgin Mary herself," he finished cheerfully, "lost her sovereignty by one vote in the Council of Trent."

Sam smiled briefly, then shook his head. The argument only went to prove that a politician must never become too confident. "This matter is not ended. It will come up in a day or a week."

There were others in the liberty party as concerned as the two Adamses. That afternoon the Massachusetts men were visited in their Arch Street lodgings by (John wrote in his diary) "Colonel Lee, Colonel Washington and Dr. Shippen of Philadelphia, who came to consult with us." They sat downstairs in Miss Port's crowded little parlor. The windows were open, the shutters drawn to keep out the flies. Noise from the street came to them: children's voices, the sound of heavy wheels passing. John laid out Madeira in two decanters. The Massachusetts men sat in their shirt sleeves; smoke from their pipes lay thick along the ceiling. Washington as usual was silent but amiable. In Congress he had not spoken once, so far, and was not on a single committee. Yet he had made his presence felt — visiting, listening, learning, endeavoring to cement the various factions, attending Quaker Meeting on Sunday morning, the Romish Chapel in the afternoon. . . . There was something reassuring in his very presence today, as he sat quiet and attentive in his stiff coat and stock.

Richard Henry Lee was spokesman and went directly to the point. They were come, he said, for the purpose of discovering once and for all the sentiments of Massachusetts concerning independence. In Congress the opinion still held that Massachusetts aimed at a complete independency. The idea was obstructive. It divided the liberty party and had, indeed, influenced many votes today in favor of Galloway's plan. Some deputies still believed that if independence were achieved, the Bostonians would seize the reins and rule the continent. . . . Lee smiled. Such a notion was indeed ridiculous, but it kept rearing its head. What answer could be given to this charge? The gentlemen might be frank; what they said would go no further than this room if they so desired.

Cushing, John, Robert Paine, all spoke at once. Independence? No — a hundred times no! "There is no man among us," John said, when he could be heard, "that would not be happy to see accommodation with Britain." What Congress could not seem to keep in mind was the present desperate condition of Boston. The city was under siege,

surrounded with troops. There had been fist fights already in the streets, fights on the guarded bridges, on the ferries. At any moment blood might be spilled, open warfare break out. Massachusetts could not afford to sit waiting while plans like Galloway's were debated in all their fine points. Something must be done immediately, to prove that America was in earnest. Some threat must be delivered to Britain, and that soon. What threat was possible but commercial non-intercourse? If Massachusetts seemed impatient, vehement, impulsive, it was due to no hidden ambition for supremacy but to the urgency of her danger and her cause.

Washington drained his glass and made as if to rise. He was happy, he said, to learn the true sentiments of four Bostonians concerning an independency. He would communicate them wherever he could. It was most important; this conversation had been a step forward. He felt sure the general fears would be allayed, the whole temper of the Congress improve.

Sam Adams, during all of this, had remained perfectly silent, not sitting with the others about the table but standing by the window, shading his eyes with his hand. Several times the Virginia men had looked toward him. When Sam made no reply but merely nodded courteously, Lee had turned to John with his questions, or to Cushing, Paine. It was as if they all knew Sam did not agree, but that he would make no trouble. He would remain silent in Congress, let the others direct this thing.

The truth was that Sam Adams was far from despising independence. Today's performance in Congress rankled sorely in his breast. He was convinced that Galloway was a Tory at heart. How lofty the arguments used — yet how insinuating, how dangerous to the cause of liberty! Had the Congress been held in Boston, as Sam himself had wished — and urged — Galloway would never have dared to make such a proposal. The Sons of Liberty, Sam told himself, would have seen to that. Yet Philadelphia had its Sons of Liberty as well as Boston; Sam had been at much pains to cultivate them, around the docks and ropeyards on the Delaware River. The trouble was, the Philadelphia Sons were not represented in this Congress of gentlemen, where nearly every member wrote "Esquire" after his name. What this gathering needed, Sam reflected, glancing at Washington's beautifully tailored blue coat, his white breeches and silk stockings, was a Captain Mackintosh, a Molineux or two —

men who forgot to shave, men whose fingernails were broken and discolored by labor. . . .

The Virginia gentlemen rose and made their farewells, bowing briefly and beautifully from the waist. Sam's lips drew in. Time was wasting and the cause desperate. Joseph Galloway must be silenced. There were other ways than voting, to close a man's mouth. Sam intended to put them to the test.*

The tabling of Galloway's Plan of Union, while it did not entirely settle the danger, at least made way for the great question of commercial boycott. This came up in Congress next day, September 29, and again on the thirtieth. Unless every colony agreed, unless every port and customhouse were closed, the thing would not work. It must be continent-wide. The Continental Association, the plan was called. Its preamble was grave, and went beyond the words of mere trade: *We, His Majesty's most loyal subjects . . . do firmly agree and associate under the sacred ties of virtue, honour and love of our country . . .*

As the plan grew, difficulties grew with it. The pockets of every American were touched, his bread and livelihood threatened. Nothing but a miracle could resolve these complications of trade. For three weeks the bargaining continued, sometimes in committee, sometimes on the floor of the house. . . . *Rice and tobacco . . . lumber, flax-seed.* Ireland could not exist without American flaxseed; the linen industry would be paralyzed, three hundred thousand Irish laborers thrown out of work. . . . So much the better, someone said; Britain would be forced to listen. . . . *Tar, pitch, turpentine, lumber . . .* England desperately needed our naval stores. *Oil, potash . . .* each colony fought for its especial product. *Molasses, sugar, coffee . . .* without the West Indian trade, our fishing towns would starve. "Thousands of New England families," a voice shouted, "will be flung into the arms of famine."

---

* About two weeks later, Galloway found a halter in his mail, followed in a day or two by an insurance policy suggesting that he would not be alive in six days. "Hang yourself or we shall do it for you." On Oct. 22, his Plan of Union was expunged forever from the Minutes of Congress. ("My Life," Galloway testified later, in England, "was in continual jeopardy. Every night I expected would be my last. Men were excited by persons from the northward, by falsehoods fabricated for the purpose, to put me to death. Several attempts were made. I declared my innocence in the public papers in vain." In 1776, Galloway openly joined the royalist forces in New York.)

In the square, bright room there was anger, and fear . . . *Tea!* Here agreement came quickly; no one desired to resume trade in tea. *Clothing* . . . could the colonies possibly manage without clothing from England? Two thirds of the people were clothed in British manufacture. . . . *Guns!* Every instrument of war, down to the very saltpeter for gunpowder, came from England. How in God's name could an arsenal be collected if there was non-importation on instruments of war?

Slaves[1] . . . This was easily settled (the question of freeing the slaves did not arise; it was not part of the matter at hand): *After the first day of December next* [so ran Section 2] *we will wholly discontinue the slave trade, and will neither be concerned in it ourselves, nor will we hire our vessels, nor sell our commodities or manufactures to those who are concerned in it.*

Rice! said South Carolina for the twentieth time. South Carolina could not live without exporting rice. Her entire planter's economy depended on it. . . . For two days, *rice and indigo* usurped the floor. The deputies from South Carolina walked out, all but Christopher Gadsden. They would sign no Continental Association, they swore, that excluded commerce in rice. In the end, rice was allowed for export to Europe, though not to England, Ireland or the West Indies.

There were fourteen sections in the Continental Association, and two thousand words. On October 18, after three weeks of debate, it was finally voted on and passed by a majority. What had been impossible was now achieved. Twelve colonies had constructed the first instrument of their union. A fair copy of the whole was ordered for the individual signatures of Congress.

On the twentieth of October, members, entering the hall, saw the document lying on the big table below the window, pens and ink conveniently placed. The delegates walked forward, some with obvious reluctance. A gentleman's signature, the liberty men said soothingly, would not commit him personally. After all, the Speaker of an Assembly signs measures he doesn't like, if they are passed by a majority.

Galloway's fingers shook, taking up the pen. To him,[2] this neatly written document changed the Congress from a mere deliberative body to a revolutionary government. The provisions for enforcement were absolute; they bound a continent: "That a committee be chosen in every county" . . . to watch the wharves and customhouses, re-

port anything suspicious, "to the end that all such foes to the rights of British-America may be publicly known, and universally condemned as the enemies of American liberty."

The words stared up at Galloway. He bent his head, and almost weeping with rage and frustration, wrote his name.*

That same evening — October 20 — there was a grand celebration at the City Tavern on Walnut Street. The whole Congress dined there by invitation of the Pennsylvania House of Representatives, who were fêting not only the "foreign" delegates but the outcome of their own just-completed annual Provincial elections. It had been a bitterly contested fight, not without influence on Congress. Mifflin, the radical Quaker, was elected to the Pennsylvania House of Representatives, and Charles Thomson with him. John Dickinson was made delegate to Congress, a severe blow to Galloway — who until now had managed to keep the famous FARMER out.

Dinner was scheduled at four o'clock, but it was growing dark by the time everyone arrived; candles were already lighted in the wainscoted room. There was to be a ball later in the evening; everyone was dressed for it. Mrs. Lynch of South Carolina had made John Adams promise to come and dance a quadrille with her, although he protested he was not a dancing man. Yet he looked well enough, John reflected with some satisfaction, smoothing his waistcoat over his stomach. The blue coat fitted nicely on the shoulders; the gilt buttons set off his canary-colored waistcoat. That French barber on the High Street surely had a knack with a wig. Catching sight of himself in a brass wall sconce, John moved his head; the powdered rolls over each ear were really distinguished.

As the guests found places at the long tables, John noted a number of Quakers. He was not overly pleased to see them. During the past week these gentlemen had done everything they could to defeat the Continental Association. Only a few nights ago they had had the effrontery to summon the Massachusetts delegation to a conference in Carpenters' Hall and actually challenge them to amend their religious laws at home, put some tolerance in them, before they at-

* Much later, Galloway, interrogated by Parliament, testified that he would rather have cut off his hand than sign the Continental Association. He said he did it partly to save his life and partly because, had the Association been defeated, Congress might have done something even worse. See Chapter Note 2 for this chapter.

tempted to legislate for Pennsylvania and the continent! John had countered hotly; he and Israel Pemberton had stood shouting angrily at each other for an hour while the others listened.

Israel Pemberton was here tonight — the old king of the Quakers, his hat firmly on his gray head, his beaked nose and rich *embonpoint* more imposing than ever. He chose, apparently, to forget the late unpleasantness; his manner was most affable. Everyone, indeed, seemed in the best of humors. The end was in sight. Surely, the Congress would break up next week and let the members go home to their families and their business! Little remained beyond the Petitions for England to be put in final shape, and the Addresses to the People of Canada and the Colonies.

Tonight the world seemed disposed to friendship; gentlemen ate and drank with appetite. The Virginia contingent were wonderful: they seemed to take over the entertainment altogether. To John there was something enchanting in their manner, so gay, so self-possessed, so easy without the slightest hint of familiarity. Bland and Harrison were everywhere, proposing toasts, raising their glasses, summoning the colored waiters who appeared like magic at their least gesture. No New England man had such a way with servants. Colonel Washington looked positively magnificent. His coat cuffs were fashionably wide, turned back almost to the elbow to show the fine white pleated ruffles. Even Patrick Henry in his homespun suit and brown wig appeared surprisingly well-brushed. He commented jovially on John's elegant coiffure, vowed he himself had spent hours at his toilet, a full ten minutes scrubbing his teeth with a rag dipped in snuff — was not his smile magnificent? Thomas McKean was in dark red velvet; the skirts of his coat were elegantly long and wide, stiffed out with buckram. He and Caesar Rodney kept together; John saw them looking for him through the room. He felt at home with them; their opinions, like Patrick Henry's, matched his own.[3]

John enjoyed himself thoroughly. The baked oysters, served hot in their shells, were especially tasty. John lost count of how many he ate; the pile of shells before him was a mountain. He drank glass after glass of Madeira and felt, he said afterward, "no inconvenience." "A most elegant entertainment," he wrote. "Near one hundred guests in the whole. A sentiment was given: 'May the sword of the parent never be stained with the blood of her children.' Two or three broad-brims over against me at table. One of them said, this is not a toast

but a prayer; come, let us join in it. And they took their glasses accordingly."

Only six days of Congress remained, to be spent entirely on various addresses, testimonials and petitions for Britain and the colonies. If the world was to be informed of what the Congress had done, the members themselves must do the informing. An Address to Canada was particularly important. Should war come it was vitally necessary to have the vast Province of Quebec on the American side. Separate letters must be written to St. John, to Newfoundland, to Nova Scotia, to Georgia, East and West Florida — and a long memorial to "the Inhabitants of the American Colonies" themselves, relating fully all procedure and suggesting future action. Richard Henry Lee composed a letter to the colonial agents in London.* Secretary Charles Thomson, putting it in the London mail, enclosed a personal note to Franklin. "I hope," he said, "administration will see and be convinced that it is not a little faction, but the whole body of American freeholders from Nova Scotia to Georgia that now complain & apply for redress. Even yet the wound may be healed & peace and love restored; but we are on the very verge of the precipice."

The Address to the People of Great Britain, in itself a daring novelty, caused much argument in Congress. Hitherto, when nations wished to communicate with each other, they addressed the monarch, not "the people." *Friends and Fellow Subjects,* the final draft began . . . *Take care that you do not fall into the pit that is preparing for us. . . .*

The Loyal Address to the King made even more trouble and delay. Patrick Henry wrote the first draft; John was on the committee with him. Congress rejected Henry's draft as too violent, more likely to insult a king than to placate him. John Dickinson was asked to write another. Congress accepted it, although even this one was far from mild. It took the tone that any truly British king would boil with indignation at the bare recital of such wrongs as were suffered by his American subjects. *As Your Majesty enjoys the signal distinction of reigning over freemen, we apprehend the language of freemen can not be displeasing. . . .* Yet if the Loyal Address was

---

* It was addressed to *Paul Wentworth, Doct*. *Franklin, W*. *Bollan* [whose house in Boston John had once rented], *Arthur Lee, Tho*. *Life, Edm*. *Burke, Charles Garth.*

defiant, it was defiant with dignity — beautifully worded, slow-moving and, like all the documents of this Congress, alive with a rhythm born of deepest feeling, utmost sincerity of purpose: *Had we been permitted to enjoy in quiet the inheritance left us by our forefathers, we should at this time have been peaceably, cheerfully and usefully employed in recommending ourselves by every testimony of devotion to Your Majesty, and of veneration to the state, from which we derive our origin. . . .*

Congress itself was innocent of the imperishable nature of its present compositions. What the members felt now was a growing impatience, a desire to be done and go home. On October 23, the Virginia men left to attend the opening of their own House of Burgesses. Only Washington and Lee remained, and even Washington's patience was growing thin. These bright frosty mornings were fox-hunting weather. At home his horses were spoiling in the stables, and if the Congress did not presently finish its business, Fairfax County would be overrun with foxes.

John himself prayed earnestly that he might never again be so long from home. Congress had agreed to convene again in the spring if Britain did not meet the American demands. In such case, John told himself that other men must carry the burden. He himself would not stir an inch from Boston and Braintree. The first excitement was gone; John was very tired. The actual daytime business of Congress, he told himself, was necessary and must be done. The evening performance was what irked. Why must it be? In New England, men managed without this perpetual ceremony. "We have dined out enough for a lifetime," John told his cousin Sam morosely. His own skin, he added, was turning green from eating turtle, and the amount of good Madeira he had consumed would make even a Rhode Island smuggler squint-eyed with envy.

John was deeply homesick. He could not get enough of writing to his wife. He would like to have sent her a dozen letters a day, and said so. But not only was he called on to read and correct articles, pamphlets and propaganda for the Southern colonies — besides all this, he and his colleagues were preparing for the struggle that lay ahead in New England. The Continental Association was yet to be ratified by every separate colonial Assembly, or by conventions called together for the purpose. Persuasion would be necessary, even in Massachusetts. After all, the Continental Congress, while it had

gained stature in the past two months, was not actually a recognized government. It was no more, indeed, than a convention of the old Committees of Correspondence. The forces against it were very strong. Probably two thirds of New York and most of Pennsylvania were Tory. Georgia had not even dared send representatives to Philadelphia; New Hampshire had barely succeeded in doing so. How powerful were the Tories everywhere? Would they prevail, as Galloway had so nearly prevailed a month ago? [4]

John felt anxious about the sentiments of New England — and even more anxious as to how Massachusetts was to govern itself, now that the Province had repudiated the royal authority. A Provincial Congress was sitting at Watertown, a sort of *pro tem* body composed of representatives from some two hundred towns. For lack of a governor they had granted executive powers to their Committee of Safety, a body of some nine patriots who had actually no more credentials than so many members of volunteer fire companies. No courts of law were functioning. So far, the Province had not disintegrated into anarchy and rioting, but there was no telling at what point this might occur.

He had been too long away, John told himself uneasily. He had lost touch with Massachusetts; it was his business to get home as fast as possible, see how affairs really stood. As for his own family, it seemed incredible that Abby had managed as well as she had, with four children and a farm to look after quite by herself. Their little savings would soon be used up; if he could not get back to the law, they would be reduced to a diet of potatoes and water. . . .

In Philadelphia the trees were golden, and along Schuylkill River the mornings dawned glorious with color. For John, no prospect pleased. Charles Thomson invited him to go shooting; the marshes were thick with rail bird. John refused; he had no heart for expeditions of pleasure. On Tuesday night the bells of Christ Church pealed as usual to announce the market on the morrow. "Butter bells," Philadelphia called them. John had been charmed with these chimes at first. Now he thought them silly. Why couldn't Philadelphia blow the conch to advertise its cabbages, like Boston? On Sunday, chains were laid across the street to prevent carriages driving by while church service was in progress. On that last Sunday John fell over one, barked his shin, turned red in the face as if he had been personally insulted and told Sam through clenched teeth that if the

Philadelphia people had any natural morality in them, they would not need such devices to remind them of divine worship.

On Wednesday, October 26, Congress perceived with a sigh of relief that its business was actually concluded. Thanks were voted "to the honourable House of Representatives of the Colony of Pennsylvania for their politeness to the Congress." Then, wrote Thomson in the Minutes, "the Congress dissolved itself." *

That evening there was feasting again at the City Tavern. The tone was buoyant, optimistic. Parliament would capitulate entirely, everyone said, repeal the coercive acts, resume the old easy policy that had prevailed before 1763. The ministry could not possibly stand out against the Continental Association. The merchants of London and Bristol would bombard Parliament with petitions to resume trade.

Against this flood of cheerful prophecy the brace of Adamses stood glum and somehow increasingly depressed. The others rallied them, booming out reassurance. Richard Henry Lee shook John's hand warmly, told him Massachusetts would be relieved of all her troubles by June. Only give the mails a chance to cross the ocean, and Dr. Franklin would see that Lord Hillsborough had the petitions in record time.

John and Sam walked silently home across the darkened city. If the Congress, John said finally, was so egregiously mistaken, what could be expected from the people at large? The real test was yet to come when the Continental Association was voted on by the separate colonial assemblies. As for Britain's reaction, that would of necessity be slow. England would not feel the pinch of commercial boycott for a year or more. Her merchants, fearing some such move, had been pouring goods into America. There was enough to supply a two years' market. Trade flourished. In the Southern colonies people were buying as if they would never buy again.

Sam Adams showed if possible even more eagerness to be gone than did his cousin. Away from Boston, Sam was always uncomfortable, constricted. He missed the more violent Sons of Liberty, desired greatly to sit with them in conclave assembled, find out exactly what they were doing to arm the countryside against Gage's possible next move.

---

* Thomson's own exertions were rewarded by the gift from Congress of "a piece of plate worth £50 sterling."

Friday, October 28, dawned dark and stormy; a cold rain fell. John rose early, groped his way to the window and threw open the shutters. Arch Street was a narrow, dismal sight. But to John, standing in his nightshirt with his nose against the damp pane, the prospect was the brightest in months. The rain water gurgled down the gutters in a song of pure triumph. Today he was going home! No matter what he found there of anarchy or of danger, no matter what problems must be wrestled with, or what defeats or triumphs might occur, home was where he longed to be.

At eight o'clock the coach was to be at the door. Descending Miss Port's staircase well before the hour, John looked for the last time on the discolored wallpaper, the bleak carpet and suffocated row of plants by the window. The rain that beat against the door invited like the gates of paradise. John went out, his greatcoat hunched about his ears, and stood while the porters loaded the coach — took a hand himself with the boxes, shouting directions to driver and servants. When all was ready, Sam Adams, Cushing, Paine, climbed into the coach. John waved gallantly to Miss Port at the window, stepped in behind his friends and slammed the door. The horses strained, slipped noisily on the wet stones. The long whip cracked, the wheels groaned; turned slowly, then faster, faster . . .

"Took our departure," said the diary cheerfully that night, "from the happy, the peaceful, the elegant, the hospitable and polite city of Philadelphia. It is not very likely I shall ever see this part of the world again."

Massachusetts is without a government. NOVANGLUS *writes on "that fiction, the British Empire," and Edmund Burke in Parliament talks conciliation. War begins at Lexington.*

T HE journey home took thirteen days; to John it was interminable. At Elizabethtown Point the coach and horses were loaded on flatboats and rowed six miles to Staten Island. It was a Sunday, and John's birthday; he was thirty-nine. Watching the men at their oars he was sure they dawdled purposefully; he had all he could do not to seize an oar himself and pull away. At New York next day, Morin Scott, McDougall and the others were waiting at the Battery; they seemed depressed. "The Sons of Liberty here are in the horrors," John wrote. "They think they have lost ground since we passed through this city." It was true: the Continental Association was not popular in New York.

Robert Paine left his companions and took the packet boat to Newport. Once the other three crossed the Connecticut border they were overwhelmed with festivities and welcome. New Haven stationed couriers twenty miles ahead, to gallop home and warn that the delegates were coming — so the bells could peal, the cannon boom and proper reception be prepared. Middletown sent word that a gala dinner was ready. "We excused ourselves with great earnestness," John wrote.

The document of Congress had already been printed and circulated. The Tories were very busy. John saw pamphlets hawked on the streets of Connecticut, written by hands he knew well, and very

violent against the Continental Association. "Could anything be more tyrannical, arbitrary and oppressive?" wrote Harrison Gray, the Boston merchant. "Can the edicts of the most despotic princes under heaven exceed it?" . . . "Its terms," exclaimed another master of commerce, "would shock the soul of a savage. It is such a system of lawless tyranny as a Turk would startle at."

Patriot Committees of Inspection and of Safety, patriot Sub-committees of Selectmen were everywhere combated by counter-Committees and counter-Associations of Tories. John's cousin, Timothy Ruggles of Hardwick, headed one of the most powerful of these. Neighbor spied on neighbor for both sides. In Falmouth, one Thomas Coulson received sails from Bristol, England, for a new vessel he was building. He refused to give them up; he had waited six months for them, he said. At Marblehead, a Mr. Lilly bought a pound and a half of tea from a Boston dealer and was forced to sign a public apology. Down in Charleston, South Carolina, a shipload of nearly three hundred slaves was returned by the consignee. Household furniture, even horses, were refused at the wharf; sometimes entire cargoes were thrown into the harbor. Itinerant peddlers gave the Committees the most trouble. Women bought British cloth, laces, gloves, at the door, then hid them and would not confess.

Short of tar and feathers, it was extremely difficult to punish the offenders. In Massachusetts, Paul Revere, Chase and Avery, the Boston distillers, headed the Committee of Inspection. Yet even with such strong partisans in command, John wondered how, lacking courts of law, violators could be held to account. Public condemnation was, actually, the only penalty. All the way from Philadelphia, John listened to tales of violators caught or violators suspected.

John did not drive to Boston with the others, but left the coach at Cambridge and rode home to Braintree on a hired horse. And when at last he reached Penn's Hill and home, he found the parlor, the kitchen with its roaring November fire, filled with people waiting to talk politics. John's brothers with their wives, his mother and her husband, Mr. Hall, were there, eager to congratulate the returned delegate, hear the news from Philadelphia. Abby herself looked splendidly. She had written that she was getting fat, and indeed she had never seemed so vigorous. Her eyes sparkled with health. She had on a dress John had not seen before, a full skirt of

russet brown wool, a blue shawl crossed over her breasts, pinned
primly at the neck; it became her vastly. Little Abby and John
Quincy followed their father up the stairs and down. Had he got
their letters in Philadelphia? they asked. Charles, at four, gazed
wonderingly at the returned stranger as at an apparition. The baby,
nearly two, had learned to walk. John lifted him, held him high in his
stiff kilts while the others laughed.

Everyone hurried to tell what had happened since John went away
in August. *August?* they repeated. Why, it seemed six months at the
least! Of course, John knew that Will Molineux was dead? A terrible loss to the liberty party in Boston. He had died suddenly, of an
inflammation of the bowels — brought on, it was said, by exertions
for his country. Had John seen *The Continental Association* in print?
Elihu led him to the wall by the mantel. Abby had tacked it up in a
conspicuous place. The words stood out: *His Majesty's most loyal
subjects, the delegates of the several colonies, do firmly agree and
associate, under the sacred ties of virtue, honour, and love of our
country* . . .

Copies were to be had very cheap at the *Gazette* office, sold by the
gross. . . . And had John heard there were lights now on Boston
streets? Fixed to pillars. If trouble came with the British troops, it
would be safer this way. Not like Massacre Night, with only the
moon as witness. The streets swarmed with redcoats; the Harbor was
filled with British men-of-war. Each time General Gage made ready
for a sortie out of town in search of powder or arms, thousands of
militia gathered across the Charles River, waited, then slipped home
again when the danger was over.

And what did John think of Josiah Quincy's sailing for England
last month in such profound secrecy? Was it by order of the Congress, and had he a definite mission? The Tories swore he had gone
to be hanged! The poor young gentleman looked wasted away; his
uncles in Braintree had said farewell with some foreboding. Did John
intend to go himself into Boston? He would be sick at heart to see it
— the bad days of '70 all over again. This time, the thing would not
stop at riot. This time the flame would spread. . . . Did the Congress at Philadelphia truly understand how dangerous it was here in
Massachusetts, and how near to war they had drifted?

John had scarcely time to reply, time to get his breath and see his
family for a few days of comparative peace, before the Provincial

Congress at Watertown sent a messenger asking urgently for his attendance. They needed him at once, they said; they were to sit only until December tenth. John was quite desperately tired, his eyes badly inflamed; it hurt him to read or write. But he got on his horse and rode to Watertown. He found two hundred and sixty men gathered in the Meeting-house, with John Hancock in the chair. They had already voted on a delegation for the next Continental Congress, due to sit in May of '75 — the two Adamses and Paine, with Hancock and Elbridge Gerry added.

Their main business was the organization of an army — "for defense," the reports were careful to add. It was agreed to raise if possible a force of twelve thousand men from Massachusetts. Three generals were named to lead them: Jedidiah Preble, Artemas Ward and Seth Pomeroy, all veterans of the French war (Preble was nearly seventy). Where arms and powder could not be bought, they must be seized from government stores. And if blacksmiths would not forge musket barrels, cast cannon balls, then a way must be found to overcome their reluctance. Expresses were sent to New Hampshire, Connecticut, Rhode Island, asking support to the tune of twenty thousand additional troops if called for. A circular letter went out also to gospel ministers, requesting their help in raising this volunteer army. Let preachers exhort and instruct their congregations as to the immediacy, the full meaning, of the British threat.

On the tenth of December the Watertown Congress dispersed. John rode home, very thoughtful and quite profoundly moved by what he had witnessed. The Provincial Congress had not been made up of lawyers, landowners, men of the caliber and background of Colonel Washington, Mr. Dickinson, John Jay of New York. Here two hundred and sixty blacksmiths, bakers, fishermen, tailors, small shopkeepers had convened, some of them representing towns of perhaps a few hundred inhabitants. Entirely without legislative authority, they had organized the raising of an army, formulated a policy of emergency government. (In the British Parliament, Edmund Burke was to express astonished admiration at the performance of the Watertown Congress.) Massachusetts, in short, was governing itself without jails or judges; Massachusetts was even collecting its taxes without penalty attached for default. Raising an army cost money, and the towns were poor.

As to our Province money [the town of Shelburne had written] *the Town's Unanimously Agreed to pay it in to Henery Gardner Esqr. of Stow but we are a New Township and money being Scarce we have it not Collected and the money is not in the place to Collect but we would Directly Hire it if we knew where to Git it, and we will Do all we can to Git it.*

At Watertown he had witnessed, John told himself, a great Province governed not by police and penalty but by, as it were, two hundred and sixty volunteer consciences. The towns seemed deeply to desire government, restraint, order.

While we profess ourselves advocates for Rational Constitutional Liberty [wrote the town of Medfield] *we don't mean to patrionise Libertinesm and Licenteousness we are sensible of the necessity of Government for the Security of Life Liberty and property and mean to vindecate and Submit to all Lawfull Constitutional authority.*

But how long, John wondered, could such a spirit, such discipline be maintained? "We have no council, no house, no legislative, no executive," John wrote from Braintree just after Christmas, 1774. "Not a court of justice has sat since the month of September. Not a debt can be recovered, nor a trespass redressed, nor a criminal of any kind brought to punishment. We are in this Province, Sir, at the brink of a civil war. Imagine four hundred thousand people without government or law, forming themselves in companies for various purpose of justice, policy, and war! You must allow for a great deal of the ridiculous, much of the melancholy and some of the marvelous." *

He and his friends, John continued, were doing all in their power to prevent an open rupture. Not that he thought ten thousand lives, including his own, too much to pay for liberty. But if even ten American lives were lost, it would be the end: America and Britain would be split, divided forever.

Tory propaganda flowed up to Massachusetts from every colony. It seemed unending, all-pervasive. John wondered if the Continental Association could stand against it. The fact that South Carolina was allowed to export rice stuck even in the radical craw. Why this

---

* Taken from (1) a letter to James Burgh who had sent John from Scotland his recently published *Political Disquisitions* and (2) letter to Edward Biddle, Speaker of the Pennsylvania Assembly, "a Reading lawyer, very high for liberty." Massachusetts liked to say that she had 400,000 inhabitants. The world accepted it.

one favored exception? And why, then, couldn't New England send
fish to Jamaica? The newspapers published à poem of eighty-two
stanzas:

> Isn't it now a pretty story,
> One smells it in a trice,
> If I send wheat I am a Tory,
> But Charles-town may send RICE.

The Tories expressed themselves as furious with their own "weak
members" who had permitted themselves to be so egregiously
"tricked" at Philadelphia. "Adams and the haughty Sultans of the
South" had "juggled the whole Conclave of the Delegates." . . .
"You had all the honors, you had all the leading cards of every sute
in your hands," said GROTIUS to his Tory friends by way of the
Massachusetts *Gazette*. "And yet you suffered *sharpers* to get the odd
trick." Everywhere, "men of the baser sort" had seized the reins of
government. It was not to be endured. These new Committees of
Inspection, Committees of Safety and Commerce, these Sub-Committees of Selectmen were made up of blacksmiths, cowherds,
leather-apron men. There wasn't a ruffled shirt to be seen among
them. "If I must be enslaved," wrote one indignant gentleman, "let
it be by a KING at least, and not by a parcel of upstart lawless Com-
mittee-men. If I must be devoured, let me be devoured by the jaws
of a lion, and not gnawed to death by rats and vermin." When a
Tory preacher was dismissed by his South Carolina congregation for
saying that "mechanics and country clowns had no right to dispute
about politics," the Newport *Mercury* commented angrily that "all
such divines should be taught to know that mechanics and country
clowns (infamously so-called), are the real and absolute masters of
king, lords, commons and priests."

In Europe, an old man sat at his desk in dressing gown and tasseled
cap. Years ago he had prophesied revolution, although he had not
foreseen that it would have its rise in North America. *History is
filled with the sound of silken slippers going downstairs, and wooden
shoes coming up.* John Adams did not yet know Voltaire. He did
not know the young New York aristocrat, Gouverneur Morris. "The
mob begin to think and reason," wrote Morris — he was twenty-
three. "Poor reptiles! It is with them a vernal morning; they are

struggling to cast off their winter's slough. They bask in the sunshine, and ere long they will bite, depend upon it."

For John something happened, one day, to bring the situation sharply into focus. It was only a trifling incident; in happier times it would have made him laugh, he said. But it did not make him laugh now. It "struck me into a profound revery, if not a fit of melancholy," he wrote later. . . . "I met a man who had sometimes been my client, a common horse-jockey, always in the law, who had been sued in many actions at almost every court. Sometimes he was in the right, and I had commonly been successful in his favor. As soon as he saw me, he came up to me. 'Oh Mr. Adams, what great things have you and your colleagues done for us! We can never be grateful enough to you. There are no courts of justice now in this Province, and I hope there never will be another!'"

Was this, John asked himself, the goal he had worked for, he who loved the law and would lay down his life to preserve it? How many felt as this wretch felt, if the truth were known? Suppose the country actually got into the hands of such men — and there was real danger that it might . . . Then to what purpose, John thought despairingly, were he and his friends risking their lives and the fortunes of their families? Such distortion of the cause was infinitely dangerous.[1]

From above and below, enemy propaganda bored in. A series of articles began appearing in the Boston *Gazette*, signed MASSACHU-SETTENSIS — smooth, logical, insidious in their appeal to the loyalty and respect for the law of "the good people of Massachusetts." John was sure he knew this voice. It could be none other than Jonathan Sewall. These were the arguments John had heard on the hilltop at Falmouth, in his Boston office the night Sewall brought the Governor's offer of a post in the admiralty court — a score of times in a score of places. They must be answered, and at once. With a green India-silk bandage shading his swollen eyelids, John, squinting miserably, took up his quill.

In a week he had composed a whole book. Sometimes Abigail wrote at his dictation while John paced the room, stopping to curse at his eyes, at Sewall, at a feeling of helplessness that came over him. What was one man's word against Tory thousands? He was

wasting his time, composing this high-sounding nonsense. Ben Edes
would refuse to print it; he would say there was too much history
in it. . . . John's voice as he dictated was high, almost querulous:
*Are we to be conjured out of our senses by the magic in the words,
British Empire?*

The first installment appeared on Monday, January 23. Ben Edes
proved only too glad to print it; he did not see fit to delete a word.
"Sign it NOVANGLUS — NEW ENGLAND," John told him. MASSACHU-
SETTENSIS answered immediately. Week by week the battle continued; it was the greatest print war the Province had experienced.
More than once, NOVANGLUS took up the entire inside of the paper,
leaving only two outside sheets for news and advertisements. John
had, in truth, set down a history of the whole dispute and a justifica-
tion for it, beginning in 1754 with the French war and taking the
story right up to 1775.*

John had asked himself if one man's voice was any use, if a handful of men could inform a nation. The truth was the American
Revolution was engineered from first to last by a handful of men,
by the sheer contagion of private correspondence: Washington, Jefferson, Lee, Henry in Virginia; Gadsden, Lynch, Judge Drayton in
the Carolinas; John Jay in New York; Dickinson, McKean, Rodney
in the middle colonies; Chase in Maryland; Witherspoon at Princeton; Roger Sherman in Connecticut. In Massachusetts the Adamses,
Hawley, Hancock and the rest talked eternally. No one within reach
of their voice or their pen was allowed to forget or to rest indifferent. In the plainest speech he had ever used, John pounded at the
attention of his countrymen. . . .

"I say, America is not any part of the British realm or dominions.
Fealty to a body politic is only a frame in the mind, an idea. The
British constitution is more like a republic than an empire. . . .

"Britain has been imprudent enough to let colonies be planted,
without ever having wisdom enough to concert a plan for their gov-

---

* In England the articles were printed (abridged) that same year of 1775
in Almon's famous *Remembrancer,* under the title, "History of the Dispute in
America, from its Origin in 1754 to the present time." In 1782, while John
was in Holland trying to negotiate a loan for America, *Novanglus* was printed
at Amsterdam in Dutch. In 1784 it was reprinted in London; and in 1819, in
Boston. Today it is available only in Volume IV of the formidable *Works.*
MASSACHUSETTENSIS turned out to be not Sewall but Daniel Leonard, the
Taunton lawyer — he who kept his own coach. In book form *Novanglus* is
166 pages.

ernment. Because she cannot make them submit, she will resort to war and conquest — to the maxim, *delenda est Carthago*. After one hundred and fifty years she has discovered a defect in her government. She has found out that the great machine will not go any longer without a new wheel. She is making it of such materials and workmanship as will tear the whole machine to pieces. We are willing to assist with artists and materials so that it may answer in the end. But Britain says we shall have no share in it; and if we will not let her patch it up as she pleases, she will tear it to pieces herself, by cutting our throats. To this we can only answer, that we will not stand still to be butchered. We will defend our lives as long as Providence shall enable us."

London had the papers of Congress just before Christmas. Franklin hurried to Lord Hillsborough with the Petition to the King. But the great Lord H. was at his Irish castle, and when he returned, Franklin visited him five times before he was admitted. Meanwhile the documents were given wide circulation. During the holidays, all London read and discussed them, waiting for Parliament to assemble in January. Samuel Johnson sat down and wrote his *Taxation no Tyranny:* a heavy, rumbling roar in the Doctor's best lionine style, blasting the "Congress of Anarchy" at Philadelphia, the Continental Association with all its attendant conventions and committees. "Their deliberations were indecent, their intentions seditious."

Poor Josiah Quincy, walking the London streets, dizzy with fever, spitting blood in his handkerchief, heard America scoffed at as a half-grown bully, a child screaming threats at its father. "The people here have got an idea," Quincy wrote home despondently, "that Americans are all cowards and poltroons." Josiah had come to London as mediator; in utmost seriousness he had crossed the ocean to interpret New England to Old England — and to discover what support America could actually count on among the British people. He visited everywhere, called on the Lords North and Dartmouth, talked with Franklin and the other colonial agents, sat in coffee-houses trying to make friends for his country and his country's cause. He had brought his best clothes; he was very attractive, his manner modest. People liked him at once, smiled at his squint, the air of desperate seriousness it gave to his peering, troubled gray eyes. "Impossible that you are an American!" they cried.

The remark threw Josiah into further desperation. He could not make himself understood. Political words had different meanings here. The word "representation," for instance. At home it was a word sacred, symbolizing British freedom, the British constitution itself. Here the word meant nothing at all. How could it, when seats in Parliament were bought outright? "Mr. Rose Fuller told me," Josiah wrote his wife in Boston, "that his election cost him ten thousand pounds sterling and more. The commonalty in this country are no more like the commonalty in America than if they were two utterly distinct and unconnected people."

And what an illusion, for New England men to persist in calling this strange island "home"! The British knew nothing about America and did not wish to know. Their ignorance would have been laughable had it not been so frightening. Major Barré told Quincy that in the year '58, when he had returned from fighting the French below Canada, two thirds of England had been surprised to learn the Americans were not Negroes! Gloomily, Josiah replied that they still seemed to think so.

Yet there were trumpet voices ready to speak for America. In the House of Lords old William Pitt, Lord Chatham, advised his peers to read the documents of the American Congress. "When your Lordships consider their decency, firmness and wisdom, you cannot but respect their cause and wish to make it your own. For myself, I must avow that in all my reading — and I have read Thucydides and have studied and admired the master states of the world — for solidity of reasoning, force of sagacity and wisdom of conclusion under a complication of difficult circumstances, no body of men can stand in preference to the general Congress at Philadelphia. The histories of Greece and Rome give us nothing equal to it, and all attempts to impose servitude upon such a mighty continental nation must be vain."

Recall the troops from Boston, Chatham urged. By a vote of sixty-eight to eighteen, his motion was defeated. Quite obviously, William Pitt did not speak for England. "The whole landed interest, Lord Camden wrote, "is almost altogether anti-American." In Parliament and out, everyone had his notion of how to manage the Americans. Dean Tucker of Gloucester Cathedral, a high Tory, was all for

granting independence. England would be well rid of the Americans, he said. Adam Smith was for independence too; *sans* feeling, as became a great economist — merely as expediency.[2] Why should Britain carry this huge annual expense? Free trade might well be more advantageous than the present disastrous monopoly.

When it came to the actual count, every measure against the Americans passed Parliament by large majorities. New England was declared in a state of rebellion, forbidden to fish on the Newfoundland Banks, forbidden to trade not only with the outside world but from colony to colony. All food and supplies must henceforth come from the mother country; no more Israel Putnams would lead sheep from Connecticut across the Neck to hungry Boston. Now surely, that stubborn spirit would bend! And what was this ridiculous talk of "starvation"? — a Member of the House asked contemptuously. "One would think the Americans were otters, and ate nothing but fish! Were we to give way, the seat of the Empire would be at Philadelphia."

For three months, Parliament debated. On March 22, Edmund Burke rose, pleading for conciliation in words America would one day get by heart. Burke was an Irishman in his middle forties; nine years of Parliament had not rid him of his Dublin accent. He wore steel-mounted spectacles; they slid down his nose while he was speaking. The House settled itself, knowing well that Burke would talk for five hours if it took five hours to say what was in his mind.

Absurd, he began now in his rapid, urgent voice — absurd to talk of "punishing" two and a half million people! Besides, while Britain deliberated methods for subduing these two million, they were grown to three! (Samuel Johnson put it more eloquently still: "The Americans multiply with the fecundity of their own rattlesnakes.") The trade of these people, Burke went on, covered the globe, their ships rode the deep from pole to pole. "No sea but is vexed by their fisheries, no climate that is not witness to their toils." Could any fleet, any army subdue such a nation? Moreover the people had a peculiar education, one that fitted them for independent action. Even their blacksmiths read law and the greater number of the delegates at Philadelphia had been practicing lawyers. "I hear the colonists have sold nearly as many of Blackstone's *Commentaries* in America as in England," Burke said. "This study renders men acute, inquisi-

tive, dexterous, prompt in attack, ready in defence, full of resources.
. . . They augur misgovernment at a distance and snuff the approach of tyranny in every tainted breeze."

Massachusetts, Burke continued — a colony of four hundred thousand inhabitants — had actually formed a government originating
directly from the people! "A vast province has now subsisted, and
subsisted in a considerable degree of health and vigour, for near a
twelfmonth, without governour, without public council, without
judges, without executive magistrates. What can arise out of this
unheard-of situation, how can the wisest of us conjecture? . . .
Obedience is what makes government, and not the names by which
it is called; not the name of a governour, as formerly, or committee,
as at present."

Give the Americans what they ask! said Burke at the end of three
hours' solid talking. "We cannot falsify the pedigree of this fierce
people. . . . An Englishman is the unfittest person on earth to argue
another Englishman into slavery." Comply with the American spirit.
Return to the former policy of "a wise and salutary neglect" — and
this people could be retained without coercion and without conquest.

Every word Burke said only hardened the Tory resolution. Should
Britain yield now, the rebellion might spread to Canada, Jamaica,
Ireland, India. Moreover, every time a group of miserable colonists
found themselves dissatisfied, must Parliament be disturbed for three
mortal months? On March 30, Parliament passed the Act to Restrain
New England, and the King began signing commissions for generals
and admirals to lead this new war. Gage's forces in Boston must be
enlarged to twenty thousand, a fleet dispatched as soon as practicable.

Vice Admiral Keppel of the Fleet refused to go. He would fight a
European army, he said, but not an American one. Lord Effingham
resigned his commission when he discovered that his regiment was
intended for America. The King called personally on Sir Jeffrey
Amherst, the great soldier; offered him a peerage. Amherst shook his
head. He could not serve against the Americans, "to whom he had
been so much obliged." (Did he remember the hills behind Worcester, his kilted troops dancing for the people, and his own long walks
over a peaceful New England farm?) The old Highland Watch,
stationed now in Ireland, balked completely at the word *Boston*.
They "would not go and fight against their brethren, who last war

fought and conquered by their side." William Pitt withdrew his son from the army rather than see him fight the Americans. Lesser men gave voice, including one Major Norris of the 27th Regiment. "He came to me," Norris's general wrote plaintively to Lord Harcourt, "and found fault with this most just and necessary war his Majesty is obliged to make against his rebellious subjects. When I would have interrupted him, he thundered out a hundred Greek lines from Homer. He then talked to me out of Plutarch's lives."

Sir William Howe, youngest of the three military brothers, agreed reluctantly to take over Gage's command at Boston. When his Nottingham constituents heard of it, they reproached him bitterly. What a choice for Commander in Chief in America! — Richmond told the House of Lords scornfully. The first thing Howe would see, landing in Massachusetts, was the monument to his brother, George Augustus, Viscount Howe, who had died fighting side by side with the Americans against the French at Ticonderoga.

Dr. Franklin never ceased his efforts. "Speaking the truth to them in sincerity was my only finesse," the master of finesse said sorrowfully, later. It was of no use. The ministerial group set him down as the "most malicious and dangerous enemy Britain possessed." *Master of mischief*, Samuel Johnson called him. On March 20, Franklin sailed secretly for home. The day before he left London he spent with Joseph Priestley the great liberal, going over American newspapers, clipping articles for reprinting in England. As he read, tears streamed down Franklin's face. Josiah Quincy sailed for home too, terribly ill but pathetically eager to get to Boston and lay before his friends the messages, the news, the grave advices from England.

Long before their two ships sighted land, something occurred to make ambassadors superfluous. General Gage sent troops to capture the powder and muskets stored at Concord, twenty miles northwest of Boston. The patriots got wind of it; Revere rode out to warn the militia. Lexington lay between Concord and Boston. And in the town of Lexington, on a clear, cold day of April, war with England was begun.

The sun had not yet risen on Wednesday, April 19, when the first shot was fired on Lexington Green. Jonathan Harrington, farmer, fell, looked at the blood on his breast with an expression of intense surprise, crawled to his doorstep across the road and died at his

wife's feet. By ten in the morning the British were in Concord, fighting on the bridge; by noon they had begun the retreat to Boston. The sun was bright, an east wind blew the smoke from their muskets back in the regulars' faces, blinding them, while from house and wall, from behind tree and ditch, single muskets cracked and cracked again, aimed by angry desperate Yankee farmers with no powder to waste.

This had been the mildest winter in New England history. The roads were dry underfoot; a messenger's horse could travel fast. The grass grew rankly a month before its time, the trees were budding out. By nightfall the roads swarmed with militia, marching to headquarters at Cambridge. All that night they came, and next day and for many days, walking by companies from Hingham, Bristol, Plymouth, Bridgewater. Men from the south coast and the east, men from far inland across Connecticut River. They came from Rhode Island, New Hampshire, Connecticut, not by the hundred but by the thousand, dressed for the most part in their work clothes, the leather breeches and checked shirts they had worn when the alarm sounded. Westward from Boston streamed riggers, shipwrights, ropewalkers who had been thrown out of work by the blockade and the occupation. They were glad to enlist — strong men, their arms burly and naked, carrying sailcloth for tents, carrying the tools of their trade in wooden boxes over their shoulder. Huts must be built for the army, barracks erected.

Out from Boston streamed also another army, converging, mingling incongruously with the volunteers: women, children, the old and the poor, terrified of the British, homeless, without food, wandering aimlessly they knew not where. (Five thousand of these were sent by the Committee of Safety to homes around Worcester.) All of Massachusetts seemed on the roads. There were people at the ferries, waiting patiently to get across; people crowded the bridges. And through them pushed persistently the army, a motley, serious, determined crew, walking fast, eating from their knapsacks as they went. One company from New Hampshire marched fifty-five miles in less than twenty hours. . . . Graybeards, their faces lined and weather-beaten, spitting tobacco, muskets slung any old way across their shoulders . . . Some carried staves, pitchforks, long-handled iron shovels; "If we cain't fight we kin dig!" they shouted jovially. Boys lugged iron kettles for the army to cook with, pulled handcarts

laden with wooden mess bowls. If the army did not eat it would go home and the local captains knew it. Wagons, drawn by horses, by oxen, carried hogsheads of flints, beef, rice, tow cloth, corn meal, flour, dried codfish in salty pungent heaps. By mid-May, twenty thousand troops would be encamped around Cambridge.

And through this river of humanity, solitary as a ship on a stormy ocean, yet with his course as firmly charted, rode John Adams, very sick at his stomach, feverish, numb with horror and foreboding — and making for Philadelphia.

The Second Congress meets. John nominates a Commander in Chief for the Army at Cambridge. There is a battle at Bunker's Hill, and John writes some very indiscreet letters.

IN the State House yard the Philadelphia Associators drilled their new-formed battalions, the bucktails on their cockaded hats standing up bravely in the early May breeze. Twenty blocks away in the Factory yard, the Quaker Blues went through the manual of arms as smartly as any veterans, aware that they had been read out of Meeting for what they did. And in John Cadwalader's garden the Silk Stocking Company drilled, determined to outdo the Blues. Their light green uniforms were crossed over the breast with white leather belts; they wore green jocky caps, and on their cartouche boxes the word LIBERTY stood out large. West of the city in a field lined with ancient trees the rifle company practiced, dressed in tow-cloth caps and belted shirts dyed the color of a fallen leaf, a tomahawk in every belt. At command they broke ranks, flung tomahawks or shot their rifles at a mark, then formed quickly, silently in line, Indian-fashion.

Crowds gathered in the late afternoons to watch them. Often enough, John Adams was among the crowd. He was touched and cheered by the martial spirit that everywhere prevailed. "Uniforms and Regimentals are thick as Bees," he wrote home. "Oh, that I were a Soldier! I will be. I am reading Military Books. Everybody must, and will, and shall be a Soldier."

Coming through New York, John had seen thousands of troops

at drill — a sight especially heartening because that large province last winter had rejected the First Continental Congress and refused to send delegates to the Second. They had even prepared Humble Petitions to King and Parliament, inscribed on paper bearing the significant watermark, *Liberty and Prudence*. But Lexington had changed their minds; they had elected a dozen delegates for Philadelphia. John hoped all twelve would not be as conciliatory as Duane and Jay. Tidings of Lexington had traveled amazingly fast. Kentucky should have it soon, and Savannah. Surely, the news would bring Georgia into the union!

Congress sat in the State House now, on Chestnut Street. Galloway had vanished no one knew where, and Lexington had made the Congress suddenly so important, so vitally necessary, that there was no need to count each move and each maneuver. The Pennsylvania Assembly had lent their room on the ground floor at the east end, a large, beautiful, white-paneled chamber, lined on two sides with windows. A handsome glass-prismed chandelier hung in the center. At the far end were twin fireplaces; the President's table faced the room. The place had an air auspicious, inspiring. And besides, thought John, entering that first morning and wiping a damp and dripping brow, the State House was comparatively cool, until they locked the doors for precaution. The tall windows were kept open only a crack from the top; insects buzzed and banged against the panes.

Forty-eight delegates answered to the roll call. (There would eventually be sixty-five.) Virginia had her old delegation. Thomas Jefferson was to come later, as alternate for Peyton Randolph, should the latter be called back to Virginia. John saw few new faces. Hancock of course was with the Massachusetts delegation now; Pennsylvania had added a distinguished young Scottish-born constitutional scholar, James Wilson. But among newcomers the most celebrated by far was Dr. Franklin, just landed from England. It was wonderful to see him, his chair at the end of the row pulled out a little from the rest, his knees crossed, tranquil and composed in his brown Quaker suit, the gray hair falling on his shoulders. Here was a man who knew the riddle of ministerial Britain at first hand, who had met Lord North face to face, a man wise in the ways of courts and empires.

The first morning, Colonel Washington created a sensation by

appearing in his uniform of the Virginia militia — blue and buff coat with rich gold epaulets, a small elegant sword at his side and a black cockade in his hat. Some, jealous of his wealth and social position, said sourly that the Virginian had found a pretty way to advertise his military ambitions. After all, Colonel Dickinson sat in Congress *sans* regimentals; so did Major Mifflin. But the New England men declared it a glorious idea. And how skillful, how natural to the man, this tacit yet open reminder that the business of this Congress might well be not negotiation but war!

It was a reminder, John discovered very soon, that was most burningly necessary. The New England men had come to Philadelphia with a program definite, immediate, practical: First, to put the continent in a state of strong defense. Second, to institute a people's government in every colony, entirely independent of Royal Governors, Parliament and Britain. They had expected to put it through without delay.

Now they found they could not even mention the word "independence," let alone the words "American Army." In spite of Lexington, the Middle and Southern colonies were not ready to accept a continental war. They had every sympathy with Massachusetts and said so with tears in their eyes. They approved the drilling, the battalions, the martial spirit out of doors. But they approved it, John discovered, conditionally — only should negotiation fail.

Sitting in the wide, white-paneled chamber, discouragement swept over John. At the expense of three precious days, Congress prepared an elaborate memorial for London, proving that Britain not America had fired the first shot at Lexington. The sworn depositions of a score of eyewitnesses were produced: "I, JOHN ROBINS, do Testifye and say, that on the Nineteenth Instant the Company under Command of Captain Parker being drawn up (sometime before sun Rise), on the Green, and I being in the front Rank, there suddenly appear'd a Number of the King's Troops huzzaing, with three Officers at their front on Horse Back and on full gallop toward us, the foremost of which cryed, throw down your Arms, ye Villains, ye Rebels! upon which the said Company dispersing, the foremost of the three officers ordered their men, saying fire, by God, fire! at which Moment we received a very heavy and close fire from them, at which Instant, being wounded, I fell . . ."

What was to be gained, John thought disgustedly, by proving who

fired first? In Congress last summer a Pennsylvania member had suggested bluntly that Massachusetts be left to conduct by herself what quarrels she chose. Was it possible Congress might repeat this proposal? *Don't let New England start a war* [Dr. Franklin had written from London] *without the approval of the Continental Congress. If they do, they may have to fight a war alone.*

John recalled it now with foreboding. Yet a display of anger, contempt, impatience, would persuade of nothing, and might lose much. Even in letters home, John told himself he must be careful, hint rather than say what he felt. "We find a great many Bundles of weak Nerves," he wrote Dr. Joseph Warren. "We are obliged to be as delicate and soft and modest and humble as possible." And to Abigail, "America is a great unwieldy Body. — Its progress must be Slow. It is like a large Fleet sailing under Convoy. — The fleetest Sailers must wait for the dullest and slowest."

After the Lexington depositions, Congress turned its attention to the Continental Association. No more goods must be shipped to Georgia, East and West Florida, Quebec. Local merchants sent pleas and claims to the floor. All were solemnly entered in the Minutes — as if, John thought, shifting irritably in his seat, as if there were no redcoats at Boston. . . .

The city of New York looked for a large detachment of British troops to land any day. Congress resolved that no resistance should be offered. The redcoats were to be received peacefully by the citizens, even given barrack room! Five men of Boston, who had seen their own town resist British troops since the year '68, sat silent, staring at their shoes. Here and again, it was true, something happened to lift the gloom of these first days. There was a knock at the door one morning and a traveler entered, his face and clothes streaked with dust. It was a Dr. Hall, from the Parish of St. John's, Georgia. The Parish — a whole county — had sent him as delegate, he told Congress a trifle breathlessly. He had ridden nearly eight hundred miles. Of course he couldn't expect to vote, he added hastily, seeing that the rest of Georgia had not joined the union. But could he sit here, that his constituents might know they were part of the union? John all but wept as the Doctor walked to the seat assigned, limping a little from six consecutive weeks on horseback.

On the eighteenth of May, Congress heard that Fort Ticonderoga had been captured from the British. Colonel Benedict Arnold of

Connecticut and one Ethan Allen of New Hampshire were responsible. With two hundred and fifty Green Mountain Boys, they had rowed across Lake George, climbed at dawn over the unguarded breech. Allen, striding ahead with sword drawn, had demanded surrender — so the story ran — "in the name of the Great Jehovah and the Continental Congress." (From neither of which, the Tories said later, had he a commission.) Ticonderoga, commanding the approach to the St. Lawrence River, was as important strategically as any point in America. Yet to Congress the affair caused more embarrassment than triumph. Badly as America needed the powder and arms taken by Ethan Allen, to advertise his victory would be to acknowledge before the world that the colonies had definitely taken the offensive against England — nullifying all the careful depositions and proofs about Lexington. Moreover, the Connecticut delegates were jealous because New Hampshire had skirmished unbidden in their territory. Had this Ethan Allen, they demanded, been authorized by headquarters at Cambridge to make such an attack?[1]

The situation was immediately and crazily complicated by the landing, at Market Street wharf, of a British Major Skene who announced breezily that he had been appointed from London as *Governor of Ticonderoga and Crown Point and Surveyor of the Woods*. Skene was clapped into custody, and laughter exploded from the city in a raucous wave. Let the gallant Major betake himself north and dispute his kingdom with Ethan Allen! On May 25, the warship *Cerberus* came into Boston Harbor, bearing three British major generals. A most unfortunate name for a frigate, people noted. Everyone barked when they said it, and a wit had composed a verse:

> Behold the *Cerberus* the Atlantic plough,
> Its precious cargo Burgoyne, Clinton, Howe —
> Bow! Wow! Wow!

It was good to laugh. Yet how strange, John thought, and how dangerous, the confusion that possessed men's minds! Down by the docks and markets of Philadelphia there was talk of omens seen by night, fearful signs like those that presaged disaster. A headless snake writhed in the heavens; when it shook its tail the earth trembled and balls of fire fell from the sky. Barns burned to the ground, ignited by this awful spark. Daily, the summer heat increased. In

the afternoon, as delegates stepped from the State House door, hot air rose from the brick footways like a blow, suffocating, demoralizing. It was a damp heat; John's woolen clothes stuck to him. At noontime the Northern delegates fanned at the flies with newspapers, threw off their heavy coats, pushed up their shirt sleeves, longed to shed their wigs and sit with shaven skulls exposed to what feeble air moved across the chamber. John envied the Southerners their light silk camlet coats and breeches.

Congress seemed blasted by the heat. Strong pleas were advanced that they leave Philadelphia and move northward. Lynch of South Carolina went so far as to ask Silas Deane to engage lodgings for him in Hartford. But the movement was quashed by the Dickinson faction, which saw a hazard that the Middle and Southern colonies would thereby become even more deeply involved with New England affairs.

Night brought little relief. John could not sleep, and his temper grew short. He marveled at his cousin Sam, who sat through the session seemingly as tranquil as Dr. Franklin, never showing what he felt. Often, John's troubled eyes turned to Washington by the window. He sat very straight in his military coat, with his hard blue eyes and silent, determined bearing. His very presence was eloquent.

Toward the last of May, something happened to push John altogether beyond his powers of self-control. The Dickinson-Duane faction moved that An Humble and Dutiful Petition be dispatched to His Majesty, including a plain statement that the colonies desired immediate negotiation and *accommodation of the unhappy disputes,* and that they were ready to *enter into measures* to achieve it.

It was too much. John sprang to his feet and lashed out. His voice, rapid, loud, penetrated to every corner. This was an act of imbecility! Were they to sit composing humble addresses, with the earth still loose over fifty New England graves, and Britain's ships of war coming ever nearer? Had not Congress wasted time enough with humble petitions that were never read, eloquent addresses that were spurned and spat upon? Let this Congress give over petitioning and memorializing, and get to the business of defending the continent! Two precious weeks had already been wasted. Before they even breathed the word "negotiation," certain matters should be tended to on this side the water.

John raised a hand, ticked off his program on his fingers: Let Con-

gress recommend to each colony that it institute an independent popular government. Let the troops at Cambridge be recognized as a Continental Army, with a Commander in Chief over all, and let Congress assume the entire burden of its subsistence and armament. England should be told of these plans, frankly and fully — and told also that if she continued this war, the colonies would seek help and foreign alliance where they could. John leaned forward, grasped the chair in front of him. "Yes," he repeated, "alliance with France, with the ancient enemy, if need be! With Spain, Holland, with any European power that cares to listen. Then and then only, Congress may enter into negotiation with Britain and her ministers. Then only we may indulge this talk of harmony, accommodation, loyalty, allegiance, love."

Spitting the last five words as if they were poison and would choke him, John sat down. Sullivan of New Hampshire rose immediately, continuing where John left off. His voice was rough, angry. John had scarcely got his breath when he was told a man wished to see him, outside the building, in the State House yard. . . . John made his way across the room. As he stepped to the pathway, the door banged behind him and a voice spoke his name, loud, peremptory. Dickinson had followed him out; he was in a violent passion.

"Give me the reason," he shouted, "why you New Englandmen oppose our every measure of reconciliation! Sullivan is in there now, haranguing against my petition to the King. Look ye, Adams! If you don't fall in with our plans, I and my friends will break off from New England, carry this Congress and this country in our own way!"

John looked coolly back at Dickinson. John was still angry, but his own speech had cleared his brain; he felt confident, exhilarated. Beyond the open window, Sullivan's voice could be heard, sharp and emphatic. Out here the midday sun blazed. Sweat poured from Dickinson's face; his lips were white and his fingers twitched at his sides.

"You are wasting your time, Mr. Dickinson," John said. "I am not to be threatened. In the name of unity, I can make sacrifices as well as you. You and your friends have seen me make them. Let the Congress judge between us. If they vote against me, I will submit. And if they vote against you, let you do the same."

Dickinson started to speak. John turned on his heel and left him.

But if John had won the encounter without-doors, Dickinson won
it within. Congress voted *Ay* to the Humble Petition. *Resolved
unanimously*, Charles Thomson wrote in the Minutes. At the last,
John submitted. He had to submit. Unity at all costs must be preserved — and even a dutiful petition need not stop America from
fighting a war. But John thought much about Dickinson and his
seeming change of front. This was a man who had done more than
any of them, back in the year '68, to wake the colonies to the reality
of their position. Yet here he was, begging, bargaining, petitioning,
praying, negotiating. John determined to fight him with all the
strength and skill he possessed. Things were in the open now;
the parties and factions defined. John and his supporters faced, he
said, "not only the party in favor of a petition to the king, and the
party who were jealous of independence, but a third party — a
Southern party which was against a Northern, with a jealousy against
a New England Army under the command of a New England
general."

On Friday, June second, Dr. Benjamin Church, the Boston surgeon, appeared in Congress, bearing an urgent letter from Watertown, asking advice and help in the formation of a new and permanent government for Massachusetts. John had expected this, had
indeed been looking for it. Before leaving for Philadelphia he had
conferred many times with the leaders at Watertown and had urged
some such move. But he watched anxiously to see how Congress
would respond.

In itself this was a request extraordinary, unprecedented. Here
was the great Province of Massachusetts voluntarily putting herself
under control of the Continental Congress, announcing she could
form no government without its consent. No central American authority had ever before been recognized by any of the thirteen colonies. As an excuse, an immediate reason for her astounding move,
Massachusetts gave the phenomenon of the vast new army of militia
in her midst. *We tremble at having an army (although of our countrymen) established here without a civil power to provide for and
controul them.* It was the old specter of military over civil authority;
New England had always feared it.

Congress received this startling communication with caution.
What they did would be a precedent. Other colonies would take it
up, make like requests. Rhode Island and Connecticut already had a

popular government, with a governor not crown-appointed but elected by the people. Three quarters of Congress were by no means sure they desired to see a republican form of government spread over the continent. Moreover, why should King George receive with favor An Humble Petition, a Loyal Address, if the same ship brought news that Royal Governors were ousted and the colonies had established separate, independent governments?

On its committee to consider the Watertown letter, Congress included no New England man. After a week's deliberation, the committee offered a cautious reply. Nothing was said about a constitution, or about a popularly elected governor. Let Massachusetts, Congress decreed, order an election of representatives to a new Provincial government in June of 1776. Then let these representatives name an upper house of twenty-eight from among their own number, to take the place of the old Governor's Council — "which assembly and council shall exercise the powers of Government, *until a Governor, of His Majesty's appointment, will consent to govern the colony according to its charter."*

Thus far Congress went, and no farther. Again the answer was conditional, again the whole thing waited on conciliation. John was at the same time elated and chagrined. Sam reminded him gently that in anything so novel and startling, a small improvement was better than none. What was it John's father, Deacon Adams, had said? *To mend the laws takes time as well as passion.*

John nodded gloomily. His father was a very practical man, he said. But his father did not live during a civil war. . . .

As a final request, the Watertown letter had asked Congress to take over entire regulation of the army at Cambridge. To this no direct answer was given. John determined to force a reply. Now was the strategic moment. His own speech and Sullivan's the other day had molded the opposition, forced it to close its ranks. The quickest way to proceed would be to name a Commander in Chief from some colony south of Connecticut. The minute a Southern general was adopted, the army automatically ceased to be a New England organization and became a continental one.

From a military standpoint the move was urgent, vitally necessary. On the way down from Braintree, John had visited headquarters at Cambridge, had seen at first hand how dangerous was the confusion. Already, since April, four thousand volunteers had got discouraged

and gone home. Sixteen thousand remained, sprawled in a line thirty miles long from Cambridge to Roxbury, subsisting precariously on gifts from the surrounding farms, living in tents, cabins, sailcloth shelters, brush-thatched huts of turf or stone. To encourage enlistment, any man that brought in forty-nine volunteers got a captain's commission. John himself had seen one of these "captains" — a wizened little shoemaker from Weymouth — order a private from his company to fetch a pail of water for the mess. "Fetch it yourself, Keptin," the man had replied without rancor. "I got the last pail."

The militia officers cared more about being liked than being obeyed. There was much boasting concerning the "equality" that marked this New England army. Colonel Israel Putnam of Connecticut carried his own meat to mess, raw, and cooked it, to show he considered himself no better than the least in his ranks.

Artemas Ward of Shrewsbury commanded these motley thousands. He was a Harvard graduate, well known for his services in the French war, and very popular. But he was nearing fifty, suffered from the bladder stone and had no experience in dealing with such vast numbers of men. John Hancock was New England's candidate to succeed him. Hancock had seen no service in the field, besides which he was frequently crippled with gout. But as Colonel of the Boston Cadets he had long cut a fine figure on the parade ground, escorting governors, officiating at civic celebrations. There was little doubt he expected the position, or at least the refusal of it. Hancock moreover had come into special prominence lately by reason of having been named President of Congress *pro tem*, when Peyton Randolph was called home to Virginia.

John had no slightest intention of nominating Hancock. George Washington was his man. Not only did John admire Washington personally, but unless a Southerner commanded the troops, there would be few enlistments south of Connecticut. Canvassing the delegates, John found little serious support for Hancock; it was Artemas Ward who was Washington's most formidable rival. Yet John felt sure he could persuade his countrymen that local pride should give way to urgent necessity.

Colonel Washington moreover could afford the job financially, having a large independent fortune. This would count heavily with the Middle and Southern delegates — men like Dickinson, Duane, the Rutledges, who considered an independent fortune the first step

to prestige. Washington had more military experience than any man in America, except, of course, the much-talked-of Colonel Charles Lee, a retired half-pay British officer who lived on his estates in Virginia and advertised himself as more American than the Americans. Many said Charles Lee would make a better leader than Washington, and in truth his military record was extremely impressive. He had served in the British Army since he was twelve, had fought in Portugal and Poland as well as with Braddock on the Ohio. At Ticonderoga in '58 he had lost two fingers. Somewhere along in this bright career, Lee had married the daughter of a Seneca chief. He was a genius at getting on with Indians; they called him Boiling Water because he was never still. Over six feet tall, he was hawk-nosed, cadaverous, slovenly in his dress, and he carried a shining though somewhat mysterious reputation as a literary man. Rumor had it he was JUNIUS, author of the notorious London letters to the King. The whole world seemed to know about Charles Lee, and about the pack of hound dogs that accompanied him everywhere. Above all men, it was said, he could whip an undisciplined army into shape.

But Lee was British-born. This alone, John told himself, must in the end tell decisively against him. The army would not fight under a British-born commander in chief. As second in command, however, Lee could be extremely useful.

From his own Massachusetts colleagues, John's plan received, at first, little support. Cushing hung back: Hancock deserved the post, he said. Robert Paine, who had been at college with Artemas Ward, declared he loved the man dearly and would be damned if he saw him superseded. Sam Adams showed no enthusiasm, but said he would go along with any sensible plan to keep the British troops from raiding Massachusetts. Even the Virginians were not united; Pendleton said frankly he did not want Washington for the supreme command. It was true the Colonel had served valiantly in the Ohio country with Braddock. But was it not true also that he had lost every battle of consequence he engaged in? There were certain circles of Virginia, Pendleton intimated, where Washington had made himself extremely unpopular after his return from the Ohio country.

John worked hard. By the middle of June, he decided the moment was ripe. On a dull, muggy morning, he walked alone to Congress, determined to nominate Washington before the noon bell sounded

from the tower. He found his cousin Sam walking in the State House yard, taking his daily exercise up and down the gravel walk under the sycamore trees. John went directly to him. Would Sam second a nomination for Washington as Commander in Chief? Didn't he agree that now was the time to strike, and that if they once got the motion actually presented, it would go through today, or at latest tomorrow? He himself, John added, was convinced the Hancock movement was mostly hollow talk, more a jealousy of Virginia than an effective, affirmative campaign.

Sam nodded thoughtfully to each question, but said absolutely nothing. John was not discouraged. It was hard to draw Sam into talk about the army on any terms; he would like to see this war won by the local militia. When any larger plans came up, Sam's face went blank and he was apt to murmur the word *Cromwell* and begin animadverting on the sacred inalienable rights of the civilian.

John left his cousin and went inside. As soon as the members were seated, he rose and spoke briefly for the establishment of a Continental Army, outlining the present dangers, chief of which was that the forces at Cambridge might dissolve entirely. What was to prevent the British from profiting by this delay, marching out of Boston and "spreading desolation as far as they could go?" As Commander in Chief of a Grand American Army he would like, John finished, to suggest "a gentleman whose skill as an officer, whose independent fortune, great talents and universal character would command the respect of America and unite the full exertions of the Colonies better than any other person alive . . ."

All the time John was speaking, Hancock wore a look of pleased, even radiant expectancy. Facing the room in his chair behind the President's table, he was plainly visible to everyone, including John, who stood near the front. No one loved glory more than Hancock; he had the vanity of a child, open and vulnerable. John saw his face and hastened on, raising his voice . . . "A gentleman *from Virginia*, who is among us here, and well known to all of us . . ."

Hancock shrank as at a blow. ("I never," John wrote later, "remarked a more sudden and striking change of countenance. Mortification and resentment were expressed as forcibly as his face could exhibit them.") Washington, who was on the south side of the room, left his seat at the word "Virginia" and slipped quietly out the door before his name was pronounced.

John finished and sat down. Sam Adams rose at once to second his motion. Hancock's face grew hard and dark with anger; he made no attempt to hide his feelings. Since the year '65, Sam Adams's open palm had received the Hancock money — thousands of pounds poured out for the use of the liberty party. Was this to be his reward? Hancock's eyes swept the room. . . . Sherman of Connecticut, then Cushing of Boston rose. The army around Cambridge, they argued, would not fight under a Southern commander. There had been trouble enough already over the local election of New England officers. Many a regiment had broken up entirely because of these local jealousies. . . .

Colonel Washington might be a splendid soldier and patriot, someone else interposed. But he could speak no French, an accomplishment that might prove indispensable should this war continue, and foreign alliances, foreign legions be sought. Colonel Charles Lee on the other hand spoke excellent French and was proficient in Spanish and Italian besides.

The debate went on. Most of the talk, John noted with relief, came from a very small group. Three quarters — perhaps five eighths — of the room sat silent. They were the Washington men. John had worked hard enough by now to know it, and know they were merely waiting for the vote. Robert Paine spoke out, testified warmly to the character and attainments of his old college mate, Artemas Ward. Nobody listened; the Southern members looked bored.

Late in the afternoon, Congress rose without taking the vote. That evening the brace of Adamses was very busy, and next morning, when Johnson of Maryland put the motion a second time, Congress voted unanimously for Washington.

John was jubilant. On paper at least, the Grand American Army had been achieved. There remained now to put it in order. Under the impetus of yesterday's debate, ten companies of "expert rifflemen" were voted, to be raised immediately in Pennsylvania, Maryland, Virginia, and sent to join the army at Cambridge. "They use a peculiar kind of Musket called a Rifle," John wrote home. "It has circular grooves within the Barrell, and carries a ball to great distances. . . . The Rifle Men are very fine fellows, the most accurate Marks-men in the World; they kill with great Exactness at 200 yards Distance; they have Sworn certain death to the ministerial officers. May they perform their oath."

Next day — June 16 — in the presence of all Congress, Washington was officially informed that he had been chosen as *supreme Commander of the forces raised and to be raised in defence of American Liberty*. Standing in his place by the window, Washington accepted the nomination. In his face and bearing there was no hint of triumph; he looked troubled, deeply serious. "I am truly sensible of the high Honour done me," he said. "I will enter upon the momentous duty, and exert every power I possess for support of the glorious cause. . . . But I beg it may be remembered by every Gentleman in the room, that I this day declare with the utmost sincerity, I do not think myself equal to the Command I am honored with."

There was something extraordinary in the way Washington said it — a simplicity, an earnest appeal that moved even those who considered themselves his enemies. Plainly, this was not the usual self-deprecatory speech of acceptance; Washington meant every word. Congress had voted his pay and expenses at $500 a month. It did not detract from his new popularity when Washington declared, as he made an end, that he could take no remuneration ("make no profitt," Thomson wrote in the Minutes). He would keep exact account of his expenses in the field, which if Congress would at the end discharge, it was all he desired.

John Adams, looking round in a glow of satisfaction, decided that, whatever Washington's military abilities might or might not be, here was a general who could unite the colonies. Every face seemed to show pleasure. Congress proceeded immediately to the election of four major generals to serve under Washington. Before ten minutes, the room was split again in violent faction. "A Tormenting Scuffle," John called it. Finally, Artemas Ward was named First Major General; Charles Lee, Second; Philip Schuyler of New York, Third; and Israel Putnam of Connecticut, Fourth. Eight Brigadiers General were settled upon, their pay voted at $125 a month; the Major Generals were given $166 — sums that John considered appallingly extravagant. But the Southern men insisted. They disapproved strongly of the leveling spirit in the New England troops. If an enlisted man would not fetch a pail of water at command, what reason was there to think he would stand against a bayonet attack? Disparity of pay would do much to improve this situation; it would fix a healthy gulf between the high command and the low, between private and officers.

A week later, on Friday, June 23, John got on his horse, and with most of Congress, escorted the Generals and their military entourage out of town on the journey northward. It was a fine bright morning, with a breeze blowing up from the Bay. The Generals were beautifully mounted. By Washington's side rode his new aide-de-camp, Major Thomas Mifflin, and the General's Secretary and close friend, Colonel Joseph Reed of Pennsylvania. The Philadelphia Light Horse looked superb in their short brown jackets, white breeches and smart high-topped boots. On the brown saddlecloths, silver braid gleamed; their flat round hats were bound with silver. The band played, the drums beat, the trees waved their green luxuriant summer plumage. A troop of little boys scurried by the road, screaming joyfully, darting almost under the horses' hoofs. It was all very gay and wonderful. On such a day and in such a company, no war could be lost, no cause betrayed.

In a cloud of dust the cavalcade vanished. John turned his horse toward town, and his spirit sank within him like a stone. Thomas Mifflin, Joseph Reed — why must these citizen-soldiers prance curvetting by the General's side while John Adams returned miserably to his lodging in the heat, doomed to perpetual drudgery, witness to eternal squabblings between committee and committee?

John sneezed loud and angrily in the dust; the sight of the military never failed to depress him. All day he brooded, and by nightfall had whipped himself into a state of overwhelming self-pity. He was thrown back twenty years, felt as he had felt at Worcester long ago when his master James Putnam marched out as Colonel of Foot, while he remained to keep school in forlorn and hopeless security.

In his boardinghouse bedroom, a future President of the United States sat at his table in the heat, while flies crawled through the shutters and the sweat glistened on a bald wide forehead. *Such [wrote John mournfully] is the Pride and Pomp of War. I, poor Creature, worn out with scribbling, for my Bread and my Liberty, low in Spirits and weak in Health, must leave others to wear Laurells which I have Sown; others, to eat the Bread which I have earned — a Common Case.*

General George Washington, Commander in Chief of the Grand American Army, had not ridden twenty miles from Philadelphia

when his little cavalcade was stopped by a very dusty courier posting down from Connecticut. . . . Gage had attacked the Provincial entrenchments. There had been a battle on the hills above Boston — Breed's Hill, Bunker's Hill. . . . Charlestown was burned by the enemy. Out of two thousand regulars, a thousand were lost, and four hundred Americans. . . . The militia were driven from their position.

Abigail Adams saw Charlestown burn that day. At dawn the guns had wakened her, a horrible sound. She got up, tried to go about her duties while in the hot, still morning the cannon boomed. She felt the eyes of the two older children upon her, round and frightened. Messengers rode by from time to time, stopped for water at the farmhouse. . . . *Warren was killed*, they said. Dr. Warren of Boston. Shot in the head. A witness had seen him fall, but none knew where his body lay.

Little Abby burst into tears. John Quincy, aged eight, clung to his mother. Dr. Warren had bandaged his wrist in Boston; Dr. Warren was his father's friend. "If we go up the hill," Abigail said, "we can see across the Bay. It will be better than waiting here, idle." She took her son and daughter by the hand; the three walked out and up Penn's Hill in the sunshine, turned off near the top and emerged through the woods to an open field. They climbed the huge gray rocks for better view. The blackberry vine was in flower; beneath their feet its small white blossoms gleamed like stars in the crannies. The smell of bayberry rose pungent in the early afternoon heat.

Abigail stood silent, gazing across the treetops and the Bay. Black smoke rose over burning Charlestown, and when it cleared she could see, above the crest of the hill beyond, a white haze hanging over the battlefield. . . . How many were dead? In what spot did Warren lie? . . . Abby laid a hand across her eyes. *Almighty God,* she prayed: *Cover the heads of our countrymen and be a shield to our dear friends. God of Israel, give strength and be a power to our people.*

The afternoon wore on and the night; the battle was done. The two armies buried their dead, shifted their position and waited. America was not proud of what happened at Bunker Hill. It was true that a thousand British had been killed or wounded, as against

four hundred Americans. Yet people murmured. Hadn't General Artemas Ward been seriously at fault in refusing to reinforce Prescott's detachment, early in the battle? And who, actually, had rallied the militia as wave after wave of British stormed the redoubt on Breed's Hill? Was it Prescott, Israel Putnam, Joseph Warren? General Ward had remained in his headquarters at Cambridge. "He never left his house all day," Warren of Plymouth wrote Sam Adams. Was it indolence that kept him there, or cowardice?

Amid the confusion, the backbiting and mutual recrimination, two things emerged, clear and convincing. The American Army was desperately in need of a Commander in Chief — and the militia could fight, not merely Indian-fashion behind walls and trees as at Lexington and Concord: they could meet and engage regular troops in the open, under continuous, bloody attack. General Sir William Howe never recovered, it was said, from that day of June 17. The vision of his men advancing in battalions to be shot down in hideous carnage would not fade.

Abigail Adams took pen and wrote her husband a long description of all she had seen and heard that day, sparing nothing of fact or feeling. John reacted in a fury of anger, not so much at the British as at his countrymen in Philadelphia. Congress was to blame for this! Congress had impeded, blocked every plan, every suggestion that might have put the army in readiness for the attack. Delay, everlasting delay, wrangling, jealousy, timidity — in God's name, was the whole continent to be lost by such tactics? A war could not be won by the moral stamina of a few, or by the gallant sacrifice of a hundred such as Joseph Warren. Poor James Otis had managed to be in the battle, too. Quite insane now, he had somehow wandered off from his sister's house at Watertown, followed the troops with a borrowed musket and was seen crouching in the trenches, his eye along the gun barrel. At midnight he had stumbled through his sister's door, weary and faint. When John heard it the tears sprang to his eyes.

After Bunker Hill, Congress, it was true, seemed to bestir itself, jolted into more decisive action. Articles of War were adopted for the Army, a hospital service organized, with doctors, nurses and such medicines as could be found. Congress scoured the country for gunpowder and for saltpeter to make it, for niter, sulphur, for brass

fieldpieces and above all for muskets that would shoot. A General Post Office was set up to facilitate communications. Loans of money were arranged to buy Army supplies; two millions of paper dollars were ordered printed and put in circulation. A Department of Indian Affairs was organized; a skillful and most necessary appeal composed, praying the powerful Six Nations to remain neutral in this war: *Brothers, Sachems, Warriors! Open a kind ear! King George, persuaded by wicked counsellors, has broken the covenant chain with his children in America!*

Yet even now, in all that Congress did, it proceeded conditionally, John noted. Always conditionally, on the assumption — the hope — the prayer that Britain would capitulate, make peace, forgive, return to the old free system of government. Early in July, Dickinson's Petition to the King went off to London, carried by Richard Penn and signed, of course, by every member of Congress. John wrote his name below Sam's, and, thoroughly disgusted, threw down his pen. The Address to the People of Great Britain, which went in the same ship, affected him as strongly. The times were too desperate, the situation too serious for such polite and fruitless trafficking. "Prettynesses," John wrote in disgust, "Juvenilities, and much less Puerilities became not a great assembly like this, the Representatives of a great People."

There was one member of Congress, a new member, who occupied himself with neither prettinesses nor puerilities. Late in June, Thomas Jefferson had arrived from Virginia. John was immediately drawn to him. ("He soon seized upon my heart," he said.) Jefferson at thirty-two was tall, thin, sandy-haired, with a fair complexion, in no way celebrated unless it was for his trick of writing fluent English. The Virginia delegates had boasted about it. Jefferson was not a speechmaker like Patrick Henry or Richard Henry Lee. His eloquence lay all on paper. He could translate into warm and even burning words the most abstract ideas concerning government, liberty, freedom. John was ready enough to believe it, having read Jefferson's pamphlet, *A Summary View of the Rights of British America*, published late in '74. The man was a natural scholar, his friends reported further, deeply read in history and natural science — "the greatest rubber-off-of-dust," Duane told John, that he had ever met, with a knowledge of French, Italian and Spanish, and the ambition to

learn German. What particularly attracted John, these first weeks, was Jefferson's quick, decisive way in committee. "He was prompt," John said; "frank, explicit as Samuel Adams himself."

Not long after Jefferson's arrival, he was put on a committee to draft a "Declaration of the Causes and Necessity for Taking up Arms," a document designed chiefly for the troops at Cambridge. Jefferson was asked to write it. He proceeded very carefully, making several drafts, striking out phrases that seemed verbose or slipshod. But the committee disapproved. ("It was too strong for Mr. Dickinson," Jefferson said later.) Dickinson went over it and though he strengthened rather than toned it down, Congress accepted his version. *Our cause is just, a final paragraph ran, our union is perfect. We fight not for glory or for conquest. In our own native land, in defence of the freedom that is our birthright, we have taken up arms. We shall lay them down when hostilities shall cease on the part of the aggressors, and all danger of their being renewed shall be removed, and not before.*

Yet the Declaration on Taking Arms, spirited though it might be, was balanced on the other side by the Humble Petition. John could not forget it. "In exchange for these Petitions, Declarations and Addresses," he wrote home, "I suppose we shall receive Bills of Attainder and other such like Expressions of Esteem and Kindness." . . . "Does every Member of Congress feel for us?" Abigail had written after Bunker Hill. "Can they realize what we suffer?" "No!" John answered. "They don't! They can't. There are some Persons in New York and Philadelphia, to whom a Ship is dearer than a City, and a few Barrels of flour, than a thousand Lives — other Men's lives, I mean."

This was the nearest John had ever come to putting on paper what he thought of Congress, although from time to time he had eased himself by entering, in his diary, vivid and caustic descriptions of individual members. He was still pledged to secrecy — and besides, the mails were far from safe. John tore up letter after letter, ended by writing home scarcely at all. Finally, one night, he broke down completely, threw care to the winds and revealed to his wife in one brief, succinct sentence the whole business of Congress past and future, as he himself wished it to be: "We have a Constitution to form for a great empire, a country of fifteen hundred miles in extent to fortify, millions to arm and train, a naval

power to begin, an extensive commerce to regulate, numberous tribes of Indians to negotiate with, a standing army of twenty seven thousand Men to raise, pay, victual and officer. . . . P.S. I wish I had given you a complete history from the beginning to the end of the behavior of my compatriots. No mortal tale can equal it. I will tell you in future, but you shall keep it secret. The fidgets, the whims, the caprices, the vanity, the superstition, the irritability of some of us is enough to . . . Yours, J. A."

This frank and passionate little paragraph was destined to raise a veritable tempest on two sides of an ocean. ("John Adams," said Franklin, "is always an honest man, often a wise one, but sometimes in some things, absolutely out of his senses.") John, happily, was unconscious of the effect he was to produce. Putting his initials to Abigail's letter, he reached for a fresh sheet:

To James Warren

PHILADELPHIA, *July* 24th, 1775

DEAR Sir, — In Confidence. I am determined to write freely to you this time. A certain great Fortune and piddling Genius,* whose Fame has been trumpeted so loudly, has given a silly Cast to our whole Doings. We are between Hawk and Buzzard. We ought to have had in our Hands a month ago the whole Legislative, executive and judicial of the whole Continent, and have completely modeled a Constitution; to have raised a naval Power, and opened all our Ports wide; to have arrested every Friend to Government on the Continent and held them as Hostages for the poor Victims in Boston, and then opened the Door as wide as possible for Peace and Reconciliation. After this they might have petitioned, and negotiated, and addressed etc. if they would. Is all this extravagant? Is it wild? Is it not the soundest Policy? . . .

One Piece of News, Seven thousand Weight of Powder arrived here last Night. We shall send some along as soon as we can, but you must be patient and frugal.

We are lost in the Extensiveness of our Field of Business. We have a Continental Treasury to establish, a Paymaster to choose and a Committee of Correspondence or Safety, of Accounts, or something, I know not what, has confounded Us all Day. . . .

You observe in your Letter the Oddity of a great Man.** He is a queer Creature. But you must love his Dogs if you love him, and forgive a thousand whims for the Sake of the Soldier and the Scholar.

* John Dickinson.
** General Charles Lee, third in command at Cambridge.

Three weeks later, both letters were in the Tory newspapers. The messenger, one Hichborne of Massachusetts, had managed to get himself captured crossing the Hudson in a rowboat. John's compositions were hawked in parody about the streets of occupied Boston, sung to music in the British camp on Bunker Hill. The world read them and laughed or swore according to its sympathies of the moment. The letters crossed the ocean, reaching London about the same time as Dickinson's dutiful Petition — nullifying word for word its tone of humble pleading and revealing for the first time the extent of the rebel plans. The next official news Congress had from England would be the King's proclamation of a state of rebellion throughout America.

John Dickinson, that *great Fortune and piddling Genius,* passed John on Chestnut Street, and cut him dead. Dickinson's Quaker friends and the whole conservative, conciliatory party cut John too. "I saw this profound and enlightened patriot," Benjamin Rush wrote years later, "walk our streets alone after the publication of his intercepted letters, an object of nearly universal detestation."

The Tories were gleeful. John Adams would be utterly ruined. His letters would cause quarrels in Congress, divisions among the colonies. . . . John himself viewed the whole matter with a kind of sour, pugnacious pleasure. At last he had given voice, said what was in his heart to say, at last come out for an American constitution, created separate from England, with an Army to back it up. Let the wind blow and the tempest rage! Why, he had experienced worse in his own home town in the year '70, when he and Josiah Quincy defended the British soldiers after the Massacre! At least the Philadelphia Quakers didn't throw mudballs, or whistle through their fingers from behind moonlit hedges.

Yet it was by no means pleasant to be shunned as a leper, to hear the conversation die when one entered a room. John grew uncomfortable. His friends rallied, some even praised him. Reed of Philadelphia said heaven itself must have got those letters published, although no one could deny their writer was prodigiously indiscreet. Independence was coming. It was inevitable, written in the stars. This happy accident enabled the continent of America to see independence written down in black and white, have time to grow a little used to the idea.

As for General Charles Lee, sitting in his quarters at Cambridge

with his hound dogs about him, he roared with delight, called his aides to listen while he read aloud about *the Oddity of a great Man whose whims must be forgiven for the Sake of the Soldier and the Scholar.* Then he wrote John a superb letter, announcing with utmost good humor that until the bulk of mankind was much altered, he would consider it a compliment to be called an eccentric. As for his dogs, as soon as he could be convinced men were as worthy of affection, he would transfer his passion to mankind. Might he add that in Mr. Adams he beheld such a biped — "endowed with generosity, valor, good sense, patriotism and zeal for the rights of humanity." He sent his respects to "the other Mr. Adams," and Spada his best hound sent love also, declaring in language perfectly intelligible that he had fared much better since the publication of the letters, being celebrated and "caressed now by all ranks sexes and ages."

CHAPTER THIRTY

*The Continental Army. Washington asks for
a Navy, and Congress is reluctant. John ad-
vises on how to frame constitutions. A London
corset maker "leads America by a thread."
Abigail Adams sees the British Fleet sail out of
Boston Harbor, and the war moves southward
from New England.*

THE British burned Falmouth in October of 1775, shelling it
from the sea — a pointed answer to Dickinson's Humble Petition to
the King. One hundred and fifty buildings, churches, houses, were
leveled to the ground. The news shocked the entire country. Here
was no midnight raid by naked, painted savages. The British had
done this. America's own brothers had done it. Captain Mowat, commander of the ship *Canceaux* that had led the shelling, showed papers
ordering him to destroy all towns from Boston to Halifax, and announced that Portsmouth would be next. "Death and desolation
mark their footsteps," General Nathanael Greene wrote to the newspapers from Washington's headquarters outside of Boston. "Fight
or be slaves is the American motto now." This was civil war with
a vengeance.

Yet there were men in the patriot party who showed little sympathy for Falmouth. One of them was John's old friend, Major Hawley of Northampton. By whose fault was it, Hawley demanded, that
Falmouth had been a "defenseless victim"? The town had refused
to arm, had taken no measures to blockade the harbor. Would its

citizens believe, at last, that Britain was an enemy not a friend, or must Boston be burned to prove it, and Philadelphia? Let Falmouth and her sister towns cease to mourn and whimper! Let them abandon their mistaken "loyalty," and enter this contest with their whole heart and strength, taking pride in the rightness of the cause. This was not the first civil war of history. The Scriptures themselves bore witness: *And the children of Israel wept before the Lord and asked counsel saying, Shall I go up to battle against the children of Benjamin my brother? And the Lord said, Go up against him.*

Go up against thy brother. . . . America was not yet ready for such counsel. America was still two thirds Tory and four fifths indifferent to the war. Thirteen colonies as yet had no conception of themselves as a nation, though they had begun cautiously to talk of a "confederacy," and newspapers used the phrase "United American Colonies." Yet even the patriots still regarded the war as an affair wholly sectional. Each colony felt justified in taking what individual stand it chose. New Jersey threatened a separate peace treaty with Britain, Massachusetts a separate declaration of independence. Congress found it necessary to pass a resolution *that it will be very dangerous to the liberties and welfare of America, if any Colony should separately petition the King or either house of Parliament.* The Middle colonies seemed more concerned over internal squabbles than over the war with Britain. Pennsylvania and Connecticut had reopened their ancient battle about the boundary line on the Susquehanna, north of Wilkes-Barre; the inhabitants were shooting it out like feudists. Down in North Carolina the mountaineers were engaged in a little war of their own against the Tidewater planters. Congress hurriedly voted to *send Gospel ministers out, at $40 a piece, to go amongst the highlanders or regulators and inform them of the nature of the present dispute between Great Britain and the colonies.*

Washington at Cambridge complained that local jealousy was destroying his Army: "Connecticut wants no Massachusetts man in their corps. Massachusetts thinks there is no necessity for Rhode Islanders to be introduced among them." The Pennsylvania and New England troops were as ready to fight each other as the enemy.

How could an Army be built under such conditions? Virginia and Carolina volunteers protested the presence of free Negroes among the New England regiments. Washington insisted that the Negroes

remain, and Congress in the end supported him. The Southern troops moreover took instant dislike to Yankee soldiers — to their faces, their nasal voices and above all their stubborn, self-righteous piety. Washington himself had trouble understanding the New Englanders. A passion for trading seemed to possess them; piety and small gains were inextricably mixed. "This Day," wrote David How of Methuen, Massachusetts, "I drawd a pare of Bretches out of the Stores price 7 shillings. Doc Langdon preached this fore part of the Day in Mica the forth Chapter & Fifth Verce. I let David Chandler Have my Breaches that I drawd out of the Stors. I sold Joseph Jackson A pare of trousers for 10 shillings. . . . John Coleman drinkt 3 pints cyder at one draught. I Ointed for the Itch this Night."

The camps covered, altogether, a line of some thirty miles. Discipline was impossible to achieve. It was the Southern riflemen that harassed Washington most. Those tall romantic fellows in hunting shirts, wampum belts and moccasins who had so bedazzled the countryside on their march northward in July were proving a fearful problem. They refused to take orders, cared for nothing but displaying their prowess with the rifle and wasted the camp's scant store of powder whizzing away at an enemy too far off to hit. Gloomily the General declared that he wished all hundred and forty of them in the backwoods again, shooting at Indians. "About eight o'clock," wrote Private Sam Haws, "their was a Rifle man whipt 39 stripes for stealing and afterward he was Drummd out of the camps if the infernal regions had been opened and cain and Judas and Sam Haws had been present their could not have ben a biger uproar. . . . This Day we turned out and went to the Larm post by order of George Washington Lesemo of the American army incampt at Cambridge and Roxbury and other places. It was very cold and we came home and there was a high go of Drinking Brandy and several of the Company were taken not well prety soon after nothing more this day."

Washington could not act without consent of Congress. His troops needed clothing, barracks, shoes, medicines. He sent express riders to Philadelphia nearly every day. Congress, instead of answering, sat down and argued. *Resumed* [said the Minutes] *the consideration of Gen. Washington's letters N.4 and 5, after some debate. A Committee appointed to prepare an answer, viz Mr. Lynch, Mr. Lee, Mr. J Adams.* What really interested Congress was the

naming of new officers and generals. John, who had seen with his own eyes the critical condition of the troops, raged and fumed while delegates fought for the distribution of rich plums. They were forever talking about what happened "last war." . . . "Last war," said Paine and Sherman, "soldiers supplied their own clothing." John ran from colleague to colleague, pleading that this great conflict could not be compared with the French wars. This war was continental; the expense must be borne by the continent. John talked so much that in his "Notes of Debates" he finally despaired of recording his own arguments. . . .

JOHNSON [the Notes read]: *Let us consider prudence.*
JOHN ADAMS: &c. &c. &c.

It seemed to John a miracle the Continental Army remained in camp at all. Sickness swept the ranks: a terrible epidemic of dysentery that had started in the hot days of late August. Ten thousand moaning, delirious men lay anywhere, in barns, stables, sheds, under bushes and fences, perished helpless in their own filth. John himself had seen them. Congress, in August, had adjourned for a brief vacation (John voted against the measure). Riding home, John had been met just outside of Braintree by a messenger with a note from Abby, warning that his brother Elihu, in camp at Roxbury, was dangerously ill. Before John could reach him, Elihu was dead. John rode to the encampment, brought his brother's body home and buried it. The earth was not dry over the grave when John was forced to travel southward again, stunned with grief, shaken with apprehension for his family as the epidemic spread to the surrounding countryside.

No sooner was he back in Philadelphia than John heard that Abigail's mother had died of the epidemic at the old Weymouth Parsonage. Abby had been with her and had seen her die. For the first time since John had left her, Abby broke down, poured out her loneliness and terror in letters that wrung her husband to the heart. A week later he heard from Mr. Norton Quincy that Abby and the four children had taken the sickness, that all had passed the danger point and were safe.

As the cold weather came on, the epidemic passed. And now a new threat assailed the Continental Army. Enlistment terms would

expire in December. Suppose the whole body of nineteen thousand should disband? All Washington's hard work and training would be wasted; he must begin again with a new Continental Army, provided one could be recruited. John urged his radical colleagues — Gadsden, Lee, McKean — to speak for longer enlistment terms. Let fresh regiments be recruited not for three months but for a year! At Cambridge, Roxbury, Winter Hill, the General walked among his troops, begged them not to desert their country at this critical hour. They merely looked back at him in silence. New England had beat the French, last war, by three-month enlistments; they could beat the British that way too. The men made one concession: a promise to sell their muskets to the Army, not take them along home when the time came.

Washington was so short of powder he dared not fire a morning or an evening gun. Fortunately, the British aim was bad; they seemed to shoot at the clouds and their balls landed anywhere. The Provincials ran after them, stuffed them in the cannon muzzle and shot them triumphantly back at Bunker Hill.

The General's messengers knocked continually on the doors of the Philadelphia State House. Could not the Congress move North, to be nearer the Army, see for themselves the desperateness of his situation? Arms, powder, ships were needed — American ships, to protect the coast, intercept the British supply line. Several privateers were already operating out of Beverly, Massachusetts, and Rhode Island in July had armed two cruisers; Connecticut voted two for herself. All these vessels did their work without sanction from Congress. The British called them "pirates," and so they were, with every man aboard subject to hang from the yardarm if captured. Nevertheless the ships were effectual, and General Washington greatly desired more of the same. When Captain Manly of Marblehead begged permission to arm his vessel and pursue two powder-laden British transports that were passing up the coast, Washington sent an express to Philadelphia, asking formal instructions.

Congress, dismayed, was struck with sudden paralysis. It was one thing for America to defend herself on land when attacked. But deliberately to engage the celebrated, the glorious Royal Navy at sea was folly "chimerical and Phantastick." It was "a child taking a wild bull by the horns." The minute Manly or any other American captain was authorized to fire a gun from his deck, the greatest Navy that ever

sailed the seas would swing to, range its guns on North America and blast the coast from Maine to Savannah. Congress resorted to such arguments as it could conjure up. Think — said Maryland, South Carolina — of the effect a privateering fleet would have on the morals of American seamen! They would grow mercenary, bloodthirsty altogether. Besides, the whole thing was too expensive. "The maddest idea in the world," said Chase of Maryland. "We should mortgage the whole Continent."

John Adams was very strongly in favor of an American Navy. Now he seized the opportunity, hurled himself into the argument, pitting himself against the opposition — Chase of Maryland, Rutledge and the more conservative of the Southern men. Hour after hour as the debate continued, John jumped up, pleading, cajoling, trotting out facts, statistics from the French war when New York alone had counted four thousand men engaged in privateering. The great white-paneled room was brilliant with October sunshine; in the two fireplaces behind Hancock's desk, flames spat and crackled. Outside on Chestnut Street the morning traffic rumbled, drays and wagons going east to the wharves eight blocks away. . . . John was entirely confident in what he said. He knew Congress by now, and he knew the problem at hand. He had lived all his life among shipowners, sailors, fishermen, had tried scores of cases in the admiralty courts and was familiar at first hand with matters of shipping and navigation.

Our coast line, he pointed out, was marvelously suited to naval defense, with its creeks and bayous, its hidden harbors and treacherous tides. Moreover, American schooners, with their long, low build and raking masts, were faster than the heavy British ships. The colonies would welcome this new occupation. He could testify by actual observation that in New England whole towns of seafaring people had lost their living by the blockade. Shipowners and shipwrights, whalers and coastal traders, fishermen, navigators, sailors by the thousand would leap at such opportunity — especially if Congress proved skillful in the framing of its Navy rules, letting common seamen as well as shipowners share generously in the prizes.

Old Stephen Hopkins of Rhode Island supported John in every argument, rising ponderously and rumbling away in his slow, deep voice. In the end, Captain Manly was instructed to mount his guns, and a Naval Committee of seven appointed, with Adams and

Hopkins among them. In record time they fitted out five vessels for privateering — two brigs, two ships and a sloop. They named the first one *Alfred*, in honor of the founder of the British fleet — "the greatest Navy," John said frankly, "that ever existed." The second was *Columbus*, the third *Cabot*, for the discoverer of New England. The fifth and last, quite simply, was the *Providence*, not after heaven but because Stephen Hopkins lived there.

Hopkins's brother Ezek was appointed first Commodore. Ezek was so old that Colonel Henry Knox of Boston, who always spoke to the point, said he would have taken him for an angel, "except he swore now and then." As First Lieutenant, Congress named one John Paul Jones, a sea captain of doubtful reputation who helped fit out the *Alfred*. Lieutenant Jones bore at his masthead the new flag, a snake with thirteen rattlers from whose mouth issued the warning, *Don't tread on me.*

The Naval Committee sat down to compose a set of "Rules for the Fleet." They were shrewd enough to know these must be made inviting. Prize money was kept separate from the scale of monthly payment, and bounties were specified: The man who first sighted the enemy ship got double his prize money; the man who first boarded her got triple. Should a sailor — a "marine," Congress called the lowest rank — lose a limb during an engagement, he would receive two hundred dollars; if he were killed, his wife or children got twice that amount.

The regulations concerning food and discipline read like a poem, compared with the brutal Old Testament of British naval tradition. Rations of ordinary seamen were generous, with the usual half pint of rum per man per day and plenty of vinegar against the scurvy. A surgeon was to look after sick men; accommodations for their care were specific and almost sanitary. The moral tone was guaranteed as high, with divine services twice every day. Punishment for offenses was lenient; a wooden collar to be worn for swearing, drunken sailors to lie in irons till they sobered. Above all, no seaman was to receive, without proper court-martial, "any punishment beyond twelve lashes upon his bare back with a cat-o'-nine-tails."

America fell joyfully into the new plan. Every householder from Falmouth down who had a dory in his back yard floated her and tried to get into the race. Captain Manly himself was forever in the newssheets. In four months he managed to capture enough stores

office was conferred under the power of his Royal Seal and signature. To deny him, dethrone him, would be not only dangerous but impious.

For King and Country! It had been the battle cry since Agincourt. Washington himself still spoke of Howe's troops as "the Ministerial Soldiers." He could not bear, he said, to call them "the King's Troops." The sentiment was not confined to the ignorant and the foolish; it is hard for even the sophisticated man to tear from him the traditions of his ancestors. Henry Laurens, the South Carolina patriot, confessed that the word "independence" cut him deep; he felt "like a child being thrust violently out of his father's house." John Rutledge, foremost citizen of his state, wept openly in Congress and said he would never give up hope of a reconciliation.

These men were not Tories. Since Galloway's departure, Congress had no "traitor" in its midst. None but liberty men could possibly have been elected, now, to a Continental Congress that since Lexington had gained enormously in prestige. Led by Dickinson, the "conciliation men" had no slightest intention of knuckling under to Britain, no intention of renouncing the fight for a free representative government in America. But they still hoped, by threat or persuasion, to gain a free government not separate from the British Empire but within it. Their position had not changed since August, 1774, when Congress first met to protest the Boston Port Bill. The trouble was, Britain had not reacted according to their prophecies or their plans. The commercial blockade had failed to force Britain's hand; the use of arms had failed to force it. Parliament and King were no nearer yielding than they had been when Peyton Randolph called the first meeting to order in Carpenters' Hall.

The radical party in Congress, the "violent men," the "independence men," were led now by the two Adamses, Gadsden of South Carolina, the two Lees and George Wythe of Virginia. Washington of course was with the Army; Patrick Henry had stayed in Virginia as Colonel of militia. Jefferson, called home by illness in his family, would not return until May of '76. Their party differed from the Dickinson-Duane-Wilson faction only in having abandoned all hope of reconciliation. This was not to say they did not still desire it in their hearts. Every one of them, except perhaps Sam Adams, would have rejoiced to see America remain — on her own terms — within the British Empire. But they were realistic, knew that separation was

now inevitable — and recognized, further, that Britain would destroy the colonies altogether, rather than yield.

To this last, the conciliatory party remained blind, preferring to deceive themselves and their followers with visions of an olive branch extended across the seas. Peace commissioners were coming from London in the spring or summer, said Dickinson, Rutledge, Duane. They had positive news of it, positive promises. What folly then and what wickedness to scream separation from England! The independence men would be guilty of plunging their country in endless, tragic civil war, compared with which the few skirmishes already fought would be nothing. A wise delay of a few months might well save the situation. . . . John Adams said openly and contemptuously that he did not believe a word of this commissioner talk. "A bubble," he called it — "As arrant an illusion as ever was hatched in the brain of an enthusiast, a politician or a maniac."

For the conciliation men, John Adams had become, this January of 1776, an adversary more dangerous even than his cousin Samuel. Sam at least was opposed to a large standing Army; Sam recognized and valued local attachments, local sentiments. One had the feeling that "the Grand Incendiary" was a Massachusetts man first, an American second. But John Adams put a Continental Army and a Continental Confederated Government over and beyond all else. There was about this Braintree Adams something maddeningly obdurate. He seemed not to care how many enemies he made, and he was sure of himself and his convictions. When he rose he spoke arrogantly, let his voice ring out with a royal impatience, thumped his hickory walking stick against the floor to make his points tell. He had a way of drawing in his lips, sucking loudly against his teeth, raising his thick powerful chest as if to gather the force of a tremendous bellows and then letting fly, repeating himself inexorably, like a bell that clangs and clangs and will not be denied: "Nothing can save us but discipline in the army, governments in every colony and a confederation of the whole. . . . *Discipline in the army!* [Thump with the hickory cane.] *A written constitution in every state!* [Thump again.] *A union and a confederation of thirteen states, independent of parliament, of minister and of king!*"

The conciliation men, in despair of shutting him up, considered ways and means to discredit Adams, get him out of Congress altogether if they could. They played a sharp game, spread such politi-

cal scandal as they could invent. John Adams was an enemy to General Washington . . . he favored an annual election of a Commander in Chief . . . he would like to force free American militia into a slavish discipline like the British regulars. Under the new Provincial government, Adams had been named Chief Justice of Massachusetts . . . *that* was why he desired independence; reconciliation with Britain would lose him his high position. A Maryland delegate, after careful conference with his colleagues, put the formal motion that no man holding lucrative office under the new government could remain a member of the Continental Congress. John rose blandly with the counter-suggestion that no man holding office under either the new *or* the old government be permitted to sit in Congress.

It was a telling stroke. Every man in the conciliatory faction bore, in his home colony, some office such as Colonel of Militia, President of the Committee of Safety, Chairman of the Inspection Committee. Amusement rippled over the room as the moderates retreated, discomfited. (In Parliament, Edmund Burke had been right. American lawyers were *dexterous, prompt in attack, ready in defence, full of resources.*)

John himself took little joy in these tactical victories, though they came, now, more and more often. He had always been ambitious, yet the stake had lately grown so great it dwarfed a man's own personal hopes, obliterating for the moment both his past and his future. For these months of 1776, John was wholly lost in the cause he supported, passionately self-forgetful. Most certainly he did not see himself in any heroic role. If he made friends, they were friends to the cause of liberty. Of his enemies he was contemptuous; their ill will concerned him, personally, not at all. Merely, he had something to do and knew how to go about doing it. The lines were drawn; there existed no alternative. . . .

State governments must be instituted at once. Without these governments, two and a half million people could not conduct a continental war. Certainly they could not expect Congress to conduct it for them. And even if, by some fluke, they staved off the enemy for another six months, the colonies, lacking firm local governments, would slide into anarchy. Victories gained against the British would be lost in hopeless, dangerous quarreling at home. Ever since June of 1775, when Massachusetts petitioned Congress to institute the first independent provincial government, John had urged the necessity

of separate state constitutions. The sooner this was accomplished, the less danger there would be of "convulsions within the states." Pennsylvania at the moment was undergoing such a convulsion, tantamount to a civil war of her own. Her Provincial Assembly sat in the State House, just across the hallway from Congress. There were continual quarrels, shoutings, surging mobs outside in the State House yard, yelling for their candidates and their faction.

"From the beginning," John wrote later, "I always expected we should have more danger and difficulty from our attempts to govern ourselves than from all the fleets and armies of Europe." Everywhere, Royal Governors were on the run. Lord Dunmore had been chased out of Norfolk, Virginia, and lived on a warship, where he complained he was "reduced to the deplorable and disgraceful state of being a tame spectator of Rebellion." In New Jersey, Governor William Franklin (Dr. Franklin's illegitimate son) was about to be arrested and put under guard by the patriots. Maryland's Governor Eden, a tactful gentleman, very much liked, was allowed to remain at large. It was gratifying to be rid of these crown officers, yet their going left no government at all. Even the conciliation men admitted that some sort of provisional governments must be constructed. They were careful to stress the word "provisional."

The great question was, What form should these governments take? In Congress and out, thirteen colonies debated it. Interest was intense and penetrated to the remotest frontier households. If the war with Britain did not touch every far-flung cabin and settlement, the question of local government most certainly did touch them. They had absolutely nothing to go by; nowhere in Europe had popular government been tried on so large a scale. People were fearful of the unknown, the untried; each man looked to his own particular interest. Landowning patriots in New York and the Carolinas ("the Barons of the South," John called these last), with thousands of acres under their personal control, were naturally inclined toward a government by the aristocracy, which meant themselves. New England, on the other hand, inhabited by small traders and farmers, fishermen, storekeepers, desired governments far more democratical. Colonies, counties, even towns sent in their stated preference. Voted [wrote Ashfield, Massachusetts, population 628], *that it is our Opinniun that we do not want any Goviner but the Goviner of the Univarse,*

and under him a States Ginral to Consult with the Wrest of the
States for the good of the whole.

In Braintree, Abigail Adams found herself the center of this lively controversy. Neighbors came to her with their questions. Not only was she the wife of John Adams, delegate to the Congress, but she was a Quincy by her own right, daughter of a family important in politics since the beginning of the century. Her house was on the great highway to Plymouth; travelers up and down the coast of necessity passed by. When politicians from Philadelphia rode to Cambridge to consult with Washington, John recommended them to the hospitality of Penn's Hill or suggested that Abby ask her Uncle Norton Quincy to take her calling at headquarters on Winter Hill. Abby met everyone, from Dr. Franklin to General and Mrs. Washington. She was "struck" with General Washington, she wrote — "You had prepared me to entertain a favorable opinion of him, but I thought the one half was not told me. Dignity with ease & complacency, the Gentleman & Soldier look agreeably blended in him. Modesty marks every line & fiture of his face. Those lines of Dryden instantly accu'rd to me

> "Mark his Majestick fabrick; he's a temple
> Sacred by birth, and built by hands divine.
> His soul's the Deity that lodges there.
> Nor is the pile unworthy of the God."

Dr. Franklin, Abby went on, had invited her to come to Philadelphia and spend the rest of the winter. . . . New England ladies, she could testify, were captivated by the gallant Major Mifflin. "My compliments to his wife," said Abby. "Tell her I do not know whether her Husband is safe here. Bellona and Cupid have a contest about him." . . . General Sullivan of New Hampshire appeared a man slow to anger, but the kind that, once roused, would not be easily lulled. . . . As for the much-talked-of General Charles Lee, "that careless hardy Veteran," he had pressed her to dine with him at Hobgoblin Hall, as he called his quarters. Placing a chair before her, he had ordered his hound, "Mr. Spada, to Mount and present his paw to me for a better acquaintance . . . that, Madam, says he, is the Dog which Mr. —— has rendered famous."

In the year and a half since John's first departure for Congress, Abby, at the age of thirty-one, had come to full maturity. The demands of her position had forced her to it. She met General Washington, Dr. Franklin, as easily as she would have met the Reverend Wibird at Sunday Meeting. Her New England reserve never gave way; it never would give way, even when she was fifty and had attained great place in the world. In Abby the fires were to burn bright and high to the end, and to the end she kept tight rein upon herself. Her intelligence, her quick perception, perhaps an unconscious fear of the strength of her own passions had caused her, in her youth and young womanhood, to seek companionship in reading and in books rather than among the immediate and narrow circle about her father's strict parsonage at Weymouth. The months with her grandfather Quincy at Wollaston Hill had been her only relief and liberation.

But she had a flair for people. There was something about Abby's reserve, her prim New England bearing that to men like Dr. Franklin, General Charles Lee, was wholly delightful, a challenge as it were to their own well-tested power of charm. At home and abroad, Abigail functioned fully now, utilizing every facet of her nature. She lived in the midst of war, within frequent sound of cannon and not three miles from a broad unprotected beach, off which the British fleet could be seen riding at anchor. Supplies were extremely hard to come by, although the countryside not fifty miles away had plenty. Without medicines, Abby had brought her household through a terrible epidemic (at one time, all four children were in bed with dysentery, and the maid Patty died in the house). Abby's shoes were worn through. Could not John send her two yards of calamanco to make new ones? she wrote. The price of cotton, wool and flax had risen prohibitively; so had corn and West India molasses. There was no coffee, sugar, pepper. It was well their grain crop had been so good last year, and they had meat salted down in the smokehouse. Not a pin was to be purchased anywhere. Life without pins, Abby indicated, was more difficult than a mere man could imagine; would John please dispatch her some as soon as possible? As for making saltpeter for powder as he suggested, she would try the experiment "after soap-making."

Abigail had four children to look after, a farm to manage. The schools were closed, and John's clerk Mr. Thaxter, who had helped

THE
Manual Exercise
AS ORDERED
By His MAJESTY

(4)

(5

Words of Command.	Num. of Motions.		Words of Command.	No. of Motions.		Words of Command.	No. of Motions.	Ex
1 Poife your Firelocks!	2	1ft. S	4 Fire!	1	Pu bring tion, the M and f the F Back	10 Draw your Rammers!	2	1ft. Draw the Ram out, feizing it at the 2d. Draw it quite Muzzle.
		2d. from juft ab upon The Body, with	5 Half-Cock your Firelocks!	1	H. the F Firel	11 Ram down your Cartridge!	1	Ram the Cartridge recovering and feizing Center, turning it and Pipe, placing at the f on the Butt-End of the
2 Cock your Firelocks!	2	1ft. place fquare 2d. down, the F	6 Handle your Cartridge!	1	Br Pouc bring Top with	12 Return your Rammers!	1	Return the Ramme Left-Hand to the Sho Hand under the Cock the Swell, turning the
3 Present!	1	Ste Right the fa be br placin Finge the M	7 Prime!	1	Sh laft F	13 Shoulder your Firelocks!	2	1ft. Quit the Left the Butt. 2d. Quit the Righ Right Side.
			8 Shut your Pans!	2	1ft Arm Cartr 2d Pofiti the l behin	14 Reft your Firelocks!	3	1ft. Seize the Firel ing the Lock outward 2d. Raife the Firelo your Left-Hand with holding the Piece righ before you, and your L 3d. Step brifkly bac it a Hand's-breadth d the fame Time bring c poffible to your Reft, (Left Knee as your R Conftraint; your Left-
			9 Chargewith Cartridge!	2	1ft the M			

"Directions for Loading and Firing"

From THE MANUAL EXERCISE AS ORDERED BY HIS MAJESTY IN 1764
used by Washington at Cambridge

out the first year, had gone now to join the Army. Little Abby was eleven, John Quincy was nine. They must be tutored, kept busy. John wrote urging the education of his sons; it was never out of his mind, he said. "John Quincy has Genius, and so has Charles. Take care that they don't go astray. Cultivate their minds, inspire their little Hearts, raise their Wishes — Fix their Attention upon great and glorious Objects. Root out every little Thing. Weed out every Meanness. Make them great and manly — teach them to Scorn Injustice, Ingratitude, Cowardice and Falsehood. Let them revere nothing but Religion, Morality & Liberty."

It was a large order; this was a generation that felt no shame at speaking in high terms. Serenely, after her own fashion, Abigail instructed her children, putting young Abby through the Latin *Accidence* and *Took's French Grammar* with her brothers. John wrote doubtfully about this. If his daughter must get the *Accidence* by heart, let her keep her knowledge to herself, lest she be considered unwomanly. Young Abby's mother ignored the thrust. John had always been bored by ignorant women; Abby had not forgotten that he had first been attracted to her with a book in her hand. Nor had she forgotten John's letter after the death of her mother last fall in the epidemic. John had hinted that while Mrs. Smith had possessed an exemplary character, yet was it not possible she had been overly narrow, overly domestic in her interests? A woman should permit her talents, her virtues, to extend beyond the walls of her house. . . . Concerning his own mother too, he wrote irritably that he wished she would stop fussing about him. Philadelphia "is as secure from the Cannon & Men-of-War as the Moon is. I had rather be killed by a Ball than live in such continual Fears as she does. *I wish she had a little of your Fortitude.*"

The content of Abby's letters, as month followed month of her husband's absence, was far from being confined to the four walls of her house. Not only was she John's most vivid, detailed and reliable correspondent concerning the military moves of General Howe and the Continental Army; she was also deeply concerned with the question of local governments and the confederacy that must necessarily be assumed before long. She knew the leaders of the Provincial Congress at Watertown from James Warren down, and carried on a spirited correspondence with Mrs. Warren (James Otis's talented sister), who was gathering material for her three-volume *History of*

Massachusetts. "If we separate from Brittain," Abby wrote to John, "how shall we be governed so as to retain our Liberties? can any government be free which is not administered by general Stated Laws? Who shall frame these Laws? Who will give them force & energy—? When I consider these things, and the prejudices of people in favour of Ancient customs & Regulations, I feel anxious for the fate of our Monarchy or Democracy or what ever is to take place."

John sent her, in reply, a piece he had written for the newspapers on this very subject. He was forever answering such questions and welcomed them with all his heart, whether they came from Massachusetts or Georgia. The very asking proved that men's minds had swung round at last; at last the political compass pointed true north. The queries were elementary, fundamental; John's colleagues in Congress brought him as it were a blank sheet of paper, asked him to fill it out. He recorded some of the conversations, both question and answer:

"What plan of government, Mr. Adams, would you advise?"

"A plan as nearly resembling the government under which we were born and have lived, as the circumstances of the country will admit. Kings we never had among us. Nobles we never had. Nothing hereditary ever existed in the country; nor will the country require or admit any such thing. But governors and councils we always had, as well as representatives. A legislature in three branches ought to be preserved, and independent judges."

"Where and how will you get your governors and councils?"

"By elections."

"How — who shall elect?"

"The representatives of the people in a convention will be the best qualified to contrive a mode."

John was ready also with ideas about the confederacy. Why should he not be ready, he asked himself. The science of government had been his greatest care since the year '55. Rising in the Pennsylvania State House he told Congress that he had looked into all the confederacies of history, from the ancient Greek city-states down to the modern Swiss and Dutch models. They would not do, he said. "They appear to have been huddled up in a hurry by a few chiefs." Surely, America could contrive far better! This was not a community of slaves and illiterate peasants led by a handful of

nobles, but a nation of curiosity and enterprise. "Our people must be consulted, invited to erect the whole building with their own hands, upon the broadest foundations. Let Congress recommend to every colony that it begin at once to call conventions and set up governments under the people, who are the authority of all power."

In January of '76, the North Carolina Provincial Assembly formally instructed its delegates to "apply to Mr. John Adams for his views on the form of government they should assume *if independence be declared*." John answered by letter, explaining quite simply how to build, he said, "a government of laws and not of men." At George Wythe's request he did the same for Virginia. The essence of his plan was the separation of powers legislative, executive and judicial — the government by checks and balances which seemed best to suit the American people and which they were to retain. Step by step, yet very briefly, John wrote down how to build this government, how to elect a house, a senate, a governor, how best to administer the courts of justice. "In this way," he added at the end, "a single month is sufficient, without the least convulsion or even animosity, to accomplish a total revolution in the government of a colony."

The letter to George Wythe was longer. And from first to last, the writing of it was for John an enormous pleasure. In his mind was not only Virginia but America: thirteen sovereign states, free and united. Had he indeed been Milton describing Paradise in immortal measures, John could not have felt himself more suitably employed. Here was the task for which life had prepared him, the goal toward which he had run his race . . . learned to read and write, gone to Harvard, read Locke and Gravesande, studied law with Putnam and Gridley . . . matched himself against a Royal Governor in the Massachusetts Council Chamber. Here was the work he loved with all his heart, the work to which not only brain but very flesh and blood responded: *I know not how it is* [he said], *but mankind seem to have an aversion to the science of government. Is it because the subject is too dry? To me, no romance is more entertaining.*

Sitting at the table in his lodging-house chamber at Philadelphia, John put on record what he knew and believed, not omitting, at the end, to recommend his favorite measures. . . . Let Virginia make careful provision for "the liberal education of youth" and for the

upkeep of a militia in times of peace as well as war. . . . Such a government and such a constitution, John finished, "introduces knowledge among the people, and inspires them with a conscious dignity becoming freemen. It makes the common people brave and enterprising, causes good humor, sociability, good manners and good morals. Compare such a country with the regions of domination, whether monarchichal or aristocratical, and you will fancy yourself in Arcadia or Elysium."

It was done. John pushed away the paper. He hoped George Wythe would approve what he had said. Wythe was an admirable man, a lawyer, brilliant, warmhearted; John had learned to like him this winter, as well as he liked any man in Congress. He reached again for the pen. "You and I, my dear friend," he wrote, "have been sent into life at a time when the greatest lawgivers of antiquity would have wished to live. How few of the human race have ever enjoyed an opportunity of making an election of government for themselves or their children! When, before the present epocha, had three millions of people full power and a fair opportunity to form and establish the wisest and happiest government that human wisdom can contrive?"

The letter to Wythe was published under the title, "Thoughts on Government." It circulated rapidly. Other colonies read it and begged advice on their own projected constitutions. There was no doubt the business was progressing. Yet the people continued hesitant, fearful. The radical leaders themselves were not fully aware of what it was that kept the body of their supporters from coming out openly for independence. To perceive it, interpret it, above all to give it voice, required not a statesman but an artist. And in the very nick of time, the very hour and second of indecision, the artist appeared. Not an American but a stranger from England; Dr. Franklin had discovered him and sent him to Philadelphia: Thomas Paine the corset maker, tobacconist, dismissed exciseman, schoolteacher, journalist. Tom Paine of London, a poor man, caring little for debts and less for credit, separated from his wife, without roots, without anchor. Sensitive, intelligent, wholly original, bowing to no man's intellectual command. Tom Paine, lover of freedom, sailed for America late in the year '74, and found his promised land.

Here in virgin territory, men could invent what form of govern-

ment, what frame of living they chose. At their fingers' ends lay freedom, yet they would not reach to grasp it but hesitated, fearful. "I came to America a few months before the outbreak of hostilities," Paine wrote. "I found the disposition of the people such that they might have been led by a thread, and governed by a reed." Thirteen months after his arrival, this defrocked Englishman, who General Charles Lee declared had "genius in his eyes," wrote a pamphlet called *Common Sense*, put it out for two shillings, unsigned — and in a month had become America's prophet.

Common Sense had forty-seven pages, which Paine offered disarmingly as "nothing more than simple facts, plain arguments and common sense." The pamphlet started off by demolishing kings everywhere, past, present and future, and it stopped at neither fact nor fantasy. Paine took hold of history and used it as he saw fit, proving his points cannily by the Old Testament. (Later he confessed to John that he had got his Old Testament out of Milton.) A pious America was pleased to learn that monarchy, far from being blessed, ranked in Scripture as "one of the sins of the Jews, for which a curse in reserve is denounced against them." This divine malediction took in also, Paine added confidently, the Kings of Israel, the Midianites, the Gideonites, the House of Samuel, Mahomet, and thence, by smooth historical transfer, George III of England. Trace any royal line to its origin, said *Common Sense* contemptuously, and the first king would be seen as "nothing better than the principal ruffian of some restless gang, whose savage manners obtained him the title of chief among plunderers."

And where, Paine demanded, was the King of America to be found? With the ruthless divination of the artist, Paine measured his audience and gave answer: "I'll tell you, friends, he reigns above, and doth not make havoc of mankind like the royal brute of Britain."

The royal brute . . . America gasped as a man gasps who hears his father damned and knows the curse is in his own heart. But Paine did not stop at bombast, fustian and cursing. For him, independence carried a significance beyond mere political boundaries: *The sun never shone on a cause of greater worth. 'Tis not the affair of a city, a country, a province or a kingdom, but of a continent — of at least one eighth part of the habitable globe. Now is the seed-time of continental union, faith and honor. A new method of thinking has arisen. All plans and proposals prior to the nineteenth of*

April * *are like the almanacs of last year. Time hath found us. Time* *hath found us! O! ye that love mankind, stand forth. Freedom hath* *been hunted round the globe. Europe regards her like a stranger.* *England hath given her warning to depart. Ye that dare oppose not* *only the tyranny but the tyrant, stand forth! O! receive the fugitive,* *and prepare in time an asylum for mankind.*

On the last page and the last paragraph, seven words stood out in large black print: THE FREE AND INDEPENDENT STATES OF AMERICA.

In three months the pamphlet sold 120,000 copies — for which the author received not one cent of profit and was even billed thirty pounds by the printer for presentation copies. COMMON SENSE *for* *Eighteen Pence:* John Adams saw it in the shop windows along Market Street. (The Tories called it *Common Nonsense.*) John sent a copy home to Abigail. Characteristically, he looked on it with caution. As a method of awakening the people, such writing was excellent. But Paine had not stopped at inspiration. He had devoted one entire section to outlining actual forms of government for the American Union to pursue — and to John, the forms chosen were anathema. Paine desired a one-chamber Legislature, without Senate or upper house, with no separation of powers executive, judicial and legislative. John did not believe in a government unrestrainedly "popular" any more than he believed in unlimited monarchy. He had seen the mob at work and knew the people were not immune to the temptations of power. Checks and balances were needed; man himself must restrain man's greed.

It was a subject on which Abigail bore him out. For a woman so frank and so religious, she was surprisingly cynical concerning the original goodness of mankind. Perhaps it stemmed from her Calvinist upbringing, perhaps from the observations of her thirty-one years. "I am more & more convinced," she wrote, "that Man is a dangerous creature. & that power whether vested in many or a few is ever grasping &, like the grave cries give, give, The great fish Swallow up the Small, and he who is most strenuous for the Rights of the people, when vested with power, is as eager after the prerogatives of Government."

John wrote back that Thomas Paine, to his mind, had "a better

* Lexington.

Hand at pulling down than building — It has been very generally propagated through the Continent that I wrote this Pamphlet. — But although I could not have written any Thing in so manly and Striking a Style, I flatter myself I should have made a more respectable Figure as an Architect."

General William Howe, youngest of the "three brave and silent brothers," sat sullenly in Boston with his seven thousand troops. "We cannot get at them," complained General Greene from Washington's headquarters, "and they are determined not to come to us." Howe was, actually, in a far from enviable position. His army was cold, hungry, sick with scurvy on a diet of salt pork, maggoty Irish beef and weevily biscuits. All his supplies came in by sea. Out of forty transports from England, only eight reached harbor that winter. The rest were either blown off to the West Indies by the prevailing northwest winds or taken by the American Navy. The face of Boston was changed. Along the Common, Paddock's elms were nearly gone, cut down for fuel. Liberty Tree itself had given fourteen cords. The North Meeting-house had been wrecked for firewood; Howe had converted the Old South church into a riding school for cavalry and set up a grog shop in the gallery. Faneuil Hall was a theater where British officers, idle, bored almost to sickness, forlornly gave plays to which Tory society flocked, eager to laugh at caricatures of General Washington and his motley army. "England seems to have forgotten us," one officer wrote home despondently, "and we endeavor to forget ourselves."

General Washington was frantic with impatience. In mid-January, some alchemy of history or of men's souls caused the tide to turn; the veterans who had left him in December returned by the thousands to camp, bringing with them new recruits. Only lack of ammunition kept the General from attacking.

In February, the longed-for ammunition appeared. Like a messenger from heaven, Colonel Henry Knox the Boston bookseller appeared one day with more than fifty cannon, mortars and howitzers, dragged by sled through two hundred miles of thickly forested wilderness over the mountains from Ticonderoga and Crown Point. Ten fresh New England regiments marched in to join the line. Washington determined to wait no longer. The British still held

Bunker Hill. But if he could command Dorchester Heights — two hills overlooking the Harbor — his new guns could cover the ships and landing parties as they approached.

Monday, March 4, was fixed as the night to occupy the Heights. On Saturday, Washington opened a cannonade, to cover his movements and confuse the enemy. For two days and nights the guns roared. In Braintree, Abigail Adams heard them; they shook her house, rattled the windows. At night she climbed Penn's Hill with her neighbors and stood looking across the Bay. Against the starry sky they could see every shell that was thrown. "The British Ships are all drawn round the Town," she wrote. "To night We shall realize a more terrible Scene still. I some-times think I cannot stand it. . . . *The Lord reigneth. He can restrain the hand of Man.*"

Monday night was clear and mild. With pickaxe and shovel, two thousand men advanced in silence up Dorchester Heights, dug trenches in ground frozen eighteen inches deep, then drove their stakes for breastworks. It was bright moonlight but a mist lay below the hills, covering operations; a northeast wind carried the sound of the picks inland between the boom of cannon. To the westward below the hill, wagoners loaded heavy guns, urging their oxen in low tones, not daring to use the long whips which cracked like gunshot. By ten that night, two forts were ready. At three in the morning the troops took their position. As the sun rose, Washington walked the lines among his men. "This is the Fifth of March," he said. "New England men, remember the day!"

Massacre Day! The men sent up a cheer. General Howe in his headquarters saw the forts and could not believe his eyes. "The rebels have done more work in one night," he said, "than my whole army could have done in months." He put his forces in motion; Lord Percy's troops marched to the wharves. From their breastworks the Continental Army watched the enemy embark, knew that when the ships moved up the river to make a landing, the attack would start.

The morning wore on and the afternoon. The hills and rooftops were alive with spectators, awaiting battle. But with the ebb tide they saw the British transports drift down the Bay to Castle Island, towing their battery. At sundown the wind rose, bringing rain, blowing in hard from the northeast. All night the storm increased, roaring above the cannon, driving against the windows where Abi-

gail Adams lay in bed with her youngest child. The surf rose, pounding the long shoreline. On their hillside the Continental Army heard it and rejoiced. The enemy fleet was helpless; should they leave their anchorage they would be blown ashore. Already three vessels lay grounded ignominiously on Governor's Island. New England soldiers who had fought at Louisburg, veterans who had been young when D'Anville's fleet was sunk off Nova Scotia in the storm of '46, remembered, marveling devoutly in their hearts. *The Lord caused the wind to blow, and they were scattered. If God be for us, who can be against us?*

After three days the storm cleared. Below in the Harbor and the Bay, Washington saw scores of British warships, frigates, transports, shift and maneuver, changing anchorage. Boats went to and fro from the wharves, laden with men and equipment. General Howe with his army was preparing to evacuate Boston.

On the seventeenth of March, the British fleet sailed out of harbor. From her grandfather Quincy's house above Wollaston Beach, Abigail Adams saw it go. One hundred and seventy sail — she counted them, moving and darting over the blue water, sloop and transport, frigate and cutter. Why was Howe leaving, people asked in bewilderment. Where was he going? To Philadelphia, to drive out the Congress? Was Boston not worth keeping, then? Abigail felt "positively deflated," she wrote. It would be wonderful to have the Province free of the enemy, wonderful to be delivered from continual threat, the terrible sound of cannonade. Their own house on Queen Street was probably demolished by now, but Abby cared not at all. Nevertheless she could not share the general elation. The burden was only being transferred to some other point, to other shoulders, "perhaps less willing to support it."

As Howe's fleet fell below the lighthouse, old Josiah Quincy stood with Abby, gazing out the window, his crossed eyes narrowed in a look that was not triumph. *Once he had had three sons*, he told himself. Two of them had loved their country — and were dead. Samuel, a traitor, died for his father the day he boarded ship and fled America. "I take a long farewell," Sam Quincy's sister Hannah had written him in bitterness and grief. "Let it not be published that a brother of such brothers fled from his country. Can you expect to walk uprightly now? Can you take fire in your bosom and not be burned?"

A thousand Boston Tories were sailing with Howe. The first of

the great migrations. A thousand bewildered civilians, crowded ignominiously in the holds, men who had lived with dignity and ease. How many, since the year '74, had gone this way! Thomas Hutchinson, Governor of Massachusetts, the most beloved, the most hated citizen the Province ever bred. Peter Oliver, the arrogant, the stubborn, the learned, doomed to live despised in a land he tried to call "home." *Chief Justice of Massachusetts,* hunted from Oliver Hall by night, fleeing on horseback through country lanes to his ship — the furnishings, the possessions of a lifetime reduced to the contents of two saddlebags.

Standing with her cousin, Abby said over the names silently: Sam Quincy, Jonathan Sewall. Friends of her youth . . . Sam Quincy had stood before the judges with John, their two hands on the Bible while they swore the attorney's oath: *To use ourselves with all good fidelity. . . .* The words were cold now upon the tongue. Jonathan Sewall, fled to England a full year ago. Jonathan the courteous, the debonair, with his sleeve ruffles and his pleasant, intimate voice. How gay they had been all three, that summer evening in the garden at Queen Street, dining in the shade of the pear tree! The scene came back to Abby, warm, poignant. . . . "Has your husband told you, Madam, how handsome you are in that rose-colored gown?" . . . John had truly loved this man. *He always called me John and I him Jonathan, and I often said to him, I wish my name were David.*

The ships wheeled, heading seaward through the green islands. Almost unconsciously, Abby raised an arm in farewell. Colonel Josiah laid a hand on hers, interrupting the gesture. "My dear," he said gently, "traitors merit no salute."

As the British fleet dropped below the horizon, General Artemas Ward, with fifteen hundred men, unbarred the gates on Boston Neck and marched in with the new Union flag flying. To show its gratitude, Harvard gave General Washington a degree;[1] at John's suggestion, Congress had a medal struck in his honor. The General asked Dr. Eliot, senior minister of Boston, for a sermon not of war but of thanksgiving, and the old man took his text from Isaiah: *Look upon Zion, the city of our solemnities: thine eyes shall see Jerusalem a quiet habitation, a tabernacle that shall not be taken down.*

And while America gave thanks, the British ministry, humiliated,

tried to pass off the evacuation of Boston as a fortunate maneuver, a master stroke of General Howe's. No one was deceived. Stocks fell, and even Lord North was heard to remark that he wished the time had come for him to be abused for having made a disgraceful peace with America. London newspapers were filled with angry questions: Who had brought His Majesty's Army into a place from which it was a triumph to escape? And if Boston was not worth defending, why had the troops stayed there nearly two years? Why had so much brave blood been shed at Bunker Hill?

In America the war moved away to the southward, left New England forever. The next campaigns would be in New York and Pennsylvania — of all colonies the most preponderantly Tory. (John Adams said later that New York and Pennsylvania would have joined the British if they had not been kept in awe by New England on the one side and Virginia on the other.) General Washington, moving through Connecticut on muddy April roads with his army, was well.aware of what he faced. Last June on the march northward his troops had been greeted in New York by cheering crowds — which later that same day celebrated with equal fervor the return from England of their Royal Governor, William Tryon.

Howe had been driven from Boston; America applauded its brave Commander in Chief. But it would be many, many months before Congress saw fit to strike another medal in his honor. Ahead lay White Plains, Brandywine and Valley Forge. . . . New York occupied by the enemy, Philadelphia occupied . . . Congress driven to Lancaster, to Baltimore. Ahead lay five years of war.

CHAPTER THIRTY-ONE

"*Every Day rolls in upon Us Independence like a Torrent.*"

MAY first, 1776. . . . Philadelphia saluted the spring in immemorial fashion. From Canada to Charleston there was war or the threat of war. But along Chestnut Street, Market Street and Second Street, May Poles flaunted their gay decorations before the shops — green branches wreathed in dogwood and cherry blossom, hyacinth, tulips red and butter-yellow. John Adams, walking to Congress, saw them. May Poling was a heathen custom certainly, long ago outlawed in New England. But heathen customs were pleasant, and a man's heart needed lifting, these days. "My Mind is overborne with Burdens," John wrote to Warren at the Massachusetts Legislature. "Cares come from Boston, from Canada, from twelve other Colonies, from innumerable Indian Tribes, from all Parts of Europe and the West Indies. Cares arise in this City and Cares spring from Colleagues — Cares enough! It would be some comfort to be pitied; but — Avaunt ye Demons!"

John had never been so busy. There were days when he worked from seven in the morning until midnight, and always in company, in committee or caucus or on the floor of Congress, conferring, planning, trying to reconcile the factions, bring Congress a step nearer to the goal. Emerging from the State House at noon for brief respite or walking a few blocks to club or tavern for a meeting with the Southern delegates, it was good to feel the warm sun, the air drifting soft and languid from Delaware Bay. Already the painted awnings were out on the big houses, and in city gardens, workmen

in striped ticken breeches trimmed the pleached alleys, pruned the arbors and set fountains going. Over brick walls the breath of lilac came dizzily sweet. How quick and how startling, John thought, were the seasons, here in this southern latitude! At home, spring did not assault a man all unprepared, while he walked in his thick woolen clothes, still armored and angry against the cold. At home the sharp salt air was a filter to this rich breath of hyacinth and lilac; New England birch buds swelled slowly against their winter background of somber evergreen and spruce. Here, spring came rushing all uninvited — riotous, loud, overwhelming, lush.

From dawn to dark the world was on the streets. Boys, carrying their masters' square wig boxes to the barbers, loitered in the shade, and out by the Northern Liberties there was cockfighting in the open air. Women stood before their doors in morning gowns of flowered chintz, walked out at noon with their cheeks tantalizingly hidden under great scooped horsehair bonnets. Around the public water pumps every block or so, petticoated serving maids lingered with their pitchers, giggling and gossiping, pretending not to notice the sailors who swaggered by three abreast, their glazed black hats tilted jauntily, faces ruddy with long voyaging. Gentlemen's coaches rattled by on the cobbles, new-varnished, harness gleaming with oil and polished silver mountings.

Walking to the State House in the mornings or home to his lodgings at Mrs. Yard's in the afternoon, John found himself a pleasing center of attention along Chestnut Street. Three times to a block, he was greeted by name. . . . "A fine day, Mr. Adams!" . . . John lifted his three-cornered hat, balanced his hickory cane jauntily on his left arm, bowed gallantly if it was a lady, solemnly if an elder senator. The barber on Second Street where John went to be shaved, had a swarming family of small sons, one of whom happened to bear the name of Johnny. His hair was flaming red, he was definitely bow-legged and he no more resembled John Quincy than he resembled Saint Nicholas. But the sight of him made John homesick and his hand went to his pocket — a gesture he would not have dreamed of making for his own son. The barber remarked briskly that the name of Johnny was a capital investment these days around Philadelphia.

When he had half an hour, John went searching for gifts to take home to his four children, finally wrote Abby in despair that he had

"walked over this City twenty Times, and gaped at every Shop like a Countryman to find some Thing, but could not. Ask every one of the Children what they would chose to have, and write it me in your next Letter." He sent a large canister of the best green tea to his wife, only to learn later that the messenger had delivered it by mistake to Mrs. *Samuel* Adams. "It was amazingly dear," John wrote indignantly. "Nothing less than 40ˢ lawfull money, a Pound. You must send a Card to Mrs. S. A., and let her know it was intended for You."

If Abigail were only in Philadelphia, John thought often and longingly — if she would bring the family and set up housekeeping, they could live pleasantly enough in this city. "I should be proud and happy as a Bridegroom," he wrote. Since August of '74, John had spent most of his time either in Philadelphia or getting himself eternally up and down from Braintree; seven times, he had made the trip. There was little prospect of release; he might remain here indefinitely. He had seen at least three houses that would do nicely to rent. One, on Arch Street, had a garden behind it with two pear trees. It reminded him of their own Boston house, and there was space to grow a few vegetables. Massachusetts paid its delegates no salary, nor did Congress. But they paid expenses, and with wise economy Abby could surely maintain the family at what it now cost to board himself and servant and make the long journeys back and forth with a pair of horses. Many delegates already had their wives with them. Hancock had lately brought his bride, Mistress Dorothy Quincy; they lived in the lodging house with John. It made him ragingly jealous. Madam Dorothy bore herself discreetly among the crowd of men, John observed. Yet she did not shine as Somebody he knew would shine, Somebody whose perceptions were keener than those of any woman he had ever met.

Abigail responded warmly to these invitations — and refused them adamantly, as she knew her husband in his heart expected her to do. She cared little for Shining; moreover it was essential she remain on the farm, raise food for the family, care for the cattle and look after their property. She would be idle in Philadelphia. How would she occupy herself? she asked — Her nature was not formed for levees and routs, those evening assemblies which even in time of war, Philadelphia ladies seemed to enjoy. John accepted her decision with a sigh. It was foolish, he knew, to compare their situation with the

Hancocks' or the Washingtons', who had set up connubial house-holds in the midst of war. These men had fortunes behind them. Hancock must by now have stored away a goodly portion of his estate in a place where it would be available in spite of the hazards of revolution. There were ways to manage such matters; Hancock had skilled advisers in the ancestral countinghouse. Whereas the Adamses, apart from two small cottages and some seventy acres of hard-worked farmland, possessed almost nothing. The Boston house still stood, it was true, having survived the occupation. But it brought no income. Their cash savings, John thought worriedly, must by now have dwindled to disappearance, and prices were soaring.

John tried his best not to think about money. But he could not help it. Anxiety dogged him, pursued and caught him at the most unlikely moments — when he sat in the State House chamber, when he walked to the tavern to eat dinner with his little club of delegates. Since the year '74, John had not made a penny. Deliberately, he had used all his influence to close the royal courts of law in Massachusetts; deliberately therefore he had done himself and his family out of a living. No matter when or how a separation from Britain were declared — or even if it were not declared at all — John was convinced the country was involved in a long and bitter war, though in Congress many thought otherwise.

Since January, since April indeed, the picture had changed. Defeat of the Continental forces in Canada was a shocking blow. Moreover the sending of an expedition against Quebec advertised to the world that the American colonies were no longer merely on the defensive but engaged in aggressive war on every front. Much depended now on the attitude of France. Suppose that powerful and traditional enemy decided to use this civil quarrel to her own advantage, turn against America as well as Britain, and in the end devour the Western World as she had tried to do before?

The possibilities of disaster were limitless. And the more a man knew of history, the more awful became the hazard. In John's mind the worst that could happen would be to see the revolution fail here at home, and the colonies defeated by their own greed and stubbornness. The patriots, so-called, had by no means shown themselves always ready to sacrifice the private in the public interest. Property, John wrote sorrowfully this spring, was still "the standard of Respect. I have seen all along my Life Such Selfishness and Littleness

even in New England, that I sometimes tremble to think that, altho We are engaged in the best Cause that ever employed the Human Heart yet the Prospect of Success is doubtful not for Want of Power or of Wisdom but of Virtue."

Suppose the war dragged on for five years, ten years, fifteen? There was no calculating it. John told himself his children would grow up penniless, obscure — and this by his own choice as it were: there had been scarcely a week since the year '65 when he had not been active on the side of revolution. His sons possessed, it was true, a mother who was not only intelligent but literate. With Mercy Warren — James Warren's wife — Abigail was one of the two women of John's acquaintance who were at the same time well read in the English classics and knew politics and the true state of the country as well as or better than most men.

But in a year or two, John Quincy and Charles would be grown beyond their mother's capacity to teach. They would need the Latin School, then Harvard College. What, John thought, would he himself have been without his university training? It had changed his life, determined his future. John Quincy, at nine, displayed not only a mind extraordinarily quick but a spirit ardent, eager and already passionately patriotic. John had attributed this to a boy's natural loyalty to his father, a boy's predilection for guns, targets, soldiers. But his son's letters, here in Philadelphia, had a tone of high and touching seriousness. "Johnny writes like a Hero," his father told Abby. Such a nature was not to be trifled with; it could be made or ruined according to the latitude allowed it. Suppose John Quincy decided to be a lawyer? It was a father's part to give such a son opportunities he himself had never enjoyed. John Quincy must study in London at the Inns of Court, see the civilizations of Europe, not be condemned forever to the narrow life of a small country farmer. It was not the hardness, the austerity of such a life that would wound and disappoint, John told himself often. It was the constriction of outlook, the rigid, terrible denial of opportunity.

John turned the thing over and over in his mind. Should the war be lost and the revolution as well, would his sons one day reproach him? Would they praise his patriotism or blame him bitterly? John could not think of it without the sweat starting on his brow. He tried to write his feelings to Abigail, but the words conveyed not a tenth of his agony: "I will not bear the Reproaches of my Chil-

dren. — I will tell them that I studied and laboured to procure a free Constitution of Government for them to Solace themselves under, and if they do not prefer this to ample Fortune, to Ease and Elegance, they are not my Children, and I care not what becomes of them — They shall live upon thin Diet, wear mean Clothes, & work hard, with cheerful Hearts and free Spirits or they may be the Children of the Earth or of no one, for me."

As war spread down the coast and the threat grew total, it became apparent even to the Tories that the character of Congress had changed. From a temporary convention which, on adjournment, voted to meet again in six months "should the situation demand," Congress had become a permanent body of State Representatives, with self-appointed powers to coin money, make loans, raise and equip an Army and a Navy. In April of '76, Congress lifted the Continental blockade, which quite obviously had failed of its purpose. American ships flung themselves blithely across the seas, trading where they could, fishing where they could and fighting when a likely prize loomed toward them over the horizon. Congress, to the world outside, appeared a united body. Because the vote was counted by colonies not delegates, there was little public conception of how sharp a difference actually existed between the members. To Dickinson, Robert Morris, James Wilson of Philadelphia, to Duane and Jay of New York, to the brothers Rutledge of South Carolina, "independence" was still a word of frightful mien, separation from England a thought deplorable — more and more threatening, it was true, but to be avoided if the brain and ingenuity of man could possibly avoid it.

With dismay the moderates saw the word "independence" bandied about freely in street, tavern and club. Since Tom Paine's pamphlet, the King's Prohibitory Act, Howe's evacuation of Boston, independence seemed to have lost its terrors. Radical newspapers, radical provincial orators discussed separation from Britain as if it were a problem merely of *when*, rather than a wholly unsolved and undecided question for gravest debate. Consider, said Dickinson, the effect such a declaration might have on Europe! From Versailles to St. Petersburg, every court, every potentate, followed move by move this quarrel within the British body politic. Russia, for instance . . . No one knew if the Empress Catherine planned to sell mercenaries

to England after the Hessian fashion or if she might by chance be induced to come to America's aid. And what of Spain — would she too view this break-up of the British Empire as a rich opportunity for plunder?

It was imperative that America borrow money somewhere, somehow, to finance the war. Perversely enough, France, the ancient enemy, was the likeliest candidate, for the simple reason that helping America was the quickest way to strike at England. Most certainly it would be well worth trying for a French loan, or at the least a commercial treaty. The question was, would Louis XVI prefer to assist rebellious British subjects, or, frankly and completely, a confederacy of self-sustaining states — in short, a free American republic?

John Adams's party in Congress, convinced that reconciliation was a lost cause and independence inevitable, thought the fact might best be advertised immediately. To Dickinson on the other hand, such a course was the height of folly. The word "republic" would instantly and irrevocably antagonize every monarch of Europe. Louis XVI was young, not yet twenty-two. Comparatively little was known about him. American radicals said they hoped he had a mind less prejudiced than his grandfather. . . . Prejudiced or no, Dickinson countered passionately, how could Louis XVI, Catherine of Russia, think it to their advantage to support a self-avowed government of three million people who had thrown off the authority of a crown? Why, these monarchs would feel their thrones tremble beneath them! Worse still, they might simply laugh at the notion of a free America, declaring — and with reason — that a few military victories would be the best proof of America's independence.

Silas Deane of Connecticut was at the very moment in Paris, sounding out Vergennes, the French minister. Congress had sent him secretly, last February. . . . Do nothing therefore, the moderates urged, until Deane's return. Above all, do not publish a defiant, bombastic declaration of independence.

The *Cool Considerate Men*, the moderates were called now, outside the State House. Their party still comprised some of the best minds in Congress, excellently trained in the law. Dickinson and both Rutledges had studied in London at the famous Inns of Court. James Wilson was educated at Glasgow and Edinburgh universities. Not

all the conservatives gave the same arguments against independence. Duane, Dickinson and Robert Morris the merchant led the bitter-enders, the men who continued dead set against separation at any time and under any guise. Their conviction seemed to spring from their very nature. The Rutledges on the other hand were radical by disposition, eager to see South Carolina set up its own independent government. Yet they were entirely certain that separation from Britain would cause serious division among the colonies, lose thousands of partisans for the liberty side. John Jay of New York 'and his law partner, Livingston, were fearful that total separation, total revolution, would result in mob rule and "democracy." Jay, more concerned at the moment with his own colony than with Congress, went home to help build the New York government. John Rutledge was in South Carolina on like business; so was the radical Christopher Gadsden. They might be gone for months.

The moderates had gained, this spring, a somewhat doubtful partisan in Carter Braxton of Virginia, sent to Congress in place of Peyton Randolph, who had died of an apoplexy. Braxton, an aristocrat to his small-boned, beruffled wrists, was an important landholder; he represented an element still very influential among the liberty party in his state. America, Braxton argued, was in too defenseless a condition to declare a separation from Britain. "A delusive Bait," Braxton called independence, "which men inconsiderately catch at, without knowing the hook to which it is affixed."

What exactly was the reason, the *Cool Considerate Men* demanded, why a declaration should be published at all? Wars can be waged without advertisement, public self-justification. Was it not suicidal to close all doors to reconciliation? Peace commissioners were certainly coming. In Admiral Howe's fleet, sailing now from England, the troop transports bore names significantly pacific: the *Father's Goodwill*, the *Felicity*, the *Amity's Admonition*, the *Three Sisters*, the *Friendship*, the *Good Intent*. Did that sound like an enemy Navy? Most certainly, commissioners would be on board one of the ships.

Nothing vexed John more than this talk of peace commissioners —"coming," he reported, reckless with his French, "to treat with Congress and to offer a Chart blanc. Their real Errand is an Insult. But popular Passions and Fancies will have their Course, you may as well reason down a Gale of Wind." Britain, John insisted, was

behaving like the farmer who, to catch a skittish colt, crosses the pasture holding out an empty hat. He had done it himself enough times to know, John told his colleagues irritably. His own position concerning separation from England was perfectly plain: Independence was inevitable. One thing alone held it back, and *should* hold it back. A hundred times, John had said it: Thirteen colonies must first construct their own thirteen independent, self-sufficient governments. Then and then only would they be able to conduct a war, seek foreign alliances, form a confederation and declare to the world that America was a republic, separate from Britain, free from Britain now and forevermore.

John had spent the past year — the past five years he told himself sometimes — trying to teach thirteen colonies how to create governments of their own. In large measure he had succeeded: one by one the states were proclaiming their desire to proceed with such a plan. South Carolina was the latest; in April she had set up law courts, elected her new Assembly and Council, named John Rutledge President, Henry Laurens Vice President and the radical Henry Drayton Chief Justice. The moment he heard of it, John reported home to Warren, who himself was about to be elected Speaker of the new Massachusetts House of Representatives. "If North Carolina[1] and Virginia should follow South Carolina's Example," John wrote, "it will spread through all the rest of the Colonies like Electric Fire. We are advancing by slow but sure Steps, to that mighty Revolution, which You and I have expected for Some Time."

In the various colonies, the governments were forming; under the old royal regime, annual elections had usually come in May and June. With closest attention, John watched for the results. Congress could make no serious move now, without sanction from its constituents. Not in Philadelphia but at home must the question of independent governments — and of independence — be decided. The Tory contention that Congress was only a minority representation remained valid of course; the country was still two thirds loyalist. Yet the Tories played of necessity an inactive, waiting role; few of them joined the British Army. Whereas the liberty party, small though it was in nearly every colony, showed itself constantly, consistently vocal. Moreover, it had behind it now three armies. The

first, under Washington, was in New York awaiting the British fleet. The second was being organized in Virginia and North Carolina by General Charles Lee. The third, under Generals Schuyler and Gates, was busy preparing a second invasion of Canada.

These three armies comprised, altogether, about thirty thousand men, every one of them radical. Their influence was enormous, incalculable. Each time a new company of fifty volunteers marched out of their home town, an equal company of citizens swung over to the liberty banner. In some colonies the militant minority was so strong it went far ahead of Congress.

Observing the state elections in May of '76, John found himself one day hopeful, the next day wildly exasperated. How slow the Middle colonies were! New York, Pennsylvania, New Jersey, could not make up their collective minds. Maryland in particular, John reported home, was "so eccentric a Colony — sometimes so hot, sometimes so cold; now so high, then so low — that I know not what to say about it or to expect from it. I have often wished it could exchange Places with Hallifax. When they get agoing I expect some wild extravagant Flight or other."

Yet if matters were unduly pushed, if some local Cassius maneuvered an Assembly against its will, in the end the business would collapse, fall through. The people must desire independence; they could not be driven to it. John had not forgotten his early political training, his father's admonitions and above all his father's invariable success with Braintree politics. . . . *Move slowly, John. Move slowly! A township is not to be pushed and shoved like a private person.*

Strange, John thought, how his father's words, even his father's tone, came back to him . . . strong, patient, with the flavor of a beneficent resignation John knew in his heart he would never achieve. If Deacon Adams were alive today, what would he think, what would he say? John was not at all sure the old man would have come along so far and wide on the road to independence.

It was necessary to keep in constant touch, now, with Massachusetts. John heard often from Francis Dana, member of the new Council or upper house, from William Cushing, one of the new judges. James Warren wrote that the Massachusetts elections were progressing nicely. They had encountered a little trouble with the Salem

members, and sent them home from the Legislature when it evolved they had been elected by a count of "corn Kernels and Pease in a Hatt" — a procedure unfitting the dignity of a great state.

Reading of it, John laughed aloud, then swore with vexation. Let Salem elect by a count of dead codfish if they pleased, but in God's name let them get on with the business of government! If states favorable to independence were so slow, how could thirteen governments be formed before the British fleet arrived and war broke in full earnest along fifteen hundred miles of coast? The time was growing short, the hour brief. Congress could not forever wait upon Instructions from thirteen governments in a state of flux, no matter how well disposed such governments might profess to be.

After earnest consultation, the radicals determined to attempt a bold stroke — nothing less than the presentation of a formal motion that all thirteen colonies abandon the Instruction procedure and free their delegates at Philadelphia for immediate, self-determined action. John himself wrote out the Resolve . . . Let the various colonial Assemblies give Congress full powers *to concert, direct and order such further measures as may seem necessary for the defence and preservation, support and establishment of right and liberty in these Colonies.*

On May sixth the resolution was proposed in Congress — and suffered instant defeat. It was too dangerous, all-embracing. The moderates saw it not only as an entering wedge to the creation of radical independent governments, but as a door to independence itself. John and his friends were not surprised at the reaction. They rewrote the measure, narrowed it to one objective and proposed it again:

RESOLVED, *That it be recommended to the respective Assemblies and Conventions of the United Colonies, where no government sufficient to the exigencies of their affairs have hitherto been established, to adopt such governments as shall, in the opinion of the representatives of the people, best conduce to the happiness and safety of their constituents in particular, and America in general.*

After two days of violent debate, the resolution passed. A committee of three was named to prepare a Preamble. *The members chosen* [the *Minutes* recorded], *Mr. J Adams, Mr. Rutledge, Mr. R H Lee.*

Only the most solemn and significant measures called for a preamble, which was a sort of preface to explain and justify the text.

Not a man in Congress underestimated the importance of this particular Resolve. The moderates still hoped to defeat it by voting against
the preamble when it should be presented, thereby reopening the
entire question and debate. The other two members of the committee, recognizing that *Mr. J Adams,* more than any man in Congress, had been behind this move to establish separate governments,
gave John what he might have called a *Chart blanc* to compose the
Preamble. They cautioned him to be brief; one paragraph would do.

John wrote his paragraph, dignified but very definite. Thus far,
Congress, in its published recitations of grievance, had aimed their
indictment always at Parliament and the British ministry, under
the stubborn assumption that George III was an innocent tool of
"wicked counsellors" — and also to avoid the charge of treason. But
that time was past; John's opening words were a blast at *George
Rex* himself:

WHEREAS *his Britannic Majesty, in conjunction with the lords and
commons of Great Britain, has, by a late act of Parliament, excluded
the inhabitants of these United Colonies from the protection of his
crown; And whereas, no answer, whatever, to the humble petitions
of the colonies for redress of grievances and reconciliation with
Great Britain, has been or is likely to be given; but, the whole force
of that kingdom, aided by foreign mercenaries, is to be exerted for
the destruction of the good people of these colonies; And whereas,
it appears absolutely irreconcileable to reason and good Conscience,
for the people of these colonies now to take the oaths and affirma-
tions necessary for the support of any government under the crown
of Great Britain, and it is necessary that the exercise of every kind
of authority under the said crown should be totally suppressed, and
all the powers of government exerted, under the authority of the
people of the colonies, for the preservation of internal peace, virtue,
and good order, as well as for the defence of their lives, liberties, and
properties, against the hostile invasions and cruel depredations of
their enemies . . .*

When the whole was ready, John rose in Congress, Preamble and
Resolve in hand. It was the fifteenth of May, a Wednesday. John
got through the first sentences and arrived at *the hostile invasions
and cruel depredations of their enemies,* when he became aware that
Duane of New York had risen to his feet, a row or two in front. The

moment John's voice ceased, words began to pour from Duane. "Congress has no right to pass such a preamble!" he shouted. "To say our petitions have all been rejected is a — mis-statement of the facts. There is no sense to it and no justice. Does not every ship bring promises of peace commissioners?" Duane looked angrily around the room, lowered his voice with an effort. "Why all the haste?" he demanded. "Why this urging, this driving? If I should vote for this measure I would be guilty of a breach of trust. My constituents have given me no such instructions. Congress has no more right to pass this Preamble and resolution than Parliament has! It is a mechanism for the fabrication of independence. As such I do protest it." Duane repeated the words, his voice rising. "I do protest it!"

One after another the *Cool Considerate Men* — not cool at all, today — rose to sustain the protest. James Wilson the Philadelphia conservative stood up, his steel-bound spectacles in his fingers. "Before we build the new house," he said in his quiet, measured way, "why should we pull down the old one and expose ourselves to the inclemencies of the season? I speak for my constituents. If this Preamble passes, Pennsylvania will suffer an immediate dissolution of every kind of authority. The people will be instantly in a state of nature."

It was reasonable enough. But the argument was shopworn. Delegates were tired of a state of nature, and as to the figure of the house and the weather, they had heard it twelve times in a week. John said nothing. These past few days his committee had canvassed the situation with utmost care; they thought they knew how the count would fall.

Late that afternoon when the vote was taken, Preamble and Resolve passed by seven colonies to five. Maryland refused to vote. John rose at once, made his way to Lee and Rutledge, stood by the window while colleagues flocked to congratulate them. Sam Adams laid a hand over John's shoulder. "Well done, Cousin," he said softly. "Well done, old friend!"

Through the crowd, John saw Duane push rapidly; men fell back to give him way. Duane's voice, when he reached the group, was clear and angry. "Adams," he said, "you are aware, I presume, of what you have done this day? You have created a machine for the fabrication of independence."

There was sudden silence while the others waited. John looked

back at his adversary. "Not a mere machine, Duane," he said. "This is independence itself."

John, of course, had exaggerated. Independence was yet to be declared, a war fought and won before the colonies would be actually free. Yet John had meant his statement every word. In his eyes the first, the hardest step toward independence was accomplished. "As to Declarations," he had lately written Abby, "be patient — what signifies a Word?"

On Wednesday night of May fifteenth, after the Resolve went through, all across the city of Philadelphia, delegates sat in tavern dining rooms and lodging-house chambers, reporting home to their constituents. Hancock, still President of Congress, sent the Resolve to George Washington . . . Considering the gravity of the situation, Congress desired the General's presence immediately in Philadelphia for conference. Stephen Hopkins reported to Rhode Island. Duane and Carter Braxton wrote home, not so much in anger as with fatalistic resignation, now the thing was done. The Easterners, the New Englandmen, were responsible mostly, Braxton said. "The wise Men of the East," he called them derisively.

This Day [John reported to Warren] *the Congress has passed the most important Resolution that ever was taken in America.* Oliver Wolcott of Connecticut sent home a transcription of both Preamble and Resolve. "A Revolution in Government is about to take Effect," he wrote. "A strange Infatuation has possessed the british Councills to drive Matters to the length they have gone. every Thing convinces me that the Abilities of a Child might have governed this Country, so strong has been their Attachment to Britain. May the Supreme Ruler of the Universe carry us thro the hardy Conflict to Liberty safety and Peace."

On Friday, May 17, Congress did not meet, having proclaimed a Day of Fasting and Prayer — time-honored method of letting the people know and share the gravity of a public situation. After Louisburg victory there had been a Day of Prayer; after Quebec was taken in the year '59; after Lexington too, and Bunker Hill. The Tories, furious at Congress's assumption of such ecclesiastical authority, called these appointed days, contemptuously, "Congress Sundays." This time, however, they were not so free with their ridicule. By the Resolve of May fifteenth, the last Tory protection was about to van-

ish. Every royal official would be outlawed; there would remain no one to whom a loyalist could legally appeal for protection not only of his property but of his life.

Congress Sunday of May 17 was sunny, very soft and warm; a light haze hung over the river. In Philadelphia some fifty delegates went peaceably to church; if there was dissension among them they did not let it show. All afternoon, John walked the city in a quiet and happy solemnity. It seemed to him incredible that at last the day was here. Friends stood together under the trees, reminiscent, talking of how this thing had come to pass. Two young gentlemen from South Carolina were in town. They had been in Charleston that morning late in March when their new Governor, Assembly and judges walked in procession to celebrate the State Constitution. The Adamses gladly heard them tell about it; John could have listened to the tale a thousand times. . . . As the procession went by on King Street, the young men said, people had stood in throngs, strangely quiet, gazing "with a kind of rapture." This Governor, these Senators marching to music behind their escort of uniformed cadets — these were men they had themselves chosen, men they knew and loved and trusted, "men they could displace if any one of them behaved amiss." As they told of it, the eyes of the young Charlestonians grew wide. "We stood on the footway," they said, "and we cried like children."

That night in his room, John wrote a long letter to Abigail. He had looked forward to this hour when he could be quiet and alone with her. He was well aware of the work that lay ahead. The Middle colonies might still balk at an actual declaration of independence, thereby imperiling the entire war machinery, from the recruiting of troops to the forming of an alliance with France. Yet tonight, John's heart was filled with thanksgiving, his fatigue for the moment lifted. The evening was very warm. At about eight o'clock a light rain set in, but it brought no relief. John sat naked except for his breeches; in the moist, still air he all but steamed. Outside there was no sound save a trickle of water from the roof. . . . "Great Britain," John wrote, "has at last driven America to the last Step, a complete Separation from her, a total absolute Independence, not only of her Parliament but of her Crown, for such is the amount of the Resolve of the 15th.

"Is it not a saying of Moses — *who am I, that I should go in and*

out before this great People? — When I consider the great Events which are passed, and those greater which are rapidly advancing, and that I may have been instrumental of touching Some Springs and turning Some Small Wheels, which have had and will have Such Effects, I feel an Awe upon my Mind which is not easily described."

On the seventh of June, a Friday, Richard Henry Lee stood up in Congress and asked leave to propose a resolution, "according to the instructions of his constituents." Fifty pairs of eyes were instantly fixed on him; not a delegate but knew perfectly what was coming. Three weeks ago, on that now fateful fifteenth of May, the Virginia Assembly had voted that its delegates in Congress be instructed "to declare for independence." Congress had had the news ten days or more; daily, the moderates had looked for the Virginians to act upon it. The tension had become almost unbearable. Over the capitol at Williamsburg, the Union flag was flying; Lee did not hesitate to advertise the fact in Philadelphia club and coffeehouse. "May God grant it never be lowered!" he said. "*Amen and Amen!*" two Adamses echoed every time. . . . What, the moderates had wondered nervously, was Virginia waiting for? What nefarious plans was she concerting with the New Englandmen, and why did they not come out with it and have done?

Quite obviously, the moment had this morning arrived; Virginia was about to "come out with it." Lee stood at ease, slim and distinguished in his light silk summer suit and breeches. Duane, Wilson, Livingston, Rutledge, Robert Morris drew in their lips, their faces set. Lee held a piece of paper in his hand; he lifted it and read slowly:

RESOLVED, *That these United Colonies are, and of right ought to be, free and independent States: that they are absolved from all allegiance to the British Crown; and that all political connection between them and the State of Great Britain is, and ought to be, totally dissolved.*

Before a dissenting voice could be heard, John was on his feet to second the motion. The moderates had but one card left to play — for postponement. They used it. The debate raged all that day and the next, a Saturday. Neither side would give an inch. Dickinson was in and out of the room, now arguing against Lee and the two Adamses, now across the hallway with the Pennsylvania Assembly, pledging himself and the other Provincial conservatives to vote

against independence. The Middle states insisted they had no authority to declare for separation from England; if the measure went through over their heads they would have no recourse but to walk out of Congress, go home and perhaps witness their colonies secede from the Union.

Congress rose with the vote still pending. In disgust, Edward Rutledge wrote that night to his conservative colleague, John Jay. "No reason could be assigned for pressing into this Measure, but the reason of every Madman, a shew of our spirit. The Question was postponed; it is to be renewed on Monday when I mean to move that it should be postponed for 3 Weeks or Months. I wish you had been here. the whole Argument was sustained on one side by R. Livingston, Wilson, Dickenson and myself, and by the Power of all N. England, Virginia and Georgia at the other."

Agreement was impossible. On Monday morning, June tenth, conciliators and radicals agreed to postpone the final decision, the final vote, until July the first, three Mondays distant. New York, New Jersey, Pennsylvania, Delaware and Maryland were still doubtful — "not yet matured for falling from the parent stem," Jefferson said. Both sides expected to use the delay to fullest advantage. Some members prepared to ride home at once; others sent urgent expresses bidding their Assemblies instruct for or against independence according to their several beliefs.

Meanwhile both factions agreed it was only prudent and sensible to prepare a Declaration of Independence — have it ready, should the final vote be affirmative. Even the moderates did not wish to see so important a proclamation "huddled up in a hurry by a few Chiefs." To compose it, a committee of five was named. *The members chosen* [wrote Thomson in the Minutes] *Mr. Jefferson, Mr. J Adams, Mr. Franklin, Mr. Sherman, Mr. R R Livingston.*

Two days later, on Wednesday evening, Congress rose sometime after six. John managed somehow to elude his colleagues and went off by himself for supper at a little ordinary he knew on Race Street out by the Common. Byrne's Tavern, it was called; the proprietor was a high Son of Liberty. John felt the need to be alone, eat a meal in peace, not be stifled by noise, smoke, the excited conversation of eight men or twenty. He had known in his heart that Lee's Resolution could not go through; things did not happen so easily. Yet in spite of political experience John had hoped for a miracle.

Sudden changes, sudden overturnings of the collective mind have been known to take place on occasion.

Tonight it seemed to John that he could not endure another three weeks of waiting, three weeks of suspense, tension, the eternal contriving of plans and maneuvers. Over and above contriving, the machinery of war and government loomed before him, appalling in its sheer weight. Since Monday John had seen his name affixed to three new committees — one to prepare the Declaration, one for foreign treaties, and a shattering affair called the Board of War and Ordnance. Of them all, the last was most formidable.

Making his way out Market Street toward Centre Square, John considered it. The Board included only five members; they had immediately thrust the chairmanship onto John. The Board's duties as outlined amounted to the management of the entire Army supply system, including munitions, arms, powder, prisoners and even the raising of money to maintain the whole vast establishment. Compared with these irksome and complicated transactions, the writing of a Declaration of Independence seemed a mere poetic pastime, a pleasing interlude in the endless and exhausting business of war.

At Tenth Street, John turned north and the city fell behind him. The country here was flat, almost barren, with scattered stretches of woodland and at intervals a small shanty with a cabbage patch behind it. In the cool of the evening, men in shirt sleeves hoed between the rows or sat before the door smoking their pipes after the day's labor. Byrne's little barroom was nearly empty. The proprietor greeted John, set a pot of ale before him and a plate of steaming ham and cabbage. After he had eaten, John called for more ale and sat alone at the table, gazing out the open door to the fields beyond, misty now with evening. He felt better, more tranquil. . . . There were letters to write, reports to make for Massachusetts. This was as quiet a place as any the city was likely to offer tonight. . . . John had his green lawyer's bag with him. He reached in, extracted paper and quill, asked the proprietor for ink. . . .

Concerning the Declaration, John thought — it would require nothing actually new or original. Congress, individual colonies — towns even — had in the past two years sent out numerous declarations of rights, carefully worded announcements and justifications of the revolutionary position. The Suffolk Resolves were the most spirited; the Declaration on Taking up Arms, published just

after Bunker Hill, the most comprehensive. A Declaration of Independence would of necessity be mostly repetition of these documents, with the inclusion of a forceful outline of America's grievances against the King. It must of course be elegantly written, strong yet simple — something a nation could subscribe to and a world might comprehend. Canada would read it and her heart even now might soften. France would read it and upon her interpretation much, very much, might depend. But look on the matter from east, west, north or south, independence was coming.

John thrust his pen in the ink:

To Francis Dana (member of the Massachusetts Council)

PHILADELPHIA, 12 *June*, 1776

We are drudging on, as usual. Sometimes it is seven o'clock before We rise. We have greater Things, in Contemplation, than ever — The greatest of all, which We ever shall have. — Be silent and patient and time will bring forth, after the usual Groans, throes and Pains upon such Occasions, a fine Child — a fine vigorous, healthy Boy. I presume. God bless him, and make him a great wise, virtuous, pious, rich and power Full Man!

CHAPTER THIRTY-TWO

Thirteen clocks strike for independence.

IT was Sunday, June 30. Tomorrow, Lee's resolution on independence would come up for final vote. The Declaration was written; Jefferson had been working at it for the past two weeks. It would be debated the moment independence was decided.

From the most violent of the liberty men to the coolest of the "Cool Devils," everyone knew that independence was coming, tomorrow's majority secure. Yet the hazard, the essential danger remained. Voting for independence meant voting for war. Those colonies which were against independence automatically would be left out of the confederation — and by that token become enemy states. A unanimous vote was necessary; a mere majority would not do. In the doubtful Middle states, political workers doubled their efforts, sending reports by every post. "I have not been idle," wrote Samuel Chase from Annapolis, Maryland. "I have appealed *in writing* to the people. County after county is instructing. Remember me to Mrs. Adams and all Independent Souls."

Maryland, however, was small and unimportant. It was New York and Pennsylvania that mattered. Their harbors, their waterways, were strategic, available. The British had no military base nearer than Halifax; they intended to strike for one at New York. Yesterday, Saturday, June 29, Howe's transports had been sighted off Sandy Hook. "*A fleet of 130 sail,*" * the message read. If Washington's forces should be driven across Hudson River, through New Jersey into Pennsylvania, the war could last fifteen years — or the war

---

* There were actually 52 large war vessels, 27 armed sloops and cutters, and 400 transports.

could be lost. Ever since April, Washington had been busy fortifying New York. City streets leading to the water were barricaded, and on Staten Island, Manhattan and Long Island, the hills were dotted with redoubts and batteries. (One such entrenchment bore defiantly the name of Bunker Hill.) Hudson River Channel bristled with obstructions. For New York, General Washington was prepared to risk his entire army.

But the great Province of New York, sitting in political convention assembled, made it plain at this late date that she was by no means ready to share the risk. New York would not instruct for independence. New York looked out to sea and remembered her motto of '74 — *Liberty and Prudence!* Gouverneur Morris continued to harp on the promised peace commissioners.* So did John Jay, Duane and Philip Livingston, who had come from Congress to sit with the home convention. It was folly, they said, not to wait for Admiral Howe's ships from England . . . the *Father's Goodwill*, the *Amity's Admonition* — worse than folly to fling away a last chance for reconciliation.

To John, such mulish blindness was almost criminal. How could New York continue to barricade her streets with one hand and with the other make welcoming gestures to the enemy? Angrily, John demanded explanation, sending off hasty letters . . . to General John Sullivan, to Colonel Parsons of Connecticut, now on Staten Island, to his old law pupil William Tudor,[1] a lieutenant under Washington. "What is the Reason that New York is still asleep or dead, in Politics and War? Have they no sense? No Feeling? No Sentiment? No Passions? New Jersey shews a noble Ardor. Is there anything in the Air or Soil of New York, unfriendly to the Spirit of Liberty? For Gods sake explain to me the Causes of our Miscarriages in that Province!"

Pennsylvania seemed even a worse case. That huge proprietary Province had not the excuse of immediate threat; no enemy ships had been sighted in Delaware Bay. To John, the local conservative patriots seemed activated by sheer greed, fear of losing their lands,

---

* As a matter of fact the "peace commission" did arrive, in the person of Admiral Lord Howe himself. Ironically enough and much to his disgust, John Adams was one of a committee of three chosen by Congress in September of '76 to go to New York and treat with the Admiral. Franklin and Edward Rutledge were the other two. From first to last it was a wonderful pilgrimage, which unfortunately does not come within the scope of this book.

their money, their high office. Thomas McKean assured John that when it came to the pinch, Pennsylvania would vote for independence rather than be left out of the Union. Yet of seven Pennsylvania delegates in Congress, only two — Dr. Franklin and Judge Morton of Ridley — were outright independence men. James Wilson desired to put off the vote till autumn. The other four, Dickinson, Robert Morris, Willing and Humphries, were dead set against independence.

Fortunately, McKean and his political cohorts were not only active but greatly skilled. Matlack, Cannon, Roberdeau, Clymer had a genius for political maneuver matched only by Sam Adams himself. When they saw that the old conservative proprietary Assembly would never instruct for independence, they called a Provincial Conference of their own in Carpenters' Hall, chose McKean for President, set up an independent government and celebrated the event by bell ringings, bonfires and huzzas.[2] Nevertheless, Pennsylvania's delegates in Congress were fixed there until a new, state-wide election could be held later in the summer. Was there not danger, John asked McKean, that this outside pressure might confirm rather than dilute the stubbornness of Dickinson, Morris *et al?* In the newspapers, Tom Paine brought angry attack, sparing no one, especially old Israel Pemberton of the magnificent hawk nose — *O! ye fallen, cringing, priest and Pemberton-ridden people! What more can we say of ye than that a religious Quaker is a valuable political character and a political Quaker a real Jesuit!*

Yet in spite of battling and maneuvering, in spite of the constant, awful anxiety of the past three weeks, John was conscious that this last delay had been, politically, a good thing. Had the vote been taken on June 7 when Lee proposed it, New York and Pennsylvania would most certainly have been lost for independence. It irritated John that his constituents at home did not share this realization. "What is your Congress doing?" Major Hawley wrote angrily from Massachusetts. "Is it dozing, amusing itself?" . . . "Remember," John wrote back reproachfully, "you cant make thirteen Clocks strike precisely alike, at the same Second."

John himself had been furiously busy. It seemed to him he was always on his feet — running to the City Tavern to meet Matlack and McKean and discuss how best to bring Pennsylvania around;[3] stopping at the printer's to deliver some article of newspaper propaganda; meeting with the Board of War upstairs in the Coffee House, then

hurrying home to write tactful letters to Army generals, explaining just why Congress could not raise and deliver troops from stated areas. John drove out to Frankford to see a manufacturer of flints for guns, to Chester in search of men and women to make saltpeter. Once or twice he looked in on Jefferson where he sat writing the Declaration in his second floor parlor at Seventh and Market Streets. Jefferson had protested this duty; he was the youngest member of the Committee save Livingston, he said. Dr. Franklin or Mr. Adams should properly be the author.

John had merely laughed. Any draft of his would be three months in revision merely because an Adams wrote it — or any other New Englandman, for that matter. "I am feared and hated in Congress," John said. Jefferson's happy talent for composition was known to all; he had a peculiar felicity of expression. "You write," John finished bluntly, "ten times better than I do."

The choice of author had proved most fortunate; John himself was delighted with the Declaration. He and Franklin made a few minor alterations and the committee of five approved the rest. On June 28 the document had been reported to Congress, and lay now "on the table" awaiting the vote on independence.

The days of doubt were nearly over; only a night remained. For John the tension had risen almost unbearably. His head ached, he felt feverish and the brief hot summer nights brought no refreshment. His appetite was gone; all meats tasted alike and when he forced himself to eat, the food lay sour on his stomach. John knew that if he permitted himself to let go, he might sink in exhaustion.

Once the vote was taken tomorrow, the politics of revolution would be finished. "Nothing," John had written home, "will remain but war." There were other men who could manage a war far better than he. Not men of ideas but men of business were needed — men who knew how to raise loans, compute debts, coin money, set prices, move supplies, manufacture arms. The whole Massachusetts delegation ought to resign and let younger men take their places in Congress. He himself was forty, nearly forty-one. Rotation of office — was it not the very stuff of which republican government was made? Since the beginning, John had preached rotation, but Massachusetts had not listened. "I will go home," he thought now, in a sudden wild upsurge of hope and homesickness, a wave of longing for a life that was his own once more, to do with as he pleased. A life secure,

defined within happy limits to the farm, the Braintree pastures, to the law courts of Massachusetts and his own most private and delightful affairs. Harvest time was coming, even now the south field must be ripe with hay. When he threw a leg over his saddle John would like to know — most urgently he would like it — that he need travel no farther than Plymouth Court House.

I will go home! John repeated the words desperately in his mind. *I will petition my constituents to let me go. I will live with my family, practice law, make money and be at peace.*

On Monday morning, July the first, 1776, John walked to the Pennsylvania State House at about half after eight. The sky was cloudless; already the bricks and cobbles gave off heat. John went up three steps and through the wide double doors that opened on Chestnut Street. The hallway was cool, the dark plank floor grateful to the eye. Through the far entrance, trees in the State House Yard showed green.

For John, every turn of this building, every room and corner was familiar. Yet today the scene was heightened; John felt each detail poignantly. To the left, over the doorway to the Assembly room where Congress sat, the carved white ornamental face stared blindly, its wide eyeballs fixed. Beneath it the doorman lounged against the wall. John walked to him and gave him good morning. If the Maryland post should come while they were in session, John said, it might be well to deliver immediately any letters for himself or President Hancock.

Turning in the door, John walked up the right aisle of the Assembly Room and found his usual seat near the front, beneath a window giving on the Yard. The room was already filling. John laid his green lawyer's bag on the wide window sill just above him, took out his papers, settled himself and glanced about with a searching, practiced eye. Across the room sat Dickinson in plum-colored coat and breeches, looking pale as death. James Wilson and Edward Rutledge leaned over him, talking earnestly. The ranks of the independence men were thin this morning, with their best debaters at home, holding the local organizations to the line. Richard Henry Lee was at Williamsburg with George Wythe, Gadsden in South Carolina, Chase still at Annapolis, Caesar Rodney in Delaware.

The actual procedure for this morning was entirely familiar to

everyone. Congress would resolve itself into a Committee of the Whole House and President Hancock would come down from the Chair, thereby making both debate and vote unofficial, a trial balloon as it were. It was an old, traditional and highly useful parliamentary device for getting the sense of a legislative body just before it took official and irretrievable action "under the mace," or seal of traditional authority.* Also, it gave the President a chance to take part in the argument. . . . When debate and vote were completed in Committee of the Whole, Hancock would resume the Chair and the final and irrevocable vote would be taken "in full Congress assembled."

To the right behind the President's chair the door opened and Sam Adams walked slowly in, caught sight of John and moved to him. By the way his head shook, John knew his cousin was agitated. He sat down and the papers in his hand rattled. "It won't go through today," Sam said. "We won't move beyond Committee of the Whole. Dickinson will have his say; I see it in his eye. That bundle of notes he holds is a speech, a two-hour harangue by any wager. . . . And you, Cousin—" Sam raised a hand—"you will have to refute him. You seconded Lee's Resolution. And Lee is in Virginia."

John turned impatiently to the back of the room. Where in God's name, he wondered, were the new representatives from Jersey? Chase's express from Annapolis should have got here long ago with the Maryland Instructions for independence. Of Delaware's three delegates, only two were present, McKean and George Read— and Read was against independence. He would surely like, John said, to see Caesar Rodney's bright wizened little apple-face back there where it belonged. It might be wiser for Hancock to delay the vote till afternoon, giving time for the radical delegates to arrive. As the vote went in Committee, so it would go in full Congress either today or tomorrow.

"If I have to talk for independence, I will talk," John told his cousin morosely. "Yet what can I say that hasn't been hackneyed back and forth a hundred times in this room? What can anyone say, including our distinguished friend in the plum-colored coat?"

Sam scratched at a hole in his stocking just below the knee. "Our distinguished friend," he repeated dryly, "can always invoke the allegory of the house and the inclement weather. Surely, you wouldn't wish him to omit that trenchant bit? Besides, he can fall back

---

* A procedure still in use in our Congress.

on the well-known New England threat. You saw the *Evening Post* article?"

John turned, smiled warmly at his cousin. A week or two ago, the Pennsylvania *Evening Post,* a radical paper, had carried a list of highly pertinent brief statements under the heading, "What Patriots Fear." John remembered it well. "Should independence be declared, I fear I shall lose my office. . . . I fear I shall lose the honor of being related to men in office. . . . I shall lose the rent of my house for two years or three. . . . The common people will have too much power in their hands. . . . *I fear the New Englandmen will turn into Goths and Vandals and overrun this country.*"

It was absurd, of course; yet the conservatives could testify to the truth of these fears. On Friday last, Edward Rutledge of South Carolina had sent a fast express to John Jay in New York, begging him by all that was sound and stable to be in Congress on July first to bolster the argument against independence and against the plan of confederacy that went with it. "Nothing less than Ruin to some Colonies will be the Consequence," Rutledge wrote urgently. "The Idea of destroying all Provincial Distinctions and making every thing of the most minute kind bend to what they call the good of the whole, is in other Terms to say that these Colonies must be subject to the Government of the Eastern Provinces. . . . I confess I dread their over-ruling Influence in Council. I dread their low Cunning, and those levelling Principles which Men without Character and Fortune in general possess, which are so captivating to the lower class of Mankind, and which will occasion such a fluctuation of Property as to introduce the greatest disorder."

For a man of only twenty-seven, Rutledge was wondrous stubborn, the Adamses often agreed. Sitting with him on committee was like sitting with a blind behemoth, Sam said — something that must be pushed and dragged and hauled along with hooks. . . .

The clock in the State House tower struck nine. President Hancock called for order, picked up a pile of papers from the table and began to read aloud. . . . Three letters from General Washington; one from General Benedict Arnold; one from Schuyler; one from the Convention of New Jersey; the Convention of New Hampshire . . . Fourteen separate letters Hancock went through slowly, painstakingly, asking the sense of Congress concerning each. It was noon before he laid the last paper down, paused briefly, then announced

that Congress would "resolve itself into a Committee of the Whole to take into consideration the resolution concerning independence."

Leaning forward, Hancock picked up the mace — he loved punctilio — and handing it to the clerk, set authority ceremoniously aside and took his seat in the ranks. Benjamin Harrison, Chairman in Committee of the Whole, moved to the vacated Chair and let his large bulk slowly down. At once, Dickinson was on his feet. His voice as he began was charged with emotion. He spoke fluently yet with a kind of halting earnestness, like a man who has thought much and painfully, rehearsing in the solitary hours what he would say. "My conduct this day I expect will give the finishing blow to my once too great, and my now too diminished popularity. Yet I had rather forfeit popularity forever, than vote away the blood and happiness of my countrymen."

In spite of himself, John was impressed. There was a deep sincerity about Dickinson's manner; his thin face showed lines of strain. As he was speaking, the door at the back of the hall opened and the doorman walked up the north aisle, gave Hancock a large, official-looking envelope, then came round by the side wall and handed John a letter postmarked Annapolis. John tore it open. "I am this Moment from the House," he read, "with an Unan: Vote of our Convention for Independence. Now for a government. *Jubeo te bene valere*, adieu . . . Your Friend, S. CHASE."

Farewell and be strong in the cause. . . . Across the room, Hancock with a quick gesture held up his own letter; his lips formed the word "Maryland." The small drama was not lost on the room. Underneath Dickinson's clear voice, whispers sounded — *Maryland for independence!*

"If we declare a separation without waiting to hear from France," Dickinson was saying, "we may be overwhelmed with debt — a debt I have computed at six millions of Pennsylvania money a year. We shall ruin ourselves, and Britain will be ruined with us. France will rise on those ruins. Britain will push the war with a severity hitherto unimagined. Indians will be set loose on our frontiers. Recollect, gentlemen, that Boston has been spared thus far. Boston will be burned!"

In the chair to John's right his cousin sat perfectly expressionless, arms folded across his breast. . . . "To escape from the protection of Britain by declaring independence, all unprepared as we are,"

Dickinson continued, "would be like destroying our house in winter and exposing a growing family before we have got another shelter."

Two Adamses by simultaneous impulse turned to each other, bowed slightly and ironically from the waist, then resumed attention, their faces bland. Dickinson went on and on; he must have talked an hour. The heat had grown stifling. Light faded in the wide room and there was a sound of thunder.

Dickinson drew himself up, raised his voice as if in peroration. Before this resolution for independence was put to a vote it might be profitable to look ahead, he said, read a little into the future, into "the Doomsday Book of America." A commonwealth of thirteen united colonies had been proposed. In twenty years or thirty, might not this great Union become unwieldy? Might it not of itself split into separate commonwealths? "I have a strong impression in my mind," said Dickinson, "that this will take place. In that case — " Dickinson paused, then spoke emphatically: "in that case, Hudson's River would make a very proper boundary for a separate commonwealth to the northward."

Handkerchief to his brow, Dickinson stood a moment, then sank to his chair. No one spoke. By their window the *par nobile fratrum* were silent, waiting. Sam continued to gaze straight before him. John's short, heavy fingers lay spread on his knees. Impossible, he thought angrily, that this thing must needs be hammered out again! Yet Dickinson, however trite his words, however specious his argument, had been impressive if only in the personal risk he took. He had spoken from the heart and in so doing had gambled away forever all chance of personal advancement, all chance of his being part of the new government of America, should independence win the day. Such a man must not be permitted to have the last word.

John drew in his breath with a long, powerful sigh. Against the windows the storm broke in a sudden flurry of rain. John stood up. . . . He could wish for eloquence, he said — all the powers of the ancient orators of Greece and Rome. The preceding speaker had been eloquent indeed; his talent for expression was known throughout a continent. And yet how simple the argument, intrinsically. How plain the issue! Was it not rather a question of man's ordinary understanding? Every honest person with open mind and senses alert, can hear the moment strike for action, knows when the path turns beneath his feet. . . .

All his life long, John was to hear this speech of July first referred to in terms of wonder, terms of praise. "He came out with a power of thought and expression that moved us from our seats," Jefferson said, years afterward. Yet no word of the speech was kept. Nobody took notes. All John himself could remember, when people asked him, were the opening words. To him indeed, the whole performance had been a waste of breath. "An idle mispence of time," he wrote Samuel Chase a few hours after the speech. "Nothing was said but what had been repeated and hackneyed in that room before, a hundred times for six months past."

But though his actual words escaped him, John never forgot the scene itself. . . . While he was speaking, the storm outside increased; John had to raise his voice against the roll of thunder. It grew dark; Hancock at his table beckoned to the clerk for candles. By then it was about four o'clock. John was still speaking when the door flung open from the hallway and three men entered, booted, spurred, rain dripping from their coats. It was the radical members from Jersey, come to vote for independence. John stopped and sat down, but Judge Stockton, speaking for New Jersey, asked to hear the affirmative argument before the vote should be taken in Committee of the Whole.

John got up, went patiently through the argument again as briefly as he could, addressing himself to the three Jerseymen who stood against the far wall. When he was done the opposition brought forth two more speechmakers, both vehement, almost abusive. One of the three Jerseymen, President Witherspoon of Princeton, ignoring the fact that he was an extremely new member of Congress, stepped boldly out from the wall. His coat, streaked with rain, was open, his clergyman's bib lay wilted against his chest. "The distinguished gentleman from Massachusetts," he said in a nasal, hoarse and quite loud voice, "remarked as we came in that the colonies are ripe for independence. I would like to add that some colonies —" Witherspoon looked pointedly at Alsop of New York,* who had just sat down — "some colonies are rotten for the want of it!"

Sam Adams, delight spreading visibly across his countenance, said

---

* When the New York Instructions for independence arrived by post on July 15, Alsop wrote his home convention an indignant letter of resignation. He could not serve his State, he said, after they had deliberately closed the door to "reconciliation with Great Britain upon just and honourable terms."

something that sounded like *Hear hear!* From the Chair, Benjamin Harrison called hastily for order, announced that the vote would be taken. One by one he called the States by name: *Massachusetts* . . . Four men stood up. *New Hampshire* . . . *Rhode Island* . . . *Connecticut* . . . Unanimous for independence. *New York* . . . Not a man rose to his feet. *Delaware* . . . McKean alone stood up; his colleague George Read remained seated, eyes fixed stolidly before him. *Pennsylvania* . . .

When the vote was counted, it was nine to four for independence. "RESOLVED," read Harrison slowly, deliberately, "*That these United States are and of right ought to be, Free and Independent States; that they are absolved from all allegiance to the British crown, and that all political connection between them and the State of Great Britain is and ought to be, totally dissolved.*"

Nine states to four. New York had refused to vote, "for want of Instructions from home." Pennsylvania and South Carolina voted *Nay;* Delaware's two deputies were divided. Harrison gave up the Chair to Hancock who adjourned the meeting — "until 9 o Clock to Morrow," the Secretary wrote. Tomorrow the final vote would be taken, "in full Congress assembled."

John Adams and Sam rose and moved quickly through the crowd, trying not to let triumph show too plainly on their faces. Much would depend, tomorrow, on Dickinson, Robert Morris and Rutledge; it would not be wise to antagonize them further. Outside the door, McKean was waiting with the Jersey delegates. The six men crossed the street together to the Fountain Tavern, talking eagerly. . . . Today's majority would in itself be a most powerful inducement to the four dissenting States. Rather than be left out of the Union, they must surely capitulate; they could play for delay no longer . . .

But Mr. Dickinson, one of the Jerseymen remarked in a positive tone, would never vote for independence. There was, McKean countered quickly, a way around that *impasse.* Dickinson could simply stay away tomorrow, and Robert Morris with him. James Wilson, when it came to scratch, would vote *Ay.* "So will that young popinjay from South Carolina," McKean added confidently. "He took me by the coat as I came out, and promised as much. 'For the sake of unanimity,' he said."

Nothing, it was agreed, could be done about New York for the

present. Witherspoon, addressing McKean bluntly, demanded what about his own State of Delaware? Could Mr. Read be persuaded before the morrow?

McKean shook his head. It was his considered opinion that men like George Read made up their minds at birth to say *No*, and descended to the grave with the pleased consciousness that they had voted against everything. "But rest easy concerning Delaware," McKean finished cheerfully. "Caesar Rodney will be here tomorrow if I have to travel to Dover myself after supper and bring him back by moonlight, riding pillion like a bride."

McKean proved right on all counts. Next morning — it was Tuesday, July second — Dickinson and Robert Morris stayed away. Wilson voted *Ay*, giving Pennsylvania a majority of three out of five. Edward Rutledge, true to promise, brought South Carolina around. Caesar Rodney, riding eighty miles in darkness and heavy rain, arrived just in time. McKean, who had sent horses at his own expense to Dover, waited for Rodney outside on the steps and brought him triumphantly in, still wiping the mud from his face and coat sleeves. When Delaware's name was called, the two stood up together. Rodney delivered his vote with a little speech. All sensible men, he said, were for independence, and so, he believed, were his constituents. Therefore he cast his vote in the affirmative. . . .

Twelve States for independence, with New York's vote guaranteed: Henry Wisner promised it. New York would not stand alone, one colony against the rest. . . . The thing was over, done, accomplished.

John Adams to Abigail

PHILADELPHIA, 3 *July*

The Second day of July, 1776,* will be the most memorable Epocha, in the History of America. I am apt to believe that it will be celebrated, by succeeding Generations, as the great anniversary Festival. It ought to be

* America celebrates the Fourth of July, when the Declaration was adopted by Congress, rather than July second, when Lee's resolution for independence was passed. To John and his colleagues, the Declaration was a mere form, the outward manifestation of that unanimous decision which on July second made independence a fact. A nephew of Abigail's (William S. Shaw) who had read the now-famous letter in John's lifetime, published it later — changing the first line to read "The Fourth day of July, 1776," rather than "the Second." Shaw also carefully altered the date at the letterhead to read July fifth instead of third.

commemorated, as the Day of Deliverance, by Solemn Acts of Devotion to God Almighty. . . . I can see that the End is more than worth all the Means. And that Posterity will triumph in that Days Transaction, even altho We should rue it, which I trust in God We shall not.

*Congress adopts a Declaration. Abigail
says Amen, and Sam Adams asks, Is it
well?*

THOMAS JEFFERSON, sitting next to Dr. Franklin in Congress, shifted his position for the fifth time in as many minutes. It was the morning of July the fourth, and the delegates in Committee of the Whole were discussing the Declaration. They had been at it since late afternoon of July second, when the vote on independence was announced.[1]

The process was quite obviously painful to the author. From time to time, Franklin glanced at him quizzically. The thing was not going at all as Jefferson had expected. It was in the Preamble that he — and John Adams too — had looked for most trouble. The Preamble contained extremely dangerous doctrines: *all men are created equal* was a hard morsel for patrician landholders to swallow. But somehow, Congress let it through, and with it the statement that men are endowed by their Creator with the right to *life, liberty and the pursuit of happiness.*

Life, liberty and property was the old revolutionary slogan. For denying it, Tories had lost their lives. *Property* was included even in the very radical Virginia Declaration of Rights, published in Philadelphia newspapers less than a month ago. Jefferson preferred his own phrase, "the pursuit of happiness."

It was when Harrison reached the indictments against the King

that Jefferson began truly to suffer. He had composed twenty separate clauses, twenty fierce "reasons" to let the world know that America was justified in what she did. Battering their way through all twenty, Congress cut and slashed, deleted, contracted, changed words and phrases — and then took out, entire, Jefferson's most cherished outburst against the slave trade. (*This assemblage of horrors,* Jefferson had called it; *this market where men are bought and sold.*)

Congress, plainly, saw no reason to lay on George Rex the blame for this deplorable but traditional trade. Had General Washington's slaves, John Hancock's slaves, been imported by order of George III? What about the late very lucrative Rhode Island traffic? New England's hands were far from clean. South Carolina and Georgia, moreover, were still importing slaves from Africa. . . . They made it instantly clear they had no slightest intention of letting CLAUSE 20 go through.

John Adams darted to his feet, shouted angrily at Rutledge — something about freedom being a mere masquerade in a country that sold humans in chains. John talked (Jefferson noted gratefully) much louder than the opposition — "fighting fearlessly for every word," Jefferson testified later. John banged with his hickory cane against the floor — and got, in the end, absolutely nowhere.

Calmly, with infinite and ruthless good sense, Congress drew the sting from Jefferson's expressed and ferocious desire for "eternal separation" from the British people as well as the British King. Why, said Congress, close the door on a people of whom a large proportion had shown great sympathy for the American cause? In the end, Harrison crossed out the word "eternal," crossed out indeed a whole page of angry accusation. America, he wrote above the lined-out sentence, would hold the British people, as she held the rest of mankind, *enemies in war, in peace friends.*

On the table before him, Harrison had one of Jefferson's copies of the Declaration. Above it the official pen hung poised as Harrison began to read aloud in a singsong, monotonous, well-bred voice. Jefferson sat near the front; his clear, steady gaze was fixed with awful intentness on the manuscript. His author's imagination reproduced each paragraph, each page with its horrid change and interlineation:

When in the course of human events it becomes neces-
                    one   *dissolve the political bands which have con-*
sary for a˄people to˄~~advance from that subordination in~~
nected them with another, and to
~~which they have hitherto remained, & to~~ assume among
                                 separate and equal
the powers of the earth the˄~~equal & independent~~ station

to which the laws of nature & of nature's god entitle them,

a decent respect to the opinions of mankind requires that
                                        the sep-
they should declare the causes which impel them to ˄~~the~~
aration
~~change.~~
                              self-evident;
We hold these truths to be˄ ~~sacred & undeniable;~~ . . .

That last change was Dr. Franklin's. Grudgingly, Jefferson confessed to himself that one word, even hyphenated, was better than
three.

Congress, in point of fact, improved the document by every
single alteration.* Moreover they shortened rather than expanded it,
a feat seldom if ever achieved by parliamentary critics. In the end
however, it was still Jefferson's composition; no one could doubt it.
His pen had written it, his spirit brooded over it, giving light to the
whole. . . . Now he sat listening as Harrison's voice droned on. This
was the final reading. When it was over, the Declaration would be
voted on in full Congress. There was no question of signing
the document today; this mutilated copy was not fit for formal
signature. It must be properly printed, "engrossed on parch-
ment." Congress moreover possessed no official seal or stamp
to honor such a document; for a hundred years the colonies had
used only the King's great seal. A stamp must be invented, and
quickly.**

We therefore [read Harrison], *the Representatives of the United
States of America in General Congress assembled . . . do solemnly*
Publish *and* Declare, *That these United Colonies are and of right
ought to be, FREE AND INDEPENDENT STATES . . . with*
full power *to levy War, conclude Peace, contract Alliances, estab-*

* See Note 1.
** Late that day, a committee was named: *Dr. Franklin, Mr. J Adams and
Mr. Jefferson, to bring in a device for a seal for the United States of America.*

lish Commerce, and to do all other Acts and Things which INDE-
PENDENT STATES *may of right do.*

*And for the support of this Declaration, with a firm reliance on
the protection of divine Providence, we mutually pledge to each
other our Lives, our Fortunes, and our sacred Honour.*

In the State House Yard there stood a round scaffold about twenty
feet high, with a little railed platform on top. From this "awful
stage," as John called it, the Declaration was first proclaimed on
Monday, July eighth, at noontime. Colonel Nixon of the Philadelphia Associators read it to a crowd that filled the State House Yard.
Troops, drawn up in formation, saluted, the people gave three great
huzzas. Forty-nine members of Congress, standing just below the
platform, cheered too, then filed through the State House door and
went back to work.

It was not a big celebration nor a loud one. Pennsylvania had
made more noise, rung more bells and lighted more bonfires when
she held her first Provincial Conference. But there was no question
that people felt deeply the significance of the Declaration. As the
days passed and post riders carried it north and south, the country
everywhere responded. In towns and hamlets men gathered, cheering
as the Declaration was read from Meeting-house steps, then ran to
tear down the King's Arms from their courthouse doors. The Lion
and the Unicorn would prance no more in these American States.

American States . . . People tried the phrase, turning it over on
their tongue. . . . *God bless the American States!* "This Declaration
has had a glorious effect," wrote Whipple of New Hampshire, who
had voted for it in Congress. "It has made these colonies all alive."
. . . A hundred King Streets changed their name to State Street;
Queen Street became Congress Way. In their dwelling houses,
men turned the King's portrait to the wall. Even the halfpenny that
bore the royal face was degraded to a farthing. On Bowling Green,
New Yorkers pulled down the dashing equestrian statue of George
Rex and melted it into — the account was pleasingly specific — "42,-
500 bullets." Worcester, Massachusetts, had a grand banquet: "24
Toasts were drank," reported the *Worcester Spy* — "Perpetual itch-
ing and no scratching to America's enemies. . . . May the freedom
and independency of America endure, till the sun grows dim and this
earth returns to chaos!"

On the nineteenth of July, 1776, the Declaration was proclaimed in Boston from the State House balcony. Abigail Adams was there. She had followed the crowd into King Street and stood across from the State House, waiting, her eyes fixed on the balcony that opened from the old Council Chamber. Troops stood at attention. The square, the streets leading from it were jammed with people. People perched on the rooftops; every window was filled with heads.

Here on this small square balcony, Thomas Hutchinson had stood on Massacre Night, pleading with the multitude . . . A thousand angry faces upturned in the moonlight, a thousand hands ready for the shedding of blood . . .

In the bright July noon sun the crowd began to shout as a man stepped to the balcony. Abby recognized him at once. It was Tom Crafts, the house painter, Sam Adams's right-hand man since 1764. "Colonel" Crafts, he was now. . . . It was Crafts who had led the little crowd of liberty boys that night when they serenaded John below the bedroom window in Cold Lane . . . JOHN ADAMS *dear, we sing to you, May heav'n its blessing show'r* . . .

The foolish, friendly words came back to Abby as clearly as if the scene were yesterday. "Why Abby," John had cried in astonishment, "they are singing my name!" Remembering, Abby felt tears start in her eyes. How long ago it was! A terrible dream, all this. Yet somehow, by God's mercy, terrible no longer. . . .

Tom Crafts had begun to read; the crowd was very still. The plain, flat Yankee voice reached easily across the square. ". . . Endowed by their Creator with sart'in . . ." Crafts stumbled, went back. ". . . By their Creator with sart'in unalienable rights; that among these are life, liberty and the pursuit of happiness . . ."

It did not take him long to finish. "God save the American States!" a voice shouted from the balcony. Crafts flung up both arms and the crowd surged forward, cheering.

"The Bells rang [*wrote Abigail that night to her husband*] the privateers fired the forts & batteries, the cannon were discharged the platoons followed & every face appeared joyfull. . . . After dinner the kings arms were taken down from the State House & every vestige of him from every place in which it appeared & burnt. . . . Thus ends royal Authority in this State. and all the people shall say Amen."

*   *   *

Three hundred miles to the southward, John Adams sat in Philadelphia City Tavern. It was dinnertime, and John had a table to himself in a far corner; Sam Adams and McKean had promised to join him. John was early; he had a full twenty minutes to wait. From a pocket he took his wife's letter and reread it. Abby, he thought with satisfaction, was a great hand at a description: . . . *every vestige of the King from every place where it appeared, and burnt.* He could see her face as she wrote — intent, serious, the lips drawn in, the fine nostrils spread a little: *and all the people shall say Amen.*

John looked up, his expression thoughtful, his blue eyes calm. James Otis[2] should be here tonight, he told himself with a little pang of sadness. Otis had worked hard and long in this business and had shared no reward. . . . A scene came back to John with sudden clarity: the old Council Chamber in Boston, with the Stuart kings framed in gold against the wall, and Otis speaking. *This writ is against the fundamental principles of English law! An act against the constitution is void.* How many men had conspired beforehand, to make that speech possible, make it come to pass! . . . Jeremiah Gridley — *I raised up two young eagles* — On the day when John first went to see him, Gridley's office had been quiet in the dark winter morning. *Pursue the study of the law rather than the gain of it,* the old man had advised. *Do not marry early.* Well, he had taken the advice on both counts. . . . Benjamin Pratt had stood in the library of his fine house, crutch under his arm. His voice had been cold as iron. *Were you sworn at Worcester, Mr. Adams? Have you read Fortescue? How far have you gone with Coke-Littleton?*

How far, John wondered now — how far with Sir Edward Coke? How far with the law, with right and wrong, with sinning and learning, with praying, rejoicing, with the cursing of God in a man's own heart? . . . Through John's mind a thousand scenes revolved, blotting out the tavern room, the tables crowded with diners, the colored waiters moving back and forth. . . . He saw his Boston office near the Town-house and the Irish Infant offering a guinea in his outstretched palm; heard his own voice: *I will defend Captain Preston and the soldiers. Mr. Forester, you may count on me.* . . . In Boston Court House, the prisoners' room had been crowded after the trial. A soldier had lifted his branded thumb. *A small price to pay for our lives, Mr. Adams.*

How far with Coke-Littleton, how far with life? What was it that young man, that young minister, declared from Braintree pulpit long ago? Briant, his name was. Lemuel Briant. *The doctrines of civil liberty, inherited from our fathers.* A wild young man, John's father had said. A man of most insidious doctrine. . . . Lemuel Briant's face was dim now, his words slipped the memory. It was another, older face John saw tonight in Braintree pulpit . . . Dr. Hancock, benign, familiar as one's father . . . *Lord, make us to see our end, that we may know the measure of our days.* . . . There had been a hymn, a Psalm they had sung often in the Meeting-house. John's mind groped for the words. Something about a people redeemed and *freed from th' enemies' hands.* . . . Great-uncle Peter used to sing it, back of the malt house when he was cleaning his gun, roaring it out full basso. *Then did they to Jehovah cry* . . . Ah, that was it!

> Then did they to Jehovah cry
> When they were in distress,
> Who did them set at liberty,
> Out of their anguishes.
>
> In such a way that was most right
> He led them forth also,
> That to a city which they might
> Inhabit they might go.

Abby knew that hymn; she liked to think it was written for New England people. . . . New England? *Where are now your land-marks,* Patrick Henry had demanded — *Where are your boundaries? I am not a Virginian but an American.*

"Thus ends royal Authority," Abby's letter said. . . . Thus ends a way of living, a way of thinking. "A new empire has arisen, styled the United States of America." Judge Drayton of Carolina had declared it from the bench, in full court assembled. The United American States. There was great power in a name, a phrase. Yet before the world would recognize this name, a terrible war must be fought. . . . *"I am well aware of the Toil and Blood and Treasure it will cost Us to maintain this Declaration, and support and defend these States."* John's own words came back to him. *"Yet through all the Gloom I can see the Rays of ravishing Light and Glory."*

I can see that the end is worth all the means. This is our day of

deliverance. With solemn acts of devotion to God we ought to commemorate it. With pomp and parade, with shows, games, sports, guns, bells, bonfires and illuminations from one end of the continent to the other from this time forward forevermore . . .

A hand fell on John's shoulder. He looked up. "Cousin John," Sam Adams said cheerfully. "You are in a very brown study. I said your name three times. . . . Is it well with you tonight?"

John smiled, filled suddenly with happiness, gratitude, a flood of deep feeling he could not have defined. With a wide, sweeping gesture of hospitality he pulled out a chair. "It is very well with me tonight, Cousin," he said.

NOTES

These notes are designed to be read all at once, either before or after the narrative — or skipped entirely. To look them up each time is to risk fatal interruption.

PROLOGUE

1. If the reader has noticed a large discrepancy in the orthography of John's letters, it is due to the fact that Charles Francis Adams, in his edition of the *Works*, "corrected" all spelling, eliminating the capitalization of nouns so characteristic of the eighteenth century. John's correspondence with James Warren, published in 1917 and 1925 by the Massachusetts Historical Society, happily escaped this unfortunate emasculation. Mr. Henry Adams, custodian of the Adams papers, kindly restored for me the original version of John's letters to Abigail. The diary, autobiography and other letters remain in C. F. Adams's "corrected" version. It is greatly to be hoped that a new, authentic edition of all John Adams's manuscripts will soon be issued.

CHAPTER THREE

1. The Reverend John Hancock was the son of a famous Massachusetts preacher and the father of John Hancock the Revolutionary patriot, who was born in Braintree two years after John Adams. The boys went to school together when they were very young. The Reverend Hancock died in 1744 and his son John was adopted by a rich uncle, Thomas Hancock the merchant. At the age of seven he went to live in Boston.

2. The Land Bank of 1741 was not a swindle but a scheme to raise money on land. It was supported by the debtor classes — town radicals and farmers all over the Province. The Adamses of Braintree being in a sound financial position, had stood with Colonel Quincy in opposition to the plan, which was opposed also by the royal gov-

ernment and such financial experts as Thomas Hutchinson of Boston. So high did excitement rise it was feared the country people would actually march on Boston. John Adams said later that the Land Bank raised a greater ferment than the Boston Tea Party. Sam Adams's father backed the Land Bank to his last shilling — and lost.

CHAPTER FOUR

1. The *Independent Advertiser* disappeared from circulation in December 1749. Nobody knew just why. What Boston did know was that Captain Samuel Adams had died in 1748 and the sheriff brought suit against the family for old debts left over from the Land Bank failure of 1741. Young Sam Adams was no longer in a position to put money in a newspaper or in anything else.

2. Rounders, or Bat and Ball, the antecedent to baseball, by 1800 was very popular in America and must have been played long before that. Cricket of course was two centuries older. As for football, the O.E.D. quotes one disgusted writer of 1532: "Footeballe, wherein is nothing but beastlie furie and exstreme violence." In a delightful autobiographical letter to Benjamin Rush, set in the third person singular, John, as an old man, reviews the pastimes of his youth:

"Fifteen years he spent at schools, Male and female Grammar and A.B.C. When he played Truant, and when he did not, he spent all his mornings Noons and Nights in making and sailing Boats, in swimming, skaiting, flying kites and shooting, in marbles, Ninepins, Bat and Ball, Football &c. &c. &c. Quoits, Wrestling and sometimes Boxing &c. &c. &c. and what was no better running about to Quiltings and Huskings and Frolicks and Dances among the Boys and Girls!!! These 15 years went off like a Fairy Tale. Apply such a 15 years to his present age and it will make 93."
— *Old Family Letters* (Alexander Biddle Collection), 1892.

CHAPTER SIX

1. Dunster, President of Harvard 1640–1654, was graduated from Cambridge University in England at the same time as John Milton. The next President was also a Cambridge man. The third was a Harvard graduate, class of 1650. The first teachers, too, were educated in England, until Harvard could raise up some native sons.

2. Wood Street became Boylston Street. The Way to the Parsonage became Massachusetts Avenue; the Charlestown road, Kirkland Street; the Connecticut highway, Brattle Street. As for the steward's gambrel-roofed house, Judge Oliver Wendell bought it in

1804 and lived in it with his daughter and son-in-law, the Reverend Abiel Holmes. Dr. O. W. Holmes was born there in 1809.

3. Charles Francis Adams once remarked that of all the New England families who flaunt a coat of arms, only two are entitled to it: the Winthrops and the Saltonstalls.

4. By act of the Massachusetts General Court in 1650, Harvard was governed by a Corporation, made up of the President, Treasurer, and five Fellows. This Corporation was responsible to a Board of Overseers, which included the Governor and the Deputy Governor of Massachusetts, six lay members and six ministers.

When John Adams was in college, the faculty members of the Corporation were Professor Wigglesworth (Professor Winthrop was not elected until 1765), old Tutor Flynt and Tutor Mayhew. The other two members were Nathaniel Appleton, pastor of the First Church in Cambridge where the students worshiped, and Joseph Sewall, another clergyman who had once declined the presidency of Harvard, and who was a bristling, hell-fire Calvinist of the strictest sect. The Treasurer, Thomas Hubbard, was a member of the Massachusetts Legislature and an excellent man of business.

Tutor Flynt, Fellow of the Corporation for sixty years, was also Secretary for the Board of Overseers.

5. Harvard was founded in 1636, William and Mary in 1693, Yale in 1701, the College of New Jersey (later Princeton) in 1746, the University of Pennsylvania (Franklin's Academy) in 1751, King's College (later Columbia) in 1754.

As for Yale's conservatism, let it be noted that in 1760, when Christ Church, an Episcopal establishment, was built in Cambridge, Harvard students were allowed to attend. But Yale forbade attendance at any but the Congregational Church until well into the nineteenth century.

6. In later life, John himself named these boys as having been his intimates at college. Of the twenty-four students who were graduated with John in 1755, a large proportion were destined for distinction. William Browne became Justice of the Superior Court of Judicature in Massachusetts, then Governor of Bermuda for the British. (In truth Browne never changed his mind; he remained Tory to the end. So did John Wentworth, Governor of New Hampshire, who became British Lieutenant-Governor of Nova Scotia.) Tristram Dalton was to be United States Senator from Massachusetts. David Sewall, brother of Jonathan, landed just where he thought he would, as Justice of the Massachusetts Supreme Judicial Court. Sam Locke became President of Harvard and was dismissed, nobody knew why. (A century later, the diary of a President of Yale re-

vealed that Locke had got a Harvard chambermaid with child.)
Moses Hemmenway became a distinguished preacher, Sam West a
chaplain in the Continental Army, then a member of the Constitutional Convention and of the convention that framed the Massachusetts Constitution. Daniel Treadwell was made Professor of
Mathematics at King's College (later Columbia) three years after
graduation. He died of smallpox before he was thirty.

CHAPTER SEVEN

1. The boy was Perez Fobes, of the class of 1762. A few leaves
from his diary and commonplace book are published in the *New
England Quarterly*, Vol. III, No. 4, 1929.

2. In 1764 Harvard Hall burned to the ground, and the library
with it. Both were rebuilt, and Boston came forward generously
with new books. After this, the rules were much stricter. All books
were locked behind brass-wire netting; there was only one day a
week for borrowing, at which time a fire was permitted in the
hearth. No more than three boys could enter at once; academic discussion groups no longer met there. No lamp or candle could be
carried in, and the only day a boy could study in the room was
Wednesday.

I have been unable to find library rules previous to the fire, but
there is reason to believe they were not nearly so strict. I myself
never yet saw a college librarian (or any librarian possessing a soul)
who would not stretch a rule when someone, young or old, showed
the genuine book hunger.

CHAPTER EIGHT

1. Arminianism was a Protestant doctrine, a Calvinist heresy
condemned by the Council of Dort in 1619 and greatly feared and
loathed by the faithful. Its five tenets are hopelessly confusing to the
modern reader, but it contained more free will and less predestination than Calvin's doctrines. What it amounted to in the end was
Wesleyan Methodism. Arminius is Latin for the Dutch name (Har-
mensen) of the man who founded the system. He lived 1560–1609.

Socianism was frankly anti-Trinitarian and therefore a step worse
than Arminianism. It combined faith in the goodness and rationality
of man with acceptance of the authority of Scripture, which was
taken as a rule of conduct. Lelio Sozzini of Italy (1525-1562) and
his nephew Faustus were its founders.

2. As late as 1829, the theological battle still raged. In that year,

the Reverend Abiel Holmes, a strict Congregationalist, lost his Cambridge parish because he stood out *against* Unitarianism.

CHAPTER NINE

1. Jacob Bailey was last man on the class list. He was twenty years old when he entered college; he kept a diary, beginning in 1753. There is an interesting account of him in the publication of the Lincoln County Historical Society for Nov. 13, 1895. Bailey, a Congregational minister, liked to dance, sing and play cards. Later, he turned Church of England. In 1779 he was banished as a Tory.

2. This is as told in John's diary. But he must have mixed two stories. Plutarch tells how Caesar, in Spain when he was thirty-nine, read a history of Alexander and wept that Alexander, who died at 33, had conquered many nations. Cicero, in one of his orations, tells how Alexander visited the tomb of Achilles and wept because Achilles had Homer to make deathless his exploits, while he, Alexander, had no Homer.

CHAPTER TEN

1. When Louisburg fell this last time, France saw the end of her power on the American Atlantic. So deeply did her statesmen feel the implications of this blow that they took the very unusual course of sending a circular letter to all the European powers:

We are advised that Louisburg capitulated to the English on July 26. We fully realize the consequences of such a grave event. But we shall redouble our efforts to repair the misfortune.

All commercial nations ought now to open their eyes to their own interests and join us in preventing the absolute tyranny which England will soon exercise on every sea if a stop be not put to her boundless avarice and ambition.

For a century past the Powers of Europe have been crying out against France for disturbing the balance of power on the Continent. But while England was artfully fomenting this trouble she was herself engaged in upsetting that balance of power at sea without which these different nations' independent power on land cannot subsist. All governments ought to give their immediate and most serious attention to this subject, as the English now threaten to usurp the whole world's seaborne commerce for themselves.

—WILLIAM WOOD: *The Great Fortress* [Louisburg]. (Toronto, 1915.)

2. This was written in retrospect, long after the French war was ended and after George III had made famous the phrase "gloried in the name of Briton."

CHAPTER ELEVEN

1. Sir Matthew Hale, Chief Justice of England under Charles II, wrote the famous *History of the Laws of England.*

Dr. Francis Dickins was Regius Professor of Civil (Roman) Law at Cambridge University in England. He was a fellow of Gray's Inn — one of the ancient legal societies, dating back to the fourteenth century.

Sir Thomas Reeve, a noted barrister in London, became Chief Justice in 1736 and died a few months later — worth, the obituaries invariably report, nearly twenty-three thousand pounds.

Robert Lightfoot, retired Judge of Admiralty, was London born and bred. Dr. Waterhouse of Harvard described him as a "very well educated, idle man, the oracle of literary Newport," adding that Lightfoot first taught him, as a young man, "to value and study Lord Bacon, Newton and Boerhave." The Judge gave wonderful dinners; people fought for invitations to share his oysters, his pheasants, his wine and his wit. He was a classical scholar, famous for his talent at reading aloud. It would seem that Mr. Lightfoot, now almost entirely forgotten, accomplished in his "very well educated, idle" way quite as much for a new country as a score of busier citizens.

CHAPTER TWELVE

1. For John's first mention of this incident, see the diary, *Works* II, p. 70:

> *1759.* Accidents, as we call them, govern a great part of the world, especially marriages. S—— and E—— broke in upon H—— and me, and interrupted a conversation that would have terminated in a courtship, which would have terminated in a marriage, which marriage might have depressed me to absolute poverty and obscurity to the end of my life; but that accident separated us and gave room for ——'s addresses, which have delivered me from very dangerous shackles . . .

Hannah Quincy subsequently married Dr. Lincoln, then Ebenezer Storer of Boston. In his *Figures of the Past,* Josiah Quincy (son of

John's friend Josiah, Junior) describes a visit to John Adams at Quincy in the year 1824, six years after Abigail Adams's death when Hannah and John met again for the last time:

> Eventful years rolled by, and I, a young man, just entering life, was deputed to attend my venerable relative on a visit to the equally venerable ex-President. Both parties were verging upon their ninetieth year. They had met very infrequently, if at all, since the days of their early intimacy. When Mrs. Storer entered the room, the old gentleman's face lighted up, as he exclaimed, with ardor, "What! Madam, shall we not go walk in Cupid's Grove together?" To say the truth, the lady seemed somewhat embarrassed by this utterly unlooked-for salutation. It seemed to hurry her back through the past with such rapidity as fairly to take away her breath. But self-possession came at last, and with it a suspicion of girlish archness, as she replied, "Ah, sir, it would not be the first time that we have walked there!"

2. Blackstone's lectures were, actually, what today would be called a "popularization," almost a layman's handbook of the law. As Jefferson in the Declaration of Independence revealed the American philosophy of government, so Blackstone's *Commentaries* with extraordinary prescience expressed the British attitude, the British feeling, toward their own constitution.

I myself was careful to read the Analysis in an old edition, one that John Adams might have used — the fourth edition, published at Oxford in 1759. So powerful, so persuasive and so charming were the words that I, a layman who knows little law, was swept with awe and excitement, as if I had set out on a voyage of discovery. Blackstone's object, he confesses, is to make law "into a science" — we would say, into a history, a literary achievement. Thus only could he give meaning, a leading thread, act as compass through the age-old maze of fact, tradition and almost incomprehensible jargon that John Adams faced when he sat at Putnam's desk and opened "Coke-Littleton."

3. From John's diary:

> *14 October, 1760.* I am beginning a new literary year in the twenty-sixth of my life. I am just entered on the fifth year of my studies in law, and I think it is high time for a reformation, both in the man and the lawyer. Twenty-five years of

the animal life is a great proportion to be spent to so little purpose; and four years, the space that we spend at college, is a great deal of time to spend for no more knowledge in the science and no more employment in the practice of law. Let me keep an exact journal, therefore, of the authors I read. This day I am beginning my Lord Hale's History of the Common Law, a book borrowed of Mr. Otis and read once already, analysis and all, with great satisfaction.

21 November, 1760. Friday. This day has been spent to little purpose. I must confine my body, or I never shall confine my thoughts: running to Doctor's, cutting wood, blowing fire, cutting tobacco — waste my time, scatter my thoughts, and divert my ambition. A train of thought is hard to procure; trifles light as air break the chain, interrupt the series. . . . Finished the History of the Common Law, the second time. The Dissertation on Hereditary Descents, and that on Trials by Juries, are really very excellent performances, and well worth repeated attentive reading.

26. Wednesday. Ten days are now elapsed since I began Hale the second time; and all the law I have read for ten days, is that book once through. I read Wood's Institute through the first time with Mr. Putnam, in twice that time, that is, in three weeks, and kept a school every day. My present inattention to law is intolerable and ruinous.

Night before Thanksgiving. I have read a multitude of law-books; mastered but few. Wood, Coke, two volumes Lilly's Abridgment, two volumes Salkeld's Reports, Swinburne, Hawkins's Pleas of the Crown, Fortescue, Fitz-Gibbon, ten volumes in folio I read, at Worcester, quite through, besides octavos and lesser volumes, and many others of all sizes that I consulted occasionally without reading in course, as dictionaries, reporters, entries, and abridgments, &c. . . .

I cannot give so good an account of the improvement of my two last years spent in Braintree. However, I have read no small number of volumes upon the law the last two years; — Justinian's Institutes I have read through in Latin, with Vinnius's perpetual notes; Van Muyden's Tractatio Institutionum Justiniani I read through and translated mostly into English, from the same language. Wood's Institute of the Civil Law, I read through. These on the Civil Law. On the Law of England I read Cowell's Institute of the Laws of England, in imitation of Justinian, Doctor and Student, Finch's Discourse

of Law, Hale's History, and some Reporters, Cases in Chancery, Andrews, &c., besides occasional searches for business; also a General Treatise of Naval Trade and Commerce, as founded on the laws and statutes. All this series of reading has left but faint impressions and a very imperfect system of law in my head. I must form a serious resolution of beginning and pursuing, quite through, the plans of my Lords Hale and Reeve. Wood's Institutes of Common Law I never read but once, and my Lord Coke's Commentary on Littleton I never read but once; these two authors I must get and read over and over again, and I will get them, too, and break through, as Mr. Gridley expressed it, all obstructions.

Besides I am but a novice in natural law and civil law. There are multitudes of excellent authors on natural law that I have never read; indeed, I never read any part of the best authors, Puffendorf and Grotius. In the civil law there are Hoppius and Vinnius, commentators on Justinian, Domat, &c., beside Institutes of Canon and Feudal Law that I have to read. Much may be done in two years, I have found already; and let it be my care that at the end of the next two years I be better able to show that no time has been lost, than I ever have been yet.

4. John's autobiography goes into some detail concerning this early crusade against pettifogging:

Looking about me, in the country, I found the practice of law was grasped into the hands of deputy sheriffs, pettifoggers, and even constables, who filled all the writs upon bonds, promissory notes, and accounts, received the fees established for lawyers, and stirred up many unnecessary suits. I mentioned these things to some of the gentlemen in Boston, who disapproved and even resented them very highly. I asked them whether some measures might not be agreed upon at the bar, and sanctioned by the court, which might remedy the evil. They thought it not only practicable, but highly expedient, and proposed meetings of the bar to deliberate upon it. A meeting was called, and a great number of regulations proposed, not only for confining the practice of law to those who were educated to it, and sworn to fidelity in it, but to introduce more regularity, urbanity, candor, and politeness, as well as honor, equity, and humanity, among the regular professors.

Many of these meetings were the most delightful entertainments

I ever enjoyed. The spirit that reigned was that of solid sense, generosity, honor, and integrity; and the consequences were most happy, for the courts and the bar, instead of scenes of wrangling chicanery, quibbling, and ill manners, were soon converted to order, decency, truth, and candor. Mr. Pratt was so delighted with these meetings and their effects, that when we all waited on him to Dedham, in his way to New York to take his seat as chief justice of that State, when we took leave of him, after dinner, the last words he said to us, were, "Brethren, above all things, forsake not the assembling of yourselves together."

5. Edmund Halley, the British astronomer (1656–1742), first saw this comet in 1682, and on the basis of Newton's theory calculated its orbit, identified it as the comet seen in 1531 and predicted its return in seventy-five years. The extraordinary accuracy of his prophecy was a stunning blow to superstition. Heretofore people had looked on comets as isolated wanderers in space, appearing and disappearing capriciously — a timely gift to pulpit preachers in need of celestial warnings for erring flocks. Halley's Comet appeared again in 1835 and 1910.

CHAPTER THIRTEEN

1. The figure for Canada's population is taken from James Truslow Adams: *Revolutionary New England*, 1691–1776, p. 223, footnote. The documents quoted by Adams show 80,000 as possibly too high. The other figures are taken from *American Population before the Federal Census of 1790*, by E. B. Greene and V. D. Harrington. This gives the population of the thirteen colonies (*in 1760*) as 1,695,-000. It quotes Pownall's Memorial (1784) for the figure 250,000 for Massachusetts (*before 1765; in 1773:* 300,000; in *1774:* 350,000).

Further figures from Greene and Harrington:

Philadelphia (1760), 18 or 20,000 people, nearly 3000 houses.
All Pennsylvania, about 250,000.
New York City (1761), 12,000 people, with 2000 houses.
Colony of N. Y., 80 to 100,000 people.
Charleston (1763), 4000 whites, 4000 Negro servants, 1100 dwelling houses.
South Carolina entire: 30 to 40,000 whites, 70,000 slaves.

Concerning Jonathan Mayhew's daring prophecy, it must be remembered that "Massachusetts herself still held to the ancient limits

from sea to sea laid down by royal patent in the Charter of 1629."
(From LAWRENCE GIPSON: *The British Empire before the American Revolution.*)

2. Lord Morton wrote this to Lord Hardwicke, the great equity lawyer who opposed Bute's peace plans. ". . . If our Governments [in North America] are properly circumscribed," the letter went on, "and care taken that the new settlements should be formed into new Governments of small extent; the mutual jealousy amongst the several Colonys would always keep them in a state of dependence and it would save a vast expense to Britain in not being obliged to keep up a great number of regular forces which must be maintained if the smallest spot is left with the French upon that Continent."
—L. B. NAMIER: *England in the Age of the American Revolution,* p. 323.

3. Carl Becker, in his *Eve of the Revolution,* gives the sworn statement of a customs man in Salem:

> I, SAMPSON TOOVEY, Clerk to James Cockle, Esq., Collector of His Majesty's Customs for the Port of Salem, do declare on oath, that ever since I have been in office, it hath been customary for said Cockle to receive of the masters of vessels entering from Lisbon, casks of wine, boxes of fruit, etc., which was a gratuity for suffering their vessels to be entered with salt or ballast only, and passing over unnoticed such cargoes of wine, fruit, etc., which are prohibited to be imported into His Majesty's plantations. Part of which wine, fruit, etc., the said James Cockle used to share with Governor Bernard. And I further declare that I used to be the negotiator of this business, and receive the wine, fruit, etc., and dispose of them agreeable to Mr. Cockle's orders.
> Witness my hand.
>
> SAMPSON TOOVEY

4. The *Gazette* carried the "Umbrilloe" advertisement every week for some time. With it the editors ran an impressive drawing of a woman holding a small umbrella above her head, stiff and straight. She had a severe expression, a stylish turban and a dress cut square and so low as to display the line, drawn black and plain as on a map, between two magnificent, round ripe bosoms.

5. As early as 1646, Edward Winslow, the agent sent to England to plead for the judicial and legislative rights of Massachusetts, argued that "if the Parliament of England should impose laws upon us, having no burgesses in their House of Commons, nor capable of a

summons by reason of the vast distance of the ocean, being three thousand miles from London, then wee should lose the libertie and freedome of English indeed."

And in 1678 the General Court wrote to the Lords of Trade: "That the Acts passed in Parliament for encouraging trade and navigation, wee humbly conceive, according to the usual sayings of the learned in the lawe, that the lawes of England are bounded within the fower seas, and doe not reach America; the subjects of his Majestie here not being represented in Parliament."

6. No register of the officers of the Province was published before 1768. This figure — twelve barristers — may be a little high. Seven years later, in 1768, there were only twenty-five barristers registered in the whole of Massachusetts, of which ten were in Boston, five in Essex County and one in Middlesex (Jonathan Sewall). (Figures from EMORY WASHBURN: *Judicial History of Massachusetts*.)

7. Benjamin Pratt had already been made Chief Justice of New York (an appointment he owed to his friendship with former Governor Powell), and was about to leave the Province forever.

8. My account of the writs trial is drawn from John's own notes, taken on the spot (*Works* II, Appendix A), and from Josiah Quincy's *Reports of Cases Argued and Adjudged in the Superior Court of Judicature of the Province of Massachusetts Bay between 1761 and 1772*. Quincy's book, published in 1865, has an extremely interesting discussion of the trial, written by Judge Horace Gray of Boston. John's autobiography (written in 1805) contains an account, and during the years 1815–1818 he wrote vivid descriptions of the trial to various friends: Dr. J. Morse, William Tudor, H. Niles (*Works* X). By this time, however (some fifty years after the event), John's enthusiasm had caused him to put into Otis's mouth as of February, 1761, every idea and argument Otis was to conjure up for the next six years concerning the rights of the colonies. For instance, "taxation without representation." There is no contemporary evidence that Otis used this phrase in 1761.

John's diary makes no mention of the trial other than the passing statement that he had taken "an abstract of the argument." For this reason, scholars suspect that John's later accounts exaggerate the effect Otis's speech had on him personally as a young man. Nevertheless, the principles Otis enunciated that day were the principles upon which John's political life was guided thenceforth. To every young man there comes a time, an hour, that sharpens and crystallizes his plan for action, reveals the path that is his to tread. Recognition of this moment may not come until much later.

CHAPTER FOURTEEN

1. This statement rests on the evidence of John's character. All that he said and did points that way. Let the reader go carefully through the excerpt below, from the autobiography. John Adams was an honest man. Why did he write the last paragraph, unless to confess his virginity and the fact that, at seventy-odd, he was still proud of it, still believed he had behaved wisely in this long and difficult constriction?

I was of an amorous disposition . . . And very early, from ten or eleven years of age, was very fond of the society of females. I had my favorites among the young women, and spent many of my evenings in their company; and this disposition, although controlled for seven years after my entrance into college, returned and engaged me too much till I was married.

I shall draw no characters, nor give any enumeration of my youthful flames. It would be considered as no compliment to the dead or the living. This, I will say; — they were all modest and virtuous girls, and always maintained their character through life. No virgin or matron had ever cause to blush at the sight of me, or to regret her acquaintance with me. No father, brother, son, or friend, ever had cause of grief or resentment for any intercourse between me and any daughter, sister, mother, or any other relation of the female sex.

These reflections, to me consolatory beyond all expression, I am able to make with truth and sincerity; and I presume I am indebted for this blessing to my education. This has been rendered the more precious to me, as I have seen enough of the effects of a different practice. Corroding reflections through life are the never failing consequence of illicit amours in old as well as new countries. The happiness of life depends more upon innocence in this respect than upon all the philosophy of Epicurus or of Zeno without it.

2. Smallpox doctors and privately owned hospitals for inoculation advertised enthusiastically in the Boston papers, careful to state at the outset whether they were prepared to treat "the rich or the plebeian." One such announcement ran as follows:

Ibrahim Mustapha, Innoculator to his Sublime Highness & the Janissaries: original Inventor & sole Proprietor of that Inestimable Instrument, the Circassian Needle, is just arriv'd from Constantinople where he has inoculated about 50,000 people without losing a Single

Patient. He requires not the least Preparation Regimen or Confinement. Ladies and Gentlemen who wish to be inoculated need only acquaint him with how many Pimples they choose and he makes the exact number of Punctures with his Needle which produces the Eruptions in the very Picquers. Ladies who fancy a favorite Pitt may have it put in any Spot they please, of any size.

CHAPTER FIFTEEN

1. In Vol. 6 of his series, *The British Empire before the American Revolution*, Lawrence Gipson disproves some pleasing national myths, notably the legend that the English colonists singlehanded drove the French from their shores, proudly repudiating British help. On the contrary, the colonies begged for it, considered it Britain's duty to protect their frontiers yet often refused maintenance to the redcoats whose presence had been implored. General Braddock's ill-fated troops were not alone in their ignorance of wilderness fighting. Only a minority of Americans — frontiersmen, mountain men, fur traders — were wise in these techniques.

2. The first appearance of the Proclamation of '63 was Shelburne's work, not Grenville's. Britain looked on it as a temporary contrivance to quiet the Indians until the Western lands could be successfully purchased for them. Pontiac's uprising, beginning with the red-stained tomahawk and war belt sent to the tribes in '62, had proven that the Indians were still a danger. There had been war along the whole line from Mississippi to Canada. Pontiac's savages besieged the fort at Detroit for five months and nearly captured it. The Proclamation would prevent a repetition of such uprisings.

CHAPTER SIXTEEN

1. Two of these letters were entitled "On Private Revenge," the third "On Self-Delusion." They appeared in the Boston *Gazette* for Aug. 1, Aug. 29 and Sept. 5, 1763, and can be found in the *Works* III. My quotations are verbatim except for the two sentences beginning "No other nation" and ending, "responsibility of every citizen." Here I condensed John's meaning, spread by him originally over many pages.

In writing this book, my knottiest problem was how to persuade people to read John's innumerable newspaper essays, speeches, Instructions, informative letters, and so on. I was at much pains therefore to invent devices of presentation. Sometimes, as above, John

"remembers" his essays of propaganda; sometimes he dictates them to Abby, as in Chapter Twenty-eight.

For John's trip to Falmouth and Pownalborough in the summer of 1765, the Maine Hist. Soc. Coll. (Vol. I, pp. 301–308) has a careful and informative paper by J. Williamson called "The Professional Tours of John Adams in Maine." Most people, says Williamson, made the journey from Boston to Maine by water, there being no roads before 1800. John, however, went on horseback, "finding his way through the woods from Brunswick to Fort Richmond by blazed trees." Incidentally, John won his case — a land case — at Pownalborough (now Dresden). "Munjoy's Hill" was where John walked at Falmouth with Sewall.

2. John's diary for 1765 has long entries concerning Gridley's law club. "The sodality," John called it — "the junto, a private association for the study of law and oratory." There were only four or five members; they met at a Boston tavern on Thursday evenings. John rode from Braintree in snow and storm to attend. The club read Cicero, Lord Kames, Blackstone, Richard Hurd's Dialogues (published 1759) — and received with coldness John's reference, one night, to Rousseau's recently published *Social Contract*. "The observation you quote," said Gridley with finality, "proves that Rousseau is shallow."

Members prepared papers to read aloud; Gridley said he would arrange to have them published when possible. "For it should be part of our plan," Gridley said further, "to improve ourselves in writing, by reading carefully the best English writers, and by using ourselves to writing. I hope and expect to see at the Bar in consequence of this sodality, a purity, an elegance and a spirit surpassing any thing that ever appeared in America."

"The sodality," John's diary continues for Feb. 21, 1765, "has given rise to the following speculation of my own. . . ." There follows the first draft of John's paper "On the Canon and Feudal Law."

3. The morning after the mob scene, someone picked out of the street the entire second volume of Hutchinson's *History of the Colony of Massachusetts Bay* and gave it to the Reverend Andrew Eliot for safekeeping. It can be seen today, part in the State House at Boston and part in the Massachusetts Historical Society, with the muddy footprints of the rioters still showing. The completed three volumes were published in Boston, 1764–1828, and in London, 1765–1828. Volume III covers the years 1760–1774. It is an excellent source book for the period, astonishingly fair and objective, considering what the author suffered at the hands of Massachusetts. Hutchinson

had the born scholar's accuracy; yet in his prim, meticulous way he brings his scene vividly to the eye.

In an Appendix Hutchinson prints the chief documents of his long quarrel with the Massachusetts radicals from 1761 to July, 1772 — each angry, sarcastic message from Boston Selectmen or House of Representatives, and Hutchinson's dignified, hortatory and quite ineffectual replies. "I wish," he told the House on one occasion, "you had spared such *coarse and indecent* epithets." Hutchinson's account of the riot against his own house and life is nothing short of superb. Remotely, in the third person singular, Hutchinson describes *the chief-justice* walking into the courtroom next morning, *in an ordinary undress, in which he was sitting in the evening when the alarm was given him; his robes and every other garment being taken out of his house, or destroyed in it.* There was something very admirable about Thomas Hutchinson. History and his biographers have not done him justice.

4. John's Essay was published in England in 1768, as *A Dissertation on the Canon and Feudal Law*. Mr. Hollis of London, Harvard's great benefactor, called it the best American work that had crossed the Atlantic. In that same year, the Reverend Dr. Chauncy of Boston wrote to Dr. Ezra Stiles (later to be President of Yale): "The author is but a young man, not above 33 or 34, but of incomparable sense, a true son of liberty and as well able to write or talk upon it as any one I am acquainted with. I esteem that piece one of the best that has been written. It has done honor to its author; and it is a pity but he should be known." The essay was reprinted in London twice before it was published as a book in America in 1783.

"On the Canon and Feudal Law" is even better than Hollis said it was. It can be found in the *Works* III, just after the article "On Private Revenge." It repays reading aloud — especially from page 462, *Let us tenderly cherish . . .* , to page 463: *In a word, let every sluice of knowledge be opened and set a-flowing.*

CHAPTER EIGHTEEN

1. "Mr. John Adams was a distant relation and intimate acquaintance of Mr. Samuel Adams. After his education at the college, he applied to the study of the law, a short time before the troubles began. He is said to have been at a loss which side to take . . . As the troubles increased, he increased in knowledge, and made a figure, not only in his own profession but as a patriot, and was generally esteemed

as a person endowed with more knowledge than his kinsman, and equally zealous in the cause of liberty; but neither his business nor his health would admit of that constant application to it, which distinguished the other from all the rest of the province. In general, he may be said to be of stronger resentment upon any real or supposed personal neglect or injury than the other; but, in their resentment against such as opposed them in the cause in which they were engaged, it is difficult to say which exceeded."
— THOMAS HUTCHINSON: *History of Massachusetts Bay*, pp. 296–297.

2. John tells this story at much length in the autobiography (*Works* II, pp. 210–212). Thomas Hutchinson's *History* gives a very different version of the affair. Sewall, says Hutchinson, promised John that if he would go over to the crown side, it would be arranged with Governor Bernard to make John "a justice of the peace." . . . "The Governor," says Hutchinson, "took time to consider of it, and having, as Mr. Adams conceived, not taken proper notice of him, or given him offence on some former occasion, he no longer deliberated, and ever after joined in opposition."

This is one place where Hutchinson let bitterness blot his usually admirable historical objectivity. Even had John possessed a character open to bribes, he would — if he were as ambitious as Hutchinson declared — certainly have aimed higher than a mere justice of the peace.

CHAPTER NINETEEN

1. Lord Barrington to Governor Bernard (Feb. 12, '69): "I am convinced the Town Meeting at Boston which assembled the States of the Province against the King's Authority, & armed the People to resist his forces, was guilty of high Crimes & Misdemeanors, if not of Treason; And that Mr. Otis the *Moderator* (as he is improperly called) of that Meeting together with the Selectmen of Boston who signed the Letters convoking the Convention, should be impeach'd. This would convey terror to the Wicked & factious Spirits all over the Continent, & would shew that the Subjects of Great Britain must not rebel with impunity anywhere. Five or Six Examples are sufficient; And it is right they should be made in Boston, the Only place where there has been actual Crime."

2. "This odious cause," John wrote in his autobiography, "was suspended at last only by the battle of Lexington, which put an end forever to all such prosecutions." Written some forty years after the event, this was one of the large symbolical statements in which

John indulged when he wished to point history toward the patriot's side. The case itself is fully discussed by Judge Horace Gray in the appendix to Josiah Quincy Junior's invaluable *Reports of Cases in Massachusetts Bay between 1761–1772*. Here John's notes, from the ledger he called his Admiralty Book, are given in full, beginning with Sewall's "information and order of process," and ending with John's own defense, which reads as vividly — and as impressively — as if written yesterday. See also Hutchinson's *History*, Vol. III, p. 189, and Gordon's *American War*, Vol. I, pp. 168, 174. A full bibliography of other sources for the case is included in Gray's discussion.

3. When John walked down the Court House steps after this trial, the boatswain of the British frigate *Rose* was waiting. He and his shipmates, the man said, were deeply grateful for John's defense of the American sailors whose ship the *Rose's* men had boarded in order to impress seamen. For twenty years, the boatswain added, it had been his business to fight "with honest men to deprive them of their liberty, I always thought I ought to be hanged for it & now I know it." (John Adams to Dr. J. Morse: *Works* X, p. 208). "This trial," John's letter goes on to say, "is a mystery never yet explained, a labyrinth without a clue! an enigma that can never be unriddled." See also the vividly descriptive letter to William Tudor, *Works* II, pp. 224–226. In the same volume, Appendix B, are John's notes for his brief in the trial. Volume X, p. 206, footnote, states that further such notes "have been found." Probably they are among the Adams Papers at the Massachusetts Historical Society.

CHAPTER TWENTY

1. Anyone desiring to know more fully what the rioters said to each other on the morning of March 2 and the night of March 5, 1770, can find it in Frederic Kidder's *History of the Boston Massacre* (1870). Kidder gives the sworn testimony of nearly a hundred witnesses, also the *96 Depositions* sent to England by Sam Adams and Co.

2. This is the summons for the town meeting of March 6, 1770, after the Boston Massacre:

In His Majesty's name, you are required forthwith to warn all the freeholders and other inhabitants of the town of Boston, legally qualified, ratable at twenty pounds' estate to a single rate (beside the poll), to convene at Faneuil Hall, on Tuesday the sixth instant,

three o'clock afternoon, to consider what measures are most proper to be taken to preserve the peace of the town at this alarming and important period.

Hereof fail not, and make return of this warrant, with your doings thereon, unto myself as soon as may be before the time of said meeting.

Dated at Boston, the sixth day of March, in the tenth year of His Majesty's reign, annoque Domini, 1770. — *By order of the Selectmen,* WILLIAM COOPER, *Town-clerk.*

On the back of the warrant is the return of the twelve constables for the twelve wards, dated March 6, to the effect that they had duly warned the inhabitants.

Although this official notice said three o'clock, people assembled in the morning, drifting quite naturally to the Old South. Perhaps Sam, seeing it, hastened to bring Dr. Cooper and hold the crowd in the church all day, rather than let them mill aimlessly and dangerously about the streets.

3. This was the greatest personal triumph of Sam Adams's life, and Sam lived to be eighty-one. John was not in the Council Chamber that day, but he knew the scene as if he had been a participant, and his old age reveled in the recollection. See especially the letter of April 15, 1817, to his former law clerk, William Tudor (*Works* X, pp. 249–253), where John describes his night watch after the Massacre: "We were all upon a level: No man was exempted, our military officers were our only superiors. I had the honour to be summoned, in my turn, & attended at the state-house with my musket & bayonet, my broadsword & cartridge box, under the command of the famous Paddock. I know you will laugh at my military figure, but I believe there was not a more obedient soldier in the Regiment . . ."

Incidentally, by cartridge-box John must have meant a case containing powder or bullets. Cartridges had not been invented in 1770.

4. On May 8, 1770, James Bowdoin had been elected Representative in place of Otis. But Bowdoin was sent up to the Council (or Senate) in a general election, leaving the place once more vacant.

CHAPTER TWENTY-ONE

1. "In truth, although no people have indulged more largely than the Americans in violent, reckless, and unscrupulous language, no

people have at every period of their history been more signally free from the thirst for blood, which in moments of great political excitement has often shown both in England and France. It is a characteristic fact that one of the first protests against the excessive multiplication of capital offenses in the English legislation of the eighteenth century was made by the Assembly of Massachusetts, which in 1762 objected to death as a punishment for forgery on the ground that 'the House are very averse to capital punishment in any case where the interest of the Government does not absolutely require it,' and where some other punishment will be sufficiently deterrent. According to Dr. Price *On Civil Liberty*, not more than one execution had taken place in Massachusetts Bay in eighteen years. The annual average of executions in London alone for twenty-three years before 1772 was from twenty-nine to thirty." (From LECKY: *American Revolution.*)

2. To the end of his life, John wondered why Attorney General Jonathan Sewall did not remain in Boston for the Massacre trials. It looked as if Sewall preferred his duties as Admiralty Judge in Nova Scotia, five hundred safe miles from the Boston mob. John wondered also why Sam Quincy and Robert Treat Paine were named as lawyers for the prosecution. Who was responsible for choosing them? (See John's letter to Jedidiah Morse, Jan. 5, 1816, *Works* X, p. 201.)

3. In his letter to Morse of Jan. 5, 1816, *op. cit.*, John mentions a stenographical report that had been sent to England. No such report has been preserved. For the incident of John's stopping young Josiah Quincy in his cross-examination, see William Gordon, *History of the American War*, Vol. I, p. 205. Concerning the surprisingly inadequate performance of the lawyers for the prosecution, Captain Preston himself bore witness in a letter to General Gage. (R. G. ADAMS: *New Light on the Boston Massacre.*) R. T. Paine and Samuel Quincy were skillful lawyers — it looked almost as if they did not want to win for the crown.

Politically, the whole affair is extremely involved. The crown was forced to prosecute; promise of fair trial was the only way to prevent the Boston mob from lynching all eight defendants. The prosecution, however, could hardly have had its heart in the argument. How could the crown desire to hang British soldiers who in the face of great provocation had fired on an unruly and "treasonable" mob of colonials? The crown lawyers included one Tory, Sam Quincy, and one liberty man, Robert Treat Paine. (Four years later, Paine was to be John's colleague at the Continental Congress.) The lawyers for the defense were the most ardent liberty men available; John Adams and Josiah were, like the prosecution, forced to argue

against their own political party. Of the four judges, three were crown sympathizers, men of great probity. Everyone knew that Lynde, Oliver and Cushing could not be tempted by threat or bribe.

As for John Adams, even had the trial been rigged, his part would have been no less dangerous. John was defending nine men whom most of Boston considered dastardly murderers, men moreover who represented a hated policy of coercion by the mother country. Our interest in the trial lies in the part John played and its effect on his character and career. My text therefore does not stress these political involutions and complications.

Besides Frederic Kidder, R. G. Adams, *op. cit.*, and William Gordon's and Thomas Hutchinson's *Histories,* my chief sources for the trials are the *Works* II, X; Boyle's *Journal of Occurrences in Boston, 1759–1778;* Peleg W. Chandler's *American Criminal Trials;* Frothingham's *Life of General Warren;* Hosmer's *Life of Thomas Hutchinson;* Wells's *Samuel Adams,* Vol. II; Esther Forbes's *Paul Revere;* Tudor's *James Otis;* Miller's *Sam Adams,* and Weldon. See Bibliography.

4. Captain Preston returned to England early in 1771. On March 5 — exactly one year after the Massacre — Lord Barrington wrote to General Gage: "Captain Preston has had all his expenses paid and a Pension of £200 a year bestowed upon him. He is a perfectly satisfied Man, which is a thing not to be found every day."

CHAPTER TWENTY-THREE

1. Concerning John's payment for the trials, he himself says in a letter to Jedidiah Morse (1816): The trials "destroyed as much of my popularity as Mr. Pitt lost by accepting a peerage and a pension. It was instantly propagated that I had been bribed by an immense fee, to sell my country. I never uttered a word or suggested a hint alluding to fees from first to last. A single guinea was put into my hand by the Irish infant, for a retaining fee; ten guineas were offered on the first trial and eight at the second, and accepted without looking at them or uttering a word. These nineteen guineas were all the fees I ever received for a whole year of distressing anxiety, and for thirteen or fourteen days of the hardest labor that I ever went through. Add to all this all the taunts and scoffs and bitter reproaches of the Whigs, and the giggling and tittering of the Tories, which was more provoking than all the rest. (*Works,* X, p. 202.)

The official expense account was as follows:

Acc^t. of Sums Expended in the Defence of Capt. Thos. Preston of the 29th Reg^t. and Soldiers of said Reg^t. at Boston, prosecuted for a Riot on the 5th of March 1770.*

To a retaining fee to C: Prestons Lawyers	£	10–10–
To ―― D^o: ―― to the mens ―― D^o:		10–10–
To a fee for pleading at the tryal to C: Prestons Lawyers		63–―
To ―― D^o: ―― to the Mens ―― D^o:		42–―
To an Attorney to assist at their tryal		10–10–
To an Attorney for taking some affidavits		3–12–
To certain people employed to enquire about town & collect Affidavits & Evidences		25–10–
To Summons's & serving them on 93 Evidences		13–19–
To Evidences for the time they waited in Court before examin:		5–19–
To Gaolers fees		15–―
To Turnkeys fees & Civility money		21–―
To a Clerk at several times		15–7–6
To small presents to particular people in Boston		21–―
To postage of Letters		2–5–
	£	260–2–6
To extra: expences in coming express from Portsmouth to London with Governour Hutchinson & Comodore Gambiers dispatches to Government		4–4–6
	£	264–7–

2. In 1774, John bought from his brother, Peter Boylston, the old house next door where he was born, also the barn and thirty-five acres that belonged with it.

CHAPTER TWENTY-FOUR

1. It was Daniel Leonard who called the Committees of Correspondence "the foulest, subtlest and most venomous serpent that ever issued from the egg of sedition." John Adams, in the Boston *Gazette*, made a nice rejoinder. "I," he wrote, "should rather call them the *ichneumon*, a very industrious, active and useful animal,

*From R. G. ADAMS: *New Light on the Boston Massacre*, Am. Ant. Soc. Proc. 1937, New Series, Vol. 47, p. 354.

which was worshipped in Egypt as a divinity because it defended the country from the ravages of the crocodiles. It was the whole occupation of this little creature to destroy these wily and ravenous monsters. It crushed their eggs wherever they laid them, and with a wonderful address and courage, would leap into their mouths, penetrate their entrails and never leave until it had destroyed them."

Daniel Leonard hailed from Taunton, the foremost town in southern Massachusetts. "Land of the Leonards," John called it when he went there to attend court. Daniel Leonard was a wit, a card player and a great swell — the first Massachusetts lawyer to sport his own coach and pair. John knew him well and liked him until Leonard turned Tory.

2. Sam Adams had never liked Franklin, and in 1770 had opposed his appointment as London agent for Massachusetts. Not only was Franklin far from pious in religion, but he was too friendly with the British ministry and had even enjoyed a visit to Lord Hillsborough at his Irish castle. John Miller in his book *Sam Adams* suggests that Franklin sent the Hutchinson letters in order to redeem his own bad reputation with the Massachusetts Whigs.

3. To the end of his life, John maintained he did not know who had taken part in the Boston Tea Party. At the time it happened, he said he did not want to know. Suppose he were called to defend these "Mohawks" in court? He must give the Solicitor General no loophole, no reason to summon him to the witness stand.

Years after the event, "Captain" Mackintosh of the South Enders boasted, "It was my chickens did the trick." Yet the trick was not done after the manner of Mackintosh's chickens. It was a movement orderly, controlled. The "Mohawks" left the ships and marched through town like soldiers, to the music of a fife. Concerning John's absence in Plymouth that night, I have my own theory. I think he stayed away on purpose and that Sam Adams wanted him to stay away. John Adams arguing for the defense would be far more useful than John as one more Indian dumping tea.

4. The Port Bill, the Murder Bill and the bill for "better regulating the government of Massachusetts Bay" were known as "the Intolerable Acts." The Quebec Act which followed strengthened colonial resistance enormously; it was in fact more significant than any colonial act passed by Parliament since 1767. Yet we are not immediately concerned with it, because it was not aimed at Boston and was in no way a consequence of the Tea Party. The Quebec Act had been under consideration in England since 1763; it was a revision of the admittedly temporary Western Proclamation — a "completion" of the new system of empire.

The bill granted to the French inhabitants of Quebec, among other benefits, complete freedom of religion; it was a highly creditable piece of toleration and statesmanship on Britain's part. But New England reacted with a veritable howl of rage: religious tolerance in this instance meant the encouragement of Roman Catholicism. Surely then, the Act presaged also the establishment of an American Episcopacy, with an Anglican Bishop, a Palace and accompanying monstrosities? Massachusetts had feared these things for some two hundred years, long before Great-uncle Peter declared to his small nephew John that he smelled incense from Braintree's Episcopal doorsill and it made him mortally sick.

The Quebec Act was not passed till June 22, 1774, five days after the Massachusetts Legislature, meeting at Salem, voted for a general American congress, to "consider measures for the recovery of rights and liberties, *civil and religious.*"

5. There is some doubt about the details of this story. The incident may have occurred sooner, on May 30, at the town meeting to appoint a Donation Committee for the Boston starving. Charles Francis Adams (*Works,* I, p. 46) says it was not Josiah Quincy but the merchant, Thomas Boylston, whom John defended with his quotation from Milton. My version comes from the diary of Josiah Quincy's son, who under date of July 10, 1820, tells of a visit to John Adams at Quincy, when John told him the tale. See *Memoir of the Life of Josiah Quincy, Junior,* by his son Josiah Quincy.

6. Peter Oliver in his *Origins and Progress of the American Rebellion,* ms. 1776, turns his sharpest strokes on Sam: "He understood human Nature so well, that he could turn the Minds of the great Vulgar as well as the small into any Course that he might chuse. . . . Mr. Hancock was as closely attached to the hindermost Part of Mr. (S.) Adams as the Rattles are affixed to the Tail of the Rattle Snake." Oliver goes on to say that Hancock, now and again, almost succeeded in freeing himself, when "Adams, like the Cuttlefish, would discharge his muddy Liquid, darken the water to such an Hue, that the other was lost to his Way. Mr. (S.) Adams was all serpentine Cunning, Mr. Otis was rash, unguarded, foulmouthed, and openly spiteful. Mr. Adams had a good Voice and was a Master of Vocal Musick. This Genius he improved, by instituting a singing Society of Mechanicks, where he preesided and embraced such opportunities to ye inculcating Sedition, 'till it ripened into Rebellion."

Of the Boston Congregational clergy — "Mr. Otis's black Regiment" — Peter Oliver calls Dr. Chauncy "hoary-haired, of exorbi-

tant Passions, resentful and unforgiving." Mayhew is "slow and awkward but powerful"; Dr. Cooper, "young, polite, of a general knowledge, attractive, Insinuating with the fair Sex. His tongue is Butter and Oil, but under it the Poison of Asps."

CHAPTER TWENTY–FIVE

1. From the *Boston Gazette* of August 15, 1774. "Wednesday morning, the Hon. Thomas Cushing, Esq., Mr. Samuel Adams, John Adams, and Robert Treat Paine, Esquires—the delegates appointed by the *Hon. Commons House of Assembly*, for this Province, to attend the General Congress to be holden at Philadelphia, some time next month, — set out from hence, attended by a number of gentlemen, who accompanied them to Watertown, where they were met by many others, who provided an elegant entertainment for them. After dinner, they proceeded on their journey, intending to reach Southborough that evening."

The editors, it will be observed, had a hard time deciding what to call their own Provincial Legislature. "House of Representatives" or "General Assembly" was no longer enough. *"Hon. Commons House of Assembly"* seemed nearer to the parliamentary status they desperately desired to attain.

2. Jonathan Sewall sailed for England early in 1775, less than a year after this farewell at Falmouth. He was formally banished by the patriots, his property declared forfeit. He lived in England about twelve years, then returned to Nova Scotia, where he had been judge of admiralty, and lived there until his death in 1796, never once revisiting his native land. But his fate was not wholly bitter; one of his sons became Chief Justice of Lower Canada, the other Solicitor General.

While Sewall was living in London, John Adams arrived in the guise of first Minister to the Court of St. James's from the United States of America and promptly called on Sewall. "When he came in," wrote Sewall later, "he took my hand in both of his and with a hearty squeeze, accosted me in these words: 'How do you do, my dear old friend?' Our conversation was just such as might be expected at the meeting of two old sincere friends after a long separation. Adams has a heart formed for friendship and susceptible of its fondest feelings. He is humane, generous and open; warm in his friendly attachments, though perhaps rather implacable to those whom he thinks his enemies. . . . Gratified in the two darling wishes of his soul, the independence of America acknowledged and estab-

lished, and he himself placed on the very pinnacle of the temple of honor, why the very devil himself must have felt loving and good-natured after so complete a victory; much more, a man in whose heart lay dormant every good and virtuous, friendly and social principle.

"If he could but play backgammon, I declare I would choose him in preference to all the men in the world for my *fidus Achates*, in my projected asylum. And I believe he would soon find it the happiest state; for, if I am not mistaken, now he has reached the summit of his ambition,* he finds himself quite out of his element, and looks back with regret to those happy days, when in a snug house, with a pretty farm about him at Braintree, he sat quiet, in the full possession of domestic happiness. He was an honest lawyer as ever broke bread but he is not qualified, by nature or education, to shine in courts. His abilities are undoubtedly equal to the mechanical parts of his business as ambassador, but this is not enough. He cannot dance, drink, game, flatter, promise, dress, swear with the gentlemen and talk small talk and flirt with the ladies. In short, he has none of the essential arts or ornaments which constitute a courtier. There are thousands who, with a tenth part of his understanding and without a spark of his honesty, would distance him infinitely in any court in Europe. I will only add that I found many Americans in London, whose sentiments and conduct towards him were by no means so liberal or polite as I could have wished."

— From *Works*, I, pp. 57, 58, *n*.

3. In *Works* II, p. 512, *n*., is printed an interesting letter from John Adams to Timothy Pickering (written August 6, 1822), giving further details of the entry into Philadelphia in August, 1774. "Cushing, two Adamses, and Paine, all destitute of fortune, four poor pilgrims . . . were met at Frankford by Dr. Rush, Mr. Mifflin, Mr. Bayard and several others of the most active sons of liberty in Philadelphia, who desired a conference with us." These particular sons, it seems, were much exercised for fear the New England men "had independence in view." "You must not," they said, "utter the word independence nor give the least hint or insinuation of the idea, either in Congress or any private conversation. If you do, you are undone, for the idea of independence is as unpopular in Pennsylvania and in all the Middle States as the Stamp Act itself. Massachusetts has long been persecuted by Britain; your feelings have been hurt, your passions excited. You are thought to be too warm, too zealous, too sanguine.

---

* About nine years later, John was elected President of the United States.

You must be therefore very cautious, you must not pretend to take the lead. The Virginians are very proud of their ancient dominion, as they call it. They think they have a right to take the lead, and the Southern States, and Middle States, too, are too much disposed to yield it to them."

CHAPTER TWENTY-SIX

1. Visitors to Carpenters' Hall today will find not two chambers but one. After the Revolution the building was used as a bank and the interior walls were taken down, the entire ground floor thrown into one room. Even so it looks about the right size for a Congress of fifty-six men. How they all crowded into the tiny East Room is a mystery.

2. The conservatives, by this time, were very tired of being confronted by *man in a state of nature*. In July of 1774 John wrote Abby a story of one such sufferer, a Salem man named Porter. While the General Court was wrangling with the Governor, Porter, John said, "came upon the floor and asked a member, 'What state are you in now?' The member answered, 'In a state of nature.' 'Aye,' says Porter, 'and you will be damned before you will get into a state of grace!'" (*Familiar Letters*, p. 12.)

CHAPTER TWENTY-SEVEN

1. Concerning the slave trade . . . There were 500,000 blacks in America in 1774, and 2,100,000 whites. In South Carolina, four fifths of the population was black. Rhode Island in 1777 was the first state to legislate against slavery. Most members of the First Congress owned slaves. John Adams's mother had given him a Negro servant of hers when he married; there is no record he had freed her. On September 24 Abigail wrote to John from Boston, "I wish most sincerely there was not a slave in the Province. It always appeared a most iniquitous scheme to me — to fight ourselves for what we are daily robbing and plundering from those who have as good a right to freedom as we have. You know my mind upon this subject." (*Familiar Letters*, pp. 41, 42.)

2. Through understatement, my account of Galloway's Plan of Union may be misleading. Galloway was no villain. Few men had worked harder over the problem of empire and commonwealth. In times of revolution, the middle-of-the-roader is always branded

"traitor." The relationship of English-speaking peoples is not settled today. Julian Boyd's *Anglo-American Union* (Pennsylvania Press, 1941) presents brilliantly "Galloway's Plan of 1774" as also his later Plans of Union, to 1788.

3. In 1817, John wrote his friend Jackson from Quincy: "In 1774 I became acquainted with Mckean, Rodney and Henry. Those three appeared to me to see more clearly to the end of the business than any others of the whole body." John wrote Jefferson that of the members of Congress in 1774, only Patrick Henry seemed "sensible of that the precipice on which he stood and had candor and courage enough to acknowledge it." *Works* X, pp. 269, 278.

4. It is impossible to know the proportion of loyalists or Tories in America, either in 1774 or later. Contemporary figures differed according to the political slant of the compiler. In 1780, John Adams stated that loyalists made up only one twentieth of the population — but when he said it he was in Holland, trying busily to prove that the colonies were united for independence. In 1813, John declared one third had been averse to revolution, one third lukewarm and one third active for revolution. This was probably as accurate as anyone's guess. Today it is assumed that the active revolutionists represented about 10 per cent of the population.

CHAPTER TWENTY-EIGHT

1. In the Autobiography, this episode of the "horse-jockey" is undated; it seems to come in the fall of 1775 — later than I give it. The recollections of John's old age were notoriously inaccurate as to dates, and I feel justified in this possible shift of timing. Incidentally, by "horse-jockey" John probably meant horse dealer, not a racing rider.

2. Five years earlier, Adam Smith had written:

> The rulers of Great Britain had for more than a century past amused the people with the imagination that they possessed a great empire on the west side of the Atlantic.
>
> This empire has hitherto existed in the imagination only. It has hitherto been not an empire but the project of an empire: not a gold mine but the project of a gold mine; a project which has cost, which continues to cost, and which if pursued in the same way it has been hitherto, is likely to cost immense expense without being very likely to bring any profit. If the project cannot be completed it ought to be given up.

CHAPTER TWENTY-NINE

1. The story about Jehovah and the Continental Congress never came out till 1779, when Ethan Allen published his *Narrative of Captivity*. In May of 1775, Congress had the first news about the capture of Ticonderoga not from Allen but from Benedict Arnold. The *Journals* for May 18 report *the surprising and taking of Ticonderoga by a detachment from Massachusetts Bay and Connecticut*. Ethan Allen's commission was necessarily from Massachusetts, Vermont not being a state at the time. Allen's Green Mountain Boys were referred to by his enemies as "Allen's *wild people*" and by his friends as "the people on the N. Hampshire Grants." In his *First Year of the American Revolution*, Professor French has an exhaustive discussion of the whole story.

CHAPTER THIRTY

1. It was Doctor of Laws, and the citation said that General Washington, "by the most signal smiles of Divine Providence on his military operations, drove the Fleet and Troops of the enemy with disgraceful precipitation from the town of Boston."

CHAPTER THIRTY-ONE

1. John wrote this letter on April 22, before he knew that North Carolina had taken the desired action, and had gone much further than South Carolina. On April 12 the Provincial Congress of North Carolina, meeting at Halifax, instructed its delegates in Congress to "declare an independency" — thereby achieving the distinction of being the first state so to instruct.

CHAPTER THIRTY-TWO

1. To date, John had accepted in his Boston office three law students; William Tudor and Jonathan William Austin came to him in 1769. (See Chapter Nineteen.) Both young men were graduates of Harvard. Austin died in 1778, having served as a major in the Revolutionary War. William Tudor (1750–1818) later became Secretary of State for Massachusetts and a member of both houses of the Massachusetts Legislature.

Some time in 1774, John took a third clerk, Jonathan Mason of Boston (1752–1830), who, incidentally, had been an eyewitness to

the Boston Massacre and testified at the trial. Mason graduated from Princeton in '74, was admitted to the bar in '77 and served repeatedly in the Massachusetts Legislature. He was U. S. Senator from 1800 to 1803, and a Representative in Congress 1817–1820.

2. What we today call Delaware, was called before the Revolution "the Three Lower Counties on Delaware," or more familiarly, "the Lower Counties." Though the Penn family held this colony as Proprietors — as they held Pennsylvania — and though the same governor usually presided over both Provinces, the Lower Counties had, since 1689, jealously maintained their own Legislature, courts, and currency. In 1776, each colony wrote its separate constitution. Political leaders frequently moved back and forth, living and holding office in both Provinces. No one thought it strange that Thomas McKean (that master of plural office holding) acted at the same time as Chief Justice of Pennsylvania, Assemblyman in Delaware, Acting President of Delaware and Congressman from Delaware. Similar ambivalence in office holding sometimes existed between Pennsylvania and New Jersey.

3. Most of Philadelphia was far more concerned, that spring and summer of '76, with the new Pennsylvania Constitution than with the Declaration of Independence. The local upheaval was terrific. There were mass meetings, bonfires, marchings and near riot. Set up in July of '76, the new Pennsylvania government provided for a unicameral Legislature with no Senate or upper house. To John Adams, this was a calamity, the very anathema of government and he made no secret of his disapproval. Nevertheless Pennsylvania's government was her own affair; John did not dream of interfering and his disapproval made no breach in his friendship with the radical leaders. In 1790, Pennsylvania overthrew her constitution of '76 and set up a bicameral Legislature providing for House of Representatives and Senate, a form of government the State retains today.

CHAPTER THIRTY-THREE

1. The student who is curious about the changes in Jefferson's composition (made first by Franklin and Adams in committee, then by Congress) will find them set out clearly and dramatically in Carl Becker's *The Declaration of Independence* (1922), with a fascinating discussion of the literary and political implications of the entire document. Julian Boyd's *The Declaration of Independence — Evolution of the Text*, reproduces in photostat Jefferson's manuscript in various forms — his own Rough Draft (now so-called by historians)

as it was before the Committee took hold of it, then the copy which John made and sent home to Massachusetts before Congress passed it. Also copies of the Rough Draft which Jefferson sent to Madison, Richard Henry Lee and Cassius Lee in Virginia.

In stating that Congress "improved the document by every single alteration," I do not except the Congressional deletion of Jefferson's "vehement phillipic against slavery" (John Adams's words). Jefferson's indictment nowhere states that slavery is a disgrace to America and should be abolished root and branch *by Americans*. Instead, he turns his anger on the wrong culprit, twists a shameful fact of American life into an instrument of propaganda against George III — condemns the slave trade, then draws the sting by putting all blame and responsibility on the King of England:

> He has waged cruel war against human nature itself, violating it's most sacred rights of life & liberty in the persons of a distant people, who never offended him, captivating and carrying them into slavery in another hemisphere, or to incur miserable death in their transportation thither. this piratical warfare, the opprobrium of *infidel* powers, is the warfare of the *Christian* king of Great Britain. determined to keep an open market where MEN should be bought & sold, he has prostituted his negative for suppressing every legislative attempt to prohibit or restrain this execrable commerce: and that this assemblage of horrors might want no fact of distinguished die, he is now exciting, those very people to rise in arms among us, and to purchase that liberty of which *he* has deprived them, by murdering the people upon whom *he* also also obtruded them: thus paying off former crimes committed against the *liberties* of one people, with the crimes which he urges them to commit against the lives of another.

2. James Otis lived until 1783. From time to time he recovered his reason; he was even able to argue one or two cases in court, but the lucid periods never lasted long. Toward the end he left the family homestead at Barnstable and went to board with a kind and pleasant man named Osgood who owned a farm on the outskirts of Andover, Massachusetts. During these two final years Otis was quiet, always gentle, shared in the farm work as he could and gave no trouble, seldom wandering more than fifty yards from the house. He had often said that when he died, he wished he might go suddenly, by a flash of lightning. On Friday afternoon, May 23, 1783, a heavy cloud came up from the west; the Osgoods took shelter in their parlor

to wait for the storm to pass. Otis, leaning on his cane, stood against the post of the hall doorway, telling a story to the family. As yet there had been no lightning and no rain. Suddenly there came a blinding flash, and thunder shook the house. The family, rigid with terror on their chairs, saw Otis fall to the floor. When Osgood reached him, Otis was already dead.

ACKNOWLEDGMENTS

INSPIRED librarians are as rare as inspired college teachers. I wish to accord deepest thanks to John H. Powell of the Philadelphia Free Library, whose scholarly eye searched every word of my manuscript and whose constant challenge sent me on ever wider quests. I want to thank Clarence Brigham of Worcester, who opened his American Antiquarian Society to a visiting worker on very hot Sundays, Richard Norris Williams of the Pennsylvania Historical Society, who likes to see historic manuscripts read as well as preserved, and Stewart Mitchell of the Massachusetts Historical Society, who performed for me many kind offices. I want to thank the ladies behind the desk at the Biddle Law Library, the Haverford and Bryn Mawr College Libraries and the Congressional Library, who signed slips and forgot to count the weeks; Mrs. Sellers, who typed and retyped beyond the ordinary limits of endurance; Mr. Elkins of the Harvard Archives, who deciphers eighteenth-century script as if it were 72-point type; my friend Charles Everitt of New York, who with unprintable expletive and infinite good nature tracked down books that the loftiest names in the bookselling business declared unobtainable. I want to thank Harold Ober for wise and patient counsel, Julian Boyd for answering specific questions; also Richard Shryock, Otto Wolff, Harold Eberlein, Dr. Samuel Newhall, McKean Downs, Thomas Adams, Gordon Bassett, Zoltán Haraszti, Judge Daniel Gillen of the Boston Municipal Court, William Edwards of the Quincy Historical Society, Charles Warren of Washington, George G. Wollems of the Massachusetts Historical Society, and especially Mr. Frank Grinnell of Boston, who taught me much about John Adams, Constitution Maker. Esther Forbes and her mother, Mrs. Harriette Merrifield Forbes, showed me new paths to old New England. Mr. Henry Adams answered questions about John's college years and himself checked various Adams quotations from the originals; Mrs. Abigail Adams Homans took me on a wonderful pilgrimage to the home of her grandsires.

A WORD ABOUT SOURCES
AND METHODS

THE facts on which my narrative is based are available to everyone. I aim not to startle with new material but to persuade with old, and I have chosen the narrative form because for me it is the most persuasive. "Fictionalized biography" is the current label; I myself do not admit a phrase which, besides being doubtful English, does not express what I have tried to do. Call it, rather, a portrait of John Adams. I have drawn a portrait and like Saint-Mémin I have used the *physionotrace;* I have found instruments with which to measure and then I have gone ahead and painted. In brief, I studied the available evidence and, on the basis of it, built pictures which to me are consistent with the evidence.

Everything that has been written on political economy or the public policy of America since 1745 bears on the career of John Adams. Books as diverse as Aristotle's *Politics,* Shryock's *Development of Modern Medicine* (1947) and Oman's *On the Art of Writing History* (1939) have helped to form this biography. Among general works, four were to me most illuminating: Randolph Adams's *Political Ideas of the American Revolution* (1922), of which Chapter 5, called "John Adams as a Britannic Statesman," was the final stimulus that determined me to write this book; Carl Becker's superb *Declaration of Independence, A Study in the History of Political Ideas* (1921); an obscure and skillfully compiled work by Harry A. Cushing called *History of the Transition from Provincial to Commonwealth Government in Massachusetts* (1896); and *The Great War for the Empire* (1946), by Lawrence Gipson, whose introductory chapter to Volume 6 is one of the most brilliantly suggestive essays in our historical literature.

All my reading and research was directed toward two goals: the understanding of John Adams's character, and of how it felt to be a citizen of the eighteenth century. My chief source is the ten

volumes of John Adams's *Works,* edited by his grandson, Charles Francis Adams, and published 1850–1856. Herein is the incomparable, self-betraying diary, and the autobiography (written circa 1805) — unreliable as to fact, invaluable for suggestion. I leaned heavily on the well-known *Familiar Letters of John Adams and his Wife* (1876) and the *Letters of Mrs. Adams* (1840). John's letters to Benjamin Rush, published by the Biddle family as *Old Family Letters* (1892), preserve John's wonderful spelling and punctuation. Written mostly in old age, these intimate letters to Rush have the tartness and affectionate, highly colored reminiscence so characteristic of John. The *Warren-Adams Letters* (1917, 1925) start in 1743 with James Otis's boyhood correspondence, and include letters by Sam Adams, by Abigail ("The Tea that bainfull weed is arrived"), and some of John's finest from 1774 to 1814. The American Antiquarian Society of Worcester, Massachusetts, has lately yielded up material for *New Letters of Abigail Adams* (1947), edited by Stewart Mitchell.

Holograph Adams letters await the student in libraries from Boston to San Marino; I have read scores of them. Never was such an articulate family, including John's wife, their daughter Abigail, their son John Quincy and their sons' sons to the fifth generation. John Quincy's diary (*Memoirs*) in eight volumes is a mere item. In that well-guarded cavern known to field workers as "the basement of the Massachusetts Historical Society" lie the Adams Papers, a rich mine of partially tapped source material. Until this great bulk is made accessible, the whole truth about John Adams will not be known. Scholars do not, however, expect sensational revelations, or anything that will alter the accepted estimate of John and his descendants.*

For the physical scene it was necessary to visit Braintree in all four seasons, look out the window of John's house onto February snow, walk by Black's Creek when November ice held the marsh grass stiff and climb Penn's Hill in June as Abigail climbed it to see the battle of Bunker Hill. In Boston, the old State House still stands; and in Philadelphia, Independence Hall. All the bustle of the twentieth century cannot efface the spirits that walk within these walls. The Frick Art Reference Library set me on the track of some twenty portraits of John. In private collections and the workrooms of museums I searched them out. If six portraits out of seven gave

* See page 673 for bibliography on *John Adams and His Family.*

John a wide brow and heavy cheeks, then I could describe him with those features.

But I spent far less time on the physical scene than on that other, harder quest. The eighteenth century is not to be trifled with. To achieve a glimpse behind two centuries is not a matter of drawing Chippendale furniture, candlewick bedspreads and gentlemen's knee breeches. What made the eighteenth century different was not man's clothing, but his outlook, his view of body and soul — a view so altered by time that only deepest immersion, a deliberate, disciplined shutting of the eyes, will bring it back. In John's day, Galen's four fluid humours still governed the body: the sanguine, the phlegmatic, the choleric, the melancholic. John's classmates at Harvard debated the truth of Copernicus's theory. The narrowing of one's mind to this strange constriction is a struggle painful, almost impossible; the Age of Enlightenment has tales to tell that wash our world away. Gone are Pasteur, Lister and the germ theory of disease. Gone is Darwin. Special creation, spontaneous generation rule the universe. Newton, Descartes, Bacon, Harvey have not yet obliterated the long medieval darkness; over our shoulders peer Ramus, Abelard and the schoolmen with Fra Castoreus and Meister Eckhart.

To help on that awful journey, I sought every avenue that offered. Contemporary newspapers were invaluable; so were funeral eulogies, diaries, the violent political pamphlets and religious tracts of the day and such laconic, prejudiced recitals as Boyle's "Journal of Occurrences in Boston 1759–1778." Zoltán Haraszti's articles in *More Books* led me to the Rare Book Room of the Boston Public Library, where some three thousand volumes from John's own collection are on the shelves. Exploring among them, I read John's inked marginal notes. "Pitifull!" he scrawls, or, in fury at a particular author, "Thou Louse, Flea, Tick, Wasp or whatever Vermin thou art!"

It made me laugh aloud. And presto! the solemn monument of our Founding Fathers fell away and John lived again in all his passionate self — his troubled ambition, restless intellect, quick perceptions, merciless irony and warm, faithful, domestic heart. "History," said Mommsen, "is neither written nor made without love or hate." I have been at pains not to let my enthusiasm or occasional deep irritation with our hero warp the factual foundation on which my scenes rest. No date is altered, no place, hour or meeting of persons contrived or manipulated.

What I have done, and often, is to use literary techniques, literary devices, to point up facts, incidents, traits of character the reader would otherwise miss. For instance, John Adams, at Harvard, by his own later testimony, was a better student at "the mathematical sciences" than at Latin, Greek and Divinity — a fact significant to his character and career. Instead of merely saying so, with sources quoted, I show John in Professor Winthrop's apparatus chamber on the second floor of Harvard Hall, studying Gravesande's great folio volume on *Natural Philosophy*. In preparation, I went to the Library Company of Philadelphia and read Gravesande in some early edition that John must have used; read also Watts's *Logick*, Gordon's *Geography* and every book in John's given curriculum. I did the same with John's law studies at Worcester. In the old, illustrated London editions of 1738 and 1759, Coke's *Institutes* and Blackstone's first slim *Analysis of the Laws of England* take on extraordinary color. Merely to handle them, to open their leather covers at the author's or publisher's apologetic first Preface, brings back the past with startling effect. Suddenly, the books are new. One sees them as their authors saw them, as John Adams saw them when he was twenty-two — matters for controversy, a daring, brand-new challenge to the intellectual world.

Instead of the conventional listing of manuscript sources, secondary sources, and so on, I have grouped these titles to follow as it were my own road back to John Adams and the eighteenth century. First of all come the great books that shaped John's thinking — inspired and timeless expressions of those broad principles that nourished the roots of Anglo-Saxon polity, and by that same token gave life to the first great familial offshoot of the British system, our own American Republic. Today we call these books classics. All of us have a vague familiarity, if not with the volumes, at least with the authors' names; every college student has "had" them in his courses in philosophy and government. Nevertheless they must be reread lovingly, with a searching curiosity, before the curtain of time will lift to vouchsafe even for a fleeting, illusory moment the images, the symbols spiritual and intellectual by which men lived two centuries ago.

These books are the indispensable preparation. Some, like Blackstone, were brand-new in John Adams's day. Others, like Newton, had been discussed for two generations. A few are native to New England and belong to John's early childhood, but most are uni-

versal and were discovered by John in his college days and his maturity. Whatever they were and whenever they came, they were John's guideposts to present and future, his breviaries of social philosophy, food for passionate argument and ultimate acceptance.

Newton, Sir Isaac, *Principia*. 2 vols. London, 1686.
Locke, John, "An Essay concerning Human Understanding." London, 1690.
—— "Two Treatises on Government." London, 1689.
—— "Letters on Toleration." London, 1692.
Hobbes, Thomas, *Leviathan*. 1651.
Hooker, Richard, *Laws of Ecclesiastical Polity*. 1593.
Harrington, James, *Oceana*. London, 1656.
Montesquieu, Charles Louis de Secondat, *L'esprit des lois*. Geneva, 2 v., 1748. *The Spirit of the Laws*. London, 2 v., 1750.
Rousseau, Jean Jacques, *Du Contrat social*. Amsterdam, 1762. *A Treatise on the Social Compact*, London, 1764.
Plato, *The Republic*.
Aristotle, *Politics* (A Treatise on Government).
Cicero, *Dialogues* ("*On the Republic*"; "*On the Laws*").
Coke, Sir Edward, *Institutes*. Commentary upon Littleton. London, 1628.
Blackstone, William, *Analysis of the Laws of England*. Oxford, 1759.
—— *Commentaries on the Laws of England*. Oxford, 1765.
Vattel, Emmerich de, *Le droit des gens*. Leyden, 2 v., 1758. *The Laws of Nations*. London, 1760.
Burlamaqui, Jean Jacques, *Principles of Natural Law*. London, 1752.
—— *Principles of Politic Law*. London, 1752.
Pufendorf, Samuel, *The Law of Nature and Nations*. London, 1749. First appeared in Latin, 1672.
Grotius, Hugo, *De jure belli et pacis*, Paris, 1625. *The illustrious Hugo Grotius of the law of Warre and Peace*. London, 1654.
Beccaria, Cesare Bonesana di, *An Essay on Crimes and Punishments*. London, 1767. First appeared in Italian, 1764.
Bolingbroke, Henry St. John, *The Patriot King*. London, 1738.
—— *Letters on the Study of History*. London, 1752.
Sidney, Algernon, "Discourses Concerning Government." London, 1698.
Tillotson, John, *Sermons*. 3 vols. London, 1752.
Gordon, T., and J. Trenchard, *The Independent Whig*. London, 1721.
Pope, Alexander, *Essay on Man*. London, 1733.

Cambridge History of the British Empire. 8 vols. N. Y., 1929–1936.

Carpenter, William Seal, *The Development of American Political Thought.* Princeton, 1930.

Catlin, George Edward, *The Story of the Political Philosophers.* N. Y., 1939.

Channing, Edward, *A History of the United States.* 6 vols. N. Y., 1905–1925.

Cooper, James Fenimore, *Notions of the Americans.* 2 vols. Phila., 1828.

Corwin, Edward S., *John Marshall and the Constitution.* New Haven, 1919.

Curti, Merle, *The Growth of American Thought.* N. Y. and London, 1943.

Cushing, Harry A., *History of the Transition from Provincial to Commonwealth Government in Massachusetts.* N. Y., 1896.

Davidson, Philip, *Propaganda and the American Revolution.* Chapel Hill, N. C., 1941.

De Tocqueville, Alexis, *Democracy in America.* 2 v. N. Y., 1900.

Dunning, William Archibald, *The British Empire and the United States.* N. Y., 1914.

—— *A History of Political Theories: from Rousseau to Spencer.* N. Y., 1920.

Dwight, Theodore W., "Harrington and His Influence upon American Political Institutions and Political Thought." *Pol. Sci. Quarterly,* Vol. II, 1887.

Eckenrode, H. J., *The Revolution in Virginia.* Boston, 1916.

Ellet, Mrs. E. F., *Court Circles of the Republic.* Phila., n.d.

—— *Domestic History of the Revolution.* N. Y., 1850.

Faulkner, Harold U., and Tyler Kepner. *America, Its History and People.* N. Y., 1938.

Fäy, Bernard, *The Revolutionary Spirit in France and America.* N. Y., 1927.

Fisher, Sydney George, *The Struggle for American Independence.* 2 vols. Phila., 1908.

—— *The Legendary and Myth-making Process in Histories of the American Revolution.* Phila., 1912.

Fiske, John, *The American Revolution.* 2 vols. Boston, 1891.

—— *The Critical Period of American History.* Boston, 1898.

—— *Essays Historical and Literary.* 2 vols. N. Y., 1907.

Fortescue, Sir John, ed., *The Correspondence of King George the Third from 1760 to December, 1783.* London, 1927.

French, Allen, *The First Year of the American Revolution.* Cambridge, Mass., 1934.

Frothingham, Richard, *The Rise of the Republic of the United States.* Boston, 1910.

Gabriel, Ralph Henry, *The Pageant of America.* 15 vols. New Haven, 1925–1929.

—— *The Course of American Democratic Thought.* N. Y., 1928.

Gibbs, George, *Memoirs of the Administrations of Washington and John Adams,* ed. from the papers of Oliver Wolcott. 2 vols. N. Y., 1846.

Gipson, Lawrence Henry, *The British Empire before the American Revolution.* 7 vols. N. Y., 1939–1949.

Greene, Evarts B., and Virginia Harrington, *American Population before the Federal Census of 1790.* N. Y., 1932.

Griswold, Rufus Wilmot, *The Republican Court.* N. Y., 1867.

Haskins, George Lee, "Court Records and History." *William and Mary College Quarterly,* 3rd series, Vol. V, No. 4, Oct. 1948.

Hazen, Charles Downer, *Contemporary American Opinion of the French Revolution.* Baltimore, 1897.

Hildreth, Richard, *The History of the United States of America.* 6 vols. N. Y., 1854–1855.

Hinkhouse, Fred Junkin, *The Preliminaries of the American Revolution as Seen in the English Press.* N. Y., 1926.

Hofstadter, Richard, *The American Political Tradition and the Men Who Made It.* N. Y., 1949.

Howard, George Elliott, *Preliminaries of the Revolution.* N. Y., 1906.

Jameson, J. Franklin, *The American Revolution Considered as a Social Movement.* Princeton, 1926.

Jensen, Merrill, *The Articles of Confederation.* Madison, Wis., 1940.

Joad, C. E. M., *Guide to the Philosophy of Morals and Politics.* London, 1938.

Johnson, Gerald, *American Heroes and Hero-Worship.* N. Y., 1943.

Jones, Howard Mumford, *American and French Culture, 1750–1848.* Chapel Hill, N. C., 1927.

Koch, Gustav Adolf, *Republican Religion. The American Revolution and the Cult of Reason.* N. Y., 1933. American Religion Series.

Larned, Josephus Nelson, ed., *The Literature of American History.* 2 vols. Boston, 1902.

Lecky, William E. H., *The American Revolution, 1763–1783.* N. Y., 1898.

Lingelbach, William E., ed., *Approaches to American Social History.* N. Y., 1937.

Lodge, Henry Cabot, *The Story of the Revolution.* 2 vols. N. Y., 1898.

—— *A Short History of the English Colonies in America.* N. Y., 1881.

Loetscher, Lefferts A., *A Brief History of the Presbyterians.* Phila., 1938.

McIlwain, Charles H., *The American Revolution.* N. Y., 1923.

McLaughlin, Andrew C., *A Constitutional History of the United States.* N. Y., 1935.

—— *The Foundations of American Constitutionalism.* N. Y., 1932.

—— "The Social Compact and Constitutional Construction." *Am. Hist. Rev.*, Vol. 5, Oct. 1899–July 1900.

—— *The Confederation and the Constitution.* N. Y., London, 1905.

Martin, Alfred S., "The King's Customs: Phila., 1763–1774." *William and Mary College Quarterly*, Third Series, Vol. V, No. 2, Apr. 1948.

Merriam, Charles Edward, *A History of American Political Theories.* N. Y., 1903.

Metzger, Charles H., "The Quebec Act. A Primary Cause of the American Revolution." *U. S. Catholic Hist. Soc. Monograph Series* XVI. N. Y., 1936.

Miller, John, *Origins of the American Revolution.* Boston, 1943.

—— *The Triumph of Freedom 1775–1783.* Boston, 1948.

—— *Sam Adams, Pioneer in Propaganda.* Boston, 1936.

Miller, Perry, *New England Mind; The Seventeenth Century.* N. Y., 1939.

Morais, Herbert Montford, *Deism in Eighteenth Century America.* N. Y., 1934.

—— *The Struggle for American Freedom.* N. Y., 1944.

Morgan, Edmund S., "Colonial Ideas of Parliamentary Power, 1764–1766." *William and Mary College Quarterly*, Vol. V, July 1948.

Morison, S. E., and H. S. Commager, *The Growth of the American Republic.* N. Y., 1937.

Morris, Richard B., *Studies in the History of American Law.* N. Y., 1930.

Muir, Pearson M'Adam, *The Church of Scotland.* Edinburgh, 1891.

Mullett, Charles F., *Fundamental Law and the American Revolution 1760–1776.* N. Y., 1933.

Mumby, F. R., *George III and the American Revolution.* Boston, 1923.

Murrell, William, *A History of American Graphic Humor.* 2 vols. N. Y., 1933.

Namier, Lewis B., *The Structure of Politics at the Accession of George III.* London, N. Y., 1929.

—— *England in the Age of the American Revolution.* London, 1930.
Nettels, Curtis, *The Roots of American Civilization.* N. Y., 1928.
Nettleship, Richard Lewis, "Lectures on the Republic of Plato," ed. G. R. Benson. London, 1901.
Nevins, Allan, *The American States During and After the Revolution.* N. Y., 1924.
Osborn, Annie Marion, *Rousseau and Burke.* N. Y., London, 1940.
Parkman, Francis, *Montcalm and Wolfe.* Boston, 1927.
—— *A Half Century of Conflict.* Boston, 1929.
Parrington, Vernon Louis, *Main Currents in American Thought.* N. Y., 1927.
Pitman, F. W., *The Development of the British West Indies, 1700–1763.* New Haven, 1917.
Pollock, Sir Frederick, "Home Rule and Imperial Sovereignty." In *Oxford Lectures and Other Discourses,* London, 1890.
—— *An Introduction to the History of the Science of Politics.* N. Y., 1890.
Pooke, Florence A., *Fountain Sources of American Political Theory.* N. Y., 1930.
Rocquan, Felix, *The Revolutionary Spirit Preceding the French Revolution.* London, 1894.
Rosenthal, Lewis, "Rousseau at Philadelphia." *Magazine of American History,* Vol. 12, No. 54, 1884.
Russell-Smith, H. F., *Harrington and his Oceana.* Cambridge, England, 1914.
Schlesinger, Arthur M., *The Colonial Merchants and the American Revolution.* N. Y., 1918.
—— *New Viewpoints in American History.* N. Y., 1926.
Schouler, James, *History of the United States of America under the Constitution.* 7 vols. Washington, 1880–1913. (Vols. 1–2, 1783–1817.)
Simons, A. M., *Social Forces in American History.* N. Y., 1918.
Smith, Margaret Bayard, *The First Forty Years of Washington Society, Portrayed in the Family Letters of Mrs. Harrison Smith.* N. Y., 1906.
Spiller, Robert E., Willard Thorp, Thomas Johnson and H. S. Canby, *Literary History of the United States.* 3 vols. N. Y., 1948.
Spurlin, Paul Merrill, *Montesquieu in America.* Baton Rouge, 1940.
Stanard, Mary Newton, *Colonial Virginia, Its People and Customs.* Phila., 1917.
Stephen, Sir Leslie, *History of English Thought in the Eighteenth Century.* London, 1881.

Trescot, William Henry, *Diplomatic History of the Administrations of Washington and Adams.* Boston, 1857.

Trevelyan, Sir George Otto, *History of the American Revolution.* 4 vols. N. Y., 1899.

—— *George III and Charles Fox.* 2 vols. N. Y., 1912.

Tyler, Moses Coit, *The Literary History of the American Revolution.* 2 vols. N. Y., 1897.

Van Tyne, Claude H., *The Causes of the War of Independence.* Boston, 1922.

—— *The War of Independence.* Boston, 1929.

—— *The Loyalists in the American Revolution.* N. Y., 1902.

Weeden, William H., *Economic and Social History of New England, 1620–1789.* 2 vols. Boston, 1891.

Wertenbaker, Thomas Jefferson, *The Puritan Oligarchy.* N. Y., London, 1949.

Wharton, Francis, *State Trials of the United States during the Administrations of Washington and Adams.* Phila., 1849.

Wilson, Woodrow, *A History of the American People.* 5 vols. N. Y., 1902.

Winsor, Justin, *Narrative and Critical History of America.* 8 vols. Boston, 1884–1889.

Wroth, Lawrence C., *An American Bookshelf, 1755.* Phila., 1934.

BIBLIOGRAPHIES AND COLLECTIONS OF DOCUMENTS (STATE PAPERS, ETC.)

Brigham, Clarence S., *History and Bibliography of American Newspapers 1690–1820.* 2 vols. Worcester, Mass., 1947.

Commager, Henry Steele, ed. *Documents of American History.* N. Y., 1934.

Commager, Henry Steele, and Allan Nevins, eds., *The Heritage of America.* Boston, 1939.

Forbes, Harriette Merrifield, comp., *New England Diaries, 1602–1800.* Privately printed, 1923.

Force, Peter, *American Archives.* Fourth Series, 1774–1776. 5 vols.; Fifth Series, 1776–1783, Vol. 1. Washington, 1837–1853.

Hart, Albert Bushnell, *American History Told by Contemporaries.* 5 vols. N. Y., 1925.

MacDonald, William, *Select Documents Illustrative of the History of the United States.* 1776–1861. N. Y., 1898.

—— *Select Charters and other Documents Illustrative of American History.* 1606–1775. N. Y., 1910.

Matthews, William, *Diaries Written Prior to the Year 1861*. Berkeley and Los Angeles, 1945.

Moore, Frank, *Songs and Ballads of the American Revolution*. N. Y., 1855.

—— *The Patriot Preachers of the American Revolution*. N. Y., 1860.

Morison, Samuel Eliot, ed., *Sources and Documents Illustrating the American Revolution. 1764–1788*. Oxford, 1923.

Niles, Hezekiah, *Principals and Acts of Revolution in America*. Baltimore, 1822.

Sargent, Winthrop, *The Loyalist Poetry of the Revolution*. Phila., 1857.

Wright, Benjamin Fletcher, Jr., *A Source Book of American Political Theory*. N. Y., 1929.

BIBLIOGRAPHY BY SECTIONS

To supplement my narrative, I have arranged a bibliography giving the sources of certain conversations or scenes. Documentation of every anecdote would require a volume: what follows can be no more than an indication of the method used.

CHAPTERS I–IV. BRAINTREE. 1745–1751

The outline of John's boyhood years comes from his own vividly reminiscent letters, such as the one to Rush quoted in Chapter Note for Chapter IV. Valuable material about John's father came from early pages of John's autobiography, beginning, "My father was the honestest man I ever knew." Here also John speaks of his first schoolteacher, Dame Belcher, of how he disliked Mr. Cleverly, gives the episode of the salt grass picking at Penny Ferry and tells of his determination to leave the Latin School and go to Mr. Marsh for tutoring. The story of Dame Belcher and the three pennies came from George Whitney's *Some Account of the Early History and Present State of the Town of Quincy, in Massachusetts* (Boston, 1827).

For schoolhouses and curricula:

Dilworth, Thomas, *Schoolmaster's Assistant*. London, 1743.

Johnson, Clifton, *Old-Time Schools and School-Books*. N. Y., 1935.

Littlefield, George E., *Early Schools and the School-Books of New England*. Boston, 1904.

Pattee, William S., *History of Old Braintree and Quincy*. Quincy, 1878.

Shaw, Charles, *Topographical and Historical Description of Boston*. Boston, 1817.

For the atmosphere and feeling of early Braintree, my best guide, after John's own accounts, was found in the writings of the later Adamses and Quincys. All of them remembered the Braintree of their boyhood; in his *Education*, Henry Adams described it lovingly. In 1948 William Churchill Edwards assembled an exhibition of historic Adams material in the First Church at Quincy. There I saw a photograph of Joseph Marsh's house (now destroyed) where John went to school, and uncovered, in letter-books and family records, dates and data unobtainable elsewhere. In January, 1946, a public auction of Quincy-Adams heirlooms was held by the Parke-Bernet Galleries in New York. Portraits, silver, furniture, helped to reconstruct the time and place. ("John Adams His Bowl," C. D. Bowen, *Atlantic Monthly*, May 1946.)

Especially helpful were:

Adams, Brooks, *The Emancipation of Massachusetts*. Boston, 1887.

Adams, Charles Francis (1807–1886, son of John Quincy Adams), *A Cycle of Adams Letters*, 1861–1865. Ed. Worthington Chauncey Ford. 2 vols. Boston, 1920.

—— "John Quincy Adams," Address, Quincy, July 4, 1856. Boston, 1856.

—— "Memoir." *Mass. Hist. Soc. Proc.* Vol. 1, 1827.

Adams, Charles Francis, Jr. (1835–1910. Son of Charles Francis Adams above), *History of Braintree*. Cambridge, 1891.

—— *Three Episodes of Massachusetts History*, Vol. 2. Boston, 1892.

—— "Some Phases of Sexual Morality and Church Discipline in Colonial New England." *Mass. Hist. Soc. Proc.*, Second Series, Vol. 6.

—— " 'Tis Sixty Years Since." Speech, Columbia, S. C., Jan. 16, 1913. N. Y., 1913.

—— *Studies: Military and Diplomatic*, 1775–1865. N. Y., 1911.

—— *Charles Francis Adams 1835–1915: an Autobiography*. Boston, 1916.

Adams, Henry (1875–   ), *The Birthplaces of Presidents John and John Quincy Adams in Quincy, Massachusetts*. Quincy, 1936.

—— Compiler, *John Adams's Book*. Privately printed. Boston, 1934.

Adams, Henry Brooks (1838–1918), *The Education of Henry Adams*. Boston, 1907.

Bates, Samuel A., ed., *Records of the Town of Braintree*. Randolph, Mass., 1886.

Edwards, William C., *Historic Quincy, Massachusetts*. Privately printed. 1945.

Faxon, Annie E., *A Brief Record of the Physicians of Quincy, Massachusetts*. Boston, 1890.

"Fiftieth Anniversary of the Ordination and Settlement of Richard S. Storrs, D.D." Discourse delivered in First Congregational Church of Quincy. Boston, 1861.

Lunt, William Parsons, Two Discourses, Delivered September 29, 1839, on the Two Hundredth Anniversary of the Gathering of the First Congregational Church, Quincy. Boston, 1840.

Quincy, Edmund, *Life of Josiah Quincy*. Boston, 1867.

Quincy, Josiah (1772–1864), "Memoir of the Life of Josiah Quincy, Junior, of Massachusetts." Boston, 1825.

Quincy, Josiah (1802–1882), *Figures of the Past*. Boston, 1926.

Wilson, Daniel Munro, "Centennial Celebration at Braintree, July 4, 1876." Boston, 1877.

—— *The "Chappel of Ease" and Church of Statesmen*. Quincy, 1890.

—— *Quincy, Old Braintree and Merry-Mount*. Boston, 1906.

—— *Three Hundred Years of Quincy, 1625–1925*. Quincy, 1926.

—— *Where American Independence Began*. Boston, 1902.

Wilson, Daniel Munro, and Charles Francis Adams, Jr., *Colonel Quincy of Mount Wollaston*. Boston, 1909.

Bartlett, J. Gardner (comp.), *Henry Adams of Somersetshire, England, and Braintree, Massachusetts* (N. Y., 1927), in spite of frequent errors, was a source of genealogical information. Useful also was Stewart Mitchell's excellent edition of *New Letters of Abigail Adams, 1788–1801* (Boston, 1947). Newspapers and broadsides gave contemporary feeling and daily items about D'Anville's approaching fleet in the summer of 1746. I used the Boston *Evening Post* for the 1740's, and for the period from January, 1748, to September, 1749, the *Independent Advertiser*. For the 1750's, the Boston *Gazette and Country Journal*, and the *News-Letter*. Dudley Bradstreet's diary, written at the siege of Louisburg in 1745, is printed in the Pepperell Papers, 2nd Series, Vol. 11, *Mass. Hist. Soc. Proc.* See also *Mass. Hist. Soc. Coll.* 6th Series, Vol. 10. Justice Winsor's *Memorial History of Boston* (Boston, 1880–1881) has the story of the Reverend Thomas Prince's dramatic sermon.

Court records, with their stenographic reports of witnesses, were my best source for authentic idiom, slang and the brief, time-

honored swear words of our language. The *Oxford English Diction-ary* gives the first recorded date for every word it lists. Diaries were useful, such as soldiers' journals and the famous brief *Journal of Madam Knight* (Boston, 1920). In addition to Noah Webster's *Grammatical Institute* and Caleb Bingham's *Child's Companion* (Boston, 1792) I used:

Krapp, George Philip, *The English Language in America*. 2 vols. N. Y., 1925.

Mathews, Mitford McLeod, *The Beginnings of American English*. Chicago, 1931.

Mencken, Henry L., *The American Language*. N. Y., 1926. Supplement I, N. Y., 1945; Supplement II, N. Y., 1948.

CHAPTERS V–VIII. HARVARD COLLEGE. 1751–1755

The story of John's journey to Cambridge for his entrance examination comes from a portion of his autobiography not included in the *Works*. In 1901, Charles Francis Adams published it in the *Massachusetts Historical Society Proceedings*. I came across it reprinted in the *Harvard Graduates Magazine* for March, 1901, entitled "A Harvard Examination in 1757," the date being an obvious misprint for 1751. The names of John's college intimates appear in early pages of the autobiography, the letter to Benjamin Rush in Biddle, ed., *Old Family Letters*, p. 331, and to Thomas Jefferson, *Works* X, 67–68. The senior discussion club also figures in the autobiography, *Works* I, 42–43.

In the Harvard University Archives at Widener Library I used *Records of the College Faculty*, Vol. 1, 1725–1752, Vol. 2, 1752–1766, *Book of Theses and Quaestiones, Records of the Overseers*, Vol. 3, and the *Admissions Book*. Here also are the manuscript diaries of Henry Flynt (1707–1747) and the Reverend John Page (1757–1780), the notebook of T. Gilman (1757–1765), and *College Laws as Copied by Meschach Weare*, Class of 1735. Other interesting diaries of the period were:

Ames, Nathaniel, "Diary." In Charles Warren, *Jacobin and Junto*. Cambridge, 1931.

Bailey, Jacob, "Journal." In Charles E. Allen, *Rev. Jacob Bailey, His Character and Works*. Lincoln Historical Soc., 1895.

Fobes, Perez, "Diary and Commonplace Book." *New England Quarterly*, Vol. 2, No. 4, 1929.

Sewall, David, "Diary." *Proc. Mass. Hist. Soc.* Vol. 16, 5–11.

Books listed in John's Harvard curriculum, available in the Library Company of Philadelphia:

Amesium, Guilielmum, *Medulla S.S. Theologias.* London, 1730.
Burgersdijk, Franco, *An Abstract and Translation of Burgeradicius His Logick, by a Person of Quality.* London, 1697.
Euclid, *Elements of Geometry.* London, 1745.
Gordon, Patrick, *The Geographical Grammer.* London, 1730.
Gravesande, Willem Jakob van's, *Mathematical Elements of Natural Philosophy.* 2 vols. London, 1747.
Ward, John, *The Young Mathematician's Guide.* London, 1722.
Watts, Isaac, *Logick, or the Right Use of Reason.* London, 1740.
Wollebro, Johannes, *Compendium Theologiae Christianas.* London, 1733.

For Dr. John Winthrop, aside from the *Correspondence with John Adams* (of much later date), I used the anonymous article "John Winthrop," from *Coll. Conn. Hist. Soc.*, Vol. 1, 1859, and Frederick E. Brasch's article, "John Winthrop, America's First Astronomer," *Pubs. Astrononical Society of the Pacific*, No. 165, 1916. Information on Commencement at Harvard I took from John Holmes's account, "Harvard Square," in *The Harvard Book* (Cambridge, 1875), his *Letters to J. R. Lowell*, edited by William Roscoe Thayer (Boston, 1917), John Pierce's "Harvard College Commencements, 1803–1848" (*Proc. Mass. Hist. Soc.*, Dec. 1889 and Jan. 1890), and Judge Samuel Sewall's recollections in a manuscript collection called *Notes on Commencement from 1704–1820* in the Harvard Archives. More general books on the Harvard background from which material was used were:
Batchelder, Samuel F., *Bits of Harvard History.* Cambridge, 1924.
Bush, George Gary, *Harvard, The First American University.* Boston, 1886.
Eliot, Samuel A., *A Sketch of the History of Harvard College.* Boston, 1848.
Historical Register of Harvard University, 1639–1936. Cambridge, 1937.
King, Moses, *Harvard and Its Surroundings.* Cambridge, 1886.
Metcalf, Keyes D., "The Undergraduate and the Harvard Library, 1765–1877." *Harvard Library Bulletin*, Vol. I, No. 1, 1947.
Morison, Samuel Eliot, *The Founding of Harvard College.* Cambridge, 1935.
—— *Harvard in the Seventeenth Century.* Cambridge, 1936.
—— *Harvard University Handbook.* Cambridge, 1936.

—— *Three Centuries of Harvard.* Cambridge, 1936.

Pierce, Benjamin, *History of Harvard University.* Boston, 1833.

Quincy, Josiah, Jr., *The History of Harvard University.* 2 vols. Boston, 1860.

Sibley, John Langdon, *Collectanea Bibliographica Harvardiana.* Harvard University Archives.

Vaille, Frederic Oznia, and Henry Alden Clark, eds., *The Harvard Book: A Series of Historical, Biographical and Descriptive Sketches by Various Authors.* 2 vols. Cambridge, 1937.

(Clifford K. Shipton's *Biographical Sketches of the Graduates of Harvard College* does not, at present publication, cover the years 1751–1755.)

The Briant controversy in Braintree figures in John's autobiography and is the subject of Samuel Niles's *Result of a Late Ecclesiastical Council* (Boston, 1753), a pamphlet reporting on the meeting of the churches at Deacon Adams's house.

Chapters ix–x. Worcester and the French War. 1755–1758

John's experiences in Worcester and his feelings about Mr. Putnam are related in Volume II of the *Works*, where also appears the story of how Thaddeus Maccarty heard John speak at Harvard Commencement and chose him as schoolmaster. Caleb A. Wall, in his *Reminiscences of Worcester* (Worcester, 1877), names John's friends of 1755–1758 and describes their families and their houses. *John Adams as a Schoolmaster* by Elizabeth Porter Gould (Boston, 1889) is a useful source of information. Further data on Maccarty I found in William Lincoln's *History of Worcester* (Worcester, 1862). The Worcester Museum has a fine large contemporary landscape of the surrounding countryside and two charming wall sconces worked in paper frills and colored shells and marked with the date 1750 which belonged to Maccarty.

Cutler, U. Waldo, *Jottings from Worcester's History.* Worcester, 1932.

Knowlton, John S. C., and Clarendon Wheelock, *Carl's Tour in Main Street.* Worcester, 1889.

"Reminiscences of the Bancroft Family." *New England Journal,* Dec. 28, 1882.

Rice, Franklin P., "Old Worcester Sketches." *Worcester Spy,* May–Aug., 1899. Collected and bound by American Antiquarian Society.

Willard, Joseph, *An Address to the Members of the Bar of Worcester County, October 2, 1829.* Lancaster, 1830.

For the deistical and medical books John read in Worcester, see his letters to Thomas Jefferson, July 18, 1813 (*Works* X, 56); Benjamin Rush, Dec. 22, 1808 (*Old Family Letters*) and Benjamin Waterhouse, May 18, 1821 (*Statesman and Friend*, edited by Worthington Chauncey Ford, Boston, 1927). For lawyers in early Massachusetts, I drew largely from Charles Warren's *History of the American Bar* (Boston, 1911). I used also his *The Making of the Constitution* (Boston, 1937); *The Supreme Court in United States History* (Boston, 1922); *Byways in American History* (Cambridge, 1942); and "John Adams and the American Constitution," an address delivered Feb. 22, 1927, at George Washington University.

Frank Washburn Grinnell's writings about Adams were greatly helpful, especially his "John Winthrop and the Constitutional Thinking of John Adams" (*Proc. Mass. Hist. Soc.*, Vol. 63, Feb. 1930). *The Massachusetts Law Quarterly* for May, 1917, is devoted entirely to Grinnell's *Constitutional History of the Supreme Judicial Court of Massachusetts from the Revolution to 1813*, of which Chapter Two, "The Place of John Adams in the History of the Court and the Background of his Mind," is particularly revealing. Grinnell's "Bench and Bar in Colony and Province, 1630–1776" (*The Commonwealth History of Massachusetts*, N. Y., 1928, Vol. 2), also supplied useful information. "An American Law Student of a Hundred Years Ago" is a long full letter from the great Chancellor James Kent of New York, telling about his early studies and the difficulties he encountered (reprinted in *Selected Essays in Anglo-American Legal History*, Boston, 1907, Vol. I). From this volume I also used:

Andrews, Charles McLean, "Conditions Leading to the Revolt of the Colonies."
Reinsch, Paul Samuel, "The English Common Law in the Early American Colonies."
Sioussat, St. George Leakin, "The Theory of the Extension of the English Statutes to the Plantations."

In his brief but enlightening introduction to *Law in Action* (New York, 1947), Roscoe Pound explains how courts and law in New England progressed from clergy to lawyers. Emory Washburn's *Sketches of the Judicial History of Massachusetts from 1630 to the Revolution in 1775* (Boston, 1840) is invaluable for law in early

Massachusetts; Francis R. Aumann's *Changing American Legal System* (Columbus, 1940) is clear and revealing.

The following were helpful:

Adams, Brooks, *The Emancipation of Massachusetts*. Boston, 1887.

Bailey, Hollis R., *Attorneys and Their Admission to the Bar in Massachusetts*. Boston, 1907.

Hilkey, Charles Joseph, *Legal Development in Colonial Massachusetts, 1630–1686*. N. Y., 1910.

Howe, Mark De Wolfe, and Louis F. Eaton, Jr. "The Supreme Judicial Power in the Colony of Massachusetts Bay." *N. E. Quarterly*, Vol. XX, No. 3, Sept. 1947.

Jones, Leonard Augustus, and Carl Reno, eds., *Memoirs of the Judiciary and the Bar of New England*. 2 vols. Boston, 1900.

Mason, Albert, "History of the Judiciary of Massachusetts." *New England States*, William T. Davis, ed., Boston, 1897.

Morison, Samuel Eliot, and Zechariah Chafee, Jr. "Records of the Suffolk County Court." *Publications of the Colonial Society of Massachusetts*. Vol. 29.

Morris, Richard B., *Studies in the History of America Law*. N. Y., 1930.

Information on Worcester lawyers who afterward turned loyalist I secured from Samuel Curwen's *Journal and Letters* (Boston, 1842) and Lorenzo Sabine's *Biographical Sketches of Loyalists of the American Revolution* (Boston, 1864), together with Sabine's article, "Life and Works of John Adams," in the *North American Review*, July, 1857.

For Thomas Pownall, aside from his own writings, listed elsewhere, I used *Old Landmarks and Historic Personages of Boston* (Boston, 1900) by Samuel Adams Drake, and William Otis Sawtelle's article on "Thomas Pownall, Colonial Governor" (*Proc. Mass. Hist. Soc.*, Vol. 63, pp. 233–287, 1929–1930). John's letter of Feb. 4, 1817, to William Tudor (*Works* X, 241–244) comments on both Pownall and Shirley. The item about the Albany people selling bloody clothes to the Indians comes from John Miller's *Origins of the American Revolution* (Boston, 1943), in a letter quoted from Jonathan Mayhew.

John's own comments on the conduct and progress of the French war appear in his letters to Jacob Bailey (Allen, *Rev. Jacob Bailey, cit. sup.*); to Dr. Bancroft of Worcester, Jan. 21, 1823; William Cranch, Mar. 3, 1815 (*Works* X, 131); William Cunningham, Oct. 23, 1809 (quoted in John Wood's *Suppressed History of the Admin-*

istration of John Adams. Phila., 1846, p. 367); Skelton Jones, Mar.
11, 1809; Jonathan Mason, July 18, 1776 (*Works* IX, 422); Dr. J.
Morse, Jan. 5, 1816 (*Works* X, 201); Benjamin Rush, May 1, 1807
(*Old Family Letters*); William Thomas, Aug. 10, 1822 (*Works* X,
403); William Tudor, Mar. 7, 1819 (*Works* X, 373); and Nathan
Webb, Oct. 12, 1755 (*Old Family Letters*).

CHAPTERS XI–XXIV. BOSTON AND MASSACHUSETTS. 1758–1774

For information about Gridley, Thacher, Trowbridge and the
other Boston lawyers, I drew on "Bench and Bar in Boston" by
John Torrey Morse, Jr., in Justin Winsor's *Memorial History of
Boston,* Vol. IV. John's own account of conversations with Gridley,
Pratt and others, and the scene of admission to the Massachusetts
Bar, appear in the diary of Oct., 1758 (*Works* II, 45–50); John's
letter of Sept. 13, 1790, to Thomas Welsh (*Works* IX, 629)
and his correspondence with Jonathan Sewall about Blackstone
(*Works* II, 79–80). Reference to Oxenbridge Thacher figures in the
letters of Feb. 13, 1818, to H. Niles (*Works* X, 283) and of Mar. 7,
1818, to William Wirt (*Works* X, 292).

For my sources on the *Writs* trial, see the Chapter Notes for Chapter XIII. George Francis Dow's *Every Day Life in the Massachusetts Bay Colony* (Boston, 1935) gives an account of the Ames
trial in which John, in 1769, defended Mrs. Ames in a murder
case at Essex, for which see also the *Essex Gazette,* Aug. 2, 1768,
and Dec. 25, 1770, a newspaper far chattier than any in Boston at
the time. The Rare Book Room of the Boston Public Library has a
scrapbook compiled by Mellen Chamberlain and entitled *John
Adams, Sketch of His Life.* In it are holograph letters and other
valuable material, including in John's handwriting his "Instructions
to the Boston Representation," quoted in my Chapter XVIII.

Documentation for the Boston Massacre is given in the Chapter
Notes for Chapters XX and XXI. I drew on almost all the sources
that have been previously mentioned; specific details came from
diverse works, such as:

Adams, Randolph G., "New Light on the Boston Massacre." *Am.
    Ant. Soc. Proc.,* V, 47, 1937.
Boyle, John, "Journal of Occurrences in Boston," *N. E. Hist. & Gen.
    Reg.,* Boston.
Chandler, Peleg, *American Criminal Trials.* 2 vols. Boston, 1844.
Frothingham, Richard, *The Life and Times of Joseph Warren.* Bos-
    ton, 1865.

Gillen, Daniel J., *Who Shot Patrick Carr?* Privately printed, n.d.
James Otis, Samuel Adams and John Hancock. Old South Leaflets,
No. 179.
Wellman, Francis Lewis, *The Art of Cross-Examination.* N. Y., 1932.

The last and best word on Samuel Adams is John C. Miller's *Sam
Adams, Pioneer in Propaganda* (Boston, 1936). *The Life and Public
Services of Samuel Adams* by his grandson, William V. Wells (Boston, 1865), is fairly correct as to fact but, by careful omissions, whitewashes the Grand Incendiary into a figure pure and colorless as Parson Weems's Washington. Other sources were *Samuel Adams and
Joseph Warren, a Sketch of their Lives, with Illustrations, Collected
and Arranged by Mellen Chamberlain* (Rare Book Room, Boston
Public Library), James K. Hosmer's *Samuel Adams* (Boston, 1896)
and Ralph V. Harlow's *Samuel Adams, Promoter of the American
Revolution* (N. Y., 1923).

The Life of James Otis by William Tudor (Boston, 1823) is often
inaccurate but filled with anecdote and color. Tudor was John
Adams's law student. For Joseph Hawley, I used Ernest F. Brown's
Joseph Hawley, Colonial Radical (N. Y., 1931).

Information on scenes and people of Boston and New England was
taken from diverse sources, among them:

Alden, John Richard, *General Gage in America.* Baton Rouge, 1948.
Allan, Herbert S., *John Hancock, Patriot in Purple.* N. Y., 1948.
Amory, Thomas C., *Life of James Sullivan.* 2 vols. Boston, 1859.
Bailey, Francis, *Journal of a Tour in Unsettled Parts of North
America in 1795 and 1796.* London, 1856.
Barnes, Viola Florence, *The Dominion of New England.* New
Haven, 1923.
Beebe, Lucius, *Boston and the Boston Legend.* N. Y., 1935.
Boyle, John, "Journal of Occurrences in Boston." *N. E. Hist. & Gen.
Reg.*, Vol. V, pp. 84, 85. 1930, 1931.
Breck, Samuel, *Recollections.* Ed. by Horace Elisha Scudder. Phila.,
1877.
Bridenbaugh, Carl, "The New England Town: A Way of Life."
Proc. Am. Ant. Soc., Apr. 1946.
Brown, Abram English, *John Hancock, His Book.* Boston, 1898.
Channing, Edward, and A. C. Coolidge, ed., "The Barrington-Bernard Correspondence, 1760–1770." Drawn from the *Papers of
Francis Bernard.* Cambridge, Mass., and London, 1912.
Crawford, Mary Caroline, *Famous Families of Massachusetts.* Boston, 1930.

Drake, Francis S., *Tea Leaves, A Collection of Letters and Documents Relating to the Boston Tea Party*. Boston, 1884.

Drake, Samuel Adams, *Historic Mansions and Highways around Boston*. Boston, 1873.

—— *Old Landmarks and Historic Personages of Boston*. Boston, 1900.

Earle, Alice Morse, *Customs and Fashions in Old New England*. N. Y., 1893.

—— *Home Life in Colonial Days*. N. Y., 1898.

—— *The Sabbath in Puritan New England*. N. Y., 1896.

—— *Stage-Coach and Tavern Days*. N. Y., 1901.

—— ed., *A Boston School Girl of 1771*, the Diary of Anna Green Winslow. Boston, 1894.

Forbes, Esther, *Paul Revere and the World He Lived In*. Boston, 1942.

Gipson, Lawrence Henry, *Jared Ingersoll*. New Haven, 1920.

Hales, John G., *A Survey of Boston and Its Vicinity*. Boston, 1821.

Hill, Hamilton Andrews, *History of the Old South Church*. 2 vols. Boston, 1890.

Howe, M. A. De Wolfe, *Boston Common, Scenes from Four Centuries*. Cambridge, 1910.

—— *Boston, the Place and the People*. N. Y., 1903.

Hutchinson, Peter Orlando, comp., *Diary and Letters of Thomas Hutchinson, Esq.* 2 vols. Boston, 1884.

Loring, James S., *The Hundred Boston Orators Appointed by the Municipal Authorities and Other Public Bodies, from 1770 to 1852*. Boston, 1853.

McClellan, Elisabeth, *Historic Dress in America*. Phila., 1904.

Minot, George Richards, *The History of the Insurrections in Massachusetts*. Worcester, 1788.

Moore, George H., *Prytaneum Bostoniense*. Boston, 1885.

Morison, Samuel Eliot, *The Life and Letters of Harrison Gray Otis, Federalist*. 2 vols. Boston, 1913.

Quincy, Josiah (1772–1784), *Memoir of the Life of Josiah Quincy, Junior*. Boston, 1825.

Quincy, Josiah (1829–1910), *Figures of the Past*. Boston, 1883.

Quincy, Josiah, Jr., *Reports of Cases Argued and Adjudged in the Superior Courts of Judication of the Province of Massachusetts Between 1761 and 1772*. Boston, 1865.

Rowe, John, *Letters and Diary*, ed. Anne Howe Cunningham. Boston, 1903.

Savage, James, *A Genealogical Dictionary of the First Settlers of New England*. 4 vols. Boston, 1860–1862.

Sears, Lorenzo, *John Hancock, the Picturesque Patriot*. Boston, 1912.

Shaw, Charles, *A Topographical and Historical Description of Boston*. 1817.

Smith, Fitz-Henry, Jr., "Some Old-Fashioned Winters in Boston." *Proc. Mass. Hist. Soc.*, Vol. 65.

Sullivan, William, *Familiar Letters*. Boston, 1834.

Thwing, Annie Haven, *The Crooked and Narrow Streets of the Town of Boston*. Boston, 1920.

Weeden, William B., *Economic and Social History of New England, 1620–1789*. 2 vols. Boston, 1891.

West, John, *Boston Directory*. Boston, 1796.

CHAPTERS XXV–XXXII. THE CONTINENTAL CONGRESS AND THE WAR. 1774–1776

Throughout these chapters I used constantly Volumes I–IV of the *Journals of the Continental Congress*, edited by Worthington Chauncey Ford (Washington, 1904, ff.). Edmund C. Burnett's invaluable *Letters of Members of the Continental Congress* (Washington, 1921–1936) and his own interpretive volume, *The Continental Congress* (N. Y., 1941). The best day-by-day account of the battle in Congress for the Continental Association is in Arthur Schlesinger's *Colonial Merchants and the American Revolution* (N. Y., 1939). The description of Edmund Burke comes from Sir Nathaniel W. Wraxall, *Historical Memoirs of My Own Time* (Phila., 1837); and of the Howe brothers, from Horace Walpole's *Letters and Journals* (ed. by Mrs. Paget Toynbee, 19 vols., Oxford, 1903–1925).

Contemporary newspapers consulted for this period were the *Pennsylvania Evening Post, Pennsylvania Gazette, Pennsylvania Journal, Pennsylvania Ledger, Pennsylvania Packet* and *Maryland Gazette*.

Sources for the battles of Lexington and Bunker Hill were:

Adams, Randolph G., and Howard H. Peckham, *Lexington to Fallen Timbers*. Ann Arbor, Mich., 1942.

Fellows, John, *The Veil Removed; or Reflections on David Humphrey's Essay on the Life of Israel Putnam*. N. Y., 1843.

French, Allen, *General Gage's Informers; New Material Upon Lexington & Concord, etc*. Ann Arbor, Mich., 1932.

Frothingham, Richard, *History of the Siege of Boston and of the Battles of Lexington, Concord and Bunker Hill.* Boston, 1903.

Martyn, Charles, *The Life of Artemas Ward.* Privately printed. N. Y., 1921.

Murdock, Harold, *The Nineteenth of April, 1775.* Boston, 1923. For the armies:

Bolton, Charles Knowles, *The Private Soldier Under Washington.* N. Y., 1902.

Dandridge, Danske, *American Prisoners of the Revolution.* Charlottesville, 1911.

Graydon, Alexander, *Life of an Officer, Written by Himself.* Edinburgh, 1828.

Heath, Major General William, *Memoirs, to which is added the accounts of the battle of Bunker Hill, by Generals Dearborn, Lee and Wilkinson.* Ed. William Abbatt. N. Y., 1901.

Heinricks, Captain Johann, "Extracts from the Letter-Book of . . ." *Penna. Mag. of Hist. & Biog.,* July 1898.

Lamb, R., *Journal of Occurrences during the American War from Its Commencement to the Year 1782.* Dublin, 1809.

Lefferts, Lieutenant Charles M., *Uniforms of the American, British, French and German Armies in the War of the American Revolution.* N. Y. Hist. Soc., 1926.

Lossing, Benson J., *The Pictorial Field-Book of the Revolution.* 2 vols. N. Y., 1857.

McClellan, Elizabeth, *Historic Dress in America.* 2 vols. Phila., 1904.

Matthews, William, and Wecter, Dixon, *Our Soldiers Speak.* Boston, 1943.

Maussion, Gaston de, *They Knew the Washingtons.* Indianapolis, 1926.

Montressor, Captain John, "Journals. 1757–1778." Collections of the N. Y. Hist. Soc., 1881.

Moore, Frank, *Diary of the American Revolution.* 2 vols. N. Y., 1858.

—— *Songs and Ballads of the American Revolution.* N. Y., 1855.

Robin, Abbé, *New Travels through North-America.* Phila., 1783.

Scudder, Horace Elisha, *Men and Manners in America One Hundred Years Ago.* N. Y., 1876.

Sherburne, Andrew, *Memoirs.* Providence, 1831.

Sullivan, Major General John, "Letters and Papers." N. H. Hist. Soc., Concord, 1930.

Tomlinson, Abraham, ed., *The Military Journals of Two Private Soldiers, 1758–1775.* Poughkeepsie, 1855.

Upham, William P., "Letters Written at the Time of the Occupation of Boston by the British." *Hist. Colls. of Essex Inst.*, Vol. 13, July 1876.

Books on Pennsylvania and Philadelphia for the period are seemingly numberless. Benjamin Rush's *Autobiography*, edited by George W. Corner (Princeton, 1948), carries descriptions of the chief characters in this book, including John Adams. Of Sam Adams, Rush says he always stood on his toes when excited, something I could not seem to work into my text. William B. Reed's *Life and Correspondence of Joseph Reed* (Philadelphia, 1847) is valuable for letters from Washington. Benjamin Davies's *Some Account of the City of Philadelphia, the Capital of Pennsylvania and Seat of the Federal Congress* (*Philadelphia, 1794*), was particularly useful for climate, background and population.

Other volumes on which I drew were:

Armes, Ethel, ed., *Nancy Shippen, Her Journal Book*. Phila., 1935.
Axelrad, Jacob, *Patrick Henry, the Voice of Freedom*. N. Y., 1947.
Barbé-Marbois, François de, The Letters of. 1779–1785. Ed. E. P. Chase under title *Our Revolutionary Forefathers*. N. Y., 1929.
Barclay, Grace, *Diary*, ed. Sidney Barclay, N. Y., 1866.
Becker, Carl, *The Declaration of Independence, A Study in the History of Political Ideas*. N. Y., 1922.
Bernard, John, *Retrospections of America*, ed. Mrs. Boyle Bernard. N. Y., 1887.
Biddle, Charles, *The Autobiography of Charles Biddle*. Privately printed. Phila., 1883.
Biddle, Gertrude Bosler, and Sarah D. Lowrie. *Notable Women of Pennsylvania*. Phila., 1942.
Birch, Thomas and William. *The City of Philadelphia in the State of Pennsylvania*. 28 plates. Springland Cot., Pa., 1800.
Boyd, Julian P., *The Declaration of Independence. The Evolution of the Text*. Princeton, 1945.
Brandt, Francis Blake, and Henry V. Gummere, *Byways and Boulevards in and about Historic Philadelphia*. Phila., 1925.
Brunhouse, Robert L., *The Counter-Revolution in Philadelphia*. Phila., 1942.
Carey, Mathew, *A Short Account of the Malignant Fever Lately Prevalent in Philadelphia*. Phila., 1793.
—— *Proofs of the Origin of the Yellow Fever in Philadelphia and Kensington in the Year 1797*. Phila., 1798.

—— The Olive Branch, or Faults on Both Sides, Federal and Demo-cratic. Phila., 1815.

Davis, John, Travels of Four Years and a Half in the United States of America. Privately printed. Bristol, 1803.

Dickinson, John, Life and Writings of John Dickinson. Phila., 1891, 1895, 2 vols. Vol. I, The Life and Times of John Dickinson by Charles Janeway Stille; Vol. 2, The Writings of John Dickinson, ed. Paul Leicester Ford.

—— "Speech of John Dickinson Opposing the Declaration of Independence, July 1, 1776." Reconstructed by John H. Powell from Dickinson's ms. notes. Penna. Mag. of Hist. & Biog., Oct., 1941.

Drinker, Cecil Kent, Not So Long Ago. N. Y., 1937.

Drinker, Mrs. Elizabeth (Sandwith), 1734–1807, Extracts from the Journal of. Ed. Henry D. Biddle, Phila., 1889.

Drinker, Henry, Papers. 1756–1869. Hist. Soc. of Penna.

Duane, William, ed., Extracts from the Diary of Christopher Marshall. Albany, 1877.

Eberlein, Harold Donaldson, Diary of Independence Hall. Phila., 1948.

Eberlein, Harold Donaldson, and C. Van D. Hubbard, Portrait of a Colonial City, Philadelphia. 1670–1838. Phila., 1939.

Eberlein, Harold Donaldson, and Horace Mather Lippincott, The Colonial Houses of Philadelphia and Its Neighbourhood. Phila., 1912.

Faris, John T., The Romance of Old Philadelphia. Phila., 1918.

Friedenwald, Herbert, The Declaration of Independence, an Interpretation and an Analysis. N. Y., 1904.

Harley, Lewis R., The Life of Charles Thomson. Phila., 1900.

Hazelton, John H., The Declaration of Independence N. Y., 1906.

Hiltzheimer, Jacob, Diary, ed. Jacob Cox Parsons. Phila., 1893.

Jackson, Joseph, America's Most Historic Highway. Phila., 1926.

—— Encyclopedia of Philadelphia. 4 vols. Harrisburg, 1931.

Lincoln, Charles H., The Revolutionary Movement in Pennsylvania. Phila., 1901.

Lippincott, Horace Mather, Early Philadelphia, Its People, Life and Progress. Phila., 1917.

Maclay, William, Journal. N. Y., 1890.

Mease, James, The Picture of Philadelphia. Phila., 1811.

Mellish, John, Traveller's Directory through the United States. Phila., 1822.

Myers, Albert Cook, ed., Sally Wister's Journal. Phila., 1902.

Oberholtzer, Ellis Paxon, The Literary History of Philadelphia. Phila., 1914.

Paine, Thomas, *Writings of*, ed. M. D. Conway. 4 vols. N. Y., 1894–1896.
—— *The Complete Writings of*, ed. Philip S. Foner. 2 vols. N. Y., 1945.
—— *See also* Brinton, Crane, "Tom Paine," *Dict. Am. Biog.*; Woodward, W. E., *Tom Paine: America's Godfather*, N. Y., 1945.
Pennell, Elizabeth R. and Joseph, *Our Philadelphia*. Phila., 1914.
Pennypacker, Samuel W., *Congress Hall*. Phila., 1895.
Peters, Judge Richard, "Correspondence." *Penna. Mag. of Hist. & Biog.*, Vol. 44, No. 3, 1920.
Repplier, Agnes, *Philadelphia, the Place and the People*. N. Y., 1898.
Roosevelt, Theodore, *Gouverneur Morris*. Boston, 1888.
Sanderson, John, and Robert Waln, Jr., eds., *Biography of the Signers of the Declaration of Independence*. 9 vols. Phila., 1823–1827.
Scharf, John Thomas, and Thompson Westcott, *History of Philadelphia*. 3 vols. Phila., 1884.
Schoepf, Johann David, *Travels in the Confederation*, 1783–1784. Phila., 1911.
Sellers, Charles Coleman, *The Artist of the Revolution, the Early Life of Charles Willson Peale*. Hebron, Conn., 1939.
—— *Charles Willson Peale. Later Life: 1790–1827*. Phila., 1947.
Selsam, J. Paul, *The Pennsylvania Constitution of 1776*. Phila., 1936.
Sharpless, Isaac, *The Quakers in the Revolution*. Phila., 1899.
Sullivan, James, "The Antecedents of the Declaration of Independence." Am. Hist. Assoc. *Report*, 1902, No. 1.
Twining, Thomas, *Travels in America One Hundred Years Ago*. N. Y., 1894.
Vaughan, Benjamin, "Letters." *Mass. Hist. Soc. Proc.*, 1903.
Watson, John F., *Annals of Philadelphia and Pennsylvania*. 3 vols. Phila., 1891.
—— "Memorials of County Towns and Places in Pennsylvania." *Memoirs*, Hist. Soc. of Penna., Vol. 2.
Willard, Margaret Wheeler, ed., *Letters on the American Revolution*, 1774–1776. Boston, 1925.

Books on Franklin, Jefferson and Washington fill whole libraries. Those I found most useful were:

For BENJAMIN FRANKLIN:

Autobiography, ed. John Bigelow. Phila., 1872.
Writings of, ed. Albert H. Smyth. 10 vols. N. Y., 1905–1907.
Letters and Papers of Benjamin Franklin and Richard Jackson, 1753–1785. Ed. Carl Van Doren. Phila., 1947.

Fäy, Bernard, *Franklin, The Apostle of Modern Times.* Boston, 1929.
Morse, John T., *Benjamin Franklin.* Boston, 1889.
Parton, James, *Life and Times of Benjamin Franklin.* 2 vols. N. Y., 1864.
Van Doren, Carl, *Benjamin Franklin.* N. Y., 1938.

For THOMAS JEFFERSON:

Autobiography, with introduction and notes by Paul Leicester Ford. N. Y., 1914.
The Best Letters of, ed. J. G. de Roulhac Hamilton. Boston, 1926.
Writings, Congress Edition. 9 vols. Washington, 1854.
Writings, ed. Paul Leicester Ford. 10 vols. N. Y., 1892–1899. Also the Memorial Edition, 20 vols. 1903–1904.
Adams, James Truslow, *Jeffersonian Principles.* Boston, 1928.
—— *The Living Jefferson.* N. Y., 1936.
Bowers, Claude G., *Jefferson and Hamilton.* Boston, 1936.
—— *Jefferson in Power.* Boston, 1936.
—— *The Young Jefferson.* Boston, 1945.
Chinard, Gilbert, *Thomas Jefferson, the Apostle of Americanism.* Boston, 1929.
Forman, S. E., *The Life and Writings of Thomas Jefferson.* Indianapolis, 1900.
Kimball, Fiske, "The Life Portraits of Jefferson and their Replicas." *Proc. Am. Phil. Soc.*, Vol. 88, No. 6, Dec. 1944.
Kimball, Marie, *Jefferson, the Road to Glory, 1743–1776.* N. Y., 1943.
—— *Jefferson, War and Peace, 1776–1784.* N. Y., 1947.
Randall, Henry Stephens, *The Life of Thomas Jefferson.* 3 vols. N. Y., 1858.

For GEORGE WASHINGTON:

Diaries, ed. John C. Fitzpatrick. 4 vols. Boston, 1925.
Writings, ed. W. C. Ford, 14 vols. N. Y., 1889–1893.
Writings, ed. Jared Sparks. 12 vols. N. Y., 1847–1852.
The Writings of. Prepared under the U. S. George Washington Bicentennial Commission. Ed. John C. Fitzpatrick. Vol. 39, 1931–1944.
Baker, William Spohn, *Itinerary of General Washington from June 15, 1775 to December 23, 1783.* Phila., 1892.
—— *Washington after the Revolution.* Phila., 1898.
Custis, G. W. Parke, *Recollections and Private Memoirs of Washington.* N. Y., 1860.

Fäy, Bernard, *George Washington, Republican Aristocrat*. Boston, 1931.
Fitzpatrick, John C., *George Washington Himself*. Indianapolis, 1933.
Freeman, Douglas Southall, *George Washington*. 2 vols. N. Y., 1948.
Irving, Washington, *Life of George Washington*. 5 vols. N. Y., 1857.
Knollenberg, Bernhard, *Washington and the Revolution*. N. Y., 1941.
Marshall, John, *The Life of George Washington*. 2 vols. N. Y., 1930.
Rush, Richard, *Washington in Domestic Life*. Phila., 1857.
Sparks, Jared, *The Life of George Washington*. Boston, 1839.

JOHN ADAMS AND HIS FAMILY

BIBLIOGRAPHY

Cronin, J. W., and W. Harvey Wise, Jr. *Bibliography of John Adams and John Quincy Adams*. Washington, 1935.

MANUSCRIPT SOURCES

Beginning with the year 1774, the Massachusetts Historical Society has holograph letters from John Adams to William Tudor, James Warren, General Heath, Henry Knox, William Cooper and others. Although many are of a later period, they were valuable as a source of information and helped to establish John's character for me. This applies also to letters in the Historical Society of Pennsylvania, notably those to Van der Kemp.

PUBLISHED WRITINGS OF JOHN ADAMS

The Works of John Adams, by his Grandson, Charles Francis Adams. 10 vols. Boston, 1856.
Richardson, James Daniel, *Messages and Papers of the Presidents*. 20 vols. (Vol. 1.) N. Y., 1897.
The Selected Writings of John and John Quincy Adams, ed. Adrienne Koch and William Peden. N. Y., 1946.
Correspondence between the Hon. John Adams and the Late Wm. Cunningham, Esq. Boston, 1823.
Correspondence of John Adams and Thomas Jefferson. 1812–1826. Selected with comment by Paul Wilstach. Indianapolis, 1925.
Correspondence between John Adams and Mercy Warren, July–August, 1807. *Mass. Hist. Soc. Col*. 5th Series, Vol. 4. Boston, 1878.
Correspondence with Benjamin Waterhouse, 1784–1822. In *Statesman and Friend*. Ed. Worthington Chauncey Ford. Boston, 1927.

Correspondence between John Adams and Professor John Winthrop.
Mass. Hist. Soc. Col., 5th Series, Vol. 4. Boston, 1878.
Familiar Letters of John Adams and His Wife Abigail Adams, during
the Revolution. N. Y., 1876.
Warren-Adams Letters: being chiefly a correspondence among John
Adams, Samuel Adams, and James Warren. *Mass. Hist. Soc. Col.*
1917, 2 vols. 1925.
Two letters to Rev. Joseph Willard, *Cam. Hist. Soc. Pub.*, Nov. 16,
1922.
Letters to Wm. Plummer, 1812, 1814. *Boston P. L. Bulletin*, Vol. 6,
1901.
Letters to Daniel Coney opposing the separation of Maine from
Massachusetts, 1819. *Sprague's Journal of Me. Hist.* Vol. XII,
No. 2, 1924.
Extracts from Letters written by John Adams (comp. by John F.
Watson), *Coll. Hist. Soc. of Pa.*, Vol. 6, 1853.

Valuable holograph letters are often printed for the first time in the
catalogues of autograph dealers or booksellers such as Goodspeed's
in Boston or the Rosenbach Company of Philadelphia — sources
never listed in bibliographies, yet not to be ignored.

EULOGIES

by John Tyler, Richmond, Va.
" Caleb Cushing, Newburyport, Mass.
" C. C. Cambreleng, City of New York.
" Samuel Smith, Baltimore, Md.
" Sheldon Smith, Buffalo, N. Y.
" John Sergeant, Philadelphia, Pa.
" William A. Duer, Albany, N. Y.
" Henry Potter, Fayetteville, N. C.
" Peleg Sprague, Hallowell, Me.
" John A. Shaw, Bridgewater, Mass.
" Samuel L. Knapp, Boston, Mass.
" Daniel Webster, Boston, Mass.
" Joseph E. Sprague, Salem, Mass.
" Edward Turner, Portsmouth, N. H.
" Felix Grundy, Nashville, Tenn.
" William Johnson, Charleston, S. C.
" Wm. F. Thornton, Alexandria, D. C.
" Wm. Wilkes, Pittsburgh, Pa.
" William Wert, Washington City.

John Adams's Library

Catalogue of the John Adams Library in the Public Library of the City of Boston, ed. Lindsay Swift. Boston, 1917.

Biographies

Adams, Charles Francis, *The Life of John Adams*. Begun by John Quincy Adams, completed by Charles Francis Adams. Philadelphia, 1871. 2 vols. Also pub. as Vol. 1 of *Life and Works*, 1856.

Adams, James Truslow, *The Adams Family*. Boston, 1930.

Chinard, Gilbert, *Honest John Adams*. Boston, 1933.

Cranch, William, *Memoir of the Life, Character and Writings of John Adams*. Washington, 1827.

Fielding, Howard, "John Adams: Puritan, Deist, Humanist." *Journal of Religion*, Vol. 20, No. 1, Jan. 1940.

Haraszti, Zoltán, "John Adams among his Books." *Bulletin Boston P. L.*, Vol. 1, No. 1–3, 1926.

—— "John Adams on Rousseau." *Bulletin Boston P. L.*, Vol. 1, No. 1–3, 1926.

—— "Madame de Stael, the Vain Woman: John Adams's Opinion of Her and Her Book." Vol. 1, No. 4, Apr. 1926.

—— "The Golden Verses of Pythagoras: Marginal Notes by John Adams." Vol. 1, No. 4, Apr. 1926.

—— "John Adams on Condorcet." Vol. 5, No. 10, Dec. 1930.

—— "John Adams on the Abbé de Mably." Vol. 8, No. 4, Apr. 1933.

—— "John Adams on Frederick the Great." Vol. 9, No. 4, Apr. 1934.

—— "John Adams on Napoleon and the French." Vol. 9, No. 6, June 1934.

—— "John Adams on Religion." Vol. 9, No. 10, Dec. 1934.

—— "John Adams on Dr. Priestley." Vol. 10, No. 8, Oct. 1935.

—— "John Adams and Turgot." *Boston P. L. Quarterly*, Vol. 1, No. 1, July 1949.

Ireland, John Robert, *History of the Life, Administration and Times of John Adams*. Vol. 2 of *The Republic*. Chicago, 1886.

McCoy, Samuel Duff, *This Man Adams; the Man Who Never Died*. N. Y., 1928.

Morse, John Torrey, Jr., *John Adams*. Boston, 1884.

Pickering, Timothy, *A Review of the Correspondence between the Honorable John Adams and the Late Wm. Cunningham, Esq.* Salem, 1824.

Smyth, Clifford, *John Adams, the Man Who Was Called "Father of American Independence."* N. Y., 1931.

Walsh, Correa Molan, *The Political Science of John Adams.* N. Y., 1915.

Warren, William Frederick, "Visits of John Adams to Lancaster in 1800." *Lancaster County Hist. Soc.,* Vol. 26, No. 8, 1922.

Wood, John, *The Suppressed History of the Administration of John Adams.* Phila., 1846.

FOR ABIGAIL ADAMS (MRS. JOHN)

Letters of Mrs. Adams, the Wife of John Adams. 2 vols. Boston, 1840.

Familiar Letters of John Adams and His Wife. Boston, 1876.

New Letters of Abigail Adams 1788–1801, ed. Stewart Mitchell. Boston, 1947.

Bobbé, Dorothie, *Abigail Adams, the Second First Lady.* N. Y., 1929.

Brown, Alice, *Women of Revolutionary Times.* N. Y., 1896.

Richards, Laura E., *Abigail Adams and Her Times.* N. Y., 1917.

Whitney, Janet, *Abigail Adams.* Boston, 1947.

Whitney, Reverend Peter, *A Sermon delivered on the Lord's Day succeeding the interment of Madam Abigail Adams, consort of the Hon. John Adams, Late President of the United States.* (Nov. 1, 1818.) Boston, 1819.

FOR ABIGAIL ADAMS, DAUGHTER OF MR. AND MRS. JOHN ADAMS

Journal and Correspondence of Miss Adams, ed. by her daughter. 2 vols. Boston, 1841–1842.

Roof, Katherine Metcalfe, *Colonel William Smith and Lady.* Boston, 1929.

FOR JOHN QUINCY ADAMS

Memoirs, ed. Charles Francis Adams, 12 vols. Phila., 1874–1877.

Life in a New England Town: 1787, 1788. Diary of John Quincy Adams while a law student. Ed. C. F. Adams, Jr. Boston, 1903.

Writings, ed. W. C. Ford. 7 vols. N. Y., 1913.

Bemis, Samuel Flagg, *John Quincy Adams.* N. Y., 1949.

Morse, John T., *John Quincy Adams.* Boston, 1882.

Quincy, Josiah, *Memoir of the Life of John Quincy Adams.* Boston, 1858.

Seward, William H., *Life and Public Services of John Quincy Adams.* Auburn, Mass., 1849.

INDEX

ACADIA, *see* Nova Scotia
Act to Restrain New England, Parliament passes, 516
Acts of Trade, British, 206, 208, 216
Adams, Abigail, daughter of John and Abigail, 267–268, 306–307, 557
Adams, Abigail (Smith), wife of John, described, 230, 291; arouses John's interest, 230–237; engagement, 237–246; marriage, 246–248; children, 263, 266–268, 298–299, 329, 370, 417–418; quoted on tree of liberty, 296; moves to Boston, 298, 299, 300, 303–307, 377; writes of arrival of tea, 434; sees John depart for Philadelphia, 450–453; writes of developments in Boston and Braintree, 482–483; watches burning of Charlestown, 535, 536; death of mother, 545; rises to exigencies of war, 555–558; on mankind, 562; watches action on Dorchester Heights and sees British depart, 564–565; declines to move to Philadelphia, 570; hears Declaration of Independence read in Boston, 604–605
Adams, Anne (Boylston), wife of Ebenezer Adams and sister of Susanna, 16, 48, 224, 227–228, 241, 248
Adams, Boylston, cousin of John Adams, 14
Adams, Charles, son of John and Abigail, 370, 557, 572
Adams, Eb, cousin of John Adams, 60, 61
Adams, Ebenezer, uncle of John Adams, 7, 16, 24, 70–71, 93; voices suspicion of Winthrop and Franklin, 94–96; demands the Reverend Lemuel Briant's dismissal, 97, 98–99; barred from Communion at church, 103–104; attends John's Commencement, 111, 115; resents John's decision on career, 149; urges John to marry, 227

Adams, Elihu, brother of John Adams, 10, 13, 19, 167, 168, 226; inherits South Precinct land, 224; marriage, 229; death, 545
Adams, Ephraim, cousin of Mr. Adams, 9
Adams, Henry, great-grandfather of John Adams, 17
Adams, John, Sr., domestic background, 7–10, 46–48; political views and activities, 7, 9, 28, 37, 38–40, 194; military activities, 9, 36; religious faith, 10, 26–27, 35; described, 15–16, 17; discusses John's future, 49–51; drives John to Cambridge, 70–71; approves John's college standing, 79–80, 96; in Briant controversy, 98–100, 103, 135; attends John's Commencement, 111–112, 115–117; declines to purchase Boylston mansion, 126; accepts John's decision on career, 149; declining years and death, 219, 222–225; on chastity, 228
Adams, John:
  BRAINTREE AND HARVARD (1745–1755) — at dame school, 7, 14; at Free Latin School, 7, 13–15, 21–23; family background, 16–17, 18–21, 125–126; youthful pastimes, 23–25, 49–50; religious training, 26–28, 29–30, 33, 35, 36, 69, 76; early acquaintance with history and government, 29–33; indifference to school, 48–50; described, 49–50, 76–77, 91, 96, 189, 227; decides to be a farmer, 50–52; Marsh accepts, as pupil, 52–55; lone journey to Cambridge, 56–57; ordeal by examination, 59–62; discovers college regulations, 69–70; Freshman year, 70–75, 70–81; friends and classmates, 75–78; studies logic with Wigglesworth, 82–86; natural philosophy with Winthrop, 86–89, 91–92; develops in-

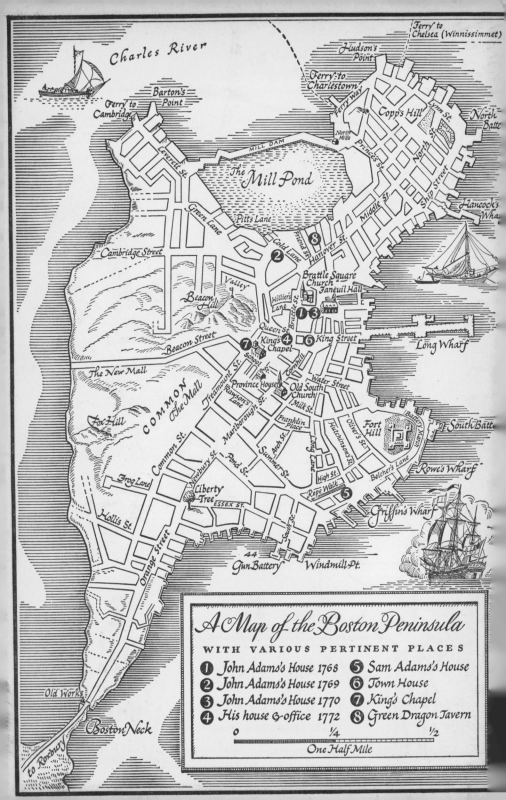

Charles River

Ferry to
Chelsea (Winnissimmet)

Hudson's
Point

Barton's
Point

Ferry to
Charlestown

Copp's Hill

North
Batte

Ferry to
Cambridge

Leverett St.

MILL DAM

The Mill Pond

North Mills

Princes St.

Inn St.

Ship Street

North St.

Green Lane

Pitts Lane

Hancock's
Wha

Cambridge Street

Cold Lane

Friend St.

Hanover St.

Middle St.

8

2

Valley

Hillier's Lane

Brattle Square
Church

Faneuil Hall

Beacon
Hill

Brattle St.

1 3

Queen St.

King St.

Long Wharf

7

King's
Chapel

4

6

King Street

Beacon Street

School St.

Cornhill

Water Street

The New Mall

The Mall

COMMON

Treamount St.

Province House

Rawson's
Lane

Marlborough St.

Old South
Church

Milk St.

Franklin
Place

Long Lane

Hutchinson's St.

Oliver's St.

Fort
Hill

Battery Marsh

South Batt

Fox Hill

Common St.

Pond St.

Arch St.

Sumner St.

Belcher's Lane

Rowe's Wharf

Roxbury St.

High St.

Rope Walk

5

Frog Lane

Liberty
Tree

ESSEX ST.

South St.

Griffin's Wharf

Hollis St.

Orange Street

44

Gun Battery

Windmill Pt.

Old Works

Boston Neck

to Roxbury

A Map of the Boston Peninsula
WITH VARIOUS PERTINENT PLACES

1 John Adams's House 1768   5 Sam Adams's House
2 John Adams's House 1769   6 Town House
3 John Adams's House 1770   7 King's Chapel
4 His house & office 1772   8 Green Dragon Tavern

0   ¼   ½
One Half Mile

Books by

CATHERINE DRINKER BOWEN

FRIENDS AND FIDDLERS

BELOVED FRIEND:

The Story of Tchaikowsky and Nadejda von Meck
(IN COLLABORATION WITH B. VON MECK)

FREE ARTIST:

The Story of Anton and Nicholas Rubinstein

YANKEE FROM OLYMPUS:

Justice Holmes and His Family

JOHN ADAMS AND THE AMERICAN REVOLUTION

John Adams and the
American Revolution

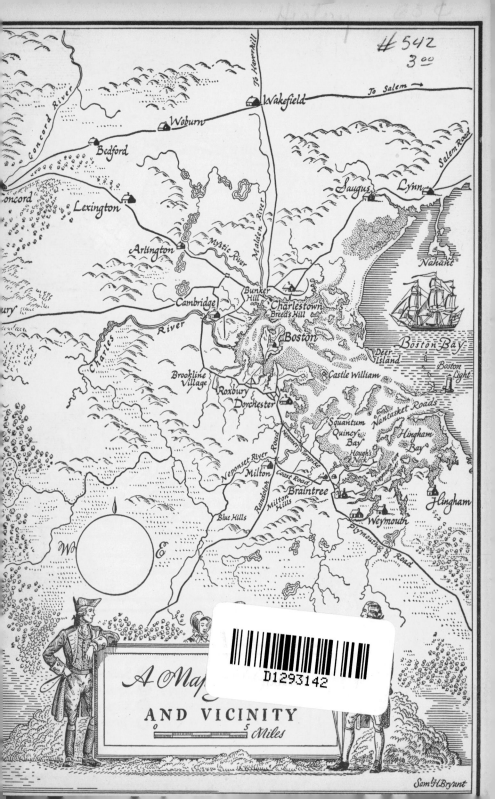

Concord River

To Haverhill

To Salem →

Wakefield

Woburn

Salem Road

Bedford

Saugus

Lynn

Lexington

Nahant

Arlington

Mystic River

Malden River

Bunker Hill

Cambridge

Charlestown

Breed's Hill

Charles River

Boston

Boston Bay

Boston Light

Deer Island

Brookline Village

Castle William

Roxbury

Dorchester

Squantum

Nantasket Roads

Quincy Bay

Hingham Bay

Hough's Neck

Neponset River

Milton

Braintree

Hingham

Blue Hills

Milton Hills

Weymouth

Plymouth Road

W   E

A Map

AND VICINITY

0   5   Miles

Sam H.Bryant